Horror Galore

300 Fantastic Fright Flicks You Might Have Missed

Nathaniel Tolle

Copyright 2023 Nathan Tolle. All Rights Reserved.

ISBN: 978-1-958842-01-0

Library of Congress Control Number: 2022941785

All rights reserved. No part of this book may be reproduced or transmitted in any form or by any means, electronic or mechanical, including photocopying, recording, or by any information storage and retrieval system, without permission in writing from the publisher or author.

All illustrations and photos are copyright of their respective owners and are reproduced here in the spirit of publicity. While we have made every effort to acknowledge specific credits and obtain rights whenever possible, we apologize for any omissions, and will undertake to make any appropriate changes in the future editions of this book if necessary.

Front Cover Design by: Kieran Curtis
Layout Design by: Tara Vermette/Tru Blu Grafix

First Published by Dark Ink Books, Southwick, MA, 2023

Dark Ink and its logos are trademarked by AM Ink Publishing.

www.AMInkPublishing.com

CONTENTS

Introduction I
Drinking Bloody Marys Until The Sun Rises 1
Universal Horror And Their Famous Monsters 13
Living Dead Ghouls Hungry For Braaaaaaaaaaains!!! 17
Totally Tubular '80s Slashers 23
Werewolves And Weird Wolves 31
Second Guessing Your Upcoming Trip To Australia 37
Must Be The Season Of The Witch And Witch Hunters 43
Cults Almost As Scary As Qanon 47
Horror Is A Dish Best Served Cold 53
Regretful Real Estate Acquisitions 59
Families That Would Give Even The Sawyers The Creeps 71
More Reasons To Get A Vasectomy 77
Occasionally, Deceased Is Superior 81
Coastal Towns With More Evil Secrets Than Saltwater Taffy .. 85
Footage Worth Finding 89
Slime, Grime, Gore, And Body Horror 93
"I Wanna Kill Everyone. Satan Is Good. Satan Is Our Pal" 101
Escaping The Horrors Of Reality
With Fairy Tales And Folklore 109
It's A Small World Of Pain and Suffering, After All:
Amusement Parks And Carnivals 119
A V/H/S Collecting Cat-Eyed Creep Shows The Darkside
Of Trick 'R Treating On The Blackest Of Sabbaths:
Overlooked Anthologies 123
Saturday Mourning Cartoons 137
A Reminder To Avoid Dinner Parties 141
Now Playing In The Heavy Metal Parking Lot 145
How To Cook Forty Humans 149
Churches With Unholy Water 153
Unfriendly Spirits With Scores To Settle 157
Frightening Initiations And Unlawful Sleepovers 165
Mad Scientists And Deranged Doctors 169
The Silent Films That Gave Our Ancestors Heart Attacks 175
Got Bugs, Rats, And Creepy Crawlies Again, Huh, Mr. Pratt? .. 177
"Love Bites, Love Dies" 183
Rubber-Suited Monster Rampage 193
"Happy Happy Halloween, Halloween, Halloween,
Happy Happy Halloween, Silver Shamrock" 197
Jingle Hells Or: Every Decent Christmas Pun
Has Already Been Taken 207
Saucy Sorcerers In Movies Beginning With S 213
Sexy Mall Madness 219
"I Don't Know How Many Years On This Earth I Got Left.
I'm Gonna Get Real Weird With It" 223
Horror Legends Sharing The Screen 231
And You Thought The Griswolds Had It Rough:
The Worst Vacations Ever 235
Cruising Down The River Styx With No Crucifix 245
No Face-Hugging Or Body-Snatching,
But Still Spongeworthy Sci-Fi Horror 249
Swimming To Your Watery Graves 257
Copyright Infringement Be Damned To Hades 261
Spirits, Demons, And Aliens Ate My Homework 267
Manic-Kin-Eti-Cuts: Let's See Andrew McCarthy
Seduce These Mannequins 271
Something Bonkers For Your 4/20 Viewing Pleasure 279
Lovecraft Adaptations For Your Cthulhu Convention 285
Ghosts And Demons That Prefer To
Downsize To Apartments 293
English Ghost Stories To Scare The Dickens Out Of You 297
Serial Killers And People Who Just
Go A Little Mad Sometimes 301
Video Nasties Telling You Not To Do Something 315
So Bad It's Essential 319
Gloves On, Knives Out, A Giallo We Will Go 323
Scream At The Beach 327
Let's All Die Laughing Like Vizzini From Princess Bride 331
Camping And Hiking Disasters 341
More Demonic Possessions To Swallow Your Souls 345
Suffering For Your Art 349
Games That Are Even Harder Than Mega Man 355
Bleak And Brutal 359
Won't Traumatize The Kiddies 365
Learning Is Fun With These Documentaries 371
Fun-Sized Horrors Of 21 Minutes Or Less 383
Something Special To Make You Feel Like
You've Just Bowled A Perfect 300 389
Acknowledgments: 393

INTRODUCTION

March 8, 2019

Welcome, creatures of the night, and thank you for letting me be your guide on this journey through foggy graveyards, abandoned mansions, subterranean tunnels, pitch-black forests and other places we weirdos equate with fun, as we shine a light on horror cinema's under-appreciated treasures.

My original plan was to write a companion piece to *Pumpkin Cinema: The Best Movies for Halloween* by focusing on Christmas, but after a few months, my heart just wasn't in a project that would force full-time yuletide spirit for two solid years at least. Such an experiment could have caused my heart to explode from excessive holiday cheer and tarnish my reverence for the holiday indefinitely, or who knows, maybe a daily visit to the North Pole would actually be good for the soul and carry therapeutic attributes. Either way, the thought of having to endure random Hallmark holiday movies through spring certainly wasn't making me feel merry inside, especially after realizing that I could be watching horror's hidden gems all through the year instead, making every night conceivably feel like a stormy Friday the 13th. As someone who became obsessed with the genre at a very young age and considers first viewings of oddities like *Spookies*, *Tourist Trap*, and *Mr. Boogedy* as defining moments of my childhood, this feels much more in my comfort zone.

As my passion for horror grows with each decade, so does the thrill of chasing after those special films that for whatever sad reason slipped under the radar of so many. I've already seen more than my fair share of grindhouse schlock, foreign shocks, direct to video cheapies, and long-forgotten creepies, but a recent visit to Portland's Movie Madness, a video store with well over 80,000 titles, proved to be a humbling, overwhelming experience. If any movie has ever been released on VHS, DVD, or Blu-ray, chances are high that this place will have it. From where I was standing in the mammoth horror section, I could turn in any direction and be faced with rows upon endless rows of horror offerings, many of which I had never heard of despite my lifelong horror devout status. In writing this book, I'll be able to relive my youth by choosing movies off these shelves impulsively without trailers, reviews, or Rotten Tomatoes percentages altering my decision in any way. I'll also be relying heavily on streaming services such as Shudder, Tubi, Kanopy, Shout Factory TV, Netflix, and Midnight Pulp to guide me along, while picking up recommendations from horror podcasts, websites, and Letterboxd members who live on the fringe. The list that I kept all throughout my middle and high school years, where I recorded and assigned a 0-5 star rating to every single movie I watched, will also probably come in handy; I'm assuming this is something that all the cool kids did, right?

There is no shortage of lists online that cater to the best of underseen horror, but I want this to be the ultimate compendium no matter what specific subgenre, era, or theme you're craving. And while I'm sure to venture into some very dark and punishing places at times, the one area that I know won't be represented is the super-ghoulish torture stuff because I'm not going to pretend to admire something like 2019's *Grotesque* just for the sake of being as inclusive as possible. The *Grotesque* from 1988, on the other hand, has a pretty good shot.

I am predicting that the hardest part will be determining whether or not certain movies fall under "hidden gem" status because some movies had moderately successful theatrical runs many decades ago but never really flourished on home video, while others languished in complete obscurity before obtaining an overdue reevaluation and sizeable cult following in recent years thanks to distributors like Shout Factory or Vinegar Syndrome. It's a fine line that I'll be measuring with my own experience and with statistics. For example, *TerrorVision* and Lucio Fulci's *The Beyond* are two borderline films on my consideration list, and I see that one has 22,000 IMDb ratings while the other has less than 7,000, and so that might end up being a factor. I realize that some of these judgment calls are going to raise a few eyebrows from the more seasoned horror fans, but if you find yourself scoffing at a few titles that are already quite revered, chances are high that you'll turn the page and see something far less familiar.

It will also be challenging to determine if certain movies like *Threads*, *Bone Tomahawk*, *Wake in Fright*, *The Night of the Hunter*, and *Hold That Ghost* are horror or merely horror-adjacent, and if laugh riots like *Tucker and Dale vs Evil* sway a little too heavy on the comedy side to be included. It's more subjective than science, but for instances when I'm straddling the fence, I'll be taking polls online and going with the majority.

With a flashlight in one hand, a shovel in the other, and a pocketful of breadcrumbs to track our path, it's time to brave the storm and get to work. Let's start with a terror tale called *Sole Survivor*, which has been creeping into my thoughts regularly since my first watch a month ago.

March 23, 2022

Forget Pinhead for a moment because this time, I'm the one who has such sights to show you!

Well, I was way off in predicting that I could complete this book in a year and a half! Under-the-radar horror, I discovered, is truly a bottomless pit and the list of potential candidates kept growing to absurd anaconda-sized proportions. There were fruitful weeks when I'd land on five winners in a row, and also some long stretches where I suffered through over 20 disappointments before finding something worth geeking out about. The most frustrating times were when I just couldn't get my hands on certain films that never received distribution in the states. I would do anything for this book but I won't do that, that being risking a computer virus by clicking on a wonky website that might illegally have them available to stream.

After three years and a sense of the finish line approaching, I looked over all 297 entries (in which I did my best to avoid spoilers) and was surprised by how little I remembered about *Hellgate*, *Robin Redbreast*, *Savageland*, *The Mansion of Madness*, *Beyond the Door*, *Kandisha*, *Prophecy*, and *Death Line*, and so I couldn't in good conscience call them fantastic fright flicks if they could fade from my memory so quickly despite initial enthusiasm. When in doubt, throw them out! Then I spent a couple more months looking for eleven final movies to write about so I could call it a day at 300, the perfect score in bowling.

Introduction

A lot has changed over the course of writing *Horror Galore*. More and more horror movies now bypass theaters entirely in favor of streaming premieres. Some that had only been available on VHS at the time I included them have since been remastered on special edition Blu-rays, and some that were easily accessible are now hard to track down with their out-of-print discs going for hundreds of dollars and no streaming service offering a lifeline. Some of the most obscure titles made the leap from Dailymotion to Shudder, and others significantly grew their audiences thanks to Joe Bob Briggs's monumental comeback and popular websites like WhatCulture including them regularly on top 10 lists.

The downside to writing first, arranging categorically later is that the book will be all over the place in terms of chronology. There could be references to the sad deaths of Betty White and Alex Trebek, the aggressively annoying new NFT trend, and the release of yet another Batman reboot in the first chapter, and then in the final one, mentions of less-timely topics like Beto O'Rourke and Kirsten Gillibrand announcing their 2020 Presidential runs, 2 million RSVPs on Facebook to storm Area 51 in search of aliens, and oh yeah, yet another Batman reboot. On the bright side, at least my slow and steady descent toward middle-aged cantankerousness won't be as easy to detect.

Thank you again, dear readers. I hope you like this book and that it steers you in the right directions on those nights when you just don't feel like scrolling for hours on streaming services as your head spins from content overload, only to choose something that puts you to sleep during the opening credits. It's such a privilege to honor the following 300 criminally underrated movies, all of which made me eternally thankful to be in this community of misfits and mutants. Happy haunting to you all, and thanks for doing your part in keeping horror alive!

DRINKING BLOODY MARYS UNTIL THE SUN RISES

Bloodstone: Subspecies II (1993)
Writer and Director: Ted Nicolaou
Cast: Denice Duff, Anders Hove, Kevin Spirtas, Melanie Shatner, Michael Denish, Ion Haiduc

It is recommended that you see the original *Subspecies* because it's a cool vampire flick with Angus Scrimm, but not a requirement in following the plot of this slightly superior sequel. This time the titular monsters, a pack of stop-motion miniature demon puppets, are only featured in the opening scene, as they work together to reunite the head and body of evil vampire Radu, who was decapitated at the end of the original by the sword of his more noble brother. Radu awakens in a typically rotten mood and locates the coffin of his doomed brother, but seconds before his imposingly long and bony fingers can snatch away the bloodstone (a mythical artifact alleged to drip the blood of saints), he's forced to go back to bed when the morning sunshine creeps into the castle, allowing Michelle, the final girl of the original and now played by longer-haired actress Denice Duff, to make an unfettered escape.

With deep puncture wounds in her neck and a dissipating tolerance for daylight, a panicked Michelle checks into a Bucharest hotel and calls her sister Rebecca, begging for her help. But before Rebecca's plane lands in the Romanian capital, Michelle has already been found unresponsive

Poster for *Bloodstone: Subspecies II* (1993), Full Moon Pictures

in the shower by a maid, pronounced dead by a doctor, and deemed resurrected by an ambulance driver whose shock results in the running down of a bicyclist. Rebecca is aided in the rescue of her sister by Professor Popescu from the Folk Art Museum, US Embassy Agent (and potential love interest) Mel Thompson, and a much less-helpful Lieutenant Marin, a Gomez Adams lookalike who equates his English skills to pop culture icons like Big Bird, Columbo, Perry Mason, and Zsa Zsa Gabor. Hot on their trail is Radu, eager to reclaim the bloodstone as well as who he perceives to be his soulmate.

Had these *Subspecies* movies been filmed in a place like West Point, Nebraska, then they would probably be remembered for nothing except the startling presence of Radu. This is a vampire that's unable to blend in with a group of mortals since he resembles Max Schreck's Count Orlok and speaks like a decaying Don Vito Corleone in *The Godfather* as blood dribbles down from his rat-toothed mouth. However, they were filmed in just about the most perfect place on the planet for a vampire movie, Romania, bringing on a level of authenticity that can't be replicated by even the most expensive movie sets. This funnier and bloodier entry takes full advantage of the old ruins, castles, crypts, monasteries, tombs, backroads, opera houses, and modern architectural wonders. I always remembered it for looking like a moody Gothic vampire movie should, and seeing it digitally remastered for the first time tonight gave me even more appreciation, for not only the locations, but also for Radu's impressive shadow-playing, the practical effects, and for the appearances of the "Mummy" character, a rotting gypsy gnome who looks like a relative of the Crypt Keeper. It's no surprise that makeup artist Daniela Busoiu has enjoyed a very extensive career, lending her talents to sequels of *Hellraiser*, *The Prophecy*, *Child's Play*, *Wes Craven's Dracula*, and *The Return of the Living Dead*, and that was all just within a 12-month span!

Much like Ted Nicolaou's (such a difficult last name to spell!) previous Full Moon picture, the often-amusing *Bad Channels*, metalheads will find plenty of opportunities to raise the devil horns. With a new bloodlust coursing through her veins, Michelle scavenges the Bucharest nightlife and settles on a strobe-lit metal club (which curiously only books one band and which constantly has more people lurking directly outside than patronaging inside) and a long-haired guy with a Megadeth patch on his jacket. The Subspecies universe continued to expand with a few more sequels and the 1997 spin-off, *Vampire Journals*, all written and directed by the *TerrorVision* mastermind with the obnoxiously spelled last name.

Captain Kronos: Vampire Hunter (1974)
Writer and Director: Brian Clemens
Cast: Horst Janson, John Carson, Shane Briant, Caroline Munro, John Cater, Lois Daine

On Day 4 of a much-needed road trip, I became starstruck at the Fargo-Moorhead Visitors Center because I got to meet the actual wood chipper used in the movie *Fargo*! It was tempting to watch the Coen Brothers masterpiece for the hundredth time after settling in to my Airbnb, but instead I decided to meet another blood-spilling force of destruction: Captain Kronos.

By the early '70s, audiences were tiring of the Gothic horror and fanged creatures of the night that the British film production company Hammer was synonymous with, an understandable reaction since they put out more than a dozen vampire features in as many years. *Captain Kronos: Vampire Hunter* was intended to shake things up a bit and birth a successful new series but instead it drove another nail into the coffin when disastrous box office numbers killed all chances of further crusades. It's one of Hammer's most underrated movies and so I was pleased to learn that it recently received a Blu-ray treatment courtesy of Shout Factory.

Written and directed by Brian Clemens (riding a career high by penning many episodes of the popular British show *The Avengers*), this movie begins with an adolescent girl sitting against a tree one afternoon and combing her hair in the picturesque countryside when a mysterious cloaked figure is suddenly reflected in her mirror—the first debunking of standard vampire mythos. Also against the norm is how the girl is found not with neck puncture wounds and a loss of blood, but with bloody lips and a gain of about 70 years. When Dr. Marcus (resembling Metallica's James Hetfield in certain shots) comes across additional teenaged girls whose attacks led to accelerated aging, he contacts his good friend Captain Kronos, a ruggedly handsome and apparently flawless swashbuckler with wit as quick as his samurai sword slicing, who has been hunting vampires ever since one took away his loved ones.

Accompanying Kronos is his trusted companion Hieronymus Grost, clearly playing the Igor role due to his hunchbacked stature but containing far more intellect. "There are as many species of vampires as there are beasts of prey. Their methods and motives for attack can vary in a hundred different ways," he reminds Kronos at one point while searching for the perpetrator. They receive additional help from a gypsy girl named Carla, whom they rescued from a pillory after she was caught dancing on the Sabbath. She is played by Caroline Munro, an actress so enchanting that it's no wonder she was chosen to be the woman that the Abominable Dr. Phibes goes on the most maddeningly labored measures to avenge.

This movie is wonderful to look at and listen to, and with its leisurely pace you have no choice but to sit back and admire every detail, my favorites being the shadow of a crucifix that curiously bends against a church's wall, the birds singing with the wind in all of the exterior scenes, and a door that opens forcefully to reveal a youth-sucker silhouetted by all shades of gray from a stormy sky—and because these vampires play by a different set of rules, it doesn't wait for an invitation!

Fright Night Part 2 (1988)

Director: Tommy Lee Wallace
Writers: Tim Metcalfe, Miguel Tejada-Flores, Tommy Lee Wallace
Cast: William Ragsdale, Roddy McDowall, Traci Lind, Julie Carmen, Jon Gries, Russell Clark

Rather than work on a sequel to his amazing directorial debut, Tom Holland focused his talents on *Child's Play* and brought along Chris Sarandon's irreplaceable presence. Stephen Geoffreys, who was somehow slated to return despite "Evil" Ed Thompson suffering the most emotional and magnificently constructed death scene in the original, read the first draft of *Fright Night Part 2* and decided to instead accept a starring role in Robert Englund's directorial debut, *976-EVIL*. Charley's girlfriend Amy was another character who disappeared in draft revisions, causing Amanda Bearse to accept another job on a certain Fox sitcom that would keep her busy for many years. We also don't get to see Charley's mom or Billy Cole (which makes sense considering he literally disintegrated before our very eyes in one of many examples of special effects wizardry from the original), but you can't say that *Fright Night Part 2* is without its interesting characters!

Even with so many principal names absent, the heart and soul of the original have returned, with Charley Brewster and "The Great Vampire Killer" Peter Vincent taking vastly different trajectories in the aftermath of the most frightening night of their lives; simply being able to spend more time with them is more than enough reason to celebrate this movie. It opens with Charley, on his third year of therapy, admitting to his psychologist that Jerry Dandridge was a master manipulator, cult leader, and serial killer, but most definitely not a vampire because vampires don't exist. He also feels sorry for Peter Vincent for not being able to cure himself of the delusions and mind control. It's a complete role reversal from the original, when Peter Vincent brushed off the "fruitcake kid" who was pleading for help in the parking lot because his neighbor was a vampire.

Charley is now a college student who reacts to the sight of nocturnal transporting of coffin-shaped objects from his window not with grave concern, but with an unimpressed headshake and a "thanks but no thanks." His change of heart feels like a betrayal, but deep down inside he's still the good ole Chuck we've grown to love, who still covers his walls with posters of cult films like *Teenage Caveman* and *Sex Kittens Go to College*, and who passionately defends horror literature like *Dracula* after his intellectual girlfriend Alex deems our chosen genre "low-grade melodrama." Since she's a speed reader, it doesn't take her long to realize she was dead wrong and that her weird boyfriend has excellent tastes.

A gang of four arrives in town and once Charley locks eyes with its multi-ethnic leader Regine, all the progress made in therapy dissolves faster than Billy Cole as he's unable to think about anybody but her, and unable to resist her even after she's plunged her fangs into his neck in dreamland. If you had to imagine in vivid detail what Jerry Dandridge's sister would be like, it's Julie Carmen's seductive Regine incarnate, in appearance, style, and cadence.

When such a miraculous piece of filmmaking in the '80s is both a critical and commercial hit, a sequel is all but inevitable, and it's possible that one of the reasons why *Fright Night Part 2* didn't capture a wider audience is because few people believed that lightning could be caught in a bottle twice. The odds were stacked against them but the casting director delivered a fortuitous roll of the dice with Julie Carmen and her fellow misfits that include Brian Thompson's herculean, bug-munching chauffeur Bozworth, Russell Clark's (choreographer for stars like Michael Jackson, Pat Benatar, Gloria Estevan, and Grace Jones) gender-bending, roller-skating mute Belle, and last but not least, Jon Cries' (*TerrorVision*, *Napoleon Dynamite*) wacky wolfman Louie, who wastes no time in taking the series into more tongue-in-cheek territory by losing his claws in an unsuccessful Peeping Tom attempt.

An even sillier scene comes after Bozworth scolds Louie for concentrating too hard on winning the affections of Charley's girlfriend, suggesting that he should amuse himself some other way… like bowling. We're then treated to a montage set to the tune of Wilson Pickett's "The Midnight Hour" as the gang shows off their crazy bowling methods like using the manager's severed head to pick up the spare. *Fright Night Part 2* might have benefitted from more scenes like this that are so far removed from the original film, or maybe it should have gone into more thought-provoking and poetic territories by giving Charley and Regine enough screen time together to make their relationship complex, complicated, and poignant rather than just a vehicle for revenge. Too often this sequel reminds us that it's inferior to the original in every way because rather than standing on its own, it keeps hitting perfunctory notes and recycling classic moments like Peter Vincent's prop mirror discovery, Charley's raging hormones getting him in trouble with his less-adventurous girlfriend, the witnessing of vampiric love bites through an open window, and a climax full of sunbeams and an open casket.

While nobody on the planet would say it's on the same level of *Fright Night*, it still delivers 104 minutes of pure joy. The makeup and special effects are once again top tier and you know that whenever a spawn of Satan succumbs to stakes, holy water, crosses, or even communion wafers, you're about to witness quite a spectacle, with the camera front and center to capture every disgusting detail. Another MVP that rejoined the army of the night was composer Brad Fiedel, and it's a real treat to once again hear those atmospheric electric violins and melancholy keyboard melodies. There's even a revamped version of "Come to Me" during the ending credits that is just as irresistible as the two Dandridge siblings.

Director Tommy Lee Wallace just couldn't catch a break at the box office with his two excellent 80's horror sequels. *Halloween III: Season of the Witch* bombed for being Michael Myers-less and too weird for mass appeal, going largely ignored for decades until an almost unprecedented reversal of fortune in recent years has made it an essential October flick and merchandise powerhouse. Father time has not been as kind to *Fright Night Part 2*, a movie cursed with tepid studio support and a distributor, Jose Menendez, who was famously murdered by his two sons shortly before the release date, causing any hope of commercial success to go up in smoke. At the time of this writing, it still has never been released on Blu-ray, and its long out-of-print DVD is on Amazon for the bargain-bin price of $116.99.

A Girl Walks Home Alone at Night (2014)

Writer and Director: Ana Lily Amirpour
Cast: Sheila Vand, Arash Marandi, Marshall Manesh, Mozhan Marno, Domonic Rains

Ari Aster, Robert Eggers, Jordan Peele, and Jennifer Kent all made modern horror masterpieces with their feature debuts, and you can add Iranian-American filmmaker Ana Lily Amirpour to that list. She showed such a high level of artistry and confidence with her first step up at bat and breathed new life into vampire lore with *A Girl Walks Home Alone at Night*. Based on her short film of the same name--which won Best Short Film at the Noor Iranian Film Festival—this movie was marketed as the first Iranian vampire western, and while it is set in an Iranian town known as Bad City and spoken entirely in Farsi, it's actually an American production filmed in Taft, California.

It opens with a young man named Arash walking through what appears to be a crumbling ghost town at the outskirts of an oil refinery, his fresh white t-shirt popping out against the bleak backdrops and black and white photography, but it's safe to say that most eyes will be glued to the adorable kitty cat that he's carrying. The breezy accordion waltz that fills the soundtrack keeps the mood light until it abruptly slows down and distorts to a demonic drone when Arash passes an open pit full of dead bodies and doesn't even react in the slightest, setting up a perfectly timed title card.

He returns to his filthy home to discover a despicable drug-dealing pimp named Saeed harassing his heroin-addicted father over money, eventually confiscating Arash's brand new flashy car (that took him 2,191 days of hard work to afford) for collateral. Saeed, with his hideous mustache, even more hideous tattoos (one of the worst offenders being the word "sex" inked poorly across his neck), and answering machine greeting that simply states "leave a message, hooker," continues to show his dominance by cruelly berating one of his prostitutes before luring a mysterious young woman to his home. She watches silently as he snorts line after line of cocaine and seductively "dances" to what he considers to be "music." I would normally consider biting off someone's finger and forcing it inside the victim's mouth to be overkill, but in this case it's an empowering display of just desserts!

After Ayash finds his car keys and a case full of drugs next to the mutilated body of his tormentor, his spirits are high enough to dress as Count Dracula and attend a chic costume party, proving that it's not all doom and gloom in Bad City. There he seemingly hits it off with a girl he likes but when an ecstasy-fueled romantic advance goes unfulfilled, agony returns and causes him to escape the party so that he can aimlessly meander down the streets in solitude instead. Hopelessly lost and too spaced out to care, he marvels at a streetlight until noticing another solo nightwalker cloaked in black. They stare into each other's eyes for lengthy periods and exchange brief but meaningful words, and then she adorably pushes him down the street on her skateboard so they can listen to music at her place while Ayash sobers up. The romance here between fake vampire and real vampire is so genuine and sweet, making this an excellent movie to watch with a significant other, and even though they don't talk much, hardly smile, or get very physical with each other, it's evident that the deepness of their connection is something an immortal being might only experience once in a thousand lifetimes (or maybe I'm just a sucker for embraces in rooms with a spinning mirror ball and Bee Gees poster).

Even if you've seen a hundred vampires on screen, it's unlikely you've seen a fanged creature of the night who wears a Chador, rides a skateboard, unwinds to alternative records, and uses her frightening vocal talents to persuade miscreant youths to change their ways. This movie has a clear understanding of how being forced to live this long would carry the burden of unimaginable regrets and torments, and why it would be in her nature to deny herself happiness, even when she's in the presence of someone special who shares her belief that sometimes, nothing quite hits the spot like a sad song. Fans of David Lynch, Alejandro Jodorowsky, and Jim Jarmusch will find plenty to like, and cat lovers will surely aww over the talents of Masuka, an exceptionally calm and curious little guy who the producer of the film urged Amirpour to cast.

The Night Stalker (1972)
Director: John Llewellyn Moxey
Writers: Richard Matheson, Jeffrey Grant Rice (story)
Cast: Darren McGavin, Carol Lynley, Simon Oakland, Ralph Meeker, Barry Atwater

Out of the entire American population watching television on the evening of Tuesday, January 11th, 1972, a whopping 54% of them were tuned into ABC's *Movie of the Week*. *The Night Stalker* not only drove a stake through its competition, but those high numbers resulted in a sequel and a short-lived television series that furthered the adventures of tenacious newspaper reporter Carl Kolchak, rarely seen without his seersucker suit and straw porkpie hat, and memorably portrayed by Darren McGavin (who many will instantly recognize as the papa from *A Christmas Story*). Legendary author Richard Matheson adapted his screenplay from an unpublished novel by Jeffrey Rice and probably made McGavin jump for joy when he realized how many precious lines he was given, whether his character was trying to get the upper hand on his superiors or supplying narration as if he were a film noir gumshoe.

After his uncompromising nature results in multiple firings at respected newspapers all over the country, journalist Carl Kolchak now works for one in Las Vegas, and when a string of unsolved murders—all involving women who have been mysteriously drained of their blood—shocks the strip to its core, he sees it as an opportunity to climb the ladder and salvage his career. The hysteria is compounded by reports of a trespasser invading a hospital and stealing the blood inventory (I was happy to see that Type O Negative was a preferred choice), but only Kolchak has the brazenness to mention the "V" word in his column, much to the fury of his boss who thinks that the public does not always have a right to know. It's only after the tall, dark-haired perpetrator is identified as a 70-something Romanian millionaire with a lengthy police record and shocking ability to remain unscathed by multiple direct gunshots that the officials start taking the speculations of an "amateur bloodhound" and "has-been big city reporter" seriously.

A great protagonist needs a great villain, and you can't ask for much more out of the bloodsucking creature played by Barry Atwater; he is legitimately terrifying as he stalks his victims and leaves them paralyzed with his piercing eyes. While it's unfortunate that the film's popularity sizzled out, hopefully those who watched the broadcast in 1972 never forgot the thrilling climax where Kolchak and the vampire face off!

Even though I've only spent a few days in Las Vegas and have no sentimental attachments, it was still a pleasure to see what it looked like back when Johnny Carson was probably making lots of Nixon jokes at the Sahara, Paul Anka was crooning at Caesars, and Bob Woods was doing whatever the hell he was known for at the Golden Nugget. Becoming mesmerized by all the casino marquees is a good way to calm down after a chilling opening credit sequence depicts an autopsy from the point-of-view of the corpse, looking up at a trio of befuddled doctors using their sharp instruments on a search for blood.

Sundown: The Vampire in Retreat (1989)
Director: Anthony Hickox
Writers: Anthony Hickox, John Burgess
Cast: Morgan Brittany, Jim Metzler, David Carradine, Bruce Campbell, Deborah Foreman

Sandwiched between the two *Waxwork* films and featuring multiple cast members from both, Anthony Hickox's horror-comedy-western *Sundown: The Vampire in Retreat* is a sun-bleached, blood-splattered romp that will please horror fans simply looking for a good time, and so I'm grateful to the crew of *Retro Movie Geek* for bringing it to my attention. You really get the sense that everyone on the set was giggling like schoolchildren after each take.

Being able to shoot in a place like Moab, Utah, is like hitting the jackpot for cinematographers, and Levie Isaacks (whose other genre works include *Leprechaun* and the indescribably bonkers *Texas Chainsaw Massacre: The Next Generation*) uses his wide-angle lens for a multitude of money shots of the rugged plateaus and slot canyons, emphasizing the isolation of the residents of Purgatory. It's an unlikely town for vampires with its average 244 days of sunshine, but this clan protects itself with super-strength sunblock, sunglasses, and sombreros. Also unorthodox is how these bloodsuckers, led by Count Mardulak (David Carradine), are trying to eliminate the feasting on outsiders as a means of survival by developing a synthetic blood substitute in their science lab. But not everybody in town is on board with these new progressive ideas, and a mutiny begins to take shape by those who want to sink their fangs into warm, soft flesh and coursing veins rather than something bland that looks like porridge.

Caught in the middle of these warring factions is a suburban family who get to stay at Mardulak's castle since Purgatory isn't exactly known for its 4-star hotels. On the first night, the wife gets molested by a bat creature and the following day, the two little girls (one of whom is a horror aficionado with an impressive collection of vampire movie posters) are scared speechless by what they discover in a secret passageway, but it's hard to cut a vacation short when the scenery looks this great. A pair of teenaged campers are also having a rough trip. Not only do they witness their friend lose his cocaine high by getting decapitated by a geriatric vampire wearing a sun bonnet, but after reporting it to the Rastafarian sheriff Quinton Canada, they are thrown in jail for the inconvenience and learn the meaning of "kill 'em or convert 'em."

You might have noticed the names Bruce Campbell, John Carradine, and Deborah Foreman listed above, but this very stacked cast also includes M. Emmet Walsh, Dana Ashbrook (who also appeared behind bars a year later in *Twin Peaks*), George "Buck" Flower, and even Gerardo Mejia—the "Rico Suave" Gerardo! Still on the fence? Well, how about some stop-motion bats conversing on their flight to the stars? An umbrella impalement? A wild west shootout with wooden bullets (uh, you probably shouldn't be shooting your limited supply into the sky in excitement, you imbeciles)? A sweet romance between the prettiest vampire in town and a clumsy Campbell looking like Ned Flanders? Yeah, that's what I thought!

Thirst (2009)

Director: Park Chan-wook
Writers: Emile Zola, Park Chan-wook, Seo-kyeong Jeong
Cast: Song Kang-ho, Kim Ok-bin, Shin Ha-kyun, Kim Hae-sook, Park In-hwan

Having already watched about 20 vampire films over the past month, I was feeling a little fanged out this evening but after learning that the South Korean film *Thirst* was from the same director of the Vengeance trilogy (which includes *Oldboy*) and a memorable segment from *Three… Extremes*, it was looking promising that the blood coursing through this one would be both plentiful and purposeful.

The fact that it stars the great Song Kang-ho from *The Host* and my favorite 2019 film, *Parasite*, made it all the more promising. He plays a Catholic priest who volunteers at a hospital to comfort patients like the portly cancer-stricken man hoping that God will remember the time 30 years ago when he made the ultimate sacrifice: giving the most tasty-looking yellow sponge cake to a couple of girls instead of eating it himself. Wanting to extend his unwavering faith and benevolence to a greater cause that could potentially save the lives of millions, the priest volunteers to be injected with the deadly Emmanuel Virus as part of an experiment to discover a vaccine. Days later, with pulsating blisters and ulcers covering his face and body, he tries to find comfort by playing his trusted flute, but ends up just coughing about a gallon of blood into it before falling to the floor. A blood transfusion saves his life and makes him the only person out of 500 to survive the experiment, earning him the moniker of "The Bandaged Saint" when he returns home looking like The Invisible Man with less stylish glasses.

After removing all the gauze, he learns that there's only one way to keep away the blisters and sizzling flesh, albeit temporarily, and it's connected to his sudden sensitivity to certain sounds, scents, and temperatures. This movie does a good job in presenting the inner turmoil and fascinating dichotomy of a priest becoming a vampire and having his pathway to heaven slowly roadblocked by sinful thoughts and uncontrollable cravings long repressed. He refuses to relent to predatory behavior to satisfy his bloodlusts, preferring to secretly drink from coma patients and seeking the miserably depressed who are desperate to have their life essences drained. But he's not as successful in resisting his friend's wife, Tae-ju, a meek, unhappy, and far younger woman.

Their love affair involves several sex scenes, equally erotic and aberrant, and with comic relief thrown in at the unlikeliest of moments, and so this is probably a movie you'll want to watch alone or with a significant other supportive of your bizarre cinema proclivities, and not in a crowded house. It wasn't until after the lengthiest and loudest tryst when I realized that my windows were open on this warm summer evening and that new neighbors were unloading a U-Haul across the street. It was tempting to immediately counterbalance this by switching to something wholesome like *Race for Your Life, Charlie Brown*, but I was digging this film too much to turn it off for the sake of neighbors who I might never really interact with anyway.

Tae-ju is initially repulsed upon learning that she's been banging a bloodsucking monster who spends his days sleeping in a crate, but once she watches him effortlessly break a coin in half and leap from rooftop to rooftop, she cheers up immensely and becomes almost giddy with the possibilities. Wanting to spend eternity together, he turns her into a vampire but soon discovers that she has entirely different attitudes on blood sources, as she wonders where's the fun in taking blood from those who give it freely, resulting in thoroughly entertaining scenes of bickering, power struggles, and geysers of blood staining their walls, painted the whitest of white in an attempt to subvert their sunlight deprivation.

While some viewers have complained of its lengthy running time, I didn't feel restless for a single second, a minor miracle considering how my attention span has experienced significant shrinkage over the past year. It was refreshing to see an entirely different take on vampiric lore, far removed from gothic castles, capes, fangs, and just about anything that could be considered derivative. It's also difficult to lose focus whenever cinematographer Chung-hoon Chung is in charge of the camera. Not only is he a long-time collaborator of Park Chan-wook, but he was also an unsung hero on why *It: Chapter One* was such a crowd-pleaser—thankfully his talents were not wasted on the lousy second chapter.

Vamp (1986)

Director: Richard Wenk
Writers: Richard Wenk, Donald P. Borchers
Cast: Chris Makepeace, Sandy Baron, Robert Rusler, Dedee Pfeiffer, Gedde Watanabe

Oh, *Vamp*, if only your teeth were just a little sharper, your blood a little sweeter, and your protagonists a tad more engaging, then this could be love instead of deep infatuation. A coin toss almost decided its inclusion in this book but ultimately, I decided that a horror-comedy vampire movie from the '80s with this much style, originality, and fun deserves to have serious flaws overlooked.

After an unsuccessful initiation, cocky college wise guys Keith and AJ make a deal with a fraternity that earns them acceptance just as long as they can supply a stripper for their next party. Their female friends refuse to help and so they persuade a wealthy classmate for the use of one of his Cadillacs, but since he's pathetically lonely, he insists on coming along to the seediest areas of Los Angeles on a search for a lady of the night. After getting into a tussle at a café with a street gang led by a lanky albino, they end up at the strip club After Dark, where AJ is bewitched by the futuristic and enigmatic Egyptian goddess Katrina in easily one of the movie's most captivating scenes, a testament to the allure of androgynous Jamaican model and singer Grace Jones, who I wish could have had much more screen time. AJ follows her backstage for an encore and when he doesn't return, Keith's quest to find his friend leads to the discovery that Skid Row has been overtaken by vampires, the kind who sleep in sewers and voraciously chew on your neck like those in a Fulci film rather than the sophisticated Count Dracula types who won't let a drop of blood spill to the floor.

Making up for the three annoying male leads is a strong supporting cast that includes friendly faces like Sandy Baron (*Seinfeld*'s Jack Klompus and *Leprechaun 2*'s Morty) as the club owner who treats his operation like an essential waste disposal service and Dedee Pfeiffer (who I've liked ever since she was the Whammyburger cashier in *Falling Down*) as a waitress that repeatedly helps Keith while expressing displeasure that he doesn't remember their fling from many years ago. The neon lighting and set pieces give each location a strong flavor and vibes of Martin Scorsese's most under-appreciated masterpiece *After Hours*, with my favorite being the hotel with chandeliers, black and white checkerboard tiles, and an elevator with a mind of its own.

The best way to appreciate *Vamp* would be as part of an all-night horror marathon because it goes down smooth and keeps you invested. And the audience members—hopped up on caffeine and alcohol and pizza and popcorn and candy—would be feeding off of each other and causing a ripple effect at jokes that probably wouldn't get much of a response during a solitary viewing.

Vampyres (1974)

Director: José Ramón Larraz
Writers: Diana Daubeney, Thomas Owen
Cast: Marianne Morris, Anulka Dziubinska, Murray Brown, Brian Deacon, Sally Faulkner

Those who showed up late to the theater in 1974 for a screening of *Vampyres* did themselves a grave disservice, for even a thirty-second delay would have cost them the chance to see two beautiful girls getting hot and heavy before a mysterious assailant barges in and shoots them dead in cold blood. These are the only gunshots in the film, but at least the late-comers would get many more opportunities to see blood and boobs. Spanish director José Ramón Larraz threw his hat in the 70's lesbian vampire ring that was already crowded with films like *Vampiros Lesbos*, *Daughters of Darkness*, and *The Vampire Lovers*, and made a film that was much more thoughtful than its eurosleeze cover art suggests.

While her husband drives their camper through the English countryside and passes a statuesque brunette hitchhiker, talented painter Harriet looks out the passenger window and notices another woman hiding behind a tree. Her husband has no interest in hearing her theories of what these two women might be up to, nor does he believe that she could possibly observe anything peculiar after setting up camp on the same grounds as a spooky castle with a cemetery for a front lawn.

The sensual brunette named Fran doesn't have to wait long for a male driver to stop, take her home, and accept her invitation to come inside for good wine, food, and something special after. "These walls have become my friends, my confidants," she tells the pasty, pudgy middle-aged man who responds with, "You're not easy to understand." She then says, "That's the way I have to be accepted. With no questions and no explanations."

And that's good enough for him as they enjoy the kind of passion where it looks like they're trying to devour each other's faces. He wakes up the next morning alone and with a nasty cut on his arm, but conveniently there's a vacationing couple right outside to provide medical care and a cup of tea. Much like the men under the spell of *The Love Witch*, he weakly returns to the castle to wait for Fran to touch him once again…and possibly drain more life from his arm. Whereas Fran patiently lets the tootsie roll pop melt in her mouth slowly, her petite blonde lover Miriam (played by former Playmate of the Month Anulka Dziubinska) bites right into hers after three licks, meaning that she gruesomely stabs the latest man she's seduced with a knife and then drinks from his many gaping wounds like a savaged animal.

Harriet spies from the comfort of her camper and tries to put the pieces together to what she's been witnessing, while the vampires inside the castle walls are quarreling over why Fran insists on keeping her new victim alive instead of draining him dry and disposing of him like so many others before him. The film hints that a previous encounter in past lives explains their deep connection but much like the ending, there are more questions than answers. Fran and Miriam aren't your typical vampires because they're free to frolic among the tombstones in the cold morning glow after a night of thunderstorms. They also don't sleep in coffins or grow elongated fangs, and unlike Count Dracula, they do drink wine and plenty of it! One of the many cigarette-smoking gentlemen wondering if this is all too good to be true happens to be a wine snob, and in a very amusing scene, he tries his hardest to pin down the origin of their mysterious nectar of the gods.

Vampyres could have easily just been another softcore porn in the guise of a horror movie considering how many love scenes and sexy close-ups there are, but it places just as much emphasis on mood and atmosphere, and will leave you with plenty to ponder afterwards. And in terms of a vampiric abode, it doesn't get more idyllic than the famous Victorian Gothic mansion Oakley Court in Berkshire, with exteriors that were also featured in *The Rocky Horror Picture Show*, *The Brides of Dracula*, *Plague of the Zombies*, and the Dudley Moore comedy *The Hound of the Baskervilles*, among others.

Horror Galore

UNIVERSAL HORROR AND THEIR FAMOUS MONSTERS

Lobby card for *Dracula's Daughter* (1936), Universal Pictures

Dracula's Daughter (1936)

Director: Lambert Hillyer
Writers: Garrett Fort, John L. Balderston, Charles Beldon
Cast: Otto Kruger, Gloria Holden, Marguerite Churchill, Edward Van Sloan, Gilbert Emery

Filmed five years after the immortal classic, this sequel takes place just hours after Count Dracula met his demise with a stake through the heart courtesy of Professor Van Helsing (Edward Van Sloan as the only returning cast member) inside the cobwebbed crypt of Carfax Abbey. A cowardly constable investigating the scene oooh's at every spooky visual and is called "chicken hearted" by his bullyish partner (turning the subtitles on confirmed that he wasn't actually saying "chicken knotted" like I thought) before they place the professor under arrest for the murder and transport him to Scotland Yard.

Dracula's body, meanwhile, stays behind at the local jail and is of great interest to a cloaked woman named Countess Mayra Zaleska. Using her ring to hypnotize the guard, she and her manservant Sandor run off with the Count's body to give him last rites at a cemetery, and it's this ceremony that causes her to believe that the curse is broken once-and-for-all, and that she can finally have a normal life. She celebrates at home by playing her first cheerful-sounding piano melody while the skeptical Sandor listens for the slightest tinges of her usual melancholy. The two have this lovely back-and-forth, exemplifying the film's rhythmic and compelling dialogue:

Mayra: Quiet, quiet, you disturb me. Twilight. Long shadows on the hillsides.

Sandor: Evil shadows.

Mayra: No, no. Peaceful shadows, the flutter of wings in the treetops.

Sandor: The wings of bats.

Mayra: No, No. The wings of birds. From far off, the barking of a dog.

Sandor: Barking because there are wolves about.

Mayra: Silence! I forbid you!

Sandor: Forbid? Why are you afraid?

Mayra: I'm not. I'm not. I found release!

Sandor: That music doesn't speak of release.

Mayra: No. No. You're right.

Sandor: That music tells of the dark, evil things, shadowy places.

Mayra: Stop. Stop! STOP!

Fully aware that a Christian jury is likely to send him to either the gallows or a mental institution after hearing his defense, Van Helsing seeks the help of former student and psychiatrist Dr. Jeffrey Garth, who turns out to be just as incredulous on the subject of vampirism. The professor reminds him that even hypnosis was considered black magic not that long ago, and asks, "Who can define the boundary line between the superstition of yesterday and the scientific fact of tomorrow?" These two paths converge at a party, when Jeffrey meets the enchanting Countess and is asked to help with personal problems that may or may not involve an addiction to blood, absence of reflections, and a history of death and destruction. Even if this man of science and medicine cannot save her soul, she plans on keeping him around anyway, possibly for eternity.

Considering how Frankenstein's reluctant bride became such an iconic figure in the Universal Monster canon, it's surprising how little attention has been given to Dracula's self-loathing daughter, who introduced herself a little more than a year after to positive reviews. Bela Lugosi didn't return for this movie, but his spirit lives on with Gloria Holden's mesmerizing performance; she inherits the mind-controlling stares and even the "I don't drink…wine" line but gives them a different flavor of gravitas. Her character falls perfectly in line with fellow tragic monsters like the lagoon's Creature and the opera's Phantom, and probably gave Anne Rice a lot of inspiration when she made a career out of chronicling a vampire's pain. Maybe the actress demonstrated the same hypnotism skills on the strict ratings board members, demanding they didn't censor the film's lesbian overtones in one of the best scenes.

Frankenstein and the Monster from Hell (1974)

Director: Terence Fisher
Writer: Anthony Hinds
Cast: Peter Cushing, Shane Briant, Madeline Smith, David Prowse, John Stratton

When Hammer Film Productions released *Horror of Frankenstein*, the horror landscape was changing so rapidly that Gothic period pieces struggled to resonate with audiences that had just been shocked to the core with the likes of *Night of the Living Dead* and *Rosemary's Baby*. That sixth entry to the series was essentially a remake of the first one, *The Curse of Frankenstein* from 1957, but instead of Peter Cushing as the mad scientist, we instead got a young university student who was just as interested in getting laid as he was with resurrecting the dead. After it was, like so many other Hammer films during its dying days, poorly received by audiences and critics, it was decided that the follow-up film would abandon the comedic tone and go back to the basics. Once again, Peter Cushing, considerably older but no less commanding, would portray Victor Frankenstein and this time he would be placed in a new frightening environment that perhaps he was always destined for: an insane asylum.

In a perfect opening scene for a *Frankenstein* entry, a grizzled man is in the final stages of a nighttime bodysnatching when a cemetery guard tries to intervene but loses the scuffle and falls in the now-empty grave. The man delivers the corpse to an aristocratic young doctor named Simon in exchange for money and then immediately heads to the pub with shaky wrists caused by a combination of chronic alcoholism and hours of exhausting manual labor, only to realize in the middle of his second shot that the guard has entered the pub and is standing directly behind him.

The guard then heads to the young doctor's home, where bottles of detached eyeballs stand beside the teachings of Victor Frankenstein, and places Simon under arrest. The judge exercises the most leniency he can muster and sentences Simon to five years in a mental institution. On his first day there, he not only uses his intellect and brashness to temporarily convince the director that he's a visiting physician instead of a patient (a very funny scene), but also makes a strong impression on Dr. Carl Victor, who jumps at the idea of having an assistant with medical surgery experience since his own heavily scarred hands have lost all sensitivity after a fire incident.

At night the institution echoes with the wailing of prisoners and, every now and then, a frightening guttural growl, prompting Simon to investigate and discover that the Baron is still up to his old experiments after all, and has his eyes set on a violin-playing mathematician with a beautiful soul and brilliant mind, as well as another aged inmate who crafted exquisite sculptures before brain atrophy robbed him of his talents. It's a pretty shocking moment when Simon discovers the creature because the setup is deftly handled and the ape-like appearance unlike any of its predecessors.

Even if you find this Frankensquatch cheap-looking and absurd (actor Shane Briant allegedly struggled to find anything complimentary to say about the costume), you'd have to be heartless not to find the overall depiction sympathetic and moving. In many ways this final Hammer Frankenstein movie, loaded with atmosphere and shocks, feels like a collection of all the strengths from its predecessors. It also served as a fitting swan song for the studio's most reliable director, Terence Fisher. The curly-haired, kidney-loving "creator of man" and his abominable creation refused to slow down, however, as Peter Cushing and David Browse would reunite just three years later in a little film called *Star Wars*, playing Grand Moff Tarkin and Darth Maul respectively.

Werewolf of London (1935)

Director: Stuart Walker
Writers: John Colton, Robert Harris, Harvey Gates
Cast: Henry Hull, Warner Oland, Valerie Hobson, Lester Matthews, Lawrence Grant

Considering how enamored I was with Frankenstein, Dracula, The Creature from the Black Lagoon, The Invisible Man, and The Wolf Man growing up—a set of homemade figurines that my dad gave me as a child were proudly displayed in my bedroom until I left for college—somehow that never resulted in a phase of ogling every single Universal monster movie I could get my hands on. I had heard of *Werewolf of London* but its pedigree of being a Universal production that predated its iconic *The Wolf Man* by six years was lost on me until tonight, and so with just a couple of hours to go on a nearly full-mooned Friday the 13th, I had just the right film for the occasion.

Dr. Wilfred Glendon and a colleague are on the mountains of Tibet for a botanical expedition to locate a mysterious plant rumored to take life from the moon. An English-speaking cleric on camelback points them in the direction of the valley but warns of superstitions and the fact that he's never met a man that managed a safe return. It almost feels like The Invisible Man is having fun with these two botanists as they feel strange forces pushing and pulling them while maneuvering through the crevices, but waiting for them under the light of a full moon is the thriving plant they desire. Unfortunately, it's being protected by a hairy, howling beast, and while it doesn't pounce and eviscerate quite like the London werewolf we're more familiar with, it does leave a mark on Dr. Glendon.

He survives and brings the Tibetan plant back home to his laboratory—equipped with the same high voltage electrical devices and bubblers that Dr. Frankenstein uses—where he works obsessively to the point that he barely reacts to his neglected fiancé reacquainting with an old flame. At a high-society botanical event, the doctor shows off his collection of plants that includes a Venus flytrap and one that devours frogs, earning the denunciation of an offended guest who gripes, "How dare you bring such a beastly thing into Christian England!" Also attending is the soft-spoken and well-dressed Dr. Yogami, beaming with curiosity and asking the host if he can take a peek at the moon-flower attempting to thrive in the laboratory. He tells Dr. Glendon that they've met before, in the dark, and that a bulb from the flower is the only antidote for a Satanic monster possessing the worst qualities of man and wolf. Another piece of advice is much more ominous: "The werewolf instinctively seeks to kill the thing it loves best."

Dr. Glendon wishes he could attribute the warnings to the rantings of a madman, but it's impossible to ignore the sudden changes to his body and the way his lethargic cat takes a break from napping by the fireplace to hiss and claw at him after exchanging glances. The "werewolfery" was superbly visualized by makeup legend Jack P. Pierce, who would take things to the next level six years later when working on Lon Chaney Jr., an actor who had no complaints about being totally unrecognizable in full lycanthrope form.

Since all prints of Henry MacRae's silent short film *The Werewolf* were destroyed in a fire a little over a decade following its 1913 release, *Werewolf of London* has the distinction of being the oldest werewolf movie available, and even while its box office numbers were disappointing, it sure set the bar high in terms of storytelling and excitement. It feels more aligned with the Dr. Jekyll and Mr. Hyde mythos, with the protagonist battling demons that refuse to submit. Eventually taking the advice of Dr. Yogami, he spends his nights far away from home so that he'll be no danger to his fiancé, but he's not exactly the ideal tenant for a couple of heavily-inebriated landladies who provide great comic relief along with fine accommodations.

LIVING DEAD GHOULS HUNGRY FOR BRAAAAAAAAAAINS!!!

The Battery (2012)
Writer and Director: Jeremy Gardner
Cast: Jeremy Gardner, Adam Cronheim, Niels Bolle

In *The Battery*'s opening shot, a man wearing shorts and a t-shirt takes a break from standing around and listening to music on his headphones to sit on the porch and replace the batteries (no, not the titular batteries) in his Discman. Just as we're identifying with his lazy sunny afternoon, his friend bursts through the door, shouting "Go! Go!" while aiming a shotgun at whatever the hell is growling from inside the house. OK, *Battery*, you have our attention, now what else can you offer besides an evocative and expertly-timed introduction? The answer turns out to be a whole heck of a lot, because Jeremy Gardner's first film, with a budget of only $6,000 and a shooting schedule of 15 days, will be a breath of fresh air to even those most burnt out on the zombie subgenre due to *Walking Dead* fatigue and disappointing indies that grow in numbers on Amazon Prime and Tubi on a daily basis.

It's not an action-packed gorefest, a terrifying thrill ride, or a cynical examination on whether humans are the real monsters in a zombie apocalypse, but it does give you little doses of all three in its quiet, thoughtful examination of a relationship between two companions travelling together simply because they've lost everyone else important to them. Ben and Mickey played on the same Minor League baseball team and that's pretty much the extent of their similarities, and despite the months of spending every waking moment together, their frames of mind remain radically different.

Jeremy Gardner performs triple duty as the writer, director, and bushy-bearded team catcher Ben, a character who's adapted well to the hunter-gatherer, zombie-brain basher lifestyle, whereas pitcher Mickey chooses to live in a constant daydream and drown out the paralyzing fear by listening to music. Ben is a realist who mirrors a shark's survival instincts of always being on the move, and Mickey is a romantic who wants to belong to a community and sleep in the same bed every night. In an early scene, they stop at the empty house of a girl Mickey used to date, and while Ben raids the garage for tools and supplies, Mickey forlornly looks around the girl's bedroom, smelling her perfume, caressing her panties, staring at her photographs, and adding her mix CDs to his collection. Ben has killed hundreds of zombies but the closest Mickey has come is masturbating in front of the least-grotesque one. These are incredibly well-written characters whose dichotomy brings fascination and entertainment to every scene, even the most leisurely and uneventful ones.

The most heated conflict centers on whether or not they should be communicating with the voices heard on a walkie talkie, which I expected would eventually derail the movie with an unwise invasion into a community like The Governor's in *The Walking Dead*, but thanks to either budgetary constraints or discipline, this movie avoids all clichés and simply allows the routines of their strange new lifestyles to play out organically.

Even in a zombie apocalypse, Ben and Mickey still manage to have fun every now and then as they scavenge through rural Connecticut, like when they get to try out their baseball bats, catching gloves, throwing arms, and taste buds at a beautiful apple orchard, or when they simply relax on folding chairs in the sunshine, getting hammered on beer and making wisecracks. But what makes *The Battery* essential viewing for anyone who thinks they haven't seen an interesting zombie flick in years is the 20-minute claustrophobic climax inside a Volvo that is surrounded by hungry zombies. As day turns into night and into day again, the two trapped friends go through a whirlwind of emotions together, and even though Ben's sarcastic quip about how the omnipresent zombie moans sound like soothing raindrops on a tin roof, it's clear that he's just as tormented and disturbed by them as Mickey. Keeping the camera inside the car the whole time in lengthy shots puts us firmly in the perspective of our protagonists, and not having any idea whether there are 20 zombies outside or 200 makes the situation so much scarier than if we were given the full picture. It was no surprise to learn that this movie won numerous Audience Awards at film festivals, but it was surprising to witness the disparity between its piss-poor Blu-ray cover and that magnificently retro work-of-art theatrical poster.

Jeremy Gardner proved not to be a one-hit-wonder with 2019's *After Midnight*, a romantic thriller that he wrote and co-directed with *Battery* cinematographer and sound editor Christian Stella. He also stars in it and instead of battling the living dead, this time the terrors come in the form of his girlfriend moving out of his rural rundown home without any warning, and a violent creature trying to move in every night afterwards by any means necessary. Most of the film poignantly scrutinizes the highs and lows of a relationship drifting apart by ego, alcoholism, and midlife crises, and while it may be too low-key for some viewers, I was highly interested in what these two characters had to say and if their paths would eventually meet right in the reach of a beast that not even a bear trap could slow down. After Gardner appeared briefly in *Spring*, it was nice seeing him repay the favor by giving a role to Justin Benson. Let's hope there will be further collaborations down the dusty small-town road between these two important indie-horror visionaries.

Let Sleeping Corpses Lie (1974)
Director: Jorge Grau
Writers: Sandro Continenza, Marcello Coscia
Cast: Cristina Galbo, Ray Lovelock, Arthur Kennedy, Aldo Massasso, Giorgio Trestini

Released under a dozen or so different titles throughout the world, including *The Living Dead at Manchester Morgue* (no such place exists in the movie) in the UK and the unimaginative *Don't Open the Window* (which is the worst advice seeing as how some characters survive dire situations only by escaping through a window) in the States, this Spanish-Italian production set in the breezy English countryside could very well be the greatest zombie movie you've never seen. It mingles Hammer sensibilities with gut-munching Romero ghouls and the results are both beautiful and shocking.

Manchester antique shop owner George is on his way to meet up with some friends in Northwest England's Lake District when his motorcycle is hit by a young woman named Edna at a gas station. With his bike needing extensive repairs, he decides that the least Edna could do is give him a lift, but also insists on driving since he worries she'll drive the whole way in reverse. As far as protagonists go, he's more smug, argumentative, and condescending than most, but he's always engaging to watch and fun to root for, especially when he's butting heads with representatives of the Midland Area Agricultural Department's Experimental Section. They're testing out a new method of pest control using ultrasonic radiation and absolutely refuse to consider the possibility that negative consequences could arise.

While a lost George is asking for directions, a creepy-looking man with tattered clothes soaked in river water tries to attack Edna and disappears once help arrives. They eventually make it to her sister Katie's house, but not in time to save her husband from getting eviscerated by the same strange man while he was taking nighttime photographs of a waterfall. When a hippy-hating police sergeant investigates and finds Katie's stash of heroin, she is immediately considered the prime suspect. Shoddy journalism allowed the picture of a drifter's dead body to take up the entire front page of a newspaper printed the previous week, and when Edna sees it, she's convinced it was the same man that attacked her by the river. The only way George knows how to shut her up and put these insane accusations to rest is to take her to the cemetery and open up the drifter's coffin to see if he's still there, leading to the scariest scene in the movie. The zombies here are quick without running, strong without overpowering, and remain alarmingly focused despite showing no emotions. As if being locked in a crypt with them weren't enough to evoke paralyzing dread, they also emanate creepy breathing noises as they inch their way closer to fresh meat.

Other goodies in this eco-horror film include a zombie baby, a streaker appearing during the opening credits apropos of nothing, a grim hospital in the Gothic Revival style, an atmospheric Giuliano Sorgini soundtrack, a surprising ending, a river-crossing that is delightful except when you're in a hurry, and as Parker Bowman from the amazing podcast *Junk Food Dinner* pointed out, a toss of the towel similar to when one of Robert Goulet's goons hilariously subdued Frank Drebin in *The Naked Gun 2 ½: The Smell of Fear*, thus proposing a very compelling double feature.

I think I'll keep the zombie theme going tonight because the video game *Zombies Ate My Neighbors*, a favorite from my middle school years, just became available to download on Nintendo Switch and thanks to this modern age of YouTube tutorials, maybe I can learn how to finally conquer that damn level at Dr. Tongue's Castle of Terror (geez, and that was only level 7 out of 44?!).

Night Life (1989)

Director: David Acomba
Writer: Keith Critchlow
Cast: Scott Grimes, John Astin, Cheryl Pollak, Anthony Geary, Alan Blumenfeld

The last Easter I can vividly recall was the one in 1996 when I received a basket containing candy and Stone Temple Pilots' third studio album. All of the others that followed are a blur of nothingness, but that's about to change because five Sundays from now, I'll be at the Hollywood Theatre seeing a special screening of horror's greatest Easter movie, *Critters 2*, with writer, director, and fellow progressive rock fan Mick Garris in attendance. If I'm lucky enough to meet him, I'll be sure to give a sincere thanks for writing the AMAZING *Amazing Stories* episode "Go to the Head of the Class." After purchasing a ticket the second they went on sale, I looked up Scott Grimes, the ginger star of the first two *Critters*, on IMDb and was happy to see an impressively long list of acting credits, the latest of which includes the Seth MacFarlane trifecta of *Family Guy*, *American Dad*, and *The Orville*. The title that intrigued me the most was *Night Life*, which came out a year after he ran away from that

Horror Galore

giant critter ball that will certainly look amazing on the silver screen. Not to be confused with the vampire horror-comedy *NightLife*, which also came out in 1989 and has never been available on DVD or Blu-ray, this night delivers a healthy, sensible diet of teenage hijinks and motivated zombies.

When we first see Grimes (or Grimey as he probably doesn't like to be called), he carries a bloody pail with a severed arm sticking out, grossing out two girls who were getting frisky with their jock boyfriends in a car parked right outside of the funeral home he works at—I guess the town of Walgren is too small to have a Lovers Lane. He plays Archie, a frequent target of the jocks' bullying behavior due to his brainiac status and ghoulish vocation, and in most movies, this type of character would avenge his tormenters by reciting a spell in a cemetery to summon a demon, but here he has the refreshingly level-headed, quick-witted, and good-natured charm of Marty McFly, and that puts the viewers in a good mood even before the toxic gas and freak lightning wake a quartet of stiffs in the funeral home.

Maybe it's because they've only been dead a few hours, but these resourceful zombies retained a substantial amount of cranial capacity. They can operate heavy machinery, drive cars (the scene in which the cops pull them over is delightful), and experience more success at playing cassette tapes than Archie. They also kill with more creativity than your average stiffs. The movie has some slow patches like when the bullies take forever in executing the most preposterous funeral home prank of all time, but it's well worth your time, from the very beginning when a stereotypical 80's meathead crushes and tosses an empty beer can before saying "Hey, gimme another brew, pal!" to the absolutely perfect ending that garnered applause at my small viewing party.

I was mad at myself for not knowing that Scott Grimes has had a successful acting career post-*Crit-*

Poster for *Tombs of the Blind Dead* (1972), Interfilme, Plata Films S.A.

ters, but was even more ashamed that I didn't recognize the great John Astin despite significant screen time portraying Archie's cantankerous uncle, "Cheap Bastard" Verlin Flanders. Sure, I was watching a 30-year-old videotape and he was without his famous mustache (and he calls himself a Flanders!), but still…Oh well, at least I recognized how brilliant all that fog looked!

Tombs of the Blind Dead (1972)

Director: Amando de Ossorio
Writers: Amando de Ossorio, Jesús Navarro Carrión
Cast: Lone Fleming, Cesar Burner, Maria Elena Arpon, Jose Thelman, Rufino Ingles

Virginia White was so looking forward to spending a holiday weekend in Lisbon with Roger because of the possibility of a romance becoming reciprocal rather than one-sided, but her hopes disintegrate when he persuades one of her old college friends to join them. Seeing Roger and Betty flirt on the train rolling through the countryside sends daggers through her heart and makes her feel like the third wheel, and so at the first sight of apparent civilization, she makes no hesitation in jumping off the train with her belongings to find that no helping hand is awaiting, only the tattered remnants of a medieval fortress that will at least put a roof over her head. She makes a roaring fire in just a couple seconds and then smokes a cigarette while listening to a jazz station that miraculously contains not even a hint of static. These shots intermingle with a less cozy situation developing directly outside, as an eerie mist drifts through the darkness where the tombstones suddenly sway to and fro, alerting their owners that it's time to grind their coffin lids against the concrete and emerge from the dirt like they do every night.

As the hoard of skeletal zombies slowly shuffle toward Virginia's camping grounds, it occurred to me that this was the most nervous I've been for a character's safety in a long time. With the possible exception of *The Return of the Living Dead*'s Tarman, these are the last zombies that I would ever want to see unexpectedly at night. Even though they are blind and slow, they can easily track their victims through heartbeats that intensify when they stretch out their bony fingers. They can also hop on their faithful ghost horses to chase down anyone who manages to run away (a spectacular visual). According to local legend, the bumps in the night at Berzano are caused by the 13th century Ancient Knight Templars that returned from the Holy Land bearing the Egyptian cross and a newfound dedication to achieve immortality by holding Satanic rituals, but they probably didn't realize that they'd be spending hundreds of these years without flesh.

Given the character dynamics, terrifying zombies, and relentlessly sinister soundtrack, writer-director Amando de Ossorio probably could have set this movie at a beige DMV office or stuffy insurance seminar and it still would have been a banger, but instead he managed to secure the Santa María La Real de Valdeiglesias Monastery in Pelayos de la Presa, a place that would strike fear in anyone even without the added atmospheric flourishes and droning Templar chants. These unfortunate characters also find themselves in a morgue with a pendulum light and a mannequin factory partially illuminated by blinking red neon, which doesn't exactly stabilize their heartbeats. Everybody knows you can't keep a good visually impaired flesh-eater down, and so De Ossorio resurrected them for three quick sequels, *Return of the Blind Dead* (1973), *The Ghost Galleon* (1974), and *Night of the Seagulls* (1975).

Horror Galore

TOTALLY TUBULAR '80S SLASHERS

Amsterdamned (1988)
Writer and Director: Dick Maas
Cast: Huub Stapel, Monique van de Ven, Serge-Henri Valcke, Hidde Maas, Wim Zomer

Turning down an offer to direct *A Nightmare on Elm Street 4: The Dream Master* so that he could make *Amsterdamned* instead probably wasn't the most lucrative career move filmmaker Dick Maas has made, and so hopefully he's enjoying the adulation of his underseen thriller receiving a Blue Underground Blu-ray and a temporary home at Shudder. This film lifts from giallos, slashers, and even *Jaws* with its underwater POV shots and Ben Gardner-like jump scare as it tells the tells the story of a serial killer (or maybe even a monster according to an eye witness) who uses the 25 miles of Amsterdam canals to his advantage, much to the dismay of the police detective assigned to the case.

The four previous films I watched this week were so joyless that I needed to take a couple days off and recuperate with *Family Guy* and Three Stooges binges. *Amsterdamned* kept the good times rolling, and its sense of humor was greatly appreciated, beginning with a scene in the Red Light District when a horny cab driver tries to compliment the prostitute in his passenger seat by saying how he really likes blondes, only for her to nonchalantly remove her wig a second later. She refuses his aggressive demands to "work on it" and jumps out of the taxi, only to become easy prey for another heavy-breather who happens to be brandishing a knife.

The following morning, groups of nuns and boy scouts are gathered in a tourist boat and learning the history of the Netherlands' beautiful capital. The boat, ever so slowly, is headed straight for what looks like a woman's corpse hanging upside down, and I absolutely loved the way the shrieks from inside get louder and louder as her bloody body scrapes and squeaks against the top of the glass roof before eventually flopping inside and giving the innocent travelers a sight they'll never be able to unsee. Hans van Dongen, frequent collaborator of Dick's, was probably laughing his head off in his editing suite putting this scene together to comedic perfection. Same goes for the scene that abruptly and randomly ends once a man opens up a packet of butter and accidentally douses his friend sitting across from him.

Huub Stapel, star of Maas' haunted elevator movie *The Lift*, is compelling as the cool and collected protagonist trying to put these gruesome murders together and hypothesizing that the subject who has been terrorizing the Amsterdam canals is a skilled diver. The film also gets a lot of mileage from its supporting characters like his best friend who may still be harboring a grudge from drawing the short straw in a love triangle long ago, his new love interest working as a guide in Rijksmuseum (in another opportunity to show off a popular local attraction), his blunt and wisecracking teenaged daughter Anneke who doesn't like French food like brains and broccoli sauce (and who I like to think was named after the goddess and greatest Dutch vocalist Anneke van Giersbergen), and the mayor who is distraught over his city once again plunging into the kind of darkness that scares away tourists.

But as effective as the characters and the scares are, what *Amsterdamned* will be most remembered for is its electrifying, gravity-defying chase scenes of cars cruising down narrow streets and speedboats careening through a labyrinth of canals, barely avoiding collisions with canoes, pedestrians, police horses, and orchestras. Huub Stapel participated in some of these crazy stunts himself and escaped with a long list of painful injuries when the boat he was in crashed into a wall.

This movie was a ton of fun, and the best Dutch thrill ride I've experienced since my 2006 visit to the Amsterdam Dungeon, an interactive adventure that also benefits from strong acting and a real sense of showmanship on how to flaunt its mangled casualties.

The Burning (1981)

Director: Tony Maylam
Writers: Peter Lawrence, Bob Weinstein, Harvey Weinstein, Brad Grey, Tony Maylam
Cast: Brian Matthews, Leah Ayres, Brian Backer, Larry Joshua, Jason Alexander, Carrick Glenn

My introduction to *The Burning* took place during a family trip to the Lake of the Ozarks, a common destination for families living in St. Louis. The brilliant Netflix series *Ozark*, which I was sad to learn is actually filmed in Georgia, might have you believe that there's nothing to do in this area except boating, gambling, and scoring drugs at religious services, but when I was growing up, the "heart of the Lake of the Ozarks" known as the Bagnell Dam Strip was a paradise of curiosities and fun attractions. On one very memorable day, my brother and I scared ourselves silly in the walk-through attraction "The Haunted Hotel," (which had a hearse parked out front with a skeleton behind the wheel), got lost in "The Maze" with its many secret wooden doors, dropped a quarter into a machine to enter a shack where a life-sized King Kong was in chains, ate ice cream, and played miniature golf as well as miniature basketball (it's a shame this novelty didn't take off because it was super fun). We also persuaded our parents to take us to a video store in town so we could rent a scary movie. How we decided on *The Burning* is anyone's guess, but the VHS cover's bold statement of "the most frightening of all maniac films" and depiction of a pair of hedge clippers threatening to slice the sun in half is probably what sealed the deal. Another possibility is that we didn't choose the movie, the movie chose us.

Thankfully we waited until our parents were well out of sight before popping it into the VCR because this was a level of "adult content" that we were not used to, and had they seen the material that led to *The Burning* being among the first inductees on England's "Video Nasties" list, then the tape probably would have been ejected immediately to the cries of "nooooo!" and "that's not fair!!!" Not only was it a significant step up the horror maturity ladder, but it turned out to be an exceptionally entertaining movie that only seemed to improve with each viewing and each decade.

Not liking to be yelled at and bossed around at summer camp, some youngsters decide to get revenge on their angry alcoholic caretaker Cropsey (a name borrowed from the New York urban legend) by placing something terrifying on his nightstand while he snores. The prank goes horribly wrong when the open can of gasoline he keeps near the bed causes an inferno that burns him to such a degree that the hospital staff are practically daring each other to catch a glimpse of this monstrosity. Cropsey is released from the hospital years later after every skin-graphing surgery fails, and he returns to the summer camp setting in an even worse mood than before.

I had forgotten just how long it takes until he brutally targets throats, fingers, stomachs, and foreheads with his powerful pair of hedge clippers, but not once did I find myself growing impatient thanks to the fun teenage tomfoolery leading up to the carnage. It also helped a great deal having one of the counselors being confidently and charismatically played by Jason Alexander in his film debut and another counselor having a voice like Joe Pesci's, which is especially noticeable during a rant about being given the non-lubricated "rubbuhs." Oscar-winning actress Holly Hunter also makes her film debut here but you probably won't even notice her since she wasn't given a single line.

Tom Savini turned down an invitation to return to Camp Crystal Lake in New Jersey for *Friday the 13th Part 2*, and instead went to a different summer camp in New York to play an integral role in *The Burning*, one of Miramax's first movies. The ways in which the teens are annihilated here make his work on *Friday the 13th* look awfully tame in comparison, with the entire makeshift raft massacre scene belonging on his career highlight reel. Another huge reason why *The Burning* stands out from the crowded pack of early '80s slashers is due to the soundtrack from Rick Wakeman, who had already proven to be a maestro of otherworldly soundscapes and technical mastery as the keyboardist for progressive rock band Yes—just listen to his contributions on the *Tales from Topographic Oceans* epic track "The Remembering" and you'll be wishing he had scored more horror.

Butcher, Baker, Nightmare Maker (1981)
Director: William Asher
Writers: Steve Breimer, Alan Jay Glueckman, Boon Collins
Cast: Jimmy McNichol, Susan Tyrrell, Bo Svenson, Marcia Lewis, Julia Duffy, Britt Leach

When one of my favorite YouTube series, *Trailers from Hell*, uploaded a piece on *Butcher, Baker, Nightmare Maker* (also known as *Night Warning*) in 2015, I wondered if I had just stumbled upon yet another standout slasher from 1981 to make me proud of my birthyear. "So shocking, so terrifying, so powerful, *Night Warning* has been named Best Horror Movie of the Year by the Academy of Science Fiction, Fantasy, and Horror," the booming voice on the original trailer confidently announces, causing me to wonder just why I've never heard of the movie that apparently defeated *An American Werewolf in London*, *Dead & Buried*, *Halloween II*, and *Ghost Story* in this category at the 1981 Saturn Awards. It turns out that it didn't win this award, nor was it even nominated. The Academy of Science Fiction, Fantasy, and Horror did, however, nominate it for Best Low Budget Film, in a category where *Fear No Evil* walked home with the golden rings. Oh well, it's tough to begrudge any deceptive trailer practices for a movie that turns out to be this good!

Even though Billy is the star of his basketball team, is dating one of the prettiest girls in school, and is a likely candidate for a full scholarship to the University of Denver, his chance of a happy adulthood is jeopardized by his aunt Cheryl, who's been raising him ever since his parents died in a car crash. Their demise is shown in a truly harrowing opening scene that was the only one directed by Michael Miller before producers replaced him with *I Love Lucy* and *Bewitched* veteran William Asher. Played by Susan Tyrrell in a brave performance that channels Bette Davis at her most unhinged, Aunt Cheryl can't bear the thought of Billy moving away and leaving her all alone, and so she tries to preemptively fill the void with another man, but when the television repairman rejects her sexual advances, she goes completely off the rails and stabs him to death.

She convinces Billy to lie during the murder investigation to Detective Carlson, a man so fueled on hatred of homosexuals that he speculates Billy and the repairman were secret lovers, and as a result, he ignores the advice of his deputy that Cheryl may have some bats in her belfry, skeletons in her closet, and some disconcerting remodeling plans for the attic loft she's preparing as a high school graduation gift. The fact that her behavior toward Billy oscillates between mildly inappropriate to downright incestuous makes it all the more unpredictable and frightening when she's about to open the door to catch Billy and his girlfriend in bed together.

It's sad but true that positive, honorable portrayals of homosexuality in '80s horror are quite rare, and so *Butcher, Baker, Nightmare Maker* deserves a ton of credit for tackling this issue at a time when the gay community was being decimated by a new virus that was at the time just referred to as "gay plague" or "gay cancer" and finding little support from politicians, the media, and even their neighbors. Throughout the whole film, Billy's basketball coach, Tom, is depicted as a likeable, average guy and not once reduced to tired stereotypes, and while it was uncomfortable to hear so many hateful gay slurs, the fact that they were only muttered by the most villainous characters makes me hopeful that this progressive movie with great characterization changed the attitudes of some viewers for the better.

Genuinely caring for most of the characters makes the last act a thrilling rollercoaster of emotions (where Ted Nicolaou gets to really show off his editing chops) since each stab, slice, swallow of poisoned milk, and drowning attempt hits so hard while we pray for catharsis. It was a surprising entry on England's Video Nasties List since none of the violence feels superfluous or even that gratuitous, but then again, it's fun to imagine ultra-conservative "monarchs" having their goofy ceremonial wigs fall off in shock after being subjected to the severing of a hand, condemnation of religious zealots, and incestuous overtones all in the same scene.

As a bonus incentive to see this underrated slasher, I'll leave it a secret which actor (who was equally beloved inside the horror genre and outside of it) plays Billy's nemesis on the basketball court—you might not even notice in the opening credits since he went by his real name in his earliest roles.

Intruder (1989)

Director: Scott Spiegel
Writers: Scott Spiegel, Lawrence Bender
Cast: Elizabeth Cox, Renee Estevez, Dan Hicks, David Byrnes, Sam Raimi, Eugene Glazer

With an atmospheric title sequence in which dark clouds pass over a full moon while your favorite Spooky Sounds for Halloween CD plays, it's easy to expect *Intruder* to be a hard-hitting, no-nonsense fright fest, when in all actuality it probably deserved a score more in line with "Fall Break" from *The Mutilator*. It's a goofy and outrageously bloody slasher that is so overflowing with bombastic energy and creative camerawork that it's no wonder writer-director Scott Spiegel is long-time friends with the Raimi Brothers and Bruce Campbell, all of whom were cast here in small roles.

It's almost closing time at Michigan's Walnut Lake Market and contrary to what the used car salesman in *Psycho* believed, it's actually the last customer of the day that proves to be the most trouble when a cashier's recently paroled ex-boyfriend storms in and demands to know why his calls haven't been returned. A scuffle breaks out and even though this man had no trouble beating up practically the entire staff at once before absconding, the store manager instructs everyone to split up in order to apprehend him. At first, the employees are simply strangled or bludgeoned with hammers, but then the killer ups the ante by incorporating some of the supermarket's specialty items like meat slicers and trash compactors, allowing a youthful group of makeup effect artists (including maestros such as Greg Nicotero, Howard Berger, and Robert Kurtzman) to show off the kind of skills that will keep them all in high demand for decades.

Filmed at an empty supermarket stocked with defective merchandise, *Intruder* might not be the first movie that shows you an eyeball in a jar of olives but it is most definitely the first one to use a magazine cover of Sting (musician, not wrestler) for a jump scare, and while most of its ilk depended on sex and ample bosoms, here we are titillated by an aisle of 80's cereal boxes. Other tasty treats include an attic where employees can smoke wacky tobaccy, a cameo from *Three Stooges* regular Emil Sitka, and a mighty-fine twist that keeps the third act running along vigorously.

Intruder was the victim of one idiotic decision after another from Paramount Pictures and its distributors, the most egregious being the removal of most of the gore. Further massacring occurred when the original title, The Night Crew, was replaced with something far more generic. And not only did the VHS cover give away a major plot point, but much like how *Trick or Treat* featured Ozzy Osbourne and Gene Simmons on its DVD cover, here we were promised a starring performance by Bruce Campbell, who plays an incompetent police officer for only about 20 seconds. But thanks to Synapse Films, *Intruder* can now be enjoyed on Blu-ray in all of its uncut, face-ripping, eye-gouging glory.

If you want to be extra productive by following up your grocery shopping with a workout, then pair *Intruder* up with *Death Spa* for a fun and gratuitous 1989 horror double feature. Also making creative use out of a seemingly innocuous location, this movie takes place at the hippest health club in Los Angeles, and despite its state-of-the-art equipment, technology, and amenities, the guests still have to put up with steam room doors locking themselves, smoothie blenders aiming for the hand, diving boards collapsing at the worst times, loose shower panels drawing blood, weight machines making sure that the ulna is no longer connected to the humerus, and the vengeful spirit of the owner's wife interrupting their sexy Mardi Gras party. *Death Spa* is a fantastic-looking movie that earns an A in nudity, creative kills, and production values, and so I'm surprised it doesn't have a bigger following.

Neon Maniacs (1986)

Director: Joseph Mangine
Writer: Mark Patrick Carducci
Cast: Clyde Hayes, Leilani Sarelle, Donna Locke, Victor Brandt, David Muir, Marta Kober

You'll find yourself asking "what," "why," and "how" countless times throughout this nonsensical but highly entertaining film, starting with the opening narration where a man who is sadly not John Larroquette says, "When the world is ruled by violence and the soul of mankind fades…the children's paths shall be darkened by the shadows of the Neon Maniacs." With the way he was reciting the tagline, surely I wasn't the only one thinking that the last word would rhyme with "fades." The children's paths shall be darkened by a game of charades, perhaps.

In a park in the heart of San Francisco, popular high school student and birthday girl Natalie is chatting about boys with her friend inside a van while the rest of the group is outside, chugging cans of beer, making out, and playing Tommy Wiseau's version of football. Spoiling their fun is a motley crew of mutated monsters, all with very distinct appearances, looking like a cross between cenobites and the baddies from *Double Dragon*, who are efficient in chopping off body parts with their wide variety of weaponry. When Natalie is the only one still alive, they surround the van and pummel it until it would take a miracle for her to see another birthday, but she gets one in the form of a phenomenon that occurs in San Francisco only once every five years (on average): a thunderstorm. They vanish and leave a traumatized Natalie to be found and questioned by a skeptical police officer who wasn't able to find any trace of her supposedly mutilated friends.

The next couple of days are grueling for Natalie as she's coping with the shock while also being accosted by her friends' family members demanding answers regarding their disappearances. With her parents away on a lengthy vacation, she has nobody to confide in except Steven (Clyde Hayes), a sensitive and sympathetic classmate who has secretly fancied her for ages, and who I immediately took a liking to since he closely resembles Todd Pettengill from WWE's New Generation Era). Sparks fly but the Neon Maniacs are just as motivated to ruin their first date as they were her birthday, surprising the lovebirds at a BART station to begin a thrilling public transportation chase sequence, and then taking the action to their high school's annual Halloween "Battle of the Bands" party.

The fact that they are seemingly impervious to everything but water, yet choose to reside underneath the Golden Gate Bridge is one of many charmingly idiotic mysteries, and the film is better for not even trying to offer any tiresome, convoluted explanations—let's hope that the scenes that couldn't be filmed due to budgetary constraints were all lengthy scientific monologues and not adrenaline-pumping attacks at the California Academy of Sciences! It's best to just turn your brain off and suffuse your soul with the sights of super-cool looking mutants stalking 1986 Bay City teenagers, some of whom possess thick Brooklyn accents.

Slumber Party Massacre II (1987)
Writer and Director: Deborah Brock
Cast: Crystal Bernard, Kimberly McArthur, Juliette Cummins, Heidi Kozak, Joel Hoffman

This was a hard day to get through because not only was I running on just four hours of sleep, but vivid images of men, women, and children suffering through a nuclear holocaust were still burned in my brain due to having watched the grueling post-apoc-

Poster for *Neon Maniacs* (1986), Anchor Bay Entertainment, Castle Hill Productions, Bedford Entertainment

alyptic nightmare that is *Threads* (1984) the night before. It's a film that takes no prisoners and leaves no viewer unscathed. Somebody with common sense probably would have suggested going to bed at a decent hour, taking a walk in the park, yoga, meditation, or therapy to get me out of this funk, but I figured the best medicine after getting home from work today would be a brew of hot apple cider, whisky, a cinnamon stick, and a drizzle of honey to go along with a different movie, one that I had the fondest memories of watching for the first time five years ago. The prescription was an immediate success so now I'm going to start recommending it to everyone I see doing the sad Charlie Brown walk (likely precipitated by *Threads*).

Even if you've never seen the original *Slumber Party Massacre*, it doesn't take long to figure out that Courtney has been suffering from post-traumatic stress disorder ever since a homicidal maniac targeted her and her older sister Valerie, who also survived but had to be institutionalized. Courtney regularly suffers from debilitating, fog-filled nightmares about a 50's rockabilly psycho stalking her, but hopes that spending a weekend with her bandmates and her heartthrob, Matt, will bring some much-needed happiness. Based on the provocative videocassette cover that my eyes darted to about a hundred times at Video Update, I was always under the impression that *Slumber Party Massacre II* was going to be a sleazy, misogynistic exploitation slasher and nothing more, but it ended up being a movie full of surprises, and perhaps the most refreshing one was just how likeable and charismatic Courtney (future *Wings* star Crystal Bernard) and her bandmates are—they're played by *Playboy*'s "Playmate of the Month" Kimberly McArthur, Heidi Kozak (who I always liked from *Mama's Family* and *Society*), and Juliette Cummins (an expert in getting topless and slaughtered in movies like *Friday the 13th: A New Beginning* and *Psycho III*). In addition to band practice (in which they actually sound great), they spend their time raiding the liquor and snack cabinets, spilling champagne on the carpet and each other, getting into feather-freeing pillow fights, and watching *Rock 'n' Roll High School*, an ironic choice seeing as how four years later, writer-director Deborah Brock would make *Rock 'n' Roll High School Forever* with Corey Feldman taking over for The Ramones.

Nightmares and hallucinations derail Courtney's weekend of fun, and eventually the poor girl can't even open a refrigerator without poultry coming to life and giving her a fright. But even scarier than an *Eraserhead* chicken is when the man from her dreams, with the sunglasses, slicked-back hair, and black leather jacket, emerges in the flesh, brandishing an electric guitar with a drill bit attached. This is not only the coolest-looking weapon in an 80's slasher film but it lends itself to irresistible music numbers as he rocks out and drills in. This movie is pure cheesy fun and I loved every second of it.

In addition to channeling Freddy Krueger with the dream demon driller killer, *Slumber Party Massacre II* also pays tribute to horror icons by giving its characters names like Courtney Bates, Officer Krueger, Officer Vorhees, and Mr. and Mrs. Craven. Another character is named Matt Arbicost, and it makes me wonder in a pre-IMDb world if they meant to name him Matt Arbogast to pay tribute to one of *Psycho*'s unsung heroes (seriously, the scene when Martin Balsam interrogates Norman should be just as famous as the shower murder). Without such resources like the IMDb, I'd still be certain that the actress playing Courtney's mom was the ice cream sample abuser in the hilarious *Curb Your Enthusiasm* episode "The Ida Funkhouser Roadside Memorial," when in fact, she portrayed another character that brought me immense joy: the heroic, nunchucking, holy water super-soaking Sister Gloria in *Night of the Demons 2*!

Horror Galore

Stagefright (1987)

Director: Michele Soavi
Writers: George Eastman, Sheila Goldberg
Cast: Barbara Cupisti, David Brandon, Robert Gligorov, Giovanni Lombardo Radice

After working as the Second Unit Director on popular Italian horror films such as *Demons*, *Opera*, and *Phenomena*, Michele Soavi was ready to make a film of his own that would stand alongside the greats from his mentors Dario Argento and Lamberto Bava. *Stagefright*, not to be confused with the 2014 horror-musical co-starring Meat Loaf, ended up being the perfect union of gratuitous '80s slashers and Italian giallo aesthetics, and maybe one of these days I'll use my time machine to travel back to its world premiere so I can pump my fists in the air during the ending credits and then present the new director with bouquets of flowers and chants of an encore.

Three nights before the premiere of their musical *The Night Owl*, a stressed-out independent theater group rehearses an elaborate dance sequence in which the spirit of a murdered prostitute rapes her killer, all while a black cat named Lucifer prances across the stage and seemingly brings bad luck to everyone involved. Leading lady Alicia disobeys her tyrannical director Peter by leaving the rehearsal so that a doctor can look at her injured ankle, and since stagehand Betty believes that all doctors are the same, they go to a mental hospital. One of its inmates is Irving Wallace, an actor known less for his performances and more for chopping up 16 people in little pieces. Desperate for a way to get back on the stage, he stabs an attendant with a syringe before sneaking into Betty's car, which looks brand new thanks to a rainfall stronger than any carwash.

With law enforcement and the media on the scene, Peter decides to capitalize on the sensational attention their production will soon be getting by signaling to his traumatized troupe that the show must go on, with increased salaries and a few changes to the script that focuses on life imitating art. Two policemen are stationed outside the theater in case the escaped psychopath decides to return, unaware that he's already inside and familiarizing himself with the set shop's many instruments of destruction like butcher knives, power drills, and chainsaws. I had only seen this movie once, many years ago, but I vividly remembered the creepy owl mask, lurid colors, Simon Boswell's music that sounds like an amalgamation of Goblin, Tangerine Dream, and John Carpenter, and the way it understood how so much slashing will make a person tired and in need of a timeout, resulting in that breathtaking shot of the killer sharing the stage with his paraded victims as feathers shower them all from above. For some odd reason the carnage didn't stick with me as much, and so I got to ooh and aah at every stylish and agonizing kill like I surely did with my first viewing. I don't think I'll be forgetting them a second time.

A maniac wearing an owl mask and wielding a chainsaw is about as good as it gets with horror villainy, and thankfully the people running from him are also pretty entertaining. David Brandon as the director responsible for locking his actors inside without knowing the key's whereabouts will be a lot of fun for anyone who appreciated Dick Tremayne's sanctimonious, fancy-lad tendencies in *Twin Peaks*, and the fact that he correctly said "couldn't care less" made him the automatic hero to me. Soavi, who even appears here as a police officer proud of his semi-resemblance to James Dean, went onto direct other genre pleasers like *Cemetery Man* and *The Church* (sometimes referred to as *Demons 3* despite having no similarities to the two previous films), as well as a recent family comedy that will surely be part of this year's yuletide festivities based on the enticing title: *The Legend of the Christmas Witch*.

WEREWOLVES AND WEIRD WOLVES

Bad Moon (1996)

Director: Eric Red
Writers: Eric Red, Wayne Smith (novel)
Cast: Mariel Hemingway, Michael Paré, Mason Gamble, Ken Pogue, Hrothgar Mathews

I vividly remember renting *Bad Moon* when it hit Blockbuster Video's New Releases shelves in 1997 because of that irresistible VHS cover, but what happened afterwards is all a blur. Either I neglected to watch it before the due date, fell asleep halfway through and never finished, or simply didn't give it a fair chance. I'm thankful for Shout Factory and Shudder for keeping this underappreciated beast alive and making me realize that I was wrong to neglect it 23 years ago because it's actually a pretty terrific lycanthrope tale.

A photographer named Ted parks his RV at a Pacific Northwest lake and surprises his sister Janet (Mariel Hemingway) with a phone call and an invitation. She and her young son Brett (Mason Gamble just three years after his debut as Dennis the Menace) arrive shortly after and at no time in the conversation does Ted mention his gnarly shoulder gash or the fact that he recently witnessed his girlfriend being torn to shreds by a werewolf in Nepal before shooting its head off with a shotgun. The family reunion does wonders for his mental state and he agrees to bring his trailer to Janet's home for more time together. Everyone seems

Poster for *Bad Moon* (1996), Morgan Creek Entertainment

happy with the arrangement except for Thor, the family's loyal and protective German shepherd, who immediately senses that something is seriously off about Uncle Teddy and his peculiar new habit of handcuffing himself to trees late at night.

Bad Moon was based on the novel *Thor* by Wayne Smith, and while it deviates from the storytelling mostly coming from the dog's point-of-view, writer-director Eric Red (who first ingratiated himself to the horror community by penning *The Hitcher* and *Near Dark*) knew that it was paramount to find just the right canine. Three different German shepherds were used to portray Thor, but most of the work was done by Primo, making his film debut. It's honestly the greatest animal performance I can recall due to how expressive and versatile he was—the scenes in which he has stare downs with Michael Paré are just as thrilling as when the massive werewolf (expertly designed by special effects master Steve Johnson) is ripping throats out and tossing humans around like snowballs.

One of my favorite scenes not involving Thor comes when Uncle Ted is watching *Werewolf of London* (1935) and finding it hilarious, much to the chagrin of his nephew who proclaims "It's not funny! He's turning into the wolfman!" I love how this reverses the norm of older audiences being the ones to grit their teeth when youngsters show irreverence to the classics, usually at late-night theatrical retro screenings. They have an interesting conversation about werewolf myths in the movies and why it's always a full moon and a silver bullet when, according to Ted, any moon and bullet will do the trick.

This is also the first film in years to make me cry, and according to Eric Red's commentary on the Blu-ray, it was difficult to find a dry eye at screenings during that particular scene. And just thinking about it now, I'm feeling so verklempt that I cannot even give you a topic to discuss.

Ginger Snaps 2: Unleashed (2004)

Director: Brett Sullivan
Writer: Megan Martin
Cast: Emily Perkins, Brendan Fletcher, Tatiana Maslany, Susan Adam, Katharine Isabelle

The original *Ginger Snaps* earned about a nickel and a hot cup of jack squat at the box office in its native Canada and in the States, but it fared much better in video stores and satisfied the craving of those seeking a stylish and thrilling werewolf film in the new millennium. As its reputation continued to grow with glowing reviews and a hyperactive IMDb message board, two sequels were greenlit and filmed back-to-back, and why it took me so long to give them both a chance I'll never understand considering how much I enjoyed the original. Rather than simply cashing in on the original's sudden popularity by rehashing the same parables, high school settings, and lycanthropy-puberty symbolism, both sequels have interesting stories to tell and exist on a world of their own.

Emily Perkins, who shined throughout the original as Brigitte but essentially played second fiddle to Katharine Isabelle, takes center stage in part two. While checking out books at the library with arms heavily scarred and a face seemingly incapable of a sincere smile, it's no surprise to the young, male librarian that she's interested in topics like bloodletting instead of *Eat Pray Love*. Smitten enough to break protocol, he delivers the book she left on the counter to her home, but finds Brigitte overdosing with a needle in her arm—an even scarier visual appears just seconds later when a werewolf gruesomely interrupts the drive to the hospital by tearing him to shreds.

She wakes up the next morning inside a rehab facility, and the staff is surprised to learn that the drug she's been injecting is not heroine, but the poisonous perennial herb wolfsbane. After failing to escape or confiscate the only drug that can downplay her metamorphosis, Brigitte relies on body mutilation to temper the cravings and disguise the initial physical transformations like elongated ears and hairy palms, but is then forced to depend on a staff member who trades sexual favors for drugs in an abandoned section of the facility, where an old crematorium collects dust.

With visions of Ginger forecasting the inevitable and a male werewolf with the hots for her lurking outside, Brigitte understands that her time is running out. Willing to help her escape is an eccentric, borderline autistic teenager nicknamed Ghost, who has been looking after her severely-burned grandmother inside the clinic, and who takes a liking to Brigitte because of her similarities to characters straight out of her favorite comic books. So off they go to grandmother's house, where charred walls clash with Christmas decorations, for an exciting, blood-soaked finale that keeps us guessing until the shocking final shot. Kudos to first-time screenwriter Megan Martin for the creative ways in which she dispels mythos and adds mystery to this most unusual friendship.

Much like the original, *Ginger Snaps 2* goes to some very dark places but offers levity with humor that comes out of nowhere but feels right at home. The biggest laugh in the room came during a group therapy session in which Brigitte describes her best-case scenario in graphic and hopelessly bleak detail, and after her painful monologue, we get a glimpse of what the counselor wrote on her notepad: "Brigitte: <u>lesbian</u>?"

Snarling wolf teeth resting a mere inch away from a very nervous character's face, an unorthodox scarecrow named Polly Ester, and a real-life abandoned mental hospital make for some deeply unsettling visuals in a movie that looks fantastic in every shot, especially ones that capture the fairytale majesty and frostbitten peril of Christmasy Calgary landscapes.

Good Manners (2017)
Writers and Directors: Marco Dutra, Juliana Rojas
Cast: Isabél Zuaa, Marjorie Estiano, Miguel Lobo, Cida Moreira, Andrea Marquee

Making its world premiere and picking up the Special Jury Prize in Switzerland at the 70th Annual Locarno International Film Festival, this enthralling horror-fantasy is unlike any werewolf movie you've ever seen. It's split into two distinct halves, one centering around the love between two women and the other between a mother and her son, with each exploring duality like rich and poor, white and black, human and monster, etc. Down on her luck but too proud to let it show, Clara shows up at a lavish apartment equipped with a remote control fireplace and picturesque city view to be interviewed for a nanny position, and while she lacks both experience and references, her nurturing instincts spring into action when the pregnant and alone Ana experiences sudden stomach pains, and is hired to not only take care of the baby once it's born, but also Ana in the meantime.

Their relationship seems awkward at first due to their differences in status, backgrounds, personality (evidenced by how Ana looks like the happiest woman in the world when doing her Zumba exercises while Clara seemingly hasn't smiled in years), and tolerance for bloody meat, and only gets more complicated with scary sleepwalking episodes and romantic rendezvouses. On her 29th birthday, Ana, in a cocktail dress and without a single message on her phone, defies medical advice and treats herself to a beer before confessing to Clara how the pregnancy was from a one-night stand with someone other than her then-fiancé, resulting in online vilification, family excommunication, and also a fetus destined to be born when the moon is full.

The second half of the film picks up when the boy, named Joel, is seven years old and asking the tough questions pertaining to his father, his restrictive diet, and his second bedroom that comes equipped with heavy-duty chains and handcuffs. Once a concerned landlady gives the protein-deficient and overly-protected boy his first bite of meat, his behavior changes, and after school the next day, he decides that rather than returning home, he'll hop on a bus with his best friend and go to the shopping mall on the other side of the river. The boys end up evading a security guard questioning the whereabouts of their guardian and hide long enough to emerge to a completely-closed shipping mall, a scenario that will have fans of *Dawn of the Dead* celebrating as if their favorite hockey team just won a crucial game in the playoffs in double overtime. And rather than high-capacity machine guns, all these boys have to protect themselves is a cardboard sword used in rehearsals for an upcoming school play. With the full moon shining through the skylights of the food court, Joel repeatedly insists that they go home immediately, his voice deepening and his teeth sharpening with each desperate plea.

Marco Dutra and Juliana Rojas (previously collaborating with 2011's *Hard Labor*) exhibit so much confidence with *Good Manners* that they even include a couple well-crafted musical numbers. No, the characters don't break out joyously into song and dance for no reason, but rather, a vagrant simply adds context to the story by mournfully singing her observances as Clara passes her on an impoverished street. Another creative curveball was thrown when Ana recounts the night she entered a cowboy-themed bar and wound up naked in someone else's car. Rather than the standard flashback, here we get an interlude of beautifully-drawn pictures, which, when combined with the breathtaking matte paintings that serve as backdrops in key scenes, give this movie such a fanciful Disney quality. Other reasons this movie rules: a sandwich vs salad lunch break comparison that reminded me of *Microwave Massacre*, confirmation that the Portuguese language has a translation for "chillax," a nighttime fair scene with impressive fireworks, a handsome orange tabby named Teobalda, a horse musical box that plays a lovely melody (written for the film), just about the best-looking baby werewolf imaginable, and did I mention the handsome orange tabby named Teobalda?

Howl (2015)

Director: Paul Hyett
Writers: Mark Huckerby, Nick Ostler
Cast: Elliot Cowan, Rosie Day, Calvin A. Dean, Sam Gittens, Shauna Macdonald

After spending a weekend uncovering some of the lesser-known werewolf offerings from the past five years, I would anoint this British indie as one of the clear leaders of the pack, mostly due to its nighttime train setting. Had I died 24 hours ago, *Night Train to Terror* would have been my last train-based horror movie in this life, and that would have been unfortunate.

A train guard and ticket collector named Joe is having a miserable night because after getting passed up for a promotion as well as a first date, he is assigned to work an overnight shift on a train departing London for the middle of nowhere. Having Joe navigate from carriage to carriage to check for proof of purchase is an excellent way of introducing our cast of characters (many of whom are tired and grumpy) as the rain pounding against the windows foretells dangerous turns up ahead. The train collides with something big and comes to a stop, putting everyone in a state of uncertainty for several minutes as the conductor mysteriously goes missing and Joe fails to communicate with the outside world due to a severed antenna. His desire to do everything by the book to protect everyone on board is undermined by multiple passengers insisting they be let outside to finish their journey by foot.

Footsteps on gravel, low rumbles of thunder, and light rain provide an eerie soundtrack to everyone leaving the safety of the train for a mist-shrouded, full moon-lit forest, but the sounds that raise their blood pressure the most are the strange howls that seem to be getting closer and closer.

The title may be lazy but the designing of these glowy-eyed werewolves and the nasty bites they leave sure weren't! It helps when your director has such an extensive background in special makeup effects, and worked on making sure those bat creatures in *The Descent* were some of the fiercest nightmare fuel in horror history. That movie's star, Shauna Macdonald, plays one of the more stressed-out travelers here, and it's lovely to see her again despite not getting enough screen time. In one of the few moments the film detours from its serious, suspenseful tone, she helps inform a man who's been preoccupied in the lavatory of all of the horrific happenings, and the way he reacts gave me the biggest laugh I've had all month.

Monster Dog (1984)

Director: Claudio Fragasso
Writers: Claudio Fragasso, Rossella Drudi
Cast: Alice Cooper, Victoria Vera, Carlos Santurio, Pepa Sarsa, Pepita James, Emilio Linder

The title *Monster Dog* probably came in post-production to take advantage of *Cujo*'s recent popularity, but unlike Claudio Fragasso's troll-less *Troll 2*, you can't really decry false advertising here because several different hounds get ample screen time. While they do look approachable most of the time, there are scenes when they snarl, growl, chase, and absolutely shred humans until they are bloody pulps, which qualifies as monstrous behavior in my opinion, but the real monsters come in the form of werewolves and grizzly gun-toting hicks straight out of spaghetti westerns.

Four years before appearing in John Carpenter's *Prince of Darkness* in a role so small you need to click on "See full cast" on its IMDb page to see it listed, Alice Cooper took the starring role in this wild and crazy Spanish horror film to try something new after being dropped by his record label. You would think the studio would want to take full advantage of having such a legendary rock star, attempting a new life of sobriety, as the lead in their low-budgeted horror film, but instead they bafflingly dubbed over all of his lines with a different actor. What in the holy hell? At least those line readings weren't a complete train wreck like some of the other character dubbings, chock-full of unnatural halts, improper emphasizing, and laughably unconvincing emotions.

The only time we get to hear Alice Cooper's real voice is during the two music video segments for songs he wrote specifically for the film, the first of which reminded me of Garfield's "What Can I Be?" routine from *Garfield's Halloween Adventure* since he tries on many costumes and sings about how he can be Sherlock Holmes, Jack the Ripper, James Bond, and Billy the Kid. His character, Vince Raven, is also a larger-than-life rock star, en route to his childhood home that he hasn't seen in two decades. Believing it to be the perfect place to shoot a new music video, he brings along a young production crew, all with such minimal character development that I don't remember anything about them despite just finishing the movie 20 minutes ago. Making a much stronger impression is the look of this town in the nighttime, steeped in so much fog that the dry ice budget must have equaled Cooper's salary. Add in the aggressive wind, all the warnings from police officers, and a delirious old harbinger of doom regarding mysterious dog attacks, and you have a highly effective horror setting for the characters to idiotically split up and become encircled by a chorus of howls, meaning a fang or claw could penetrate the fog at any given second. The story is senseless and the dialogue laughable, but the film is competently directed and at times genuinely creepy.

Vince Raven and company arrive at the mansion and find a welcome sign and a plate full of the kind of sandwiches that Nigel from Spinal Tap would curiously keep folding, but no sign of the caretaker. Later that night, after one of the girls has the kind of nightmare that more than justifies waking everyone up to incessant screaming, Vince reveals to another friend the tragic childhood story of what happened to his father after a vigilante mob blamed his rumored lycanthropy curse for a string of gruesome murders, and wonders if it was a good idea to return to his hometown that clearly still dreads sundown.

Monster Dog is a rocking good time with strong atmosphere and music, fist-pumping moments of catharsis (especially during a gunshot scalping), and charismatic dogs whose real names were disgracefully omitted from the ending credits. It was also a pleasure to find another Claudio Fragasso movie where characters mention how it's nighttime even while they're practically squinting from excessive sunshine.

SECOND GUESSING YOUR UPCOMING TRIP TO AUSTRALIA

Long Weekend (1978)
Director: Colin Eggleston
Writer: Everett De Roche
Cast: John Hargreaves, Briony Behets, Mike McEwen

Now here is a movie that will be of great comfort to single people because experiencing a volatile relationship that's hanging on by a thread is far more unpleasant than spending a Friday night alone in sweatpants, eating almonds and drinking Coconut rum and Coke Zero, and scribbling down notes while watching a 70's Ozploitation nature vs human psychological thriller at an excessive volume since you don't have subtitles and are struggling at times with the thick Australian accents.

Resentment and rage are rife in Peter and Marcia's relationship but they're hopeful that a weekend away from suburbia will bring them close together once again. The trip gets off to a miserable start with the car ride from hell, in which Marcia—upset that they're going camping on Phillip Island instead of staying in a nice luxury hotel—is breaking the world's record for longest scowl. She also leaps down Peter's throat at every opportunity, complaining about the rain, how he's not completely sure where the beach is, and how they've just run over a kangaroo.

A brief reconciliation occurs in the light of morning because it's hard to stay in a rotten mood when you're lounging on a beautiful and secluded beach under the sun, but the toxicity rolls in with the tide. He wants to swim, surf, and indulge in demonstrations of masculinity by shooting his rifle and chopping down trees while all his wife does is sulk and read steamy romance novels, repeatedly reminding him that she's not the outdoorsy type. It was supposed to be a romantic weekend together but she packed her vibrator and he, his Playboys. Their complexities and flaws cause our allegiances to shift throughout this movie, written by Everett De Roche, who would go onto pen *Road Games*, *Razorback*, and *Patrick*. For example, I despised Peter immediately because he jumped into his convertible rather than opening the door, a sin in my book unless you're one of the two Coreys, but when he at least made attempts at amiable small talk during the long drive and she could only bicker and stare at him contemptuously while he read his map, I was squarely on Team Peter for a while.

When he shoots to death a dugong, a slow-moving marine mammal related to the Steller's sea cow that was hunted to extinction in the 1700s, Mother Nature deems this the last straw and wages war on the couple who would seemingly rather die than work together. While we don't get attacks from the more typical Australian terrors like sharks and snakes, atypical offenders like eagles and possums are more than ready for their close-ups. In between these unexpected attacks, Peter and Marcia are haunted by the wailing cries of what they expect might be the dugong's children and also by their true feelings which had been bubbling below the surface. Instead of being entwined in each other's arms, they soon find themselves entwined in a labyrinthine forest filled with creepy crawlies and an abandoned tea party (!), and the results are just riveting. Also, there aren't many horror films out there that devote shots to koala bears, wallabies, ducklings, and pelicans. Army ants get plenty of screen time too, and while the presentation isn't on the visually mesmerizing levels of the underrated masterpiece *Phase IV*, they will get your skin itching nonetheless.

Next of Kin (1982)

Director: Tony Williams
Writers: Michael Heath, Tony Williams
Cast: Jacki Kerin, John Jarratt, Alex Scott, Gerda Nicolson, Charles McCallum

In the summer before my junior year of high school, I started working at Video Update, and on my first day, my manager gave me a roll of paper towels and a bottle of cleaning solution for the alleged newbie tradition of making all of the shelves sparkle. Given the layout of the store, it made little sense logistically to start with the horror section, but it also made little sense to ignore the gravitational pull that's existed ever since my earliest video store days. It was nice to become formally introduced to each videotape even with the clouds of dust, and one of the covers I remember being intrigued by was for *Next of Kin*, where a bloody arm reaches down from an apocalyptic red sky to a silhouetted manor. For some idiotic reason I never took it home with me after a shift, and for years I had forgotten all about it, but then I heard that Quentin Tarantino referred to it in an interview as one of his three favorite movies from Australia, stating that it contained the same "mesmerizing tone of dread" found in *The Shining*. It's hard to imagine a more complimentary comparison, and so I went to a video store that, unlike Video Update, is still alive and well, and picked it up in the "Dysfunctional Families" rows of Movie Madness' incredible horror section.

After spending the past few years in a university, Linda returns home when her mother passes away and bequeaths the entire estate to her. It's a large property that's been converted into a retirement home, and when Linda starts reading her mother's many diaries, she begins to wonder if there's something sinister lurking within the walls or trying desperately to get in. During a storm, she reads a page in which her mom wasn't able to sleep a wink because somebody was wandering around the house, and then she looks out the window just as a lightning bolt illuminates a strange figure lurking outside in the rain. Maybe it was one of the Wet Bandits because the next day she finds that one of the bathrooms is flooding due to plugged drains.

Next of Kin was originally intended to be the kind of darkly comedic slasher that was all the rage in the States, but director Tony Williams instead molded it into a more sophisticated thriller with a highly European feel, and despite the script leaving plenty to be desired, he and cinematographer Gary Hansen (who was tragically killed in a helicopter crash shortly after production) crafted a movie that you simply cannot take your eyes off of. Using an ambitious arsenal of overhead cranes, steady cams, dolly shots, slow-motion, dreamlike imagery, and juxtapositions, their inspirations were presumably Hitchcock, Kubrick, and Giallo giants like Argento and Bava.

In addition to looking incredible, this movie is also quite frightening, with psychological horrors wrapped up tightly in an impeccably detailed house that you wouldn't want to tip-toe through late at night. It has high ceilings that cast eerie echoes with every cat's meow and startling grandfather clock chime, a dizzying spiral staircase, and rooms occupied with senile souls knocking on death's door. It swings for the fences with early daytime scares (one in particular spooked me so badly that I literally shouted "Oh my God!") and so I became a nervous wreck when nighttime came and the electricity went out in the nursing home. There are also some soothing respites, such as when Linda reconnects with her charming ex-boyfriend (played by "Double J" John J-a-double r-a-double t) with a field frolic, cemetery stroll, and pond dip, all set to proggy electronic music from ex-Tangerine Dream member Klaus Schulze. Not as successful are the scenes where Linda, rapidly losing her marbles, researches old medical records to solve the mystery regarding her supposedly deceased aunt, but the terror returns in a climax that is so satisfying, it even manages to make sugar cubes unsettling.

After its initial festival screenings, *Next of Kin* lived a very unappreciated life until Severin Films gave it a special edition DVD in 2019. Loaded with extras, it will tell you why Tony Williams left the industry for decades, how some of the most creative shots were achieved (such as when Linda looks out the window to see a drowning man knocking on it), and what happened during an explosive stunt near the ending that caused an unlucky crew member to suffer a nervous breakdown.

Wake in Fright (1971)

Director: Ted Kotcheff
Writers: Evan Jones, Ted Kotcheff, Kenneth Cook (novel)
Cast: Gary Bond, Donald Pleasence, Chips Rafferty, Sylvia Kay, Jack Thompson, Peter Whittle

A slow pan across the sun-bleached landscapes of Tiboonda shows us everything that the dusty town has going for it. On one side of the train tracks is a single-room schoolhouse, where our discontent and understandably bored protagonist,

Poster for *Wake in Fright/Outback* (1971), NLT Productions, Group W Films

John Grant, teaches children of varying ages, and on the other, the air-conditionless hotel in which he is surely the only guest, and probably spending most of his earnings in its bar since there's nothing else to do in this godforsaken part of the world that he was sent to as part of Australia's education program for new teachers. With Christmas and Boxing Day approaching, John's holiday begins with a train ride where he's quickly offered a beer by a boisterous group of inebriated men pausing their singalong, and he'll be experiencing so much more of this aggressive hospitality in the city of Bundanyabba before he's to be reunited with his civilized and intellectual brethren in Sydney.

Horror Galore

Even late at night, it's so miserably hot in the 'Yabba, and John tries to alleviate the discomfort by joining the proud citizens in drinking beer at a staggeringly fast rate. He learns much about the town from its police officer, who asks, "How about another beer?" at every break in the conversation, and then waits for John to chug his mostly full glass. Among the customs are a nightly memorial for fallen veterans and a rowdy game of Two Up, in which the patrons gamble over how two tossed coins will land. Hoping that lady luck (the only lady that might appear in this establishment) will shine on him and give him enough money to get out of his teaching contract, John presses his luck again and again until he loses everything, an indicator that he's simply not cut out for life in the 'Yabba. He wakes up the next morning completely naked, hungover, drenched in sweat, and attracting flies in his dingy hotel room, and it's the most comfortable he'll be for the following few hellish days.

Not having any choice but to rely on the kindness of strangers, he is welcomed by a group of men whose typical day begins with waking up on the floor, clutching a can of West End beer from the previous night and finishing it off before breakfast, and even though it's not in his nature to sink to levels of degradation and abhorrent living conditions, he does his best to emulate their masculinity and be accepted. John Grant (played to perfection by the late British actor Gary Bond) can be somewhat unlikable at times, but he's an easy character to sympathize with. Pale, blonde, and educated, he is simply not suited to this brutal environment and every minute spent there is slowly eating away at his soul as he descends into madness. One of the men he begrudgingly befriends has acclimated to the vacuous lifestyle despite being a doctor of medicine, and is one of the only people in town who admits that the 'Yabba might not be the best place in Australia after all; he's played by Donald Pleasance and so if you ever wondered how Dr. Loomis would behave had he drank the entire flask of liquor that was offered to him while hitchhiking in *Halloween 4*, then this movie is for you.

Much like Tobe Hooper achieved with *The Texas Chainsaw Massacre*, the attention to detail here really maximizes the discomfort and makes you crave a shower afterwards. Kotcheff was insistent that all of the sets and wardrobes be shades of red, yellow, sienna, and orange to compliment the climate and make John feel even more trapped. This terrifying film was beloved by critics and warmly received at festivals, but its American distributor, United Artists, was lukewarm on its chances in the States. Not only did they change the title to the innocuous *Outback*, but they released it without any publicity whatsoever. The only place where it was successful was France but now decades later, it seems like the rest of the world is drinking the midnight oil in excess, giving it new life in the festival circuit. It even had the extremely rare re-screening at the Cannes Film Festival, largely thanks to one of its most passionate supporters, Martin Scorsese. *Wake in Fright*'s editor, Anthony Buckley, was also instrumental in its rebirth because he spent almost ten years trying to locate the negatives, which were eventually tracked down in a Pittsburgh warehouse—they had been languishing in several shipping containers labeled "For Destruction." With the celluloid saved just in the nick of the time, a painstaking restoration took place to make the movie look as good as the most golden of ales, and all horror fans need to drink it up!

I'd be remiss for not warning you about one particular scene that you may prefer to experience with your eyes closed since it involves the hunting of actual kangaroos. Kotcheff, a Canadian visiting the land down under for the first time, was a vegetarian who was appalled by the idea, but understood that it was integral to the plot and so he and his director of photography accompanied a group of local hunters on a nightly excursion.

Horror Galore

MUST BE THE SEASON OF THE WITCH AND WITCH HUNTERS

Il Demonio (1963)
Director: Brunello Rondi
Writers: Ugo Guerra, Luciano Martino, Brunello Rondi
Cast: Daliah Lavi, Frank Wolff, Anna Maria Aveta, Dario Dolci

Right around the time he was co-writing the Oscar-winning Fellini films *8 ½* and *La Dolce Vita*, Brunello Rondi was embarking on a directing career of his own, and one of his earliest works was just included on Severin's mammoth box set *All the Haunts be Ours: A Compendium of Folk Horror*.

The combination of black and white photography, mountainous landscapes, Italian baroque architecture, and forebodingly overcast skies paints an enticing world for our disturbed protagonist to wreak havoc in. When we first meet Purif, she's adding drops of her blood and strands of her dark, flowing hair to a special concoction intended for Antonio, the man she vows will be hers even though he's about to marry another woman, someone more respectable. When he eventually takes the bait, she doesn't even wait for him to swallow before laughing in his face and mockingly shouting, "With that wine you have drunk my blood! You have drunk my body and my substance. I have bewitched you! Now you will love me whether you want it or not, even if you're scared of me. Fear will make it worse. Bad luck will befall you. You will die! I have bewitched you!" Lucy Van Pelt being one of my favorite Peanuts characters probably made me appreciate these conniving, bratty outbursts from Purif, and the fact that she's so antagonistic and prone to laughably bad decision making prevents *Il Demonio* from becoming yet another sorrowful, unjust tale of a free-spirited young woman driven to the stake by an ancient community with their ancient religious beliefs.

Purif's family tries hard to protect her but despite dire warnings to stay away from Antonio, she still escapes to perform a ceremony on a cliff overlooking the church where another ceremony is taking place. Since this wedding mostly consists of people sitting in silence watching candles burn, it's easy for her to interrupt the proceedings with cries of "Antonio! Antonio!" and the baaa-baaaing from a herd of goats. She also attempts to thwart their honeymoon night, even after all the trouble the elders have gone through to cover the bed in dried grapes to absorb evil and to place a scythe underneath for protection against the devil.

When further discipline and religious interventions fail to cure Purif of her wicked ways, they arrange an exorcism. *Il Demonio* came out a decade before the scariest movie of all time, and being able to witness another freaky spider crawl, elongated and in a church no less, was just the kind of extra oomph to put this movie over the top.

Palestinian actress Daliah Lavi would later work with Mario Bava and on big productions like *Casino Royale*, but she has stated that *Il Demonio* was her finest movie, even though it left emotional and physical scars lasting for weeks. To give the most believable performance, she walked straight into barb wire with the fearlessness of Mick Foley and spent a day in a mental asylum to visit the possibly possessed woman who this story was based on.

Viy (1967)

Directors: Konstantin Ershov, Georgiy Kropachyov
Writers: Konstantin Ershov, Georgiy Kropachyov, Nikolay Gogol (story)
Cast: Leonid Kuravlyov, Natalya Varley, Aleksey Glazyrin, Nikolay Kutuzov

It's easy to be furious and disgusted with Mother Russia these days, but for all 77 minutes of watching its very first horror movie, you'll be feeling nothing but gratitude because it's such a magnificent sight to behold. Often cited as a precursor to *The Evil Dead* due to dizzying, maniacal camerawork and ingenious special effects, *Viy* exemplifies what pure talent behind the camera can pull of notwithstanding budgetary restraints. It opens with a speech from a monastery beacon to his monks about having a safe vacation and not getting into trouble. Khaliava the Theologian, Khoma the Philosopher, and Gorobety the Orator were clearly not paying attention because they immediately embark on a night of mischief before finding themselves lost in darkness where even the devil would lose his way.

The three young men stumble upon a farmhouse owned by an elderly woman who, after hearing their pleas on how it's unforgivable to let Christian souls perish into the night, allows them to enter under one condition: they must sleep in separate sections of the house. As Khoma, a goofy bastard with an unfortunate Lloyd Christmas hairstyle, is getting ready for bed, the old woman approaches him with arms outstretched and hypnotizes him so that she

Poster for *Viy* (1967), Artistic Association-Luch

can ride him into the night sky like a broom; it's not quite as heartwarming as the snowman and the little boy flying hand-in-hand though the Aurora Borealis in the Oscar-winning short film *The Snowman* (1982). Khoma later finds the strength to repeatedly bludgeon the witch, but stops and backs away in shock as she transforms into a young woman, crying out for help.

Back at the monastery, Khoma receives word from the beacon that a young woman is on her deathbed and has specifically requested for his presence in praying for her soul. Refusing to go will result in a public lashing but by performing the ritual, he will be rewarded handsomely by the girl's wealthy father. He takes his chances and returns to the farmhouse only to discover that the girl has passed away and that per tradition, he'll need to spend three consecutive nights locked inside her mausoleum (which casts such brilliant echoes that even the slightest of footsteps could wake the dead) to pray for her safe travels into Heaven. He tells nobody that he was responsible for her death but plants the seeds within the townspeople that her soul was possessed by witchcraft. On the first night, her body rises from the coffin but is unable to penetrate the chalk circle that Khoma drew for saintly protection.

With escape from the farmhouse futile and with the threat of a hundred flesh-ripping lashings, Khoma spends the following days drinking a seemingly endless supply of vodka and engaging with the equally sloshed townsfolk who occasionally break into song to pass the time, all while a restless night alone with a living corpse looms over his spinning head. The second night scares him so badly his hair changes to Leland Palmer white, but his faith remains intact and he believes that no demon can possibly harm him as long as he speaks the holy words and remains inside his chalk circle.

Anchored by a wonderful soundtrack that works wonders whether it's providing a mournful dirge or making the things that go bump in the night even more threatening, *Viy* wisely waits for the third night to lay all its cards on the table, and results in a monster mash of a climax (much like *The Cabin in the Woods*) that will warm your pumpkin-coated heart even more than a gallon of vodka could. *Viy* was loosely remade into the fantastical *Forbidden Kingdom* in 2014, a movie that has its fair share of appealing scenes, like when a flying coffin chases Homer around and when a decapitated head shouts instructions to its sightless body, but feels more connected to the *Pirates of the Caribbean* sequels with its flashy style, zany spirit, and unjustifiably long running time.

Witchfinder General (1968)

Director: Michael Reeves
Writers: Tom Baker, Michael Reeves, Louis M. Heyward
Cast: Vincent Price, Ian Ogilvy, Rupert Davies, Hilary Heath, Nicky Henson

Another holiday season has sadly come to an end. Not wanting to go out of my way to let the darkness of 2020 seep into the new year, I chose the delightful *Bon Voyage, Charlie Brown* as my first movie of 2021. With that whimsy and charm out of the way, it was time to go back to work and embrace the misery of inquisitions.

You would think that a 24-year-old director with only a couple features to his name would have jumped for joy upon learning that horror legend Vincent Price had been chosen to play the villain in his next movie, but instead, Michael Reeves was upset at this decision by distributor and co-producer American-International Pictures, believing that Price's string of hammy performances in his collaborations with Roger Corman would be detrimental to the hard-hitting *Witchfinder General*. He had his heart set on Donald Pleasence playing the role of Matthew Hopkins, who in real life was a British lawyer during the English Civil War travelling from town to town at the request of mental magistrates to brutally interrogate and execute citizens suspected of witchcraft. Reeves and Price clashed on set throughout the production but walked away with mutual respect for each other, with Price later stating in interviews that it was the finest role of his lengthy career.

Bereft of the campy style that he was known for at the time, his depiction of the superstitious witch-hunter is determined, sanctimonious, and effectively low-key, and even though we horror fans are unconditionally trained to love this man (the fact that he's from St. Louis gives me more hometown pride than anything else), we can't wait to see his character receive an almighty punch to the face from Parliamentarian soldier Richard Marshall. The sky was the limit for filmmaker Michael Reeves, making it all the more tragic that just nine months after *Witchfinder General*'s world premiere, he died of a drug overdose at age 25.

After saving the life of his captain (wearing a ridiculous helmet that makes him look like a purple rooster) and killing his first enemy soldier, Richard rides his horse to the home of his lover, Sara, whose uncle has given his blessing of marriage under one condition: that he take her away from their town that is in the midst of Satanic paranoia. After a brief rendezvous, he returns to his comrades but along the way, gives directions to two men who unbeknownst to him, have been hired to force a series of confessions in Sara's town by any means necessary.

With a mid-17th century English countryside setting and a fair amount of romance, war casualties, well-staged chase scenes, and equine clip clops, the sweeping soundtrack performed by a 55-piece orchestra is appropriately epic. I couldn't get enough of a particular score that was so beautiful, it was of no surprise to learn that composer Paul Ferris was inspired by the heavenly folk song "Greensleeves" when writing it. It really tugs at your heartstrings and also makes you totally unprepared for scenes where innocent people are drowned, burned, stabbed, beaten, hanged, raped, and imprisoned. *Witchfinder General* tested the limitations of many critics appalled by its gratuitous depravity and sadism, but like with so many other challenging pieces of cinema that were initially met with outrage, this suspenseful and engaging film stood the test of time and basks in the glory of reassessment. Just make sure your windows are closed because the amount of screaming that takes place could result in neighbors making false accusations about what in God's name you're up to.

CULTS ALMOST AS SCARY AS QANON

Apostle (2018)
Writer and Director: Gareth Evans
Cast: Dan Stevens, Michael Sheen, Mark Lewis Jones, Bill Milner, Kristine Froseth

Revisiting the bleak and savage world of *Apostle* wasn't something I was looking forward to for this project, but after suffering through five clunkers in a row and wanting to write about something this week, I decided to finally cross this one off the list. Right away I was feeling guilty about subjecting my girlfriend to such a nerve-frazzling, emotionally-exhausting suckerpunch on week four of quarantine with no end in sight, when perhaps something light and cheery like *Funny Farm* would be better for our mental health. She ended up liking it a lot and didn't seem the least bit traumatized, and so maybe it's time I introduce her to *The Texas Chainsaw Massacre* since it's one of the most gratifying endowments a horror fan can bestow.

It boggles the mind why *Apostle*, so epic in scale with its production designs and set decoration (kudos to Tom Pearce and Sue Jackson-Potter), didn't get theatrical distribution and a chance to become a horror juggernaut, but I suppose in this day and age, the next best thing is being picked up by the world's most successful streaming service. The reviews were fantastic, but there wasn't much word of mouth, making it easy for this gem to get lost in the shuffle of Netflix's sea of mostly underwhelming offerings; both the title and poster are powerful but easy to skip over because of how little they tell us. The long running time must have scared some people away but those who took a chance probably didn't glance at their phones or watches once. It's kind of incredible how writer-director Gareth Evans established such a mercilessly tense tone right from the opening scene and not once lifted his foot off the gas for 150 minutes. Known mostly for *The Raid* action series, he was also one of the two filmmakers responsible for the scariest segment of the *V/H/S/* series, "Safe Haven," and *Apostle* further demonstrates that very few things in the world are scarier than a cult.

Already skilled at depicting early 20th century hardships and tragedy with his stints as Matthew Crawley in *Downton Abbey*, actor Dan Stevens here plays a former missionary named Thomas who has lost favor with his wealthy family for abandoning the Lord for a bedraggled, godless junkie lifestyle. He learns that his sister has been kidnapped and that he must travel to a secluded island off the English coast to pay the ransom to the cult that stole her. Trying his best to mask the burning intensity in his eyes and blend in with the flock of converts on the raging seas, he makes it to the island and infiltrates the cult, and even though nobody seems to recognize him from the prayer meetings, he's accepted into the community by Prophet Malcolm (Michael Sheen), who promotes compassion and equality during his fervent sermons before slitting the throat of a suspected blasphemer.

Horror Galore

With the island's animals no longer breeding and crops no longer thriving, Malcolm and his two co-founders have been feuding over how to keep their paradise alive and their worshippers fed, a dilemma that Lord Summerisle from *The Wicker Man* could identify with. Thomas earns the trust of the prophets' sympathetic teenaged children who warn him not to pay the ransom if he wants to return home with his sister, and so after the nightly bell rings and everyone leaves the cozy pub in a drunken stupor to return to their weathered log cabins, he goes on a desperate search where each peek through a window reveals something that makes us increasingly terrified for him, especially thanks to an *Insidious*-style score that follows him every step of the way. And as unsettling as a nightly bloodletting is, that's nothing compared to what feasts on the drops that fall between the floorboards.

"The promise of the divine is but an illusion," Thomas tells Malcolm's daughter. "God is pain, God is suffering. Beware of false prophets that come to you in sheep's clothing but inwardly they are ravening wolves." He's about to learn that the wolves here bite even harder than the ones he experienced many years ago while trying to introduce Christianity to China during the Boxer Rebellion. Anyone who expected a typical Jonestown Massacre retelling was undoubtedly shaken to the core with *Apostle*'s nasty surprises, mean-spirited violence, and determination to make just about every other cult look like Sunday school in comparison. Even the hoods worn in sacrificial rites seem taller, sharper, and more menacing than any we've seen before.

Apostle didn't need to shed a drop of blood to be one of the scariest films in years, but it really goes for the jugular in the second half, showing carnage like deep wounds, eviscerations, stabbings, skull-drilling, body-stretching, hand-mangling, and mechanical cranium-squeezing. The island's children even take delight in prodding the kidnapped victim with sticks while their parents work on salvaging materials from shipwrecks. Some of the violence is upsetting, some cathartic, and each act hits so hard due to how invested we are in the story and its characters. I have now seen the light and will be open-minded to all Netflix-exclusive horror flicks going forward.

The Endless (2017)

Directors: Justin Benson, Aaron Moorhead
Writer: Justin Benson
Cast: Aaron Moorhead, Justin Benson, Callie Hernandez, Tate Ellington, Shane Brady

To follow up their well-reviewed romantic horror movie *Spring*, Justin Benson and Aaron Moorhead returned to the universe from their 2012 debut film, *Resolution*, and produced, wrote, directed, edited, shot, and starred in this slow-burning, low-budgeted science fiction-horror mindbender. The fact that they knocked it out of the park in all of their roles shows that they were blessed with a level of talent that is simply unfair.

They play brothers appropriately named Justin and Aaron, who receive a videotape in the mail that was made in Camp Arcadia, where they spent their childhoods as members of a cult. The woman speaks of the final ascension, leading the brothers to hypothesize that it's code for mass suicide. After escaping a decade ago and sharing unflattering stories to the media, their lives haven't been easy in the outside world. They are currently working as housecleaners and eating the cheapest kind of Ramen noodles for sustenance. Aaron is especially unhappy with his life and persuades his brother to return to Camp Arcadia for one day to reconnect with their former friends and get closure. To him it wasn't a cult but a loving commune that he misses terribly. Justin, on the other hand, believes it's a

UFO crackpot operation steeped in nefarious objectives but he's willing to return just for one day if it will pull his brother out of his funk.

They are welcomed back with open arms by the members—who haven't seemed to age a day in ten years—and assured that all is forgiven. It doesn't take long for us to understand why Aaron longed to return to this lifestyle of spending days with fishing, archery, painting, target shooting, and beer-brewing, and the nights with bonfires, karaoke, marijuana, magic tricks, and a ritual called The Struggle where you play tug-of-war with a rope ascending from the inexplicably double-mooned night sky. Opening with the H.P. Lovecraft quote "The oldest and strongest emotion of mankind is fear, and the oldest and strongest kind of fear is the unknown," the film takes its time revealing what makes Camp Arcadia such an otherworldly place and thankfully never overexplains. It is goosebump-inducing whenever characters go out on their own in the final act and journey to areas yet unexplored—often with the pleasing aural combination of gravel footsteps and crickets—because literally anything could be right around the corner. *The Endless*, which made its debut at the Tribeca Film Festival before being released to Netflix, is confusing for sure, but like some of the best work from David Lynch and Don Coscarelli, we just feel privileged to bask in such delightful weirdness and intoxicating auras.

Even without any knowledge of their first film, I still found *The Endless* to be a fulfilling masterpiece, but now that I'm updating this review a year later, I'm kinda wishing I had started with *Resolution*, which tells the story of the two men (played by Peter Cilella and Vinny Curran) living inside a broken-down house who appear to be trapped in a time loop. That movie opens with graphic designer, husband, and soon-to-be-father Michael driving to an Indian reservation where his best friend, Chris, has been squatting for the past year, unwilling to leave his miserable existence in squalor for a stint in rehab. Michael uses a taser and a pair of handcuffs to ensure that Chris goes an entire week without drugs in an attempt to save his life, but they strongly disagree on whether or not this life is even worth saving. In between deeply personal conversations on how their lives were destined to veer off in opposing trajectories, Michael discovers that they picked a terrible place for a week of detoxification with the introduction of strange locals, photographs, and the kind of videos that would make someone living a clean lifestyle understand what it's like to have drugs turn on you in the most horrifying of ways. While not really a horror film, the poignant and puzzling *Resolution* confirmed that whatever Justin Benson and Aaron Moorhead (whose appearances as a couple of polite and friendly prophets of the celestial Messiah add another fascinating connection between the two films) are selling, I'm buying!

Kill List (2011)

Director: Ben Wheatley
Writers: Ben Wheatley, Amy Jump
Cast: Neil Maskell, MyAnna Buring, Harry Simpson, Michael Smiley, Emma Fryer

With my head currently spinning like a top, it might be wise to process everything and get some zzz's before tackling this entry, but at the same time, I'm in no rush to go to bed with the trepidation of Mr. Sandman bringing a dream under the influence of Mr. Ben Wheatley.

Nominated for eight awards at the 2011 British Independent Film Awards, this expertly shot and acted genre-bending thriller received much attention in England but in the States, was only given the smallest of theatrical releases. It centers on a former British soldier named Jay who has been out-of-work for eight months after botching an unspecified assignment in Kiev, putting pressure on his marriage now that he and his Swedish wife no longer have the funds to repair their jacuzzi. One night over dinner, she criticizes the way he eats and he questions why in God's name she served the gravy in a "fucking Pyrex," leading to a shouting match for the ages that their young son has no choice but to suffer through. Even though he's reluctant to get back into the game, Jay accepts the high-paying proposal from his best friend, Gal, and all they need to do is murder three people.

With the first assassination, I couldn't help but be reminded of the Queensryche song "Suite Sister Mary," with the lyrics "The priest is cold and dead, on his knees he fed from my barrel of death, he turned the holy water red, as he died he said 'thank you,' I just watched him bleed." Jay goes off the deep end when it's revealed that the next person on their list is connected to child pornography and decides to ditch his shotgun for the much more agonizing hammer, much to the disapproval of Gal, who despite being a hitman, never loses his charming everyman quality. The first half of *Kill List* presents itself as a character-driven drama, the darkest of comedies, and a crime thriller in the vein of *In Bruges* and *Sexy Beast*, and even though I was loving the hell out of it, I was curious as to why Bloody Disgusting editor Brad Miska declared it the best horror movie of 2011. Well, I would find out once the third person on the list enters the fold and opens up an entirely new realm of darkness, turning this film into a ruthlessly suspenseful nightmare that will leave you in stunned silence as the credits roll.

When digging up these hidden gems, I've been actively scribbling down notes but I was so involved with *Kill List* that I dropped my pen after only three words: TURN SUBTITLES ON! For more Ben Wheatley horror and heavy accents, I recommend his 2021 movie *In the Earth*, written during lockdown and set in another pandemic. It's about a scientist who, with the help of a forest ranger, takes a nightmarish two-day trek through the forests to the government-controlled site where his ex-girlfriend has been obsessively conducting experiments on plants and trying to communicate with them. Those of you who enjoyed the trippy nature elements of his civil war oddity *A Field in England* will feel right at home in these woods, and those who didn't might be fighting back seizures during the impressive onslaughts of psychedelic cosmic horror energy.

The Spider Labyrinth (1988)

Director: Gianfranco Giagni
Writers: Riccardo Aragno, Tonino Cervi, Cesare Frugoni, Gianfranco Manfredi
Cast: Roland Wybenga, Paola Rinaldi, Margareta von Krauss, Claudia Muzii, Stephane Audran

Taking inspiration from giallos, creature features, and the H.P. Lovecraft's story "The Shadow Over Innsmouth," *The Spider Labyrinth* is an underseen Italian horror movie that delivers on both style and substance. Hollywood rightfully called the name of production designer Stefano Maria Ortolani, and she would go onto serve as the art director in *Gangs of New York*, *The Talented Mr. Ripley*, and *The Life Aquatic with Steve Zissou*.

After being jolted awake by a recurring nightmare recounting the time as a child when he found himself locked in a closet with a very large spider, Alan Whitmore is summoned to the office of his superiors. They are leading the secretive Intextus Project, and a researcher named Professor Roth who was sent to Budapest to gather critical information on a cult has suddenly ceased communication, so they need Alan, a linguistics specialist, to travel there to check in on him and bring back his research.

Alan, with a dubbed voice that doesn't match his face whatsoever but is still pleasant to the ears, arrives in Hungary and is greeted by Professor Roth's assistant Genevieve, whose legs he can't resist taking sneaking glances at while she drives him into town. At Professor Roth's residence, his wife warns Alan that he's recently suffered a complete nervous breakdown and may say some awfully peculiar things that aren't to be taken seriously, which softens the impact when the professor offers a few cryptic words before insisting that he return later that night without anyone else knowing. After settling into his room at the nearby inn and noticing in a cold sweat that he has a perfect view of Genevieve's bedroom, he grabs dinner and then returns to the professor's home while a lightning storm spooks the city. Law enforcement circles the property and takes him inside to where the professor hangs by a cobwebbed-covered noose, while Genevieve smokes a cigarette in shock.

Not heeding the warning of a concerned stranger who accosts him around the corner and says, "You have to escape this very night. You'll get sucked into the vortex and they won't let you go," Alan is quickly entangled in a web of hallucinations, paranoia, ancient secrets, uproariously misleading driving directions, and violent murders, and spinning from above is a Nosferatu-like creature with deadly saliva tendrils.

The cult's motives and magical powers are a whole lot of hocus pocus but thankfully *The Spider's Labyrinth* is more successful at creating an intoxicating atmosphere with moodily lit set pieces (including caves, tunnels, and the most gothic spa ever), a richly diverse soundtrack by Franco Piersanti, and dreamlike action scenes like when a character runs for her life into a maze of windblown white sheets. It even melds into shapeshifting body horror and climaxes with a grotesque creation that wouldn't have looked out of place in Brian Yuzna's highlight reel.

Horror Galore

HORROR IS A DISH BEST SERVED COLD

Grotesque (1988)
Director: Joe Tornatore
Writers: Mikel Angel, Joe Tornatore
Cast: Linda Blair, Tab Hunter, Donna Wilkes, Brad Wilson, Nels Van Patten, Guy Stockwell

Even though only two people are credited as writers, it's easy to imagine a crowded and chaotic writers' room where everybody was steadfast in honoring a different subgenre until the exhausted producer relented and agreed to make *Grotesque* a brutal home invasion thriller, a slasher with a monster chasing a group of youngsters, a police procedural drama, and a revenge-centered tragedy. And instead of one shocking twist, there are maybe four or five, each one more absurd than the last.

Your opinion of the movie will probably hinge on whether you criticize it for not having any clue what it wants to be or you praise its unrestrained, enthusiastic kitchen sink approach. And if you happen to be on the fence, then best friends played by Linda Blair and Donna Wilkes (*Jaws 2*, *Angel*) should be enough to turn that stubborn thumb of yours up! They're visiting Linda's parents when the lovely mountain cottage is seized by "a bunch of punkers" who are under the impression that the patriarch—who has made a good living as a makeup effects artist in Hollywood—has either a bunch of cash or a bunch of dope hidden somewhere in the house and they want it. They eventually uncover the

VHS cover for **Grotesque** (1988), United Filmmakers

secret room they were looking for but are shocked to find out what is actually inside.

Led by the bleached-mohawked Scratch, shouting all his lines like he's on angel dust, these are some of the most outrageously over-the-top punks you'll ever see. One of its members is even played by Robert Z'Dar, who had a very busy year with appearances in the cult classics *Maniac Cop* and *Samurai Cop*! It's just unfortunate that he's monosyllabic and given very little screen time, playing second fiddle to Gibbs, a character whose defining trait is cackling loudly after every single thing he says, which is especially irritating inside an echoey mine shaft.

Much of the soundtrack is disappointing, a girl not naming her doll because it's an orphan makes no sense, and a tedious scene where a posse searches for survivors in the woods cries out for an "Intermission" title card. But on the bright side, *Grotesque* features a character named Orville Krueger, an anachronistic Burger King product placement, and tons of thunder, lightning, *and* snow! It's one of a handful of films I vividly recall watching on *USA Saturday Nightmares* back in the late '80s, when I was probably a little too young to be watching the senseless terrorizing of a family inside their home. Certain moments are still powerful and upsetting to watch thirtysomething years later, despite the fact that the cartoonish punks, amusing good cop/bad cop parody, and berserk ending (which feels like it belongs at the end of a *Simpsons* "Treehouse of Horror" episode) confirms that it isn't meant to be taken that seriously. In fact, the ending was so confounding that some lame-o with no understanding that ghouls just wanna have fun had the audacity to remove it from certain versions.

Knuckleball (2018)

Director: Michael Peterson
Writers: Kevin Cockle, Michael Peterson
Cast: Luca Villacis, Michael Ironside, Munro Chambers, Kathleen Munroe, Chenier Hundal

With my post-Halloween depression now mingling dangerously with the pre-election anxiety that's been boiling for months, this first of November has been an odd day all around. Having to navigate a shopping cart around 50 other masked shoppers all seemingly determined to stand in my way in the busy produce section of Winco certainly didn't help my sanity, but what did help immensely was a combination of a mostly funny new Simpsons "Treehouse of Horror" episode and the taut 2018 thriller Knuckleball. With Samhain appearing smaller and smaller in the rearview mirror and a sad Corona Christmas up ahead, it felt appropriate to watch a movie that veers into Home Alone territory with just as much snow and a lot more blood.

Before a married couple leave town to attend a distant relative's funeral and also spend some much-needed alone time together (potentially making or breaking their marriage), they drop off their young son Henry at the rural farmhouse of his grandfather (Michael Ironside) whom he has previously spent little-to-no time with. "You said you were dropping off a boy, I see a full-grown working man here," the gruff and grunting old man says with a smile when he realizes that he'll have help with a long list of chores in the bitter cold. Later that afternoon, Henry takes a break from shoveling manure to throw snowballs against a shed, which is witnessed by the grandfather, but rather than the scolding orders to get back to work like we might suspect, he instead teaches Henry all the different baseball pitching styles; the two will continue to bond over baseball by listening to a game on the radio together.

Henry continues to prove that he's a considerate, sweet, and very self-sufficient kid when he wakes up the next morning to surprise his grandfather with a French toast breakfast, but even the smartest kids can sometimes forget to pack the charger to the phone they're glued to, and as a result, he has to use the last seconds of battery power to frantically call his parents to let them know, in a garbled and panicked voice message, that his grandfather is dead. He then seeks help from the nearest neighbor, a polite but suspicious young man named Dixon who was previously described as being "like family." After saying, "We'll just have to have some fun so we don't get all sad," he seems far too eager to challenge Henry to see who can drink their glass of Coke the fastest, and while he does win the race, he loses the duel of the intellects and ends up poisoning himself. Among the many smart touches in the film is establishing early on how Henry is all too familiar with the sound of pills jingling!

A good portion of the running time is devoted to an absolutely thrilling cat and mouse chase that takes full advantage of the jarring contrast between the Canadian wilderness and a cheerless old house with stained piano keys and dusty photographs of soldiers and horses. And with so much snow and madness on display, it's hard not to think of Jack Torrance when somebody shouts maniacally while clutching a baseball bat.

Knuckleball reunites two stars of the nostalgic and endearingly oddball cult movie *Turbo Kid*, because in addition to Michael Ironside, the yellow-toothed psychopath in this movie is played by the Kid himself, an all-grown up Munro Chambers, who shows that he's just as convincing playing the detestable hunter as he was the sympathetic hunted. Kathleen Munroe also gives a strong performance as the mother who shows crippling vulnerability when she sees the home where she spent her childhood and where her post-traumatic stress disorder stems.

Pontypool (2008)

Director: Bruce McDonald
Writer: Tony Burgess
Cast: Stephen McHattie, Lisa Houle, Georgina Reilly, Hrant Alianak

The first time I saw this Canadian slow-burner, I was fascinated by its first half and let down with the second, and then a couple months later on a night where the temperatures were expected to fall to single digits, I found myself unable to resist taking another trip to this tiny, unincorporated Ontarian village about to become the epicenter of a brand-new type of virus. My appreciation grew with the second viewing and it wouldn't take much longer until I watched it yet again. As a lifelong horror fan, it's just such a pleasure when you discover a film that frightens you in such inventive ways! So many times I've been scared by sharks, ghosts, vampires, psychopaths, zombies, and spiders, but to have my spine chilled by the English language was an entirely new experience.

Stephen McHattie, whose lengthy IMDb page has surely elicited many "oh yeah, that guy!" reactions, plays a radio personality named Grant Mazzy, looking very much like Lance Henriksen did in the must-see "Cutting Cards" episode of *Tales from the Crypt*. While most everyone in town is still asleep, he drives through a dangerous combination of heavy snowflakes and pitch darkness—receiving quite a scare along the way from a mysterious pedestrian in a state of distress—to the station where's he greeted by his producer Lisa, technical assistant Laurel-Ann, his Joey Ramone figurine, and a bottle of alcohol to make his coffee extra special.

He's new to the area and suffering bigtime from its endless winter, opening his weather report with "It's a big, cold, dull, dark, white, empty, never-ending, blow-my-brains-out, seasonal affective disorder, freaking kill me now weather-front that will last all day, or maybe, when the wind shifts later on, we'll get a little greenhouse gas relief from the industrial south." The fact that he uses the unapologetic Rush Limbaugh approach of growing a loyal listener base by pissing people off so they'll stay alert and maybe even tell their friends puts him at quandaries with Lisa, who wishes he would just stick to the traditional formula of school closures and mundane local news. It's fascinating to watch him react in real time to breaking news that's a tad more crucial than a woman's missing kitty cat, Honey, and a group of drunk ice fishermen getting into a disagreement with a group of drunk policemen.

When it's time to check in with Ken Loney from the "Sunshine Chopper" for a traffic report, he instead shares details of a large group of people gathered outside of a doctor's office, where what initially seemed like a protest generates into mass hysteria and an unruly mob. Since nobody but Ken has been able to confirm the story and share more insight, Lisa decides to go ahead with the scheduled musical number from a cast of actors, in town and also fully in costume for a production of *Lawrence of Arabia*, and I loved how this scene goes from goofy to terrifying in an instant when the girl playing Farraj suddenly becomes confused while on the air, saying, "I can't remember how it ends, I can't remember how it ends. It just keeps starting over and over. Pra-pra-pra-pra-PRA-PRA-PRA." Additional reports begin to trickle in about how this group of disturbed Pontypoolians, growing larger by the minute, have started to engage in cannibalistic behavior, all while chanting incoherently, and Grant (who previously accused his coworkers of playing an elaborate prank on him) has to tell a curious BBC reporter that nobody understands the reason why.

This film makes the case that one of the many adaptations of *War of the Worlds* should have stuck to the original concept and set the whole damn movie inside the radio station because close-ups of talented actors simply reacting to the shocking eye reports and ghastly sounds can be much more evocative (and millions of dollars cheaper) than a hundred extras running away from a myriad of explosions. As appropriate as it was to watch it on a freezing cold night in February, it was perhaps even timelier on the sunny afternoon of May 9th, 2020, now that I can better appreciate how maddening it would be to have this kind of exchange with somebody you've been quarantined with: "Do you have a sample?" "A sample of what?" "Just a sample, I think, a simple kind of sample." There's still plenty of research to be conducted pertaining to the Coronavirus, but thanks to *Pontypool*, we can all be eternally grateful that words don't seem to be inspected. And thanks to *Pontypool*, I can be unsettled by how I just typed inspected rather than infected.

The Snow Woman (1968)
Director: Tokuzo Tanaka
Writers: Fuji Yahiro, Lafcadio Hearn (story)
Cast: Shiho Fujimura, Akira Ishihama, Machiko Hasegawa, Taketoshi Naito

I first heard the term "Snowpocalypse" when a snowstorm hit Portland, Oregon in 2008, trapping commuters in their cars for many hours and completely shutting the city down for days. People in New England and Minnesota would have referred to it as a "light dusting," but for us it was a very big deal, and that's why the weather reports this week have stirred up so much excitement for some and dread for others. It was all leading up to today, Snowpocalypse Part II. I stayed up really late last night because it was all but guaranteed that I'd wake up to a beautiful text about how work was canceled for today and then fall back asleep until noon. I was hoping to hear my feet crunch last night in a wintry wonderland walk in the woods, but then the forecasts kept annoyingly delaying the start of the first snowfall. Eventually I decided to just get some zzz's and save the celebrations for tomorrow. It was utter heartbreak to wake up at the usual time of 7:42 without a text notification, and to then look out the window and see nothing but blues and greens. Rather than the 6-10 inches of snow everybody was expecting, we didn't even get enough to make a single snowball the size of a dot.

After a workday where I felt especially morose and defeated, I collapsed on the couch and figured that since I couldn't enjoy real snow, I might as well get lost in the television's white stuff and finally cross off *The Snow Woman* from my watchlist.

Just after master sculptor Shigetomo and his orphaned apprentice Yosaku have found a tree magnificent enough to be carved into a Buddha statue for the Kokubun-ji Temple, a winter storm chases them through the forest until they eventually find shelter. A warm fire and plans for their best creation yet keep their spirits high, but then the cabin door opens in the middle of the night and a ghostly figure in a white kimono glides inside. Without saying a word, she scans the cabin with a deep stare and turns the walls, floors, and master sculptor to ice. When she sets her witchy eyes on the young man, her cold expression changes as she floats closer and closer to him. Not wanting to kill someone as young and innocent as him, she agrees to spare his life as long as he never tells a single soul about their encounter.

It's agreed by the religious leaders that Yosaku will carry out his deceased master's work and create the holy statue, although he's threatened by both corrupt officers and a lack of faith in his own abilities. He finally gets some good luck when he meets a wonderful woman in the rain who later takes his hand in marriage, but there's no forgetting the fact that one foolish word can cost him everything, and so we watch every scene with bated breath. Since this was based on the same Japanese folktale (originating from the 1300s) that inspired my favorite segments from *Kwaidan* and *Tales from the Darkside: The Movie*, I was more than happy to see a longer interpretation.

The ceremonial rituals from the local shaman were some of the most intriguing moments, especially when two sets of eyes intensely lock on each other while a slow, ominous drumbeat reverberates and the bad kind of sparks fly. Scary scenes like this are few and far between though and so this won't be everyone's cauldron of tea, but if you find yourself feeling blue because your snow day has been replaced by a low day, then it should hit the spot. With its visual grandeur that brings witches and snowstorms to life, lovely soundtrack from Akira Ifukube (of *Godzilla* notoriety), and haunting story filled with love and compassion, I became so immersed in this movie that my skin felt icy cold while my soul was practically burning. Or maybe I just have a sickness caused by unfulfilled Snowpocalypse II expectations.

Horror Galore

REGRETFUL REAL ESTATE ACQUISITIONS

Amityville 1992: It's About Time (1992)
Director: Tony Randel
Writers: Christopher DeFaria, Antonio Toro
Cast: Stephen Macht, Shawn Weatherly, Megan Ward, Damon Martin, Jonathan Penner

As of now, there have been 12 official entries in the *Amityville Horror* series that opened its doors in 1979, and you would be forgiven for believing there are even more after you've been scrolling through Amazon Prime's horror selection aimlessly for 20 minutes. Deep down in the muck and mire you'll find totally unrelated movies with misleading cash-grab titles like *The Amityville Haunting*, *Amityville: Mt. Misery Road*, *Amityville: Vanishing Point*, and *Amityville: No Escape*. Having only seen the first four official entries and only really liking Part II, I felt like it was a daunting task to search for a diamond in the rough of this never-ending series, but it turned out to be a piece of cake because I jumped ahead to Part 6 after learning that it was directed by none other than Tony Randel, who made *Hellbound: Hellraiser II* and one of the most underrated horror films of the '90s, *Ticks*. Adding to the intrigue was the childhood memory of flipping through a *TV Guide* one afternoon and staring at the magnificent advertisement for *Amityville 1992: It's About Time* and wondering if it was going to bear similarities to the novel *The House with a Clock in its Walls*. For some reason I didn't bother to tune in or program the VCR to find out, and so I'll never know how the 11-year-old me would have reacted to this film, but the 39-year-old version sure enjoyed the hell out of it!

It's been a distressing week for Oregonians because entire towns have disintegrated from the wildfires that show no signs of being contained. Portland hasn't been greeted by an eerie red sky reminiscent of Mars and *Night of the Comet* like other parts of the Beaver State have, but according to CNN, Newsweek, and Bloomberg, we do officially have the worst air quality in the world at the moment. I usually like to wait until it's cloudy and gloomy to look at Halloween decorations at Michael's, but this year I might have to settle for smoky and apocalypticy. Tonight for 95 joyous minutes, I forgot all about the death, destruction, and eye-stinging smoke, and remembered what pure fun feels like. My spirits were lifted almost immediately because this movie opens with thunder, lightning, and rain (three things I've been wanting to experience more than anything this week) before introducing us to a housing developer named Jacob Sterling who returns home from a business trip to Suffolk County, New York. He greets his two teenaged children and their babysitter, Andrea, who happens to be his ex-girlfriend, and then shows off the souvenir that he brought back: an antique clock that used to live above the fireplace in a house addressed 112 Ocean Drive. With its insomnia-inducing ticking, it fits right in with Jacob's microwave that beeps with each second and also his wonky doorbell.

Jacob and Andrea make love later that night and then disagree over whether she should leave her boyfriend and move back in, but things are even more complicated downstairs when his metalhead son discovers that with a simple flick of the light switch, the living room takes on a sinister transformation equipped with candelabras, windblown curtains, and instruments of torture. The clock makes for a much better manifestation of evil than the lamp in *Amityville 4: The Evil Escapes* because not only does it drill itself into the mantle and take on additional parts on the opposite side of the wall, but it cleverly plays around with the perception of time for the family members while producing crazy hallucinations.

It's unclear how exactly the clock manages to possess the neighbor's dog Peaches (or create an evil clone of it) so that it attacks Jacob while he's on a morning jog, but you probably shouldn't overthink a Part 6 to any franchise, much less this one. It's better to just celebrate the sheer viciousness of this attack and the outrageousness of his doctors quickly sending him home without stitching his open wounds, so that by the time Andrea drives him back home, his bandages are already drenched in oozing blood and pus. His mental state begins to deteriorate as rapidly as his legs, and soon he's obsessing over his work much like Jack Torrance in *The Shining*, and creating something that's almost as shocking as the "All Work and No Play Makes Jack a Dull Boy" manuscript. Given how the family dynamics were already unconventional to begin with, the powers contained within the clock have a lot of juicy material to work with, especially when Andrea's current boyfriend shows up for a surprise visit and realizes that his many years practicing psychology simply didn't prepare him for this. "You have a pyromaniacal Nazi down the hall, you've got a toxic lunatic in the master bedroom. The only one around here who seems normal is Lisa and that's because I have not met her yet!" he amusingly shouts in vexation right around the time the aforementioned teenaged daughter goes to second base with her own reflection.

Bones (2001)

Director: Ernest R. Dickerson
Writers: Adam Simon, Tim Metcalfe
Cast: Snoop Dogg, Pam Grier, Michael T. Weiss, Clifton Powell, Ricky Harris, Bianca Lawson

Man, 2001 was such an unjust year for horror at the box office. *Frailty* played to empty theaters for a couple weeks before having its run truncated, and Stuart Gordon's *Dagon* was relegated to direct-to-video. *Bones* also failed to attract crowds, most likely due to being released just a few weeks after September 11th, when most people weren't really in the mood for bloodthirsty hounds, Snoop Dogg proclaiming that he's got "a natural high, a supernatural high," and a severed head complaining about being dropped on the ground.

A couple of frat boys find themselves way out of their league when trying to acquire drugs in a dangerous neighborhood. They lose their car to the dealers and after entering an abandoned brownstone, their lives to a devil dog that's been lurking there ever since the 1979 murder of previous owner Jimmy Bones (Snoop Dogg), a gangster that was too loyal and benevolent for his own good. The dog with the glowing red eyes receives more company the following day and is much friendlier to a young man named Patrick, who has just purchased the property with plans to renovate it into a hip nightclub with his brother and two friends. His prosperous father, on the other hand, is furious at the acquisition because he had worked hard so that he and his family could escape that ghetto and never go back.

With cobwebs covering the spiral staircase, animal jaws on the floor, and rats hiding in every crevice, Patrick's friend jokes that the last person left alive by the end of the week will inherit all of Vincent Price's money, but then he goes and makes the cardinal mistake of stealing a piece of jewelry from the skeleton they find buried in the cavernous basement. Weeks later, it looks like their swanky dance club is going to be a big hit but then thousands of maggots begin raining down from the ceiling into everyone's drinks, indicating that the dog has finally taken enough blood and flesh from others to regenerate Jimmy Bones a'la Frank from *Hellraiser*. He wakes up in an understandably foul mood and vows revenge on everyone that played a role in his death, no matter how small, and so it remains to be seen how he'll treat former sweetheart Pearl (the always welcome Pam Grier) during their reunion.

Ernest R. Dickerson directed the Bruce Springsteen music video for "Born in the U.S.A." and worked as the cinematographer on Spike Lee's best film, *Do the Right Thing*, before introducing himself to horror fans as the director of *Tales from the Crypt: Demon Knight*, in which he demonstrated the same kind of manic energy, fluid camerawork, and outrageous gross-out gags that makes *Bones* such a rib-tickling good time. With nods to blaxploitation and Italian horror, this is a very stylish film that gets the most out of flashbacks, shadows on the wall, and splattered blood of the deepest red. And we never have to restlessly shuffle in our seats waiting impatiently for scenes involving Snoop Dogg and Pam Grier because the teenagers are pretty engaging, especially once Grier's daughter Cynthia (Bianca Lawson) enters the fray. It was a treat to just listen to car banter that goes like:

"I'm the melting pot"

"Nah, you've been smoking pot."

"I'm the tossed salad. I am Martin Luther King's dream, all I gotta do is hold my own hand. I am post racial!"

"Post-apocalyptic more like it."

Other reasons to give yourself a supernatural high include the all-time best projectile vomiting from a dog, a billiards table gushing blood after a switchblade slice, a catchy Jimmy Bones nursery rhyme, a psychedelically dizzying montage of sensual bloodbaths and scary psychopaths, and a really effective vision of hell with slimy bodies writhing in agony against the wall they've contorted themselves into. Considering the volume of their perpetual wailing, it's safe to say this is one of those extra-bad hells without the brief respite of naps.

Burnt Offerings (1976)

Director: Dan Curtis
Writers: William F. Nolan, Dan Curtis, Robert Marasco (novel)
Cast: Karen Black, Oliver Reed, Burgess Meredith, Eileen Heckart, Lee Montgomery

Three years before serving as the Morningside Mortuary in *Phantasm*, the stunning Oakland property known as the Dunsmuir Hellman Historic Estate housed the Rolf Family in *Burnt Offerings*, winner of the Best Horror Picture at the Saturn Awards. It also should have won the award for Biggest Title Credit Size; I like Dub Taylor as much as the next guy, but I don't think his name should take up half of the screen, especially when we're trying to focus on a car that looks a lot like the Griswold Family Truckster!

Karen Black, who previously worked with director Dan Curtis in *Trilogy of Terror*, and Oliver Reed, coming off an appearance on *The Tonight Show* when Shelley Winters poured whiskey on his head for making misogynistic comments, star as married couple Marion and Ben Rolf, who believe they've gotten the bargain of a lifetime when they're able to rent a beautiful remote mansion for the summer for only $900. The reason for the low price is because the owners of the house, a pair of siblings played by Burgess Meredith and Eileen Heckart, ask that they look after their mother, who is 85 but could apparently pass for 60, by bringing her food to the upstairs bedroom that she never leaves, a task that Marion happily takes on single-handedly. They are joined by their 12-year-old son, David, as well as Ben's aunt Elizabeth, played by Bette Davis.

Marion immediately falls in love with the house and everything inside, feeling a strong inner peace by running her fingers along the many trinkets, staring into the old photographs, and winding the old clocks. Shots of her listening to the lovely music box melody are effectively intercut with Ben and his son horsing around in the swimming pool. Despite having to share the screen with such heavyweights, Lee Montgomery more than holds his own as the pre-teen Davey. Because he's just about the nicest kid ever (Montgomery was just as likable in 1985's made-for-TV Halloween film *The Midnight Hour*), it's both shocking and upsetting when Ben uncharacteristically snaps and violently throws his son around, even submerging his head underwater, much to the horror of Aunt Elizabeth, also experiencing strange troubles of her own. Known for being the most energetic member of the family, she suddenly finds herself feeling weak and frail, sleeping more and painting less.

Burnt Offerings burns slow but trusts its character dynamics and marvelous setting to keep you invested, never feeling obligated to punctuate every ten minutes with a scare (however cheap) like so many movies do; there are many dark closets in this movie and not a single one contains a cat ready to shriek and pounce on nervous protagonists. All the scares are legitimate and they last a long time, such as the scene in which Aunt Elizabeth and Ben are sitting in a room together, not uttering a word but watching each other's increasingly agonizing facial expressions, as if an unknown entity is driving nails, one by one, into their cerebral cortexes.

When watching haunted house films, it can be very frustrating if the characters don't make an honest effort to just get the hell out of there already, but that's not a problem you'll face here because the house doesn't frighten with shadows in the night or floating candlesticks—it attacks its inhabitants mentally. For the instances when they find the strength to run away, it can even bequeath its power to outside elements like vines. But on the bright side, the kitchen is always fully stocked, much to the delight of David, who ecstatically shouts out "Hey, I think I see some Ding Dongs! Hey, they *are* Ding Dongs!"

The Evil (1978)

Director: Gus Trikonis
Writers: Galen Thompson, Gus Trikonis, David Sheldon (story)
Cast: Richard Crenna, Joanna Pettet, Andrew Prine, Cassie Yates, George O'Hanlon

The generic title hasn't done this film many favors in standing out among a crowded pack of Evil Deads, Evil Eds, Evil Eyes, Evil Spawns, and Evil Bongs, but it's right on the money in terms of accuracy because the mansion depicted in this film is so damn evil, the Devil himself has a luxury suite beneath the basement.

The location scout struck gold with the finding of an abandoned and unfurnished health spa and resort because it doesn't look like any haunted house we've seen before; it breathes unease high up on the balcony, underground in the cellar, and everywhere in between. Even the caretaker is nervous about entering, and mumbles to himself about how he'll be safe in the daytime while sweeping the floors in preparation for potential new tenants. He carefully avoids the mass of cobwebs while following the sounds of whispering children, and learns that the house doesn't much care for double negatives because "You ain't nothing" are his last words. If I were just a little more vocal as a movie-watcher, this would have been the first occasion among many in *The Evil* to provoke a loud, startled "Holy shit!"

A psychiatrist named C.J. (a bearded Richard Crenna and looking nothing like his appearances in *Summer Rental*, *Leviathan*, and the *Rambo* movies) and his wife Caroline buy the 200-room property, and with the help of their friends, they start renovating it to become the first upscale rehabilitation center with a cemetery for a front lawn. Their first day on the job gets off to an unsteady start when Caroline spots apparitions, C.J. makes the mistake of removing an iron cross in a crypt, and the cute German shepherd Kaiser returns from a howling fit with a new aggressive demeanor that brings his lifelong owner to tears.

Noticing your own reflection is unavoidable when watching a movie outside during the day on a Fire Tablet, and mine looked notably shaken, surprised, amused, and delighted during this movie in which characters are electrocuted, strangled, buried alive, mangled via self-inflicted bandsaw, and sexually assaulted to the sounds of ghostly cackling over the course of one stormy night. They sure as hell try to leave the premises like any sane person would, but much like room 1408, this hellhole seems to have an answer for everything.

Gus Trikonis, whose name had appeared on many drive-in screens for his low-budget 70's New York City exploitation movies, demonstrates impeccable timing with his first horror film and given the shocking ways in which dead bodies are revealed

here, I think he would have been a perfect choice for a *Friday the 13th* entry. The cast also includes Andrew Prine playing a psychologist who's sleeping with one of his students, and while scrolling through his long list of acting credits, the one role that caused me to cheer was for portraying the titular character in Al Bundy's favorite show, *Psycho Dad*! And now I shall revisit the catchy *Psycho Dad* theme song thanks to a YouTube compilation that surely exists.

His House (2020)

Director: Remi Weekes
Writers: Remi Weekes, Felicity Evans (story), Toby Venables (story)
Cast: Sope Dirisu, Wunmi Mosaku, Matt Smith, Malaika Wakoli-Abigaba, Javier Botet

I spent the first cold November rain of 2020 watching *His House* and I didn't bother taking any notes because it was a Netflix exclusive that had been generating buzz ever since it premiered at Sundance, and so how could it possibly fall under the underseen/underrated banner? Well, despite earning universally glowing reviews, it didn't really make much of a splash with the horror community and was conspicuously absent from a lot of yearly top ten lists from horror journalists the following month. Given its timely subject matter and ability to stay grounded in heavy real-world horrors even while scaring the holy hell out of us with perfectly executed haunted house scares, it seemed like if any movie were destined to break through in a year like 2020, it would be *His House*. Being released so close to Election Day, when its socially conscious demographic was constantly glued to the news for weeks, might have doomed its chances with us damn Yankees. On a rewatch more than a year later, I was happy to discover that it was every bit as entertaining, eerie, and poignant as I remembered.

Horror Galore

Married couple Bol and Rial are fleeing from war-torn South Sudan and after promising to protect their young daughter along a treacherous journey that will lead to a new home, they lose her to the angry waters of the English Channel. Many heartbreaking weeks later, they are granted probational asylum in the United Kingdom and are given a new place to live and a lengthy list of strict guidelines, where even the slightest infraction could result in deportation. Even with faulty electricity, peeling wallpaper, and a host of unsanitary conditions, Bol and Rial are relieved to have a house of their very own, a house that happens to have more square footage than the one belonging to their case worker Mark. The jubilation of a new life full of hope and opportunities is short-lived when the ghosts from their past manifest in various forms to terrorize them from every nook and cranny and from both sides of the walls. Still, Bol remains determined to succeed and to assimilate to his new community—he even updates his wardrobe, joins the pub regulars in their boisterous soccer celebrations, and brings home silverware for Rial and him to try for the first time. But every attempt is met with a challenge twice as strong and soon he's forcefully pressing his hands against his ears in a hopeless attempt to silence the trauma echoing in his head and then smashing holes in the walls to locate the evil spirit that his wife believes followed them all the way from Sudan.

The screenplay cleverly circumvents the common "But why don't they just leave?" haunted house complaint by giving its desperate and sympathetic protagonists no easy solutions after being told by Mark that it just wouldn't look good to his supervisors if they were to complain about the conditions. In one of my favorite scenes, Rial tries to calm her nerves by exploring her neighborhood for the first time but even with a map, she can't find the main road that will take her outside of the littered cement squalor, as sidewalks turn into twisting alleys where every dead end reveals the same child robotically kicking a ball against the wall; it's as unsettling as Spinal Tap's "Hello Cleveland" venture is hysterical. It's easy to see why she begins to miss the familiarity of her home village even after the unending tribal wars there have left her physically and emotionally scarred. Another one of my favorite moments occurs when a mundane meal around the dinner table morphs into something else entirely when the camera zooms out ever so slowly with the confidence of a magician pulling back the curtain.

Year after year the Academy Awards go out of their way to ignore independent horror cinema at all costs, but England's equivalent, the BAFTA Awards, proved once again how they aren't as closed minded when they nominated *His House* (as well as A24's religious shocker *Saint Maud*) for Outstanding British Film of the Year and gave a much-deserved award to Remi Weekes in the Outstanding Debut by a British Writer, Director, or Producer category.

Superstition (1982)

Director: James W. Roberson
Writers: Galen Thompson, Michael O. Sajbel, Bret Thompson Plate, Brad White
Cast: James Houghton, Albert Salmi, Lynn Carlin, Larry Pennell, Jacquelyn Hyde, Heidi Bohay

It's unlikely that any of the video stores I frequented in my youth carried a copy of *Superstition* because that brilliant cover surely would have won me over instantly and created a magnetic reaction leading straight to the checkout counter. It's all for the best though because in these October days where the pandemic has shut down my favorite Halloween attractions in Portland and replaced them with a Cinema of Horrors drive-in that charges $59 to see the 2010 remake of *A Nightmare on Elm Street* and another $59 for *The Nun*, as well as a drive-through haunted house that costs $79 just so three monsters can circle your car for 12 minutes (the scathing reviews were priceless), I needed something like an obscure and gory 80's haunted house film to come along and put me in the Halloween spirit, especially one that features a man's severed head exploding in a microwave and another man cut in half by a possessed window. And that's just in the opening scene!

This large house has been the center of ghost stories and murders ever since 1692 when a witch was found guilty and sentenced to drown, her demonized voice cackling and vowing revenge seconds before being plunged into the adjacent lake. Hours later, the church belonging to her accusers burned down and the minister was mysteriously crushed in his own torture device. Despite all of the blood of Christ spilled, this piece of property that is still owned by the church is deemed an adequate home for their new preacher, a tortured alcoholic who moves in with his wife, two pretty daughters (whose short shorts draw the attention of men of law and men of the cloth alike), and son played by Billy Jacoby (*Bloody Birthday*, *Just One of the Guys*).

Aside from one scene in which a character tiptoes around the house shouting "Hey Arty" for what feels like forever, *Superstition* moves at a fairly quick pace and never leaves you waiting long for the next kill, always creative and vicious, like when stakes are pounded through foreheads, a dislodged circular saw blade slices through chest cavities, and an elevator shaft subsequently strangles and bruises those who fall. I haven't read any reviews but I'm assuming that several people alluded to these death scenes being selling point A-Z for this movie because the story is disjointed and the characters not all that memorable, and while it would be hard to argue, I also found plenty to admire in the secret rooms of rotting flesh, the soundtrack that makes a strong impression in nearly every scene, and the stylistic and tonal similarities to the works of Argento and Fulci.

There was also a shot of a creepy demon hand grabbing the bludgeoned face of a woman and dragging her away that I had to rewind a few times because it looked so damn cool! James W. Roberson only directed three other films, but his career as a cinematographer is extensive, shooting everything from the 1976 Texarkana classic *The Town that Dreaded Sundown* to 103 episodes of an ABC sitcom starring Melissa Joan Hart and Joey Lawrence, creatively titled *Melissa and Joey*.

Terrified (2017)

Writer and Director: Demián Rugna
Cast: Maximiliano Ghione, Norberto Gonzalo, Elvira Onetto, George Lewis, Julieta Vallina

As experienced horror fans, we can sometimes go many months searching for the next big thrill only to find a slight shiver here and there, and so it's a big deal whenever a film comes along that makes us feel as vulnerable as something like *Poltergeist* did when we still had our training wheels on. It's good to know that just when we thought we've seen it all, a movie like *The Descent* and *Insidious* can shake us to our core and reduce us to quivering casualties as we stumble out of the theater into the night and look over our shoulders every ten seconds to make sure nothing is following us. It's unfortunate that we weren't given the pleasure of being spooked by *Terrified*—a relentlessly nerve-jangling export from Argentina—on the silver screen but at least at home we can find protection with a warm blanket or purring feline.

A young woman named Clara has her cooking plans ruined when she keeps hearing strange noises emanating from her sink drain—sometimes they are distorted clangs and sometimes they are voices threatening to kill her. Her husband, Juan, awakens to odd noises of his own, which he attributes to the neighbor who's been acting strangely for days. But the shifting noises leads to the bathroom, which is now covered in blood as a result of Clara being violently thrashed against the walls by an invisible force, *à la* Tina from *A Nightmare on Elm Street*. While imprisoned for her death, he is visited by a trio of experts from the paranormal and criminal investigation fields who believe his story and want to help.

It's not only his house that is haunted, but the entire unassuming Buenos Aires street he lives on, explaining his neighbor's disheveled state and abnormal behavior. The man had been pleading for help from one of the investigators for weeks, and after seeing what he had to put up with on a nightly basis, I can no longer complain about my lovely cat Marmalade's middle-of-the-night demands for attention and fresh food. Another neighbor and her ten-year-old son experience an even worse fate in what may be the most potent nightmare fuel you'll experience all year!

Terrified produces more legit scares in its first 20 minutes than most horror films do in 90 and somehow never runs out of steam. I appreciated how they came in such a wide variety of forms and how they're occasionally anchored by such portent dialogue. For example, when a forensic pathologist responds to a call in the middle of the night, he is asked by a deputy at the front door, "Nothing really scares you, right?" to which he replies, "You never know. Let's see." In a lesser film, such a warning would probably be detrimental to the final reveal but here it just takes the tension to a new level.

Make sure you blast some music or have the TV playing at a loud volume for the hours following your viewing of *Terrified*, because this is a night where you won't want to hear your home making strange noises! In my case, I was startled by a sudden crackling of ice that ignited as I reached for my glass of cheap Canadian whisky, and had I been listening to Dream Theater's new album a little louder, perhaps I wouldn't have heard it, or all the threatening voices from my kitchen sink.

The Vagrant (1992)

Director: Chris Walas
Writer: Richard Jefferies
Cast: Bill Paxton, Michael Ironside, Marshall Bell, Mitzi Kapture, Colleen Camp

This is one I remember seeing on the video store shelves growing up, but a screaming Bill Paxton on the cover showing off every gleaming tooth wasn't enough to lure me in, which is a shame because I would have really dug *The Vagrant*'s cartoonish sensibilities, steady blend of dark comedy and horror, and undeniably creepy villain; it would make a damn fine double-feature with Steve Miner's *House* (1985). I wouldn't appreciate the awesomeness of Paxton until the high school years. It would take me even longer to realize the cover is mimicking Macaulay Culkin in *Home Alone*, which makes me feel like a total square considering the tagline "He's not home alone" is clearly visible.

Approximately a year removed from playing the weirdest character of his entire repertoire in *The Dark Backward*, Paxton starts off *The Vagrant* playing a boring financial clerk named Graham Krakowski (one of many silly names in the film) who thwarts off the sexual advances from an eccentric real estate agent by buying the house she's showing him, a house on the outskirts of urban decay that has the word "potential" written in bold, bloody letters. At first, he's only stressing out about mortgage payments and home repairs, but a new concern takes over on his first day there when he witnesses a homeless man, as disheveled and squirm-inducing as possible, using his kitchen sink. He sees him again in his bedroom later that night.

Graham takes out a second mortgage so that he can purchase a top-of-the-line home security system, but nothing he does frees himself from the vagrant's presence, and with every horrifying encounter he loses a chunk of sanity. With amplified night terrors, paranoia, and sleepwalking, it remains unclear if his visions of a vengeful and possibly homicidal drifter are real or if Graham is the one who's been hacking the fingers off elderly women. The movie calls his craziness and raises it considerably, taking so many bizarre turns and eventually leading us to a courthouse, an RV park in the middle of nowhere, and a Southwestern tourist trap.

Much of the humor comes from an odd assortment of supporting characters, such as some of the worst policemen (one of whom is Michael Ironside) in horror history and Graham's cubicle decoration-hating boss played by Stuart Pankin, who has gotten to showcase more of his comedic chops in everything from *Arachnophobia* to *Curb Your Enthusiasm*.

Produced by Mel Brooks, *The Vagrant* is absolutely bonkers, but the kind of bonkers we horror fans require from time to time to maintain a healthy balance and radiant glow.

We Are Still Here (2015)

Writer and Director: Ted Geoghegan
Cast: Barbara Crampton, Andrew Sensenig, Lisa Marie, Larry Fessenden, Susan Gibney

Just a year after Snowfort Pictures released *Starry Eyes*, they cemented their status as a production company that horror fans should pay attention to with Ted Geoghegan's *We Are Still Here*, in which the writer and director paid homage to one of his favorite films, Lucio Fulci's *House by the Cemetery*, in his story about a married couple named Paul and

Poster for *We Are Still Here* (2015), Snowfort Pictures, Dark Sky Films

Anne (terrifically played by Andrew Sensenig and genre favorite Barbara Crampton) who move to a large, old house in New England that unbeknownst to them, might already be occupied by something. They are still very much in mourning over the tragic death of their teenaged son and hope that escaping the city to live in the small town of Aylesbury will help them cope. Their neighbors pay them a visit one night and while drinking a round of Scotches, inform them about the house's sordid history, dating back to when it was constructed for the Dagmar Family in 1859 for the purpose of being a funeral home. After it was discovered that Mr. Dagmar had been selling the corpses and burying empty coffins, the townspeople united in an angry mob and drove them out of town.

Anne senses a strong presence in the house and wonders if it may be the spirit of their son, prompting an invitation to her sister and brother-in-law, both of whom are spiritualists with an uncanny ability to make contact with the dead; they are played by Lisa Marie and the prolific Larry Fessenden (certainly no stranger to snowbound horror whether he's in front of the camera or behind it). Paul, a skeptic who chalks it all up to hippy stoner mumbo jumbo, is far more concerned about their temperamental boiler in the basement—a menacing and cavernous cesspool that flummoxes the unfortunate electrician assigned to the house. After the two couples go out for dinner and are given a Slaughtered Lamb type of reception by the locals, they return back to the house for more drinks and Paul loosens up and admits what everybody is thinking, "I gotta say, this is one weird fucking town!"

Taut and efficient, Geoghegan (the most complicated last name of a horror director named Ted since Mr. Nicolaou) still wisely allows the camera to occasionally linger to give us a better sense of the surroundings. As someone who hasn't experienced a New England winter in almost two decades, I was grateful for the beautiful shots of snowflakes gently landing on the camera lens, blocks of ice flanking a brook, and 19th century architecture lining up quaint neighborhoods. And unlike Tim Allen who comfortably parades around in the snow wearing his boxers in *The Santa Claus*, here we can actually see characters' breaths and understand why they'd want to fight off this degree of bitter cold by drinking whisky by the fire as soon as they get home. I'd recommend saving *We Are Still Here* for the dead of winter, and extra layers of clothes are encouraged because this is a movie that will scare the pants off of you, especially during that séance scene, good god almighty!

It also delivers unsuspecting carnage that hits hard, is faithful to its 1979 setting, and presents a very convincing haunted house with a lot of character. The owners of this remodeled farmhouse in upstate New York were told that the filming crew would clean up afterwards, but considering how many gallons of blood were splashed against the walls, surely a drop or two still remains.

The Witch in the Window (2018)
Writer and Director: Andy Mitton
Cast: Alex Draper, Charlie Tacker, Arija Bareikis, Carol Stanzione

Let's say it's around 11 pm and you've just finished watching the dreadful *The Human Centipede III*, which has made you feel so defeated that you're tempted to call it a night. What if you died in your sleep and found out that there is some ridiculous stipulation in the afterlife that states that the only movie you'll have access to for the rest of eternity is the last one you watched on Earth? Rather than take this enormous risk, you should probably just stay up for another 79 minutes and watch the Shudder exclusive *The Witch in the Window*. You'll still get to bed at a reasonable time and will have quickly eliminated the chances of that centipede sequel being the final movie you watch in this life.

Andy Mitton followed up his collaborations with Jesse Holland (*We Go On*, *Yellowbrickroad*) with this classic New England haunted house thriller that achieves a tremendous lot in its brisk running time. Tensions rise in a small New York City home when a mother catches her 12-year-old son Finn looking at something inappropriate on the internet, and being overwhelmed and distraught at the situation, she asks her ex-husband Simon to take Finn along to his new house-flipping project in rural Vermont. Finn responds to the size and decaying façade of the farmhouse with "Tell me people got chopped up here," and so he's happy to hear from a neighbor that the previous owner was a woman named Lydia, considered to be a witch by the locals. After her husband and son were mysteriously killed in a haybale accident, she was often seen in the upstairs window, staring motionless and seeming to feed off the fear of those who noticed her, something she managed to achieve weeks after passing away in her favorite chair.

Racked with guilt for being an absent father due to sheer cowardice, Simon attempts to connect with the son he's spent such little time with over the years by teaching him the tricks of the home repair trade (while making me feel incompetent in the process) and offering to answer any questions about what Finn saw on the world wide web, even though the actual subject matter ends up being far more concerning than the usual. Desperately wanting to make it feel like home, he even filled a bedroom with his son's favorite toys, and while Finn initially scoffs for being too old for them, he eventually reconnects with his old teddy bear once the electricity goes out and Lydia makes her presence known.

Actors Alex Draper (who kept reminding me of Paul Giamatti) and Charlie Tacker have terrific chemistry together that will resonate with many viewers who've experienced family turmoil. You would think that a 79-minute haunted house movie in 2018 would speed along at a breakneck pace, caring more about a jump scare quota than character development, and so it was refreshing how *The Witch in the Window* takes its time to simply allow its characters to talk, listen, react, and grow. It also doesn't rush the scary moments, preferring your hair to rise strand by strand rather than all at once, and as a result, the lingering dread of the scene involving the discovery of the former owner might even remind you of the first time seeing the library apparition in *Ghostbusters.* There's another scene involving a phone call that earns at least a 9 on the terrormeter! And those with wandering eyes will be further rewarded with some menacing spooks camouflaged in the background. This film might not reinvent the wheel but it's superbly made, and much like the 2004 masterpiece *Sideways*, starring the aforementioned Paul Giamatti, it ends on an absolutely perfect note with a simple knock.

Horror Galore

FAMILIES THAT WOULD GIVE EVEN THE SAWYERS THE CREEPS

Blood Massacre (1991)

Director: Don Dohler
Writers: Barry Gold, Dan Buehl, Don Dohler
Cast: George Stover, Robin London, James DiAngelo, Thomas Humes, Lisa DeFuso

After having a jolly time with the rubber-suited alien adventures *Nightbeast* and *The Alien Factor*, I was eager to see a list of Baltimore director Don Dohler's entire filmography, and while it was sadly short, one title was practically glowing as if an angel above was reminding me that on this night, a good old-fashioned massacre with some blood was the ticket to a soul-enriching evening at home.

Actor George Stover isn't his usual affable self here, playing a man named Rizzo who clearly doesn't like getting kicked out of bars. His longings to be back in Vietnam where he could kill without repercussions causes him to fly off the handle at every opportunity, even during a routine mid-afternoon video store robbery. With his fellow gang members (one of whom resembles Tommy Lee while another proudly wears a Kim Carnes "Mistaken Identity" 1981 tour t-shirt) annoyed that somebody had to die for a measly $720, they all flee into the night only for their car to run out of gas in the middle of nowhere. They flag down an approaching car and take hostage a young woman (Robin London in the film's best performance), who seems strangely calm and sassy about taking them all back to the rural home she shares with her sister and parents and offering them bowls of the family's award-winning stew—*Motel Hell*'s Farmer Vincent and *Texas Chainsaw Massacre*'s "Cook" Sawyer could probably guess the secret ingredient.

Considering all the years that passed between *The Alien Factor*'s completion and eventual distribution, you would think that Don Dohler's luck would have improved by his fourth feature, but instead, *Blood Massacre* is filled with the kind of nightmarish backstories that would make amateur filmmakers consider another line of work. He had already shot the majority of the film on video before investors liked the footage so much that they pressured Dohler into starting over from scratch and shooting on 16mm film instead. He acquiesced and shuffled around the cast since some of the performers had already committed to other projects, and as a result, Stover went from playing a secondary character to the lead. After the second version was completed, the investors took the reels and seemingly vanished into thin air, only for the film to resurface a few years later under a different title. The ultimate heartbreak was that for God knows what reason, a work print was ultimately released instead of the finished project. Understandably fed up with the whole industry, Dohler wouldn't make another film until ten years later, and just like all of his previous films, there was a sizable gap in between the year *Alien Factor 2: The*

Horror Galore

Alien Rampage was reportedly completed and the year it became available to the public.

With the exception of a boring stretch in which an unlikeable character sets traps in the woods and ever-so-slowly pokes holes in Maxwell Coffee cans, *Blood Massacre* flies by at 72 minutes and has enough ludicrous twists, memorable characters, savage scenes of people being stabbed to death, and fearlessly random tonal shifts to sustain a film three times as long. It also repeatedly tickles our funny bones with exchanges like:

"Look, we're looking for three men and a woman. Strangers."
"That's four people."
"That's correct."
"Young lady, I'll have you know this is an old family recipe."
"Oh really? Well, you should have buried it with the old family."
"You go back down this here road about ten mile 'til you come to a place where four roads meet."
"Uh huh."
"But be sure you just take one of them."

It had been quite a while since a scene filled me with so much joy that I had to rewind it over and over, and so I rejoiced during the video store robbery. I'm guessing it was intended to be one of the most suspenseful parts but it ends up being the funniest because the audio track went missing during post-production and the meager budget was already too squeezed to allow for dubbing, resulting in dialogue that is abruptly, inexplicably muted and replaced by a Benny Hill-type musical number that only seems fitting during the quick succession of close-ups of local extras looking more confused than afraid (one of several occasions when the soundtrack becomes this movie's MVP). In addition to pressing rewind, I also pressed pause several times to sentimentally stare at every detail in this video store, even though the quality of this transfer was too damn lousy to make out most of the posters and VHS covers (or what was even happening in some of those nighttime woods scenes).

Come for the bloody massacre, stay for the tummy-grabbing shower seduction!

Basket Case 2 (1990)
Writer and Director: Frank Henenlotter
Cast: Kevin Van Hentenryck, Annie Ross, Heather Rattray, Kathryn Meisle, Jason Evers

"I understand your pain, Belial, but ripping the faces off people may not be in your best interest." It's safe to say from all the Jolt Cola product placement that the incomparable Frank Henenlotter was well-caffeinated during the dying days of the 1980s, giving him enough energy to shoot *Frankenhooker* and *Basket Case 2* back-to-back, and firing on all cylinders in both creativity and style. The grindhouse classic *Basket Case* ended with Duane and his formerly conjoined deformed twin brother falling seven stories from the Hotel Broslin during a fight, and this sequel, despite coming out a long eight years later, picks up from the very same night of the accident.

Both brothers managed to survive the fall and are taken to a hospital under a flurry of sensational media coverage, with shocked television reporters trying their best to describe the murderous Belial— "small grotesque monstrosity, "strange little being that might be human," and "small twisted deformity" being a few examples. They even interview the original's delightful character Casey, played by the late Beverly Bonner, who follows up her summary of the events with "Do you believe that shit, man?"

The brothers manage to escape and are picked up by the nurturing Granny Ruth, who gives them much better accommodations than they received on gritty, sleazy 42nd Street. Also living inside her upstate New York mansion are a collection of unique individuals who need protection from the outside world. The movie almost plays out like a cartoonish version of Tod Browning's *Freaks*, with each member of the community inheriting exaggeratedly goofy characteristics like oversized piano key-teeth and a scaly crescent moon-shaped noggin. There's even one from South America with a ridiculously oversized head, ridiculously undersized body, and remarkably lovely opera-singing voice. Bigger-budgeted Belial, no longer relying on stop-motion animation to move around, almost looks normal in comparison, yet he still delivers the film's most monstrous moment when he laughs sinisterly at his twin brother for thinking he can just move out of the home and start a normal life. It's an interesting role reversal because it's now Duane who feels like he doesn't belong, a vulnerability that an ambitious tabloid reporter resembling Jennie Garth would love to capitalize on to bring her closer to Belial and the biggest story of her career.

Annie Ross as the godmother to the freaks is so much fun and she helps us accept the fact that the colorful side characters from the original aren't coming back, and neither are those great curly locks of star Kevin Van Hentenryck. In one of the best scenes, she pays a late-night visit to the owner of a dusty sideshow attraction promising an unforgettable collection of freaks that include a living fetus, a two-headed boy, and the featured star, Belial, and it reminded me of a hilarious sketch from MTV's *The State* in which Ken Marino recites carnival barker adulations for the "Medium Head Boy" in his freak-show rip-off.

A love scene near the end pushes absurdity to new levels, and the fact that no protection was used sets up an angle for *Basket Case 3*. This final entry, which also comes highly recommended, veers even further away from horror and feels more connected to the zany dark comedy *Freaked* than to the original *Basket Case*. The first half of the film consists of such light-hearted and goofy material that it's hard to imagine anyone dying, much less in gratuitously gory fashion. Dimwitted characters eventually get in the way of Belial's happiness and experience tiny teeth of fury and a whole lot more.

Needing some time to recuperate after the events of Part 2, Granny Ruth and her entourage pile into a school bus (amusingly marked with the words "no one you know") and drive to a mansion in Peachtree Valley owned by a friend of the family, just in time for the birthing of a dozen tiny Belials. A couple of police officers break into the house and after witnessing the freakiest celebration in town, confiscate the unholy brood and bring them back to the station, where it's debated on whether or not these fanged little monsters would make good pets. It's here where we also get this great line from the sheriff: "You boys have been through a lot tonight. Bailey, you book the Bradley boy. Baxter, take the bassinet of baby Belials in back and get Brody to come by. Where's Brannon and Banner?" Even if the storyline is only marginally compelling, I still had fun seeing Annie Ross display characteristics of a motivational speaker, televangelist, drill sergeant, and loving grandmother to inspire her strange foster children (the same unique individuals that Gabe Bartalos lovingly designed for Part 2 plus a few new additions) to fight back at a daytime talk show taping and at a fast-food restaurant managed by someone very near and dear to the Henenlotter universe.

Horror Galore

Skinned Deep (2004)
Writer and Director: Gabriel Bartalos
Cast: Les Pollack, Aaron Sims, Kurt Carley, Linda Weinrib, Eric Bennett, Lee Kociela

I wish I could remember who recommended this utterly out-of-this-world horror-comedy to me so I could extend a proper thank you. Hell, it might take a kidney donation to make it a commensurate show of appreciation considering how much enjoyment Gabe Bartalos' feature film debut brought me this afternoon, and after perusing his IMDb page, it's only natural that I should react this favorably. The mile-long list of awesome horror films this man has contributed special effects and/or makeup effects for include *Fright Night Part 2*, *From Beyond*, *Dolls*, *Gremlins 2*, *Friday the 13th Part VI*, *Basket Case 2*, *Brain Damage*, *Leprechaun 1-3*, and *Darkman*, but the one that impressed me the most was at the very bottom of the list: special makeup effects for *Spookies*! And he even played one of the muck men!

We open with an elderly man careening down a rain-slicked country road at night, and even more frustrating than the uncooperative defroster is the way a truck passes with blinding high beams and a whip-swinging psychopath leaning out the window. This exhilarating scene is much more than an homage to the first kill in *Texas Chainsaw Massacre 2* (yet another Bartalos credit!) because it's mysteriously intercut with shots of an oily bodybuilder flexing his muscles and showing off his "Josh" tattoo and "Dyno Mite" crotch.

The following day sees another bearded man struggling down the same road, as a punctured tire derails his family vacation to a "historic old town where there's all the activity from the last century and all." As gullible as he is friendly, he accepts the invitation of a strange woman at the general store who offers him, his wife, and two teenaged children a place to stay while their car gets worked on. Her labyrinthine house's interior design is about as unsettling as it gets and yet, the father remains unphased the whole time, smiling and telling his family, "See, I told you this place was normal," as he chooses to focus on standard features like doors and hallways rather than doll heads on sticks. Frank Henenlotter-levels of absurdity are matched with a dinner scene in which we meet the strange woman's family: a young man whose cartoonish deformity earns him the nickname Brain, a steampunk Dr. Satan with the mouth of Gwar's Balsac the Jaws of Death, a plate-throwing psychopath named Plates played by Warwick Davis (he and Bartalos must have developed a strong bond after countless hours of makeup application during the *Leprechaun* productions), and last but not least, The Creator.

Given the cheap and grimy presentation, one would assume *Skinned Deep* is a forgotten straight-to-video relic of the late '80s, rather than a 2004 release from Fangoria's short-lived Gorezone label, and that only adds to the charm of a film in which each and every dollar of a $600,000 budget seemed to be prudently allocated. Even if the actors weren't allowed to have second takes because of limited 16mm reels, it totally works to the film's advantage because when you have a plot this nonsensical, you might as well double down with perplexing line readings from people that behave as if they're brand new to Planet Earth and the art of conversing.

The fact that it sort of piggybacks on horror traditions makes it all the more surprising when not a single scene materializes the way you're trained to expect. It's a daffy, disorienting, and impressively gruesome smorgasbord of body-melts, finger soups, exploding body parts (both external and internal), Gilliam gadgets, and naked sprints down Manhattan streets (resulting in an actual arrest during a permit-less production). It's every bit as strange as *Nothing but Trouble*, another film that envisioned what *The Texas Chainsaw Massacre* might look like as a comedy, but a million times more fun. There's even a clever gag involving spelling blocks that makes *Insidious: Chapter 2*'s Boggle séance even lamer in retrospect.

Fans of *Spookies* will have another reason to celebrate when they see just who plays one of The Surgeon General's potential roadside victims. I was Facebook friends with the great Peter Iasillo Jr. and wish I had seen this movie before his unfortunate passing in 2017 so I could let him know just how happy his appearance in this film made me. He was listed third in the credits to Bartalos's other directorial effort, 2013's *Saint Bernard,* and I kept waiting for him, only to find out afterwards that he was unrecognizable under layers of prosthetics and makeup in what was easily the film's greatest scene, set in a police station so strangely located that it might as well be up a beanstalk.

For aficionados of surrealism, avant-garde, and Terry Gilliam-style weirdness cranked up to 11, *Saint Bernard* (also featuring Warwick Davis) will implant happy dollar signs on your cartoonishly sized eyeballs, but for those who demand a somewhat coherent plot to follow, it will feel like frustratingly searching for a set of keys in a river of glass bottles. Our protagonist's odyssey unfolds in a series of fragments (all of which would make for unforgettable modern art installations) that are connected only by how one strange location can reveal the next, like a curtain on the grimiest bus in existence functioning as a barrier between two completely different worlds. Watching that dystopian film, so full of ambition, silliness, and creativity, feels like trespassing through a forbidden funhouse that seems harmless until one wrong turn gives you sneak previews of hell and few opportunities to turn around. It's as if Bartalos kept a list for the ten years since *Skinned Deep* to write down every single weird thought and

Poster for ***Storm Warning*** (2007), Film Finance Corporation Australia, Film Victoria, Darclight Films

vision, and then dared himself to include them all for his follow-up.

Storm Warning (2007)

Director: Jamie Blanks
Writer: Everett De Roche
Cast: Nadia Fares, Robert Taylor, David Lyons, Mathew Wilkinson, John Brumpton

Writer Everett De Roche, who also penned *Long Weekend* and *Razorback*, decided that he wasn't done making Australia seem like the scariest place on Earth when he dusted off a 30-year-old screenplay that seemed to take inspiration from hard-hitting thrillers like *Deliverance* and *Straw Dogs*. This movie isn't going to win any medals for originality but if you're craving yet another tale of yuppies having their idyllic adventure suddenly ruined by a wrong turn leading to hillbilly country, then this movie more than delivers on thrills, gore, and terrifying villains you won't soon forget.

It opens with a lawyer named Rob and his French artist girlfriend Pia taking a small boat out for a romantic day of sailing and fishing, but what kills the mood even more than the bludgeoning of a fish under dark grey skies is his decision to drift down the marshes before heading back to their Volvo. Going into this movie completely cold led me to believe that a crocodile, shark, or something else with sharp teeth was about to make its presence known, but instead, the couple choose to ditch the boat and seek assistance from the first house they see on land, opening a whole new realm of horrific possibilities when the lightning reveals scarecrows and dozens of decaying automobiles.

With the rain pounding down and nobody answering the door, they sneak in through the back and start an unsuccessful search for a telephone inside this nearly-inhabitable farmhouse that would scare anyone with common sense back to the black waters. With so many red flags present, it's not until Rob discovers a marijuana grow house on the property that he realizes they may be in serious danger, and then an angry pair of headlights all but confirm that their night is about to get so much worse. The heavily-armed drunken homeowners demand (with vulgarity galore) that whoever is inside their house show themselves immediately, racketing the tension to almost unbearable levels.

The elder of the brutes is in no condition to communicate as he clumsily makes his way upstairs to pass out, leaving his sons in charge of dealing with their uninvited guests. It would have been easy to make these characters one-dimensional monsters who waste no time in tearing apart their victims with as much nuance as a wild boar, but the film is just as focused on their personalities as their poor dental hygiene, and some of the scariest moments come during conversations around the dinner table after they've agreed to let the couple stay for the night. David Lyons does such a good job playing the terrifyingly unhinged older brother, mocking his guests' situation every chance he gets, that it's hard to imagine this actor playing anyone remotely stable.

What follows is a punishing night of sexual humiliation, broken legs, bashed brains, tables turning, stomachs churning, and all male viewers squirming as Pia recalls a piece of advice a relative once gave her: to beat a mad dog, you have to think like a mad dog. Oh yeah, and there's also a bloodthirsty Rottweiler named Honky in this mix from the director of *Urban Legend* and *Valentine*.

MORE REASONS TO GET A VASECTOMY

Bloody Birthday (1981)
Director: Ed Hunt
Writers: Ed Hunt, Barry Pearson
Cast: Lori Lethin, Julie Brown, K.C. Martel, Elizabeth Hoy, Billy Jayne, Andrew Freeman

It's easy to get *Bloody Birthday* confused with *Happy Birthday to Me* because they both came out in 1981 and had memorable VHS covers—the former suggests death by shish kabob and the later presents a bloody cake with lit severed fingers as candles—but the stories they tell aren't the least bit similar. *Happy Birthday to Me* is a fairly formulaic, methodical slasher with fun kills, impressive stunts, and a whopper of an ending in which the killer is revealed after almost two hours, whereas *Bloody Birthday* lies in the killer kid subgenre and wastes no time in showing a ten-year-old gleefully bashing in a police officer's head with a baseball bat. It moves along with the energy of a prepubescent on a sugar rush at Chuck E. Cheese, suggesting a violent outburst is possible at any moment, yet it knows just when to pull the trigger and when to hold back to let the strong performances and genuinely uneasy feel transcend the mayhem.

In many ways, *Bloody Birthday* feels like the chemically unbalanced stepsibling of *Village of the Damned*, replacing a mysterious mass blackout pregnancy for three different births at the same hospital during the zenith of a total solar eclipse. It's unclear how long these three children have been best friends and mass murderers, but when we catch up to them on the eve of their tenth birthday, they're receiving high marks at school during the day and teaming up at night to disrupt some cemetery sex (these doomed teenaged lovebirds clearly learned nothing from *Phantasm*) with shovels and nooses. This trio of hellions are terrifically cast, with one serving as the beauty, one as the brains, and one as the brawn, creating an unlikely and unsettling alliance as they get away with murder on a seemingly daily basis and take great pride in their creativity. When they play a game of hide and seek in a junkyard with one of their classmates who suspects they're up to something, I couldn't help but think of an episode of *Punky Brewster* that traumatized me as a child, and I'm sure at least a couple of you know what I'm talking about.

In an early scene, the little girl who's referred to as "angelface" by her relatives collects some cold hard cash from her two friends and allows them to look through a peephole to spy on her older sister undressing. Not only is she stripping to a hilariously cheesy rock song ("My Darlin Don't You Cry" by John Jones) that is full of "Na-na-na-na-na-na"s, but the actress is none other than Julie Brown in one of her first film roles! Not MTV's "Wubba wubba wubba" Downtown Julie Brown, but the comedian and future star of parody films like *Plump Fiction* and *Attack of the 5 Ft. 2 Women*, and the underrated

Horror Galore

Fox sketch comedy show *The Edge*. The fact that there is so much nudity in a film about ten-year-old kids is strange to say the least, and a clown who randomly appears wearing a shirt that says "I can't say no" doesn't help, but *Bloody Birthday*'s veneer of sleazy exploitation is no match for the goofy '80s sensibilities that keep you chuckling through the discomfort. You also get the sense that director Ed Hunt has a penchant for horror, naming one of his characters Chief Brody and borrowing the mask from *The Town that Dreaded Sundown* (or *Friday the 13th Part 2*, take your pick). A really sweet poster of Blondie also makes an appearance, and it's left unscathed during a shootout in which the bullets fly through the Ted Nugent poster instead.

The Pit (1981)

Director: Lew Lehman
Writer: Ian A. Stuart
Cast: Sammy Snyders, Jeannie Elias, Sonja Smits, Laura Hollingsworth, Andrea Swartz

When recalling the creepiest kids in horror movies, Isaac from *Children of the Corn*, Esther from *Orphan*, and Damien from *The Omen* are a few that get the most recognition, but they would probably all be easier to babysit for than Jamie Benjamin from *The Pit*.

Imagine if Charlie Brown grew up to be five maladjusted years older and struggled with the tribulations of puberty in the worst ways possible. Strange and pathetically needy, Jamie is scorned by just about every single person he comes into contact with, whether it's the little girl who lives next door or an elderly woman confined to a wheelchair, and so it's no wonder why he's always in a bad mood. I expect he also receives rocks while trick or treating. Under his bed is a pornographic magazine and on top of his bed is a teddy bear that is his only friend—a teddy bear that gives him terrible advice

Poster for *The Pit* (1981), Amulet Pictures

on how to attract the opposite sex. But while it hurt us immensely to see bad things happen to other horror loners like Carrie White, Jamie is such a creep that it's hard not to laugh hysterically when his classmate and neighbor Abergail (no, I did not intend to write Abigail) plays a bicycle-related prank on him that, while not as cruel and methodical as dumping a bucket of blood on someone at the prom, took a fair amount of time and effort to execute.

His parents are concerned with his peculiar, obsessive behaviors around girls and so they hire a babysitter working toward a psychology degree who has experience with exceptional children. Maybe they should have looked for someone a little less drop-dead gorgeous. Not only does she wake up one morning to find Jamie staring longingly at her ("I was just watching you sleep!"), but she also has some of her money stolen so that he can buy tons of meat to feed the tra-la-logs that live in the titular pit.

In Ian A. Stuart's original screenplay, these mythical beasts with glowing eyes and razor-sharp teeth were restricted to Jamie's wild imagination, but Lew Lehman, to whom *The Pit* is his only directorial credit, said to hell with that and made them real. After the meat is gone and Jamie proves unsuccessful at luring cows to the big hole in the ground, he decides to let the monsters feast on those who have tormented him, setting up the funniest moments of the movie when people clumsily walk right into the large pit in broad daylight. Other resounding laughs come at the expense of a librarian's ugly-as-sin eyeglasses and a swimming scene that might have inspired a completely dry Michael Caine in *Jaws: The Revenge*.

Filmed in Oshkosh, Wisconsin, *The Pit* eventually loses steam because the tra-la-logs aren't nearly as entertaining or charismatic as star Sammy Snyders, who previously played Tom Sawyer in the short-lived series *Huckleberry Finn and His Friends*, but it regains its footing and ends in pretty much the best way possible.

Horror Galore

OCCASIONALLY, DECEASED IS SUPERIOR

The Autopsy of Jane Doe (2016)
Director: André Øvredal
Writers: Ian Goldberg, Richard Naing
Cast: Brian Cox, Emile Hirsch, Ophelia Lovibond, Olwen Catherine Kelly

I should have been more responsive to this movie from the moment it came out, seeing as how it's a horror film from the director of Norwegian found-footage fantasy *Trollhunter* and starring one of our finest living actors in Brian Cox. It also earned a coveted Stephen King endorsement with the tweet "Visceral horror to rival *Alien* and early Cronenberg. Watch it, but not alone." Instead, I kept procrastinating on it and getting it confused with *The Taking of Deborah Logan*. The biggest reason why I wasn't in a hurry to see it is because its morgue setting was likely to bring back unpleasant, borderline-traumatic memories from the years I spent working in the death industry, where operating a cremation oven became a dreaded part of my daily routine; having a degree in Film Studies in a competitive job market often requires someone to venture way outside their comfort zone. Thankfully I never had to get anywhere close to an autopsy table because despite a lifetime of horror fandom, just the thought of observing such things in person has always made me queasy, and this was reiterated by the film's stomach-churning closeups of Jane Doe's body being sliced open and fully dissected, layer by layer. This is far from a ghoul movie, but it's certainly not one you'll want to watch while eating.

Law enforcement officers swarm the Virginia home where multiple homicides have just taken place, and instead of the usual signs of a break-in, in this case it appears that people attempted to escape. The most puzzling discovery is a halfway-buried corpse of a young woman in the basement.

Tommy Tilden (Cox) operates the morgue that's been in his family for generations, and he's taught his teenaged son Austin (Emile Hirsch, looking like a young Michael Shannon) all the tricks of the trade, like to never assume that a horribly burned corpse died from smoke inhalation. Austin's girlfriend Emma stops by before their date and he's reluctant to entertain her morbid curiosity about what takes place there, warning that certain things cannot be unseen, but fortunately for her, the elder Tilden is totally game and asks her in the most charming way which of the day's casualties she'd like a closer look of.

When the mysterious, cloudy-eyed "Jane Doe" is brought to the morgue by authorities in a late-night emergency to appease reporters who are bound to have questions the next morning, Austin postpones their midnight movie date at the Strand Theater so he can help out his dad (who hasn't seen a movie since he fell asleep five minutes into *The Notebook*) with the autopsy. This endearing father-son dynamic keeps us fully invested in these characters as they struggle to make sense of how this porcelain and clean body belies the charred organs and extensive damage under the skin. Adding to the confusion are the flickering lights and how the crackling handheld radio keeps insisting on leaving the classic rock station for The McGuire Sisters' version of "Open Up Your Heart (and Let the Sunshine In)," and this brought back fond memories of John Cusack being tormented by The Carpenters in the masterpiece *1408*. While the incisions' revelations get increasingly sinister and mystifying, so does the storm brewing outside, and soon the Tilden men find themselves trapped inside their own morgue. And "we've only just begun…"

Some podcasters I listen to weren't too keen on the third act but it played out just fine to me; I can't really think of any moment when I was anything less than fully engrossed. Surely you have watched Brian Cox (whose rant in *Adaptation* is just as epic as Clark Griswsold's in *Christmas Vacation*) battle Sam Hain in *Trick 'R Treat* on numerous Halloween seasons, so maybe now it's time to see how he fares against a set of restless stiffs eager to leave their cold slabs and stretch their legs.

Poster for ***Deathdream/Dead of Night*** (1974), Quadrant Films, Dead Walk Company, Impact Films

Deathdream (1974)

Director: Bob Clark
Writer: Alan Ormsby
Cast: John Marley, Lynn Carlin, Richard Backus, Henderson Forsythe, Anya Ormsby, Jane Daly

After Bob Clark (*A Christmas Story*, *Black Christmas*) and writer Alan Ormsby made the highly entertaining *Children Shouldn't Play with Dead Things*, they stuck around Florida for a little longer to make another film with much of the same cast and crew members, but this time they abandoned all campiness and dark humor with an emphatic declaration that playtime is over and death is serious business. The serious tone is captured right from the opening credits, when soothing nature sounds are drowned out by bombs and artillery.

We're introduced to a typical American family sitting at the dinner table with eyes closed and hands folded while the mother prays for the safe return of her son, Andy, who is fighting in the Vietnam War. The dreaded and unexpected knock on the door interrupts their meal and it's from the last person they want to see: a US Army Sergeant with unfortunate news. Andy's father and sister weep, but his mom insists in complete denial that it's all a lie. Later that night they are awakened by another visitor who they at first suspect might be a prowler, but instead, miraculously, it's Andy, alive and seemingly unharmed. What had been the darkest night of their entire lives is now the happiest, but the newly reunited family faces nothing but turmoil in the following days due to Andy's increasingly bizarre behavior that drives them apart.

Actor John Marley, who is mostly known for sharing a bed with a horse's severed head in *The Godfather*, is outstanding as the father who is losing patience over his son spending all his time up in his room, in a rocking chair, not speaking to anyone. Irritation turns to utter heartbreak as the situation worsens, with his wife exploding at the mere mention that something might be wrong with their son who was proclaimed deceased just days ago. Even when all signs point to Andy being the culprit in a truck driver's murder that's been the talk of the town, she insists that everything is fine and he just needs a little more time to acclimate to everyday life after experiencing the horrors of war.

Released at a time when the Vietnam War was still in the daily headlines, *Deathdream*, also known as *Dead of Night*, addresses post-traumatic stress disorder of the young men who return home as well as the unimaginable grief that their relatives experience when they don't. It's heavy stuff and at times, so sad that you might want to keep a box of tissues handy, but it's also a thrilling horror movie that will make your skin crawl and force your hand to cover your mouth in disbelief. The soundtrack consists of drones, distorted whispers, hisses, and shrieking violins that make you easy prey for what happens in the shocking third act, where Andy reunites with his adorable and affable girlfriend, played by Jane Daly, in hopes that a fun night out will make him normal again. Just like in the good old days, they go to Coney Island Drive Inn (which remains a popular establishment in Brooksville, Florida) and then to 41 Drive-In Theatre (which has sadly been demolished) for a grindhouse double feature. It's tough to imagine a more perfect time for Tom Savini to make his feature film debut as a makeup artist, and the fact that his effects are used so sparingly here make them all the more indelible.

It's a sophisticated and haunting take on "The Monkey's Paw" that confirms Jud Crandall's claim in *Pet Sematary* that sometimes dead is better, no matter how grief-stricken you may be.

Sole Survivor (1984)

Writer and Director: Thom Eberhardt
Cast: Anita Skinner, Kurt Johnson, Robin Davidson, Caren L. Larkey, Andrew Boyer

When *Final Destination* hit theaters in 2000, it was praised for its originality in exploring the possibility that when you escape death by the narrowest of margins, you are cheating an angry and vengeful Grim Reaper out of a soul that was rightfully his. It's a thoroughly entertaining and fascinating thriller but it doesn't quite feel as original after watching *Sole Survivor*, made 16 years prior.

When a young television producer named Denise survives a plane crash that killed everyone else on board, she begins to wonder if her survival was a mistake that will be rectified sooner rather than later. Unlike the jaw-dropping plane crash shown in excruciating detail in *Final Destination*, the much smaller-budgeted *Sole Survivor* could only afford to show the aftermath, but it's every bit as effective, as a slow camera pan reveals fires, mangled bodies (one man is severed at the waist), luggage contents strewn about, and finally, an emotionless woman clutching both armrests and without a scratch on her. Also, instead of playfully making every household item seem like a potential harbinger of a ridiculously elaborate death, this film takes a more cerebral approach and relies more on atmosphere and escalating dread. Denise nearly gets crushed by a driverless truck in a parking garage (one of several naturally spooky settings) and later begins to see strange people out in public, standing still and staring at her with unblinking eyes; *It Follows* (2014) is another modern horror movie that you can't help but compare this to. Her fragility is tested further when one of them follows her into an elevator of all places, and when she receives a phone call from an aging Hollywood actress with an uncanny ability of predicting the future, who warns her to keep her doors locked.

Among the extra goodies is a flummoxed mortician, a pervy cab driver, a game of strip poker (where Scream Queen Brinke Stevens is predictably dealt the worst cards), and lots and lots of rain, but the quieter moments are just as engaging because of likeable characters who have interesting things to say. The conversations between Denise and her studmuffin doctor/lover is especially fun to listen to, whether they are playfully teasing each other or discussing the characteristics of survivor guilt, a real-life mental condition that causes many people who miraculously survived traumatic episodes to die soon after, not by suicide or physical effects, but by behaving in a reckless manner and unwittingly putting themselves back in danger. Both Anita Skinner and Kurt Johnson give such impressive performances that I had to pause the film just to research them on IMDb and was saddened to learn that she never acted in anything again and he tragically passed away from AIDS at only 33 years old.

With the help of composer David F. Anthony and his eerie, minimalistic score reminiscent of *Night of the Living Dead*'s, director Thomas Eberhardt (making his feature debut) sets the mood during the opening credits with shots of lonely rain-slicked streets, flashing red streetlights, and department store mannequins. He would go on to create an equally mesmerizing montage for his follow-up, the outstanding *Night of the Comet*, which has deservedly received a large cult following and special edition Blu-ray in recent years. He sustains a high level of tension throughout the film and keeps us guessing all the way until the final shot, which is a real doozie. Also making his feature film debut is cinematographer Russell Carpenter, whose career never really took off because he continued shooting really cheap, obscure movies like *Titanic*, *Ant-Man*, and *Avatar*.

Sole Survivor was shown theatrically in December 1983, an appropriate time given the Christmas imagery and amusing "Jingle Bells" rendition a character gives while making a phone call. While the numbers quickly surpassed its $350,000 budget, the cast and crew never saw much of that money because this is one of those sad examples of inexperienced filmmakers that probably should have had an extra set of eyes on the contract they signed with the distributor International Film Marketing, who even re-edited the film against Eberhardt's wishes. Also sad is how quickly the 2008 DVD went out of print, and considering how difficult it is to find these days, I'm going to assume the Grim Reaper bought every copy and requires souls for currency.

COASTAL TOWNS WITH MORE EVIL SECRETS THAN SALTWATER TAFFY

Dead & Buried (1981)

Director: Gary Sherman
Writers: Ronald Shusett, Dan O'Bannon, Jeff Millar, Alex Stern, Chelsea Quinn Yarbro (novel)
Cast: James Farentino, Jack Albertson, Melody Anderson, Dennis Redfield, Lisa Blount

Considering all of the horror credibility this movie has, with a screenplay from the writers of *Alien*, an off-kilter performance by Robert Englund, and ghastly makeup effects designed by Stan Winston, it's bewildering that it never really found a wide audience.

It takes place in the sleepy coastal town of Potter's Bluff, bathed in atmosphere so oppressive that you can practically taste the sea salt, and with an omnipresent foghorn that sounds like it's trying to warn travelers to stay the hell away, people like George Le Moyne, a photographer visiting from St. Louis who is taking pictures on the beach while a devastatingly sad piano score plays. His camera eye spots a beautiful woman on the beach who proceeds to charm, flatter, and seduce him, leaving him weak-kneed and unable to detect the angry mob forming around him. George is bashed with crowbars and shovels, tied up, and then set on fire. This won't be the first time the viewers are played like marionettes and subjected to horrifying, disturbing acts of violence at the unlikeliest of moments, for *Dead & Buried* is a movie that waits until you're most vulnerable to pounce.

Lobby card for *Dead & Buried* (1981), Aspen Productions

Much is asked of actor James Farentino, who plays the sheriff investigating the murder and whose shoulders the film rests upon, and he brilliantly portrays the nuanced protagonist with everyman sensibilities that you can't help but root for. To see him melt down with increasing despondence as each mortifying layer to the mystery is revealed is both soul-crushing and exhilarating. It's easy to imagine this character drinking brewskies with Chief of Police Martin Brody at the end of a very long shift, sharing tales of their respective New England coastal towns. But while Chief Brody only had to worry about "a large predator that supposedly injured some bathers," this poor sap can't help but clench his fists and scream "What the hell is going on in this town?!" when murders pile up and remain unsolved, when buried coffins are missing their skeletons, when the new gas station attendant bears an uncanny resemblance to the deceased photographer (and also to actor Peter MacNicol in my opinion), and when his loving wife develops a fascination with witchcraft. Equally captivating is Jack Albertson as the dapper town mortician with questionable practices, macabre humor, and a sizeable collection of Big Band Era records. With over 180 acting credits to his name, Albertson remained at the top of his game until the very end, even when he was dying from cancer while filming *Dead & Buried*. He was able to attend the premiere with an oxygen tank, but passed away just ten days later, and a few months before children got to hear him voice the trigger-happy lunatic Amos Slade in *The Fox and the Hound*.

The only noticeable misstep is a scene involving a family of three whose decisions are infuriatingly idiotic after passing the "Welcome to Potter's Bluff" sign. Nobody can blame poor George because his only mistake was thinking that an attractive stranger flirting with him and then disrobing on the beach was within the realms of probability, but these people are lured to a creepy house simply because the mother thinks she saw a light for a split second, and then once they see that it's covered in cobwebs and long-abandoned, decide to split up so the father can investigate that unsettling noise coming from the basement.

The final act is especially powerful as Sheriff Gillis' world shatters with the revelations of Potter's Bluff, and then the return of that sorrowful score from composer Joe Renzetti allows us to grieve and process with him. *Dead & Buried* was more than deserving of that killer poster and the tagline "It will take your breath away…all of it," both of which were preserved in Blue Underground's 2016 Blu-ray that features three different commentary tracks and additional features.

Hour of the Wolf (1968)
Writer and Director: Ingmar Bergman
Cast: Max von Sydow, Liv Ullmann, Gertrud Fridh, Georg Rydeberg, Erland Josephson

While many of Swedish filmmaker Ingmar Bergman's masterpieces have crossed into horror territory, only one has its roots planted firmly in the genre, and it was the follow-up to arguably his greatest achievement in 1968's *Persona*. Drawing influence from some of his own nightmares along with Mozart's opera *The Magic Flute*, Bergman cast his former lover Liv Ullmann (who at the time was pregnant with their child) and his longtime muse Max von Sydow as a couple who move to a secluded island only to have their relationship emulate the rocky waters.

No, Max von Sydow's character Johan Borg, a painter looking forward to a life of isolation, doesn't get bit by a werewolf under a full moon like the title might suggest. Instead, Bergman stated that he named the film after "The hour between night and dawn … when most people die, sleep is deepest, nightmares are most real. It is the hour when the sleepless are haunted by their worst anguish, when ghosts and demons are most powerful. The hour of the wolf is also the hour when most babies are born." One afternoon while Johan is out painting landscapes and macabre interpretations of other island citizens, his sad-eyed pregnant wife Alma is visited by an elderly woman claiming to be "216, no, 76 years old" who suggests that she read his diary hidden under the bed, containing passages of nightmares, childhood traumas, regrets, ghosts from the past that refuse to flee, and other things that would explain his insomnia-fueled fragility. The fact that Johan previously joked that if this aged woman ever removed her hat, her face would probably go along with it makes her surprise visit all the more unsettling.

The owner of the island invites Johan and Alma to his castle for a dinner party, and the way Bergman circles the table and captures a dozen different conversations concurrently (a nice callback to the score-less opening credits) will disorient anyone with a shred of social anxiety, especially since each glass of wine causes the other guests to appear more eccentric and mysterious. Johan's dizzy state, intensified by a surreal puppet show, leads to pure madness when another man suggests they've met before under disturbing circumstances, and when a painting on the wall depicts a long-lost love, Veronica Vogler, who is later rumored to appear at the next castle gathering much to an increasingly jealous Alma's displeasure.

This majestically shot film on the windy Baltic island of Fårö is just about as philosophical and mesmerizing as Bergman's more acclaimed films like *The Seventh Seal*, *Wild Strawberries*, and *Cries and Whispers*, and the fact that it's nowhere near as emotionally draining means that you can still cheer when plucked-out eyeballs land in glasses of wine, when gravity is defied by wall-walking, and when bratty vampiric kids are thrown off cliffs.

Messiah of Evil (1973)

Writers and Directors: Willard Huyck, Gloria Katz
Cast: Marianna Hill, Michael Greer, Joy Bang, Anita Ford, Royal Dano

A young free-spirited drifter named Toni pays 50 cents to see a screening of the 1950 crime thriller *Kiss Tomorrow Goodbye*, a very apropos title considering the unsettling menace that greets her the moment she enters the theater. There's not a soul in sight in the lobby or behind the concession stand, and so she helps herself to a bag of popcorn and walks into the massive auditorium to dead silence, a blank screen, and a man sitting in the front row despite the fact that there are about 300 better seats available. As Toni leans back and munches on her popcorn, she notices a couple of other patrons and then looks straight ahead to see that the man in the front row is no longer staring at the blank screen, but right at her. Then the lights abruptly fade and the trailer for *Gone with the West* projects, distracting Toni to the point where she doesn't notice hordes of people piling into the theater and around her, getting closer and closer. Taking place near the middle of *Messiah of Evil*, this is a perfectly executed scene that slowly raises the tension with each impeccable shot and clever edit, and tempts you to scream at Toni to climb over the seat in front of her before it's too late. And it's far from the only moment of this movie that will be floating around your subconscious for the next several days to threaten any hopes for pleasant dreams.

This surreal 70's horror film was made by the husband-and-wife team responsible for *Howard the Duck* and the screenplay for *American Graffiti*! It opens with a young girl introducing her razor blade to the neck of a sweaty, feverish man—the title credit appearing in mid-slice—and a wide-pitched narrator warning that "they're waiting for you, they'll take you one by one and no one will hear you SCREAM!!!" It uses dream logic and a color palette reminiscent of Italian horror films popular at the time to tell the tale of a woman named Arletty traveling to the coastal town of Point Dume, California, in search of her father, whom she hasn't heard from in a while. A gifted and eccentric artist, he has a bizarrely decorated house that the film gets great mileage out of, with its depth murals and furniture swinging from chains. Art director Jack Fisk went on to provide further orgiastic feasts for the eyeballs in *Phantom of the Paradise*, *Carrie*, *Mulholland Dr.*, and *The Straight Story*, and even earned Academy Award nominations for his work in *The Revenant* and *There Will be Blood*.

Horror Galore

An unsuccessful afternoon of locals shaking their heads and backing away at questions regarding her father's whereabouts takes an interesting turn when she meets a dreamy aristocrat with charismatic cult-like appeal, who claims to have been born in a Portuguese castle. He's been staying in town with his two traveling companion groupies to investigate the strange local legends that might be related to her father's sudden disappearance following weeks of mental anguish, evidenced by a recent journal entry that describes the images of ghouls that he wrestles with while walking alone on the beach at night.

Point Bume harbors secrets so unimaginable that it's impossible not to lose at least a few marbles while driving through…or something far worse if you happen to run into the local mice-eating, truck-driving towering albino. You might even find yourself spitting out beetles and maggots at the next rest stop if you're lucky enough to survive. And if you prefer to avoid the crowds by doing your grocery shopping late at night, you'll be in for quite a surprise.

FOOTAGE WORTH FINDING

Butterfly Kisses (2018)
Writer and Director: Erik Kristopher Myers
Cast: Seth Adam Kallick, Rachel Armiger, Reed DeLisle, Kelsey June Swann, Matt Lake

In the basement of his new home, struggling filmmaker Gavin York finds a mysterious box of mini DV tapes under the stairs and ignores the cryptic message: DON'T WATCH. The tapes contain many hours of rough-cut footage from a student documentary about local myth The Peeping Tom, a Bloody Mary-like spirit that can be conjured up by staring down the Ilchester Tunnel for a solid hour without blinking. Teenaged filmmakers Sophia and Feldman are hoping that by exploiting the talents of a staring contest champion, they can prove the legend is real even if it means that Peeping Tom will then appear closer and closer to the man every time he blinks until he's close enough to perform an eyelash kiss and then something gruesome.

Gavin becomes convinced that the teens, who he's unable to track down, were onto something with their disturbing documentary that went mysteriously unfinished, so he hopes to continue their work and finally catch his big break in Hollywood. By having Gavin (wonderfully played by Seth Adam Kallick) be a pretentious, self-righteous twat who loses his patience at interviewees who don't give the desired responses, the movie is able to poke a lot of fun in the found footage subgenre without once coming across as forced or overly meta, and despite his insufferable nature, we can't help but feel sorry for him when he's mocked and ridiculed in public for insisting that the footage contains proof of the Peeping Tom's existence. Maybe I'm just easily swayed by the sight of a guy in a Rush t-shirt, but my favorite scene would have to be when Gavin desperately tries to enlist the services of the local paranormal and ghost investigators by making his case in what looks like a high school gymnasium. It's never a good sign when a presentation ends with someone inquiring about your medication habits.

From the quaint locals who are interviewed in the bitter cold outside a wagon wheel store to its examination of a tortured artist who's losing his marriage, money, and his sanity, everything feels authentic as the movie playfully peels off the layers to this mystery (while probably leaving you with more questions than answers when all is said and done). *Butterfly Kisses* is a fun exploration of uncharted mockumentary waters, and by having writer and director Erik Kristopher Myers appear on screen as the producer of Gavin's project, it plays like a documentary within a documentary within a documentary. Myers, a fixture of the independent film scene in Baltimore, sadly took his own life at age 45, just three years after *Butterfly Kisses* won top prizes at the GenreBlast Film Festival and the Silver Scream Famous Monsters event.

Horror Galore

In addition to the author of Weird Maryland and the director of the documentary *Divine Trash*, this movie also features the clever participation of Eduardo Sanchez, a godfather to found footage horror.

Gonjiam: Haunted Asylum (2018)

Director: Beom-sik Jeong
Writers: Beom-sik Jeong, Sang-min Park
Cast: Yoo Je-Yoon, Seung-Wook Lee, Ye-Won Mun, Ah-yeon Oh, Ji-Hyun Park, Sung-Hoon Park

Sometimes I leave the lights on because it's easier to take notes that way, but in this case, I was just feeling cowardly. Not since the last 30 minutes of Adam Wingard's underappreciated *Blair Witch* has a found footage film scared the holy bejesus out of me to this degree for long stretches of time.

CNN posted an editorial on their website years ago revealing the seven freakiest places on the planet, and joining the ranks of Pripyat Amusement Park, the Catacombs in Paris, Sedlec Ossuary in the Czech Republic, and Akodessewa Fetish Market in Toyo was the Gonjiam Psychiatric Hospital located in Gwangju-Si, South Korea (about a 40-minute drive from Seoul). When it was abruptly shut down and left abandoned in the '90s, local legend suggested that many patients had died from secret experiments conducted by psychotic doctors, and even though it was probably something far less sinister like costly structural damages and sewage problems, the rumors continued to circulate. The locals were apparently unhelpful in revealing the exact location to morbidly curious tourists, but that didn't stop the massive and decaying Gonjiam building from receiving hundreds of visitors year after year, some of whom were lugging expensive video and audio equipment with them much like the characters in this movie.

Poster for *Gonjiam: Haunted Asylum* (2018), Hive Mediacorp

Wi Ha-Joon, the host of a YouTube program called *The Horror Times' Terror Squad* hires a small crew of videographers and influencers to accompany him to the haunted asylum for a live video broadcast on October 26th with the intention of breaking a million views and being the first group to open the door to Room 402, the only room sealed shut following the hospital's closure and owner's mysterious disappearance. The mood is lighthearted and jovial on the drive up, as the youngsters crack jokes, show off their hi-tech video equipment, and take slight detours to jump into bodies of water. Some are fueled on adrenaline (especially a girl named Charlotte who has already been to three of the places on CNN's list and is anxious to cross off another one) and others on internet vanity, but are all determined to make this episode a success while not vanishing off the face of the earth like many others who had bypassed security and found a way inside.

The group of seven sets up a tent in the woods outside the property and enjoys a quick ramen feast before Wi Ha-Joon mans the editing suite and the others fasten their dual-facing GoPro cameras that capture their point of view as well as their reactions as they walk toward the creepiest building they've ever seen, graffitied with message like "Enter and you will die. Fuck it." They split up into pairs once inside and as they explore the four floors, the fear shoots up as rapidly as their view count, all while their director warns them not to leave under any circumstance until they can reach a million, which reminded me of *Tales from the Crypt*'s scariest episode, "Television Terror."

Director Beom-sik Jeong and his cast and crew didn't film at the infamous asylum, but instead gave the Maritime High School in Busan a makeover to mirror the façade and floor plans. In addition to the GoPro cameras, the characters also employed drones and motion-detector cameras to give us a much wider variety of angles and perspectives than in a typical found-footage film, taking full advantage of the décor as well as the wide pools of darkness that cause our eyes to dart back and forth knowing that anything might be approaching from any corner. During post-production, a court in Seoul dismissed a lawsuit from the actual asylum owner who declared that the chances of selling the building would be harmed by the film's release. One year later, *Gonjiam: Haunted Asylum* had become the third most-watched Korean film of all time, following *A Tale of Two Sisters* and *Phone*, and one of the ten freakiest places in the world had become completely demolished.

Willow Creek (2013)

Writer and Director: Bobcat Goldthwait
Cast: Alexie Gilmore, Bryce Johnson, Laura Montagna, Peter Jason, Timmy Red

Comedian-turned-filmmaker Bobcat Goldthwait originally intended to make a satirical Christopher Guest-style mockumentary set at a Bigfoot convention, but being a lifelong outcast with passions that would be considered strange by the majority, he found it difficult to poke fun at the community. Plan B became a found-footage horror film about a young couple named Jim and Kelly who are traveling to Northern California to make a short documentary. This excursion to Bigfoot territory has the folksy charm of *Legend of Boggy Creek*, the light-hearted humor of *Missing Link*, and the escalating danger of *Abominable* (2006) packed in a tight 80 minutes that never goes off course.

Jim has been passionate about Sasquatch lore since childhood and is extremely excited about visiting the location of the famous footage that Roger Patterson and Robert Gimlin captured in 1967. Even though Kelly says at one point, "Honey, I'm afraid of a lot of things but I'm not afraid to admit that I don't believe in Bigfoot," she's happy to go along for the ride because it means spending time together. Along the way they stop at small towns which have embraced the Bigfoot gimmick as a means of survival, and interview some of the locals. Out of all the interview segments, my favorite is with a woman who has worked at the Willow Creek Visitor Center for 20 years but has no idea where the famous site actually is. When Jim asks if she believes in Bigfoot, she answers "Not at all" without hesitation. Jim and Kelly are fully realized characters with their own idiosyncrasies (Jim struggling with the "Action!" cues is funny), and it's a pleasure to listen to them discuss the merits of the famous Bigfoot Burger and the questionable nuances of murals and redwood-carved statues. At one point I noticed that my jaw was hurting from all the smiling this movie was making me do.

When they leave their car behind and make the long hike into the forest, he's having the time of his life but her patience starts to wear thin, causing them to set up camp earlier than expected. The highlight of the film is an almost 20-minute unbroken stationary shot from inside the tent that is an absolute juggernaut of tension-building. It wasn't divulged to the actors what would be happening and so they're just as terrified as the rest of us are during this scene—well, probably even more so since they witnessed the presence of mountain lions near the set shortly before shooting!

If you find yourself hungry for more tent terror off the beaten path, then I recommend the 2014 survival thriller *Backcountry*, in which a man's plans to propose to his girlfriend during a camping getaway are disrupted by a creepy tour guide played by Eric Balfour from *The Texas Chainsaw Massacre* remake, a wrong turn, and a ferocious bear that likes to take advantage of those who are heavy sleepers.

SLIME, GRIME, GORE, AND BODY HORROR

Baby Blood (1990)
Director: Alain Robak
Writers: Serge Cukier, Alain Robak
Cast: Emmanuelle Escourrou, Christian Sinniger, Jean-Francois Gallotte, Roselyne Geslot

Being foolishly under the impression that ultra-gory horror films from France didn't exist before the boundary-pushing movement that included *Martyrs*, *Inside*, *Frontier(s)*, and *High Tension*, I was very intrigued to learn about *Baby Blood*, which came out shortly after Frank Henenlotter's *Brain Damage* (1988) and also features a conversational slug-like parasite in need of a new host.

With a harsh, demonic shrill of a voice, the parasite narrates to open the film: "In the beginning, the world was no more than a cooling star covered with hideous vegetation and foul gargoyles who fought each other for their sustenance under the star-spangled sky. In the beginning, the very first life form appeared somewhere around the forgotten edges of a bog in Africa. All these life-forms started reproducing, all but one that is… me. I only needed one thing to happen to me…to be born!" It finally starts implementing this grand scheme by hiding inside the body of an African cheetah and waiting until it arrives at a circus in Northern France to cause the beautiful animal to explode (mercifully offscreen) so that it can crawl inside the trailer of a sleeping performer named Yanka and then inside her uterus to take over the fetus that she most likely wasn't even aware of.

When the abusive husband that Yanka escaped from manages to track her down inside of the scariest apartment complex in all of France, she doesn't hesitate to plunge a butcher knife into his chest. She'll need to keep the killing spree going to placate her little problem, who warns that it will tear her body apart if she doesn't feed it properly with the freshest of blood. Often either completely naked or covered in blood, Emmanuelle Escourrou gives a daring performance that covers so much ground in its 88 minutes of lunacy. Her character picks up a different profession with each phase of pregnancy, and after an unsuccessful suicide attempt, ultimately submits to a symbiotic relationship and a lifestyle of inflicting artery-slashing geysers to the hornball men who follow her. Even the monstrous slug shows some growth (and not just in the physical sense) when it admits to also being unhappy from time to time and asking Yanka if she ever feels any affection for it.

Cronenbergian body horror meets a high body count in a viscera-soaked climax that will make gorehounds feel like Dracula whenever a nocturnal bloodmobile drives through Whitby Abbey. Speaking of the Count, Academy Award-winner Gary Oldman supposedly voiced the nicotine-hating creature in the English-dubbed version of this movie just a couple years before his Transylvanian twist.

Horror Galore

Beyond the Darkness (1979)

Director: Joe D'Amato
Writers: Ottavio Fabbri, Giacomo Guerrini (story)
Cast: Kieran Canter, Cinzia Monreale, Franca Stoppi, Sam Modesto, Anna Cardini

Last week's movie-watching itinerary included *Sweetheart*, *Curtains*, and *Planet of the Vampires*, and I wish I had saved one of them for today because with temperatures reaching 100 degrees for the first time all year, perhaps looking at the ocean, Canadian winter landscapes, or outer space could have made me feel a couple degrees cooler. Instead, I treated my sticky skin to a layer of grime and subjected my sweat-stung eyes to disgusting acts of depravity courtesy of the notoriously ghoulish Italian film *Beyond the Darkness*.

With a directing pedigree that includes post-apocalyptic action flick *Endgame*, gory video nasty *Anthropophagous*, softcore porn thriller *Annabelle and Francoise*, and the hardcore *Porno Holocaust*, you never know what you're going to get with a Joe D'Amato film. Even before I learned that he also produced the best worst movie of all time, *Troll 2* was already on my mind, not just because Claudio Fragasso made another movie called *Beyond Darkness*, but also because the title sequence of this movie includes a music credit to The Goblins. As Margo Prey would ask with the blankest of expressions, "Michael, who are the goblins?" Turns out that just like in the European version of the soundtrack for *Dawn of the Dead*, the progressive rock soundtrack gods known as Goblin were given a The and an S for some reason, and as recently as 2017, their live setlists included the funky score for *Beyond the Darkness*.

No stranger to death after his parents died in an accident 11 years ago, Frank tells his hospitalized fiancé that "Death has no power to separate us," unaware that the catalyst for both her illness and final breath is his housekeeper Iris gleefully sticking needles into a voodoo doll. Returning to his luxurious villa a heartbroken man, he is quickly comforted by Iris and a suckle from her breast, suggesting that this might not be the most professional of relationships. He fulfills a promise by returning to the cemetery hours after the funeral and digging up Anna's body, conveniently only buried about six inches under, but the drive back home isn't so easy when he has to deal with a flat tire, a police officer, and an adamant Cockney hitchhiker all within the span of about a minute.

After a quick succession of drags from her joint, the hitchhiker passes out in the passenger seat and Frank takes advantage by carrying his fiancé inside to an operating table, slicing her up, and taking an even bigger bite out of her heart than in the most memorable shot from *Jason Goes to Hell*; her other organs are simply tossed into a bucket. The hitchhiker wakes up just in time to see him replace a set of eyeballs, and despite having plenty of time to escape or look for a weapon, she just attempts the weakest of strangulations, and for her poor decision making, she gets chopped into pieces by Iris' meat cleaver and then tossed into a bathtub full of acid. It's a very messy procedure but nothing compared to what Walter White and Jesse Pinkman experienced.

Shades of *Psycho* are revealed in how Iris dresses, wears her hair, and brandishes a butcher knife, and how Frank desperately relies on his taxidermy skills to preserve the most important person in his life while avoiding a fate that doesn't include her. As ghastly as his actions are, it's hard to ignore the levels of tragedy and obsession whenever that sad piano melody plays, even when he's pacing around the bedroom trying to figure out how he can have consensual sex with another girl right beside Anna's corpse. This film, also known as *Buio Omega* and *Blue Holocaust* among others, is more than simply a mire of bad taste and perversion, but it also doesn't hesitate to zoom in on the nipple of a woman burning alive inside a cremation oven.

The Demon's Rook (2013)

Director: James Sizemore
Writers: James Sizemore, Akon Tidwell
Cast: James Sizemore, Ashleigh Jo Sizemore, John Chatham, Melanie Richardson, Josh Gould

It was fortuitous that my cat Mr. Marbles Tigerpants was sleeping on my lap and making the remote control difficult to reach as I was watching *The Demon's Rook*, because at the 25-minute mark, I was so close to pressing the home menu button to consider other options. While I was digging the practical effects, monster designs, and overall look of the film, the story of young Roscoe losing his carefree existence when the demon monk he draws every night abducts him to the underworld to be a guardian of the cosmos for an inevitable battle between good and evil wasn't really grabbing me. This bout of uncertainty didn't last much longer because once the unearthed and adult Roscoe reunites with his childhood friend Eva while the scary demons that followed him above ground start turning the town into a slaughterama, it became every bit as enjoyable to watch as I'm sure it was enjoyable to make.

A scene featuring partygoers chanting "Cake! Cake! Cake!" aroused my sweet tooth and prompted an intermission where I had to wake up my lap cat and drive to Wendy's for a large chocolate frosty, and on the way back I was practically giddy about returning to the couch and seeing more Fulci-level zombies, jaw-dropping gore, mind-controlling antics from a demoness that could be the distant cousin of *The Unnamable*'s Alyda, and Southern stereotypes so cartoonish that, of course, there's an impromptu harmonica hoe down. *The Demon's Rook* has a really fun rhythm the way scenes with the two leads alternate with the wide-ranging annihilation of side characters that were just introduced, and to be honest it had been months since I so enjoyed the simple pleasure of watching goofy characters get killed.

Writer, director, and star James Sizemore (producer of one of 2016's greatest horror films in *The Void*), filled the cast and crew with friends, relatives, and even household pets like Butterbean the Dog and Dweezil the Rat, and so he was able to allot nearly all of the $70,000 budget to makeup, prosthetics, and geysers of blood, which are all confidently paraded in closeups and daylight. Despite the fact that it shimmers in crystal clear 2013 digital photography, it's rooted in the same bad-tasting, deceased-yet-lively soil of youthful Peter Jackson, where talented artists could be as outrageous as possible without having to worry about studio interference. It's just the kind of movie you prayed about stumbling upon while channel-surfing late at night in simpler times.

While scrolling on Tubi, you'll encounter many other independent horror movies from 2013 that also revel in gratuitous gore, nudity, and redneck stereotypes, but *The Demon's Rook* aims to do so much more than just shock, titillate, and offend. There is a lot of heart to this apple-bobbing, eyeball-popping adventure, and the beautiful shots of dogs and butterflies (if only they could have afforded the music rights to one of Heart's best songs) fit in just as well as the savage throat tears and disembowelments.

Evil Dead Trap (1988)

Director: Toshiharu Ikeda
Writer: Takashi Ishii
Cast: Miyuki Ono, Aya Katsuragi, Hitomi Kobayashi, Eriko Nakagawa, Masahiko Abe

OK, where the hell do I begin with this one? I'm still trying to process the past 102 minutes and not sure if the formation of complete, coherent sentences is even a possibility after the insanity waffles crooked have sometimes chumbawumba sad actually. I had heard of this Japanese movie for years but didn't make it a priority until the boys at the Horrorble Podcast spoke highly of its weirdness and ability to surprise even the most jaded of horror fans who think they've seen it all. It's an amalgamation of slasher tendencies, Cronenberg body horror, Fulci-flavored gore, atmospheric tones of Argento, and eerie Giallo-like synth music, all working together in perfect harmony inside of a dilapidated factory that can crush you with crumbling walls or sizzle your brain matter with errant electrical charges. And while there is zero connection to the *Evil Dead* series, we do get some accelerated point of view shots from demonic forces who are in a big hurry to feast on human souls.

A late-night television host named Nami, after asking viewers to send in homemade videotapes to be used in future segments, has her curiosity peaked when a package arrives at her door with a note reading "For those who suffer sleepless nights." The accompanying video is of the snuff film persuasion and features a woman who bears a striking resemblance to her getting her eye gouged out. Usually somebody would go to the police with a piece of evidence like this, but Nami is in a desperate quest for ratings and so she brings four of her crew members to the location where the video was shot, ignoring the signs at the gate to keep out. One member of the team thinks that they'll be hotter than Madonna overnight if they can find a body, and so they unwisely split up to explore the giant property, occasionally running into snakes, bugs, maggots, metal spikes, and the occasional dirty blanket to make love on top of. Nami encounters an enigmatic, well-dressed gentleman who provides no answers, just a simple warning to be careful and alert in these dangerous army base remnants, as if she couldn't have already figured that out.

After our remorseful TV host sees another comrade depicted on rows of television, her face covered in white makeup and crying out for help, she ventures deeper into the building (with tilted shots giving it a disorienting funhouse vibe) and eventually inside a subterranean passageway that looks like it could be a portal to hell. The events that follow don't really make a lick of sense but in a movie this unconventional, it's best to just sit back and let the evil dead trap do its thing. Few people will complain about the lapses in logic but I suspect some will feel restless by the long running time, especially when a few minutes are totally wasted by an unnecessary rape scene that does nothing for the plot other than make it even more convoluted. Still, this is an inventive and stylish creepfest that is well worth seeking out.

The Incredible Melting Man (1977)
Writer and Director: William Sachs
Cast: Burr DeBenning, Myron Healey, Alex Rebar, Ann Sweeny, Michael Alldredge

Three months after getting central air-conditioning for the first time since moving to Oregon in 2004, the universe congratulated me by giving the Pacific Northwest its most extreme heat wave in history. Today was the third day in a row where Portland has broken its all-time highest recorded temperature. It reached an ungodly 116 degrees earlier, and because I was morbidly curious to get a tiny taste of what those weirdo hikers in Death Valley, California voluntarily subject themselves to, I went for a little walk. Stepping out into the heat dome at first caused me to chuckle in disbelief, but then I became overwhelmed with sympathy at remembering the governor's State of Emergency declaration. There are hundreds of thousands of Oregonians without air conditioning and the death toll could be staggering when this heat wave is all over.

The power cables hadn't melted and the pavement hadn't split apart like in other parts of the city, but there was such an eerie silence that made me feel like I was the last person on earth. I only encountered one other person outside, and to make the scene even more surreal, this young and healthy-looking man was wearing an N95 mask as if it weren't already hard enough to breathe out there. For the first five minutes I was feeling OK thanks to my ice water, but on the way back home my energy started to rapidly deplete to the point where I was tempted to seek shelter under a tree and slowly melt into the ground. It made me think of an incredibly fun and humorous movie that I could watch again if I made it back home in one piece.

"Magnificent! You've never seen anything until you've seen the sun through the rings of Saturn," proclaims Astronaut Steve West just before being blasted by a solar flare. When we next see him, he's back on Earth somehow, unconscious in a hospital bed and flabbergasting the hospital staff who have never seen anything quite like this in all their years in the business. He wakes up on the wrong side of the bed and when he removes the bandages and gets a look in the mirror, he flies into a mad rage that causes one of the nurses to run away screaming in slow motion in a scene that I'm sure was championed when *The Incredible Melting Man* appeared on *Mystery Science Theatre 3000*. Steve escapes from the hospital and through the woods, where he decapitates a man for choosing the most miserable-looking puddle to go fishing in. The sight of his severed head floating merrily down the stream, tumbling down a waterfall, and then buckling against a rock is much more magnificent than the sun through the rings of Saturn.

By this point, Steve is experiencing the absurdly advanced stages of radiation, where he's constantly producing globs of goo, blood, and slime that spill to the ground and take chunks of flesh, and occasionally a body part, with it. And the reason you can't take your eyes off the horrific state of him is because the producers managed to land the one-and-only Rick Baker for the makeup effects despite having a budget much, much smaller than his previous projects like *Star Wars*, *King Kong* (1976), and *The Exorcist*. Following the path of blood that leads to several subsequent victims is Steve's very concerned friend, Dr. Ted Nelson, but he's a mostly ineffective hero as if he never fully got over the disappointment of not having any crackers with his supper.

B-movie actress Cheryl "Rainbeaux" Smith (*Lemora: A Child's Tale of the Supernatural*, *Revenge of the Cheerleaders*) and future Oscar-winning director of *The Silence of the Lambs* Jonathan Demme appear in minor but noteworthy roles in this movie where there were daily arguments behind the scenes over what the tone should be. The director wanted to make a goofy parody but the producer insisted on a serious horror picture. They both probably walked away unhappy with the final results but this gooey horror-comedy compromise sure landed well on my palate. If you only have room in your heart for one incredible man, then it should probably be reserved for *The Incredible Shrinking Man* from 1957, but everyone else would be wise to seek the acquaintance of this incredible melting man when looking for a good time on summer evenings when you can fry eggs on the sidewalk.

Horror Galore

Silent Night, Deadly Night 4: Initiation (1990)

Director: Brian Yuzna
Writers: Richard Gladstein, Arthur Gorson, Woody Keith, S.J. Smith, Brian Yuzna
Cast: Neith Hunter, Tommy Hinkley, Clint Howard, Hugh Fink, Richard N. Gladstein

I saw the first two *Silent Night, Deadly Night* films but never bothered with the others because nobody talks about them, and their straight-to-video status and zero critical acclaim more than hints at diminishing returns. After revisiting the surreal and slimy *Society*, I perused Brian Yuzna's IMDb page and was shocked to learn that he directed the fourth *Silent Night, Deadly Night* installment, and despite the fact that the Christmas tree had just been dismantled and returned to the garage two weeks prior, I decided that a Yuletide encore was in store because a Brian Yuzna Christmas horror movie wasn't something I wanted to wait 11 long months to experience.

Taking a cue from *Halloween III: Season of the Witch*, this sequel keeps the holiday cheer intact while substituting all slashing with strange cults and large bugs, and completely ignores the previous installments. After a fun title credit sequence that juxtaposes 90's PowerPoint templates with the musical arrangements of 60's crime thrillers like *Charade*, a homeless man in Southern California played by Clint Howard (!!!!!) finds a half-eaten burger on the ground and objects not to the fact that it's covered in maggots, but to the lack of cheese. Then a woman seemingly jumps to her death from a tall building and spontaneously combusts on the pavement, prompting Clint to get so close that we don't know whether he'll stare in strange fascination, use the flames to warm his hands, or declare her a superior alternative to a maggot hamburger.

Kim, an ambitious young newspaper staffer whose journalist aspirations are repeatedly beaten down by rampant sexism decides to defy her boss (played by Reggie Bannister!!!!!) by investigating the strange suicide on her own. Inside the building of the tragedy is where she meets the enigmatic bookstore owner Fima, who gives her a complimentary book that explores feminism and the occult. Her boyfriend's father isn't nearly as generous, giving her only a string of nasty insults about her being Jewish and wanting a career rather than celebrating Christmas and the joys of cooking and cleaning. Her night gets even more annoying when an army of cockroaches invades her apartment, and one of them is so gigantic that it must have come from Gordon Shumway's home planet of Melmac.

Special effects maestro Screaming Mad George was no stranger to roach scenes, having recently worked on Debbie's memorable metamorphosis in *A Nightmare on Elm Street 4: The Dream Master*, and he succeeds in making us squirm repeatedly with the bugs and also the gnarly body horror that one expects in a Brian Yuzna picture. Fingers bend and twist independently, larvae swim around ferociously beneath the skin, mutant slugs try their damndest to escape out of a terrified woman's mouth, and yet perhaps no visual is more disconcerting than Clint Howard putting on a dildo mask and partaking in a cult ceremony.

Had this feminist cult set up their headquarters in ice-cold New England rather than sunny Southern California, and had this bizarre and amusing movie stood on its own with a simple Initiation title, then it surely would have gotten more fanfare due to the fact that holiday horror was slim pickings until recent years. To this day it still hasn't received a stand-alone DVD release, only included in a collection with parts 3 and 5, but it's easy to imagine a future in which it gets the kind of royal treatment that causes horror fans to flock to it like Ricky Chapman flocked to naughty miscreants.

Slime City (1988)
Writer and Director: Gregory Lamberson
Cast: Craig Sabin, Mary Huner, T.J. Merrick, Dennis Embry, Dick Biel, Jane Doniger Reibel

If you were awestruck by the radiant body-meltings in *Street Trash* but were a little turned off by the ugly tone and unlikeable characters, then you deserve to take a trip to Slime City, where among the gratuitous goo, grindhouse sensibilities, and NYC slums are people worth giving a damn about. In this case, it's an artist named Craig who, with the aid of his girlfriend, finally finds a vacant apartment where the fridge is free of roaches and the windows actually open. One of his new neighbors, a vegetarian poet, offers him blue Himalayan yogurt and a mysterious elixir strong enough to kick any acid habit. Craig also receives an invitation from the attractive goth down the hall whose late-night moans and stripteases through the enticingly paper-thin walls bring back memories of Sergeant Howie being tormented by Willow in *The Wicker Man*.

As a result of ingratiating himself with the fellow occupants, he awakens from a nightmare the next morning covered with a greasy residue from head to toe. It seeps through his clothes as the day goes on and eventually materializes into a chlorophyll green epidermis covered in boils of gushing yellow puss, and he discovers that the only way to get his normal appearance back for a limited time is to commit atrocities like bludgeoning a hobo with a baseball bat and slashing the face of a prostitute, the kind of acts that would normally be distasteful to watch, but here, in a slimy city full of derelicts reacting atypically to everything, any scene is likely to make you smile. Unlike some inexplicably popular brats on YouTube, I don't make a habit out of pointing a video camera at myself just to record instant reactions and so I have no evidence of when my smile reached a crescendo, but I'm willing to bet it was during the scene when a gang member quickly regrets punching what looks like a cenobite dressing up as The Invisible Man.

A terrific soundtrack, an actor who resembles *Re-Animator*'s David Gale, a video store that delivers, a book titled Flesh Control, a quintessential 80's comic relief sidekick, the greatest stabbing scene so far this year, and a girl that has the courtesy to wait while her attacker collects his intestines from the floor gave me more reasons to don't worry, be happy for 81 minutes. The *Street Trash* connections expanded as I fooled around on the IMDb and learned that Scott Coulter worked on the makeup in both films before enjoying a lengthy and successful career as a visual effects producer. He puts on quite a show in *Slime City*'s climax, a splattacular jubilee where the black and white checkerboard floors get coated with blood, guts, and body parts that refuse to accept the fact that they've just been severed. I also learned that Craig's girlfriend and neighbor were played by the same actress, something I never considered for a second; Mary Huner even returned for the 2010 sequel *Slime City Massacre*!

Horror Galore

"I WANNA KILL EVERYONE. SATAN IS GOOD. SATAN IS OUR PAL"

Alucarda (1977)

Director: Juan L. Moctezuma
Writers: Alexis Arroyo, Juan L. Moctezuma, Yolanda Lopez Moctezuma, Sheridan Le Fanu (novel)
Cast: Tina Romero, Claudio Brook, David Silva, Susana Kamini, Lili Garza, Tina French

Being a friend of Alejandro Jodorowsky and associate producer of one of his weirdest masterpieces, *El Topo*, was a clear sign that when Juan Lopez Moctezuma got his chance to direct, his goal was not to appease mainstream audiences. His third picture, the Mexican supernatural horror film *Alucarda*, fuses together the melodramatic and lunatic blasphemy of Ken Russell's *The Devils* (1971), the moral quandaries of European's nunsploitation subgenre, and the stylish eroticism of the lesbian vampire movies of the '70s.

The first few minutes play out more like a Jim Henson movie, where a teenaged girl asks an enigmatic gypsy to protect her newborn son in what looks to be Fraggle Rock, but when she pleads, "Don't let him take her away," she's not referring to Jareth the Goblin King, but to the cloven-hoofed Beezlebub, who is described as many things throughout the film such as the transgressor, the seducer, the enemy of virtue, the perpetual persecutor of innocence, the arch enemy of almighty God, and the foul receptacle of sin. The baby grows up to be a 15-year-old girl named "A Dracula" backwards who lives in a catacomb-like convent run by nuns whose nurturing ways contradict their peculiar mummy outfits. She's a striking presence with a beautiful black Victorian dress suitable for funerals and with middle-parted dark hair flowing well past her shoulders.

She quickly befriends an orphan girl (played by an actress who must be in her mid-30s) who just moved into the convent and they spend the afternoon together rolling down hills and exploring the woods. They come across an enormous mausoleum, and Alucarda, being a curious creature fascinated by death, can't resist wandering inside, where she confesses to the new girl, "Darling darling Justine, I live in you. Would you die for me? I love you so. I have never been in love with anyone. I never shall unless it's with you." Justine is kind of a spoilsport because not only is she reluctant to make a blood pact with a scary-looking knife, but she doesn't even want Alucarda to open up a coffin where the lid may be the only thing protecting them from a Satanic infestation!

What follows is an insane phantasmagoria of holy and unholy rituals, orgies and bloody kisses, flagellations, leech-bloodlettings, beheadings, naked bodies, quakes, smoke, fog, and Jesus statues engulfed in flames, all set to a chorus of screams loud enough to tempt your neighbors to alert the authorities, and so this probably isn't the best movie to watch with open windows. Just imagine 20 Sally's from *The Texas Chainsaw Massacre* all suffering under the same roof and that's what the third act of this movie sounds like. And the best vocal cords of all belong to Tina Romero. So much is asked of her in the titular role, and the movie very well could have been a slog to get through were it not for her magnetic performance. Also superb is Claudio Brook in a dual role as the Atticus Finchish voice of reason and the alchemist gypsy, two characters that are polar opposites in every way.

Anything for Jackson (2020)

Director: Justin G. Dyck
Writer: Keith Cooper
Cast: Sheila McCarthy, Julian Richings, Konstantina Mantelos, Josh Cruddas, Yannick Bisson

With their long list of credits mostly consisting of Hallmark holiday cheer like *Baby in a Manger*, *Christmas in Paris*, and *Christmas with a Prince: Becoming Royal* (and that's just from 2019), the team of director Justin G. Dyck and writer Keith Cooper decided to take a well-deserved vacation from yearlong yuletide and commercial act breaks, and instead soak in the sinister seas of Satanism with this Shudder exclusive and easily one of horror's nicest surprises of 2020.

Anything for Jackson spins an intriguing web involving a likable elderly couple named Henry and Audrey Walsh who are so grief-stricken over the tragic loss of their grandson that they require something far more effective than simple "thoughts and prayers," even if they have to attend occult classes in the local community center, travel around the globe to acquire a book similar to the Necronomicon, and kidnap a pregnant woman with the hopes of performing a ritual that brings back their beloved Jackson. "Trust me, we've thought of everything. No one has more time than a grieving family," Audrey reassures the terrified woman who they've shackled in a soundproofed room, but even with all of their meticulous planning, they still find themselves way over their heads with both the kidnapping and the incantation.

With a mountain of problems piling up and a tenacious police officer at his heels, I couldn't help but be reminded of Jerry Lundegaard in *Fargo* when Henry ultimately has a meltdown in a wintry landscape that can only conceal evidence for so long. This was a depressing day for sure, with my cat Marmalade having to be hospitalized for kidney failure, and so I was thankful that this movie, even with its tragic story and tortured characters, could still make me laugh on multiple occasions. *Anything for Jackson* has a wicked sense of humor but it also takes the concept of demonology seriously, with deranged spooks vying for the right to be reborn and innocent bystanders becoming corrupted for taking just one step too close to the portal that is the Walsh's upper-class home.

Dyck has since returned to his comfort zone with *Christmas in the Rockies*, *Christmas in the Wilds*, and *A Christmas Exchange*, which is actually a great thing because he has proven that living inside a Hallmark snow globe for years makes a filmmaker uniquely qualified to construct horror at the highest level after shattering the glass. And considering how *Anything for Jackson* contains the most menacing "trick or treat" greeting ever heard, I'm personally hoping his next foray into horror takes place on the nightmare before Christmas.

The Devil Rides Out (1968)

Director: Terence Fisher
Writers: Richard Matheson, Dennis Wheatley (novel)
Cast: Christopher Lee, Charles Gray, Nike Arrighi, Leon Greene, Patrick Mower, Sarah Lawson

Director Terence Fisher delivered the first major horror hit for Hammer Studios with *The Curse of Frankenstein* back in 1957, which cast Christopher Lee as the monster. The two men would see a lot of each other over the next decade with *Horror of*

Dracula, *The Hound of the Baskervilles*, *The Man Who Could Cheat Death*, *The Mummy*, *The Two Faces of Dr. Jekyll*, *Sherlock Holmes and the Deadly Necklace*, *The Gorgon*, and *Dracula: Prince of Darkness* before bringing Dennis Wheatley's 1934 novel to life with the help of screenwriter Richard Matheson. Not only had Matheson previously written screenplays for *Tales of Terror*, *The Incredible Shrinking Man*, *House of Usher*, *Pit and the Pendulum*, and *The Raven*, but he also wrote 16 episodes of *The Twilight Zone*, including "Nightmare at 20,000 Feet." So yeah, it shouldn't surprise anyone to learn that *The Devil Rides Out* is a delightfully devilish treat!

Christopher Lee stated multiple times that out of all of his 100+ movie credits, his absolute favorite performance was Lord Summerisle in the masterpiece *The Wicker Man*, but he gave one of his runner ups to the immaculately dressed Duc de Richleau in this film, which gave him the rare opportunity of embracing the holy cross rather than shielding his eyes from it. When he discovers that the young man to whom he feels like a father figure has been flirting with the occult, he does everything he can to save his soul before it's doomed forever with a Satanic baptism. Even when he's providing loads of exposition that might come off as dull by any other actor, in this case we're hanging on each and every syllable. These scenes are traded off with the devil's minions having fun and demonstrating their powers, and it is excitement galore when their worlds ultimately collide with the highest of stakes. The Devil himself even makes an appearance so memorable that it would later be spliced into Iron Maiden's video for "The Number of the Beast." But an even more menacing presence is from the cult leader Mocata, played by Charles Gray, determined not to surrender his young prospects. After an attempt at hypnosis fails due to inopportune interference, he departs with a chilling and confident warning: "I won't be back for Simon—but something will."

Since it's a Hammer film, the sets are lavish and luxurious, and they offer plenty of space for monstrously sized tarantulas to stretch out their legs and for phantom horses to run laps around a protective chalk circle. The American distributor was worried that audiences would expect much more equine screen time with a western-sounding title like *The Devil Rides Out*, so it was given the alternative title *The Devil's Bride*.

Grave Robbers (1989)
Director: Rubén Galindo Jr.
Writers: Carlos Valdemar, Rubén Galindo Jr.
Cast: Fernando Almada, Edna Bolkan, Erika Buenfil, Ernesto Laguardia, Maria Rebeca

Man, I'm really kicking myself for not buying the *Cemetery of Terror/Grave Robbers* double feature DVD sooner because the original $15 price has sky-rocketed to monstrous proportions in just a couple of years, now going for $99 on Amazon. This movie opens with a screaming woman tied down to the floor atop a pentagram, and after her stomach is emblazoned with the number of the beast, her capturer tells her that she'll be giving birth to the new king before nine moons. A group of monks rudely interrupts the ceremony and gives the brute a little torture of his own in the form of a good stretching. An axe is fatally plunged into his chest when he refuses to admit his pact with Satan, and similar to the Sanderson Sisters' final warning, he vows to return with even more power once someone removes the axe, even if takes a century.

In present day, a young gang of "tomb sackers" climbs over the gates of a cemetery looking for just the right grave to rob when one of them has a clairvoyant episode and insists she's found the spot where gold was surely buried (as an offering for heaven's path). With six painstaking feet of soil dug and the coffin lid opened, they find only a boring old skeleton inside the coffin, but then one of the girls suddenly falls much farther underground and ends up in a large crypt where every corpse is decked out in fine jewelry that sparkles through even the thickest of cobwebs. Her friends join in on the pocket-filling party but then one of the guys decides to take one more special souvenir that he's quite fond of. This special axe won't be in his possession for very long.

They emerge from their graveyard shift only to discover they're working overtime thanks to their truck tires becoming stubbornly encased in mud, making it all the harder to escape from a vengeful Satanic zombie with both the strength and versatile killing methods of Jason Vorhees, as well as the ability to shockingly appear out of nowhere when all guards are down to force heads through metal bars, chop off hands, gruesomely saw through necks, fill lungs with water, and cause stomachs to explode. If you ever wanted to see the Nostromo crew members try alleviating the situation by shoving the alien back inside John Hurt's chest, then this is your movie!

With a friendly skeletal hand landing on a shoulder and a not-so-friendly floating knife ruining a priest's hand modeling career, *Grave Robbers* will scratch you right where you itch, unless of course you have a phobia of subtitles or spaces in a movie's title, in which case you'd be better served with *Graverobbers* from 1988. That one is about a former prostitute turned graveyard shift waitress who accepts a marriage proposal from a handsome man despite having known him for literally only a minute, not quite long enough to know about his two deceased ex-wives or about his experimentations on corpses at the family business. Written and directed by Straw Weisman, *Graverobbers* feels like a goofy parody of *Dead & Buried* with its town of evil secrets and reanimated bodies, and I had a lot of fun with the hammy performances, idiotic char-

acter decisions, baffling lines like "It's safe sex now, because we can't get AIDS from dead people," and the hilariously out-of-place autopsy music.

Poster for *The House of the Devil* (2009), Constructovision, Glass Eye Pix, MPI Media Group

The House of the Devil (2009)

Writer and Director: Ti West
Cast: Jocelin Donahue, Greta Gerwig, Tom Noonan, Mary Woronov, AJ Bowen, Dee Wallace

Throwbacks and homages to the 1980s are a dime a dozen these days but very few feel as dedicated to authenticity as *The House of the Devil*, with its use of 16mm, freeze-frames, and yellow roman numeral copyright in the opening title credits.

Anyone who was lucky enough to experience the decade will find plenty of nostalgia in the fashion, furniture, automobiles, and even the cans of Coca Cola, and the movie's intentions are evident by how quickly it became available to purchase in a clamshell VHS following its successful festival tour and not-so-successful limited theatrical run.

Coming out just in time to be included on many Top 10 Horror Movies of the Decade lists, *The House of the Devil*'s positive reaction surely helped writer-director Ti West cheer up after failing in the attempts to get his name removed from the disastrous *Cabin Fever 2: Spring Fever* and replaced with the popular pseudonym Alan Smithee. My first viewing was met with some mixed emotions but it ended up being one of those rare movies that I couldn't stop thinking about. In addition to the time period, I kept craving its winter atmosphere, slow burn, brilliant piece of cover art, and natural performances from a cast of favorites including Greta Gerwig, Mary Woronov, AJ Bowen, Tom Noonan, and Dee Wallace. I ended up seeing it three more times in a span of six months, with my appreciation growing more and more.

Jocelin Donahue (who would reunite with AJ Bowen and Satan a decade later with *I Trapped the Devil*) plays Samantha, a college student trying to earn enough money to escape from her miserable dorm existence and incompatible roommate. After accepting a babysitting gig, she is driven by her best friend Megan through mid-Connecticut backroads (which is where I happened to learn about the usefulness of high beams) leading to a massive, isolated house that contains no child. Upon learning from the kind but slightly eccentric Ulman couple, who are eager to experience the Lunar Eclipse later that night, that she'll actually be babysitting an invalid permanently residing in an upstairs bedroom, Samantha nervously declines but is lured back with the promise of more money.

Samantha is such an engaging and sympathetic character that when the Ulmans leave, we feel terrified for her as she explores the house alone. This movie is polarizing for just how much time it spends on her snooping from room to room and finding no immediate danger, and while these mundane moments don't further the plot, they really help establish the film's unique personality and add so much realism with the way Samantha fumbles around for a light switch, plays with the phone cord while ordering pizza, or instinctively presses down on the harpsicord. Not even a *Risky Business*-like dance with her Walkman is able to subdue the gradual unease, and by the time the alarming discoveries are made, the house seems to possess an evil every bit as spectacular as seeing the moon disappear into the earth's shadow at the stroke of midnight.

In what could have easily been a throwaway supporting sidekick role, Greta Gerwig steals every scene with the same magnetism and adorable goofiness that made so many viewers of the masterpiece *Frances Ha* wish she could be their best friend. I loved the way she was so sick to death of everyone in town talking incessantly about that stupid eclipse. Ti West would further his status as a modern master of horror with the very scary *The Innkeepers* (2011), set in a haunted hotel during its final week of operation, *The Sacrament* (2013), an entertaining found footage take on the Jonestown Massacre, and *X* (2022), a refreshingly different take on the gritty and sleazy '70s slasher formula, which received excellent reviews and a wide theatrical release that will hopefully open the doors for further collaborations with studio A24.

Horror Galore

Night of the Eagle (1962)

Director: Sidney Hayers
Writers: Charles Beaumont, Richard Matheson, George Baxt, Fritz Leiber Jr. (story)
Cast: Peter Wyngarde, Janet Blair, Margaret Johnston, Anthony Nicholls, Colin Gordon

Considering the script was co-written by Richard Matheson and Charles Beaumont, who contributed a combined total of 36 episodes of *The Twilight Zone*, including some of the all-time greats like "Nightmare at 20,000 Feet," "The Howling Man," and "The New Exhibit," it would seem natural for Rod Serling and his spiral of cigarette smoke to emerge from the darkness to formally introduce *Night of the Eagle*. They had also been taking turns writing those well-known Edgar Allan Poe adaptations for Roger Corman when they decided to collaborate with a third writer, George Baxt, for this engaging and thrilling movie that was later re-named *Burn, Witch, Burn!* by American International Pictures prior to its US release.

Released just a couple of years after *Psycho*, this was also filmed in black and white and features a main character named Norman who finds himself in all sorts of trouble thanks to a woman with short blonde hair. This Norman works as a psychology professor known for his lectures debunking superstitions and belief systems that can't be backed up by tangible evidence, and despite being relatively new on campus, he's already earned the respect of his superiors and is the clear favorite for the next promotion. His wife, Tansy, senses the petty jealousy coming from the spouses of his fellow professors, and so she's not looking forward whatsoever to their weekly game of bridge and having to comb over their house afterwards to make sure that none of these "middle-aged medusas" left something dangerous behind, like a doll used to cast spells.

When Norman discovers that she's been casting spells of her own regularly (after studying the Obeah practices in Jamaica) and attributes them to his recent successes, he flies into an emasculated rage and demands that she stop believing in such mumbo jumbo. She is terrified of the consequences but nevertheless acquiesces to her husband's insistence on burning every doll, herb, token, trinket, and dried spider in her collection, and in no time at all, a hellacious storm severs their electricity and rains down misfortune upon them. The next day is a no good, terrible, very bad one for Professor Norman, who is accused of rape by one of his students, threatened at gunpoint by her boyfriend, almost run over by a car, and I'm sure that if he put his lunch in the teacher's lounge refrigerator, somebody else got to it first. Having just read Stephen King's novella "Fair Extension," included in the book *Full Dark, No Stars* and about a man whose seemingly perfect life is upended after being cursed by his jealous and cancer-stricken best friend, I was feeling a tad nihilistic and would have liked a couple additional scenes of Norman's day from hell before he returns home to find a devastatingly cryptic note from Tansy. It's a clear sign of a terrific movie when you wish it could be longer.

Norman then speeds off to their coastal cottage, the kind that seems tailor-made for Vincent Price's tortured characters in those aforementioned Poe adaptations given how it features one of those high balconies overlooking the rocky shores, in a desperate attempt to reconnect with his wife who has proven that everything she does, she does for him. Peter Wyndgarde and Janet Blair succeed in making us care about this couple put to the test by their contrasting convictions, pressures of societal-ranking, and universal black magic, but the real scene-stealer has to be the wild-eyed Margaret Johnson who is playing with her own deck of cards after hours in the university. I'd be a real jerk to spoil the fun of how the eagle comes into play, because it's one of the most exhilarating spectacles I've witnessed all year.

"I Wanna Kill Everyone. Satan Is Good. Satan Is Our Pal"

Warlock: The Armageddon (1993)

Director: Anthony Hickox
Writers: Sam Bernard, Kevin Rock
Cast: Julian Sands, Chris Young, Paula Marshall, Joanna Pacula, Bruce Glover, Steve Kahan

October 20, 2019 will go down as one of the best days of my life because most of it was spent with my close friends Summer and Ben at Silver Dollar City, an utterly charming amusement park in Branson, Missouri, that I hadn't seen since childhood. I was thrilled that it hadn't lost any of its wholesome Southern charm or 1880's mining town gimmickry, and the fact that it was now decorated with thousands of beautiful pumpkins—arranged in enormous piles or constructed together in elaborate works of art—made me feel like I had been transported to the Halloween episode of *Little House on the Prairie* ("The Monster of Walnut Grove"). Their Pumpkin Nights festivities proved to be a Shangri La for Halloween enthusiasts, but I was given an equally memorable gift later that night when an unexpected thunderstorm rolled through and lit the sky in an apocalyptic strobe for a solid hour. Living in the Pacific Northwest makes the sight of a single measly lightning bolt a rare pleasure, so this was a magical cause for celebration. I stood outside and while getting drenched in torrential rain, looked up at the electrified sky with arms outstretched and shouted "Is this the best you can do!?!?!" all while knowing I could never look or sound anywhere near as cool as Julian Sands.

This was the only line from *Warlock: The Armageddon* I could remember despite owning it on VHS; I just couldn't get enough of Julian Sands' irresistibly devilish performance and over-the-top murder methods. For some stupid reason I hadn't gotten the urge to seek it out as an adult, but if I instinctively quoted it during my happiest moment in many years, then I figured it

Poster for *Warlock: The Armageddon* (1993), Trimark Pictures

would be a wise idea to save one of the 11 remaining October nights for a trip down memory lane to watch Satan's son being reborn and traveling the country to collect the seven ancient stones needed to bring Lucifer back to Earth. And much like Silver Dollar City, the first sequel to Steve Miner's 1989 campy horror-fantasy was just as delightful to a jaded adult as it was to an innocent kid.

Disappointing box office numbers for the original film didn't deter Trimark Pictures from moving forward because they understood the potential for a new horror series and a new horror icon. *Warlock: The Armageddon* feels more like a reboot than a sequel because it picks up a new story, new characters, and new setting, and places much more emphasis on violence, gore, and special effects. Everything was bigger except its budget.

Horror Galore

Throughout history it's been up to the druids to protect the world from evil by using the magic of their sacred rhinestones to prevent the birth of Satan's son once the sun aligns with the moon, but the stones were stolen in a battle with Christian soldiers long ago. A young woman possesses one of them and is planning to wear it for her hot date with *Gremlins* star Zach Galligan (star of director Anthony Hickox's two *Waxwork* films) but while getting ready, she suddenly succumbs to the most extreme case of stomach pain that causes her to give birth to a disgusting embryo that morphs into a nude Julian Sands. With only six days between solar and lunar eclipses, he's on a tight schedule to acquire the additional stones but he'll make time to ensure those who get in his way suffer in the worst ways imaginable.

In another part of the country, a high school student named Kenny, played by *PCU* star Chris Young, learns from his father that he's a descendent of the druids and has the ability to stop the warlock by mastering powers he never knew he had, a daunting task considering he can't even stand up to the mulleted school bully. Paula Marshall, who should be recognizable to fans of *Seinfeld* and another Anthony Hickox film, *Hellraiser III: Hell on Earth*, plays his love interest and willing warrior. Her father is the town reverend trying to console a frenzied town after a string of bizarre incidents like blood and dead birds falling from the sky, and thanks to the IMDb, I now know why this actor reminded me so much of Crispin Glover. Fortunately, when the young lovers embrace in the woods and accept their calling, they are showered by thousands of leaves rather than blood and birds.

Sands proves why he was one of the most entertaining, charismatic, and devilishly dashing actors to watch in the early '90s. He had recently appeared in *Arachnophobia*, *Boxing Helena*, *The Turn of the Screw*, *Naked Lunch*, and *Tale of a Vampire*, always with long blonde hair and his natural British accent. Just as satisfying as his inventive kills are scenes in which locals simply interact with this strange traveler, sometimes poking fun at his speech patterns and expressing incredulity when he insists that they give him the stone freely and willingly because those are the rules—it reminded me of how the Leprechaun communicates during his blood-soaked quests for gold.

One of the best scenes has the Warlock visiting a fair in a dusty Western town and getting into a dispute with the man operating the Horror Chamber attraction, eventually chasing him into the house of mirrors and mocking his every move. Another fun highlight has him demonstrating arts and crafts skills to create a living Picasso. It's also pure joy to watch him fly, whether it's to chase an automobile or show a smitten fashion designer in Chicago a good time after making a deal that "Faust would be proud" of.

Further boasted by religious choral chants in the soundtrack, *Warlock: The Armageddon* hits all the right notes but much like its predecessor, was a box office bomb. Still, that wasn't enough to silence Satan's son, as a Warlock video game was released in 1995 on Super Nintendo and Sega Genesis. It's borderline sacrilegious to think of anyone besides Julian Sands as the Warlock, putting Bruce Payne in the unenviable position to inevitably fail with *Warlock III: The End of Innocence*. Sands reportedly declined to return after reading the script, which was probably a wise move given how much the film bored my friend Summer and me when it came out in 1999, with the exception being a single hilarious line reading that made us giggle: "YOU DON'T HAVE THE PPPPPPOOOOWWWWWEEEEEERRRRRR!!!"

Maybe I'll scream that to the heavens if I'm ever lucky enough to witness another cataclysmic lightning storm.

ESCAPING THE HORRORS OF REALITY WITH FAIRY TALES AND FOLKLORE

The Company of Wolves (1984)
Director: Neil Jordan
Writers: Angela Carter, Neil Jordan
Cast: Sarah Patterson, Angela Lansbury, David Warner, Stephen Rea, Tusse Silberg

Coming out in the heyday of cinematic lycanthropes, *The Company of Wolves* tends to get overshadowed by *An American Werewolf in London* and *The Howling*, but to a youngster browsing the video store shelves, there was no looking past its eye-catching cover art. Despite not being able to make heads or tails out of the story-within-a-story narrative at this young age, I always held it in extremely high regard due to its special effects, fun Angela Lansbury performance as the grandmother, and essences of my favorite Brothers Grimm fairy tales. What horror-loving child with bedroom posters of *Labyrinth* and *The NeverEnding Story* wouldn't love a movie that opened with a dream sequence where owls, creepy dolls, towering mushrooms, a menacing and mega-sized teddy bear, and a rapidly spinning grandfather clock distract a young woman running through a forest to get away from a pack of wolves with eyes that "shine like candleflames, yellowish, reddish"?

I had forgotten just how visually breathtaking Neil Jordan's episodic take on *Little Red Riding Hood* was, and while watching it tonight (after returning from a satisfying Thanksgiving feast at Cracker Barrel) for the first time in many years, I kept getting the hypnotic urge to press pause and soak in every detail. The temptation was also there to run full-speed into the 55-inch TCL television as if it were platform 9 ¾ quarters at King's Cross Station and hope for the best. Sure, it wouldn't be fun to bite into a windfall apple, mingle with gentlemen who don't believe in the separation of eyebrows, struggle to find a Cracker Barrel in this peasant village, and be torn apart by ravenous beasts after straying an inch or two off the path, but dammit, I would much prefer that foggy forested world where dreams are real as opposed to the one I'm in at the moment, where my employer is asking me to waste 45 minutes of my precious Thanksgiving vacation to download an app and have a stranger stare at me awkwardly while I take yet another weekly COVID test even though I'm fully vaccinated and boosted and masks are already mandatory, ugh. Madness!

The Company of Wolves was the beginning of a multi-picture collaboration between Jordan and fellow Irishman Stephen Rea, which also led them to the world of vampires in *Interview with the Vampire* and the world of prestigious award ceremonies in *The Crying Game*. The always-captivating actor sadly doesn't get a whole lot of screentime here, but he makes the most of it and is even involved in one of the greatest and most savage werewolf transformations you'll ever see.

It turns out that most of the wolves in this movie were actually played by Belgian Shepherd dogs with dyed fur, surely a relief to the cast, crew, and the hundreds of other animals on set that must have provided endless entertainment between takes. I expected the list of animal wranglers and handlers to consume half of the ending credits but to my amazement, only four people were in charge of this critter country.

Dolls (1986)

Director: Stuart Gordon
Writer: Ed Naha
Cast: Carrie Lorraine, Stephen Lee, Ian Patrick Williams, Guy Rolfe, Carolyn Purdy-Gordon

Filmed between his two popular H.P. Lovecraft adaptations *Re-Animator* and *From Beyond*, Stuart Gordon's *Dolls* hearkens back to the Brothers Grimm, morality tales, and EC comics where despicable people get their comeuppance and the kind-hearted learn an important lesson.

Much like an episode of *Tales from the Crypt*, *Dolls* sets up its story quickly and effectively when a violent thunderstorm forces a family of three to abandon their vehicle and seek shelter in the looming castle that appears from out of nowhere. The walk up to the front door tells us everything we need to know about their dynamics, as young Judy can't help but fantasize of a giant teddy bear (looking like it escaped from Bjork's "Human Behavior" video) gobbling up her greedy father and wicked stepmother because of how they treat her. The owners of the house, an elderly couple played by Guy Rolfe and Hilary Mason, specialize in the art of handcrafted toys while the rest of the world obsesses over mass-produced items. They are very kind to Judy and even give her a doll, believing that a little girl without one is somehow incomplete. Also spending the night in their castle (the perfect place for those with an active imagination) are a young man named Ralph, who is taken right back to the innocence of childhood as he gazes upon the thousands of toys, and a pair of punk rock hitchhikers, one of whom was cast largely because of her daily MTV appearances in A-Ha's "Take on Me" video.

Dolls is the kind of movie that, while it doesn't necessarily take place during autumn, is an absolute no brainer for perfect Halloween viewing. It has just the right balance of the sweet and the sinister, where two characters could be conversing about toys in a way that's just as warm and sincere as the *Toy Story* series, while in another room, dolls could be working together like barracudas to gruesomely punish someone who has refused to surrender to the goodwill that toys provide. Stuart Gordon was intent on making this a movie that just straddled the line between PG-13 and R, so he wisely left a sequence where a woman's intestines were pulled out via pitchfork on the cutting room floor.

David Allen, Gabriel Bartalos, and John Carl Buechler lead a team of brilliant special effects artists, and the way they make the dolls come to life, whether by a subtle eye shift or a full-on grisly attack involving biting, stabbing, bludgeoning, drilling, shooting, and sawing, is still as awe-inspiring to watch as a 40-year-old as it was when I was Judy's age. This marriage of traditional puppetry and stop-motion animation would prove to be so time consuming that Gordon's next film, *From Beyond*, managed to get released six months before *Dolls* ended its post-production phase. And even though production designer Giovanni Natalucci was extremely busy around this time with *Troll*, *TerrorVision*, and *Crawlspace*, he meticulously combed over every inch of the sets until they looked straight out of our wildest, most gothic fairy tale fantasies.

Predating *Child's Play* by a couple of years, this movie succeeded so well at making dolls terrifying that executive producer Charles Band resurrected the formula when he made the transition from Empire Pictures to Full Moon. Actor Guy Rolfe would join the *Puppet Master* party too, concluding his seven-decade career by portraying Toulon in four sequels.

Like many other horror aisle browsers, I found the VHS cover to be simply irresistible, so much so that I would rent it repeatedly as a kid. Santa must have known this because under the tree in 2014 was the just-released special edition Blu-ray from Shout Factory! Once all the relatives were asleep, I made myself cozy that Christmas night with Chex mix, a couple Schlafly beers, and hours of special features for one of my all-time favorite horror movies. It was a bittersweet experience because the tremendously likable star of *Dolls*, Stephen Lee, had just passed away four months ago at 58. Whether he is subtly realizing that Judy's crazy stories about dolls coming to life might have some validity, playing with the toys with the same enthusiasm as a kid on Christmas, or exasperatingly trying to defend himself against Judy's enraged father, Lee hits all of the right notes and steals every scene he's in. It's almost a miracle how the friendship between Ralph and Judy never seemed cringy and creepy for a single second, and you can chalk that up to great acting and the magic of fairy tales.

P.S. I took the hitchhikers with me.

Eyes of Fire (1983)

Writer and Director: Avery Crounse
Cast: Dennis Lipscomb, Guy Boyd, Rebecca Stanley, Sally Klein, Karlene Crockett, Fran Ryan

It would behoove anyone who listed Robert Eggers' directorial debut *The Witch* as one of the greatest films of 2015 to seek out another super-

Poster for *Eyes of Fire* (1983), Elysian Pictures

natural horror film in which English settlers are forced to leave their community and venture out into the mysterious woods in search of a new home. In writing the script, Kentucky-born filmmaker Avery Crounse drew a lot from his knowledge of Daniel Boone, native Americans, fundamentalist preachers, and mythology in the woods in his story about a group led by preacher Will Smythe, who miraculously survived a public execution after he was found guilty of sleeping with another man's wife. He leaves town for a new promised land and brings along the trapper's wife, her children, and a group of worshippers as they sail down the river through territory owned by the Shawnee tribe. They come across a passage aligned in feather-covered trees—the first of many fantastical set pieces—which local legend claims is where the lost blood gathers. Believing the Native Americans are too afraid to travel down this path, Will sees it as a perfect place to construct a new settlement, even if the occasional severed head obstructs the sowing of the seeds.

Crounse makes superb use out of his background in experimental photography and magical realism, and you'll be thankful for every time he allows the camera to linger on the creative composites. I was stuck with a crummy VHS transfer on YouTube because of its unavailability on DVD or a streaming service, but no layers of grain were able to conceal its astonishing beauty. It started off as a perfect choice for a summertime watch outside with my recently purchased Fire tablet, with shots of a Union Jack-bowed ferry floating leisurely down the river to the sound of Celtic folk music, leading its passengers to forests of swirling mist and sunbeams shining like diamonds. It made me feel like I was exploring the great outdoors of Missouri's Lake of the Ozarks through the comfort of my own backyard. As a child I spent many vacations in the Ozarks and so it was neat to see it represent the American frontier in 1750. It didn't take long, though, to sense the limitations of my new piece of technology when I kept struggling to find the shapes and the faces under a blinding sun—all I could really see clearly was my own reflection. My thick black-curtained bedroom and computer monitor gave me only slightly better results.

Eyes of Fire unfolds like a Lynchian nightmare of psychedelic hallucinations and bizarre nighttime visitors like cat demons and naked swamp phantoms. The special effects are terrific considering the miniscule budget, especially when human heads are grotesquely imbedded in a tree planted in what looks like a witch's earth cauldron, and when lightning does considerable damage. Will Smythe is memorable for being smug and charismatic but sadly none of the other characters (and there are many) ever get to shine. I became so disoriented while keeping track of who they were and how they were related that I began to wonder if each character was played by three different actors without rhyme or reason. It didn't detract from the enjoyment of the film, however, because plot is secondary to the bizarre and beautiful visuals.

Update: It's now two and a half years later and Severin Films has come to the rescue by releasing *Eyes on Fire* on a Blu-ray that looks out of this world! Watching it again, this time in the proper format, gave me a new appreciation of the art direction by Gregg Fonseca, who worked as the production designer in popular films such as *A Nightmare on Elm Street* 1 and 2, *House* 1 and 2, and *Wayne's World* 1 and 2. As a very special feature, the Blu-ray also includes an alternative version of the film that is over 20 minutes longer and which goes by the original title, *Crying Blue Sky.*

Hansel and Gretel (2007)
Director: Pil-sung Yim
Writers: Pil-sung Yim, Ji-hye Kim, Min-sook Kim
Cast: Jeong-myeong Cheon, Eun Won-jae, Eun-kyung Shim, Ji-hee Jin, Hee-soon Park

Once upon a time a young salesman named Eun-Soo was on his way to visit his ailing mother when he crashes his car just moments after his pregnant fiancé abruptly ends their phone conversation. Coming to his aid is a young girl resembling Little Red Riding Hood with her deep red shawl, and she brings him back to her family's isolated home, which has a sign out front reading "House of Happy Children." While the construction is neither confectionery nor edible, the interiors are an unnatural jubilation of lush candy-colors and wintry cheer, making it seem as if the man can relax and recover from his injuries inside a living snow globe where it's Christmas every day.

The girl's parents and two siblings are friendly and hospitable, but without a means to contact his loved ones, Eun-Soo leaves the next morning, only to return several hours later when the forest brings him right back where he started. After a couple more failed attempts to escape the maze, now covered in sparkling snow, he learns that the parents have had to travel into town for an emergency and that the three children (who now lovingly refer to him as Uncle) are depending on him to take care of them. He follows a trail of strange sounds into the attic where he discovers something that's every bit as startling as an old witch with a large oven.

This South Korean fantasy-horror, recommended by my friend Jenne, is such a loose adaptation that the Brothers Grimm tale merely exists as one of many books these three kids cherish, but it's impossible to be angry with a misleading title when the storytelling, acting, and atmosphere are this effective at reeling you in and hooking you up for twists most macabre. In a whimsical world where trees come alive, humans transform into dolls, and an unplugged television plays weird cartoons on a loop of a bear and a rabbit pulling off each other's body parts, the promise of Santa Claus arriving to grant everybody's wishes at first comes across as a horror fan's idea of a fun time. But just like a pair of siblings abandoned to rot in a forest, there's nothing funny about the situation these characters find themselves in, and a happily ever after ending cannot be guaranteed in the slightest. I certainly won't be forgetting about this gem anytime soon.

Lemora: A Child's Tale of the Supernatural (1973)

Director: Richard Blackburn
Writers: Richard Blackburn, Robert Fern
Cast: Cheryl Smith, Lesley Taplin, William Whitton, Hy Pyke, Maxine Ballantyne

Richard Blackburn intended to make his feature film debut a bizarre comedy but when he couldn't drum up enough interest, he shifted gears to take advantage of the popularity of the recent Count Yorga films, and thankfully was able to raise enough money to make a vampire film like no other, one seemingly inspired by the haunting southern Gothic tranquility of *Night of the Hunter*, surreal nighttime terrors of *Tourist Trap*, and countless Grimm fairy tales in which vulnerability is preyed upon by strangers with deceitful smiles.

Far removed from Transylvania, this vampire tale begins in the deep South during the Prohibition era when a gangster shoots his wife and her lover in cold blood before driving into the night, accidentally hitting a woman with his car along the way. Soon after, his thirteen-year-old daughter Lila Lee receives a letter from him, asking her to join him in Astaroth, a town steeped in folklore and epidemics. Despite her father's dastardly deeds, Lila is considered by the citizens of her small town to be the most innocent creature on god's earth due to her strict devotion to the Lord and how her beautiful singing voice graces every Sunday sermon. But when she's alone at night and trying to get to the bus station, she notices that all the men she's seen at church are suddenly behaving in a different way.

"If I was him, I'd sure have one hell of a time keeping my mind on Bible studies," one man says about the kind reverend who has taken the "ripe and ready to go" girl into his home; the taboo temptations of an otherwise virtuous man of the cloth did not go unnoticed by the Catholic Film

Horror Galore

Board because this film was on their list of condemned titles for decades. The lecherous behavior continues when a man outside the bus station calls out to her, "Are you looking for a good time, girlie?," when the ticket taker offers her chocolate while smiling into her angelic face, and when the possibly-inebriated driver (who some will know as the grandpa in *Hack-O-Lantern*) suggests charging her a little something extra for being the only passenger.

Things get even creepier as the bus teeters through a forest surrounded by mist and howls, and is then overtaken by a ravenous, snarling group of man-beasts straight out of *The Island of Dr. Moreau* who bark like Dobermans while dragging the driver to his death and chasing Lila further into the fairy-terror land. The girl with the braids and white dress is then caught, imprisoned, and looked after by an old woman with the cadence of Disney's Witch Hazel. In one of the film's spookiest moments, the woman encircles Lila while singing the classic Halloween song "Skin & Bones," which was inspired by the director being traumatized when his grandmother sang it to him as a child. Hopefully the scenes involving hallway paintings warning someone to escape and creatures fighting to see who gets to devour the child stuck in a tree weren't also autobiographical.

It's rare to find such a low-budgeted horror movie that is this convincing in its period piece setting as well as its beastly creatures in prosthetics and heavy makeup. It was also spectacularly lit for its many nighttime scenes, something I repeatedly mentioned in my notes, probably because the other movie of the night was Full Moon's *The Gingerdead Man*, and its lighting setups were somehow even lamer and flatter than Gary Busey's offscreen one-liners for a deranged gingerbread cookie.

Since Lila Lee is in pretty much every scene, the film could have been a disaster with a less convincing lead, but Cheryl Smith makes you truly believe that she's a singin' angel, a symbol of purity, and only 13 years of age, despite the actress being 17 and living off of the innocence-stealing Sunset strip. Nicknamed Rainbeaux due to her frequenting L.A.'s historic rocker hangout Rainbow Club, Smith would go on to appear in many cult-exploitation films and also perform with rock groups including The Runaways before passing away at 47 from hepatitis, caused by a lengthy heroin addiction.

This is sadly Blackburn's only film but a decade later, he finally got the chance to work on a bizarre comedy when he co-wrote *Eating Raoul* with Paul Bartel, who also directed the film and starred alongside cult movie queen Mary Woronov. Now if you'll excuse me, I'm going to make a drunken late-night online purchase because why the hell do I not own *Eating Raoul* on DVD? That cannibal comedy rules!

But who is the titular Lemora, you may be wondering?

A. A beautiful vampire Queen who says to a potential blood sister "The mirror is broken but you can see how lovely you are in my eyes."

B. A guardian to a bunch of creepy kids who all start and stop cackling in unison

C. A very proud bathtub-owner who insists that Lemora take a soak in front of her

D. A manager of Little League Champions the Astaroth Angels of Death?

E. All except D

Watch this underseen gem and find out for yourself!

November (2017)

Director: Rainer Sarnet
Writers: Rainer Sarnet, Andrus Kivirähk (novel)
Cast: Rea Lest, Jorgen Liik, Arvo Kukumagi, Katariina Unt, Taavi Eelmaa, Heino Kalm

Adapted from Estonian writer Andrus Kivirähk's popular novel *Rehepapp ehk November* from 2000, this film has one of the strangest opening scenes you'll ever see, as tranquil shots of icy ponds and trees reflecting into puddles prelude the shocking and unnatural sight of what looks like a piece of Ed Gein's artwork somehow moving on its own toward a barn. After it traps the cow inside and literally flies it back to its new owner, we learn that this strange contraption made out of an animal skull and rusty farmhouse scrap metal is known in these parts as a Kratt, an inanimate object magically brought to life to be subservient to its owner, but prone to lashing out if not given enough work to do. It's one of many fairy tale elements incorporated in this otherworldly film that stays incredibly true to itself while also throwing viewers off guard time and time again, unafraid to snap the neck of a character in the midst of an otherwise languid scene. At times it might recall the comic edge of Terry Gilliam, the poetry of Ingmar Bergman, and the episodic pace of Jim Jarmusch, but much of the time you'll struggle to compare this to anything you've seen before.

Monochromatically shot with the contrast amped up to emphasize beauty and darkness, *November* maximizes the power of desperate peasants venturing deep into the forest to sell their soul to the Devil, lovesick loners visiting the local witch in hopes of obtaining a romantic potion, families pretending to be asleep while the goat (Black Phillip's distant cousin, perhaps) that hosts the plague circles them methodically, a heartbroken woman stripping naked and howling at the moon while an actual wolf mirrors her actions, a snowman continuing to tell fanciful and poetic tales even as it melts, and the deceased casually reuniting with their loved ones in a candlelit cemetery on All Souls Day for food and conversation. There might also be a sauna that turns people into beasts or human-sized chickens.

At times it feels like *November* was designed as a pilot of the weirdest TV series since *Twin Peaks* because many side characters get their own vignette to suggest that every single person living in this precarious village has quite the story to tell, but the main storyline concerns Liina and Hans, who seem destined to live happily together until a German baroness moves to town and becomes the object of all of Hans' hopes, fantasies, and desires. He sees a way out of his life of poverty by somehow meeting her and ingratiating himself to her father (played by Dieter Laser of *Human Centipede* fame), but the burden of a low-class status makes that kind of dream unlikely without the help of some witchcraft. Liina is terribly burdened by her inability to murder the baroness in cold blood and by the arranged marriage her father promised to an older drunken brute, but the unrequited love hurts her the worst.

It's safe to say that this movie is not for all horror fans, but if you're looking for a surreal and quirky visual treat that takes you back to the early days of thumbing through Grimm Fairy Tales, then any witch with a lick of common sense would suggest eating up this tasty Estonian folklore broth.

Horror Galore

Tumbbad (2018)

Directors: Rahi Anil Barve, Adesh Prasad, Anand Gandhi
Writers: Mitesh Shah, Adesh Prasad, Rahi Anil Barve, Anand Gandhi
Cast: Sohum Shah, Jyoti Malshe, Anita Date, Ronjini Chakraborty, Deepak Damle

After his mom rushes his younger brother, unconscious and bleeding badly after falling from a tree, to the local doctor, it's up to Vinayak to feed Grandmother, a nightly ritual he's never been allowed to conduct due to the dangers involved. He is told that she usually sleeps through the feedings but just in case she should wake up, all he'll have to say is "Sleep, or else Hastar will come for you." As he tiptoes down the hallway to the dungeon where she's kept locked and chained, her ungodly snores get louder and louder until they suddenly dissipate, and then she croaks "Who is this little prince? Come here my child" in a voice that would have harmonized well with Mercedes McCambridge's Pazuzu from *The Exorcist*.

In the past 16 months of searching for hidden horror gems, I've encountered so many creatures, zombies, witches, vampires, ghouls, neon maniacs, and cannibalistic humanoid underground dwellers, but in this rare Indian horror film serving as a cautionary tale against greed, I think I've found the most unsettling character yet in The Grandmother, with grisly makeup effects, terrifying toenails, and iron rods impaling her cheeks. When she woke up, so did the long-dormant childhood fears from reading the German book *Der Struwwelpeter*, especially when she mockingly shrieks "Or should I just eat you?!?!"

Fifteen years later, a down-on-his luck Vinayak living poorly in the city of Pune breaks a promise he made to his mother and returns to their hometown of Tumbbad, still cursed with perpetual rain. His childhood home is abandoned and falling apart, but inside he finds something that makes him howl with laughter: his grandmother, with a barely-beating heart and with a tree literally growing inside of her. He demands to know the family secrets and how they're connected to Hastar, the first of 160 million gods that the Goddess of Prosperity gave birth to, who was doomed to be forgotten for all eternity after being caught trying to steal all of her gold and food. The Grandmother agrees to show Vinayak "the womb" where Hastar and his treasures lie just as long as he can end her suffering once and for all, and inside these dark, dripping, breathing caves is where he finds his fortunes—he just needs to grab coins off the bodies of *Descent*-like cave creatures and escape before facing a fate worse than death. And much like the Pet Sematary, this inherently evil place has a way of possessing, clouding judgment, and tempting visits time and time again to reclaim what has been lost.

Containing Bollywood trademarks like upbeat song lyrics filling in the blanks of the narrative and a surgeon general warning appearing whenever characters are shown puffing away at opium dens, *Tumbbad* became the first Indian film to be screened at the 75th Venice International Film Festival, and the road to get there was long and tumultuous. Production commenced a full decade before this world premiere, and took twice as long as anticipated because the producers were unhappy with the first attempt and decided that the film needed to be completely re-written and re-shot. Thankfully this decision didn't turn out to be an *Exorcist* prequel fiasco in which two equally-flawed versions competed against each other because the level of perfectionism and a decade of hard work are immediately noticeable. It looks and sounds sensational, whether we're soaring above picturesque Indian countryside or scavenging in the bowels of hell.

Valerie and Her Week of Wonders (1970)

Director: Jaromil Jires
Writers: Jaromil Jires, Ester Krumbachova, Vitezslav Nezval (novel)
Cast: Jaroslava Schallerová, Helena Anýzová, Petr Kopriva, Jirí Prýmek, Jan Klusák

Fans of Neil Jordan's *A Company of Wolves* seeking another quest into fairy tale imagery and dreamlike logic will definitely want to dip their toes in this surrealistic horror from Czechoslovakia, featuring a girl blossoming into womanhood and confronting predators in the form of men, monsters, priests, vampires, and even wicked grandmothers.

While having breakfast with her grandmother, young Valerie looks out the window to see a parade of missionaries and actors marching into town. She catches the eye of a man who removes his mask and takes great pride in his ability to scare her by what's underneath. It's the kind of face that recalls Klaus Kinski's Nosferatu and *Salem's Lot*'s Barlow, and belongs to the town's Constable, who is determined to steal Valerie's pair of magical earrings while others in town would like nothing more than to steal her youth.

The film can seem a bit inconsequential at times since these magical earrings routinely get her out of horrible situations like being raped or burned at the stake, and it almost seems like you could shuffle all the scenes around to be played in any order and it wouldn't make any difference. But I was still in no rush to wake up from this carnivalesque, immersive dream, largely thanks to its rhythmic editing, gorgeous shots, and enchanting soundtrack by Czech composer Luboš Fišer where flutes, harpsichords, church bells, choirs, music boxes, bells, organs, and foot-tapping military march anthems gently mingle to unite Renaissance fairs with fairy tales.

Inside this dream you'll also find bubbling cauldrons, lesbianism, well-behaved birds and horses, cobwebs, dolls, coffins containing polecat victims, truly gnarly teeth, and the kind of church service that might have influenced the Swedish rock group Ghost for their stage ambiance. In recent years it has been given a Criterion Collection release, a *Trailers from Hell* segment hosted by Joe Dante, and an entry in the book *101 Horror Movies You Must See Before You Die*, and so hopefully the film's stocks will continue to rise to the point where this Valerie is as well-known as the late Mrs. Harper.

Horror Galore

IT'S A SMALL WORLD OF PAIN AND SUFFERING, AFTER ALL: AMUSEMENT PARKS AND CARNIVALS

Clownhouse (1989)

Writer and Director: Victor Salva
Cast: Nathan Forrest Winters, Brian McHugh, Sam Rockwell, Michael Jerome West

In the midst of the Halloween season, a town so quaint that its residents include an Officer Friendly and a Mrs. Applebees is hosting the Jolly Bros Circus, much to the apprehension of young Casey, who suffers from extreme coulrophobia. Not wanting to be treated like a scaredy cat, he agrees to go to the circus with his supportive and understanding older brother Geoffrey and his mocking and bullying eldest brother Randy (played by the great Sam Rockwell in his first movie role). His first of many spooks in the night takes place inside the tent of a fortune teller whose glass eye clouds with fear over his severed life line, but that's nothing compared to the crippling fear Casey experiences at a show when a clown offstage locks eyes with him in a first-rate pantomime act to mock his nervousness while everybody else in the bleachers is staring straight ahead at the performers. The clown later zeroes in on the poor boy when it's time to select a lucky audience member to join him and his two clown brothers on stage. It's a scene so masterfully directed and edited, made all the more effective by the performances of Nathan Forrest Winters as Casey and Timothy Enos as Cheezo the Clown.

After the show, while Cheezo, Bippo, and Dippo are back in their quarters removing their makeup, a trio of recently escaped inmates from the local asylum barge in and take their lives and also their identities. Then they make their way to a house with three boys left home alone on this stormy night where screams are muffled by winds carrying swarms of dead leaves. Because of the authenticity of its sibling rivalry and adolescent behavior, the film really takes you back to your childhood and those precious nights of freedom wisely spent with sugar rushes, make believe, and scary stories, and it makes you wonder how you would have reacted to looking out the window and seeing three scary clowns playing with your disturbing Halloween decorations.

Among the many hair-raising moments are a chase scene along the wooded path leading to the convenience store, the drawing of straws to see which unfortunate sap has to change the fuse in the scary cobwebbed attic, and a freaky blink-and-you'll-miss-it shot of one of the clowns sneaking across the frame during a disorienting strobe.

The disturbing incidents of what transpired behind the scenes have been well-documented but those capable of separating the artist from the art (certain uncomfortable shots will put you to the test for sure) will find so much to admire about *Clownhouse*, a film funded by none other than Francis Ford Coppola. The director of *The Godfather*, *Apocalypse Now*, and of course, *Jack*, was so awed by Salva's short film, *Something in the Basement*, that in addition to putting up $250,000, he also offered the use of his home in Napa Valley for filming as well as the very same cameras that George Lucas used to make *American Graffiti*.

The Incredibly Strange Creatures Who Stopped Living and Became Mixed-Up Zombies!!? (1964)

Director: Ray Dennis Steckler
Writers: Gene Pollock, Robert Silliphant, E.M. Kevke (story)
Cast: Ray Dennis Steckler, Brett O'Hara, Atlas King, Sharon Walsh, Pat Kirkwood, Erina Enyo

Lobby card for *The Incredibly Strange Creatures Who Stopped Living and Became Mixed-Up Zombies!!?* (1964), Fairway International Films

Back in 2004, a company called Multicom Entertainment Group put out the hour-long DVD *The 50 Worst Movies Ever Made*, and taking the top spot was this cult oddity, originally titled The Incredibly Strange Creature: Or Why I Stopped Living and Became a Mixed-up Zombie until Columbia Pictures threatened a lawsuit against writer and director Ray Dennis Steckler for sounding too similar to their upcoming *Dr. Strangelove or: How I Learned to Stop Worrying and Love the Bomb*. Simply being noticed by Stanley Kubrick is already a feather in the cap of such a young filmmaker working with a budget of only $38,000, and the fact that he made a film memorable enough to rank above movies like *Bela Lugosi Meets a Brooklyn Gorilla*, *Leonard Part 6*, and *Ishtar* on this list is even more impressive. But in truth, this isn't a bad movie at all, and that Worst Movies documentary had already discredited itself for including the original *Troll*.

Much like fellow *Mystery Science Theater 3000* favorite *Santa Claus Conquers the Martians*, I hesitate to call this movie "so bad it's good" because it achieves everything it set out to do and even its schlockiest moments display a certain level of craft and creativity in both shooting and editing. The Pike Amusement Park in Long Beach, California makes for a perfect setting, and even though we sadly don't get to spend any time inside the infamous funhouse where the corpse of outlaw Elmer McCurdy was discovered (by a cameraman during the filming of *The Six Million Dollar Man*) posing as a dummy 65 years after his death, we still get the kind of seedy carnival immersion that made Tobe Hooper's *The Funhouse* so unforgettable. Until we have the ability to transport back to when The Pike was a popular destination for thrillseekers, we should savor all the 35mm footage of it that exists and be thankful that cinematographer Joseph Mascelli managed to hold such a bulky camera steady enough to get impressive POV shots from The Cyclone Racer rollercoaster during the day and night.

In a cool opening scene inside of Madam Estrella's fortune-telling tent, a man is more interested in swigging alcohol and hurling insults than having his palm read, and as a result, gets acid thrown in his face before being forcibly taken to the back to become one of her pets. But because this is billed as the first "monster musical" by securing a release date just a few weeks before *The Horror of Party Beach*, the tone is kept light and inoffensive. The main storyline concerns a rebellious teenager named Jerry (who I was a little disappointed to learn was played by the director and not the father of Nicolas Cage based on his appearance) who takes his girlfriend

Angela to the carnival for some beach-prancing and a variety of rides. Their evening takes a dark turn when Madam Estrella foretells that someone close to Angela will die, and a carnival barker successfully lures in Jerry by promising a show unlike any other. After the beautiful stripper Carmelita cuts through him like a knife with that seductive stare, he insists on buying a ticket to see more of her even if it means losing Angela, and once inside he ends up seeing something else that sends him into a violent rage. Scenes of hypnotism, psychedelia, on-stage stabbings, teenage romance, disapproving mothers, and animatronic chimpanzees are intercut with a host of toe-tapping musical and dance numbers worthy of joining the applause for at home.

Much like a day at The Pike, *The Incredibly Strange Creatures Who Stopped Living and Became Mixed-Up Zombies!!?* (repeating the title is probably a better way to increase my page count than my usual nonsense) is pure escapism back to a simpler time, when men didn't get laughed at for asking a psychic inside her tiny tent, "Which is the way out of this place?" with a clearly visible door you entered from directly behind you, and when you could leap from rock to rock on the shore without worrying about being included on a YouTube fail compilation when a mighty wave knocks you off.

Scream Park (2012)

Writer and Director: Cary Hill
Cast: Wendy Wygant, Steve Rudzinski, Kevin 'ohGr' Ogilvie, Alicia Marie Marcucci

I can't help but root for every horror slasher set in amusement parks or carnivals because there's something about teens being slaughtered there that creates the ultimate dichotomy, especially when their screams start to blend with the sounds of rollercoasters, laughter, and calliopes. Sometimes all it takes is a simple camera manipulation to make one of the happiest places on earth look more like Satan's personal playground. *The Funhouse* and *Hell Fest* are the two films that have used this setting to its fullest, seediest potential and it's hard to imagine anything even coming close to dethroning them, but with a setting so ripe for possibilities, I'm more than willing to take a chance on micro-budgeted, direct-to-video thrillers when scrolling to the cellar dwellers on Amazon Prime and Tubi. My second book was all about the most amazing, terrifying, amusing, and wacky true stories that have taken place inside amusement parks, and had the events of *Scream Park* been based on a true story, it would have been almost as astonishing as Fabio's unfortunate rollercoaster goose collision at Busch Gardens in Virginia.

Writer-director Cary Hill didn't need to spend any of the $40,000 raised on Kickstarter to construct elaborate sets or sneak around incognito like the very ballsy director of *Escape from Tomorrow* did at Disney World and Disneyland because for *Scream Park*, he was given full permission to film inside an actual amusement park. He also saved some money by not using proper audio equipment, which may explain how he was able to afford a surprising cameo from Doug Bradley. In this 80's slasher throwback, the employees of Fright Land decide to give their bankrupt park a proper sendoff after its final day of operation, but the party is spoiled by two masked intruders—one with a burlap sap and the other wearing one of those medieval plague doctor masks with the protruding beak—who didn't get notified by the moose out front that the park was closed forever. Fans of industrial rock band Skinny Puppy might recognize one of these hillbilly hellions once the body count starts rising.

The movie sounds terrible but has a good soundtrack, looks lousy but has a nice composition every now and then, and is sorely lacking in the scares department, but I certainly didn't regret paying the $1.99 rental admission. You can tell Hill had his heart in the right place and was inspired by the same movies we hold so dear, and he managed to make an entertaining little film that stands out from the crowded pack of retro homages. It's an underdog that is fun to root for, just as long as a blatantly tone-deaf murder scene doesn't kill the buzz—c'mon, they couldn't pick literally anyone else in the movie to show hanging from a rope, for fuck sake!? The opening montage of rollercoasters, scramblers, tilt-a-whirls, carousels, fried food, games, funhouses, and a rather lethargic group of bumper car drivers exudes charm immediately, as does the cast whose performances are just the right amount of awkward—their characters aren't multi-dimensional by any means but they kept me entertained. The best performance belongs to Wendy Wygant, who makes for a likable and strong final girl, and maybe it was her long curly hair but I kept getting vibes of Jensen Daggett from *Friday the 13th Part VIII: Jason Takes Manhattan*.

It makes perfect sense that *Scream Park* was filmed in Conneaut Lake Park in Pennsylvania, one of America's oldest amusement parks, and owned by people who probably shared the sentiments of Doug Bradley's character, about how the changing times result in many people no longer being able to afford going to amusement parks and others preferring to ride the sofa and brave the commercials rather than ride rollercoasters and brave haunted houses. Now in its 129th year of operation, it has miraculously persevered through numerous instances when it seemed like a complete demolition was inevitable, and is currently managed by the non-profit organization The Trustees of Conneaut Lake Park, who repaired two of its most iconic rides, Devil's Den (with its infamous wall of gum) and Blue Streak Roller Coaster just in time to be showcased in this splatter fest.

A V/H/S COLLECTING CAT-EYED CREEP SHOWS THE DARKSIDE OF TRICK 'R TREATING ON THE BLACKEST OF SABBATHS: OVERLOOKED ANTHOLOGIES

After Midnight (1989)
Writers and Directors: Jim Wheat, Ken Wheat
Cast: Jillian McWhirter, Pamela Adlon, Marg Helgenberger, Tracy Wells, Ed Monaghan

Right now, I'm hoping to find more hidden gems that prominently feature sharks, amusement parks, or churches. If there is one category that has already surpassed its quota for this book, it's horror anthologies. The problem is that I can't seem to go a week without hearing about some obscure collection of terror tales that I curse myself for not knowing about, but when the product is such a fun ride like *After Midnight*, it's a good problem to have.

After some playfully creepy music, we're introduced to a pair of college students about to attend their first course of the semester. Allison, groggy from a restless night, is trepidatious about crossing the threshold and confronting Psychology of Fear 101, but her friend Cheryl is giddy about this popular class and the unorthodox methods of Professor Edward Derek. Their first homework assignment involves going over to the professor's home later that night because to understand fear, one has to experience fear.

Once everyone is gathered, the professor tells the first scary story, "The Old Dark House," in which a woman tries to give her husband a happy birthday by suggesting they take a long, romantic drive down Old Coast Road like they used to do years ago. But while they are passing the old Griffith house and seeing its attic lit up for the first time since the notorious murders rocked the seaside town, their tires get rocked by tacks strewn all over the road, leaving the couple stranded. Not wanting to just stand out there and shiver all night, she approaches the murder home against the birthday boy's wishes. Her aggressive knocks at the front door are ignored and so she climbs through the window to look for a phone inside, and is greeted by classic haunted house motifs like skulls, bugs, white sheets draped to the shape of ghosts, and a grandfather clock that almost functions as a watch dog. A deliciously twisted reveal seals the deal and solidifies "The Old Dark House" as my favorite of the three and one I'm going to include on my next Halloween movie night for sure.

Fans of *Adventures in Babysitting* and *After Hours* will find plenty to admire in the next story, "A Night on the Town," in which suburbanites find themselves way out of their element with a late-night drive downtown. Unable to sneak their way into a nightclub, four underaged females improvise on a plan B but wind up in an industrial district with their gas tank nearly bone dry. Inside an abandoned gas station, they find no gasoline, Hostess snacks, or a phone, just a knife-wielding rapey hobo and his wild pack of hounds. Annoyingly, these "devil" dog actors are not honored in the ending credits and so I couldn't find out if their real names were actually Sunshine, Fluffy, and Lil' Fufu; their eight trainers, on the other hand, were all listed. I hadn't recognized any of the names in the opening credits, but there were several familiar faces that I was happy

Horror Galore

to see again–hey, there's Pamela from *Louie*, there's Samantha from *Friday the 13th: The Final Chapter*, and there's Catherine Willows from *CSI*! But the one that made me happiest was Penelope Sudrow, who I had developed a little childhood crush on after seeing her in *A Nightmare on Elm Street 3: Dream Warriors* and an episode of *Mama's Family* where she played Iola Boylen's bookish niece.

"All Night Operator" centers around a woman named Alex whose late-night shift at a telephone answering service gets off to a sour start when a disturbed man keeps calling and demanding to speak to Mrs. Birch, one of their clients. The calls are nowhere near as creepy as the ones heard in *Black Christmas* or *When a Stranger Calls*, partly because we clearly see the individual on the other end of the line and he's not particularly threatening, but when it's cleverly revealed that he's a stalker and getting closer and closer to his prey, *After Midnight* becomes that rare anthology in which each segment, including the wraparound, is pretty dang strong, and it's such a blast to see them all linked together in a climax that also features a circle of fire and an animatronic axe-wielding skeleton!

Ken and Jim Wheat's directing chops sadly weren't given commensurate esteem with *After Midnight*, which made only $59,260 in its opening weekend before finding availability in only the largest of video stores, but the brothers have proven that the pen is mightier than the sword with their scripts for *A Nightmare on Elm Street 4: Dream Master*, *The Fly II*, and *The Chronicles of Riddick*, among others

Campfire Tales (1997)

Directors: Matt Cooper, Martin Kunert, David Semel
Writers: Matt Cooper, Martin Kunert, Eric Manes
Cast: Glenn Quinn, Christopher Masterson, Ron Livingston, Alex McKenna, Jacinda Barrett

Originally intended for a theatrical release shortly after *Are You Afraid of the Dark?*'s final season, *Campfire Tales* seemed destined to be a hit among younger audiences going through midnight society withdrawals, but sadly this was not a prosperous time for the horror genre and the studio decided to just put it out on video instead. I quickly snatched it off the shelves because how could I possibly resist a horror anthology starring Mark from *Roseanne* that pays tribute to some of the creepiest urban legends ever told? I found it very entertaining and was looking forward to this rewatch, only to find out that now, 23 years later, copies of the DVD are going for $125.98 on Amazon and it isn't available to stream anywhere. Thankfully I got to relive my youth and snatch it off the shelves once more thanks to Movie Madness being just a 30-minute drive away.

For a second I was afraid they gave me the wrong DVD because I had no memory of its grand introduction set in the 1960s and shot in black and white. A couple played by Amy Smart and James Marsden are listening to the radio at Lovers Lane when, in between R&B hits "Ya Ya" from Lee Dorsey and "Mama Said" from The Shirelles, a news report warns of a psychopath with a hook for a hand roaming the area. This nostalgic segment lasts only a few minutes and ends at a classic malt shop and so you may want to have some ice cream handy to avoid jealousy.

The wraparound story concerns four high school friends who crash their car on scenic backroads while driving home from a concert–I'm assuming a metal show seeing as how Francis from *Malcolm in the Middle* is wearing an Iron Maiden t-shirt. As they wait for help, they build a fire in the ruins of a nearby church from the 1830s and add to the mood by sharing scary stories. The first one is about two newlyweds on their way to Las Vegas who park their RV for the night in the middle of nowhere, only to be quickly warned by a rifle-toting survivalist that when the moon is full, "they" come out to haunt (or maybe he was saying "hunt" with this segment's heavy New

York accents), and that they should return to the highway as soon as possible. With their RV mysteriously out of gas, they find themselves at the mercy of strange creatures who must have been taking notes during *The Hills Have Eyes*. An unsatisfying ending cements this one as the weakest of the three, but you'll still be heavily invested simply because of which universally adored actor plays the new husband who can't resist a nighttime detour to see some historic caverns where three pioneers survived by eating the other nine.

The second story strikes a far more sinister tone, harkening back to the early days of chat rooms and instant messages. A girl named Amanda has the house to herself on the eve of her 12th birthday (when her older sister ditches her babysitting duties for a hot date), unaware that the person she's talking to online, asking questions like "U'll be alone?" and "Are u scared?" isn't her best friend, but a grown man who secretly videotapes her playing in the yard with her dog, Odin. Creepy dolls, startling bumps in the night, and the joy of a brand-new bicycle add plenty of fun to this heavily disturbing premise.

The final tale isn't just the best of the three, it's a work of art that deserves to be mentioned on any list celebrating the greatest horror anthology segments. Glenn Quinn, who would sadly pass away from a heroin overdose just five years later at age 32, stars as a young man aimlessly travelling on his motorcycle on a whim that he's getting closer and closer to his destiny, but like every other motorist in this movie, he is left stranded on the side of the road without a phone or a AAA account. Just as a thunderstorm is rolling in, he spots a house in the distance and asks the beautiful mute woman who opens the door for assistance. She can't offer a phone or electricity, but she invites him inside this warm and cozy lantern-lit home and uses gestures, a chalkboard, and even a round of charades to tell him that she lives there alone with her father, who is riding horses and isn't expected to return anytime soon. With a magical lightning strobe and mournful music box melodies that sound strangely familiar, he comments that it feels so much like a dream as he stares lovingly into the eyes of the mysterious woman wearing a choker necklace, but it begins to feel more like a nightmare when the house fills up with hallucinatory images, sounds of a struggle, and the bloody aftermath, all seemingly occurring on a time loop. The woman only explains the phenomena by pressing a fingertip against the raindrop-splattered window and writing "ghosts," but the ghastliest of secrets is up to him to discover on his own.

My exhilaration from this dark fairy tale segment continued all the way until the DVD main menu reappeared, because the wraparound story (also featuring the always-delightful Christine Taylor) reached a surprising, satisfying conclusion and then a very cool cover of "The Monster Mash" played over the ending credits, one final clear sign that the filmmakers really knew their target audience.

Dead of Night (1945)

Directors: Alberto Cavalcanti, Charles Crichton, Basil Dearden, Robert Hamer
Writers: John Baines, Angus MacPhail, T.E.B. Clarke
Cast: Mervyn Johns, Roland Culver, Mary Merrall, Googie Withers, Frederick Valk

Horror films were banned from production in England during World War II, but an exception was made for the brilliant anthology *Dead of Night*. I'll make an exception for it as well, because normally I wouldn't consider something highly regarded as a bona fide horror classic for this book, but it does seem like it's one of the lesser-known movies containing the words "night" or "dead." I can practically see a question mark floating above the heads of my horror companions whenever I've brought it up.

Horror Galore

It begins with an architect arriving at a remote cottage in the country for a new assignment, and feeling dumbfounded when the inhabitants turn out to be the very same folks he's been having recurring dreams about for ages. He's even able to predict with astounding accuracy when particular events will occur, like a brunette showing up at the house in need of money, much to the entertainment and intrigue of the group. After making light of the strange situation by suggesting they are merely the leading characters in his dream, and that they'll cease to exist the moment he wakes up, they take turns sharing their own personal encounters with the supernatural.

The first tale is about a race car driver who is hospitalized after an accident, and while he makes great progress in the coming weeks, he suffers a mental setback when he looks out the window one night and sees something rather unsettling: a hearse with a driver telling him that there's room for one more.

Next, we're taken to a large house during Christmas, where a teenaged girl is looking for the perfect hiding place to win at the game Sardines, a version of Hide and Seek. The spooky attic has potential, but she ventures a little too deep and gets a hands-on demonstration of the house's tragic past.

In my favorite of the five tales, a man is gifted an expensive antique mirror by his new wife and begins to question his sanity when it reflects things that are not there. We're not talking about *Oculus*-levels of torment here, but it still succeeds in making a simple image like a Victorian room with a fireplace deeply disturbing.

It's full-on silliness with the delightful fourth segment, which reunites Basil Radford and Naunton Wayne's characters from Alfred Hitchcock's *The Lady Vanishes*, and this time, the comedy duo are golfing buddies competing on the greens for a woman's hand in marriage. When the loser suspects his opponent of dirty tactics, he enacts the best and most amusing type of revenge he can muster.

They saved the most popular and influential tale for last, and it concerns a ventriloquist losing control of his dummy who seems intent on breaking up the act. We've seen this story interpreted before, as it inspired the movie *Magic* and episodes of *The Twilight Zone* and *Tales from the Crypt*, but no abundance of versions or passing decades can dull the spooky presence of Hugo the dummy.

Back at the country cottage, the architect is jolted when he remembers just how this recurring dream always becomes a nightmare, and this generates an intelligent, ambitious freakfest of a conclusion that feels so ahead of its time. Wraparound threads don't spin any finer than in this essential horror anthology. Not essential is the 1977 made-for-TV horror anthology that annoyingly shares the same name. Even though it's only been a couple months since I saw it, I couldn't tell you a single thing about the first two tales. However, it recovered with a magnificent finale about a grieving mother haunted by the spirit of her drowned son Bobby. Despite its obscurity, this segment was given a ton of appreciation in *Tales of the Uncanny* (2020), an entertaining and informative documentary from Severin Films that explores the history of horror anthologies, going all the way back to the German silent films *Eerie Tales* (1919) and *Waxworks* (1924). Pandemic-related restrictions actually worked to the documentary's advantage since more filmmakers, writers, and horror experts were willing to participate through Zoom in the comforts of their own homes. I can't get enough of those talking head horror tributes like Bravo's *The 100 Scariest Movie Moments* and the *In Search of Darkness* series, and so I was more than happy to shell out a few bucks to hear the 61-member panel single out some of their personal favorites, like Federico Fellini's segment in *Spirits of* the Dead for Richard Stanley, *Creepshow 2*'s "The Raft" for Rebekah McKendry, *Black Sabbath*'s "The Wurdulak" for Ernest R. Dickerson, *Tales from the Crypt*'s "And All Through the House," for Larry Fessenden, *Cat's Eye*'s "Quitters Inc." for Eli Roth, *Necronomicon: Book of the Dead*'s "The Drowned" for Ted Geoghegan, *V/H/S 2*'s "Safe Haven" for Michael Gingold, and *Trilogy of Terror*'s "Amelia" for Brian Yuzna.

All the heavy hitters like *Creepshow*, *Twilight Zone: The Movie*, *Tales from the Darkside: The Movie*, and *Trick 'r Treat* are featured of course, but thankfully everyone involved did their homework and discussed lots of lesser-known examples like *Grim Prairie Tales*, *The Monster Club*, *Screamtime*, *Three…Extremes*, *The Offspring*, and more recently, *Holidays* and *XX*. And they also had nothing but kind words to say about the next movie in this book…

Dr. Terror's House of Horrors (1965)
Director: Freddie Francis
Writer: Milton Subotsky
Cast: Peter Cushing, Christopher Lee, Neil McCallum, Ann Bel, Bernard Lee, Roy Castle

Given the title, I expected the six tales of this British anthology to be linked to a home fit for a Cryptkeeper, and so the introduction of a train was surprising. It also exacerbated my feverish state since it brought horrible flashbacks of *Night Train to Terror*, the most unintentionally incomprehensible anthology I've ever seen (but with jaw-dropping musical numbers that almost make the movie worth checking out). To say that Dr. Terror's tracks are smoother would be an understatement. Director Freddie Francis would even go onto win two Oscars and serve as cinematographer for two of David Lynch's greatest films, *The Straight Story* and *The Elephant Man*.

An intriguing quintet of strangers—which include Christopher Lee and Donald Sutherland—gather in a passenger car and sit in silence until a mysterious psychic (played by Peter Cushing) joins them and uses a deck of tarot cards to tell their futures, setting up tales involving werewolves, killer vines (this is 1965 so don't be expecting those horrifying, modern *Ruins* vines!), vampires, voodoo, and vengeful disembodied hands. With each segment at a fun-sized 11-20 minutes, this is a perfect movie to watch on those days when your attention span is low or if you're feeling under the weather.

A couple endings are a tad anti-climactic but it's so hard to stay disappointed when you're back to those clever and amusing wraparound segments in the train carriage, with scene-stealing Christopher Lee sanctimoniously dismissing the practice of fortune telling. It's no surprise that when he eventually taps the deck thrice to prove that it's all rubbish, it's revealed that he makes his money as an egotistical art critic. After he's publicly humiliated by one of the artists he's repeatedly slammed in his column, he takes revenge by running the man over with his car, which severs the hand he used for painting. The critic is tormented by his actions and eventually faces the kind of ironic punishment straight out of EC Comics. In the other standout story, a musician performing in the West Indies witnesses a voodoo ceremony and unwisely steals the tune of the song for his upcoming jazz concert.

Dr. Terror's House of Horrors isn't top-tier but it's still a lot of fun, and was successful enough for Amicus Productions to continue down this path with a string of films that include *Tales from the Crypt*, *Asylum*, and the next film on deck…

Horror Galore

The House that Dripped Blood (1971)

Director: Peter Duffell
Writers: Robert Bloch, Russ Jones
Cast: Denholm Elliott, Peter Cushing, Christopher Lee, Jon Pertwee, Ingrid Pitt, Tom Adams

Way before Letterboxd offered the most convenient method of film chronicling, I was doing it the old-fashioned way in my teenage years: with pen and paper. While combing through all 17 pages of 0-5 star ratings to see which obscure horror movies might be worth revisiting for this book, I noticed my 3-star rating for *The House that Dripped Blood* and wondered why I couldn't remember a single thing about it except that banger of a VHS cover where a grinning female skeleton proudly offers a severed head on a plate. I can barely remember yesterday, and so the list of movies I've completely forgotten about is lengthy, but surely a horror anthology written by Robert Bloch (*Psycho*) and starring Christopher Lee and Peter Cushing should have left more of an impression. Maybe my eyelids were just really heavy at the time? In any case, tonight I had the odd combination of fresh coffee and a watermelon for sustenance and was ready to give this movie my undivided attention.

In the wraparound story, an inspector from Scotland Yard investigates the disappearance of a film star. He is dissuaded from entering his residence by the estate agent who believes that while the old country house may not be haunted, it is indeed cursed due to the horrible fates that befell those who have gotten too close.

The first former tenant we meet is a horror novelist named Charles, played by Denholm Elliot, who I had only known as the aged alcoholic in the very funny *Noises Off*. He's naturally charmed by a realtor with the name of Stoker, and by how the fully furnished house dedicates bookshelves to the works of Edgar Allan Poe, so he deems it the perfect place to live in while he probes the darkest realms of his imagination. Inspiration strikes on the first night, when staring out the window provides a clear vision of his next villain, Dominic, who will be committing the most gruesome murders imaginable. Much like an actor getting dangerously lost in a role, Charles starts identifying more and more with Dominic, whose appearances continue with increased vividness and malice, especially when accompanied by lightning illumination and the startling chimes of a grandfather clock. Titled "Method for Murder," this is such a strong and suspenseful opener with an ironic ending that I, a hopeless cynic, assumed the movie would be all downhill from here, but fortunately, the waxworks waiting in the wings were ready to strike while the iron was hot.

A retiree named Philip, played by Peter Cushing, becomes the next tenant, and his plans of a simple, carefree existence involving gardening, reading, and listening to music are threatened by a visit to Jacquelin's Museum of Horrors while strolling through town. Amongst the waxworks depicting grisly acts is one modeled after Salome that bears an uncanny resemblance to a woman from his past. The museum's proprietor admits that other lonely men have also been bewitched by this redheaded sculpture that carries a man's decapitated head on a plate, frequenting the establishment repeatedly just to stare at her. Philip gets an unexpected visit from an old friend in town for business, and they finally make amends after once fighting over a woman they were both in love with, but the past continues to haunt them with another visit to the wax museum. OK, *The House that Dripped Blood*, you've clearly positioned your two strongest segments out front, and now it's time to kill the momentum with some *Creepshow 3*-level bullshit, right? Nope, once again I was dead wrong, because not only does the next story, "Sweets to the Sweet," star the great Christopher Lee, but it's the best of the bunch!

Lee plays a widowed father who moves into the house with his young daughter, Jane, for whom he hires a tutor since this troubled child is forbidden from going to school or even socializing; he insists that he has his reasons for such strict parenting. The concerned homeschooler teaches Jane how to read (it's cute seeing her try to pronounce "adventures") and then helps her overcome her intense fear of fire by showing the beauty of the colors changing and the shapes forming within the flames. She even gives her some toys to play with, but her father absolutely freaks out when he sees the doll and immediately throws it into the fire, causing Jane to cry and consider reading books about witchcraft rather than *Alice in Wonderland*. This story does a great job in keeping us guessing, and waiting until a wicked storm knocks out the power to reveal its true horrors.

The final segment is more on the comedic side, and while it's a shame that scheduling conflicts kept Vincent Price from playing a character seemingly tailormade for him, Jon Pertwee does a fine job portraying a veteran actor with hundreds of horror credits to his name, who is quite unhappy to be on the set of his latest picture, Curse of the Bloodsuckers. He criticizes the flimsy sets, dime store wardrobes, and lack of realism while professing his desire to return to the glory days of Universal Horror, with films like *Frankenstein*, *The Phantom of the Opera*, and *Dracula* ("the one with Bela Lugosi, of course, not this new fella" in a playful dig at the star of the previous segment). On a night drenched with fog, he stops at a costume shop owned by an excitable geriatric who has just the right vampire cloak for someone of his distinction, one that will grant him the level of realism he so desires. It works like a charm, so well in fact that the actor no longer requires fake fangs to sink into the neck of his co-star.

This Amicus Productions anthology, originally titled *Death and the Maiden*, concludes with the inspector not taking Mr. Stoker's dire warnings seriously and deciding to see the insidious house for himself, producing one final fun jolt that will cause you no hesitation in awarding this film a very generous rating on Letterboxd or a piece of paper.

Kwaidan (1964)

Director: Masaki Kobayashi
Writers: Yoko Mizuki, Lafcadio Hearn (novel)
Cast: Rentaro Mikuni, Tatsuya Nakadai, Tetsuro Tamba, Keiko Kishi, Michiyo Aratama

I've been such a scrooge on my birthday for the past several years and considering how this one was especially Bah humbuggy, I was eager for the sun to stop reflecting off my television screen so I could escape reality for a while with a movie. I didn't have any cake, ice cream, or marijuana, but at least the astonishingly beautiful-looking Japanese horror anthology *Kwaidan*, which won the Special Jury Prize at the 1965 Cannes Film Festival before earning an Oscar nomination for Best Foreign Film, was the equivalent of the strongest, tastiest edible on the market.

These four unrelated segments, all meant to represent the four seasons, were based on the stories from Lafcadio Hearn. After moving to Japan in 1890, this Greek writer married the daughter of a samurai family and became fascinated by their traditions, superstitions, and ghost stories, which he would introduce to the Western world in his writings. "The Black Hair" is about a swordsman who is so frustrated with his life in poverty that he leaves his wife and gets married to a wealthy woman in order to achieve higher status in the world. It doesn't take long for him to regret this decision, as his days are spent noticing all the ways in which his new wife is cold and selfish, and being haunted by memories of the faithful and loving woman he abandoned. Desperate to atone for his cruelty, he returns to his old home after a few years and finds that his former wife, still with the same beautiful black hair, hasn't aged a day, and while she is quick to forgive him, there's something awfully sinister that prevents them from singing "Reunited and it feels so good."

Kwaidan feels dreamlike due to how it mixes beautiful cinematography with techniques more associated with theater, and nowhere are the color palettes more dynamic and the painted backdrops more spellbinding than in "The Woman of the Snow." In a majestic forest, two woodcutters fight through the snow and frost-biting blizzard winds, eventually finding refuge in an empty fisherman's hut which happens to have a door just as uncooperative as the one in Minnie's Haberdashery from *The Hateful Eight*. The younger of the two men wakes up on the floor hours later to see a female spirit hovered over his companion, her breath cocooning his face in ice. Before she can do the same to him, she takes pity on his youth and offers to let him live just as long as he never tells a single soul what he's witnessed that night. It's like the greatest segment from *Tales from the Darkside: The Movie*, but replacing the gargoyles and New York City grime for attractive ghosts and a winter wonderland with skies of cosmic swirls and eyeball suns.

The lengthiest segment, "Hoichi the Earless," starts out with a fantastical recreation of a Genpei Civil War battle fought between the Taira and Minamoto clans for dominance of Japan at the end of the 12th century, all while a young blind man narrates the action through song with the help of his trusted biwa. One night while playing his instrument in the courtyard, his talents are noticed by a samurai who requests a private late-night performance at his lord's estate, which can only be reached by passing through the cemetery gates. Warriors diving headfirst into their red watery graves, a massive storm soaking a city of the dead, and a young man being given a makeover to look like WWF's underrated New Generation wrestler Hakushi are among the many visuals that reiterate how *Kwaidan* is simply one of the greatest looking films you'll ever see.

In the much more comical "In a Cup of Tea," a writer hypothesizes why so many pieces of Japanese folklore were curiously unfinished, not knowing whether to point the finger at an impatient publisher, a quill-grabbing grim reaper, or something else entirely. One example is the story of an aristocrat's guard whose teatime is ruined when reflected in his Matcha is the face of another man he's never seen before, grinning mischievously. This unsettling phenomenon doesn't go away with the filling of another cup, and only gets worse when later that night, the guard receives an uninvited guest that knows all too well about his sudden tea dilemma. Even worse than seeing something scary reflected in your tea is realizing that you don't have a single teabag or Matcha latte around, and so I pressed pause to revitalize myself in other ways. After returning to the couch with a smoothie consisting of steel oats, Greek yogurt, almond milk, a banana, celery, and frozen berries, I realized that I chose a foolish time for an intermission because before I could even take a sip, "The End" appeared. That's what I get for not going out to the lobby to get myself some snacks during this marathon movie's "official" intermission. Just how much of a marathon will this be, you ask? Well, because the running time might unfortunately scare some people away, I'll make you work for it: take 13 baker's dozens and add the number of lines in a sonnet.

The Mortuary Collection (2019)
Writer and Director: Ryan Spindell
Cast: Clancy Brown, Caitlin Custer, Jacob Elordi, Barak Hardley, Ema Hovarth, Sarah Hay

On this day it was announced that the short-form video app Quibi will be shutting down just six months after launching, and it remains to be seen whether its content will be available anywhere else except its subscribers' memories; it's a reminder of the fluctuation of streaming services and the importance of physical media. The streaming service Shudder, which rose from the ashes of Fearnet and recently reached the impressive milestone of 1 million subscribers, has been doing such a great job lately with their acquisitions as well as their original productions. But because this is a cruel world, there's the chance that the years ahead could cause Shudder to vanish in a gust of demon wind, taking all episodes of *The Last Drive-In with Joe Bob Briggs* with it. But for now, I'll just be thankful every day for its fortunes, and how it also makes an effort to give some of their exclusives, like the *Creepshow* series, a secondary home on Blu-ray.

Writer-director Ryan Spindell made his feature film debut with another Shudder exclusive, *The Mortuary Collection*, which became available to stream on October 15th, 2020, a time when so many of us have experienced an insatiable hunger for fun thrills to compensate for stupid Covid keeping so many beloved Halloween attractions from opening. It feels awfully premature to categorize it as a hidden gem already but no audience could be big enough for a horror anthology this good and so I am including it in the book anyway, dammit!

Clancy Brown, making a case that nobody on earth would do a better job as The Tall Man if *Phantasm* were ever remade, stars as a decrepit funeral home owner named Montgomery Dark in the wraparound segment set in a rainy Oregon town that might also be home of the Goonies. He interviews potential assistant Sam and acquiesces to her desire to hear some dark, twisted, and awesome true stories from all of his decades of mortuary experience. He begins with a tale set in the 1950s about a woman who escapes to the bathroom during a fancy party so that she can better organize the contents of the multiple wallets she's stolen from smitten gentlemen. Still wanting more treasures to stuff into her bra, she's intent on opening up the medicine cabinet that was deliberately sealed for a very good reason. Sam thought this story was fun but expected something more meaningful with a twist about sinful people paying for their sins. In a slight and smart use of meta humor, Monty assures that he was just warming her up.

Macabre-obsessed Sam gets her wish with the next story about a womanizing and charismatic college student who uses his charm to convince a freshman girl to attend a big party his fraternity is hosting. They end up in his bedroom later that night for a love-making marathon that includes a well-practiced maneuver of him flinging the condom across the room while she isn't looking, and he'll regret this deceitful act in the following days in which his studies and sexual pursuits must take a backseat to humiliation and repulsive body horror.

In the film's strongest segment, a once-blissful marriage teeters delicately on the "'til death do us part" provision when a sympathetic man named Wendell (Barak Hardley) has to devote his entire existence to caring for his vegetative wife. Her illness has put them hopelessly in debt. With no end to the nightmare in sight, he decides to poison his wife on a night when Murphy's Law mocks his every desperate move and forces him down an even bleaker path with obstacles involving broken elevators, leaking crates, and devastating confessions.

Noticing a pattern in Montgomery's tales where people are punished for their evil deeds, Sam decides to tell a true story of her own, set on a stormy night inside a house inconveniently located close to a mental institution with slipshod security. She is babysitting a young child asleep in his upstairs bedroom when an escaped psychopath shows up at the door. It's a bloody and stylish battle to the death that doesn't quite play out the way you might expect. With four out of four stories ranging from very good to great, and a wickedly entertaining wraparound thread, *The Mortuary Collection* is one modern anthology that, along with *Ghost Stories* (2017), *Southbound*, and

Horror Galore

V/H/S 2, deserves to be remembered and revered for many decades to come. It also cannot be overstated just how entertaining Clancy Brown is in this movie! His previous horror stints include *John Dies at the End*, *Pet Sematary 2*, *The Burrowers*, *Little Evil*, and the *SpongeBob SquarePants* episode where Mr. Krabs (who he voices) and a terrified Spongebob attempt to bury the corpse of a food inspector.

Phobia 2 (2009)

Writers and Directors: Paween Purijitpanya, Visute Poolvoralaks, Songyos Sugmakanan, Parkpoom Wongpoom, Banjong Pisanthanakun
Cast: Jirayu La-ongmanee, Danuwong Worrawech, Nicole Theriault, Wiwat Kongrasri

Considering I hadn't yet reached my quota for sequels, anthologies, or films from Thailand, it was exciting to possibly check all three boxes with this poorly titled follow-up to the even worse-titled 4BIA, a surprise hit from 2008 that contained four unrelated terror tales.

There are five segments this time, and once again are all helmed by different directors, three of whom also contributed to the original. It's a sign of a strong anthology when even during the weakest story you're fully invested and in no rush to see it end. Things get off to a pretty wicked start with "Novice," where a teenaged boy is sent by his mother to live incognito among a group of monks in a secluded forest to avoid being caught by the police after a night of mischief results in the death of someone behind the wheel. He is taught to pray and meditate for peace of mind, but that might not be enough to ward off a hungry ghost whose offerings at the sacred nibung tree have been tampered with. This segment benefits from breathtaking locations, a spirit with a good throwing arm, and the striking image of a D.A.R.E t-shirt amongst the Buddhist robes.

"Ward," the scariest of the five, centers on another teenager involved in a nighttime crash, but this time he's the victim, and sharing a hospital room with a comatose patient about to have his plug pulled once his family says their final goodbyes, and by family we aren't talking blood relatives, but rather, disciples. With his legs fractured, there's not much the kid can do when he awakens to television static (never a good sign) and then experiences hellish torment similar to that of the poor girl from *Drag Me to Hell*.

"Backpackers" opens promisingly as a couple of hitchhikers accept a ride from a trucker and his son, and then wish they had kept on walking when frantic bangs are heard from the back of the truck that has suddenly veered off into the middle of nowhere. The gore ramps up as a stomach is cut open on a search for drugs and various arteries are severed from vicious zombie bites, and while it all looks terrific and the action scenes well executed, I honestly couldn't make heads or tails out of what was happening in this story.

A car dealership after hours proves to be an effective horror setting with "Salvage," as a saleswoman with questionable tactics is about to call it quits for the night, only to be forced into an impromptu game of "Hide and Seek" with her young son who's made it a habit of using the fleet as his playground. After looking through the security camera footage, she walks over to the spot where her son mysteriously vanished and instead encounters a woman justifiably hysterical considering the horrifying state her body is in. It probably won't be anyone's favorite but it's still a tense entry that reiterates how the characters in this movie get their comeuppance in unreasonably cruel ways.

While I haven't read any reviews for this film, I'd bet money that a large majority have stated that the best segment was saved for last. "In the End" is about a young film crew who are just a few scenes away from wrapping up production on a sequel to their horror hit *Alone* when the actress playing the ghost becomes seriously ill and has to be rushed to the hospital. Determined not to leave any business unfinished, she vows to complete her final scene by any means necessary, even if she has to free herself from a body bag. Makeup artists complaining about an actress' long hair covering up their hours of hard work and cast members pontificating of the pointlessness of this sequel just seconds before pretending to champion the film's integrity for the DVD's behind-the-scenes footage are a couple examples of this entry's wit, and its satirizing comes from the heart since the director, Banjong Pisanthanakun, actually made a horror film titled *Alone* that stars Marsha Wattanapanich. While I think we should have retired the dumb line "This is just like in a bad horror movie" decades ago, pretty much all of the other jokes, as well as the appropriately ludicrous twists, landed solidly.

Phobia 2 fared even better at the box office in Thailand than its predecessor, even breaking opening weekend records, and so it's surprising that this series didn't continue. Maybe it's for the best because now we don't have to feel guilty about giving two hours of our lives to a movie titled 4BIA4.

Southbound (2015)

Directors: Radio Silence, Chad Villella, Roxanne Benjamin, Matt Bettinelli-Olpin, David Bruckner, Justin Martinez, Tyler Gillett, Patrick Horvath
Writers: Matt Bettinelli-Olpin, Roxanne Benjamin, Susan Burke, David Bruckner, Patrick Horvath, Dallas Richard Hallam
Cast: Fabianne Therese, Mather Zickel, David Yow, Hannah Marks, Hassie Harrison

For many years the anthology subgenre was but a barren wasteland but then *Trick 'R Treat* was finally released in 2009 after a maddeningly incompetent delay from Warner Brothers studio executives, and quickly sowed the seeds for a rebirth of films including *All Hallows' Eve*, *Ghost Stories*, *XX*, *A Christmas Horror Story*, the *V/H/S trilogy*, and so many others.

Poster for **Southbound** (2015), Willowbrook Regent Films, The Orchard

With such a resurgence for these delectable and miniature slices of horror, it's understandable that a gem like *Southbound* would get lost in the shuffle.

The prolific Larry Fessenden channels his inner Wolfman Jack as he entertains the unfortunate souls traveling down a stretch of desert highway in what can only be described as the twilight zone, and where the FCC clearly has no jurisdiction over radio DJs who let the expletives fly from time to time. "Well, we all know the past can be a piece of shit sometimes and when it catches up to you, you better be ready to keep your eyes on the road and let that engine roar so loud that you can't hear the demons screamin' in your ear," is one of many affirmations about regret, remorse, amends, and atonement that the characters in *Southbound* all must confront.

The makers of the original *V/H/S'* standout segment, "10/31/98," reunite for *Southbound's* first pitstop, in which two bloodied men arrive at a café that is desolate and creepy, but which deserves five stars on Yelp simply because it plays *Night of the Living Dead* on the TV. After washing up and wondering why nobody else is reacting to the café shaking violently in sudden bursts, they hit the road in a rush to go home, but the road keeps presenting the very same café with the very same hostess, causing Matt Bettinelli-Olpin's character (resembling Lance Guest in the years between *Halloween II* and *Jaws: The Revenge*) to react like any of us probably would: with an exasperated and loud "WHAT THE FUCK?!" Oh yeah, and they're also being stalked by…hmm…what shall we call these things…ten-drilled alien-bat skeletal phantoms? Whatever they are, they look bloody awesome!

One of *Southbound*'s strongest attributes is its creative interweaving of the segments, where a character has his/her story ended by metaphorically passing the reign to someone new. This strategy keeps the film moving quickly since we're not treating it as five individual short films competing against each other, but rather one episodic nightmare that is probably your average day in this desert town. In Roxanne Benjamin's superb section, a trio of female rockers are on route to their next gig when their van breaks down. They cautiously accept help from a couple of locals who seem to belong to a different decade and are given shelter for the night, as well as a carnivorous dinner preceded by a creepy saying of "Grace," but what creeps band member Sadie (played by *Starry Eyes*' Fabianne Therese) out the most are the insinuations on how their music group used to be a foursome.

David Bruckner has proven with *The Signal*, *The Ritual*, *V/H/S*, *The Night House*, and episodes of Shudder's *Creepshow* series to be a modern master of horror, and so it's no surprise that his contribution is considered by most to be the scariest. When a distracted driver plows into a woman in the middle of the road late at night, he calls for an ambulance but isn't able to give a location other than "the middle of nowhere." The dispatcher, played by another impressive actress from *Starry Eyes*, instructs him to take her to the nearest town for help. He speeds to the lights up ahead but can't find any signs of life in the town, not even inside the hospital despite the fact that the lights and televisions are on and half-eaten meals remain on the tables. Given the severity of the woman's injuries, a compound fracture and partially collapsed lung for starters, the dispatcher tells him that he needs to follow all of her medical instructions in order to save her life, and sadly it was at this gruesome and hard-to-stomach scene when my chicken pot pie was finished baking in the oven and ready to consume.

It only makes sense that this town would have a bar even more depressing than Moe's tavern, and in the riveting penultimate tale, a hysterical man with a rifle bursts inside and demands to know the whereabouts of his beloved sister, who was traveling through 13 years ago when she disappeared. The film creatively comes full circle with a home invasion on a vacationing family by a trio of men wearing plastic presidential masks, and given the nature of the film, the motive is much more understandable than a simple "because you were home."

Terror Tract (2000)

Director: Lance W. Dreesen, Clint Hutchison
Writer: Clint Hutchison
Cast: John Ritter, Rachel York, Bryan Cranston, Brenda Strong, Will Estes, Allison Smith

I'm pretty sure that the year 2000 was the first time I ever had to go without cable, and so I missed out when USA premiered *Terror Tract* during its Shriek Week lineup, which is such a shame because this fun and occasionally vicious anthology starring John Ritter and Bryan Cranston would have made that Halloween season more eventful. It stayed under my radar for two decades until Paul Le from *Bloody Disgusting* wrote an editorial called "30 Standout Segments in Underseen Horror Anthology Movies" and included *Terror Tract*'s "Come to Granny." But this is one of those rare anthologies where each segment could be considered the standout.

Taking a cue from David Lynch's *Blue Velvet*, this movie opens with a sardonic view of a typically idyllic suburbia, where beneath the freshly mowed blades of grass a bird devours a worm, who is then killed by a cat, who becomes startled at the sight of a human and dashes onto to the street where it's run over by a real estate agent's fancy car. He's played by John Ritter, and it's such a joy watching this beloved and terribly missed actor show off a trio of homes to a newlywed couple anxious to participate in the American dream, and having no choice but to honor the full disclosure clause at the expense of reaching his severely crucial sales quota.

The couple seem enamored with House #1 until they hear all about what happened to the previous owners, trapped in the kind of love triangle that may remind you a little of "Something to Tide You Over" from *Creepshow*. A wealthy man catches his wife in bed with another man and has a diabolical plan for revenge but the tables keep getting turned ever so violently in this thrilling opener that features the scariest moment of the whole film. I'm always a sucker for a foggy late-night canoe ride to desperately cover up a crime, and this one delivers on more than one occasion.

The second house viewing also seems to be going well until John Ritter spills the beans on what happened when a little girl who used to live there found something peculiar in the backyard: a small capuchin monkey wearing a red suit. She names it Bobo and persuades her father to let her keep it until they are able to find its owners. Displaying characteristics of both Hal (from *Malcolm in the Middle*) and Walter White, Brian Cranston plays the father whose eagerness to keep his little princess happy clashes with an initial distrust of the monkey that boils over to downright hatred. He even hires an animal control specialist (played by WCW's Buff Bagwell of all people) to take care of the little problem but it goes about as well as Buster Poindexter trying to eliminate "the cat from hell" in *Tales from the Darkside: The Movie*. Considering how the story calls for Bobo to go from a playful pet with a heart of gold to a little hellraiser with fangs of fury, the producers were very lucky in being able to cast Crystal the Monkey in the early days of a successful acting career that would include much bigger films *American Pie*, *George of the Jungle*, *Dr. Dolittle*, *The Hangover Part II*, *Failure to Launch*, the *Night at the Museum* trilogy, and many others, prompting the *Los Angeles Times* to call her "the most powerful pet in Hollywood." Crystal would even reunite with her co-star Bryan Cranston in the appropriately titled *Malcolm in the Middle* episode "Monkey" from season 3.

Frustrated by the grisliness of the last two stories, the newlyweds demand to see a normal house that isn't cursed, with previous owners who are nice, upstanding, and still alive. An equally frustrated John Ritter tells them, "If you want something this nice, you're gonna have to take something with a little history" and then drives them to the third house, previously owned by a couple and their deeply disturbed teenaged son, whose desperation prompted an unscheduled visit to a therapist (played by another *Seinfeld* alumni in Brenda Strong). For reasons he cannot explain, he's being tormented by visions of the notorious "Granny Killer." The therapist begins to feel just as edgy as her patient while the session goes on, culminating at one of the most reliable places for thrilling cinema climaxes: an elevator.

The wraparound also ends on an extremely satisfying note, although I was really hoping the final shot would be a closeup of John Ritter's repeated screams of "MAKE ME AN OFFER!!!" in the vein of Tom Atkins in *Halloween III: Season of the Witch*.

Horror Galore

What Happens Next Will Scare You (2020)
Director: Chris LaMartina
Writers: Jimmy George, Chris LaMartina
Cast: Melissa LaMartina, Rachel D. Wilson, Kalima Young, Kathy Carson, Troy Jennings

This hasn't been the most celebratory of Halloween seasons with the pandemic keeping most attractions closed, and with election anxiety creeping into our minds as we're trying to fixate on fall foliage and the unmistakable scents of October spirits. But even though the Great Pumpkin's arrival is not scheduled for another week, it kinda feels like he paid an early visit to those who purchased a ticket to the virtual Nightmares Film Festival: Masquerade because it premiered the new film from the team that blessed us with 2013's *WNUF Halloween Special*. That perennial favorite now has a new double-feature soulmate with *What Happens Next Will Scare You*.

This razor-sharp satire focuses on the formerly prestigious, award-winning website Clik Clique that has attempted to stay socially relevant by shedding all traces of journalistic integrity for the kind of trashy content that generally receives far more hits. Constantly crabby owner June is being forced to make a few layoffs, and rather than give her hipster staff a "coffee is for closers only" ultimatum, she offers them a chance to present the scariest viral videos they can find for an upcoming Halloween listicle (grrr, you're not going to underline "listicle," Microsoft Word, but you have a problem with "kinda"?!). Everyone takes turns presenting their findings, which include a little girl's birthday party possibly being crashed by an apparition, the hosts of a local fishing show not taking the screams of their cameraman seriously, an Italian priest conducting an exorcism, and a drunk driver confronting something even worse than the police officer about to arrest him. But ultimately making the biggest impression of the night is a video that had only received two views so far. It's a close-up of a record player spinning a rare "Native American death song," but before we get to hear any of it, a character is forced to skip the mood-killing advertisement in a very clever gag.

Fans of *WNUF Halloween Special* are rewarded by Paul Fahrenkopf (still with Frank Stewart's terrific mustache) playing the corny joke-telling janitor and, in a viral video centered on a possibly possessed teddy bear, the return of Dr. Louis and Claire Berger, who sadly aren't joined by Shadow because the very pretty kitty passed away between films. This semi-anthology plays to the strengths of writer-director Chris LaMartina and writer-producer Jimmy George, with their youthful energy and ocean of ideas, because it gives them freedom to bounce around the entire spectrum of the horror genre and lovingly pay homage to a wide host of influences while also including so many visual gags at the expense of internet culture that you'll be tempted to press pause to catch them all. They even found the perfect time to recycle the memorable line "Don't fuck with the Chuck!"

Even during the least impressive segments, the excitement of what will happen next never wanes over the 72-minute runtime. My personal favorites would have to be Vera's Very Very Vlog, which is watched in slow-burning segments over the course of the evening and focuses on a bratty teenaged girl who learns the hard way that she shouldn't have been making fun of her classmate with the silly name, and the video dating profile that delivers the most captivating monologue from a clown since Richard Brake in Rob Zombie's *31*. The final act is another highlight, bringing back the level of gooey gore and over-the-top splatter that exploded all throughout their previous film, *Call Girl of Cthulhu*, and causing us to wonder just how the hell this was all made for only $6,000.

SATURDAY MOURNING CARTOONS

The Curse of Kazuo Umezu (1990)
Director: Naoko Omi
Writers: Shiira Shimazaki, Kazuo Umezu (comic)
Cast: Shinobu Adachi, Ikuya Sawaki, Narumi Aoki, Takehito Koyasu, Osamu Hosoi

I was having the most wonderful dream of Warner Bros announcing they were making a sequel to *Daffy Duck's Quackbusters* with Stephen King writing the screenplay and the band Pulp providing the soundtrack, but then my alarm jolted me back to this cruel world where the Looney Tunes characters are instead being wasted in a Pulp-free sequel to *Space Jam* that has one of the most irritating and soul-sucking trailers I've ever seen. To cheer myself up, I decided to devote the next week to the world of animated horror, starting with *The Curse of Kazuo Umezu*, which was such a unique trip that I'm starting to wonder if it was also just a dream.

For those of you who watched the animated series *Tales from the Cryptkeeper* growing up, this 43-minute Japanese movie, recommended to me by horror journalist and anthology specialist Paul Le, might take you back to those carefree Saturday mornings when weekends seemed to last much longer than they do now, even though it's doubtful that show ever lopped off body parts from children and then sewed them back together only so they can be re-dismembered.

The first of two shorts based on the works of "grandmaster of manga horror" Kazuo Umezu opens with a high school girl named Masami who feels otherworldly sensations when staring into the eyes of a new female student whose beauty makes all of the boys salivate over their desks, earning them smacks to the back of the head from their teacher who looks a lot like Phil Donahue. Masami can't explain the hypnotic power this new girl seems to have over her, nor the mysterious mark that appears on her neck after screaming herself awake from a nightmare. When her condition worsens with each subsequent nightmare, she begins to wonder if this new girl is a vampire who creeps into her bedroom each night while she sleeps, prompting one of her friends to set up a video camera to possibly catch the intruder in action. Even with a payoff involving shocking body transformations, what I liked best about this segment is the buildup of her friend being scared speechless by the footage, and poor Masami being too nervous to watch. I would probably be just as hesitant considering there have been occasions when I had to psyche myself up for hours just to click on an email, listen to a voice mail, or open an envelope if it carried even the slightest possibility of bad news.

With the possible exception of "thunderstorm warning," there are no two words that please me more to see together than "haunted" and "mansion," so my hopes were through the roof when learning the title of the second story, which begins with two teenaged girls hanging out with mountains of sugar and horror videocassettes. Even though I can count the number of anime and manga-inspired movies I've seen on one hand, I think I've already encountered the very best character they have to offer in Nanako because not only is this girl a horror movie addict who pretends to be Vampira sucking the blood out of her cowardly friend, but she's so full of life that she spontaneously decides to explore a haunted mansion that night...just because. Her friend cries out, "Objection! Major objection!" to the change in itinerary but is eventually persuaded when they meet up with a couple other friends from school and Nanako says how this adventure will be "a memory of our youth." The soundtrack continues to impress as they enter the house that's became notorious for "suicide by fire" headlines and instantly lose the power of their flashlight. Thankfully there's a lantern to illuminate the many creepy dolls, the teddy bear rocking in his chair, and the blood raining down. The traditional haunted house motifs end right here because what happens next is so unexpected that you and your friends are going to harmonize beautifully when you all channel Joey Lawrence and say "whoa!" at the same time.

It doesn't appear that *The Curse of Kazuo Umezu* has ever gotten the DVD treatment or been available on a streaming service, so I'll just be over here praying that the English-subtitled version currently on YouTube never gets taken down, because this is a really fun one that I'm already looking forward to spending more time with.

Fear(s) of the Dark (2007)

Writers and Directors: Blutch, Charles Burns, Marie Caillou, Pierre Di Sciullo, Richard McGuire
Cast: Gil Alma, Aure Atika, Francois Creton, Guillaume Depardieu

Released the same year as another parenthesized horror movie from France, *Frontier(s)*, this ominous and unsettling black and white anthology was col-

Poster for *Fear(s) of the Dark* (2007), Diaphana Films

laborated by a total of six different graphic artists throughout Europe and America.

One of the best segments was constructed by Charles Burns and is about a boy who traps a mysterious insect in a jar, only for it to escape and go unseen for many years, sporadically disturbing his sleep by making strange noises in the middle of the night. It even follows him to college, where he is now a painfully shy young man struggling to make connections with other people. After meeting a girl in the library one day, he battles the fear of making that first phone call to ask her out on a date, only for an entirely new fear to take over when she spends the night and wakes up with a strange gash on her forearm.

Another standout, directed and co-written by Richard McGuire, is scarier in the traditional sense because it takes place in a haunted house during a late-night blizzard. It is cleverly shrouded in pitch black where a small section of the frame is illuminated by a candle held by a deservedly nervous traveler who may or may not have an insidious spirit following him every step of the way as he explores the gloomy abode giving him shelter.

Other fears in this movie that Guillermo del Toro described as "thrilling, disturbing, and haunting" involve a girl who is confronted by the ghost of a samurai, an unnamable creature that feasts on a village, and a psychopathic aristocrat that repeatedly unleashes his pack of snarling hounds from hell on random people in public. In another repeated motif, we're treated to abstract-expressionist images as French actress and filmmaker Nicole Garcia describes phobias such as aging, sex, politics, cancer, and isolation.

Violence Voyager (2018)

Writer and Director: Ujicha
Cast: Saki Fujita, Kellen Goff, Derek Petropolis, Tomoro Taguchi, Nao Hanai

Just before the title credits, the narrator says about our main character Bobby, "the poor boy had no idea at all," but he really could have been referring to me because I had no idea what I was getting myself into with *Violence Voyager*. All I knew was that it was an animated film from Japan that was about to be reviewed on the *Junk Food Dinner* podcast. Considering how formulaic and bland the previous three movies I watched this week were, it was as if they were working together to soften me up for an experience like this, where I was blindsided by the shocking turn of events and forcefully thrown into a universe I didn't know could exist.

To say this film isn't for everybody is an understatement. It was made using the "gekimation" technique where all of the characters are essentially hand-painted cardboard cutouts puppeteered in front of painted storybook backdrops. Some will find it jarring but thankfully I settled in right away and got used to the characters' mouths not moving because there was enough variety to their static expressions and because the story was instantly engaging.

Bobby, an American boy who recently moved to Japan with his parents, wants to have one final adventure before the new schoolyear begins, and so he convinces his pal to go exploring across the mountain. They find a run-down theme park and agree to participate in its hands-on, role-playing adventure game in which they suit up and choose water guns to defeat the aliens and their militarized robots. They both enjoy the game at first, even if it's a little corny, but the fun ends when they run into some other children who have been trapped there for days, and discover that that the park is run by a mad scientist intent on horrifically modifying their nude bodies. Yes, this movie is seriously messed up, and despite these kids being made of paper, they're still capable of dripping blood onto the carpet.

Even in a world where *A Serbian Film* is easily assessable, it's difficult to imagine *Violence Voyager* as a live-action movie because of all its degradation towards minors, but when it's presented in such a unique and painstaking form of animation as this, even the ugliest of acts were works of art to be watched with wide-eyed fascination. The unconvincing dubbing in the American version makes the experience even more surreal but I was actually appreciative for how it muddled the tone and provided levity in these trying times. This movie also gave me a chance to see what my cat Marmalade would look like in "gekimation" form due to the uncanny resemblance between her and Derek the Cat, who bravely assists a bat, a chimpanzee, and Bobby's father in a rescue attempt.

Horror Galore

The Wolf House (2018)

Directors: Joaquín Cociña, Cristóbal León
Writers: Alejandra Moffat, Joaquín Cociña, Cristóbal León
Cast: Amalia Kassai, Rainer Krause

In the middle of my one and only experience with hallucinogenic mushrooms, I made the mistake of watching the animated Beatles film *Yellow Submarine* and it legitimately made me feel as if I were sinking deeper and deeper into the pits of hell, with demons berating me with horrible insults and ugly truths. What I saw when my eyes weren't on the television screen was even scarier. My friend's face melted while his body contorted unnaturally. Layers of paint were being stripped off the walls and forming a multi-colored quicksand puddle on the floor. The lamp's bulb was shooting out lasers while its base thumped as if to mock my fear-induced rapid heartbeat. No sir, this drug was simply not for me, but thanks to a new animated film from Chile called *The Wolf House*, I can now experience the most gobsmacking hallucinatory visuals possible without having to worry about Satan taking my soul.

Stop-motion animation is the most tedious filmmaking technique and while it wouldn't have surprised me to learn that brilliant artists worked laboriously for decades to make this movie, it turns out that filming lasted approximately five years and functioned like a traveling art installation, giving guests in art galleries and museums all over Europe the rare chance to observe the process in person.

It's filmed to look like a single continuous sequence as well as a 70-minute magic trick, as the characters and the house they're trapped inside are in constant metamorphosis. A matte painting of a little girl can sprout solid limbs and transform into a 3-dimensional lifelike figurine who then wilts to Paper Mache form only to unravel and disintegrate in a process that took several weeks to create for 20 seconds of screen time.

The Wolf House initially takes the form of a propaganda film from The Colony, an isolated group of Germans living in southern Chile under the mantra of "Helping makes happiness." Renown for the "unparalleled flavor and texture" of their honey but also unflattering local legends, they aim to dispel the unfounded criticism by sharing with you a film uncovered from their vaults about a little girl named Maria who chose to spend her days daydreaming and playing with animals as opposed to working. She is punished for 100 days of isolation for allowing two pigs to escape from their pen, but decides to escape from the colony herself. In the wilderness she finds an abandoned house and is reunited with two of the escaped pigs, who she names Pedro and Ana.

"I don't miss anyone. Here I can play and sing. I will transform my little pigs into beautiful creatures that will never leave me. A magic ball will help me and no one will punish me," she declares shortly before her beasts open up their presents under the Christmas tree and undergo their first of several dazzling transformations. Despite finally having a loving family, happiness continues to elude her with a predatory "wolf" lurking outside, with brainwashing skills and taunts of "you're burning, be careful" that are every bit as effective as a series of huffing and puffing. He is based on the real-life German fugitive Paul Schäfer—nowhere near as likable as David Letterman's former bandleader—who in 1961, emigrated to Chile to escape multiple charges of child molestation. There he founded the cult Colonia Dignidad ("Dignity Colony") to continue a reign of evil that would last for decades until he was finally imprisoned for the final five years of his life.

Even with a brief running time, you'll be forgiven for taking multiple intermissions to rest your eyes from a constant state of disbelief. This visual pageantry can be a lot to process but it's a trip that all horror fans would be wise to take.

A REMINDER TO AVOID DINNER PARTIES

Coherence (2013)
Director: James Ward Byrkit
Writers: James Ward Byrkit, Alex Manugian
Cast: Emily Baldoni, Maury Sterling, Nicholas Brendon, Lorene Scafaria, Elizabeth Gracen

The movies have depicted some mighty disastrous dinner parties but the one in *Coherence* is on a whole different level due to a comet passing overhead while the appetizers are served, causing a chain of events so mysterious that at one point, our main character hopes that the food was drugged because at least that would explain the hallucinations and heightened paranoia. To get the most out of this uniquely absorbing movie and wild ride towards existential dread, you should eschew from watching the trailer or reading reviews that are more detailed with their plot descriptions.

With a budget of only $50,000, James Ward Byrkit's directorial debut is a fantastic achievement in storytelling suffused with dread. The guerrilla filmmaking makes us feel like we have a seat at this dinner table and so at first, it's a little overwhelming as social anxiety starts creeping in, but it doesn't take long to settle in and assimilate. The guests are Hollywood yuppies for sure but they're mostly pleasant and witty, and even though there are eight of them, they all manage to stand out without being reduced to one-dimensional stereotypes. The director cast friends of his that did not know each other,

Poster for *Coherence* (2013), Bellanova Films, Ugly Duckling Films

intuitively predicting who would have the kind of chemistry that the camera lens can capture. Much like an episode of *Curb Your Enthusiasm*, these gifted actors were not given scripts, just notecards that

Horror Galore

roughly outline the scene and detail their motivation, and so the reason why the dialogue sounds so natural is because most of it is improvised. Whether they are discussing how missed opportunities altered the course of their lives, how much Ketamine it would take for someone to lose their grip on reality, or the Tunguska event—where a meteor entered the atmosphere over eastern Siberia in 1908 and leveled over 700 miles of forest due to the air pressure—these characters are always entertaining to listen to.

In an age where attention spans are low and all it takes is one uninvolving scene for moviegoers to reach for the phone and check something, anything, movies like *Coherence*, with their myriads of sonic twists and turns, remind us of the raw power of cinema because not for one moment will you think of anything other than what's on the screen and how you would react in this dinner party from hell. It weaves a tapestry of weirdness as new layers of the mystery are revealed at a playful rate, each one proposing possibilities so intriguing that it may take a double dose of Melatonin later that night to stabilize your brainwaves enough to fall asleep.

If *Coherence* gives you time loop fever, then continue the hysteria with the 2009 Christopher Smith film *Triangle*, about a group of friends who are out sailing when a storm capsizes their boat and leaves them at the mercy of a mysterious ocean liner. The characters aren't nearly as compelling as the ones in *Coherence*, but it's fascinating to watch them climb aboard and explore every nook and cranny, not running into any captain or crew while experiencing a chilling case of déjà vu. Much like the 1980 film *Death Ship* starring George Kennedy demonstrated, there is something intrinsically unsettling about a ship sailing the seas unattended, preying upon doomed souls.

The Invitation (2015)
Director: Karyn Kusama
Writers: Phil Hay, Matt Manfredi
Cast: Logan Marshall-Green, Tammy Blanchard, Michiel Huisman, Mike Doyle, Jay Larson

Logan Marshall-Green leads a very strong cast as Will, who arrives at a swanky, warmly-lit house in the Hollywood Hills with his girlfriend for a dinner party hosted by his ex-wife, Eden, and her new husband, David. It's a reunion between several old friends who haven't seen each other in two years, and in that time, Will has remained shackled by grief, guilt, and anger over the death of his son. He's disheveled, withdrawn, and seemingly incapable of smiling; it's clear right from the start that attending such a social event in a place he used to call home might be too overwhelming for him, but he does his best to be cordial instead of a party-killer. Eden, on the other hand, is all smiles and positivity as her friends comment on how she seems like a completely different person since returning from a sabbatical in Mexico, where she and her new husband had a spiritual awakening that expelled every negative emotion from their bodies and cleansed them from all that useless pain, and she hopes that by sharing a short video explaining the teachings of her new-age guru, her friends will then be persuaded to join them on their new path.

The presentation makes her friends a tad uncomfortable, who say in private that while Eden and David are saying some really batty things, they're just exhibiting the kind of weirdness that's harmless and commonplace in Los Angeles. The only one taking it seriously is Will, who grows increasingly skeptical of the bars on the windows, locked doors, lack of phone service, and the two invited guests from that Mexican sabbatical, one being a hedonistic, manic pixie girl named Sadie and the other played by John Carroll Lynch as if he envisioned what his character in *Zodiac* would be like after serving a prison sentence. Eden and David (the perfectly cast Tammy Blanchard and Michiel Huisman) have reasonable answers for everything and are hurt by the repeated implications of a nefarious agenda, causing us to wonder if the likable but mentally fragile Will, shocked that his former wife has managed to free herself from the agony of the tragedy while he remains tormented, is a reliable narrator or if he's just the only one willing to use the c-word.

The Invitation is director Karyn Kusama's first feature film since 2009's *Jennifer's Body*, and is Hitchcockian in its twists, slow-building suspense, and clever camerawork that keeps you glued to the screen for all 100 glorious minutes, culminating in a monster of a climax and the kind of brilliant final shot that can make you feel uneasy for days! Its world premiere took place at the South by Southwest Film Festival, where strong word of mouth propelled it to a limited theatrical release and a home at Netflix among other streaming services to the delight of those willing to take a chance on the oddest of party invitations.

Horror Galore

NOW PLAYING IN THE HEAVY METAL PARKING LOT

Black Roses (1988)
Director: John Fasano
Writer: Cindy Cirile
Cast: John Martin, Ken Swofford, Sal Viviano, Julie Adams, Frank Dietz, Carla Ferrigno

With my ears still ringing from having just attended an Opeth/Mastodon co-headlining show, I was ready to keep the devil horns raised, as well as the volume bar on my television, with my first viewing of *Black Roses* in decades.

Those with an affinity for the glammier side of '80s hard rock (I refuse to use the disrespectful "hair metal" label) and those curious to see the most boring-looking box of Raisin Bran in existence will have a friend for life in *Black Roses*, one of several heavy metal horror films that came out in the later half of the decade to parody the Satanic Panic outcries. While it's never been as popular as 1986's *Trick or Treat*, few could resist running their fingers against that iconic raised plastic VHS cover! My first exposure to the film took place when I was about nine years old watching *USA Saturday Nightmares*, around the time I started amassing a decent-sized collection of cassettes for bands like Stryper, Def Leppard, Europe, Motley Crue, and Whitesnake. Since I had never been to a concert before, it was enthralling seeing this movie open with a live performance of a kickass metal tune—the fact that the musicians are all legitimate monsters and the audience members legitimate zombies who are ready to trample the uptight, suited older gentleman intent on shutting the concert down was just icing on the cake. I'm a fan of *Trick or Treat* too, but if *Black Roses* is vastly superior in any way, it's definitely with the music (mostly performed by Lizzy Borden).

The teenagers in Mill Basin (apparently a real-life residential neighborhood in Brooklyn) are feeling hometown pride for the first time when up-and-coming rock band The Black Roses have curiously chosen to open their first ever tour with a string of dates at the local high school auditorium, much to the chagrin of many parents concerned with the band's lyrical content. At a public forum, a woman played by *Creature from the Black Lagoon*'s Julie Adams tries uniting all of the church-going citizens of Mill Basin in a protest against the town's first-ever rock concert because it will corrupt the youth and turn them into disciples of Satan. The mayor shuts her down by simply reminding everyone that the musical artists from their own childhoods—Chuck Berry, Little Richard, Elvis, and The Beatles—were similarly targeted by out-of-touch adults who feared the tiniest bit of rebellion or progression in popular culture.

When The Black Roses hit the stage for the very first time and open with an inoffensive power ballad about their hometown, even Julie Adams' character admits that she may have been wrong about them, and so all of the adults decide to leave and

Horror Galore

let the kids have their fun, not noticing the sinister grin slowly forming on lead singer Damian's face. The following morning, the high school literature teacher with a 4-star mustache sees a change in his students (perhaps the oldest-looking teens in film history) that he generally has a good rapport with. They have zero interest in learning about the works of Ralph Waldo Emerson because Damian has touched their souls more than any dead writer ever could, and they can't wait to attend the next concert even if a couple of them will have to rock out in skeleton-form.

In an early scene, a kid pathetically attempts to paint the town red with one stolen can of paint, but the concerts inspire more determination and creativity out of the youngsters, and soon they are pushing people out of windows and slitting throats. They also get some help from silly-looking ghoulies in all shapes and sizes. In the greatest scene of all, The Sopranos' Big Pussy Bonpensiero's multiple attempts of turning off his son's record player results in the vinyl and the speakers bubbling *Videodrome*-style and birthing something that wants to chew his face off.

Black Roses is a jubilant time capsule capable of being just as serious or silly as you desire. Given the Canadian flavor, hard rock anthems, and ridiculously cartoonish fight scenes with weapons no more harmful than sock puppets, it makes sense that this is from the same director as *Rock 'n' Roll Nightmare*, and yet I was surprised to learn this because one looks like it was made by someone who has never seen a movie before and the other looks mostly competent; you laugh at one and laugh with the other.

Poster for ***The Day of the Beast*** (1995), Sogetel Iberoamericana Films

The Day of the Beast (1995)

Director: Alex de la Iglesia
Writers: Jorge Guerricaechevarria, Alex de la Iglesia
Cast: Alex Angulo, Armando De Razza, Santiago Segura, Terele Pavez, Nathalie Sesena

A year before Trans-Siberian Orchestra formed as a side project for the members of Savatage (one of my all-time favorite metal bands) and showed the world how beautifully the worlds of heavy metal and Christmastime could intertwine, Spanish filmmaker Alex de la Iglesia was headbanging on the holiest night with his horror comedy *The Day of the Beast*.

Roman Catholic priest Father Angel Berriartua has finally, after many years of trying, deciphered a numerical code contained in St. John's Book of Revelation, and just in the nick of time too. He calculates that in just a couple of days, the antichrist will be reborn somewhere in Madrid, and he figures that his best chance to prevent the Apocalypse is to travel there and commit as many sins as possible. By tricking the devil into thinking he's joined the dark side, he can then perform the ultimate betrayal for the love of God. The priest succeeds in spreading his version of unholy terror in the Spanish capitol sparkling with Christmas cheer by pushing over mimes, keying cars, stealing books, and performing a terribly rude last rites, and then he visits a record store to immerse himself in the world of heavy metal like any heretic would, bringing along a shopping list that includes Napalm Dez, Iron Maiden, and Hace de Ce. I also got a kick out of the shop's display window featuring merchandise from Iron Maiden, Scorpions, Metallica, Kiss, Def Leppard, Sepultura, and…Green Jelly. I couldn't help but look for Ministry as well, since the movie's kickass theme song sounded a bit like their song "Scarecrow."

To help him carry out his mission, he recruits the burly, long-haired, tattooed store owner who takes a dab of acid during breakfast time, and a phony occult television show host who stages exorcisms to the gullible public. They make for an extremely unlikely, entertaining trio as their Christmas eve gets increasingly bonkers with the aid of pentagrams, magic mushrooms, a goat, and virgin blood. While confidently straddling the horror-comedy divide and also incorporating social unrests and crises of faith, *The Day of the Beast* hits all the right notes and sends you on an action-packed sleigh ride to hell. Alex Angulo is a lot of fun as the priest who's completely oblivious to how batty his mathematical proclamations sound, and who is so inexperienced with criminal behavior that a simple apartment chase veers into Benny Hill absurdity. The physical comedy is also outstanding when it involves the metalhead's perpetually stern mother.

Braveheart and *Apollo 13* may have won big at the 1996 *Academy Awards*, but taking home the most prizes at Spain's equivalent, the Goya Awards, was *The Day of the Beast*. It was also a huge hit in theaters, proving that the heavily Catholic population of Spain could withstand a little blood-soaked blasphemy every now and then.

Rock 'n' Roll Nightmare (1987)

Director: John Fasano
Writer: Jon Mikl Thor
Cast: Jon Mikl Thor, Jillian Peri, Frank Dietz, David Lane, Teresa Simpson, Adam Fried

It's always a thrill to check out the website for Portland's Hollywood Theatre and scroll down on the Coming Soon section because absolutely no film is off limits, even the most obscure and maligned titles you can think of, and through programs such as B-Movie Bingo, Mondo Trasho, and Repressed Cinema, fans of cinema at its schlockiest can feel like kids on Christmas morning multiple times a year. One of my fastest ticket purchases came when with the announcement of a *Rock 'n' Roll Nightmare* special screening on July 19, 2014. As if a rare 35mm presentation wasn't enough, the star, producer, screenwriter, Mr. America, Mr. Canada, and self-proclaimed "legendary rock warrior" Jon Mikl-Thor was going to be in attendance to answer questions and perform "We Live to Rock" and "Energy" just in case you weren't tired of hearing them in their entirety during the film. As someone who's gotten a kick out of this movie since high school, I found it equally surreal and satisfying to see it projected on a massive screen with hundreds of people energized on pizza, beer, and questionable filmmaking. Director

Horror Galore

John Fasano was originally scheduled to appear on stage with Thor for the Q&A, but it was announced that an illness prevented him from making the trip. Shortly after returning home, I was scrolling through my Twitter feed and saw the terribly sad announcement that he passed away that night from heart failure at just 52 years of age.

To describe the plot of this movie is a lost cause, and waiting for such plot to materialize is quite the endeavor because after five boring minutes of title credits and demon POV shots that show every inch of an unremarkable house, we get five even duller minutes of Thor—doing his best to look like the muscular Greek god he's named after—driving a van in what feels like slow motion. But even while we're screaming for the film to "do something!" we're somehow charmed by the ineptitude on display, and that goodwill carries on for scene after scene where nothing consequential happens (and where just about every single shot goes on for three seconds too long), making the eventual appearance of hilariously cheesy alien sock puppets all the more rewarding. This is simply one of the best examples of "so bad it's good" out there, as you're constantly shaking your head in amazement and unable to take your eyes off the screen.

Thor, his bandmates and their girlfriends arrive at a secluded farmhouse in Canada to rehearse their new album and come up with ten minutes of new material. For an over-the-top '80s metal act, they are remarkably well-behaved; it must be all of that Canadian spirit. All goes well until their manager goes missing, leading to a line that got one of the loudest reactions at my Hollywood Theatre screening, where Thor says "But it sounded like the scream came from down here............You're right, let's go upstairs." More people go missing, some get possessed, but most everybody gets laid at some point, the standout love scene being an awkwardly staged shower tryst with Thor and his girlfriend. Oh yeah, and everyone also drinks a lot of Coca-Cola in the most blatant of product placements, and the actors probably spent most of the rehearsals learning how to set the cans on the table so the logo faces the camera dead on.

Rock 'n' Roll Nightmare might not have a fanbase or a special edition DVD if it weren't for having perhaps the craziest ending in horror history, which comes completely out of left field and tosses away logic much like how Satan tosses stuffed animals. It's mind-numbingly stupid and contradicts everything that came before it, but it's also the perfect conclusion for a movie like this, substantiated by the deafening laughter and applause from the Hollywood Theatre audience that night.

HOW TO COOK FORTY HUMANS

Flesh-Eating Mothers (1988)
Director: James Aviles Martin
Writers: James Aviles Martin, Zev Shlasinger
Cast: Robert Lee Oliver, Donatella Hecht, Neal Rosen, Valorie Hubbard, Terry Hayes

It's quite possible that as a little kid, I should have been watching more Disney titles about talking animals and fewer horror-comedies about adulterous suburban moms contracting a venereal disease that turns them into cannibals, but back then I had a date every Saturday night with the cable station USA, and it made all the plans. *Flesh-Eating Mothers* was every bit as weird as I remembered, and funnier now that I'm old enough to detect crummy acting, boring sets, irritating music, awkward editing, and sexual innuendos.

Howls of laughter erupted from the first few seconds when a hunter walking around in the snow casually looks down and then starts screaming incessantly when he sees a stump where his arm should be. The campiness becomes official when the title credit is gobbled away bit by bit to the exaggerated sounds of chomping and a cheery theme song about living happily in the ideal home of suburbia.

On a sunny afternoon, a middle-aged woman holds her baby innocently and then decides to see whether or not this holy infant is so tender and mild, a side effect from a disease transmitted by a man slightly resembling Fred Ward, who sleeps with

Poster for *Flesh Eating Mothers* (1988), Academy Entertainment

every dissatisfied housewife in the neighborhood. Anotha mutha (as the 38-year-old actors playing teenagers would say in their thick New York accents) chews her son out for his poor performance at

Horror Galore

school and then reveals her new Joker-sized mouth and razor-sharp sets of teeth; it was a wise move to allocate much of the shoestring budget to scary facial prosthetics, even if it meant sacrificing proper lightning and the freedom of second takes when the actors screwed up their lines.

In one of the best scenes, a teenaged girl meets up with a friend and after they take a couple hits off a joint, she confesses that in a single afternoon, she saw her father kiss another woman inside a bar and then saw her mother eat her baby brother, something that automatically sounds hilarious when stoned. After more body parts have been severed and devoured like chicken wings all over town, she runs into a group of similarly affected schoolmates for this witty exchange: "My mother, she ate my brother." "Our mothers too." "My mother ate your mothers?"

It's corny and dumb, but with characters named Hitchcock and Eisenstein, and miscommunications over cannibals and cantaloupes, there is a level of charm to the script loaded with head-scratching lines like "My mother is on the rag, it's all society's fault" and "Everybody's mother is after our meat!" The youthful fresh-out-of-film-school energy is so contagious that you can practically hear the director and editor giggling hysterically in the editing suite after agreeing on what the final shot would be. If Troma and John Waters is your bread and butta, then you'll probably enjoy these satirical and sleazy flesh-eating muthas.

Microwave Massacre (1979)

Director: Wayne Berwick
Writers: Thomas Singer, Craig Muckler
Cast: Jackie Vernon, Loren Schein, Al Troupe, Marla Simon, Claire Ginsberg

On the night of December 7, 1969, many millions of people tuned into CBS to watch the debut of Rankin/Bass Productions' *Frosty the Snowman*. Some may have been a little incredulous by how the magical and virtuous snowman was being voiced by none other than Jackie Vernon, a popular comedian known for his deadpan, self-deprecating style, and whose occasionally raunchy punchlines made him a hit at celebrity roasts. But for some younger folks who knew nothing of Mr. Vernon's work outside of those Frosty specials, a similar state of disbelief was shared while experiencing *Microwave Massacre*, an extremely low-budgeted cult film where you can hear the wholesome voice of Frosty the Snowman spout vulgarities like "I'm so hungry I could eat a whore."

Jackie Vernon plays Donald, a miserable construction worker in a hapless marriage that is getting worse every day now that his wife, May, has purchased a Major Electric Microwave Model X1-74A and uses it exclusively for worldly cuisine. Her delusions of a sophisticated life in high society clash with schlubby Donald, who just wants to find a simple baloney and cheese sandwich in his lunchbox. If WatchMojo ever gets desperate enough to make a video of the Top 10 Weirdest Cinema Sandwiches, they should save room for this king-sized crab sandwich that seems impossible to take a bite out of. Rather than having to force-feed himself another hoity toity French dish straight out of the microwave, he chooses to fill up his belly at a bar after his shift, getting so drunk that when he returns home, trashing the living room and urinating on the recently vacuumed carpet seem like perfectly natural reactions. Oh yeah, and he also bludgeons his wife to death with a pepper grinder and then stuffs her inside of the microwave (I had to do a little research just to confirm that microwaves were never actually this big!).

The next day, he chops her into pieces and shows us that a huge portion of the film's $75,000 budget must have gone to aluminum foil. Half of the refrigerator is stuffed with May's leftovers and the other half the leftovers of her meals, and when Donald wakes up in the middle of the night with a grumbling tummy, he unintentionally munches on one of her hands, and it turns out to be the best meal he's had all year. This triggers a ravenous new hunger that he satisfies by luring prostitutes over to his house for a round of thumpety thump thump thumpety thump thump, look at Frosty go, thumpety thump thump thumpety thump thump, over the hills of ho. But he's not such a bad guy, because he shares his mouth-watering meals with his co-workers.

Microwave Massacre knows exactly what kind of movie it is, proudly showing off its drive-in sleaziness right from the opening credits with close-ups of a woman's breasts and butt as she struts to the construction site (with arms flailing so much I was reminded of Mr. McMahon). It aims low with cheap and repetitive gags, crude humor, and groan-inducing one-liners, but thanks to Jackie Vernon's loveable presence and Rodney Dangerfield-esque deliveries, I was more than happy to put up with them; he is the sole reason why *Microwave Massacre* is such a guilty pleasure. This is the kind of movie that Al Bundy and his No Ma'am buddies would have enjoyed watching after their meetings while cracking open cans of Girlie Girl beer.

Horror Galore

CHURCHES WITH UNHOLY WATER

Dark Waters (1993)
Director: Mariano Baino
Writers: Mariano Baino, Andy Bark
Cast: Louise Salter, Venera Simmons, Mariya Kapnist, Albina Skarga, Valeriy Bassel

It's easy to scroll past this one when scouring Tubi's horror selections because of its generic title, but all the other films with a similar name might as well be called Crystal Light Lemonade, because these are easily the darkest and most unholy waters around. It's an art-house horror film of the highest degree, opening with a ten-minute wordless prologue consisting of one spellbinding shot after another in a remote island and its ancient convent, starting with a cow's skull tied to a tree swaying in the breeze, a sunset silhouetting a group of cross-carrying cloaked figures, and ocean waves crashing with an eerie red tint. A church window collecting raindrops behind a statue of Jesus soon explodes and invites violent floodwaters to drown the statue and hundreds of candles. Outside in the storm, a nun stands beside a cliff and clutches a mysterious carving which precedes to shatter against a large rock when she is mysteriously pushed to her death.

Twenty years later, a young woman named Elizabeth is traveling in a bus that seems about as uncomfortable as the air-condition-less van after Sally Hardesty and her friends picked up the head-cheese-loving hitchhiker. All of the other passengers are positively off their rockers, perhaps none more than the man who finds comfort in spiders crawling all over him. She's on her way to visit a convent that her recently deceased father had allocated payments to over the years, and which served as her home for the first seven years of her life, of which she remembers nothing except how much the nuns frightened her. After quite an ordeal to reach the islanded convent, she receives a chilly reception by the blind Mother Superior, but ultimately given access to its library and a young nun eager to assist her with anything she needs. In addition to finding out if further payments are warranted, Elizabeth wants to see an old friend, but her timing stinks as bad as the hundreds of fish rotting outside.

Director and co-writer Mariano Baino was inspired by the works of Lovecraft and it shows, because this island could be a dead ringer for Innsmouth with its perpetually stormy state, ancient gods, secretive evils, and artwork of tentacled monsters. At many times it reminded me of Stuart Gordon's creepy-as-hell *Dagon*, especially when Elizabeth encounters drenched locals incapable of offering a reassuring smile.

There is a relentlessly creepy tone anchored by its heavy atmosphere, exploration of cavernous locations in candlelight, effective nightmare sequences, the occasional self-flagellating nun, and sound mixing that is out of this world—any haunted house would be lucky to echo these demonic wall grumblings and prepubescent wails. One of the only moments of levity comes when Elizabeth and Sarah (played respectively by the lovely-accented Louise Salter and Venera Simmons) are figuring out a game plan after witnessing something gruesome—Elizabeth says "We should stick together," but Sarah replies, "I won't be gone long" before walking away, earning a much-deserved "Shiiiiiiit."

If unsettling religious imagery is your thing, then you'll be easy to forgive a plot that grows more flabbergasting with each scene. Sometimes it feels like key moments are missing, such as Elizabeth's first day at the convent where I would have preferred less reading and more interacting with the nuns, and the ending doesn't make a lick of sense. But overall, this movie more than lives up to that brilliant prologue. And because Baino—who sadly only made one other feature film—knows exactly where to position the camera for maximum effect, a simple shot of a hand slowly entering the frame will elicit gasps, and he doesn't even require an accompanying loud and cheap stinger like nearly every modern theatrical film would use.

Despite the movie receiving the quietest of releases, it's a miracle it got released in the first place considering how tumultuous the production was, being the first Western film shot in Ukraine after the Soviet Union's collapse. Severin Films did the lord's work when they gave it a Blu-ray release bursting with special features, where stories about awaking to gunfire from a Russian coup could be told.

Incubus (1966)

Writer and Director: Leslie Stevens
Cast: William Shatner, Allyson Ames, Eloise Hardt, Robert Fortier, Ann Atmar, Milos Milos

Shortly after creating the inventive anthology program *The Outer Limits*, Leslie Stevens continued to experience the awe and mystery that reached from the deepest inner mind by writing and directing *Incubus*, which is a curiosity for many reasons. Imagine if Ingmar Bergman crafted a moody love story in which a succubus targets a noble soldier played by a pre-*Star Trek* William Shatner and filmed it primarily in Esperanto. Stevens thought that using this language created in the late 19th century for the purpose of bringing the world together to speak as one would add another layer of eeriness and intrigue.

In a DVD commentary track, William Shatner recounted an incident when a hippie approached the crew in Big Sur, California, and when he didn't much care for their demeanor, put a curse on them that some people later speculated was legitimate. Yugoslavian actor Milos Milos, as the titular character, was found dead shortly after production wrapped as part of an alleged murder-suicide with a woman he was having an affair with (who happened to be the estranged wife of Mickey Rooney). And right around the time the film was scheduled to be released, actress Ann Atmar (playing Shatner's endearing and kind-hearted sister) committed suicide. All of the tragic news made *Incubus* problematic to market, and the final nail in the coffin was believed to occur after a theatrical run in France, when a lab reportedly burned all of the prints and all of the negatives as part of a big mix-up. As a result, the film was considered lost until one print was miraculously discovered in Paris decades later. A genie might have visited the set along with the hippie gypsy and granted wishes to both William

Shatner and cinematographer Conrad Hall, whose careers absolutely skyrocketed the following year with an iconic reoccurring role and first of many Oscar nominations respectively.

Incubus opens in a village named Nonem Tuum, home to an ancient Deer Well rumored to contain healing waters that restores health and beauty, and that is often secretly monitored by a pair of demonic temptresses who habitually prey on the vain and vulnerable souls before damning them to hell. When one man uses the magical water to remedy his open sores, the younger succubus, named Kia, appears and uses her intoxicating beauty to lure him out to the beach and into the ocean, where he grows weaker with each step until he's no match for the waves. Kia is getting bored with the simplicity of morally corrupt men falling at her feet so easily and vows to corrupt someone who might put up a better fight—someone pure and saint-like, someone who would use the magical waters to treat battle wounds instead of wrinkles, and someone who wouldn't think twice about protecting a small town against a kingdom of the spiders.

She visits the soldier named Marc at the cabin he shares with his sister, and at first, all goes according to plan. Assisted by a sudden eclipse that creates otherworldly excitement and romantic mood lighting, she bewitches Marc but later finds herself developing feelings of her own, and as you can imagine when a woman of Satan and a man of God fall in love, things get extremely complicated. There's even the strong possibility of Black Phillip showing up at the chapel to rain on their parade! Just get past the languid early shots of characters walking and walking and walking and thou shall be rewarded most deliciously.

Romanian poster for ***Mother Joan of the Angels*** (1961), Studio Filmowe Kadr

Mother Joan of the Angels (1961)

Director: Jerzy Kawalerowicz
Writers: Tadeusz Konwicki, Jerzy Kawalerowicz, Jaroslaw Iwaszkiewicz (novel)
Cast: Lucyna Winnicka, Mieczyslaw Voit, Anna Ciepielewska, Maria Chwalibog

Recently selected by Martin Scorsese to be digitally restored for his *Masterpieces of Polish Cinema* series, the moody and existential *Mother Joan of the Angels* is based on the same true story that inspired Ken Russell's *The Devils* (a film so controversial that Italian lawmakers threatened stars Oliver Reed and Vanessa Redgrave with a three-year prison sentence if they ever stepped foot in their country), where in

Horror Galore

17th-century Loudon France, the Catholic Church burned one of their priests at the stake after his libertine behavior with the Ursuline nuns allegedly resulted in mass demonic possession. Despite predating *The Devils* by a decade, *Mother Joan of Angels* feels like a spiritual sequel, since it picks up just a few days after the accused priest was executed, with village children now casually playing right next to the burned pyre that portentously stands before Father Jozef Suryn. He arrives at the Polish convent with the belief that he can do something the previous four priests couldn't: cleanse the nuns of their evil spirits.

Opening the gates for him is Mother Joan, a nun with a wicked smile and supposedly eight different spirits living inside her. Her angelically white garments make for a stark dichotomy with his none-more-black cassock. The comforting choirs are silenced as the two discuss faith and all of the sinning within the hallowed halls, and ramping up the tension is how she keeps turning her back to him in these very long shots because we can't help but wonder if she'll have the same face when she rotates again. The progress of Father Suryn, who had been fasting and mortifying his body for days to prepare for this mission, is much-gossiped about at the nearby inn, where Sister Malgorzata makes nightly visits and entertains the vodka-guzzling men with her song about how she'd "rather be a nun and saved from his stick" while sneaking flirtatious glances with a travelling guest. She may succumb to temptation but the father prefers to flagellate himself with every impure thought, and it's possible he threw a couple extra lashes in there for his demon-exorcising methods being mostly ineffective. On a late, desperate night, he visits a rabbi's cabin in one of the film's greatest scenes, with the two men clashing over their beliefs to the crackling of fire, and ultimately agreeing that neither of them truly knows a damn thing.

It might try the patience of some people in the mood for more violence and vulgarity in their exorcism films, but I think most will find themselves immersed in this beautiful world created by director Jerzy Kawalerowicz, cinematographer Jerzy Wójcik, and editor Wiesława Otocka, where every shadow, unnatural movement, closeup, and juxtaposition unsettles as well as dazzles. The ways in which the nuns resemble ghosts on a field about to be swept up in the wind, sternly march to the sounds of birds and church bells (ringing to help the men lost in the forests ruled by hungry wolves), spin around after doses of holy water, or tumble to the church floor in the sign of the cross with their outstretched arms, it's as if the powers of God and Satan united to create the mightiest of ballets.

UNFRIENDLY SPIRITS WITH SCORES TO SETTLE

Demon (2015)
Director: Marcin Wrona
Writers: Pawel Maslona, Marcin Wrona
Cast: Itay Tiran, Agnieszka Zulewska, Andrzej Grabowski, Tomasz Schuchardt, Tomasz Zietek

While scouring the very impressive horror category on the streaming service Kanopy—free for just about anyone with a library card—I'm awfully glad that on this night I didn't automatically pass on films with the blandest of titles. Having just seen the stunning Argentinian anthology *Wild Tales* and the episode of *It's Always Sunny in Philadelphia* where everyone loses their minds after being spiked with bath salts during Maureen Ponderosa's wedding, I was itching to attend another wedding from hell, and the one in the Polish masterpiece *Demon* was the craziest of them all!

On the eve of his wedding, a man named Piotr permanently leaves his home in England and arrives at a large dilapidated estate in Poland owned by his fiancé Zaneta's family. He plans to fix it up and make it the home of their dreams, but in the meantime, it just has to look nice enough for the ceremony. Even though her relatives hardly know Piotr and wish their daughter hadn't rushed into marriage so quickly, they are eager to make their special day the grandest event the town has seen in decades. Envisioning a perfect place to install a swimming pool, he ignores the fact that it's pitch-black and raining, and decides to start digging. As if finding a human skeleton wasn't alarming enough, he then sinks into the mud and is completely submerged in an instant, only to wake up the next morning inside his car. Both his friends and his fiancé can tell that something besides typical wedding day jitters is troubling the groom who is suddenly prone to nosebleeds and outbursts. His soon-to-be father-in-law, Zygmond, pays little interest to the claims of a skeleton being buried at his property, insisting that "the whole country's built on corpses."

As the ceremony takes place and Piotr's behavior only becomes more erratic, Zygmond's only real concern is to keep the vodka flowing all night long so that everyone will be too sloshed to remember the groom screaming in Yiddish and befalling to epileptic seizures. He announces that Piotr is just suffering the side effects of food poisoning, of course unrelated to the food being served at the wedding, when in reality his body has been invaded by the spirit of a Jewish girl who disappeared decades ago.

Based on Piotr Rowicki's 2008 play *Adherence*, this film is a wicked and clever take on Jewish folklore where the spirit of a dybbuk languishes and possesses until it's able to find closure, but the fact that the locals choose not to recognize the horror unfolding before their very eyes—due to a concoction of alcoholism and shame—makes any kind of solace unlikely. This rural Polish town seems frozen in time, as if it's understandably still shellshocked

Horror Galore

from the horrors of the holocaust where some of the most notorious concentration camps operated nearby. Even its sole bridge has yet to be repaired or replaced. It's no surprise that even the most joyous of nights in this town must end with a speech that mentions collective hallucinations and closes with "Everything will be clear to us. We just need to sleep it off. We must forget what we didn't see here."

Demon is a movie I know I'll be revisiting soon because it's equally fun and profound, and gave me so much to mull over in the hours that followed. By laughing so hard at the drunken antics from wedding guests that my eyes filled up with tears, I was made to feel oddly complicit because much like everyone else there, I was just having a wonderful time and choosing to ignore the severity of the situation, preferring vodka over confrontation. As the perpetually rainy affair begins, those with social anxiety will be reminded of why their eyes roll upon receiving invitations in the mail, but as the night gets crazier and crazier, we're more than happy to be in the company of any one of these guests, whether they are mumbling about Descartes' theories, spinning about the floor as an ambulance pulls in, or randomly breaking out into song. Fans of *Trainspotting* will also be pleased with the lead actor's resemblance to Ewan McGregor's Renton, especially when covered in sweat and fighting a losing battle with himself.

As the ending credits rolled and I prepared to dive down a rabbit hole in the form of wedding fail videos, I decided to first look up Marcin Wrona's Wikipedia page to see what else that super-talented director has made, only to sadly learn that he committed suicide when he was only 42 years old and busy promoting *Demon* around the world at film festivals. Being unable to keep personal demons at bay even during what should have been one of the most rewarding periods of his young life is unbelievably tragic, and I just hope he was given some measure of comfort during these painful times by how much audiences were enjoying his haunting and beautiful film.

TV Guide advertisement for ABC's ***Don't Go to Sleep*** (1982), Warner Bros Television, Spelling Television

Don't Go to Sleep (1982)

Director: Richard Lang
Writer: Ned Wynn
Cast: Dennis Weaver, Valerie Harper, Robin Ignico, Kristin Cumming, Oliver Robins

It's easy to imagine 12-year-old actress Robin Ignico inviting all of her friends from school over on December 10, 1982 to see her star in the television broadcast of *Don't Go to Sleep*, only for someone to ask during a commercial break, "Gag me with a spoon, this movie is bogus to the max, can we watch the tubular new show *Silver Spoons* instead?" The reason is because there are a lot of youngins out there who prefer not to see mental illness, alcoholism, post-traumatic stress disorder, overwhelming grief, vengeful spirits, and the tragic deaths of children their own age on TV during Christmastime. It's also easy to imagine her peers feeling quite startled by her presence the following Monday at school. When the IMDb message boards were around, I'm assuming that the vast majority of posts for this movie came from people who were traumatized by this movie as children, unaware that ABC's primetime lineup had such a dark side, and some of them might even have an irrational fear of pizza cutters to this day.

Advertised with the tagline "Mary thinks something is alive under her bed—Mary is right," this movie begins with a scene that will make some men thankful for their vasectomy, as two children in the backseat complain, bicker, and play pranks involving fake tarantulas while their parents (Valerie Harper in between her popular sitcoms *Rhoda* and *Valerie* and Dennis Weaver from *Duel* and *Gunsmoke*) are already feeling stressed by the long car ride to their new home possessing an ominous 13666 address. While Mary is at first happy to have her own room for a change (with stained glass windows and a collection of creepy dolls that watch her every move), her first night there is anything but restful when she wakes her parents up in the middle of the night with incessant screaming. It's for a reason far more legitimate than a silly nightmare or an invisible monster in the closet: her bed is literally engulfed in flames! She escapes physically unharmed but becomes mentally unbalanced later that night with a visit from the ghost of her older sister, Jennifer, who harbors ill will against the other members of the family over her death and manipulates Mary to seek revenge.

Ned Wynn's script does a really effective job of enlightening us on the tragedy by having each relative provide a small piece of the puzzle through brief confessions throughout the film, merely hinting at who, if anyone, was to blame, before an action-packed climax places us directly inside the car on that fateful night. I also appreciated the realistic quarrels between the family members, whether it's brother vs sister, husband vs wife, or husband vs mother-in-law, where a small disagreement turns into a shouting match, and just as it's reaching a boiling point, someone relents by offering the use of toys (some, not all) or assistance with household chores, and all returns to normal.

Despite all the nihilism, death, and unhappiness on screen, there is still much fun to be had with *Don't Go to Sleep*, and you'll find yourself giggling nervously over scenes of Mary's brother Kevin (Oliver Robins continuing his year of apparitional family destruction after *Poltergeist*) tip toeing on a rooftop to retrieve a frisbee, and a pet iguana creeping its way up the bedsheets to say hello to the sleeping grandmother (Ruth Gordon!). Mary voicing her displeasure over the "slimy monster" iguana's stupid name and snapping at her psychologist over an even stupider question provide further levity. I have no idea why it's called *Don't Go to Sleep* but I know you shouldn't sleep on this legitimately scary and merciless made-for-television thriller.

Kuroneko (1968)

Writer and Director: Kaneto Shindo
Cast: Kichiemon Nakamura, Kiwako Taichi, Nobuko Otowa, Kei Sato, Hideo Kanze

Out of the 20 horror fans I polled, only four had heard of *Kuroneko* (which translates to The Black Cat) and only one had actually seen it. The numbers were slightly higher for its counterpart, *Onibaba*, another exquisitely shot slice of Japanese folklore helmed by the same director and featuring key cast members, and which benefits from having its grotesque demon mask on the artwork to tantalize horror fans at first glance. Both films are about a young woman who lives in a cottage with her mother-in-law, and while her husband is fighting in a bloody civil war, she spends her time spilling the blood of samurai warriors. *Onibaba* places its characters in fields of tall grass and allows sunlight to shine on their sexual desires, jealousy, and petty manipulation, but *Kuroneko* paints a more mysterious, tragic picture, with bamboo groves at nighttime, a constant wind conjuring the supernatural, and the desperation to make the ultimate sacrifice for true love. They are opposing sides of the same brilliant coin and are both worthy of your full attention.

Kuroneko opens with a large group of samurai descending on a modest cottage one afternoon. They quickly shed their traditionally heroic depiction by raping the two women who live inside before killing them and setting the home ablaze. On the nights that follow, samurai warriors who travel alone near Rajomon Gate are preyed upon and slaughtered, and their leader insists that it's the work of phantoms. Newly trained war hero Gintoki is instructed to slay them back to hell, but first he returns home for what he assumed would be a joyous reunion, only to find the cottage reduced to charred remains and no signs of the whereabouts of his wife or his mother. It's a beautifully told fable that also makes room for themes on class systems and the traumas of returning soldiers, both of which were important to legendary filmmaker Kaneto Shindo, a Hiroshima-born socialist who was one of only six men in a 100-troop squad to survive 18 hellish months fighting in World War I. He passed away in 2012 at the age of 100, just a couple years after his final film, the critically acclaimed *Postcard*, was released.

Even with the darkest of subject matters, *Kuroneko* and all of its phantasmagoric imagery is a pleasure to watch. In a time where horror films usually showcase ghosts by having them appear out of nowhere with arms aggressively outstretched and accompanied by an ear-piercing bang, it was refreshing to see melancholic spirits connect with the outside world in understated and interesting ways, saving most of the kinetic action for the last act.

Mystics in Bali (1987)

Director: H. Tjut Djalil
Writers: Jimmy Atmaja, Putra Mada (novel)
Cast: Ilona Agathe Bastian, Yos Santo, Sofia W.D., W.D. Mochtar (yes, there are actually two W.D.s in the cast!)

This film opens with a family of bizarre demon masks shaking and clattering their jaws to ferocious tribal music, and the fact that they're unconnected to their bodies is a sign of things to come for one of the strangest horror films you'll ever see, one that didn't get North American distribution until the new millennium when the studio Mondo Macabro gave it the remastered DVD it deserved. It was also deserving of the accolade "The Holy Grail of Asian Cult Cinema" as printed on the cover to go along with a review snippet stating, "Some of the most bizarre supernatural horror elements I have ever seen in a motion picture." I'm sure similar sentiments were shared by the lucky bastards who got to see it screened at the Alamo Drafthouse in 2016 as part of a celebration of *The Witch*'s release.

Cathy, an American tourist in Bali working on a book about the black arts, persuades her native boyfriend to accompany her to a cemetery where not even the mightiest of thunder and fiercest of wolf howls can drown out the cackling of The Queen of the Leyak, a decrepit witch with fingernails even longer than Freddy Krueger's. Cathy displays several bottles of fresh blood, and the witch's tongue grows 50-feet to lap it all up. She then says "Mmmm, delicious, that's some good blood" before agreeing to take her on as a temporary disciple of black magic. In her first lesson, Cathy masters the Disney's Witch Hazel Art of Laughter and is then deemed ready for more ambitious tasks like transforming into pigs and snakes, and detaching her head so that it can fly around like a kite with the internal organs serving as the string. She soars the skies in search of young blood that will make her new master appear younger, and no blood is fresher than that of a baby about to be born, a gruesome act steeped in Balinese folklore. It's safe to say that Cathy has the most inappropriate severed head since David Gale in *Re-Animator*. A witness to the madness would later say that "It seems that this thing is a flying head but the funny thing was, this flying head had light-colored hair," which is a ridiculous sentence even without the fact that Cathy's hair isn't light.

She wakes up the next morning with no memory of the night before, but with the realization that something is seriously wrong when she starts throwing up live mice. The nonchalant way in which her boyfriend responds to this act is consistent with the baffling ways in which these characters behave, communicate, and react. Whether the blame should be placed on the actors, the voiceovers, or the writing, the film is all the better for these unintentionally hilarious moments that mesh so well with cartoonish special effects like green laser fingertips and the voice of the witch, a merging of Yoda and Bill Skarsgård's Pennywise. Mystics in Bali also features some legitimately impressive practical transformations scenes, set to strobes and swellings of static electricity.

Retribution (1987)
Director: Guy Magar
Writers: Guy Magar, Lee Wasserman
Cast: Dennis Lipscomb, Leslie Wing, Suzanne Snyder, Jeff Pomerantz, George Murdock

On this Friday night in September, it mercifully rained in Beaverton, Oregon, for the first time in almost four months, and adding to my good mood was a slice of supernatural horror known as *Retribution*.

It's Halloween night and a police car speeds down rain-slicked city streets, the camera occasionally mounted behind its flashing lights *Naked Gun*-style. It joins other emergency vehicles at the towering Don Hotel, where people wearing unbelievably cool Halloween costumes are gathered outside and staring up at the roof. The sight of a Frankenstein monster watching in horrified silence a man plummeting to his own demise is both poetic and a perfect way to hook viewers, especially when it's accompanied by pulsating synths reminiscent of Giorgio Moroder's "The Chase" from *Midnight Express*. Seeing the composer and frequent John Carpenter collaborator Alan Howarth's name listed in any movie is an immediate cause for optimism.

George, the miserable shlub with glasses and a bowl cut, crashes hard through a parked car before spilling onto the pavement, and as paramedics try to save his life, we see his spirit ascend to a tunnel of life before it's blocked by a mammoth and monstrously burned screaming head that senses an opportunity. He survives the suicide attempt and spends the next several weeks in a hospital, making significant progress both physically and mentally but certainly not having the best of times in dreamland. It feels like a Frank Henenlotter universe when he returns to his home, a run-down hotel with permanent residents who are all so friendly and supportive, especially the attractive prostitute named Angel who genuinely likes spending time with him.

But when his fever dreams become increasingly disturbing and his art canvases literally start spewing blood (there are no happy accidents with this red paint!), he loses his grip on reality. Desperate for answers, he follows his sudden impulses to take a bus to a neighborhood he's never been to and talk to a woman he's never met, and maybe through her he can discover whether or not he's somehow linked to the recent deaths in downtown Los Angeles that are so grisly a slaughterhouse worker stuffed inside a cow carcass and sawed in half is just par for the course.

Often bathed in candy-colored Day-Glo, *Retribution* oozes with '80s decadence and fashion, where even the diviest of bars has a full color palette and plush carpeting. When George and Angel smoke a joint and visit a neon museum, I decided to join in on the fun and fill a pipe with some Ghost Train Haze sativa. I also used this intermission to look up the actress playing Angel and find out why she looked so dang familiar. Shame on me for not having cherished Suzanne Snyder since childhood because she was also in *Return of the Living Dead II*, *Killer Klowns from Outer Space*, *Night of the Creeps*, and *Weird Science*. She was also one of those rare performers who appeared on *Seinfeld* playing two different characters (pointing a gun at Jerry in a limousine in one episode, bending his mind into a pretzel by refusing a bite of apple pie in the other). There are many other familiar faces peppered throughout this frenzied and tortured tale of possession, and they all had so much faith in the project that they agreed to accept the minimum Screen Actors Guild fee.

Director, co-writer, and co-editor Guy Magar faced hardships right from the beginning with this passion project. Being known as a television director, he struggled to find a producer and then years later, struggled to find theaters that would screen it, even after extensively trimming the gore scenes to change that unwarranted X-rating into an R. But he'll be receiving the ultimate gift from The Great Pumpkin on October 26, 2021 because that's when *Retribution* will make its North American Blu-ray debut, courtesy of Severin Films in a 3-disc special edition. I'm hoping one of the special features will be devoted to the guy at the bar with a Jack Daniels t-shirt and a helmet with the name Jim written on it. He only had a few seconds of screen time but I'd like to see how he's doing these days. It will also be fun hearing stories about that glorious dog costume.

Satan's Slaves (2017)

Writer and Director: Joko Anwar
Cast: Tara Basro, Bront Palarae, Dimas Aditya, Endy Arfian, Nasar Annuz, M. Adhiyat

Minutes after taking down the Christmas tree and sending all tinsel, garland, and snow globes back to their garage tombs, it was time to turn off the lights and welcome my first horror movie of 2020. It got off to a wicked start thanks to a marvelous score featuring a harpsichord, violin, and melancholy female wails. The previous few weeks had been devoted to holiday programming, and I had to go back even further to find an example of a movie truly scaring me, and so *Satan's Slaves* sure hit me pretty hard tonight. Much in the style of James Wan's *Insidious* and *The Conjuring*, this Indonesian film exists solely to scare the living daylights out of you, and while the scare techniques aren't anything you haven't seen before, they are rarely executed this effectively.

Set in 1981, a golden year for horror if there ever was one, the film centers on a large family who has been caring for their cancer-stricken matriarch for the past three years, depleting their savings and selling personal possessions to keep her alive, a problem that many American viewers will have no difficulty relating to. With her body, mind, and beautiful singing voice that made her a household name years ago deteriorating more each day, her youngest children can't help but dread the sound of her ringing the bell from upstairs to request assistance--the way they look at each other nervously at each ring is haunting. When she eventually passes away, the townspeople all gather to show support for the family and give her a proper Islamic funeral, a refreshing departure from the usual Christian practices in spiritual supernatural horror films. It soon becomes apparent that it will take a much stronger ceremony to put her to rest as her spirit seems intent on giving heart attacks to her survivors on a nightly basis; one particular scene involving an apparitional request for hair-combing nearly gave me one as well.

As the aforementioned Wan classics showed, you need well-established characters to get the most impact from your scares, and even though it sure takes a while to figure out how everyone here is related to one another, the family members are all personable and cause the viewers to sympathize with their situation. Having them live adjacent to a cemetery was a nice touch, because not only does it serve as a constant reminder of the inevitable, but it gives the youngest children an incredibly discomforting bedroom view and a damn fine excuse why they want to sleep in a different room after the funeral. And it's probably a good thing they didn't choose to sleep in the room containing a well that people make a habit of falling into! Ah, and I just learned that this is a remake of a 1982 film, also from Indonesia. Oh well, who the hell needs sleep? Let's check it out!

Satan's Slave (1982)

Director: Sisworo Gautama Putra
Writers: Sisworo Gautama Putra, Naryono Prayitno
Cast: Ruth Pelupessi, W.D. Mochtar, Fachrul Rozy, Simon Cader, Siska Widowati

Well, a cinematic amalgamation of the remake's suspense and the original's style would be the ultimate, but until the advent of such a magical piece of technology, let's just be thankful that both of these films exist. Not wasting any time, this version opens right at the funeral for the matriarch of a wealthy family whose agnosticism clashes with traditional Muslim mourning. The camera even puts us inside the coffin as the dirt is shoveled over it, a strange sensation I've become accustomed to thanks to Portland's Freakybuttrue Peculiarium's burial simulation. The deceased's son Tomi awakens later that night to a tapping against his bedroom window (much like in *Salem's Lot*'s most memorable scene) courtesy of a spirit who beckons him outside and back to the cemetery, leaving him understandably shaken and disoriented the following morning. His empathetic friends recommend coping mechanisms which leads him down a path of fortune tellers, flirtations with black magic, and an impressive collection of horror magazines, much to the chagrin of his father and older sister.

Several people in town, including the family's severely asthmatic servant, encourage them to pray daily and find God because their religion states that when a person dies, the spirit has a 40-day haunting grace period. The one tormenting this family masters all the basics in no time and even instructs the piano to play itself in the style of the latest victim. In the greatest scene of all, the devil seems to be getting closer to infecting the whole family when Tomi is led down what appears to be the cleanest subway tunnel in existence to a Satanic celebration where he's the main attraction, and the best part about it is how everyone is wearing Halloween masks, and not the kind you can acquire at Spirit. No sir, these are like the vintage cardboard and crepe paper masks you might have seen in galleries like Buzzfeed's "21 Terrifying Old Photos That Prove Halloween Was Once Scary AF."

When you see so many of Satan's Slaves in a single night, every change is a welcome one and so I really appreciated how the two houses look nothing alike. The one in this movie contains beautiful stained-glass windows and eclectic artwork that are hard to take your eyes off of, even as a character foolishly swings a pillow against the midsection of a demon as a means of defense. The posters in the children's bedrooms deserve a paragraph of their own, but I have to be at work in a few hours and so I'll give you the CliffNotes version: freaky cat, eyeball, thong, Linda Ronstadt.

FRIGHTENING INITIATIONS AND UNLAWFUL SLEEPOVERS

Hell Night (1981)

Director: Tom DeSimone
Writer: Randy Feldman
Cast: Linda Blair, Vincent Van Patten, Peter Barton, Kevin Brophy, Jenny Neumann

Hell Night didn't make much of a splash at the box office when it hit theaters just a week after I was born, but its VHS cover depicting Linda Blair screaming at the gates of a gothic manor sure caught the eyes of many lurkers in the horror aisle. I was probably in 3rd grade or so when I persuaded my parents to rent it for me at our local video store in Affton, Missouri that was promoting the deal of a lifetime with 555 (eat your heart out, Herman Cain Zombie): 5 tapes for 5 days for $5. I remember being entertained by the movie, but unlike fellow 1981 slashers *The Funhouse*, *The Burning*, *Halloween II*, and *Friday the 13th Part 2*, it didn't become a repeat childhood rental, and I wouldn't see it again until three decades later when its costumed characters and strong autumnal presence made it an obvious inclusion for *Pumpkin Cinema: The Best Movies for Halloween*. It didn't take nearly as long for a third viewing, thanks to the special edition Shout Factory Blu-ray that became a late Christmas '17 gift to myself.

It begins with a scream of the youth gone wild variety as Alpha Sigma Rho's annual shindig is in full swing, and it looks like it must have been a ton of fun for all the actors despite the chilly temperatures. Among the hundreds of partiers are four pledges who are about to undertake the initiation of spending the entire night inside Garth Manor, a gothic mansion left uninhabited ever since its walls were splattered with the blood of Ramon Garth, his wife, and their severely deformed children 12 years ago. This fraternity/sorority ritual is a setup we've seen so many times before but rarely is it presented with this much showmanship, production value, and artistic flair.

Dressed as a dancehall flapper girl, prosperous cowboy, Victorian beauty, and Robin Hood, the four leads are refreshingly distinguishable and competent, and they have every right to feel nervous when they get their first look at the menacing estate. After the front door slams and locks behind them, they take the edge off by indulging in Jack Daniels, Quaaludes, and each other. With tall ceilings, castle walls, cavernous tunnels, and about 5,000 lit candles, this house looks good enough to have hosted a Vincent Price party for the ages, and it's very suspenseful watching them investigate the source of strange noises, whether it be a Halloween sound effects cassette or a freshly decapitated head rolling on the floor courtesy of the towering tenant who looks like a relative of the *Hills Have Eyes* mutants. Nearly every jolt is powerful and perfectly timed, evidenced by my startled girlfriend spilling some of her drink on the couch during a monstrous reveal.

A few years ago, I had the rare pleasure of expressing my fondness for this movie to Linda Blair herself at an autograph signing at Movie Madness (to raise money for her animal sanctuary), and in my usual nervous state, I think I said something lame but innocuous like "Hi Linda, how are you? Nice to meet you. You know what movie of yours is really terrific and doesn't get enough recognition? Hell Night!" She smiled and said she was very happy to hear that because of how enjoyable it was to work on it. While walking out of the video store, I thanked my lucky stars for not saying anything too foolish that I'd be annoyingly reminded of every time I saw one of her films, but I couldn't help but curse myself at forgetting to ask her about the ultimate curiosity that is *How to Get...Revenge*, a 49-minute video she starred in from 1989 that the Found Footage Festival generously unearthed for their hilarious and fascinating Volume 5 tour.

The Lamp (1987)

Director: Tom Daley
Writer: Warren Chaney
Cast: Andra St. Ivanyi, James Huston, Deborah Winters, Scott Bankston, Red Mitchell

I'll admit that my expectations were pretty low on this one. For starters, *The Lamp* is such a lame title for a horror movie and so is its alternative name *The Outing*. Equally lame is its tagline "Don't say see you later, say goodbye." My pals on Letterboxd had many other issues with the movie and gave it scores that were mediocre at best. However, I ended up being granted a bloody good night at this museum!

It was charming right from the start as a trio of cartoonishly Southern drunks drive to the middle of nowhere at night and break into a house similar to the one in *Spookies*. Rather than a sorcerer and his ultimate monster mash, the only inhabitant here is a decrepit woman who looks so old that I bet when she was in school, they didn't have history class (sorry, I don't know why that ancient joke just popped in my head). Underneath the many layers of makeup is thirtysomething Deborah Winters (a decade after co-starring in *Blue Sunshine*), who plays a total of three roles in this film. "Inconspicuous" is not in the hillbillies' vocabulary as they cause a ruckus that nobody could sleep through, and when the old woman refuses to divulge the whereabouts of the secret treasures she's rumored to be hiding, she gets an axe through her skull for her troubles. The axe also goes through the wall where a magic lamp from 3500 BC and a very bloodthirsty genie with a death metal voice have been hiding, resulting in an unholy mess for the police to discover the following day.

Both the lamp and a special bracelet found on the old woman are taken to the local natural science museum to be researched by Dr. Wallace, whose workaholic tendencies are getting on his attention-starved teenaged daughter Alex's nerves, so much so that she lashes out and regrettably mutters "Sometimes I wish you were dead." She then experiences more pressing concerns like an ancient bracelet that stubbornly won't come off, a psychotic and racist ex-boyfriend that violently shoves her against school lockers after he fails to run her off the road, and a group of friends who pressure her into letting them spend the night inside the museum following a school field trip.

As goofy as the teenage hijinks are—the school brawl being the comedic highlight—it's no laughing matter when the genie is out of the bottle and ready to throttle. Unlike its witty, charismatic, and manipulative younger brother the Wishmaster, this one uses its powers in no-nonsense fits of rage, as its victims are thrown into ceiling fans, ripped in half underwater, impaled by spears, and devoured by the museum's mummified corpse (by far the most trauma-inducing thing that any kid could observe on a field trip). There's even a rape scene that, while mercifully brief, is so surprising to see just 15 minutes after a security guard with opera aspirations hilariously tests the after-hours museum acoustics with a jovial round of "Figaro." And as a common man who's never been given a VIP tour at a science museum, I also didn't expect to see one of the girls take a bubble bath in the museum's basement following a minor beer explosion, but I'm so glad she did because it becomes the scariest sequence in the movie when a pair of snakes insist on getting zestfully clean as well. Even if the ending and a character's supposed possession didn't make any sense, I still think my friends on Letterboxd were far too harsh on this fun gem and perhaps they should spend more time rubbing lamps instead of other things.

While looking far too mature to convincingly play high schooler Alex, Andra St. Ivanyi has a really nice presence, a resemblance to 80's pop star Tiffany, and a lovely Southern twang, and so it's a shame this is her only acting credit. It's also the only film directed by Tom Daley, who would later write a screenplay for a movie called *The Toy Factory* in 2004, and act in a thriller called *Killing Uncle Roman*, both of which have sadly never seen the light of day.

One Dark Night (1982)

Director: Tom McLoughlin
Writers: Tom McLoughlin, Michael Hawes
Cast: Meg Tilly, Melissa Newman, Robin Evans, Leslie Speights, Donald Hotton, Adam West

The many people who fell in love with Meg Tilly when watching *Psycho II* will be happy to know that a year before moving in with Norman Bates, she starred in an obscure horror film that offers a glimpse of what heaven might be like: taking her

Poster for *One Dark Night* (1982), Comworld Pictures

on a date to a boardwalk arcade with bumper cars, air hockey, photo booths, and romance-detecting machines (where "Fantastic" ranks even higher than "Sexy" and "Passionate"). For that alone this movie would be worth seeing but what makes it a real hidden gem is how it elevates the classic college sorority/fraternity initiation storyline by placing the action inside a mausoleum. Tilly's character, Julie, has to spend the night alone before she can be officially accepted by The Sisters, whose knowledge of Peter Lorre films was perhaps the least plausible thing about this movie.

As if the group being led by her boyfriend's vindictive ex Carol wasn't problematic enough, the newest addition to the mausoleum is the infamous occultist Karl Raymarseivich, recently found deceased in his apartment along with the bodies of six missing women crammed and contorted in a closet. The knives and plates curiously imbedded into the walls add credence to the rumors that his "psychic vampirism" gave him the ability to expel the bioenergy from others by scaring the living daylights out of them, and then using that adrenaline to move objects at will.

Determined not to be intimidated by Carol's theatrical taunts of what it would feel like to be "surrounded by the dead, nothing but dead bodies!" for an entire night, Julie enters the mausoleum with a sleeping bag, a flashlight, and a good attitude. She even laughs when the flashlight reveals itself to be a springy snake gag, but she doesn't find it amusing when what she thought was a sleeping pill turns out to be Demerol, stimulating panic with every bump in the night. I couldn't help but be reminded of *Phantasm*'s Reggie when Carol says "Let's get up to that mother!" and prepares to enter the mausoleum to cause some bumps of her own and smoke a little weed.

As much as I was enjoying Carol's weird one-liners (like "Do you prefer your corpses fresh or rotted?") and Dottie from *Pee Wee's Big Adventure*'s presence, at the halfway point I had doubts that *One Dark Night* could deliver on its exciting premise because this mausoleum, so brightly lit and identical at every hallway, simply wasn't succeeding in the creep factor; the "Baby Murray" chamber was a nice touch, though. But once the lights started dimming and the coffins started tilting, I lost my Charlie Brown/Doubting Thomas persona and became a full-blown cheerleader for this film, celebrating the loudest whenever the corpses (all oozing with terrific and distinctive makeup) would just float over to the women understandably frozen in fear, choosing not to chew on their brains but just to crowd them in a corner, which is somehow even more unnerving.

Much like Jamie Lee Curtis in *Halloween 2*, Meg Tilly doesn't get as much to work with after her character enters a drugged state, but if you enjoyed hearing her recite The Lord's Prayer, then I recommend checking out her Academy Award-nominated performance in *Agnes of God*. It's a damn good thing for us horror fans that first time screenwriter and director Tom McLoughlin's talents wouldn't go unnoticed, as he was deservedly chosen for his next gig to resurrect the Friday the 13th series after a disappointing part 5, and boy did he ever succeed because *Jason Lives: Friday the 13th Part 6* is considered by many to be Jason's finest hour and a half.

MAD SCIENTISTS AND DERANGED DOCTORS

The Black Pit of Dr. M (1959)
Director: Fernando Méndez
Writer: Ramón Obón
Cast: Gaston Santos, Rafael Bertrand, Mapita Cortes, Carlos Ancira, Carolina Barret

As Dr. Jacinto Aldama wheezes and trembles on his deathbed, his friend and colleague Dr. Mazali leans in and reminds him of their sacred oath to each other, and how eternal rest won't occur until the promise is fulfilled. These two men of science have spent their careers being tormented by the mysteries of the afterlife and have agreed that the first one who passes on must do whatever possible to return and tell the other what lies beyond death. It's at least commendable that they choose to torture their own souls rather than go the sickening *Martyrs* route and flay the innocent. Hours after being buried, Dr. Aldama's spirit returns during a séance and forecasts doom on the horizon much like Jacob Marley, but his partner in death remains fearless just as long as it brings him closer to the answers that have eluded mankind for all eternity.

A struggle ensues between the staff at Dr. Mazali's sanitarium and an imprisoned gypsy, resulting in a bottle of acid being hurled at an orderly named Elmer, who goes into a homicidal rage days later when the bandages are removed and he meets the beast that he's become. A knife inscribed with "May the fires of hell consume the one who uses

Poster for *The Black Pit of Dr. M* (1959), Alameda Films

me for evil" impales the gypsy and incriminating evidence points to the doctor as the murderer. He's convicted and sentenced to death at the gallows, and even with the rope tightening around his neck, is still convinced that a stay of execution is guaranteed—the cosmic forces of fate may have other plans. This utterly fascinating story by Ramón Obón, who passed away in 1965 at only 47 years old, also finds the time to include a love triangle featuring two participants who have dreamed of each other for ages before ever meeting in the flesh, sort of like Mike and Liz in *Phantasm II*.

The Black Pit of Dr. M is a brooding black and white Mexican movie with classic Universal horror atmosphere and stellar performances, and it left me spellbound to the point where I totally forgot that my Coke Zero was becoming a solid block in the freezer eager to explode (a price to pay whenever you protect yourself with chilled beverages in an air condition-less house in July). I also appreciated an organ being used as peaceful background music for a change, an entrance reminiscent of The Shockmaster's infamous WCW debut, a lazy afternoon chance encounter inside a church, a courtyard that looks brilliant in the dead of night, a man complaining about the "horror of death inside this flesh," the rare sight of gravestones tilting down a steep hill, the melodramatic reveal of a painted portrait, an afterlife that gives you a free cape at orientation, horrifying facial disfigurements, a corpse's arm poking out from the soil and touching the creeping fog, and a shockingly good climax that ties together the many threads just perfectly. Boils and ghouls, do not let this one stay away from you, even if you have to clean up chunks of frozen Coke Zero for several minutes afterwards.

Dead Kids (1981)

Director: Michael Laughlin
Writers: Bill Condon, Michael Laughlin
Cast: Michael Murphy, Louise Fletcher, Dan Shor, Fiona Lewis, Arthur Dignam, Dey Young

Whether you know this movie as *Dead Kids* or *Strange Behavior*, you can't accuse either title of false advertising because in the first scene, the teenaged son of an Illinois mayor gets stabbed repeatedly after the power goes out in their house, and in the next scene, Chief of Police John Brady is talking on a rotary phone in the bathroom while shaving (and of course cuts himself) when his teenaged son Pete walks in completely naked. More deceased youngsters and peculiar actions will follow in this highly entertaining thriller that proves that New Zealand can look an awful lot like a small Illinois town when it wants to.

High school senior Pete attends an "Independence" party at a classmate's house in which everyone is wearing a strange costume and joyfully dancing to Lou Christie's "Lightning Strikes," a supposed favorite of Oscar-winning screenwriter Bill Condon. Also striking is a psychopath wearing a terrifying Tor Johnson mask who slices through a "kid" resembling George Wendt in his 40s. When a local pathologist examines the two deceased boys and determines they were killed by different perpetrators, Chief Brady suspects that the Galesburg University psychology department is somehow responsible, due to the fact that they've been conducting unregulated secretive experiments for years. And unbeknownst to him, his strapped-for-cash son has just volunteered to be a test subject there for Professor Gwen Parkinson, who for their first appointment, administers a pill that will allegedly increase his brain activity and make the world feel like his oyster for a few days. The follow-up appointment isn't quite as rosy.

As anyone who has seen *Sorcerer*, *Legend*, and *Near Dark* knows, a soundtrack by Tangerine Dream is an enormous gift for a film, and *Dead Kids* takes full advantage of their cold, ambient soundscapes, giving scenes of a coffin slowly being opened and a disturbingly human scarecrow bleeding over cornstalks so much extra impact.

Another reliable gift is the acting talents of Louise Fletcher, another Oscar winner, who plays Chief Brady's adoring girlfriend who does her best not to allow the recent tragedies to stir up old demons and painful memories. Also noteworthy is the set design, where a seemingly ordinary, brightly lit hospital suddenly becomes a futuristic Big Brother portal with a turn of the doorknob.

I giggled like a schoolgirl when Pete and his new girlfriend are driving around at night and he suggests eating at Steak n' Shake, a beloved restaurant chain that has tragically never made its way out to Oregon. I've probably been to over 50 different Steak n' Shakes in my day, and none of them looked anything like the one depicted in this film, but it still looked like a restaurant that would serve a damn fine milkshake in the middle of the night! Another giggle occurred when a witness described the murderer as a chubby 20-year-old girl, prompting a thorough examination and the line, "Here are the files from the college—135 overweight girls!" And while I didn't giggle, I definitely smiled when the film honored the golden age of television sitcoms by naming characters Brady and Haskell.

Depraved (2019)

Writer and Director: Larry Fessenden
Cast: David Call, Alex Breaux, Joshua Leonard, Ana Kayne, Chloe Levine, Owen Campbell

While looking through Hulu's Huluween picks, I was about to settle on a rewatch of the 2017 British anthology *Ghost Stories*, but then the artwork for *Depraved* caught my eye, and once I saw that it was directed by indie horror icon Larry Fessenden (his first since 2013's aquatic creature feature *Beneath*), it became easy to look past that boring title. Yet another modern retelling of Mary Shelley's *Frankenstein* might not sound like the most exciting proposition, but Fessenden, who also served as producer, writer, and editor, takes this movie in many fascinating and unexplored territories while also showing a clear understanding of what makes this story so powerful after more than two centuries.

Alex and Lucy, fresh out of college and coping with uncertain futures, are having a romantic evening together until a casual remark about having a child sparks a lover's spat that they have clearly experienced on multiple occasions. Overwhelmed birthday boy Alex decides to leave and on his way home, is suddenly attacked by a stranger in a vicious opening scene that left me staring at the opening credits in a shocked silence, much like how Alex stares at his unfamiliar reflection in the makeshift laboratory he finds himself in afterwards. The makeup artists earned their paychecks with this grotesque patchwork of multi-toned flesh, each stitch and scar jostling for attention. A young doctor, whose name is of course Henry, enters the room and is overjoyed to see his creation taking its first steps. Alex has no memory of his past, but through clever digital effects, we're able to watch his synapses rejuvenate as a very proud Henry restores his brain activity through puzzles, stories, and music therapy. He even picks up the game of ping pong faster than Forrest Gump!

When Henry's business partner Polidori believes that Alex is ready to experience the outside world, they visit the Metropolitan Museum of Art in New York City in one of the most compelling scenes, where Alex learns about French Classicism canvases and the madness of Van Gogh before stopping in the gift shop and experiencing split-second flashbacks when he locks eyes with the cashier. Polidori then eagerly plays the role of "cool uncle" by introducing him to the pleasures of cocaine, whiskey, and strip clubs, a modern update of The Monster's tobacco lesson in *Bride of Frankenstein*.

While the finale is a celebration of carnage and lightning-lit gothic imagery, *Depraved* spends most of its two-hour running time as a slow-brooding drama that successfully integrates parenting struggles and post-traumatic stress disorders into the Frankenstein lore, and so be prepared for heavy material that will probably leave you depressed afterwards. My only complaint was how it feels the need to focus on a pharmaceutical subplot near the end because it shifts attention away from something we're far more invested in: the relationship between doctor and monster, terrifically played by Alex Breaux and David Call, who put their own spin on these classic characters.

Mad Love (1935)

Director: Karl Freund
Writers: P.J. Wolfson, John L. Balderston, Guy Endore, Florence Crewe-Jones, Maurice Renard (novel)
Cast: Peter Lorre, Frances Drake, Colin Clive, Ted Healy, Sara Haden

Sweets were plentiful on this Sunday in October, starting with a six-pack of mini cider donuts at a pumpkin patch. Then with a pocketful of Hi-Chews, I took a walk around the neighborhood to admire the fall colors and decorations and catch whiffs of Halloween spirits in the air. I also tried a little of the limited-edition Monster Mash cereal, which contains pieces from Count Chocula, Franken Berry, Boo Berry, Frute Brute, and Yummy Mummy during a commercial break for *The Simpsons*' "Treehouse of Horror XXXII", but as someone who had never tasted any of those cereals before, it was a bit confusing on the taste buds. With tomorrow already gearing up to be a salad and exercise day, I figured I might as well indulge once more, this time with two shots of Jim Beam Orange (nectar of the gods) as I watched tonight's movie. As if watching Peter Lorre in his prime wasn't enough of a treat!

Mad Love was based on Maurice Renard's novel *Les Mains d'Orlac* (which was also filmed as *The Hands of Orlac* in 1924), and stars Lorre as Doctor Gogol, an ingenious surgeon with a gentle demeanor and penchant for performing life-saving surgeries on children free of charge. Inside the Theatre des Horreurs, modeled after Paris' real-life Grand Guignol, the doorman has a scary head and the coat checker is completely missing his, and it's where the doctor has been spending every evening for the past few months so that he can watch his favorite actress Yvonne Orlac being tortured on stage with body-stretching racks and hot coals courtesy of her tyrannical, jealous husband.

On the night of the final performance, he purchases the lifelike mannequin of her that has stood in the theater lobby. He also gathers the courage to go backstage and meet the woman of his dreams. While Yvonne does her best to be polite to the man with a ghostly pale melonhead and bulging eyes that never blink, she's understandably unsettled by his insistence that they must see each other again. Having Frances Drake play her own wax figure, much like the actors did in *Mystery of the Wax Museum* a couple years before, really added to the creep factor when the obsessive doctor takes it home.

Yvonne's husband Stephen is traveling home to Paris when his train crashes, and at the hospital he is given the worst prognosis a famous pianist could receive: mangled hands that will need to be amputated. She is so desperate and panicked that she visits Dr. Gogol, who vows to do whatever he can to save her husband's hands. Not wanting to disappoint her after initial methods are unsuccessful, he decides to secretly give Stephen a brand-new set of hands courtesy of the knife-throwing murderer who was recently guillotined at an event the doctor watched with the same fascination as Yvonne's pretend torture. One of the comical side characters mentions how "he never misses one of those head choppings!"

The following weeks are unsettling for Stephen because not only does he struggle at the piano, but he demonstrates a dangerous new talent with his hands when overcome with anger. With him being played by Colin Clive only a few years after famously crying out "It's alive! It's alive!," it's almost like we're seeing Dr. Frankenstein become a patient in his own laboratory. Adding to the rare thrill of this illusion is how many other tie-ins there are to the Universal Monster universe, with the narrative themes of *The Phantom of the Opera*, writing talents of John Balderstone, and visions of Karl Freund.

Mad Love, which flies by at 68 highly entertaining minutes, was Lorre's first American picture. It crashed and burned in theaters (probably for being a little too weird for the time), but the critics were just as awed and complimentary of his performance as they were of his star-making role as the murderer in Fritz Lang's *M* in 1931. There weren't many leading men in Hollywood who could make a line like "I, a poor peasant, have conquered science! Why can't I conquer love?" sound this convincing, tragic, and repulsive, and so it was fitting that he would become a mainstay in horror cinema until his death in 1964. In one of Lorre's final performances, he got to star alongside fellow genre icons Boris Karloff and Vincent Price in Roger Corman's fun-filled *The Raven*.

And since it's past midnight and I'm still wide awake, it looks like I'll be needing one last sweet for this very sugary Sabbath: a yummy Melatonin gummy.

The Manster (1959)
Directors: George P. Breakston, Kenneth G. Crane
Writer: William J. Sheldon
Cast: Peter Dyneley, Jane Hylton, Tetsu Nakamura, Terri Zimmern, Norman Van Hawley

Drive-in aficionados were given one hell of a creepy night when Lopert Pictures released *The Manster* and *Eyes Without a Face* as a double feature. While the latter film would gain a healthy reputation in the following decades, the former quickly fell into the public domain and was given so many alternate titles that moviegoers might have had a difficult time tracking down the source of those grisly and indelible images from that memorable night in their car. A horribly disfigured woman begging for help by sliding her claw-like hands through the bars of her cage and a man shrieking as an eyeball protrudes out of his shoulder must have seeped into the unconscious for many unsuspecting youths back in the day, much like how the images of *Pet Sematary*'s Zelda and the Brundlefly transformations scarred the youngsters of the '80s.

Known also as *Nightmare*, *The Two Headed Monster*, and *The Split* (the name of Jean Redon's novel it was based on), this movie was shot entirely in Japan with all of its characters fluent in English. Before a foreign correspondent named Larry can finally return to the States and be reunited with the love of his life, he has to interview the reclusive Dr. Suzuki at his mountaintop home where he experiments with chemicals to uncover the next step in human evolution. He tells Larry about how sporadic cosmic rays in the atmosphere have mutated his plants and fungi, but leaves out the part where he turned his brother into an abominable ape-creature and had to throw him down a volcanic elevator shaft after the reveal of unfortunate side effects.

The good doctor perceives Larry to be the perfect subject for his new experiment, so he prepares

Horror Galore

a Cosby cocktail and a syringe filled with his new and improved chemical concoction. In the following days, Larry's behavior changes drastically and he no longer has any desire to return to his wife or continue his journalistic assignments. He prefers to accept the pleasurable invitations from Dr. Suzuki that involve partying in Tokyo with geishas and unlimited sake, and soaking in hot springs with his irresistible laboratory assistant, Tara. The celebrations are interrupted with confrontations by his wife (who travels to Japan after being unable to reach him) and shocking physical transformations that send the jerk wandering the nighttime streets alone in a mad panic, finding momentary solace in the chanting of a Buddhist monk before exploding in a fit of rage at being ignored. The audience of angry-eyed Oni statues would put anyone on edge, especially if you've discovered just hours before a grotesque monster permanently attached to the side of your body and growing larger by the hour.

At only 72 minutes, *The Manster* would have benefitted from more character development from our protagonist in the early scenes so that the mental mutation would be just as unnerving as what happens to him physically. To actually care about this character would have carried so much weight, rather than just witnessing a very marginal and uninteresting man with arrogant tendencies become a full-fledged heel. It's still a very entertaining movie though, and if you happen to watch this with a group, I implore you to press pause after Dr. Suzuki asks Larry how old he is at the beginning of the film so that everybody can take a guess. Chances are everyone will be off by a decade or two and then erupt in befuddled giggles. The same kind of laughter will be triggered by the end title card because the conclusion is so hilariously abrupt that you'll have to rewind just to make sure it wasn't a technical difficulty.

THE SILENT FILMS THAT GAVE OUR ANCESTORS HEART ATTACKS

Häxan (1922)

Writer and Director: Benjamin Christensen
Cast: Elisabeth Christensen, Maren Pedersen, Clara Pontoppidan, Oscar Stribolt, Tora Teje

Oscillating between documentary and dramatization, *Häxan* investigates witchcraft from a cultural and historical point of view while showcasing groundbreaking special effects (including the use of double exposures, stop-motion animation, shadow play, and reverse motion) that still hold up well to this day. This Swedish silent film's cult following has continued to grow over the decades thanks to easy public domain accessibility (much to the delight of rock bands eager to project it behind them during shows), and with its 100th birthday coming up next year at the time of this writing, it seems that more and more independent theaters have made it an October tradition to screen the film with either an organist or music group providing the live soundtrack.

Once you get past the opening chapter, which is essentially a 13-minute PowerPoint presentation (the type that plays on a loop in museums) about how primitive men blamed everything that was incomprehensible to them on sorcery and evil, *Häxan* more than lives up to its reputation to shock with its gnarly visuals and upsetting subject matter. An old woman breaking off the finger of a corpse, witches-in-training lining up to literally kiss Satan's ass, an infant being tossed into a boiling pot, demons forcing people to dance over a cross, a nude woman sleepwalking through the forest, the devil seducing a woman while her husband sleeps, and Inquisition judges torturing an innocent woman until she falsely confesses aren't usually attributed to silent cinema, especially

My ticket stub from a Haxan screening

since it hadn't been that long since audience members fainted at a simple stationary shot of a train speeding toward the camera.

Writer and director Benjamin Christensen, who appears on screen as both Christ and Lucifer, spent years working on the film after studying extensively *The Malleus Maleficarum*, a 1486 how-to-condemn-and-sacrifice-witches guide for dummies written by German Catholic clergyman Henrich Kramer. His jovial sensationalizing of Satanic stereotypes blends well with his condemnation of witch-hunting through the ages. It's extraordinary and oddly inspiring that a movie like this could have even existed back in 1922 and that so many people flocked to see it, helping to lay the foundation of a long-term, reciprocal relationship between Satan and the box office.

Horror Galore

The Phantom Carriage (1921)

Director: Victor Sjöström
Writers: Victor Sjöström, Selma Lagerlöf (novel)
Cast: Victor Sjöström, Hilda Borgström, Tore Svennberg, Astrid Holm, Concordia Selander

On New Year's Day 2021, this silent film from Sweden celebrated its 100th birthday, and even though the newspaper says differently, I'd like to think that the Grim Reaper himself took the whole day off to soak in the majesty and moodiness of one of Ingmar Bergman's personal favorites. The director who would also include Mr. Death in *The Seventh Seal* claimed to have watched *The Phantom Carriage* at least once every year and so when it came time to direct *Wild Strawberries*, he extended his appreciation by casting Victor Sjöström in the starring role as a narcissistic professor confronting his mortality through a series of disturbing nightmares and painful memories. Bergman wasn't the only person heavily influenced by *The Phantom Carriage*, as its nonlinear narrative—in which flashbacks have their own flashbacks—and special effects were groundbreaking in their day, and still impressive to this day.

On New Year's Eve, a dying woman named Edit requests the presence of David Holm, who's busy drinking and smoking in a graveyard with two friends. "It's a spooky place to await midnight, here among the dead. You gentleman are not afraid of ghosts, I hope," he says before recounting the disturbing legend that states the final person to pass away before the clock strikes midnight would be forced to drive Death's carriage for an entire soul-snatching year, meaning that getting into a drunken brawl at the worst possible time could potentially lead to a meeting with a Grim Reaper eager to relinquish the reins.

Much like in another holiday-themed morality tale where Death shows a Scrooge of a man the error of his ways, David is forced to confront a pattern of destroying lives with his hostility, pettiness, and selfishness. Even taking into account the inflation of shadiness over the past century, he's still a truly detestable man who repeatedly betrays the trust of his wife, intentionally spreads his tuberculosis to those trying to help him, and gives alcoholics a very bad name!

In one of the most powerful scenes, David is forced through Edit's bedroom door so forcefully that he tumbles to the floor, hesitating to stand back up because then he'll be painfully reunited with a woman under the most tragic of circumstances. Just one year ago, she was hopeful and strong, but had her life essence stolen just because her path had to unfairly cross his. The last time they saw each other, she wished him a happy new year and he mockingly laughed in her face as if he could foretell their doomed fortunes through the clouds of his cigarette smoke. We feel every bit of his remorse and her sorrow because the acting is grounded and believable, mercifully avoiding the exaggerated melodrama common in films of this era. Sjöström is also quite good in scenes that accentuate his alcoholism, whether he's lost in his own world at the bar and unable to mask his utter contempt for humanity, kicking a jacket that falls to the floor because of his lack of coordination to hang it properly, or repeatedly slamming an axe against a door that separates him from his petrified wife, so many decades before Jack Torrance notified his significant other that Johnny had, in fact, arrived.

While it's improbable that I'll be revisiting these languid and bleak 107 minutes (where the word "Slut" fills the screen in the dying seconds for a logical reason) with the voracity of Bergman, I can definitely see myself watching on a yearly basis the hauntingly beautiful shots of the grim reaper steering his rickety carriage through the dead of night and into the ocean, perhaps searching for lost souls amidst the flotsam and jetsam.

GOT BUGS, RATS, AND CREEPY CRAWLIES AGAIN, HUH, MR. PRATT?

Kingdom of the Spiders (1977)
Director: John 'Bud' Cardos
Writers: Richard Robinson, Alan Caillou, Jeffrey M. Sneller (story)
Cast: William Shatner, Tiffany Bolling, Woody Strode, Lieux Dressler, David McLean

Intense fear of spiders is something I apparently inherited from my mom, but as a youngster it never stopped me from enjoying movies where they were the stars. *Kingdom of the Spiders* was something I watched with friends on a couple different occasions back in the day because we had a fun time watching a town seized upon by thousands of tarantulas that crawl over everything and everybody, including a crop duster screaming at the top of his lungs like a girl when his helicopter is invaded.

My arachnophobia hasn't subsided at all three decades later, and in fact, has only gotten worse, compounded by a dreadful sleeping disorder called hypnagogic hallucinations, which occurs every six months or so and causes me to wake up and immediately hallucinate that spiders are right next to me. After jumping out of bed in a panic, I'll watch the spiders scramble away and suddenly disappear, and then I'll spend the next 30 seconds turning over pillows and inspecting the walls until I resign to the fact that they were imaginary and not worth losing more zzz's over. After a few of these episodes, I nervously typed "waking up and thinking" before Google continued with the most popular search: "you see spiders." It was gratifying to learn that this was a common occurrence and not evidence that I was losing even more marbles than I thought. But just as unfortunate as these rude awakenings is how I no longer want to look at a tarantula on television in any capacity. Thankfully I've seen Home Alone enough times to know exactly when to close my eyes. In a more recent example, I had to shield my eyes during an excruciatingly long and terrifying scene from Fulci's *The Beyond*—I still have no idea what all those tarantulas were doing to that poor man but it sure sounded repulsive! As a result of my cowardice, *Kingdom of the Spiders* now seems impossible for me to enjoy, but that won't stop me from recommending it whole-heartedly to horror fans!

In a rugged and dusty Arizona town, a veterinarian played by William Shatner investigates the deaths of a prize calf and a dog in which blood tests determined the cause to be spider venom. His skepticism flees when a stretch of farmland reveals a hill covered in tarantulas, a rare sight seeing as how arachnids tend to be solitary creatures, even cannibalistic in nature. Due to an overuse of pesticides that has ridden them of their natural habitat, the spiders prey on large animals and humans instead, attacking them in numbers and giving the veterinarian much more to worry about than his busy love life.

The producers of the film offered $10 for each live tarantula brought to them, and ended

Horror Galore

up spending about $50,000 in a deal that clearly didn't require a return stipulation because in an action-packed, out-of-control montage, several hundreds of them are shown getting crushed by running feet and car tires—the lucky ones just got to stretch out their long legs on the faces of screaming women and children. Donna Mills (*Play Misty for Me*) was originally considered for this brave cast but backed out after more details were revealed to her; this wasn't going to be like encountering gigantic ant animatronics or a normal-sized spider in a bowl of popcorn. Fortunately for her, none of the 236 episodes of *Knots Landing* she appeared in required getting a massage from 80 hairy legs.

Even though it's been over 25 years since my last *Kingdom of the Spiders* viewing, certain scenes must be ingrained in my hippocampus, especially that hard-hitting doozy of an ending! A sequel never came, but it was oh so close. There was even a full-page ad in *Variety* in the late '80s that announced that William Shatner was going to both star in and direct *Kingdom of the Spiders II*, but sadly Cannon Films went bankrupt before production began and all the ambitious spider thespians would have to wait a couple more years for *Arachnophobia* to be greenlit.

Of Unknown Origin (1983)

Director: George P. Cosmatos
Writers: Brian Taggert, Chauncey G. Parker III (novel)
Cast: Peter Weller, Jennifer Dale, Lawrence Dane, Kenneth Walsh, Shannon Tweed

Even though the poster art leaves much to be desired, I feel this will be an easy sell to you, dear readers, because in addition to being a favorite of Stephen King, it also stars Peter Wellers (four years before wowing the world with *Robocop*) as a man whose world turns upside down when a monstrous rat invades his newly renovated New York City brownstone and refuses to be outsmarted.

With two weeks to complete a lucrative new assignment that might further his climb to the very top of the corporate ladder, he struggles to stay focused when every day he returns home to find that the rat has done something terrible like chew through the dishwasher line (causing the kitchen to flood), gnaw at every item in the pantry with her "teeth like chisels," puncture the furniture, and avoid every single trap, from the antiquated to the supposedly foolproof. His calls to various exterminators have also been ignored because it's tough to convey urgency when they're all living in a giant open sewer like NYC where armies of rats rule the subway.

He learns a great deal more by flipping through books Chief Brody style, staring in horror at severely scarred victims, and soon he's able to recite to uncomfortable dinner party guests a litany of facts regarding rats' involvement in the Bubonic plague and how they're viewed as a tasty delicacy in South East Asian countries. Also similar to *Jaws* are the clever ways the film makes the rat's initial presence known, with point-of-view shots, extreme close-ups of various body parts, and frightening manipulation of objects both animate and inanimate (those bedsheets! AHHHHHH!!!), leading up to a full reveal that will have your heart drop to the floor, and once you get over the shock, you can't help but laugh about how effective it was. Weller's descent into madness is such an entertaining spectacle, whether he's pounding his copy of Moby Dick against the ceiling or drinking J&B Scotch from the bottle in a scalding hot bathtub fully clothed.

A plot this simple would have you expecting just another cheap creature feature, but this Montreal-shot movie punches far above its weight in every department. It also has the distinction of a title credit reading "Introducing Shannon Tweed," which is fair because she probably didn't get much of an introduction playing "Beautiful Woman" in the 1982 TV-film *Drop-Out Father* starring Dick Van Dyke, sandwiched at the bottom of the IMDb credits with "Satisfied Customer" and "Announcer #1."

Director George Cosmatos (*Cobra*, *Rambo: First Blood Part II*) would give Weller another chance to be mercilessly terrorized five years later for the aquatic cult favorite *Leviathan*, placing him against a Stan Winston-designed creature that has the ferociousness of the rat with a Kaiju-sized body.

Phase IV (1974)

Director: Saul Bass
Writer: Mayo Simon
Cast: Nigel Davenport, Michael Murphy, Lynne Frederick, Alan Gifford

If you go to a video store and simply ask for that intellectual sci-fi horror movie about killer ants, you're going to be handed a copy of the classic *Them!* (1954). But if it's a really good video store, then you'll be pressured into taking a second movie home for an ultimate double feature.

To the annoyance of many, Saul Bass's *Phase IV* has been completely bare-boned in all of its releases on DVD and Blu-ray, but maybe it's a good thing that no extensive "making of" special feature has been produced because it might take away some of the magic. I quickly turned off a documentary included on the Blu-ray for *2001: A Space Odyssey* after realizing that I preferred not having any idea how the hell Stanley Kubrick achieved those sequences that take my breath away every time, and *Phase IV* is similarly mysterious and superhuman in its artistry. It's just about the only movie that will hit the spot when you're craving a horror movie as well as an episode of *Planet Earth*. But it's a downright travesty that no physical release has included the lost ending—which I finally saw for the first time after some kind soul recorded it at a special screening and uploaded to YouTube—because it's a mesmerizing and challenging piece of filmmaking that fans of Alejandro Jodorowsky and avant-garde would go gaga over. It's easy to imagine a lame studio executive, however, seeing it and screaming, "What the fuck was that about? Cut it! Cut the whole damn thing! *Blazing Saddles* just grossed over $100 million and you know how many far-out montages it had? Notta! This is a film about killer ants, not an acid trip!"

Following an unexplainable cosmic event, two scientists named James Lesko and Ernest Hubbs set up a computerized lab in Paradise City, an Arizona desert development that never developed and is now a ghost town. They are studying its ant population that has suddenly inherited the ability to communicate and make decisions. The ants have also been ganging up on their predators like tarantulas and mantises, and using their newfound intelligence to combat insecticide and every other trick the humans have at their disposal. They've even found a way to construct monolith-like structures to deflect sunlight onto Lesko and Hubbs' lab so that the intense heat overwhelms their air conditioning and electrical equipment.

It's pretty silly how infallible the ants and scientists are throughout this serious movie, but you won't find much opportunity to nitpick over narrative flaws because you'll be too distracted by all the beauty and psychedelia. Much like in the 1996 French documentary *Microcosmos*, the camera gets so close to these insects that you can practically hear them breathe, and whether they are being drenched in a neon yellow poisonous waterfall, marching to Tangerine Dream-esque prog music in a rainbow-colored underworld, or crawling one-by-one out of a hole in a corpse's hand, you simply won't be able to take your eyes off of them while they carry out their ambitious plans for the future. Nor will you want to blink during shots of flowers quickly wilting under a full moon and desert sunrises peaking over cornfields. Apparently, its geometric crop circles are the first to ever be shown on film, and it's been long-rumored that *Phase IV* influenced the crop circle phenomenon that began a couple years after its release.

This is the only feature film that Saul Bass ever directed but his mark was left all over pop culture in many different avenues from the '50s until his death in 1996. For starters, he created the title sequences for *The Man with the Golden Arm*, *Vertigo*, *Big*, *The War of the Roses*, *Goodfellas*, *Casino*, and about 45 other films. In addition to handling the memorably intense credits for *Psycho*, he was also credited as a visual consultant for his storyboards in the movie's most famous scene. He proved to be invaluable from a marketing perspective as well, designing posters for *Anatomy of a Murder*, *It's a Mad, Mad, Mad, Mad World*, *The Shining*, and so many others. And you probably can't even open your kitchen pantry without seeing one of the iconic logos that he created for various companies! It's extraordinary how in the same year his existential arthouse horror film about killer ants hit theaters, United Airlines introduced his "tulip" logo to the world, and held onto it for 38 years until merging with Continental Airlines.

Slugs (1988)

Director: Juan Piquer Simon
Writers: Ron Gantman, Shaun Hutson (novel)
Cast: Michael Garfield, Kim Terry, Philip MacHale, Alicia Moro, Santiago Alvarez

Throughout my life I've enjoyed films about killer spiders, ants, cockroaches, serpents, and ticks, and so it was exciting to learn that the director of *Pieces* gave slugs their chance to terrorize a small American town. And just like in that awesome cult classic which proved "you don't need to go Texas for a chainsaw massacre," several Spanish-speaking cast members were later dubbed to occasionally shoddy results. Line readings and character reactions will have you scratching your head in nearly every scene, starting with a pre-credits moment where a teenaged boy on a raft dangles his legs in the water and says "There's something slimy down there. I don't like it!"

The slugs find their way inside greenhouses, bedrooms, faucets, salads, and eye sockets, and by the time the cops make it to the scene of the crime, their victims are but pulpy skeletons. Health inspector Michael Brady spends most of the film trying to convince people that unnaturally large and aggressive slugs are the possible culprits, but he's constantly ridiculed and dismissed, all while the evidence piles up and no other plausible explanation can be found. The chief of police is particularly condescending as he wonders if Brady will bring up

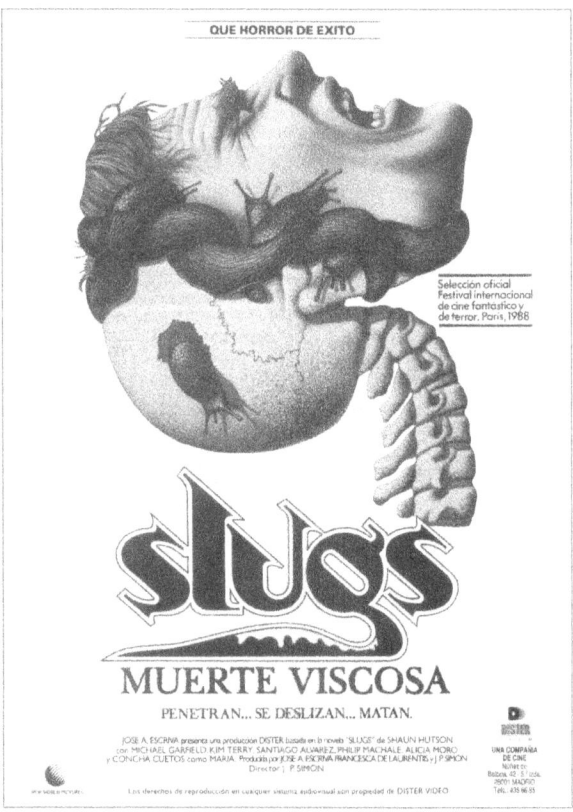

Spanish poster for *Slugs* (1988), Dister Films

other preposterous ideas like killer mosquitos, while the mayor barks, "You don't have the authority to declare 'happy birthday!' Not in this town!"

This is the kind of movie made for late-night theatrical screenings with pizza and beer because audiences will be howling with laughter over the dialogue and cheering triumphantly after each elaborate kill. Much like *Ticks* accomplished five years later, *Slugs* gets a solid A in the body horror and makeup department, with the highlights consisting of a character chopping off his own hand when a slug doesn't relinquish its grip, an important business meeting ruined after an embarrassing face explosion, and a couple making love only to discover that about 50,000 vicious voyeurs were watching from the floor.

As much as I enjoyed the film, the highly-anticipated Halloween party was a colossal letdown because it involved only about 20 teens dancing outside in the middle of nowhere without a single costume in sight, but hey, at least the music wasn't horrible and there was that one pumpkin to confirm that it was, in fact, the season of the witch.

Update: Uhhh, you know how I was saying a year and a half ago how *Slugs* is the kind of movie made for late-night theatrical screenings with pizza and beer because audiences will be howling with laughter over the dialogue and cheering triumphantly after each elaborate kill? Turns out I was right on the money because on October 23, 2021, Portland's Hollywood Theatre screened it as part of their annual All Night Horror Marathon (which has legitimately become the hottest ticket in town), and even in a stacked '80s lineup that also featured *The Gate*, *Rawhead Rex*, and *Chopping Mall*, it got by far the loudest reactions. It was a smart and observant audience because not only did they cheer the condescending bastard chief and all the gore, but they also noticed how the soundtrack would find goofy ways to wrap up just in time for a character to start speaking.

Ticks (1993)

Director: Tony Randel
Writer: Brent V. Friedman
Cast: Seth Green, Rosalind Allen, Ami Dolenz, Virginya Keehne, Alfonso Ribeiro, Peter Scolari

The quickest and easiest visit I ever had at Blockbuster Videos was in 1994, when I immediately headed to the New Releases, and for some reason, started at the end of the alphabet. Once I got to the T's and saw a closeup of Ami Dolenz being terrorized by giant mutant insects, my mind was made up. It wouldn't be the last time I excitedly snatched *Ticks* off of the shelves. Always a crowd pleaser, this throwback to the giant insect movies of the 1950's has its tongue firmly in cheek, pushing up against a throbbing abscess until it explodes with pus, blood, and eight black legs.

An even fresher-faced-than-usual Seth Green stars as a solemn teenager named Tyler who is prone to panic attacks and episodes of crippling fear stemming from an experience years ago when he was lost in the woods. His father, thinking it would be prudent for him to join an inner-city wilderness getaway, drops him off at a meeting location that is naturally a filthy vacant lot below an overpass. Tyler is all alone until he's confronted by a switchblade-carrying street tough who forces him to shoot some hoops with possibly his life on the line. The fact that he's played by *Fresh Prince of Bel Air*'s Carlton and that he introduces his character by saying, "They call me Panic cuz I never do" (maybe this is how they allocate nicknames in the bizarro world) will make your heart bleed for this movie instantly. The rest of the smorgasbord of troubled teen stereotypes includes a Latino meathead, a ditzy valley blonde, and a solemn girl who prefers to be mute. Along with the adult couple running the organization with their reluctant daughter, they head to the San Bernardino National Forest for some team-building exercises in the fresh air, unaware that marijuana plants are ubiquitous and their cabin closets have permanent residents in the form of gelatinous embryonic sacs.

One of the weed farmers is played by b-movie icon Clint Howard, whose only purpose in the movie is to die, and you won't find anyone at the Academy Awards that can die on screen in a more entertaining fashion. To get the upper hand on his competitors, he foolishly mixes water with an herbal steroid to accelerate growth, and its seeping into the ground results in an army of mutant ticks. The late, great Rance Howard (father of Clint and Ron) also makes an appearance as a police officer.

In addition to roided-up ticks determined to tunnel through the hypodermis, the campers also have to worry about a couple of locals who are ready to pounce if you get too close to their beloved crop. With Jerry channeling the *Deliverance* hicks and ascot-wearing Sir always armed with a pocket comb and French salutations, this is the ultimate odd couple and it makes me wish they had their own spinoff!

Revisiting *Ticks* as an adult and being just as entertained by the cast of characters, impressive creature effects, hilarious nonsense, creepy sounds of bugs quickly crawling across the floor, and a seriously messed up-looking Clint Howard yelling "I'M INFESTED" (which inspired an alternative title) makes me eager to introduce *Ticks* to current friends and relive some of the best sleepovers from my youth, when my mentioning of Seth Green and Ami Dolenz both appearing in the comedy *Can't Buy Me Love* was met with mutant cricket noises.

"LOVE BITES, LOVE DIES"

Buried Alive (1990)

Director: Frank Darabont
Writers: Mark Patrick Carducci, David A. Davies (story)
Cast: Tim Matheson, Jennifer Jason Leigh, William Atherton, Hoyt Axton, Jay Gerber

If you start watching a movie from 1990 called *Buried Alive* and it begins with a teenaged girl escaping from a boarding house late at night only to run into a masked maniac in the woods who pushes her down a chute leading to his secret lair where he walls up victims like in Edgar Allan Poe's "The Cask of Amontillado," then turn it off before wasting any more time. You have the wrong *Buried Alive* from 1990, silly rabbit! Streaming services often get these two movies mixed up by posting the wrong cover art and synopsis, and it makes me wish that the good one, the one that premiered on USA Network on May 9, 1990, had kept its working title, Till Death Do Us Part to avoid the confusion. Thankfully, Kino Lorber Studio Classics has made the search easier by releasing it on a 2K-mastered DVD/Blu-ray with extras and awesome new cover art for a low price.

Clint Goodman is the happiest he's ever been. He's back in his hometown with a beautiful wife, successful construction company, dream home, and good friend to go fishing with. His wife Joanna, a city girl at heart, is far from content though, and has been cheating on him with the local doctor who promises her a luxurious life in Los Angeles, far away from the hick town she now feels trapped inside. All it takes is a little help from his exotic fish to make their problem go away.

At the dinner table the following night, Clint makes a toast and drinks a glass of wine while Joanna stares daggers into him and offers no help when he falls to the floor in an excruciating struggle for air. He's pronounced dead at the scene but since the funeral home is given strict orders to skip the embalming process and bury him immediately in the cheapest coffin available, there may still be hope for Clint yet.

Demon Knight was super cool and all but I think something like *Buried Alive* would have been a more appropriate film for the Crypt Keeper to present on the silver screen. It really feels like an extended episode in how it's a morality tale involving greed, infidelity, murder, revenge, and a poor sap clawing his way out of a claustrophobic hell during a thunderstorm. And check out this list of impressive participants:

Jennifer Jason Leigh – Seeing this actress' name in the credits of any movie you're watching should be celebrated as if you just discovered that the next Halloween falls on a Saturday. She rules!

Hoyt Axton – The name might not be familiar to you but the face and smooth bass-baritone voice most certainly will. "Rand Peltzer, fantastic ideas for a fantastic world, I make the illogical logical."

Horror Galore

William Atherton – Walter Peck from *Ghostbusters* and Thornberg from *Die Hard* is back with his wickedest, smarmiest role yet!

Jacques Haitkin – Cinematographer of *A Nightmare on Elm Street* parts 1 and 2, *The Hidden*, *Shocker*, *Maniac Cop 3: Badge of Silence*, and *Wishmaster*.

Mark Patrick Carducci – Screenwriter of *Pumpkinhead* and *Neon Maniacs*.

And last but not least…

FRANK freaking DARABONT! – Before getting his well-deserved strolls on the red carpets of Hollywood for his work as both writer and director of *The Shawshank Redemption* and *The Green Mile*, Darabont had already given the horror genre so much by writing one of the best horror sequels, *A Nightmare on Elm Street 3: Dream Warriors* and one of the best remakes, *The Blob*. The popularity of his more recent contributions like *The Mist* and *The Walking Dead* makes it all the more surprising that the first feature he ever directed has remained so obscure.

"Oh, this is great. This is just great. We've got Jason upstairs and Cujo in the front yard!"

Cemetery Man (1994)

Director: Michele Soavi
Writers: Gianni Romoli, Tiziano Sclavi (novel)
Cast: Rupert Everett, Anna Falchi, Francois Hadji-Lazaro, Mickey Knox, Fabiana Formica

It was exciting to find a VHS copy of *Cemetery Man* at Fenton Missouri's Video Update one sunny afternoon in the late-90's, not only because it was my introduction to Italian horror, but because one of my high school friends gave it a glowing recommendation. A couple hours later, as the videotape kindly rewound itself, I just sat there trying to process what I had just seen and wondering how I was going to be able to put my reaction into intelligible words when I saw him at school the next day. And tonight, on this 20-year-reunion with the handsome cemetery man, I am once again feeling so weirdly distanced to planet earth that I can just be thankful it's a holiday weekend and I don't have to deal with social interactions and small talk for a few days.

I'm still struggling to put my finger on why this movie affects me so, as it should be a walk in the park compared to far stranger films like *Eraserhead*, *Begotten*, *Liquid Sky*, and *Santa Sangre*. Maybe it's the way in which such a fearlessly zany attitude manages to coexist with ruminations on love, sex, obsession, and loneliness, and whether there's a point to anything when death remains inevitable. I'm pretty sure the quote "I'd give my life to be dead" was featured on my AOL member directory profile for a bit. Or maybe it's just because of the indelible scenes involving forced impotence and a nervous idiot savant resembling Curly from The Three Stooges vomiting on a teenaged girl he's attracted to. Or the off-putting score that makes me wish that Tangerine Dream provided the soundtrack as originally planned. Or the juggling of Michele Soavi's visual senses that hearkens back to Hammer horror, Fellini, Evil Dead, and the works of his mentor, Dario Argento. While the thought of revisiting *Cemetery Man* always fills me with a mysterious trepidation, I think it's something that all horror fans should experience at least once because few films are this unforgettable.

Known to the rest of the world as *Dellamorte Dellamore* (which translates to "of death and of love"), *Cemetery Man* was loosely based on the Italian comic strip *Dylan Dog*, which had its titular character illustrated to resemble Rupert Everett, and so the film's star was practically written in the stars. Here he plays a cemetery caretaker named Francesco Dellamorte, who has no idea if there's a worldwide epidemic going on that's affecting other cemeteries—he just knows he has a job to do at his. The brilliantly shot opening scene shows this unusual addition to his list of responsibilities, when Francesco casually pauses a phone conversation to respond to the knocking at the front door. Shirtless, sweaty, and with a cigarette dangling from his mouth, he opens the door and stares at the man with a briefcase, a tattered suit, and a bug crawling on his face for several seconds in complete silence before blowing the man's brains out. Those who are buried in this Buffalora, Italy cemetery rise from their graves on the seventh night after their death, often with a ferocious appetite, and it's up to the caretaker to put them back where they belong.

The following day, as fresh soil is shoveled onto a marble casket, Francesco approaches a mourner (Anna Falchi) who he believes to be the deceased's daughter, only to find out that she was his much, much younger wife, and that his attraction to this woman is about to dominate every decision for the rest of his life. After a couple failed flirting attempts throughout the week, he finally gets her attention by mentioning the cemetery's ossuary, and it's in this subterranean pond of human bones when they kiss for the first time, resulting in a lovemaking session right on the newest gravesite, observed by the naturally occurring ignis fatuus fire flames. The dead, cuckolded husband crawls out of his coffin and fatally bites the woman who earned the top spot on Arrow in the Head's "Top 10 Boobs in Horror" list, forcing an agonized Francesco to send them both to their eternal slumbers twice and for all.

Guilt-ridden and heartbroken, he faces further mental turmoil with a visit from the Grim Reaper himself, who tells him to stop killing the dead and focus on the living instead. He also keeps running into the girl of his dreams, always with a new name, new way of complicating his life, and no signs of decomposing. His assistant, Gnaghi, is similarly troubled when he forms a relationship with the severed head of a recently deceased teenaged girl (who encourages him to take advantage since there's nothing she can do to stop him), which is somehow just as endearing as when he chases after the dead leaves that the wind blows away. The film feels every bit as free and fleeting as these leaves, reinventing itself with each act until it's time for these two lovesick cemetery men to discover whether or not the outside world really does exist.

A Chinese Ghost Story (1987)
Director: Siu-Tung Ching
Writers: Kai-Chi Yuen, Songling Pu (novel)
Cast: Leslie Cheung, Joey Wang, Wu Ma, Wai Lam, Siu-Ming Lau, Zhilun Xue

Spawning two sequels, a television series, an animated adaptation, and a 2011 remake, *A Chinese Ghost Story* was a major hit in several Asian countries but has never received much Western attention. Seeing it again after eight years was a great way of capping off my holiday break and making sure that I wasn't too depressed the night before returning to work. It was just as special as I remembered, and hopefully someday it will be given the kind of region 1 physical release it deserves, with subtitles that aren't riddled with typos.

A kind-hearted young debt collector is having a tough time collecting fees after heavy rains soak his book and smudge all the ink, forcing him to venture deep into the woods for free lodging at a temple that is deserted and rumored to be haunted. After he is chased by a pack of hungry wolves and clumsily falls into an icy lake, his night gets even more eventful when he meets a beautiful girl with skin even colder than his. Love at first sight prevents him from entertaining the possibility that she may be a ghost that is forced to seduce men for the evil Tree Demoness with a milelong tongue to feast on, and it also prevents her from carrying out a mission that is closely monitored by her tormentors. A Taoist swordsman and a basement full of hideous ghouls add even more complications to their sweet and innocent romance, but that's not enough to stop them from enjoying one of the most electrifying first kisses in cinema history. *A Chinese Ghost Story* also depicts perhaps the quickest body decomposition you'll ever see, where the camera travels down a man's throat and through his stomach in just a couple amazing seconds.

The mood is kept light with dazzling, gravity-defying martial arts choreography, frequent slapstick comedy, fireballs, head soup, obvious *Evil Dead* influences, and a character randomly breaking out into song where he tries to come up with rhymes for "Dao." At one point, our main character cries in frustration, "Why is the world such a ridiculous place?" and we can't help but be thankful for every ridiculous visual on display, whether it's above ground or in the underworld. *A Chinese Ghost Story*'s music, a mixture of pretty pop ballads and droning synths that would fit right in on Super Mario Brothers' castle levels, allows the film to be just as easy on the ears as it is on the eyes.

Deadly Friend (1986)

Director: Wes Craven
Writers: Bruce Joel Rubin, Diana Henstell (novel)
Cast: Matthew Labyorteaux, Kristy Swanson, Michael Sharrett, Anne Ramsey, Anne Twomey

It's surprising that one of the more overlooked titles in Wes Craven's filmography was released just a couple of years after the one that made him a household name. "If you enjoy being really scared, if you're not afraid of the unknown, if you've found a friend in fear, then we have a friend for you: Samantha," says the foreboding narrator in the trailer. "The director who unleashed Freddy in *A Nightmare on Elm Street*, Wes Craven, now brings you his most frightening creation, *Deadly Friend*. She can't live without you." With a trailer as spooky as this and a prime October release date, it seemed likely that Craven's first big-budgeted film for a major studio would be a hit, but it bombed at the box office and also with critics. Craven himself even wanted to disown himself from the project due to studio interference, a common occurrence for young directors in Hollywood, and in this case his frustrations were more than justified because "his most frightening creation" wasn't even intended to be a horror film at all.

Based on Diana Henstell's science fiction novel *Friend*, this movie was Craven's opportunity to venture outside of the horror genre and try something different, but once more studio executives at Warner Bros eventually caught onto his repertoire, they kept demanding for his calling cards like intense dream sequences and gory kills for what was supposed to be a PG-rated "macabre love story with a twist." The audiences for test screenings clearly took the side of the executives, and wanted to see even more action, more blood, and more scares, resulting in reshoots that jettisoned scenes of teen romance and friendship to make room for elaborate death scenes.

Originally titled Artificial Intelligence and later A.I., this could have been one of Craven's greatest achievements had he been given more creative freedom thanks to the compelling characters and the complex situations they're forced into, but I personally won't be lamenting too much over what could have been because I consider *Deadly Friend* to be a really fun horror movie with plenty of depth. Where else are you going to find shades of *Short Circuit*, *Pet Sematary*, *Frankenstein*, *Starman*, *A Nightmare on Elm Street*, *Return of the Living Dead III*, *E.T.*, and even *Misery* (with that poisoning scene) all contained in a 90-minute running time, where basketball decapitations and crotch-grabbing robots can peacefully coexist with child abuse and the unwillingness to accept the death of a loved one?

Paul, a brilliant teenager on a science scholarship, moves with his single mother to the town of Welling, and has no trouble making friends (as well as enemies) thanks to BB, the adorable robot he created that can communicate, follow demands, plug itself into electrical outlets, sing while mowing the lawn, and even ogle lab skeletons—it's just a tad peculiar that he was given a voice that sounds just like Stripe from *Gremlins*. Paul, BB, the newspaper boy named Tom, and next-door neighbor Samantha (Kristy Swanson in her first starring role) make an extremely likable foursome, and early scenes of them playing ball and celebrating Halloween together are full of sweet Spielbergian charm, but then the evils of humanity float to the surface and it starts looking more like Stephen King's suburbia.

Despite Paul being even smarter than his professors, he's not smart enough to realize that "sometimes dead is better" when a tragic accident causes him to do the unthinkable. Actor Matthew Labyorteaux (who previously played Albert Quinn Ingalls in 89 episodes of *Little House on the Prairie*) does a convincing job in showing the inner turmoil of this lovesick teen with mad scientist capabilities. Sweetness, silliness, and suspense all abound in this underrated gem from one of horror's all-time greatest directors. Trust me when I say there's more to this movie than the popular gif of Kristy Swanson throwing a basketball at the cranky lady from *The Goonies* and *Throw Mama from the Train* so furiously that it causes her head to literally explode and what's left of her body to comedically waltz around the room with outstretched arms.

"Love Bites, Love Dies"

The Iron Rose (1973)

Director: Jean Rollin
Writers: Maurice Lemaitre, Jean Rollin, Tristan Corbiere (poem)
Cast: Francoise Pascal, Hugues Quester, Natalie Perrey, Mireille Dargent

Aimlessly browsing through Kanopy's bottomless pit of horror brought me to a film titled *The Iron Rose* with a synopsis starting with "Two lovers have a tryst in a vacant tomb, only to find themselves trapped within the graves and crypts of the massive cemetery," causing me to nearly squeal with excitement. The intrinsically unnerving concept of people experiencing a night of terror inside a cemetery should be every bit as common as the "cabin in the woods" formula, yet few movies have really taken full advantage of it. Some viewers might lose patience over its lack of scares and logic, but if one of your happy places involves walking through a cemetery on a bed of crunchy autumn leaves, then you won't mind being the third wheel on this rendezvous.

This was French filmmaker Jean Rollin's follow-up to a string of erotic arthouse vampire films that included *The Nude Vampire* and *The Rape of the Vampire*, and he would later call it the strangest movie of his long career. It opens with a melancholy piano melody and powerful images of ocean waves and architecture from the Northern France city of Amiens. This was the home of Jules Verne until his death in 1905, and his real-life resting place is the actual cemetery used in the movie.

A couple of lovebirds decide to explore the cemetery on their first date after engaging in some train track tomfoolery. While conversing about death and what happens to the soul, the man explains to his trepidatious date how this is the perfect place to be because there are no cars, litter, or disturbances, and she eventually warms up to the idea and follows him down an open crypt for extra privacy from a woman in mourning, a man in a cape, and an actual clown. How many other movies have been able to offer you a clown walking in a graveyard for no apparent reason?! Stamina must have been on their side because by the time they're ready to leave, nighttime has fallen and prepared to wreak havoc on their sense of direction. As hour after hour passes with them struggling to find an exit, sanity slips away and prompts a lovers' spat.

Because their behaviors become so schizophrenic and the dangers remain unclear, *The Iron Rose* begins to feel a tad inconsequential in the second half, but thanks to lovely little touches like flowers melting in a fire, a "singin' in the cemetery" dance, and an open grave for miscellaneous skulls, I was never bored. Music doesn't play much of a role until the end, but this symphony of weirdness is worth waiting for as spacey synths swell with the additions of clangs, coughs, Gregorian chants, wailing, and church bells to chilling effects.

One of my most cherished Halloween season traditions is visiting a cemetery on a sunny October afternoon to read random sections of *October Dreams: A Celebration of Halloween* (and its sequel) while junking out on caramel apple lollipops and being showered by falling leaves. As a diehard horror fan, I'm always secretly craving a good scare there, and while I've had the pleasure of searching for a pair of lost keys in the middle of a cemetery during a rainstorm and exploring a curiously unlocked mausoleum after hours, nothing elicited the kind of paranoia and panic that being unable to find a way out would, and so this movie still managed to feel like an adrenaline rush despite its slow pace. It also helps that this is one of the best-looking cemeteries I've ever seen, where the statues with heads are somehow even creepier than the decapitated ones.

Possession (1981)

Director: Andrzej Zulawski
Writers: Andrzej Zulawski, Frederic Tuten
Cast: Isabelle Adjani, Sam Neill, Margit Carstensen, Heinz Bennent, Johanna Hofer

This was a strange day indeed. I woke up to a text announcing that the workday was being preempted by three hours due to an unexpected dusting of snow, and after failing to fall back asleep, I retreated to the couch to watch the last of the four movies I rented a few days ago. Because I had seen it years ago, I should have known better than to watch it right before having to interact with a ton of people because this movie puts you in a headspace not equipped for Earthlings. It made me wish I could wear a shirt reading "No, I'm not on drugs, I just watched *Possession*."

This English-speaking French-German co-production was filmed in West Berlin with a Polish director and stars from France and New Zealand, and it's unlike anything you've ever seen before. Sam Neill plays a secret agent named Mark returning from a mission to learn that his wife Anna (Isabelle Adjani) wants a divorce because she has found somebody new. A meeting at the local café to discuss the terms of separation and parental rights dissolves into hysterical screaming, tables pushed over, and the entire staff having to separate them even further. This heightened level of madness fills up so much of the running time that I was thankful to have the house to myself so that nobody would inquire about all that screaming.

Mark spends the next three weeks in a delirium similar to Renton's heroin withdrawals in *Trainspotting*, while Anna descends into a different state of insanity, causing all of their subsequent interactions to somehow be both uncomfortably intense and wickedly entertaining. Some of the most extreme moments play out with lengthy shots where the camera smoothly whirls around the actors, gets right in their faces, and follows them from room to room as they scream, cry, beg, self-mutilate, and destroy inanimate objects. Both actors went through hell to deliver these performances and it took a long for them to fully recover, with Neill stating in interviews, "I think I only just escaped that film with my sanity barely intact" and Adjani swearing that she would never take on a similar role because of what she went through.

The film doubles down on its vibes of otherworldly craziness with carnivalesque music and the introduction of Anna's eccentric new lover Heinrich. When it's revealed that he hasn't seen her in days, Mark hires a private investigator to find her whereabouts. This takes us down the streets of West Berlin (the most striking of '80s settings that several films were wise to take advantage of) to a derelict, unfurnished apartment where a big surprise waits for anyone who enters, courtesy of Italian special effects artist Carlo Rambaldi, who also worked on *E.T.*, *Alien*, *The Neverending Story*, and *Silver Bullet*.

"Mortal terror, inhuman ecstasy, soon you will know the meaning of…Possession. The darkness is forever," the forbidding voice warns in the movie's trailer. Hopefully by the time you're reading this, the meaning will cost less than $154.95 on Amazon or be available to stream somewhere legal. From being classified as a Video Nasty and banned in England to its physical formats going out of print repeatedly, *Possession* hasn't been the easiest movie to track down but boy is it worth the effort, even if you have to put down a $200 deposit to rent it at a video store like I did. Sam Neill absolutely going berserk in *In the Mouth of Madness* and *Event Horizon* was beyond incredible, but *Possession* proves that not even the scariest New Hampshire town or a black hole leading straight to Hell can compete with the maddening mysteries of love.

The Return of the Living Dead III (1993)
Director: Brian Yuzna
Writer: John Penney
Cast: J. Trevor Edmond, Melinda Clarke, Kent McCord, James T. Callahan, Sarah Douglas

The first sequel to Dan O'Bannon's horror-comedy masterpiece was a nonstop party with fun gags like the Michael Jackson "Thriller" zombie electrocution and the Southern-drawled severed head with that dang screwdriver in her head. You would expect more of the same from a straight-to-video Part 3, but all bets are off the table when Brian Yuzna is the dealer, as we've learned from his collaborations with Stuart Gordon and his unforgettable directorial efforts like *Society*. After just taking the *Silent Night, Deadly Night* series into radical new territories, he was clearly given carte blanche to ignore the predecessors completely if it meant giving a much-needed jolt to the zombie sub-genre, and so this movie chooses not to ask "Do you wanna party?!" this time, but rather, "Are you ready to be heartbroken?"

The reliable Trimark Pictures logo flashes ever so briefly and gives way to the most thunderous of scores—epic and commanding, and with a tinge of sadness to serve as a proper warning that this isn't going to make you smile like the first two did. In fact, it's one of the hardest-hitting and upsetting zombie films you'll ever see, offering no respite and insisting you feel every bit of the misery its unfortunate characters do.

The disastrous barrels of Trioxin are now in a US military base, where Col. John Reynolds is leading a team (which includes the dad from *Charles in Charge*!) to prove its usefulness in warfare, unaware that while he's using the chemicals to bring an angry cadaver back to life, his teenaged son, Curt, is secretly observing the horror from above along with his morbidly fascinated girlfriend, Julie.

The experiment ends in disaster and Col. Roberts has to tell his son later that night that he's being transferred to Oklahoma City and they'll have to move in a week, a volatile lifestyle they are both used to. But this time, Curt defies his father and escapes into the night with Julie to begin their new lives together where nothing can tear them apart, not even a fatal motorcycle accident. Curt once again uses the security key card stolen from his father to sneak them both inside the building, but this time he experiments with the Trioxin on his own. Julie wakes up, sentient and coherent, but right away she can tell that something is seriously wrong with her. She's experiencing numbness and hunger like never before, and it won't be until she mutilates her own body and takes her first bite of human brains that she discovers a way to take all the discomfort away, if only for an instant.

J. Trevor Edmond and Melinda Clarke give terrific performances essentially playing Romeo and Juliet in Hell, and each scene of their disintegration is more devastating than the last, with Curt feeling increasingly disgusted by Julie's behavior, while she resents him for turning her into a monster. As if this wasn't heartbreaking enough, writer John Penney also makes Curt's father and a homeless man named Riverman into sympathetic and tragic figures. But don't let the gloom and doom deter you from watching this movie because above all else it's thrilling, suspenseful, and smart, and once again, Yuzna employed a motivated special effects team to deliver topnotch gore and creature effects. This is a zombie picture that calls for quality over quantity in its brain-munchers and so each one looks quite distinctive and scary, with my favorite resembling a violent Jack in the Box. Oh yeah, and fans of *Curb Your Enthusiasm* will be happy to see who plays the convenience store owner!

Trimark sadly pulled the plug on a theatrical run once it saw how another horror sequel, *Warlock II: Armageddon*, was underperforming at the box office, all but killing the series until it was eventually brought back to life and beaten mercilessly with two lousy Sci-Fi Channel sequels in 2005, *Necropolis* and *Rave to the Grave*.

The Signal (2007)

Writers and Directors: David Bruckner, Dan Bush, Jacob Gentry
Cast: Anessa Ramsey, AJ Bowen, Justin Welborn, Sahr Ngaujah, Scott Polythress

Not to be confused with the annoyingly titled 2014 science-fiction film *The Signal*, starring Laurence Fishburne and ubiquitous on streaming platforms, this hugely ambitious apocalyptic *The Signal* is divided into three segments with different filmmakers. It truly runs the gambit in terms of radical tone shifts yet somehow never loses focus of the bigger picture: that on this day, citizens of the city of Terminus are being infected by a hypnotic frequency in the airwaves, causing distorted perception and heightened paranoia. All it takes is a few seconds of zoning out in front of the aggressively psychedelic images from the TV for you to join the mass psychosis. It's easy to call this a horror anthology, but essentially, it's telling the same horrific story from different perspectives.

The first transmission, titled "Crazy in Love," was directed by David Bruckner, who has gone onto make other acclaimed horror films like *The Ritual*, *Southbound*, and *The Night House*. It opens with two lovers named Ben and Maya, bathed in blue lighting and imagining a world where they can be living happily together instead of in secret. As Maya returns home later that night—trying to think of an excuse of why she was out so late—she has a couple terrifying encounters with total strangers in a parking lot. It's a masterful exercise of building tension when Maya enters her apartment building and hears numerous arguments coming from the paper-thin walls and sees other residents roaming the hallways, seemingly drugged out of their minds. She makes the long, uneasy walk to her apartment and is immediately quizzed by her intense husband Lewis, played by the beautifully bearded AJ Bowen, one of horror's most dependable actors in recent years. Like so many others in the building, Lewis succumbs to uncontrollable rage, which raises the stakes and the fear factor even further as Maya tries to escape, finding solace and strength in the mix CD that Ben gave her earlier that night.

We're introduced to entirely new characters in "The Jealousy Monster," which takes a much more satirical and comedic approach, centering on a woman (played by Cheri Christian) who kills her husband in self-defense just moments before her New Year's Eve party commences. The circumstances get increasingly absurd with each new guest that arrives, and it's a lot of fun watching them sit on a couch in awkward silence while trying to enjoy pretzels and cocktails as if everything is normal and the carpets are not stained with blood. Lewis shows up, gravely concerned over the safety of his wife and demanding to know where she is. Creative camerawork emphasizes the delusional state he's in when one character is suddenly replaced by another without any edits. Bowen leads a stellar cast and portrays a type of villain we're unaccustomed to—psychopathic and deranged, yes, but also quite complex because he always thinks he's doing the right thing since protecting his wife is paramount when everyone around him appears to be suddenly, mysteriously stuck on stage one of the Rage Virus from *28 Days Later* and cannot be trusted.

The final segment, "Escape from Terminus," reveals existential horror and centers on Ben's bruised and bloody journey to a train station where he thinks Maya might be, but Lewis remains one step ahead of him. A love triangle is heated enough on a day when the world isn't ending and when the unfortunate participants aren't losing their minds to a bad sector in the electromagnetic spectrum that obliterates logical thinking while leaving memories intact, and *The Signal*

Poster for ***The Signal*** (2007), Shoreline Entertainment, Magnolia Pictures

takes full advantage of this fascinating scenario and remains unpredictable and intense to the very end.

As smart and imaginative as this movie is, it's also unflinchingly violent, and you'll be feeling every baseball bat to the cranium and pesticide to the corneas. Filmed in Atlanta for only $50,000, *The Signal* is a chilling masterpiece that deserves to be at the top of your watchlist. While it didn't receive the wide theatrical release it deserved, it got a 2-disc DVD release that is absolutely stacked with extras, even one that simply contains the dizzying transmission so you get the crazies anytime in the comfort of your own home.

Horror Galore

Spring (2014)

Directors: Justin Benson, Aaron Moorhead
Writer: Justin Benson
Cast: Lou Taylor Pucci, Nadia Hilker, Francesco Carnelutti, Nick Nevern, Jeremy Gardner

Even if you're dating someone who sadly doesn't share your passion for the horror genre, *Spring* will be the kind of movie you can watch together without having to worry about mental scars or sleepless nights. Just imagine if you were watching Richard Linklater's *Before Sunrise*, and Ethan Hawke and Julie Delpy had to overcome something so much more bizarre and complicated than long distance after discovering they were soulmates.

Lou Taylor Pucci, looking like a *Core*-era Scott Weiland and bearing no resemblance whatsoever to the character he played a year prior in the *Evil Dead* remake, stars as an aimless and affable 20-something named Evan who in the opening scene, says a tearful goodbye to his cancer-stricken mother who is breathing her last breath. His emotions are put through the ringer even further when he loses his job after brawling with an unruly customer at a bar, and rather than spend the next days in a paranoid stupor and awaiting a visit from either a cop or a gang, he decides to use his inheritance money and previously neglected passport to go somewhere far away. In one of many delightful scenes that put a big, goofy grin on my face, he calls the airport to book a flight but has no idea where to go, instantly taking the advice of an agent who posits that "white people seem to love Italy." Directors Justin Benson and Aaron Moorhead (*The Endless*, *Resolution*, *Synchronic*) once again prove what's possible with very small budgets, as they use the most modern of filming equipment and even a helpful drone to produce a majestic montage of a picturesque Italian coastal town that will take your breath away. The way they employ slow-motion effectively conveys what it feels like to be a stranger in a strange land.

With the film's beautiful locations, natural dialogue, and slice of life narrative, it was both fun and challenging to imagine what was going to turn *Spring* into a horror movie. Was the trio of fun-loving British tourists going to parlay that initial invitation for Evan to have a drink with them ("to see if the Yank can fucking keep up") into a week of chugging beers until they go insane and Evan "Wakes in Fright?" Was the beautiful, mysterious, and strangely-accented Louise (played by German actress Nadia Hilker) going to lure Evan into her "House of 1,000 Corpses?" Was the kindly and elderly Italian farmer who serves as a mentor to Evan secretly harvesting a field behind his "Motel Hell" where people are buried up to their slashed throats? Or were the horror websites that championed *Spring* just overly thrilled to see Jeremy Gardner from 2013's impressive zombie film *The Battery* in something new, even if it was a scare-less, bloodless Richard Linklater love letter?

When the horror elements do come along at around the 36-minute mark, they're pretty damn spectacular, but don't expect them to stick around for long. The third act mostly consists of Evan and Louise talking in ancient Italian ruins and just romantically watching the sunset together, and while I can understand some horror fans feeling a bit restless and asking, "Where's the beef?," for me it was just a pleasure to spend the evening with these interesting people and hang on their every word as they discuss history, their surroundings, and the awfully strange predicament they find themselves in. It was the perfect movie to enjoy with a glass or two or three of red wine, and the advantage of having an unrefined pallet is being able to pretend that a bottom-shelf Safeway Sauvignon is a Masseto from Tuscany!

The thoughtful and beautifully poetic *Spring* understands grief, love, anger, isolation, self-discovery, and disconnection, as well as how simply observing the world around you can sometimes be the best medicine of all, especially when it includes a canal under a full moon and a tentacle or two.

RUBBER-SUITED MONSTER RAMPAGE

The Alien Factor (1978)

Writer and Director: Don Dohler
Cast: Don Leifert, Tom Griffith, Richard Dyszel, Mary Mertens, Richard Geiwitz, George Stover

Shot in Baltimore for approximately $50,000, *The Alien Factor* was intended as a satire of '50s science fiction movies and so it's difficult to gauge how much of the silliness was intentional. Whether you and your friends (this isn't the kind of film meant to watch alone) choose to laugh at it or with it, you'll still have heaps of fun and appreciate the earnest effort from first-time filmmaker Don Dohler, whose inexperience is immediately overt in a clunky sequence featuring a young couple who seemingly can't decide whether to make out or drink hard liquor while something mysterious approaches their car. He does get slightly better with shot compositions as the film goes on, and even though the first big monster reveals are hilarious in framing and timing, there was a genuinely startling one in a basement later that earned an audible gasp from me.

For a movie that required long walks in the woods, multiple phone conversations, and a pointless dive-bar musical act to pad out a brief 80-minute running time, one would expect a fairly straightforward plot, but instead we're practically assaulted by long, confusing expository monologues from out of nowhere that at least help us identify more with the town journalist when she responds to all this mumbo jumbo with "I don't understand!"

All you need to know about the story is that a spacecraft crashes one night and the three intergalactic zoo creatures inside escape and cause a whole bunch of trouble for the citizens of a small town. The doctors become flabbergasted by recent autopsies that reveal everything from deep wounds to symptoms of progeria, a rare disease that causes the rapid aging of children. The mayor, whose last name sadly doesn't sound anything like Vaughn, Murray, or Hamilton, is far more concerned about negative publicity because without those summer dollars, what will happen to their sweet new entertainment complex? The acting, editing, and cinematography made it an easy candidate for Joel Hodgson's project *Cinematic Titanic*, but hopefully the creature designs were at least spared from riffing because it's obvious that a lot of talent and hard work went into these rubber-suited monstrosities, especially the open-chested tusked, cloved bigfoot on stilts!

If you're in the mood for something harmless and bewildering, then let this *Alien Factor* into your heart at the same time you let a hot chocolate with peppermint schnaps into your mouth and your night will be well spent. Several scenes set in the snow might have you craving a warm cocktail but for the sake of your tomorrow morning, just don't try to outdrink one flannelled gentleman who, in a bar scene in which every single shot is bewildering, manages to empty his glass at least half a dozen times in as many minutes. A regional production from this time period that wears '50s science fiction B-movie reverence on its sleeves is an extremely rare pleasure, and so Dohler's 1982 *Nightbeast* should be celebrated as well.

Lobby card for *Equinox* (1970), Tonylyn Productions

Equinox (1970)

Directors: Jack Woods, Dennis Muren, Mark Thomas McGee
Writers: Jack Woods, Mark Thomas McGee
Cast: Edward Connell, Barbara Hewitt, Frank Bonner, Robin Christopher, Jack Woods

Fourteen years before winning his first of nine Academy Awards for his achievements in visual effects, Dennis Muren was a college student working on his first short film, *The Equinox…A Journey into the Supernatural*, along with his friends David Allen and Jim Danforth. It's no surprise that all three of these men went onto do very big things in the film industry because on their first attempt with a micro-budgeted short film, they managed to woo a production company hoping to turn it into a feature film for theatrical distribution. Additional scenes were directed by Jack Woods, who later pursued a career as a sound editor in some of your favorite sequels like *Naked Gun 2 ½*, *Phantasm II*, *Critters 2*, and *Star Trek III: The Search for Spock*. With multiple directors, the intermixing of scenes shot three years apart with the same actors, and a kitchen sink approach to the horrors and the rules of this universe, it's a wonder that this film, simply re-titled *Equinox*, feels so cohesive. It made its DVD debut in 2006 as an unlikely entry in Criterion's library, and as a very special bonus feature, the original short film became available for the first time.

Equinox's title credits appear over the close-up mechanisms of a grandfather clock, and as far as I can tell it has nothing to do with a story about a man named David surviving an explosion and running frantically through a forest canyon. He eventually makes his way to a public road and waves down the first car he sees, which unfortunately for him, has nobody behind the wheel. The driverless car runs him down and he spends the next year and one day at a hospital in a catatonic state.

Through flashbacks, we see that David had been out in the country with his girlfriend and another couple to have a picnic and visit David's old geology professor, only to find his cabin abandoned and obliterated. The mystery deepens when a cackling old man beckons them into a pitch-black, skeleton-occupied cave and demands they leave with his Sulphur-smelling copy of the Necronomicon. This film has the jolly spirit of a *Scooby Doo* episode and several narrative similarities to *Evil Dead*, and with that kind of automatic goodwill, you can't help but cheer for every irrational decision the protagonists make, especially since it's likely to lead to awakened curses or a confrontation with stop-motion animated monsters in the style of Ray Harryhausen. The fact that it takes place almost entirely in daylight and has plenty of laughable overdubbing lends itself well to a lazy afternoon viewing experience when you can be as invested as you want to be and then afterwards still have plenty of hours left in the day to recite bizarre lines like "I wouldn't know a catatonic coma if it bit me," or "My cross! Mmmmmyyyyyyy croooooooossssssss, wheeeeeeeeeeeeeere iiiiiiiiissss mmmmmyyyyyyy cccccccrrrrrrrrroooooooooosssssssssssssss? M m m m m m m y y y y y y y y y ccccccccccrrrrrrrrooooooosssssssssssssss!"

More fun is had with a park ranger with the distrustful eyebrows of R. Lee Ermey (and whose kissy face closeups will haunt your dreams), a castle that appears out of nowhere, three monsters, one giant, and an alternate dimension with the sepia-toned cliff barriers of *Phantasm*. Oh yeah, and perhaps most fearsome is a little hill that is apparently too steep for women (even young and healthy ones) to even attempt walking up.

Rawhead Rex (1986)

Director: George Pavlou
Writer: Clive Barker
Cast: David Dukes, Kelly Piper, Hugh O'Conor, Cora Venus Lunny, Ronan Wilmot

The first screenplay Clive Barker ever wrote was for *Transmutations*, about a doctor whose experimentations result in a family of mutants living underground in East London, and its producers made so many drastic revisions to the script that Barker felt it was no longer his story. For his second screenplay, he adapted the short story "Rawhead Rex" from his recently published third volume of *Books of Blood*, but once again he was severely disappointed with the final film, so much so that he vowed to never again give up so much creative control over his material. He learned his lessons and wasn't going to let anyone interfere with his next baby, *Hellraiser*.

Most of the critics back in the day and most Letterboxd members in present day also gave *Rawhead Rex* the cold shoulder, and much of the ridicule has to do with the monster's silly appearance. Rather than the 9-foot-tall phallus that Barker envisioned, this Rex would look natural playing on stage with Gwar (or appearing alongside Eddie on Iron Maiden album covers), with its Mad Max jacket ripped open to expose a muscled rubber suit, and its gorilla-ogre head with a mouth permanently open wide enough to fit members of the audience. Even though it can't physically express an emotion other than pure rage, I thought it was balls-to-the-walls awesome, much like the film as a whole. If I can't have the demonic stained-glass window depicting his image, then maybe I can somehow get my hands on a poster of him standing under the stars on a freezing cold night, raising a severed head in triumph.

In addition to completely changing the design of the titular character, the film also departs from Barker's English setting and moves the action to the rural countryside of Ireland (hence an opening title screen featuring two different actors named Niall), where a trio of farmers are attempting to move a monolith-structure that stubbornly refuses to budge until it's struck by lightning. Billows of smoke then rise from the ground and allows a pagan deity to make a Godzilla-like entrance. This gives plenty of material to an American writer who is in town researching ancient religious sights, even if it means he and his family running into a ferocious giant that sometimes subscribes to a "women and children first" policy when it comes to mealtime.

At one point in the film, a kind police officer says to the American, "The Inspector will see you as soon as he can. In the meantime, can I get you a cup of tea?" and he responds with, "Why don't you go fuck yourself?" This exemplifies the sheer unlikability of our main character and also the head-scratching dialogue that infects so many scenes in a movie that I didn't expect would be this funny. Adding to the humor is ten seconds of the goofiest music you'll ever hear (when Jenny's friend parks his car), a roaring fireplace in an unoccupied upstairs bedroom, a bloodthirsty monster that takes pleasure in destroying kitchens, a character that somehow gets locked inside a trailer, and a bit of laughably gratuitous nudity right in the middle of a medley of total mayhem.

With the possible exception of Creedence Leonore Gielgud from *Troll 2*, it's hard to think of a role that would be more fun to play than the shady priest and Rex sympathizer Declan O'Brien, who provides most of the comedy and campiness and so I'll forever be jealous of actor Ronan Wilmot. Like it says in the Bible, "You can't piss on hospitality, but you can certainly get pissed on by Rawhead Rex," and this lovable villain of opposing faiths will learn that firsthand.

"HAPPY HAPPY HALLOWEEN, HALLOWEEN, HALLOWEEN, HAPPY HAPPY HALLOWEEN, SILVER SHAMROCK"

Cemetery of Terror (1985)
Director: Rubén Galindo Jr.
Writers: Rubén Galindo Jr., Carlos Valdemar
Cast: Hugo Stiglitz, Servando Manzetti, Rene Cardona III, Maria Rebeca, Andres Garcia Jr.

With the grinning jack-o-lantern lovingly carved a couple days ago now staring back at me with teary disdain as its insides rot away at an alarming rate, today I had to go through the painful ritual of bidding a final farewell by placing it inside the yard debris bin with as much dignity as possible; I lacked the energy to give it the ultimate riverside sendoff like Joe Pera did in his Adult Swim program. Just hours later, I received a package in the mail that made it seem like the Great Pumpkin was still feeling generous in the cold November rain. So rather than take down all my yard decorations (the most I've ever put up), I decided to give Halloween one hell of an encore performance by finishing off the candy bestowed by the lack of trick-of-trickers while watching Vinegar Syndrome's brand-new *Cemetery of Terror* Blu-ray.

One of my most enthusiastic entries for *Pumpkin Cinema: The Best Movies for Halloween* was for this Mexican horror film, causing a couple of readers to reach out to me and inquire about its accessibility. Since it wasn't available to stream anywhere, I could only direct them to an out-of-print DVD that was becoming about as expensive as a lock of Elvis Presley's hair. Much like Vinegar Syndrome's wonderful release of *Spookies* the previous year, it was such a gratifying feeling to cradle this Blu-ray in my hands, my eyes vacillating between the playfully morbid artwork on the front and the enticing list of special features on the back.

Oh, what a pleasure it was to revisit this story in which three young men convince their girlfriends (one of whom curiously brought a plastic *Creature from the Black Lagoon* mask) that they are about to attend a "jet set party" with limousines, celebrities, and television crews, only to drag them to an abandoned house adjacent to a cemetery under the impression that, given the spooky setting, they will be perceived as macho and irresistible protectors. The girls, however, are understandably put off by this deception and retreat to the dusty couch, where they sit together with scowls and crossed arms. Like we've all done in this situation when our romantic partners are being cold and fussy, the lads double down on the scare factor by heading to the local morgue so they can steal the ugliest and most gruesome corpse with the intent on bringing it back to life by reciting Latin incantations in a cemetery. That'll put 'em in the mood, dammit!

"Satan! Give me proof of your existence! Listen, lord of hell, this is our night!" one of the guys shouts just before the angry skies bawl upon a dead body twitching back to life, much like in fellow '85 zombie flick *The Return of the Living Dead*. Back in the morgue, a professor is panicking over the sudden disappearance of the infamous Satanic serial killer Devlon, who was to be cremated that night, and then possibly have his ashes sealed in a tomb and dropped at the bottom of the ocean to make sure that his reign of terror was over for good. *Cemetery of Terror* takes a radical tonal shift at the halfway point when what had been a gory slasher suddenly morphs into a *Scooby Doo*-type adventure involving a group of much-younger kids following the glow of their jack-o-lanterns while singing a cheerful Mexican Halloween jingle. They decide to circumvent the usual trick-or-treating routine by hitchhiking to the cemetery and walking among the tombstones that are sure seeing a ton of action this coincidental Halloween night. The film loses a little bit of steam when it's clear that none of these children are in any real danger and when a golden opportunity for a good scare is missed as two of them hide inside a crypt, but these are the most trivial of nitpicks for a very special movie that deserves to be on everyone's radar during our favorite time of year.

This was the feature film debut of Ruben Galindo Jr., who was only 23 years old at the time and clearly full of inspiration from the "Thriller" music video given the amount of fog in the graveyard, the appearances of the zombies, and the fact that one of the characters is wearing an unlicensed Michael Jackson jacket. Watching closely over his shoulder during production was his father, an established filmmaker and producer, who found it unacceptable that the early shoots were going so slowly and that the original cut ended up being only 83 minutes. With 90 minutes being the magic number at the time for theatrical screenings, the young director was pressured to add the cheerful opening scene that required one more day of shooting for the older group of kids, who were probably relieved to find out that instead of being drenched in a cemetery or covered in cobwebs from a dilapidated house in southern Texas, they would instead be boating, waterskiing, and sunbathing on a beach in Mexico, while also debating the merits of rock concerts and jet set parties. Currently a producer for soap operas and reality shows, let's hope the filmmaker whose career began with three bangers in *Cemetery of Terror*, *Grave Diggers*, and *Don't Panic* will someday choose to follow the light of a will-o-the-wisp leading back to his horror roots.

Dark Night of the Scarecrow (1981)

Director: Frank De Felitta
Writers: J.D. Feigelson, Butler Handcock (story)
Cast: Charles Durning, Robert F. Lyons, Claude Earl Jones, Larry Drake, Jocelyn Brando

As far as made-for-television horror films go, it's hard to think of one that's been more successful than *Dark Night of the Scarecrow*, which premiered a week before Halloween '81 on CBS. Not only was it replayed multiple times over the decades, but unlike most of its ilk, it made the transition to VHS, DVD, and even a 30th Anniversary Blu-ray with a pristine transfer and many special features. Not even an onslaught of recent Halloween-themed movies has been able to devalue its stock, as it seems to appear on more lists of recommendations every October. And so I was conflicted on whether or not it even belongs in a book of "hidden" gems, but then I asked the nine people I know at work who are really into horror movies if they had seen *Dark Night of the Scarecrow*. Only one person said yes, and the Halloween-obsessed girl in her 20s with the *Trick 'R Treat* Sam tattoo had never even heard of it. That was clear indication that this movie hasn't permeated enough horror circles just yet.

I caught bits and pieces on TV growing up but the only scenes that held my interest were the early ones with Larry Drake, who I knew primarily from

Dr. Giggles and one of the best episodes of *Tales from the Crypt*. As a teenaged channel surfer, I guess I just expected a movie titled *Dark Night of the Scarecrow* to be a slasher where a scarecrow relentlessly mutilates people with scythes and pitchforks until the sun came up, and not an atmospheric whodunit with really heavy themes and a pace that moves every bit as slow as the small Southern farming town where it's set. It took quite a while for me to give this movie my undivided attention but once I did, I was completely drawn into the mystery, allured by the old-fashioned Halloween imagery, fascinated by the performances, lulled by cicada singalongs, and downright giddy for the death scenes—especially the one that takes place in a grain solo!

Larry Drake plays Bubba, a mentally challenged gentle giant whose innocent and sweet friendship with a little girl raises the suspicions of four men in town, and when word gets around one day that she's been gravely injured, they rush to judgment and form a lynch mob. Led by the town postman Otis P. Hazelrigg (what a name!), they find Bubba in the cornfield and fire 17 rounds into him, just before finding out that he was innocent and that a dog was to blame for the girl's injuries. The way in which the camera revealed Bubba's special hiding place is unbelievably intense and probably left viewers too shocked to get a snack during the next commercial break. The men are found not guilty by a jury of their peers and set free to the disgust of Bubba's mother, the district attorney, and possibly someone/something else. Boy is it ever fun watching their paranoia intensify as they discover that there are other forms of justice in the world!

Charles Durning (*Dog Day Afternoon*, *When a Stranger Calls*) not only carries the mailbag, but he comes close to carrying the whole movie on his shoulders in a performance that is nothing short of perfection. Otis very easily could have been a stereotypical, one-dimensional bigoted hick villain, but he's written as more of a deeply troubled soul whose mostly calm demeanor belies the personal demons constantly at war in his head, and Durning captures the nuances and complexities of this character in every scene, even the most mundane ones like when he's simply enjoying breakfast at his boarding house. One of my favorite scenes involves a Halloween party at an elementary school, where a witch serves punch, adults in cowboy hats dance to country music, and children bob for apples and play hide and seek. The small-town Samhain charm comes to an end, however, when Otis surprises a little girl in the hallway and suggests a very disturbing backstory.

Also, The Grand Pumpkin from *The Simpsons* would be horrified by all of the pumpkin atrocities that take place in the climax of this movie and would certainly vow revenge on that tractor.

Haunt (2019)

Writers and Directors: Scott Beck, Bryan Woods
Cast: Katie Stevens, Will Brittain, Lauryn Alisa McClain, Andrew Lewis Caldwell, Shazi Raja

Much like how the studios Laika, DreamWorks Animation, and Warner Bros Animation were undoubtedly cursing each other upon discovering that they all had an animated Yeti feature slated for release within a year of each other, there was probably some friendly competition and some agitation between the talented crews of *HellFest* and *Haunt*, two recent movies that had its protagonists enter commercial haunted houses on Halloween to discover that animatronic ghouls were the least of their concerns.

Seeing *HellFest* on a rainy October opening night was one of the most satisfying theatrical experiences I've had in years. While the same special treatment couldn't be given to *Haunt*, I have zero

Horror Galore

regrets about streaming it on a sunny Monday in June because it managed to turn a totally worthless day into something exciting and dangerous, and I went to bed feeling hopeful and excited about the autumn nights that now seem close enough to smell the pumpkin spices and burning leaves.

Haunt, which had the most limited of theatrical screenings before premiering on Shudder, opens on Halloween night in Carbondale, Illinois, a town that, in real life, banned Halloween celebrations for almost two decades after riots broke out in 2000 near the campus of Southern Illinois University, and so the eerie silence on these pumpkin-lit streets is fitting. Nursing a facial bruise and ignoring the texts from her alcoholic boyfriend Sam, Harper agrees to go out with her friends to celebrate All Hallows' Eve, and after getting buzzed in a club and winning awards for most disappointing costumes, they plan their next move. The haunted corn maze and scary movie on campus are both nixed for something more thrilling: an extreme haunted house. Blinded by headlights, Harper worries that they are being followed by her angry boyfriend and requests that they turn on the next road, in which a haunted house just so happens to be open for business. Skepticism grows since there's only one other car in the lot and just a single review on Yelp, but they end up signing the required liability wavers, surrendering their phones to the mute clown out front, and walking through the doors for the most extreme scares of their lives.

Much like *HellFest*, we feel like we're part of this surprisingly likable group of youngsters tiptoeing through the dark in a labyrinth of horrors, unsure if our perceptions are just being twisted by brilliantly macabre theatrics or if we're all actually in serious danger. Popular haunted house motifs like the psychedelic spinning bridge and funhouse mirrors are on display until the group decides to separate when confronted by two different mazes, safe vs unsafe, and then the terror (and violence) escalates to ridiculous levels. Not since Wes Craven's *The Serpent and the Rainbow* has a movie so effectively exploited fears of spiders and tight places at the same time! Still, these are the fun kind of scares, unlike my last experience at a haunted house attraction where I became disoriented by the dizzying strobes and with my outstretched arms, accidentally and very gently touched the face of one of the teenaged actors, who preceded to freak out and call a trio of security guards to drag me away—I was so confused that I assumed this was all part of the act. I haven't been to a haunted house since.

Leading this terrific cast is Katie Stevens as Harper, a sympathetic character whose memories of a childhood spent inside a very different type of "haunted house" fuels the determination and resourcefulness needed to survive to see another Halloween, and she knows that making just one wrong turn can end in disaster. As you would expect from a film produced by Eli Roth, *Haunt* doesn't shy away from splatterpunk sentiments. The red-hot pokers to the face, cinder blocks to the hand, flesh-tearing adhesives to the arms, nails to the foot, sledgehammers to the skull, and backs of hammers ripping faces clean off will have you hooting, hollering, squirming, and covering your eyes in equal measure.

With only 20 minutes to go, I paused to refill my coffee mug and then saw that the notes I had been taking on my phone had disappeared. I can only hope that the haunted house designers across America had better luck with their scrupulous observations because then we all might be treated to a super fun happy slide set to the echoes of chainsaw revs! *Haunt* may have the most uninspired of titles but you certainly can't accuse filmmakers Scott Beck and Bryan Woods of laziness because at the same

"Happy Happy Halloween, Halloween, Halloween, Happy Happy Halloween, Silver Shamrock"

time they were writing this script, they also penned another film they weren't sure would ever see the light of day, *A Quiet Place*. I thought this movie was a kickass thrill ride, but a more rousing endorsement comes from my girlfriend, someone who recently watched *The Exorcist*, *Insidious*, and *The Texas Chainsaw Massacre* for the very first time (yeah, I was as shocked as you are), but found *Haunt* to be even scarier!

The Midnight Hour (1985)

Director: Jack Bender
Writer: William Bleich
Cast: Lee Montgomery, Cindy Morgan, LeVar Burton, Dedee Pfeiffer, Jonelle Allen

Nothing cures a midlife crisis better than pure enthusiasm for the Halloween season, and few films capture the excitement and endless possibilities that Halloween brings better than *The Midnight Hour*, which premiered, oddly enough, the day after Halloween 1985 on ABC. It opens on an appropriately crisp morning at the corner of Elm & Maple, where the newspaper delivery boy is putting on a skeleton mask and a beanie cap on top for added warmth before riding through the small New England town, throwing papers with great accuracy despite his impaired visibility. Everybody from the milkman to the gravedigger seems impressed with his skills and also his Halloween spirit, for this is a town that much like Salem, takes Halloween very seriously.

The high school kids are also feeding off the pumpkin-spiced energy by presenting slideshows about the history of Halloween and coming up with Hangman phrases like "Ghouls just want to have fun," but it's after school when the real festivities begin. Lee Montgomery (*Ben*, *Burnt Offerings*) stars as the lovesick brainiac Phil, who is the only one in his very eclectic and charming

October 26-November 1 1985 TV Guide ad for ABC's *The Midnight Hour* (1985)

group of friends not so keen on breaking into the Pitchford Cove Witchcraft Museum to borrow some historical costumes for the big Halloween party. He's also apprehensive about trying the costumes on in the confines of the cemetery and then reading from an ancient scroll. The utterance of the final syllable provides a spook that sends them running out of the cemetery, and then in a really pleasing crane shot, the camera lowers through cumulus fog and pans over to an angel statue just as a gust of wind, so forceful that it sounds like a guttural growl, sends a pile of leaves flying like bats out of hell.

The creative camera choices continue when the zombies are first shown waking up from inside their coffins and bursting through *Kill Bill: Vol 2* style.

Horror Galore

Some of the undead want to spend their Halloween night partying and engaging in "Thriller"-inspired dance numbers, others want to settle old scores (like the werewolf who is thrown in to the mix for good measure), and one, a 1950s cheerleader named Vicki, wants to do something she never experienced when she was alive: fall in love. She also reminisces about the demolished malt shop of her youth and wonders why in the world anybody would remake a song as perfect as "Sea of Love."

Much like ghouls just wanting to have fun, so do moviegoers every once in awhile, and this is such a wholesome and uplifting time that it even fills a coffin with popcorn. The supporting cast is full of familiar faces, and adding to the sweet-natured nostalgia is how the one-and-only Wolfman Jack provides the night's soundtrack just like he did in *American Graffiti*, another film featuring a 1954 Cadillac Convertible. It's banger after banger in a soundtrack that features Wilson Pickett's "In the Midnight Hour," Creedence Clearwater Revival's "Bad Moon Rising," Sam the Sham and the Pharaohs' "Lil' Red Riding Hood," Three Dog Night's "Mama Told Me Not to Come," Barbara Lewis' "Baby I'm Yours," and in a scene where red wine spills along with vampire bite blood, The Smiths' "How Soon is Now." If that weren't enough, the film's score was written by Brad Fiedel right around the same time he composed the much-adored music for *Fright Night*.

Aside from the exaggeratedly angry town judge played by Kevin McCarthy, who decries all the damn kids and their loud music after bashing his son's radio to pieces, the (living) characters in *The Midnight Hour* are all so charming, especially the leads Lee Montgomery and Cindy Morgan. Even with one of the most spirited Halloween parties of all time, I found myself just as invested in their romance blossoming on the empty streets of town, becoming more poignant and complicated as the sun prepares to officially welcome November. Long out of print on DVD and unavailable to watch on any streaming service except YouTube, *The Midnight Hour* has still been gaining fans over the years since it's becoming clear that no list about the most festive horror movies to watch during the Halloween season is complete without it. It also features Macaulay Culkin's first-ever film appearance, although he's uncredited and probably one of the trick-or-treaters hidden behind a mask.

Murder Party (2007)

Writer and Director: Jeremy Saulnier
Cast: Chris Sharp, Stacy Rock, Paul Goldblatt, William Lacey, Sandy Barnett, Macon Blair

Just a few months after *Pumpkin Cinema* was published, I heard about a 2007 movie called *Murder Party* that for whatever reason never showed up during my years of researching Halloween-themed movies. And then I found out it was written and directed by the man who made *Green Room* and *Blue Ruin*, and started to get worried that my book was already missing an important ingredient. I was rooting for the film's failure to justify the oversight, and so when the opening minute showered me with an arresting medley of Halloween festivities, I blurted out a panicked "Oh shit!" because it was clear Jeremy Saulnier was a remarkable filmmaker even in his debut, and that he knew exactly where to position the camera to make the most of every shot.

Included in this montage is a pumpkin getting pulverized, cupcake eyeballs, trick-or-treaters roaming the streets in the afternoon (a practice I've only witnessed in film and television), a puppy enjoying the fragrance and flesh of a jack-o-lantern, decorations toing and froing in the breeze, the renting of horror videocassettes, and finally, a fancy black envelope blowing in the breeze and passing many people on the sidewalk until it's eventually stepped on by a man named Christopher, who we later learn is the owner of the doomed gourd and the renter of the movies ScareWolf, Zombie Vs Unicorn's Horn and Xanthachroid. His Halloween plans consisted of watching them alone in the small Brooklyn apartment he shares with his cat Sir Lancelot (played by a feline named Puff Snooty) while munching on candy corn, but then the lonely sad sack who ruins the days of others by administering parking violations decides to accept the invitation that he stepped on—a vague invitation to a murder party.

After making pumpkin bread from scratch and constructing a knight costume mostly out of cardboard, he makes the journey downtown where he's like a fish out of water, his nervousness compounded by everyone he encounters. He walks down a dark and sketchy street and finds that the party is being held inside a dilapidated warehouse loft, occupied by pretentious artists flabbergasted that someone would voluntarily show up to a murder party. Rather than offer libation to their new guest, they just tie him to a chair and discuss the ways in which they can murder him for the sake of art. Whoever's proposal is most appealing is promised an exorbitant grant by their wealthy and sinister companion, Alexander, who arrives at the party with his Russian drug dealer. While waiting for the midnight hour, they pass the time by reciting Edgar Allan Poe's "The Raven" and sharing a syringe during an extreme version of truth or dare, seemingly forgetting about their trapped victim until our lovable protagonist motions to the gag in his mouth when he has something witty to contribute to the conversation. He also manages to escape from his chair at one point but fails hilariously to make it much further, suggesting that his survival skills are equally as inept as his social skills.

Murder Party straddles the line between comedy and horror so effectively without ever venturing far in either direction, so even when a character dressed as a werewolf chases somebody around with a chainsaw, he has to be mindful about making sure it's plugged in first. The art students are all satirized mercilessly but the fact that they remain in their Halloween guises gives them an extra layer of personality and individualism—not only do we get the aforementioned werewolf, but there's also a 19th-century vampire, Pris from *Blade Runner*, and a Baseball Fury from *The Warriors* who actually gets in some wicked licks this time, and that is something I think we can all dig!

Night of the Demons 2 (1994)
Director: Brian Trenchard-Smith
Writers: Joe Augustyn, James Penzi (story)
Cast: Cristi Harris, Robert Jayne, Merle Kennedy, Johnny Moran, Christine Taylor

July 28, 2018 was a special night because I got to celebrate *Night of the Demons*' 30th Anniversary with a 35mm presentation at Portland's Hollywood Theatre, followed by a Q&A from horror icon Linnea Quigley! To see this childhood favorite for the first time on the silver screen with a rowdy sold-out attendance was a big deal, but at one point during the screening I couldn't help but wonder how much rowdier everyone would be if they were instead watching the superior Part 2.

It's been six years after Angela's party inside the demonic walls of Hull House, and her younger sister Melissa, attending a Catholic boarding school for troubled teens, is still emotionally shattered by her disappearance. Some of her classmates have been disciplined by the strict Sister Gloria and forbidden to attend the school's Halloween dance, but they decide to sneak off campus to attend a very different kind of party, one in which a succubus' younger sibling would be the perfect invitee.

Horror Galore

Night of the Demons 2 is a ghoulishly witty, no-holds-barred sequel that brings back the debauching hostess Angela to spread her wicked ways onto an even more entertaining group of sexy partygoers (the most recognizable face belonging to Christine Taylor). When all hell breaks loose and students start playing basketball with their severed heads, it's up to Sister Gloria to prepare for the inevitable battle between good and evil. She spends the first half of the film being the ultimate curmudgeon, placing a yardstick in between couples and insisting they leave a little room for the holy ghost, but is so easy to cheer for once she starts kicking ass for the lord by practicing kung fu moves and filling up balloons with holy water, much to the disapproval of Father Bob who refuses to entertain the possibility that something other than typical Halloween teen mischief is to blame. These authoritative characters played by Jennifer Rhodes and Rod McCary are so engaging that they almost give Bret Hart and Steve Austin a run for their money as the greatest heel-face double turn of the '90s.

With spectacular effects courtesy of Steve Johnson, fun characters, the return of a famous tube of lipstick, and an organ-heavy soundtrack that includes two songs from death metal giants Morbid Angel, *Night of the Demons 2* guarantees a truly rocking Halloween movie night for you and your heathen friends.

Scary Movie (1991)

Director: Daniel Erickson
Writers: Daniel Erickson, David Lane Smith, Mark Voges
Cast: John Hawkes, Suzanne Aldrich, Ev Lunning, Mark Voges, Zane Rockenbaugh

No, no, no, you won't see Carmen Electra running through a sprinkler in slow motion and losing a breast implant to Ghostface's butcher knife in the opening scene. Nor will you hear a vulgar rap song play over the ending credits. This *Scary Movie* is much more my cup of tea, opening with a thunderstorm of biblical proportions waking a man up from terrifying nightmares, and ending with Roky Erickson's festive 1981 song "I Walked with a Zombie." Discovering this shoestring-budgeted regional film felt like being a kid again and finding a king-sized version of a favorite candy bar a week after Halloween, when you were absolutely certain that only the lowest-of-the-low treats like Good & Plenty remained in the sack. *Scary Movie* was filmed in Austin, Texas and seemingly adhered to a "for locals only" policy for decades until American Genre Film Archives allowed outsiders to finally join in on the southern-fried Halloween party in 2019 with a 2K preservation from the original 16mm camera negative.

"This is so exciting, Warren, Halloween night, the most thrilling holiday," Warren's much-cooler blind date whispers in his ear while they wait in line for the local haunted house attraction. "Christmas is too expensive, Thanksgiving's for turkeys. Easter is for when you wanna believe rabbits lay eggs, but Halloween, creatures of the dark reign supreme." A very young John Hawkes plays the hopelessly nerdy Warren, who doesn't share her enthusiasm in the slightest and seems to be caught in a perpetual panic attack that makes us wonder how he's able to function at his job at the movie theater. He struggles to find the words to say to his date. Beads of sweat converge on his forehead with every chainsaw sound and scream coming from inside the house. Rowdy people in line point and laugh at every dumb and awkward thing he does. By the time it's their turn to walk through the door decorated with the warning "Abandon hope, all y'all who enter here," he's an even bigger scaredy-cat than Don Knotts in *The Ghost and Mr. Chicken*, and has to be physically shoved inside.

"Happy Happy Halloween, Halloween, Halloween, Happy Happy Halloween, Silver Shamrock"

Some of my happiest moments of the '90s took place inside haunted attractions and so I felt truly honored to join Warren and his group as they navigated through this earnest, lovingly crafted house of horrors furnished with a pumpkin pit, rope bridge, pendulum, and tunnel of hanging chains. But what scares Warren even more than the mummy skeletons is the very real possibility that behind any door and around any corner is the homicidal maniac that has just escaped from a nearby facility.

Daniel Erickson makes his feature film debut both a nostalgic Halloween adventure and a psychological thrill ride where we're not sure what is real life and what is make believe. His passion for the holiday can also be explored in his 1986 short film *Mr. Pumpkin*, available for free on the Texas Archive of the Moving Image website. It features a scene in which a blonde boy sneaks a candy bar from his stash to eat in bed while his glowing jack-o-lantern stares at him menacingly and raindrops smack against the pavement. What happens next will give you the willies for sure, and what happens after that will give you the giggles.

I had never even heard of *Scary Movie* until this afternoon, when Gillman Joel recommended it on the podcast *Jay of the Dead's New Horror Movies*. Finding more hidden gems just days after turning in my final draft of this book to the publisher was annoyingly inevitable, but at least it's not too late to make this one final change. Horror Galore: 301 Fantastic Fright Flicks You Might Have Missed doesn't quite have the same cachet, and so I'll need to cross something off the list…

67 minutes later:

I'm sorry, *Anthropophagus* (from notorious Italian director Joe D'Amato), but you've been chosen as my sacrifice. You're still a good movie and you have more to offer than just your infamous scene of a cannibalistic madman strangling a pregnant lady, ripping out her fetus, and then devouring it in front of her shocked husband. A few examples are:
-an entertaining opening scene with Greece's Changing of the Guards ceremony and a meat cleaver hacking of a couple on the beach—an unlikely one-two punch combo.
-the most startling introduction of a blind woman since 1959's *House on Haunted Hill*.
-one of the most endearing jump scares because not only does the adorable kitty cat leap from the corner of the screen, but it lands on a piano and then playfully contributes to the aggressively weird carnivalesque soundtrack by Marcello Giombini.
-a terrifying villain with a clever backstory. It's not unusual to be loved by anyone, and it's not unusual to have fun with anyone, but it is unusual to find a movie where the killer is played by the screenwriter; thankfully, George Eastman is more than competent at both roles.
-a nice performance from Tisa Farrow, sister of Mia, who retired from acting after this movie to pursue a career in nursing.
-a deserted island that would be creepy even without cannibals tearing jugulars open with their bare hands.

WNUF Halloween Special (2013)

Director: Chris LaMartina
Writers: Chris LaMartina, Jimmy George, Pat Storck, Michael Joseph Moran
Cast: Paul Fahrenkopf, Richard Cutting, Leanna Chamish, Brian St. August, Helenmary Ball

For their first project since 2011's horror-comedy *Witch's Brew*, Baltimore director Chris LaMartina and his longtime producing collaborator Jimmy George decided to tap into the popular found-footage subgenre as well as the recent VHS revival to make an experimental film with such painstaking authenticity that it would appear as if someone taped their local news broadcast one Halloween in the late '80s and allowed it to circulate for decades among collectors at video conventions. *WNUF Halloween Special* allows you to revisit a part of your childhood taken for granted as it serenades you with corny local commercials and even cornier Halloween jokes (told by newscasters in costumes), and the fact that it looks so real makes the evil slowly simmering beneath the innocent façade all the more impactful.

Exactly 20 years ago in the summer of '67, the Webber house "was the sight of ghastly depravity" when a teenaged boy decapitated his parents at the alleged suggestions of demonic spirits he summoned through a Ouija board. With numerous reports of paranormal sightings raising its infamy over the years, snarky reporter Frank Stewart (Paul Fahrenkopf in a role written with him in mind) hopes to make television history by giving the public their first tour inside these walls while making sure to avoid the kind of anticlimactic fiasco that occurred the previous year when Geraldo opened Al Capone's vault. Along for the ride are a husband-and-wife paranormal team whose names might as well be De and Eniarrol Nerraw, their clairvoyant kitty cat Shadow, and a priest that caresses a Bible as unconvincingly as Trump and who clearly wasn't informed on Frank's plans for an on-air exorcism.

With a central storyline similar to that of *Tales from the Crypt*'s scariest episode, "Television Terror," *WNUF* avoids one of the most common complaints about found footage films because it's the characters' job to keep the cameras rolling no matter what. The cast members all do an excellent job in reacting to the unpredictability of the night while bantering in a way that feels improvised rather than scripted, especially whenever Frank asks questions to the locals gathered outside who are ecstatic and nervously unprepared to be interviewed on live television, and when an on-air séance surprises everyone for the wrong reasons.

Advertising dollars were more important than the public's right to know even in simpler times, and so commercial breaks often interrupt the suspense inside the house, giving the film a real playful energy. LaMartina acquired mountains of content from royalty free websites, libraries of inexpensive stock footage, and the shot-on-video projects from his fellow filmmaking friends, and he worked with an editing team to put together the kind of ads that you would catch on your local networks late at night. Some of my personal favorites were for Phil's Carpet Warehouse (probably because it reminded me of the Southern-styled Bargain Barn ads that ran in St. Louis throughout my childhood), 1-900 Monster Hotline (inspired by Freddy Krueger's hotline and Creeptalk), the heavy metal compilation Feel the Steel, Gordon's Petting Zoo, a pumpkin patch and hayride, the most antiquated version of Turbo Tax, Tokens Video Arcade and Pizzeria, incumbent State Senator Mike Barlow and his challenger Robert Dandridge (lovingly referencing two of the all-time greatest vampires), late-night creature feature host Dr. Bloodwrench, and all of the fake movie spots. They even made the smart decision to save the more risqué advertisements for late into the broadcast because just like in real life, networks aren't likely to advertise strip clubs and suicide prevention hotlines while the kiddies are still awake.

Because it knows its target audience to an uncanny degree, *WNUF Halloween Special* is an absolute triumph and the most charming of oddities for channel-surfers of the '80s and '90s. Same goes for LaMartina's terrific 2022 spiritual sequel *Out There Mega Halloween Tape*, which also succeeds in scratching an itch you didn't realize you've been carrying for years.

JINGLE HELLS OR: EVERY DECENT CHRISTMAS PUN HAS ALREADY BEEN TAKEN

Better Watch Out (2016)
Director: Chris Peckover
Writers: Chris Peckover, Zack Kahn (story)
Cast: Olivia DeJonge, Levi Miller, Ed Oxenbould, Aleks Mikic, Virginia Madsen

In the Halloween season of 2017, I took a solo road trip through Idaho, Utah, New Mexico, and Colorado, and one of the highlights was attending a meetup with the hosts and fans of the podcasts *Horror Movie Weekly* and *Retro Movie Geek*. We gathered in the University of Utah's theater (which took me about 30 frustrating minutes of wandering around campus to locate) and watched a double feature consisting of *Tremors* and a special screening of a new film directed by a man I didn't know who happened to be sitting one chair away from me. Even though everybody's heart was bleeding for beautiful fall foliage and pumpkin patches at this time, we had to make an unexpected leap into Christmas Town with *Better Watch Out*, and after only 25 minutes or so, I was certain that it was going to be the feature attraction of my annual Christmas movie night a couple months later. I couldn't wait to show my friends what was the most subversive, edgy, and twisted yuletide flick in ages.

While his parents are attending a Christmas party, 12-year-old Luke is being babysat by a high school student named Ashley, someone he's always had a bit of a crush on. In an ill-conceived attempt to appear more mature to her, he raids the liquor cabinet, lights some candles, and puts on a scary movie for them to watch together on the couch. She predictably rejects all his advances but is then confronted by something far scarier: a masked man who breaks into the house carrying a shotgun. Even if this took the route of a traditional home invasion slasher, it would probably still be a homerun due to the incredible performances by the small cast, confident direction, festive Christmas atmosphere, and ability to creep you out and make you laugh in the same scene, but *Better Watch Out* wickedly defies all expectations time and time again, so it's imperative that you avoid trailers and major spoilers!

Not having any idea what was going to happen made this one of the most powerful moviegoing experiences for me, and it was such a rare privilege to be able to reach out during the ending credits and shake the hand of director Chris Peckover (I'm pretty sure the first words out of my mouth to him were "Holy shit!!!"). Among the many fascinating bits of trivia shared in the Q&A was how he wanted to include Wham's "Last Christmas" during a crucial scene but unfortunately wasn't able to acquire the rights in time—at least he found a suitable replacement in the Ramones' "Merry Christmas (I Don't Wanna Fight Tonight)." He also informed us why two of the leads looked so familiar—Olivia DeJonge and Ed Oxenbould played the brother and sister in M. Night Shyamalan's *The Visit* just a year prior, and thank heavens there would be no impromptu rapping with this reunion.

As predicted at my Christmas movie night, my friends did a lot of hooting and hollering for Patrick "David Puddy" Warburton's appearance, but the most enjoyable part was looking around the room right after a certain moment at the top of the staircase to witness everyone's expression change. By the end of the movie, the crowd was split down the middle, allowing me to see who the true ghouls were in my social circle. I did feel like a bit of a masochist for subjecting them to possibly uncharted territory of discomfort during the holidays, and for replacing their visions of sugar plums with horrific acts of violence, and so I immediately cleansed their pallets with *A Garfield Christmas* and strong servings of Hot Buttered Rum!

A Christmas Horror Story (2015)

Directors: Grant Harvey, Steven Hoban, Brett Sullivan
Writers: James Kee, Sarah Larsen, Doug Taylor, Pascal Trottier
Cast: William Shatner, George Buza, Zoe De Grant Maison, Adrian Holmes, Amy Forsyth

With that cover depicting a muscular and almighty Krampus swinging a chain at Santa Claus as snowflakes fall from a gray sky to land on fir trees and piles of skulls, it was an easy click when it suddenly appeared during my holiday scrolling. My expectations were tempered due to its direct-to-streaming status and all the years that passed since the last truly memorable Christmas horror movie (this predated Michael Dougherty's modern classic *Krampus* by a year), and I also worried that the brilliant concept of Krampus and Santa dueling to the death would prove to be a massive letdown much like when Abraham Lincoln battled all those vampires. Despite being titled *A Christmas Horror Story*, what we get here is actually an anthology consisting of four separate stories, and the way they intermingle together makes it clear the filmmakers were attempting to create a *Trick 'R Treat* for the Yuletide season, and for the most part they succeeded.

After a rendition of the always-intense "Carol of the Bells," we're taken to the North Pole to discover that Santa's Headquarters is surprisingly lacking in the merry department, what with the overworked elves and Santa being preoccupied by the weather. It's nowhere near as bleak as *Family Guy*'s interpretation of the North Pole in season 9's must-see "Road to the North Pole," but it does involve an epidemic that turns the elves into ravenous, foul-mouthed monsters hungry for the blood of their master. Unlike the other tales which are far more subdued, here the action is kinetic and nonstop, with over-the-top kills and wall-splattering gore.

In my favorite segment, a family of three ignore a Private Property sign in a forest on a quest to find the perfect Christmas tree. It's an idyllic winter wonderland outing until the little boy goes missing, and after a frantic search, is found hiding inside of a tree. There is no apparent physical harm, but the father suspects something may be wrong when his child shows no interest in conversing or using the inhaler that he's always depended on—he only seems focused on eating pasta and stabbing people with forks who try to interfere. Tensions continue to rise on Christmas eve for this family as the quarrelling parents decide to sleep in separate rooms and their son's facial expressions grow more unsettling by the minute.

In another part of town, a far more dysfunctional family is paying an unexpected visit to Aunt Edda, whose house would be just perfect for Paul Bunyan and Count Dracula if they were madly in love with each other, according to one character. It's an unpleasant reunion all around, with the last straw coming as the bratty sociopath son intentionally breaks an antique figurine of Krampus, and on Krampusnacht of all nights! On the way home their car becomes trapped in snow and forces them on foot through the forest where spooky sounds and painful traps await.

The fourth story concerns a trio of high school students, working on a web series called "Horror in the Halls," who sneak into St. Joseph Academy on the one-year anniversary of a tragedy that shocked investigators and the entire town of Bailey Downs to the core. They take their equipment down to where those two mutilated bodies were discovered, recounting the sordid details and then having no choice but to go for extra credit when the doors lock behind them, trapping them with creepy Nativity Scene statues in a school that is still a week away from opening again. If this particular tale is winning any awards, it's for the Best Executed Jump Scare in Recent History category.

None of these segments are spectacular but they're all good enough, and are anchored by marvelous wraparounds in which William Shatner plays a radio DJ named Dangerous Dan, who is once again pulling double duty on Christmas Eve to get everyone in Bailey Downs into the holiday spirit. While all the other characters are cold and fighting for their lives, he's inside a cozy studio, keeping himself warm with a Christmas sweater and lots of alcohol. In between the nostalgic tunes, he waxes poetic about his love of Christmas--occasionally stumbling with lines like "let's throw another eggnog on the fire"—before having to announce yet another Christmas tragedy as reports come in detailing a massacre at the shopping mall. *A Christmas Horror Story* automatically earns an extra half star, or maybe even a whole one, for that whopper of an ending!

Poster for *Christmas Evil* (1980), Pan American Pictures

Christmas Evil (1980)

Writer and Director: Lewis Jackson
Cast: Brandon Maggart, Jeffrey DeMunn, Dianne Hull, Andy Fenwick, Brian Neville

About ten Decembers ago, a very thoughtful co-worker was telling me about her evening of digging though Walmart's bargain bin of $1 DVDs and finding a title that she correctly assumed would be right up my alley. She then gave me a copy of *Christmas Evil*. I was genuinely excited to extract this DVD from its unusually thin case (the legitimate-looking Digiview Entertainment logo gave me assurance that this wasn't just some unauthorized bootleg copy) the second I got home, but not before cranking up the space heater and plugging in the Christmas tree, of course.

My thumb was barely up for it afterwards and I never got the urge to watch it again when scanning my movie collection. The case was practically swallowed whole by the normal-sized DVDs of *A Christmas Carol (1984)* and *Christmas Vacation*, and I also had myself believing that "there was more gravy than grave to it," as Scrooge would have said, and that it was just a cheap-looking, marginally entertaining slasher about a lonely man who goes on a killing spree dressed as Santa Claus. It would be easy to blame the poor transfer and the inexplicably missing parts on that DVD version for my lukewarm reaction, or the simple fact that tastes can change over the course of a decade, but the likeliest explanation is that I decided to smoke pot so that a silly movie would be even sillier—why expect anything short of a laugh riot with a goofy cover like that and the tagline "He'll sleigh you!"? I was probably just a little let down by how *Christmas Evil* wasn't a dark comedy, a goofy slasher, or a "so bad it's good" *MST3000* contender, but rather, a deeply disturbing examination of a man scarred for life from a childhood incident that damaged his psyche beyond repair. His mental state gets worse when he notices all injustices of the world, the mistreatment of the weak, shady business practices, and especially naughty children! As someone whose eyes flood with tears at every viewing of *Falling Down*, it makes sense that *Christmas Evil* would finally resonate with me on a profound level, and now I consider it to be one of the greatest Christmas movies ever.

On Christmas Eve 1947, Santa Claus descends down the chimney of a suburban New Jersey home, and after indulging in a milk and cookie display so elaborate that there's even a handwashing station for him, he lays the wrapped presents under the tree with care. Two young boys and their mother secretly watch the magic unfold from the staircase. Harry, the older of the two brothers, would see Santa again later that night and never recover from the trauma. It would be a disturbing image for any child to witness, but Billy from *Silent Night, Deadly Night* might have scoffed at their Santa support group and responded to the story with "Is that it?!"

Now, as an adult, Harry begins every morning by prancing around his apartment in a Santa Claus suit to the tune of "Winter Wonderland." His routine also includes giving himself an impressive shaving cream white beard and spying on the neighborhood children with his binoculars, chronicling every good and bad deed in his book; one child will receive positive marks for taking out the trash while another will be punished for flipping through a *Playboy* magazine with Blondie on the cover, for example. Stepping outside his perpetual Christmas wonderland changes his demeanor considerably, where he spends his days working at a joyless toy factory with people who disrespect him and don't subscribe to his "If it's not a jolly dream, it's not worth having" philosophy. As the misery builds and builds to Frank Grimes levels, a haunting piano melody repeats and chaotically blends with the sounds of broken music boxes and ghostly female "ahhh's" to let us know what Christmas sounds like in hell.

You're not going to find a better performance in a Christmas horror film than Brandon Maggart (father to Fiona Apple) as Harry, especially when he tries on the fake white beard and stares in the mirror that now reveals the man he was always meant to be. After seeing him as a put-upon, dejected sad sack for the first half of the film, it's equally chilling and heartwarming when he's suddenly unable to stifle his bursts of jubilation while staring at his own reflection. With his van painted like a sleigh, he pretends to be steering his reindeer as he drives to a children's hospital with sacks of stolen toys. His first interaction as Santa Claus gets off to a rocky start when the elderly security guard asks, "At this hour? What are you, wacko?" but then the snow begins to fall just as he's perfected his "Ho Ho Ho" and he quickly wins the hearts of the hospital staff who all salute in unison, "Merry Christmas Santa Claus!" One of the nurses even kisses his cheek and it's just delightful.

He's also a major hit at a local Christmas party, triumphantly dancing with children to the tune of "Jingle Bells" on the accordion while all the adults clap along. He's not as warmly received outside of a church, however, especially after one worshipper loses an eye to a sharp nutcracker figurine and another losing the top portion of his skull to repeated axe swings. As a media frenzy reports on a homicidal Santa Claus terrorizing the town, the home belonging to Harry's younger brother fills with paralyzing, soul-crushing dread.

Writer-director Lewis Jackson, who spent many years collecting discounted Christmas merchandise to be used in the film, was forced to make difficult financial sacrifices to ensure that his labor of love turned out just as he hoped, with professional cinematography and sound design, painstaking attention to detail, and a cast that was up to the task of going to some extremely dark places on the holiest of nights. For a long time the film's distribution seemed as tortured and troubled as its main character, but thanks to a Special Edition DVD from Synapse Films (featuring a commentary track from John Waters who calls it the greatest Christmas movie ever made), a 4K-mastered Blu-ray loaded with extras from Vinegar Syndrome, and easy accessibility on various streaming services, *Christmas Evil* is gaining legions of new fans every year.

Dial Code Santa Claus (1989)

Writer and Director: René Manzor
Cast: Louis Ducreux, Brigitte Fossey, Patrick Floersheim, Alain Lalanne

The streaming service Shudder made its subscribers feel all warm and jolly in December of 2019 when it added a French Christmas horror film from 1989 that few people had ever heard of. While it features a homicidal Santa Claus, it has much more in common with *Home Alone*—which it predates by one year—than *Silent Night, Deadly Night*, and a few of the similarities were so jarring that writer-director René Manzor even threatened legal actions.

Also known as *Game Over* and *Deadly Games*, the movie opens with a sentimental quote about kids' belief in magic sparring with the disappointments of reality, and then the sight of a beautiful Eiffel Tower snowglobe exploding under the wheel of a garbage truck. It's a joyously white Christmas Eve and all of the neighborhood children are engaged in a snowball fight (that comes to an abrupt end when a shaggy-haired grownup attempts to join in) with the exception of Thomas, a privileged whiz-kid with a mullet that would make Billy Ray Cyrus envious. He is busy living out his action-hero fantasies by dressing up as Rambo and running around one of the coolest-looking mansions in cinema history. His mom owns a department store that is doing record business for the holidays, keeping her busy at work and relegating most of the parental duties to Thomas' diabetic and half-blind grandfather.

Even with all of the toys a kid could ever want, Thomas's mood is souring due to a sudden case of agnosticism so strong that he's not only questioning the existence of Santa Claus, but also if cavemen or Napoleon were made up as well. He decides to use the altruistic Minitel, France's groundbreaking telecommunications system that served as an appetizer to the world wide web, to try to contact the real-life Santa Claus. His instant messages are quickly responded to by Jolly Ole Saint Nick himself, who answers a couple basic questions about elves and the North Pole before asking a couple questions of his own: "What is your address?" and "Do you want to play with me?" in a cautionary scene that feels a decade ahead of its time.

The skinny and dark-haired Santa Claus manages to creep out another child when at the department store, he strokes her cheek repeatedly while gazing intently into her eyes. "I don't like your face. You're not the real Santa," she says before yanking off his beard and receiving a white-gloved slap to the face. Fired on the spot, the disgruntled Santa decides to spread his unique version of holiday cheer by making a personal house visit in which maneuvering down the chimney is the only part that goes relatively smoothly.

The MVPs of this movie have to be the set designers, who have constructed a castle-like funhouse full of labyrinthine passageways, tunnels in the unlikeliest of places, and magnificent décor in every room (Thomas even has posters for *Texas Chainsaw Massacre 2* and *Critters* in his bedroom). It almost feels like the brilliant artists responsible for the Meow Wolf museum in Santa Fe got direct inspiration for this film, especially when Thomas and his grandfather open what appears to be a normal refrigerator door. There's even a massive cave that not even Thomas' mother knows about, where his father, grandfather, and great grandfather's toys are preserved. The relationship between grandson and grandfather is the heart and soul of the movie and it's a pleasure watching them work together ingeniously to save each other from a Santa slay—the usage of a wind-up train toy and a knight costume are especially clever.

What prevents *Dial Code Santa Claus* from being an absolute Christmas classic is its frustrating tone where the misguided soundtrack (which includes a rip-off of Survivor's "Eye of the Tiger") gets in the way of scenes that are shot to elicit suspense, and where the home intruder is only vicious and intimidating for the first minute or so before becoming mostly ineffective—just imagine if the Wet Bandits had stabbed a dog to death before slipping on toy cars. Yeah, the dog death is another strike against it. It won't become an annual tradition like *Gremlins*, *Krampus*, and *Black Christmas*, but it's still a unique hidden gem for the holiday season and a reminder that Shudder is definitely worth subscribing to.

SAUCY SORCERERS IN MOVIES BEGINNING WITH S

Seeding of a Ghost (1983)
Director: Kuen Yeung
Writers: Yee-Hung Lam, Kamber Huang (story)
Cast: Norman Chu, Phillip Ko, Maria Jo, Jung Wang, Mi Tien, Hussein Abu Hassan

Mostly known for popularizing the kung fu genre, Hong Kong's Shaw Brothers Studio produced approximately 1,000 films until switching to the television medium in 1987. One of its final cinematic offerings was *Seeding of a Ghost* (kindly recommended by my buddy Nelson), which takes the sorcery and accelerated combat of previous horror titles but adds to the cauldron a powerful rape-revenge angle and special effects seemingly inspired by *The Thing*.

It begins when a cab driver accidentally hits a graverobbing occultist who tells him, "It's your rotten luck to run into me. You know, it's bad luck to break up black magic. If you are lucky, you'll at the most be sick, if not, you and your family might die." Seemingly on cue, his unhappy wife begins a passionate affair with a married man she met at her blackjack table, and while she pontificates on the wonderful life they could have together if they just left their partners, the man makes it clear that he has no intentions on divorcing his wife. This causes her to jump out of his car in anguish and telephone her cab-driving husband. She is then pursued by a couple of young thugs and chased into an abandoned house where, after a grueling struggle, she is raped and accidentally murdered.

When discovering that the police consider him a suspect in his wife's murder, the cursed man takes matters into his own hands by visiting the sorcerer for a little tutorial in black magic. Together they perform a ritual on her corpse, now looking ghoulish and horrifying, which sends her ghost on a path of revenge to all who wronged her. Worms are vomited up, tasty coconut treats turned into brain stews, arms bitten off by tentacled creatures, spines pulverized, and stomachs exploded by satanic spawns in this smorgasbord of inventive practical effects. The strange title is visualized with a dazzling black magic show in which a levitating animatronic corpse has sex with her unwitting and injured mate—who's undergoing a strange transformation of his own—and thankfully this love scene doesn't play with cliched softcore porn saxophone music like the others do. This is a film in which the camera repeatedly lingers on its nude actresses (including full frontal) and isn't ashamed to capture them running topless on the beach in super-super slow motion.

As someone who has probably watched *Tourist Trap* at least 30 times and owns Pino Donaggio's soundtrack, I was triggered on three separate occasions during *Seeding of a Ghost* and wondered how tiny sections of *Tourist Trap* music managed to escape from the universe of Mr. Slausen and his

The Seventh Curse (1986)

Director: Ngai Choi Lam
Writers: Jing Wong, Kai-Chi Yuen
Cast: Siu-Ho Chin, Chow Yun-fat, Maggie Cheung, Ken Boyle, Yuen Chor, Sibelle Hu

From the director of *Riki-Oh: The Story of Riki*, this composite of action-adventure, martial arts, fantasy, and horror will give you such an adrenaline rush that after 30 minutes, you may require an intermission to catch your breath. It oozes the same madcap energy, bombastic camerawork, and gooey practical effects that made the *Evil Dead* trilogy and Peter Jackson's earliest work such an experience. I loved it almost instantly because one of the first characters we meet is named Alf, and even though he gets killed after about 20 seconds, my joy remained intact for the entire picture.

When his legs suddenly pulsate with deep veins and convulse until blood spurts from the kneecap, Dr. Yuan wonders if this mysterious affliction is related to that time he traveled to Thailand and had his assignment of acquiring special herbs for an AIDS treatment derailed by falling in love with a woman who was to be sacrificed by the Worm Tribe. He succeeded in rescuing her from the sorcerer in charge and a glowy-eyed animatronic skeleton, but not before a horrible curse was placed on them both. The evil sorcerer, with his Mickey Mouse voice, could probably make certain lines like "Hi, ya pal, gosh golly, everything must be so new and exciting for ya!" work but certainly not "You have blasphemed Old Ancestor. That was a very big mistake. And now we have no God. I shall punish you both."

Realizing that one more bloody leg spasm could seal his fate, he returns to Thailand in hopes of finding a cure, and much to his displeasure, an opportunistic and overbearingly upbeat young reporter insists on tagging along for a series of adventures that wouldn't feel out of place in *Krull* or *Indiana Jones and the Temple of Doom*.

The plot is the least-important aspect of *The Seventh Curse*, so be sure to leave your brain at the door and just revel in the blood-splattered nonsense and blazing choreographed fight scenes. In addition to that bad-ass skeleton, Dr. Yuan and his friends also must battle a creature that looks like a flying fetus relative of *Basket Case*'s Belial, a dinosaur bat, a Xenomorphic monster, cruising coffins, and martial artist monks that protect a humongous Buddist statue during an impressively staged climbing scene. There's even a grinder that turns abducted little kids into juicy pulp to appease God!

The characters of Dr. Yuan and his best friend Wisely originally existed in a shared literary universe, as Hong Kong writer Ni Kuang had a series of novels devoted to them. With 145 different novels written from 1963-2004, hopefully somewhere within is a backstory on the Alf character that died in *The Seventh Curse* even before I could take my first bite of popcorn.

Spookies (1986)

Directors: Thomas Doran, Genie Joseph, Brendan Faulkner
Writers: Thomas Doran, Ann Burgund, Frank M. Farel
Cast: Nick Gionta, Felix Ward, Peter Dain, Peter Iasillo Jr., Anthony Valbiro, Maria Pechukas

One Monday in the second grade, I had the hardest time concentrating on schoolwork because I kept thinking about that incredible horror movie that aired a couple nights ago on *USA Saturday Nightmares*. Social studies and arithmetic could get bent because all I wanted to do was replay random scenes in my head, doing my best to remember what the monsters looked like and what the synthesizer melodies sounded like. It wouldn't be long until the unforgettable film *Spookies* aired again on television and this time, I was armed with a blank videocassette and a remote control where I could pause the film during commercial breaks so that it looked almost as good as the VHS copy from Blockbuster Video, thus saving my parents plenty of bucks in rental fees (and late fees when I wasn't ready to relinquish it).

I probably watched *Spookies* over 20 times before learning of its troubled production and how it was essentially two different movies spliced together. I couldn't believe it, nor could I believe how otherwise excellent books like *Creature Features* and *Terror on Tape* gave it such negative reactions. It became a challenge to find any critical appreciation for it whatsoever. Every now and then, I would find a review from someone who liked it in an ironic sense as "so bad it's good" shlock, which only caused more irritation since it was crystal clear to me that this was a legitimately great movie that only seemed to get better and better with age. Throughout my life it has remained one of my favorite things to introduce friends to because whether we've all been adolescents, college students, or middle age, the collective response in the room has always been glowing and enthusiastic. And then, after the ending credits, I reveal the mysteries behind the production known as *Twisted Souls* to a chorus of "Wooooaaaah's!" and "Whaaaaaaaaat's?!" because like me, they also didn't question why the sorcerer and the partiers never interact inside the haunted mansion. My eternal gratitude went to the kind soul who uploaded the entire movie on YouTube in a quality far better than my ancient VHS tape because for the longest time, *Spookies* was one of those sad examples of a movie never making the transition to DVD, despite my monthly Twitter pleadings to various distributors of cult cinema.

Poster for ***Spookies*** (1986), Sony Video Software Company

Long-suffering spookies like me finally got reasons to celebrate when in January 2015, Austin's Alamo Drafthouse screened a rare 35mm print of the movie and invited a few cast and crew members to participate in a Q&A afterwards. About a year later, the recording label Terror Vision released Ken Higgins and James Calabrese's official soundtrack on vinyl, cassette, and mp3, and it was such a treat to hear remastered themes like "Attack of the Lizard People," "Kreon's Bride," and that wonderful opening theme in their entirety. But the biggest news came on November 29, 2019, when Vinegar Syndrome surprised everybody by announcing that

Horror Galore

headlining their Black Friday sale was a *Spookies* Blu-ray, restored in 4K from the long-lost original negative and with several special features, the most enticing one being a feature-length "making of" documentary. They were even selling *Spookies* t-shirts! It also finally became available to stream when Shudder acquired it in 2021 to be featured on an episode of *The Last Drive-In with Joe Bob Briggs*. You knew that its time had finally come when Joe Bob himself participated in a "Spookies rap!"

For those scared of the dawk and late to the pawty, this movie is set on "a night of unrelenting terror" where a group of friends, in search of something to do, take the back roads leading to an abandoned mansion that appears to fertilize its front lawn with a cemetery. They break inside but the party is short-lived when one of them becomes possessed and the others discover that zombies have surrounded the perimeter, trapping them inside. They split up to look for another escape, all while the sorcerer living inside prepares to transfer their life essence to his bride (who died 72 years ago) with the help of a fantastical battalion of monsters summoned by a weird Ouija board. Got all that? The titular spookies include an icy-breathed cackling witch, a hook-handed cat-man, a combustible grim reaper, a slimy little lizard-gremlin thing, an Oriental spider lady, an adolescent druid with fangs, a towering fleshless creature with face-melting electrical tentacles, wind-breaking muck men, and others. It's honestly hard to pick a favorite from this bunch because they're all works of art that really shine in high definition!

It's easy to lament over what could have been had executive producer Michael Lee not fired directors Thomas Doran and Brendan Faulkner during production of the movie *Twisted Souls* after one too many clashes behind the scenes. It really sucks that they, along with their talented crew and cast, weren't allowed to complete the movie they all worked unbelievably hard on because it was shaping up to be bona fide creature feature classic, especially when you hear details about specific scenes from the original script co-written by Frank M. Farel that were never shot.

Lee ended up hiring a new director, writer, cast, and crew to film about 45 minutes of additional scenes to somehow blend with the *Twisted Souls* footage, and it's kind of remarkable how seamlessly these two completely separate storylines managed to coexist, sometimes even in the same scene. This unorthodox Frankenstein monster-style of filmmaking gives *Spookies* such a confounding, otherworldly quality, and as someone who whole-heartedly loves every single second of this movie, it's really hard to imagine it being as memorable without the half written by Ann Burgund and directed by Genie Joseph. While watching the Blu-ray extras, I was hoping to see an inspirational mending of the fences between these two *Spookies* camps after decades of animosity, but sadly there still remains much resentment and hard feelings, which is totally understandable.

If I ever make it out to New York, the first line of my itinerary would be "Visit 210 Boston Post Road in Rye." The Peter Augustus Jay House, constructed in 1838, is a popular place for history buffs because it's a National Historic Landmark, but for us weirdos it will always be known as the Spookies House, inside and out. Its façade looks exactly the same 35 years later, even when photographed on a sunny afternoon without a single thumping tombstone out front or grim reaper falling from the balcony.

It's unlikely that the fine folks over at WatchMojo will ever make a **"Top 10 Greatest Spookies Moments"** list and so you'll have to settle for my choices.

10. Kreon opens up Isabelle's coffin to confess what he's done to revive her

Saucy Sorcerers In Movies Beginning With S

9. Cat-man doesn't care that it's Billy's 13th birthday

8. Duke gets angry at a closet door for not opening

7. Very bad things happen to Carol when her chess pawn changes color

6. Lonely grim reaper just wants to participate in the upstairs brawl

5. In a long, dark hallway, "David" returns to congratulate a terrified and bloodied Adrienne on her victory, but another round is about to commence. Pretty much every moment with Anthony Valbiro and Charlotte Alexandra as this bickering young couple fills me with joy, and I wish they had more screentime.

4. Rich (the late, great, scene-stealing Peter Iasillo Jr.) drunkenly bumps into multiple friends and gets yelled at by Duke. His struggles with mops, buckets, and electrical cords were also hilarious.

3. Isabelle's bewitching dungeon journey

2. Adrienne can't enjoy her cigarette thanks to her napping boyfriend and a violent lizard creature

1. Spider transformation and balloon head combo pack

Horror Galore

SEXY MALL MADNESS

Chopping Mall (1986)

Director: Jim Wynorski
Writers: Jim Wynorski, Steve Mitchell
Cast: Kelli Maroney, Tony O'Dell, Russell Todd, Barbara Crampton, Karrie Emerson

Legend has it that after an early screening of a movie called Killbots, the audience made it clear that they weren't thrilled with the title, and it was the theater's janitor who suggested the name *Chopping Mall* to schlockmaster Jim Wynorski. I would like to think the same man was responsible for coming up with the provocative titles for later Wynorski projects like *Big Bad Mama II*, *Scream Queen Hot Tub Party*, *Munchie Strikes Back*, *The Bare Wench Project 3: Nymphs of Mystery Mountain*, *The Witches of Breastwick*, *The Hills Have Thighs*, and *Sharkansas Women's Prison Massacre*.

Many moviegoers were initially turned off by how the film wasn't the typical slasher the title suggested, and that no actual chopping was to be found. It was just a matter of time before people realized the unlimited potential of killer robots terrorizing teenagers in a shopping mall—now it has quite the cult following.

Four couples decide to have an after-hours party inside the mall where most of them are employed, and because the main agenda involves drinking and having sex, they congregate in the furniture store. It would have been a perfect plan had it not been for

Hollywood Theatre's marathon participants finished strong thanks to *Chopping Mall*

the three recently purchased Protector 101 security robots who, on their first night on the job, have their computers struck by lightning. This causes the kind of minor malfunction where a robot that's supposed to scan your security card and then wish you a good day instead projects a laser beam that causes your

219

head to explode and then wishes you a good day. They are also capable of electrocutions, body-burnings, throat-slittings, disgusting slop bucket-spillings, and chasing humans out of the safety of their furniture store so that they run around in a state of mall madness, if you will. But since this is a mall in the mid '80s, at least the teens can defend themselves by breaking into the sporting goods store and taking the semiautomatic weapons and large quantities of bullets on unprotected display.

Oh man, there are so many friendly faces here if you're a cult cinema aficionado, starting with cameos from Mary Woronov and Paul Bartel, reprising their roles of Mrs. and Mr. Bland from the gut-busting and gut-munching dark comedy *Eating Raoul*. And if you know Woronov best as the foxy matriarch of the Putterman family in *TerrorVision*, you'll be happy to know that Mr. Putterman (*Phantom of the Paradise*'s Gerrit Graham) also appears later in the picture as a security guard who has to get used to double-takes and triple-takes when foolishly reading a book in front of potentially dangerous robots. The man, the myth, the legend, Dick Miller himself, also shows up as the same dejected janitor he played in *A Bucket of Blood* (1959), a nice homage courtesy of producer Julie Corman to her husband Roger. And be sure to keep your eyes open for a certain Dream Warrior in the early montage of mall behavior that includes balancing a tray of six cups of soda in the food court, fighting over arcade games, and participating in escalator fails decades before YouTube made them famous.

Playing much larger roles are scream queen legend Barbara Crampton as well as Kelli Maroney, who had filmed scenes in that same shopping mall two years prior for *Night of the Comet*. Maroney doesn't play her usual ditzy cheerleader self, but rather a shy girl named Alison, set up on a blind date by her outgoing friends to the even shier Ferdy (Tony O'Dell). While their friends get frisky on the inventory, they bond in front of a television showing Roger Corman's 1957 film *Attack of the Crabmonsters*, cementing themselves as the two characters to root for. Yet another fun Corman tribute comes in the form of a store called Roger's Little Shop of Pets, easily the worst place in the mall to hide because you're putting four-legged friends at risk (thankfully the robots pay no attention to dogs and cats) and because you also have to hide from hairy eight-legged freaks. Sherman Oaks Galleria has also been used in films such as *Fast Times at Ridgemont High*, *Valley Girl*, *Commando*, and Joe Dante's *Innerspace*.

Sorority Babes in the Slimeball Bowl-O-Rama (1988)

Director: David DeCoteau
Writer: Sergei Hasenecz
Cast: Andras Jones, Linnea Quigley, Robin Stille, Hal Havins, Brinke Stevens, Michelle Bauer

The horror community received the ultimate Friday the 13th gift in July 2018 when on the streaming network Shudder, legendary host Joe Bob Briggs made his television return nearly 20 years after the final episode of TNT's *MonsterVision*, a series that gave fans of cult cinema something fun to do on Friday nights. To say that he was sorely missed would be an understatement, as Joe Bob "broke the internet" when an overwhelmingly large audience tuned in at the beginning of the 24-hour marathon and obliterated Shudder's servers for hours. While it was really frustrating to miss out on the opening film *Tourist Trap*—easily one of my five all-time favorite fright flicks—it was beyond comforting to witness the staggering demand from other weirdos excitedly embarking on this ambitious watch-a-long with me. Reading comments on Facebook and Twitter entertained me a great deal as I waited for Shudder's I.T.

crew, surely on the verge of a nervous breakdown, to save the night. The comment that got the biggest laugh out of me came from my friend Matt Faure, who posted a screenshot of Cousin Eddie and kidnapped boss Frank Shirley from *Christmas Vacation* with the caption "Hey Shudder, you about ready to do some kissing?"

The spinning wheel of agony finally vanished from my TV screen right around the time Pino Donaggio's heartbreakingly beautiful score accompanied the ending credits of *Tourist Trap*, serving as an unlikely starter's pistol for a marathon. Armed with blueberries, grapes, almonds, chips, and Jack & Cokes, I watched *Sleepaway Camp*, *Rabid*, and *The Prowler*, and then my eyelids gained mass and started to betray me. Fortunately, the next film was *Sorority Babes in the Slimeball Bowl-O-Rama*, instantly giving me rushes of adrenaline and putting me back into blissful sprinting mode. Starring three seminal scream queens in Linnea Quigley, Brinke Stevens, and Michelle Bauer, this horror comedy packs so much fun into 80 minutes that its obscurity is perplexing. I mean, how many other movies take you inside a shopping mall's bowling alley that is being terrorized by a jive-talking, wise-cracking imp that had been imprisoned in a bowling trophy for 30 years?

The movie, which was shot in nine days for only $90,000, opens with a trio of lovable losers in their dorm room: Keith is lying in bed gawking at a *Penthouse* magazine, Jimmie is lounging with a 6-pack of Budweiser resting on his stomach, and Calvin is sitting inches away from a TV with his eyes fixated on a monster movie. Their plans change once they realize it's Initiation Night for Tri-Delta, a sorority so prestigious they currently only have three members. Spying through the window and then sneaking in the house to get a better view, they watch in amazement as the two pledges—played by Stevens and Bauer—are bent over and having their backsides paddled for a ridiculous amount of time. Next, they are covered with whipped cream, seemingly for no other reason than to warrant a shower scene. The boys are caught peering through the bathroom door and are then ordered to accompany the pledges for the final stage: breaking into the local bowling alley and bringing back a trophy.

As you would imagine in a movie like this, the guys are total horndogs, but what is surprising is just how amiable they all are; it's clear that their hearts are in the right place. They remind me so much of Elliott (that no-good son of the Coopers) and his friends in *Troll 2* and that's pretty much the greatest possible compliment of all time. The bowling alley is located inside a shopping mall, which *Chopping Mall* and *Dawn of the Dead* has taught us is a marvelous setting for horror, but *Sorority Babes* never focuses on fear, just good-natured fun as the teens unexpectedly run into a hearing impaired janitor (hilariously played by George "Buck" Flower with his trademark southern drawl) who has accidentally locked himself in the closet, a street-tough girl named Spider on a mission to break into every cash register and pinball machine she sees, and a mischievous little imp who likes to grant wishes and turn innocent bystanders into bloodthirsty demons. Cast members Linnea Quigley and Hal Havins would experience further demon possession that same year in the crowd-pleasing *Night of the Demons*. Amusing gags include a severed head attempting a strike, a body being pulled apart like taffy, the Bride of Frankenstein gleefully wielding an axe, and magic radiation that causes escape to be futile.

Just as long as you shut your brain off and embrace the weirdness, *Sorority Babes in the Slimeball Bowl-O-Rama* will be a highlight in any movie marathon and with its zany, idiosyncratic charm, give you a second wind to stay awake for another two films.

Horror Galore

"I DON'T KNOW HOW MANY YEARS ON THIS EARTH I GOT LEFT. I'M GONNA GET REAL WEIRD WITH IT"

Anguish (1987)
Director: Bigas Luna
Writers: Bigas Luna, Michael Berlin
Cast: Michael Lerner, Talia Paul, Clara Pastor, Zelda Rubinstein, Angel Jove

I was feeling a bit of anguish when in early October 2017, the Hollywood Theatre finally announced the date for their 2nd Annual All-Night Horror Movie Marathon. Attending the first one, which sold out just a couple of hours after tickets went on sale, was an unbelievably cool experience. We entered Portland's most beautiful theater not having any idea what films we would be watching, and were then treated to rare 35mm prints of *Race with the Devil*, *Burial Ground*, and two of my favorites, *Psycho II* and *The Funhouse*, as well as a scattering of fun, obscure horror trailers while gorging on popcorn, pizza, candy, donuts, beer, and of course, coffee. Just before the sun started to peek out, we were all deliriously lumbering out of the theater as if we were imitating the Italian gut-munching zombies from the final feature. Feeling so excited about participating in another marathon, I knew the risk when I made vacation plans for the Halloween season several weeks in advance, and that there was a 25% chance that this year's all-night marathon would take place on the one Saturday where I'd be several hundred miles away. Of course that's what ended up happening.

After returning from my vacation and finding out that the lineup had included my beloved *Tourist Trap* (which I've never seen in a theater before), and an '80s slasher I had been wanting to see for years, *Anguish*, I could at least take comfort in knowing that on the very same day this event took place, my itinerary consisted of something even more epic: driving around the Salt Lake City area, heavily graced in autumn's majesty, and seeing the filming locations of *Troll 2* and *Halloween 4: The Return of Michael Myers* in person! Hollywood curator Dan Halstead once again did an excellent job in finding films perfect for the occasion because tonight, nearly three years later, I discovered just how appropriate *Anguish* is for a crowded movie theater. It's on the same level as seeing *Jaws* projected while floating on a raft, *The Shining* at The Stanley Hotel in Estes Park (another iconic and unforgettable stop during my road trip), and *Night of the Living Dead* in a cemetery.

Anguish opens with William Castle-like showmanship as a title card reads "During the film you are about to see, you will be subject to subliminal messages and mild hypnosis. This will cause you no physical harm or lasting effect, but if for any reason you lose control or feel that your mind is leaving your body, leave the auditorium immediately." A voice provides one final piece of advice: not for one moment should you speak to someone you don't know during the projection. Then a slow ticking of a grandfather clock and even slower snail crawling to the edge of a table take us inside the home of nerdy adult John (played by character actor Michael Lerner), kissing one of his many pet birds while his mother crochets in her rocking chair. She's played by Zelda Rubinstein and she uses her trademark whispery rasp and visuals like the spinning spiral from a record and an eyeball taped to the clock's pendulum rod to hypnotize her son, an optometrist's assistant who is ironically losing his own sight, into committing murders and removing the victim's eyes for a strange collection. "All the eyes of the city will be ours," she proclaims while ensuring that the woman who verbally abused John at the eye clinic will understand what true suffering is all about. So will some of the people who decided to see an afternoon screening of the 1925 silent adventure *The Lost World*.

Elsewhere, two teenaged friends discover that there are far worse problems than seeing their bag of popcorn reduced to the final few kernels, and… Nah, I can't in good conscience reveal anything more about the plot because this was one of those occasions where I thanked my lucky stars for not having seen any trailers or reviews beforehand. It may seem like your typical throat-slashing, eye-plucking sleaze-fest at first, but it doesn't take long before this movie lays its cards on the table and you discover it's playing an entirely different game. According to Microsoft Word, I'm on page 185 of this book and haven't written WTF once (god knows how many *Seinfeld* references I've already used), and so I'm glad I could save this prestigious euphemism for *Anguish*, a deserving and underseen movie that continues to beguile even while the ending credits roll. If you want to feel like a wild and crazy guy or gal while watching this film, then either take a shot whenever you see a terrible mustache or an adult consoling a terrified girl.

The Boy from Hell (2004)

Director: Mari Asato
Writers: Seiji Tanigawa, Naoteru Yamamoto, Hideshi Hino (comic)
Cast: Mirai Yamamoto, Mitsuru Akaboshi, Baku Numata, Hanae Shoji

Being alone with my negative thoughts is something I try to avoid whenever possible and so I've always needed some source of noise to help me sleep. Through various stages of my life, I've depended on The Weather Channel, new age music, a fan, DVD commentary tracks, a sound machine set to thunderstorms or ocean waves, and most often these nights, podcasts. Late last night I was listening to an episode of the *Horrorble Podcast* from 2017, and just when the Melatonin started kicking in, the witty guys from Kentucky started reviewing an hourlong Japanese curiosity called *The Boy from Hell* which left them in a state of shock—their descriptions of the insane plot were more than enough to make sure that my dreams were even stranger than usual. But as crazy as my dreams ended up being (visiting my childhood home to discover there's an ocean in the backyard and that Judge Reinhold lives next door?!), it's nothing compared to actually watching the movie the following day.

It's based on a story from popular manga artist Hideshi Hino, who actually introduces the film much like R.L. Stine did for the *Goosebumps* series. I only learned the word "manga" recently after perusing a Barnes & Noble large enough to accommodate an escalator and finding entire shelves devoted to these Japanese graphic novels, but it turns out I was already familiar with one of Hino's earlier works. Way back in 1985, he wrote and directed *Guinea Pig: Flower of Flesh and Blood*, which gained a little bit of notoriety when Charlie Sheen alerted the FBI after a viewing because he was certain he had just witnessed a kidnapped woman being chopped into

"I Don't Know How Many Years On This Earth I Got Left. I'm Gonna Get Real Weird With It"

pieces. Stupid curiosity got the better of me one day and I regrettably subjected myself to a couple nauseating scenes, on a sunny weekend afternoon, no less, when I should have been out frolicking through a sprinkler instead. Never would I have guessed that the filmmaker would go onto have such a successful career as an artist, and that one of his works would inspire a movie that filled me with such glee.

Being a manga virgin might have made me more susceptible to the nuances and imagery of *The Boy from Hell* because I kept having to pause it just to do research on what the hell I was witnessing. Repeatedly I needed confirmation that this was technically a movie. I can't wait to show this one to friends because it'll be fun seeing what aspect from the opening scene, depicting a casual drive in the countryside, will make them laugh the hardest. Will it be the hilariously cheap green screen effects? The soap opera overacting? Or the little boy who gets Hereditaried when the car swerves? Considering the ultimate gut-punch that was Charlie's demise, something that makes me terribly sad just thinking about it, it was strangely fulfilling to react to another minor dying the same way with an incredulous gasp followed by howls of laughter. And if that sounds the least bit insensitive, then let's just see you keep a straight face during this scene! No chance in hell!

The boy's mother, a well-respected surgeon, is devastated over the accident and chooses not to listen to her devoted servant reminding her that no medical science could have saved him, but to the haggard woman in the cemetery who might know how to bring him back. The following day, she tricks a cancer-stricken boy into thinking that he's finally leaving the hospital (which looks more like Dracula's Castle), and just after he expresses his delight at returning home, the film abruptly cuts to a shot of the boy hanging upside down in a cemetery and crying directly over the grave of her son.

With a quick slash of the throat, the blood spills and awakens the corpse beneath the soil. Mother and son may be reunited, but he's hideously deformed, fanged, and addicted to flesh and blood (which doesn't make him particularly accepted by other kids on the soccer field), and she's considering other options like a brain transplant.

This 50-minute film also finds time for plastic ducks, a detective with a cartoonishly large nose, and an acid-tripped vision of hell where women and children are first to be mallet-mangled and snacked on in a story essentially about a grief-stricken young mother who'll do anything to keep the light of her life shining no matter how much darkness it spreads to the rest to the world. There's also a score that's blatantly derivative of Goblin's "Profondo Rosso" from *Deep Red*, but once it infuses electric guitars during the ending credits, it suddenly sounds less like a rip-off and more like a new and improved remix.

Dementia: Daughter of Horror (1955)
Writer and Director: John Parker
Cast: Adrienne Barrett, Bruno VeSota, Ben Roseman, Richard Barron, Ed Hinkle

It wasn't until I scrolled through the YouTube comments of Faith No More's video for "Separation Anxiety," from their 2015 comeback album *Sol Invictus*, that I learned all of the clips came from the same silent horror-noir that was shown during the iconic theater sequence of *The Blob* (1958). Then I saw that it was available to watch for free online, and so I cut my solo Faith No More party short and watched this bizarre 55-minute movie, hoping that the strawberry-banana smoothie I was drinking wasn't going to morph into face-melting jelly from outer space.

While none of the characters utter a single word, *Dementia: Daughter of Horror* isn't your typical silent picture because instead of intertitles, it has dubbed sound effects and a narrator, whose booming voice tells us in the beginning, "You, you out there. Do you know what horror is? Smug, confident, secure because you're sane, do you know what madness is or how it strikes?" After director John Parker repeatedly clashed with the New York Censor Board and was only able to get his movie screened a single time in two years, producer Jack H. Harris took over the distribution and added all of that narration, which many reviewers called unnecessary, goofy, or distracting. But when this voice comes from Ed McMahon himself and he's personally inviting us "into the tormented, haunted, half-lit night of the insane," I personally wouldn't want it any other way.

First-time actress Adrienne Barrett (looking a little like Arcade Fire's Régine Chassagne) plays a woman waking up from bad dreams alone in a hotel room. A light outside her window provides a pulsating strobe that would drive anyone bonkers after a few minutes, and so it's understandable why she's anxious to leave and wander the streets, but not before spying on a drunken neighbor down the hall being arrested for domestic abuse. While all the normal people are slumbering under the covers, she joins the seedy nightlife and its colorful after-hours cast of characters that include pimps, doped-up flower peddlers, vagrants in dark alleys who grasp a liquor bottle in one hand and grope passersby with the other, cigar-smoking men flaunting their wealth, and a newspaper boy (here played by Angelo Rossitto from *Freaks* and *Mad Max Beyond Thunderdome*) who finds morbid amusement in the "Mysterious Stabbing" cover story.

The newspaper's front page seems to follow the woman along her odyssey—where she trades off being the hunter and the hunted—through penthouse balconies, libertine jazz clubs, limousine rides, streets patrolled by corrupt policemen, and a misty graveyard that conjures up disturbing flashbacks of drunken Father shooting to death the flagrantly adulterous Mother before receiving a knife to the back from a little girl discovering that her secret talent is stabbing.

Cinematographer William C. Thompson, who shot Ed Wood's most famous films, captures the haunting nuances of film noir and gets the most out of vulnerable characters being followed by their shadow, chased by blinding headlights, and preyed upon by black-masked "ghouls of insanity." And much like another black and white nightmarish journey through expressionism, *Carnival of Souls*, this movie has just the right score to make viewers feel as mentally unstable as its heroine; right from the beginning it reminded me of *Creepshow*'s "Something to Tide You Over" music with its wailing ghostly female moans, but maybe that's because when we first hear it, someone is being gulped up by ocean waves.

The Evil Within (2017)

Writer and Director: Andrew Getty
Cast: Frederick Koehler, Sean Patrick Flanery, Dina Meyer, Michael Berryman, Brianna Brown

Even before I knew any details of the fascinating backstory, it was evident from the meticulously shot and edited opening scene—a dream sequence centering on a little boy named Dennis and his mother wandering around a dusty carnival—that *The Evil Within* was created by a unique voice and uncompromised vision. The boy is ecstatic that the lack of guests means they don't have to wait in line for the haunted house dark ride that boasts to be the scariest one in the world, only to be let down as it reveals itself to be just a short dark tunnel without a spook in sight. Feeling justifiably ripped off, the boy looks up at his mother and suggests they ask for a

"I Don't Know How Many Years On This Earth I Got Left. I'm Gonna Get Real Weird With It"

refund, and what happens next officially makes this one of the most satisfying dream scenes in years.

Dennis grows up to be a man suffering from mental disabilities and the same types of nightmares that haunted him as a child. John is his older brother and legal guardian, loving and dedicated, but being persuaded slowly but surely by his girlfriend to place Dennis in a facility so that he can focus more on their future together. "I said I wanted a baby. I meant the small kind, the cute kind, not the 30-year-old masturbating kind," she protests. While in the midst of renovating their large house, John asks if he can store an antique mirror in Dennis' room just for a couple of days, and it turns out to be a colossal error when Dennis' articulate and confident reflection starts persuading him to do very bad things to prove that he's just as smart as everyone else and unwilling to be lied to any more.

Watching a mentally challenged man kill animals and little kids before moving on to the people he genuinely cares about sounds about as fun as the straight-to-video horror films from the early 2000s named after the most notorious serial killers, but *The Evil Within* is an entirely different beast. It's unsettling for sure, but it's safe to say you've never seen anything quite like it. Some will find it grating like I did for a short time, but then the central story materializes and reveals a thoroughly compelling, mystifying, and head-scratching descent into depravity.

Not only will horror fans rejoice in seeing a fingertip-biting demon played by Michel Berryman terrorize a house of mirrors and literally unzip someone's body to crawl inside, but Matthew McGrory (who played Tiny Firefly in *House of 1000 Corpses*) even makes a cameo, a surprising reveal considering this larger-than-life actor passed away over a decade before *The Evil Within* made its world premiere at Fantasporto Film Festival in Portugal. Writer and director Andrew Getty, grandson of Getty Oil Company founder and kazillionaire J. Paul Getty, began production of his debut film The Storyteller all the way back in 2002, basing it on some of the nightmares he experienced as a child, as well as brainstorm sessions exploring the possibility that David "Son of Sam" Berkowitz's claims of a dog telling him to commit murder were true. Illnesses and lawsuits halted production numerous times, but those delays were nothing compared to the amount of time he spent inside his mansion working on elaborate special effects and making every cut, sound effect, and visual effect just right. It's commendable that anyone would devote so many years to a single project, but the downside is that there's no guarantee of staying alive long enough to see its completion. Getty, who had been working on The Storyteller for 13 years and who had become addicted to methamphetamine, passed away in 2015, leaving producer Michael Luceri in charge of the finishing touches and a title change to this strange, strange movie.

For a film that took over 15 years to get made, it's a real shame that the cover art was designed so blithely. I love Michael Berryman as much as the next guy and I'm glad he's in this movie, but when a 2017 movie shows him front and center and shirtless with a boring gray background, it's easy to assume it has little else going for it. It's the kind of cover you're conditioned to pass over on Tubi before even checking out the synopsis, so maybe they should have showcased something like the animatronic octopus percussionist (who would be too massive to play with the Rock-afire Explosion at Showbiz Pizza) or giant head-deflating spider instead.

Horror Galore

Lobby card for *Private Parts* (1972), MGM, Premier Productions

Private Parts (1972)

Director: Paul Bartel
Writers: Philip Kearney, Les Rendelstein, Paul Bartel
Cast: Ayn Ruymen, Lucille Benson, John Ventantonio, Laurie Main, Stanley Livingston

To pay tribute to cult cinema icon Paul Bartel on the 20th anniversary of his passing, I finally watched his first directorial feature, the horror-comedy *Private Parts*, which has absolutely nothing to do with Howard Stern. It was produced by MGM but then delegated to a subsidiary once the initial test screenings proved to be disastrous, and its theatrical run was so disappointing that it took decades before it even received a VHS release. But now these private parts are ready to fill the desire of so many people in 2020 who are clamoring to be transported to a simpler time of twisted psychosexual '70s sleaze.

Those of you who found the colorful background characters in *Basket Case*'s Hotel Broslin to be every bit as memorable as Belial will surely enjoy your stay at Skid Row's King Edward Hotel, where teenaged Cheryl escapes to after running off with her grouchy roommate's wallet following an argu-

"I Don't Know How Many Years On This Earth I Got Left. I'm Gonna Get Real Weird With It"

ment. It's owned by Cheryl's elderly aunt Martha Atwood, who agrees to let her stay for a few days just as long as she doesn't wander around the hotel alone since it's no place for little girls, a stipulation that is quickly ignored. While Martha is away at a stranger's funeral, fulfilling a hobby of trying to photograph the exact moment when the spirit leaves the body, Cheryl steals the set of keys so that she can enter the rooms of the residences and learn of their peculiar eccentricities and fetishes.

There's a flamboyant and heavyset reverend interested in astrology, numerology, and a BDSM lifestyle, and there's also a senile old woman who goes to great lengths to convince herself that her beloved Alice wasn't murdered in the same hotel years ago, but the guest that Cheryl is most interested in is the mysterious, good-looking photographer George with nudie mag wallpaper and a water-filled sex doll (with oddly appropriate facial expressions). She also notices that the room next to hers contains holes in the walls so that its voyeuristic occupant can spy on her in her bedroom and the communal bathroom, a revelation that provokes more excitement than revulsion, even as her stalker becomes increasingly brazen and creepy. What she doesn't find during her rounds, however, is the body of her roommate's boyfriend who, while searching for her and the stolen money, was decapitated and incinerated in a shocking scene that gives this impossible-to-categorize movie some real horror legitimacy.

A role like Cheryl is a demanding one for any actress, especially one making her film debut, but Ayn Ruymen was up for the challenge and she's a huge reason why this movie is so damn entertaining. The fact that she looks ten years older than the girl she's playing is no problem for a movie as weird as this. Lucille Benson is also a lot of fun as the mysterious Aunt Martha, sermonizing about how the body is a prison for the soul that longs to be somewhere else, and about how this rundown hotel that collects oddballs is the last respectable establishment in the city. Given the professionalism of the camerawork, I had a feeling that cinematographer Andy Baker would have an impressive IMDb list, but I wasn't expecting anything quite on the epic level of a directorial credit for *The Fugitive*, a movie so perfect that it could have only been improved with one of those classic cameos from Paul Bartel. Now I can't help but fantasize about Paul's sanctimonious characters in *Rock 'n' Roll High School*, *Piranha*, or *Eating Raoul*, for example, interacting with a very annoyed and stone-faced Deputy Samuel Gerard.

Shrunken Heads (1994)

Director: Richard Elfman
Writers: Matthew Bright, Charles Band
Cast: Julius Harris, Meg Foster, Aeryk Egan, Rebecca Herbst, Darris Love, Bo Sharon

After several days of wallowing in the depths of Full Moon releases and being pulled down to the muck and mire by evil bongs, weedjies, killer eyes, and ooga boogas, my sunken treasure chest eventually shined on a trio of shrunken heads. Had I picked this off the video shelves when it came out in 1994, it probably would have been an instant favorite because it seems especially catered to nobody else in the world except middle schoolers with a very dark sense of humor. While clearing out the doldrums this morning, I had to convince myself that *Shrunken Heads* was an actual film that I watched last night and not just the craziest dream I've had in years. As much fun as it would be to go into the all the WTFs and describe this absurd plot in great detail, I feel this is a movie you'll want to go into as cold as possible, and so I'll keep the synopsis brief.

Three kids in New York City spend an afternoon discussing whether Green Lantern is better than Crypto when the local gang The Vipers, led by greaser Vinnie Benedetti, stop by to rip up their comic books and call them terrible names. Vowing revenge on these thugs, they videotape the gang wreaking havoc on the neighborhood late at night and give the evidence to the police. Crime boss Big Mo (Meg Foster in a role she clearly enjoyed) is furious to see the gang members arrested and orders a hit on the three kids responsible. She'll need to be watching over her shoulder though because local Haitian voodoo priest and newspaper stand owner Mr. Sumatro has the most unorthodox methods for fighting back against injustice in the world.

With zany sensibilities and a playful soundtrack by Danny Elfman and Richard Band (often sounding strikingly similar to "Jack and Sally Montage" from Elfman's *The Nightmare Before Christmas* soundtrack), I almost paused the film so I could doublecheck online that *Shrunken Heads* was in fact a horror movie, but then something so shocking happened at about the 32-minute mark that answered my question definitively.

Shrunken Heads is a movie I can't believe ever got greenlit but you could always count on mid '90s Full Moon to go against convention at every opportunity. This was only Richard Elfman's second film, coming a whopping 12 years after *Forbidden Zone*, a musical fantasy that features performances of the band he formed with brother Danny, Oingo Boingo, and much like *Texas Chainsaw Massacre 2*, *Shrunken Heads* also features their song "No One Lives Forever" over a hazardous nighttime driving sequence. Yet another Elfman (Richard's son Bodhi) plays one of the gang members who may or may not contract a mysterious disease with side effects such as a "peculiar shuffling gait, a total loss of bowel control, and a compulsion to pick up litter and clean graffiti," as a newscaster describes. Also leading the cast is Rebecca Herbst, playing a 15-year-old girl named Sally (hey, another *Nightmare Before Christmas* connection) who wears tube tops, hangs out with ruffians that look twice her age, and whose virginity plays a pivotal role in the climax, and so that's a little weird, but then again, so is everything else in this movie. If she happens to be signing autographs at a convention, it's more likely for a soap opera convention due to her appearances in about 2,000 episodes of *General Hospital* than at a horror convention for the time a flying severed head nestled up against her chest.

For further excursions into horror at its weirdest, you might want to consider the surreal 1982 French film *Litan*, about a couple whose vacation takes an unexpected turn when they get wrapped up in the Festival of the Dead, a holiday that inspires the locals to wear the creepiest masks they can find and act all loony. I was in love with the first half of the movie, a fever dream involving waterfalls, caves, tunnels, a hospital that looks like a spaceship one floor and a torture dungeon the next, a coffin cruising down the river, hundreds of unsettling costumes on adults and children alike, and fog so thick that our main characters keep accidentally bumping into frightening things. But then the confusion kept mounting and the movie became less fun when I wasn't able to understand with my shrunken head the extraterrestrial bodysnatching masterplan involving glowing blue worms in the water.

HORROR LEGENDS SHARING THE SCREEN

Black Friday (1940)

Director: Arthur Lubin
Writers: Curt Siodmak, Eric Taylor, Edmund L. Hartmann
Cast: Stanley Ridges, Boris Karloff, Bela Lugosi, Anne Nagel, Anne Gwynne

Black Friday opens with a newspaper headline reading "Condemned Man Refuses to Break Silence Held During Sensational Trial." We're then introduced to the eminent surgeon Ernest Sovac (Boris Karloff) as he walks the green mile and hands his journals over to the one reporter who treated him fairly. Through flashbacks it's revealed that his best friend, Professor George Kingsley, was an innocent bystander during a hit on one gangster by another. With the gangster paralyzed and Professor Kingsley left brain-damaged, the surgeon decides to secretly perform the first-ever human brain transplant in hopes of saving his best friend's life and quite possibly learning the whereabouts of a hidden $500,000. Screenwriter Curt Siodmak would revisit the reliable theme of brain-transplantation in films such as *House of Frankenstein*, *Creature with the Atom Brain*, *Earth vs. the Flying Saucers*, and *Donovan's Brain*.

It all goes down like fine wine and serves as a pleasant reminder of why Lugosi and Karloff, previously working together on *The Black Cat* (1932) and *Son of Frankenstein* (1939), were Universal's two biggest icons, even though at this point, Bela was on a downward trajectory and relegated to a supporting role here. Notwithstanding his limited screen time, his face and name commanded just as much of the frame as Karloff's in the marketing materials, and most of the trailer was devoted to a publicity stunt in which Lugosi was purportedly hypnotized before shooting a scene to accentuate the horrors of suffocating in a locked closet. The two legends don't share a single scene together, sadly, but the story is strong enough to keep you from yearning for a monster mash rematch, and to be honest, Stanley Ridges is the real star of *Black Friday*. With his seamless duality in a Dr. Jekyll and Mr. Hyde spectacle, we're often forgetting that it's the same actor playing both roles. He's a meek and mild-mannered professor trying to get his life back together, but every now and then the war inside his head is won by the smooth-talking criminal Red Cannon, determined to get revenge on the mobsters who double-crossed him and a former lover who may have been culpable.

Watching this film on the titular "holiday" wouldn't be a bad move at all, as it's a gentle and engrossing thriller that the whole family can enjoy together in between rounds of Thanksgiving leftovers, but it's even more appropriate for Friday the 13th, the actual setting. As we learned from *Freddy vs. Jason*, Mr. Vorhees doesn't mind a little healthy competition.

Poster for *The Gorgon* (1964), Hammer Film Productions, Columbia

The Gorgon (1964)

Director: Terence Fisher
Writers: John Gilling, J. Llewellyn Devine (story)
Cast: Richard Pasco, Peter Cushing, Christopher Lee, Barbara Shelley, Michael Goodliffe

As someone who is for the most part unmotivated and aimless, it boggles the mind how anyone could be as productive as Terence Fisher was when he managed to direct 18 Hammer films in a span of only 15 years. Considering the majority of his works were quite good, I can only assume he had either sold his soul to the devil or discovered the most amazing drugs and refused to share. In any case, *The Gorgon* is one of his very best, and the only Hammer film inspired by Greek mythology.

In the early 20th century, a strange string of murders cripples the backwoods European village of Vandorf, and rather than entertain the possibilities of gods, monsters, and curses, everyone there turns a blind eye and grasps only for logical explanations and conspiracies. The father of the latest victim, however, is determined to discover the truth, and he finds it within the crumbling ruins of Castle Borski (a set recycled from a couple of Hammer Frankenstein films), long abandoned and always welcome to autumn leaves and doomed souls. Locking eyes with a snake-haired lady sends him running for the hills, and also for a pen and paper so he can quickly write a letter to his other son before it's too late. Having to hurriedly document such critical events all while your body is turning to stone is a kind of horror I hadn't seen before.

The very dashing Richard Pasco makes for a likable and sympathetic protagonist as Paul, losing both his father and brother in the same week and receiving one of the scariest letters imaginable, which brings him to Vandorf to find out just what in the hell is going on. He doesn't get much cooperation from Dr. Namaroff, cryptically played by Peter Cushing, but his beautiful assistant Carla is seemingly the only one in town willing to accept the fact that bodies turning into stone is not normal. Christopher Lee, who gets top billing, doesn't appear much at all until the final 30 minutes but he definitely makes excellent use of his screen time, whether he's mocking an officer for using long words that don't suit him or threatening anyone that tries to get in his way.

Even if you're among those who complain about Hammer films being slow and overly talky, a good gorgonizing might hit the spot. Heavy on dread and atmosphere, and filmed in lush Technicolor, this is a beautiful world created, and even the characters seem to think so because at one point, Paul pauses his nighttime stroll just to stare longingly at a fountain, with dead leaves mingling with the reflection of the full moon. *The Gorgon* also tells a compelling and spooky story that wisely sacrifices comprehensive explanations to keep its running time at a brisk 83 minutes. Some of the special effects are disappointing and I wish Medusa's sister had made a stronger impact at the climax, but this film still stands out in Hammer's extensive catalog.

Tales of Terror (1962)

Director: Roger Corman
Writers: Richard Matheson, Edgar Allan Poe (stories)
Cast: Vincent Price, Peter Lorre, Basil Rathbone, Maggie Pierce, Joyce Jameson, Debra Paget

You really can't go wrong with any of the eight films that Roger Corman produced and directed from 1960-1965 based on the works of Edgar Allan Poe. *The Masque of the Red Death* and *The Pit and the Pendulum* seem to be the most popular and best-reviewed of the bunch, and out of the remaining six, my highest recommendation goes to *Tales of Terror* because it's nearly impossible to compete against Vincent Price starring as three different characters!

In the first of three tales adapted by Richard Matheson, Price plays a man living alone in a cobwebbed and dilapidated mansion that's in constant danger of being swept away by the angry ocean. One day he receives an unexpected visit from his long-lost daughter who he blamed for the death of his beloved wife Morella 26 years ago. "When she died, I died with her," he tells her, "All that remained of me was this walking corpse, this shell, this ghost of flesh." His cold demeanor changes upon learning of his daughter's terminal illness, and then he tearfully apologizes for his neglect and begs for her to stay with him for a while, even though happy reunions are nearly impossible in gloomy houses where spirits refuse to be restfully entombed. "Morella" contains excellent performances, production design, and music to distract from the confusing plot.

My favorite of the three segments is "The Black Cat," which also incorporates elements of another Poe tale, "The Cask of Amontillado." Peter Lorre plays Montresor Herringbone, a man who certainly won't be winning any "Husband of the Year" awards with his abhorrent behavior and nightly routine of taking his wife's money to appease his alcoholism. After getting kicked out of a tavern during his latest binge, he stumbles into another one that is hosting an event for wine connoisseurs, and challenges the esteemed Fortunato Luchresi in a tasting competition. Price's facial expressions during this scene, whether he's extracting as much flavor as he possibly can with his dandy sips or reacting in horror at his challenger's unorthodox method of tasting, will bring sunshine to even the darkest days. Same goes for when he, after helping Montresor get home safely and meeting his wife Annabelle, affectionately lights up at the sight of their cat, to whom he calls "that lovely cat" and "that handsome fellow." As it purrs on his lap, Annabelle stares into the eyes of this handsome stranger and suddenly the drunken snores coming from her obnoxious brute of a husband seem a million miles away. Chances are very slim they could live happily ever after in a Poe tale, even one that is loosely adapted, but I still couldn't resist cheering them on. In a clever publicity stunt that resulted in a photo in *Life* magazine, the studio held a casting call in which hundreds of people brought their handsome black cats in for an audition and the chance of a lifetime to be affectionately held by Price and abusively yelled at by Lorre.

I suspect that most people will declare that the best was saved for last, as "The Facts in the Case of M. Valdemar" is a reliably terrifying premise that would be further explored by George A. Romero to great results in 1990's *2 Evil Eyes*. Price plays the gravely ill Valdemar, who employs a hypnotist to alleviate the pain while on his deathbed, much to the displeasure of his loving wife and dedicated doctor, sharing a mutual distrust of this man who may have a couple of ulterior motives. Valdemar, he who can be named whenever you desire, ends up passing away while in a trance, leaving him trapped in a tiny, painful gap between life and death that the hypnotist (played by Basil Rothbone in great villain form) refuses to release him from.

Roger Corman, Richard Matheson, Vincent Price, and Peter Lorre proved to be such a dream team with *Tales of Terror* that they joined forces again a year later with *The Raven*, easily the goofiest of Corman's Poe pictures but one of the most entertaining.

AND YOU THOUGHT THE GRISWOLDS HAD IT ROUGH: THE WORST VACATIONS EVER

American Gothic (1987)

Director: John Hough
Writers: Burt Wetanson, Michael Vines
Cast: Sarah Torgov, Rod Steiger, Yvonne De Carlo, Janet Wright, Caroline Barclay

One of my more successful movie nights in high school transpired after finally renting *American Gothic*, which had a VHS cover that caught my eye ever since the earliest days at the horror aisle. It's a faithful replica of the iconic painting of the same name, but with lightning in the sky, a group of youngsters screaming in the upstairs window, and blood dripping off farmer Rod Steiger's pitchfork. I've always been appreciative of this movie for being such a hit with me and my three guests on a celebratory occasion, but it's one I've been hesitant to revisit since it could never be as much fun as the first time. Thankfully, I would learn that it's simply impossible to feel maudlin when watching Rod Steiger, Yvonne De Carlo, and their three "children" clash with a group of Seattleites.

Now with a much larger television and a Shout Factory Blu-ray full of glorious pixels, I was able to notice just how lovely the overhead footage of the Pacific Northwest looks during the opening credits, but not even the most enchanting of shots could distract from that absurdly out-of-place, 80's sitcom-reject theme song. It was filmed at Bowen Island near Vancouver, British Columbia, the same

Poster for **American Gothic** (1987), Virgin Vision, Vidmark Entertainment

location used in *The Fog* and *The Wicker Man*, and the reason this sentence won't end with a trio of exclamation points is because we're talking about the remakes.

Horror Galore

A group of six are forced to make an unexpected landing after plane trouble derails their camping trip, and while the pilot tends to the mechanics, one of the women decides to go scuba-diving. Cynthia, the most likable of the bunch, watches her slip off a rock and land so rough that her head submerges underwater for a dangerous amount of time, triggering a traumatic flashback of the accidental drowning death of her baby, an event that sent her to a mental institution. While her doctor hesitated to officially declare Cynthia cured, he felt she was ready for this idyllic vacation with her husband and friends, and so it's a cruel twist of irony when the island she gets trapped on is crazier than just about any asylum in existence.

A charming-looking house presents itself on this island they feared might be completely abandoned, and even though their knocks go unanswered, they enter anyway and immediately laugh at how it looks straight out of the 1920s. A phonograph and a closet full of old-fashioned attire inspires an impromptu dance session that ends when the gray-haired homeowners return. Ma and Pa, believing that any dance outside of the Charleston is sinful, aren't exactly pleased with their shenanigans but are willing to open their home to the strangers like any good Christians should.

At the dinner table, one of them is scolded for reaching for the bread before the Lord's prayer and another for not becoming a member of the "clean plate club," but the real weirdness comes with the introduction of their daughter, Fanny, who's about to celebrate her 12th birthday despite being about 50 years old. The tagline of the movie is "The family that slays together stays together," a sentiment proven the next day when Fanny and two other fully adult children (one of whom is played by familiar face Michael J. Pollard) add some malice to playtime, starting with pushing one of the guys a little too hard on a swing overlooking a cliff and continuing with a round of jump rope that's trickier than Double Dutch. The sanity that Cynthia recently reclaimed starts disappearing along with her dear friends, setting up an unpredictable, clever, and exciting battle of the crazies that ends perfectly.

You can't ask for more engaging villains than Pa and Ma, played by Rod Steiger and Yvonne De Carlo (no stranger to atypical families since she famously portrayed Lily Munster), declaring that there will be no devil's play in this house all while keeping a creepy mummified grandchild and a cellar full of mutilated corpses. They also refuse to believe in news stories or "contraptions" like telephones. It's a riot just seeing them interact with a bunch of well-educated city folks who see nothing wrong with sex before getting hitched.

Filmmaker John Hough was no stranger to the horror genre, having previous directed *The Legend of Hell House* and Disney's *Watcher in the Woods*, and just a few months after *American Gothic* came out, so did his poorly received fourth entry to *The Howling* franchise.

Bloody Pit of Horror (1965)

Director: Massimo Pupillo
Writers: Romano Migliorini, Roberto Natale
Cast: Mickey Hargitay, Walter Brandi, Luisa Baratto, Ralph Zucker, Rita Klein, Alfredo Rizzo

Even if an Italian film inspired by the Marquis de Sade where scantily-clad beauties are elaborately tortured in a castle isn't your cup of tea, this delicious slice of sleazy '60s Eurotrash will put a smile on your face. Irrespective of the dark subject matter, it just wants to have a good time, and clearly so did the voice actors who were cast to dub it in English. They aren't quite on the jaw-dropping level of Bob in Fulci's *House of the Cemetery*, but so many of these exchanges will have you in stitches. Another reason to have your volume turned up is for the groovy retro score, which is probably more suitable for a spooky beach setting than a torture dungeon.

A group of male photographers and their female models (sporting some unfortunate hairdos even for 1965 standards) arrive at a medieval castle in hopes of using it for a sexy Gothic photo shoot. They naturally decide to break in when nobody answers the door, much to the displeasure of the owner, a former actor who just wants to live in solitude. He eventually allows them to spend the night to complete their work, but his stern warnings to stay away from the dungeon are disobeyed even before he finishes his sentence since they can't resist utilizing devices like the pendulum for their seductive shoots. Suddenly, one of the models remembers that this castle used to belong to The Crimson Executioner, a sadist who delighted in torturing and butchering innocent people until he was caught and sentenced to death via one of his very own contraptions. Played by Hungarian actor and 1955 Mr. Universe Mickey Hargitay, the Crimson Executioner will pump you up with laughter thanks to his bright red tights, even brighter red hood, Zorro mask, and penchant for speaking in the third person, which can only be a good thing when you're named The Crimson Executioner! It's a rarity to find a villain who could pull off a line like "Mankind is made up of inferior creatures, spiritually and physically deformed, who would have corrupted the harmony of my perfect body!" while flexing to the camera.

One by one the trespassers are dispatched for their lascivious behavior, and while the gore is kept at a minimum to complement the strangely cheerful tone, this well-oiled and chiseled Crimson Executioner has a wild imagination and prances around in childish glee while unveiling diabolical methods that make the iron maiden look like amateur hour. Just wait until you see what he does with a poisonous spider! It's a contraption so confusing to the viewers that it has to be explained in meticulous detail by the trapped victim, one of many moments that's bound to elicit a big round of laughter from you and your fellow sadists.

Calibre (2018)

Writer and Director: Matt Palmer
Cast: Jack Lowden, Martin McCann, Tony Curran, Ian Pirie, Kate Bracken, Therese Bradley

Well, my trusted St. Louis Botanical Gardens notebook isn't going to be very helpful here, because after five minutes of frantically scribbling notes about how beautiful the remote Scottish countryside looked and how I wanted to travel there and stay at the same bed & breakfast, I was too invested in *Calibre* to look away from the screen for a second. Winner of Best British Film at its premiere at the Edinburgh International Film Festival and picked up by Netflix to very little publicity, it follows a similar path to thrillers like *A Simple Plan*, *Shallow Grave*, and *Deliverance*, where characters are overwhelmed by bad luck while trying to cover up a crime.

Soon-to-be husband and father Vaughn celebrates his last days of freedom by taking a weekend hunting trip with his old friend from boarding school, Marcus, who is now a businessman full of confidence and swagger. The first evening in the Scottish Highlands is spent inside the local pub, The Stag's Head, where they make a friendly acquaintance in a community leader named Logan, participate in a drinking game, dance to Aztec Camera's great 1987 hit "Somewhere in My Heart," and against the advice of a concerned patron, court a couple of attractive ladies, one of whom looks exactly like Clea DuVall (making it feel like an *American Horror Story: Asylum* reunion since Jack Lowden is the doppelganger of Evan Peters). Fighting off hangovers the next morning, our two leads head out to the mountain ranges and notice a deer in no time at all. A timid Vaughn, who has never hunted before in his life, doesn't notice the little boy standing directly behind it when he takes a shot.

Devastated and enraged, the boy's father aims his gun at Vaughn but ends up being shot and killed by Marcus. Believing that he'd never be able to make it in prison, he persuades Vaughn to go along with his plan that involves making their presence known as soon as possible further up the glistening mountain, having dinner at the pub as if nothing was wrong, and then returning to the scene of the crime at night to bury the bodies along with their camping supplies. Even with these dastardly deeds, we want so badly to see them survive this vacation from hell, but the locals, wrapped up in planning the annual solstice festival, keep interfering and causing their lies to unravel like a windsurfing mummy.

The award for Worst Night of Sleep for a Character in a 2018 Film would obviously go to poor Peter in *Hereditary*, but taking the silver medal would be *Calibre*'s Vaughn. I slept pretty horribly last night come to think of it, probably because I was temporarily denied closure from this adrenaline-pumping, nail-biting thriller when my girlfriend asked, with 17 minutes to go, if we could finish it tomorrow since it was getting late. With my eyes closed and all of the possible outcomes swimming in my head, I eventually had to take a Melatonin, figuring that five and a half hours of sleep is better than nothing. You wouldn't expect a production company with a quaint name like Wellington Films to deliver something this bleak and intense!

Dead End (2003)

Writers and Directors: Jean-Baptiste Andrea, Fabrice Canepa
Cast: Ray Wise, Lin Shaye, Alexandra Holden, Mick Cain, William Rosenfeld, Amber Smith

Several years ago, when writing for the website Geek Legacy, I had a recurring column called The Netflix Horror Shuffle Experiment, where I'd close my eyes and spend at least 30 seconds scrolling up and down on Netflix's horror offerings, moving the cursor all over the screen before randomly clicking on something to watch and review. The only requirement was that it had to be a title I was unfamiliar with, which was easy to achieve since Netflix's horror selection at the time specialized in titles that few people outside of the cast and crew cared about. A few of the films I selected must have gone in and out of my head like vapor because I cannot recall a single thing about them, but one movie that I'll never forget for as long as I live is *Dead End*, written and directed by first-time filmmakers from France. It pains me to realize that if my cursor had been just an inch away in any direction that afternoon, this incredible mind-trip of a movie might still be eluding me to this day.

On Christmas Eve, Frank Harrington is driving his family to the annual gathering at his mother-in-law's house, and decides to take the back roads for the first time in hopes that a change of scenery will make the drive less boring. For the most part it definitely feels like your typical American family, balancing sincerity and sarcasm, and indulging the mom when she requests a rendition of "Jingle Bells" to get her in the holiday spirit. With each passing minute they become increasingly mystified by how they aren't seeing a single car, intersection, or sign of civilization, and it's easy to imagine Rod Serling appearing on the side of the road, the smoke from his cigarette spiraling into the December sky as he explains just where these labyrinthine forested roads have taken the Harrington Family on this fateful Christmas Eve. Instead, on the side of the road appears a strange woman in white, cradling her baby, and apparently too shocked to answer any of Frank's questions.

This is essential viewing for *Twin Peaks* fans because Ray Wise practically relives the entire complicated, tortured spectrum of Leland Palmer, trying to maintain composure in impossibly stressful situations before succumbing to violent outbursts that quickly trigger remorse. Few actors can charm, delight, and frighten you to this degree in a single scene, and when he's intensely staring at the road ahead, guzzling whiskey that was intended to be a Christmas present and calling out to Laura, it seemed like this road was leading to the Black Lodge. In this case, the Laura he's calling out to is his wife, and you can't ask for a more entertaining and endearing actress to play her than the great Lin Shaye, who gets to be sympathetic, hilarious, and frightening as she sporadically loses her marbles throughout the night. One of many funny squabbles takes place in a forest ranger station when he tries to use the telephone to call for help. After saying "Damn!" she asks, "Was there no dial tone?" and he sarcastically shouts, "No, Laura, I just forgot the number for 911!"

There have been many horror movies that have depicted loving families dissolving amidst a night of terror, but few have benefitted more from its setting than *Dead End*. Their attempts at rationalizing the unexplainable turn fruitless, as is their ability to get off of that damn road. Being too weakened from heightened hysteria to keep their true feelings for each other (and their Christmas traditions) hidden creates utterly absorbing character arcs and added layers of dysfunction. The only thing holding this movie back from perfection is the character of the son, who has the exaggerated mannerisms and unabashed vulgarity of the kind of brat that was ubiquitous in raunchy '90s teen comedies. Not only is he played by an actor who looks 15 years too old for the part, but much like Jonesy in *Wrong Turn 2: Dead End*, he's so damn irritating (when he's not listening to his "Marilyn Bronson" CDs) that you can't wait for someone or something to shut his mouth for good.

If you have enough wintry drinks to keep you warm for a double feature, *Wind Chill* from 2007 also features characters who have their Christmas ruined by making an unwise detour to the middle of nowhere. Emily Blunt plays a student who uses the university rideshare board to find a ride home to Delaware for the holidays, and along the way her suspicions of the driver mount (the backstory of these two characters is easily the film's biggest strength), especially when he makes a spontaneous decision to take a more scenic route through the snowy countryside. Unable to maneuver through the winter wonderland, the car breaks down, making its passengers easy prey to frigid cold temperatures and all of the angry, charred spirits who haunt the road, but at least the radio is still capable of playing all their favorite Christmas carols.

Death Weekend (1976)

Writer and Director: William Fruet
Cast: Brenda Vaccaro, Don Stroud, Chuck Shamata, Richard Ayres, Don Granbery

It seems lately I've been blessed with the strange ability to grant new releases to films that have only been available on VHS or on Daily Motion with an audio track off sync by a couple seconds. All I have to do is write about them for this book and complain about their unjust neglect, and then in less than a week, a company like Synapse will announce a special edition Blu-ray and force me to go back and edit the reviews. I could save some time and not even mention how this is a really difficult film to track down, but what's the point of having a superpower if you don't use it? Besides, I'm really looking forward to having this on the shelf someday snuggled up against *Death Sentence* and *Death Wish*.

Long before Ivan Reitman directed marshmallow fellows, kindergarten officers, and unlikely twins in Hollywood, he was freezing in Canada while directing Eugene Levy in *Cannibal Girls* and producing David Cronenberg's *Shivers*. Another low-budgeted Canadian thriller he attached himself to was *Death Weekend*, later retitled to *The House by the Lake* in America so it could be the perfect dancing partner to *The Last House on the Left* on a rape-revenge drive-in double feature. It's more like a palette cleanser to Wes Craven's shocking debut because it offers all the thrills and catharsis without any of the unspeakable depravity that sends you to the shower or the Prozac bottle afterwards.

Wealthy dentist Harry and fashion model Diane are on route to his luxurious lakeside home to spend a weekend partying with a bunch of his friends and blossoming their newfound romance when she asks if she can take a turn driving his Corvette. She is skilled under the hood and also behind the wheel, and this comes in handy when a rowdy group of "goddamn greaseballs" terrorize them with their '67 Camaro. "Jesus, this broad can drive! That pisses me off!" barks the leader of the gang when his fragile male ego is left in the dust…and then in the lake.

Following this pedal to the medal adrenaline rush, a different kind of tension develops at the house due to Harry, with a soothing baritone that reminded me of Alan Alda, proving in so many ways that he's not exactly Mr. Right material. He repeatedly brags about liking "the biggest and the best of everything" and having total privacy on "his lake" since there are no other houses around. He also lied about inviting other people to the house for the weekend. Oh yeah, and he also spies on Diane through a one-way mirror and secretly photographs her while she showers. Yikes!

Thankfully, Diane is such a refreshingly headstrong character that even on a boat "with implications," she refuses the increasingly lecherous Glenn Quagmire in the flesh and stands up for herself. And if a gang of middle-aged drunkards were to say, storm onto the property *Straw Dogs* style and hold them hostage for a weekend of hell, as well as a feather-filled pillow fight that is anything but sexy, she's definitely not the type to meekly submit or depend on a boyfriend for protection. She might not be a skilled survivalist like Erin in *You're Next* or capable of rigging a house with boobytraps in under 15 minutes like a sleep-deprived Nancy Thompson, but she has a great head on her shoulders and it's riveting to watch her navigate through these ultra-realistic and unpredictable scenes of twisted mayhem. We can thank the movie gods that Brenda Vaccaro got over her hesitancy about starring in such a violent movie at a time when she was establishing herself as a friendly face on television because she absolutely shines in this multifaceted role that feels decades ahead of its time.

Director William Fruet's other horror contributions include *Spasms*, *Blue Monkey*, *Funeral Home*, and ten episodes of *Friday the 13th: The Series*. He has also directed far more episodes of the R.L. Stine anthology *Goosebumps* than anyone else, and seeing as how it's now September 21st and officially autumn, maybe revisiting his "The Haunted Mask II" and "Attack of the Jack-O-Lanterns" adaptations would be a fun way to kick off the Halloween season.

Demon Wind (1990)

Writer and Director: Charles Philip Moore
Cast: Eric Larson, Francine Lapensee, Lynn Clark, Jack Forcinito, Stephen Quadros

In the opening minutes of this fascinating mess of a movie, a woman has her farmhouse seized by evil forces that include her recently demonized husband. She defends herself by grabbing a sad-looking snow globe and smashing it against the floor, somehow knowing that it would cause everybody and everything in the vicinity to explode for some insane reason, a microcosm of the baffling and disjointed plot that makes *Demon Wind* such a guilty pleasure. Due to the nonsensical story and occasionally awful acting, it's easy to include it in the "so bad it's good" canon, but with the top-tier makeup effects, interesting locations, genuinely good cinematography, and several funny moments that were actually intentional, it might just be so good it's good. Even after two viewings in under 48 hours, as well as a few special features from the pristine Vinegar Syndrome Blu-ray, I still don't know what exactly to make of this movie other than that I'm certain to recommend it to anyone who thinks they have seen it all.

Shortly after the suicide of his father, a young man named Cory takes a road trip to the remnants of his grandparents' farmhouse to get a clearer understanding of the strange legends surrounding his family, but first he makes a stop at a secluded café that he had previously only seen before in dreams (sans clothing). Despite not knowing if this establishment actually existed, he deemed it an appropriate meeting place for his many friends, showing up in separate cars, who volunteered to show their support in his time of need. Among the group is a magician who makes the kind of entrance that Gob Bluth from *Arrested Development* envisioned in his delusions of grandeur, and although the movie is full of highlights, his hacky sack skills with the soda can is on a whole other level! With such an epic introduction, it's baffling how he loses the flamboyant outfit, live dove in pocket, and all traces of showmanship by the next scene, but a thousand times more baffling is how the group of friends react so lackadaisically to the first death they witness that day, when one of their own is transformed into a bloody doll whose final cryptic words should have haunted them to the core, but instead they just casually decide it's best that they go back inside the charred remains of the farmhouse.

Much like *Night of the Demons*, the characters are picked off by evil forces one by one and return with oozing pores and death metal vocals. Even those who manage to distance themselves from the farmhouse are magically transported right back by mysterious waves of fog, a creative element that I wish the movie had taken advantage of more. Demon Fog might have made for a more accurate title, but you sure can't fault the movie for being windless because the howls grace nearly every scene. Bonus points go to the creepy gas station attendant and his "What can I do you for?" greeting, an idiom I've admired ever since Dick Miller said it in *Night of the Creeps*. He even manages to provide helpful and accurate driving directions for a change!

Lisa and the Devil (1973)

Director: Mario Bava
Writers: Mario Bava, Alfredo Leone, Giorgio Maulini
Cast: Telly Savalas, Elke Sommer, Sylva Koscina, Alessio Orano, Gabriele Tinti

After a mesmerizing title sequence and score from Italian composer Carlo Savina puts us in a most delightful trance, we're further spellbound by the sights of Toledo, the "Imperial City" of central Spain, where a tourist named Lisa is traveling with a tour group. While everyone else is learning about a Medieval Christian painting depicting the Devil hauling away a man to meet his own version of hell, she is lured by a siren song coming from a music box and follows it to a nearby antique shop, where she has an unsettling encounter with a strange man and his lifelike mannequin. Nobody can blame Lisa for wanting to hear the Adagio section of Joaquin Rodrigo's *Concierto de Aranjuez* more closely because it's a magical piece of music that takes you to another world.

To say I'm directionally challenged would be an understatement, so my anxiety went through the roof as Lisa exits the gift shop and doesn't recognize any of her surroundings. She hopelessly scavenges through the twisty Visigoth alleys in hopes that the central square and traveling companions will appear, receiving no help from the joyless locals until she shrouds herself in headlight beams and flags down a car. A wealthy man (bearing an uncanny resemblance to Boris Karloff), his much-younger wife, and their driver agree to help Lisa but they don't make it far, as engine trouble leaves them stranded in front of a mansion owned by a blind Countess and her desperately lonely son, Maximilian, who invite them all inside just in time for an elaborate feast.

"The entire setting is so right for a tall tale of gloom and perdition," the young wife excitedly proclaims. "We can make one up as we go along. We have the right ingredients. The dark night, the house, it's all so spooky, don't you find, your ladyship?" And at times, it does feel like *Lisa and the Devil* is making everything up as it goes along, as a growing number of plotlines intersect with wild abandon, but rather than being frustrated that I couldn't follow the overly ambitious plot, I was just appreciative of the level of earnestness and passion to everything being said. Bava's exquisite style and the meticulous set arrangements are all wrapped up in a morbidly decadent package that touches on heavy topics like unrequited love, extramarital affairs, the desire to bring back a departed loved one at whatever cost, vengeful jealousy, and the torture of repeating the same mistakes to grasp a glimmer of elusive happiness.

As much as I would love to see this gorgeous movie presented in 35mm, I feel the personal themes would lose a little power if experienced with an audience, especially if it's filled with the kind of annoying Gen Z-ers who find hilarity in the sight of a rotary telephone. The occasional snicker is certainly warranted, however, due to lines of dialogue that look better than they sound, ridiculous reactions to finding a dead body (Nobody is going to ask how this happened?!), and having a goofy name like Maximillian said ad nauseum. Watching a man try to make love to a woman while the skeletal remains of his former lover mockingly cackle inches away is probably preferable in the comfort of your own home, and maybe that's why an early test screening went disastrously and prompted producer Alfredo Leone to do something drastic. Directing such masterpieces like *Black Sunday* and *Black Sabbath* should give a filmmaker carte blanche to do whatever he or she wants, but *Lisa and the Devil* was butchered unrecognizable when Leone decided to remove scenes like the awesome and terrifying airplane finale and inject new scenes that blatantly tried to capitalize on the success of *The Exorcist*, and with the assistance of Bava's son Lamberto (who would go onto direct the much-adored *Demons*), *Lisa and the Devil* was turned into *The House of Exorcism* in America, which flopped at the box office and depressingly became the de facto version of this film for many years. But now Bava's original vision is available on DVD and streaming services like Kanopy, and when you search for *The House of Exorcism* on Wikipidia, it takes you directly to something far better.

Wither (2012)

Directors: Sonny Laguna, Tommy Wiklund
Writers: Sonny Laguna, David Liljeblad,
Tommy Wiklund
Cast: Patrik Berg-Almkvisth, Lisa Henni, Patrick Saxe, Johannes Brost, Amanda Renberg

Coming out a year before Fede Álvarez's powerful, intense, and insanely violent *Evil Dead* remake, this Swedish film also features a group of young adults in a secluded cabin who find something sinister in the cellar that initiates a possess-a-thon. It also glorifies in the chopping up of bodies and dispensing viscera by the bucketloads, but wants you to cheer instead of cringe. Heads are caved in, mouths drilled, arms hacked off, eyeballs shot out, and bodies mangled in a wide variety of ways, and thanks to the majority of the film's budget seemingly allotted to the special effects crew and makeup department, the carnage looks absolutely terrific and makes the shortcomings all the easier to forgive.

There aren't even any attempts at character development (with the exception of an annoying couple defined by how much they like kissing each other at every single opportunity) as the group of seven are herded into the cabin and don't even get a chance to relax or enjoy a meal before one friend goes bonkers and gruesomely bites off the lips of another—a side effect from locking eyes with the mythological Medusa-like creature hiding beneath the floorboards. Why the hell this character journeyed down to this creepy basement, unannounced and alone, in the first place is anyone's guess, but this is a movie you'll want to turn your brain off for and just enjoy the psychotic ride. Suspecting that the youngsters have befallen a similar fate to that of his wife and daughter, a gun-toting man responds to the ruckus and demands to be let inside to examine the situation and blow the brains out of anyone dripping blood from every orifice and sporting shiny cataract-colored eyes.

Originality be damned, the relentlessly paced and action-heavy *Wither* really hit the spot on this Friday night in May 2020, as I'm losing patience with this quarantine and craving a woodsy cabin getaway (or any type of adventure) with friends, even if one of us has no choice but to bury another alive under a ferocious thunderstorm.

Horror Galore

CRUISING DOWN THE RIVER STYX WITH NO CRUCIFIX

Dark Angel: The Ascent (1994)
Director: Linda Hassani
Writer: Matthew Bright
Cast: Angela Featherstone, Daniel Markel, Charlotte Stewart, Nicholas Worth, Milton James

There was one year in the early '90s where I had a hard time exiting a video store without a videocassette from Full Moon in my hands because at a time when the horror genre was not exactly thriving with major studios, these strange and small-budgeted movies, often with eye-catching covers, were providing harmless and stupid fun on a consistent basis. I feared the relationship was souring when *Dollman vs. Demonic Toys* and *Lurking Fear* left me feeling cold, but fortunately Full Moon won me back, if only for a few more months, with *Dark Angel: The Ascent*, a major departure that felt fresh and relevant, and that actually had important things to say for a change.

Angela Featherstone, who would later make appearances in *The Wedding Singer* and an episode of *Seinfeld*, much to my delight, is perfectly cast as Veronica, a demon whose lifetime yearnings to see the world above Hell leads to face slaps from the authoritative, horned torturers. Her own father (who I thought I recognized as the racist, homophobic shop owner in *Falling Down* until IMDb proved me wrong) attempts to kill her when she refuses to apologize for her blasphemy and insubordination, but her mother (played by David Lynch regular Charlotte Stewart) intervenes and allows her a chance to escape. Veronica runs along the river Styx with her loyal hellhound, Hellraiser, and finds an unguarded crevice that allows them to enter the living world through a sewer, disproving the myth that the only way her kind can escape is through demonic possession.

The dreamy Dr. Max Barris notices her walking down the street, and the two get lost in each other's eyes until a car ruins the moment and knocks her unconscious. For many reasons she turns out to be a medical mystery to him, with a stethoscope not registering a heartbeat but instead amplifying Hell's soundtrack of eternal suffering. When she is to be discharged at the hospital, she asks Max bluntly to accept her into his dwelling and he is powerless to refuse.

Now living in Max's apartment, Veronica spends a forlorn and soul-crushing first night glued to the television news stations and realizing just how much evil exists in this world. She responds by venturing outside and ripping the spinal cord out of a rapist and then the heart out of a racist, but her ultimate goal is to cleanse the city from its sinful mayor. All of her anger melts away whenever she's in the presence of Max, who she genuinely cares for and wants to get closer to. In an utterly charming and bizarre sequence, she asks that he accompany her to a theater so that she can see a movie for the first time in her life, and it ends up being the kind of cinema that Travis Bickle from *Taxi Driver* takes his dates to. He can only smile and shake his head in disbelief by how enigmatic she is, but since he's so bewitched, maybe he can look past the horns, nails, and wings that belongs to her true self.

Dark Angel: The Ascent is successful as a touching love story and cathartic obliteration of the unjust, and it also knows just the right moment to insert some screwball comedy, like when an oblivious detective falls into a pothole. The scenes in Hell, which were all filmed inside a 17th century Romanian castle, look absolutely stunning and will make you salivate for a good ole fashioned bowl of tongue stew.

Highway to Hell (1991)

Director: Ate de Jong
Writer: Brian Helgeland
Cast: Chad Lowe, Kristy Swanson, Patrick Bergin, Richard Farnsworth, Pamela Gidley

Always the bridesmaid, never the bride was this movie when I frequented video stores in the '90s. The sight of a grinning Lucifer on a dusk-saturated stretch of highway with the tagline "Where the toll is your soul" made for an alluring cover but for some reason I always took something else to the checkout counter. It's a real shame because I would have adored this movie at any age due to its unabashed free-spirited silliness, high-speed desert chases, exceptional production design by Philip Dean Foreman (whose credits include *Killer Klowns from Outer Space*, *Sometimes They Come Back*, and all four *Critters* films), and makeup effects from one of the horror genre's elite artists, Steve Johnson.

On their way to elope in Las Vegas, Charlie and Rachel decide to take a back road just in case a concerned parental call to the police puts them at risk. They stop at Last Chance Service Station,

Poster for *Highway to Hell* (1991), Hemdale, Goodman-Rosen Productions

which might have appeared in even more horror movies than Steve Johnson's makeup, but for once, the owner isn't a snaggle-toothed, crotchety old man wearing a soot-caked wifebeater and informing them of a secret road that will save them considerable time on their journey; rather, he is played by Richard Farnsworth, who anyone that has seen *The Straight Story*, *Misery*, *Anne of Green Gables*, or coincidentally, an episode of the Michael Landon-starring series *Highway to Heaven* knows could play kind and benevolent old men like nobody else. The kids ignore his smart advice and continue down the backroad, but still end up seeing the flashing red and blue lights of a police car in their rearview mirror. Their fears intensify when they notice the officer's hulking frame and aggressive gait (it's no wonder the same actor portrayed Jason Vorhees in series standout *Friday the 13th Part VI: Jason Lives*), and the way his face is heavily scarred with Satanic scripture. After attacking Charlie, he straps a pair of handcuffs (still attached to the severed hands of a previous victim) onto Rachel and steals her away into seemingly another dimension.

A panicked Charlie returns to the gas station to get more information and is given a customized gun and pristine 1940 Ford Coupe by Farnsworth's character, who lost his soul mate to the Hell Cop decades ago and has been warning travelers ever since. In order to rescue Rachel, Charlie has to literally drive into the depths of hell—looking conspicuously just like the deserts of Arizona—and outsmart the devil and his many minions. We get our first glimpses of the movie's berserk, pun-riddled style of comedy reminiscent of films like *Stay Tuned* and *Nothing but Trouble* when the Hellcop makes a stop at a diner. Not only are the patrons covered in cobwebs and reading the latest edition of the 666 Times, but the diner seems to be fully employed by members of the Stiller family—Ben is outside offering headcheese omelets straight off the pavement while his parents and legendary comedy duo Jerry Stiller and Anne Meara demonstrate that the art of bickering continues after death. Amy Stiller makes her cameo later on at a strip club where Cleopatra has dinner with Adolf Hitler (played by Gilbert Gottfried!) and Attila the Hun (Ben Stiller again, whose connections with Attila would continue 15 years later in *Night at the Museum*).

Coming right off the heels of his unpleasant *Drop Dead Fred*, director Ate de Jong gives a playfully weird approach to *Highway to Hell*, and it's easy to imagine it being rated PG-13 and serving as a gateway to horror for younger audiences. It's almost miraculous that a movie this bonkers could be greenlit by a studio and given a $9 million budget, and so you should savor every second, lest you find yourself in line to be pulverized and paved on the road of good intentions.

Jigoku (1960)

Director: Nobuo Nakagawa
Writers: Nobuo Nakagawa, Ichiro Miyagawa
Cast: Shigeru Amachi, Utako Mitsuya, Yoichi Numata, Hiroshi Hayashi, Jun Otomo

After trying for over an hour to fall asleep, I decided to start watching a foreign film in hopes that my eyelids would grow heavy after a few minutes of subtitles. Stopping *Jigoku* proved to be impossible and as a result, not only did I get just a few hours of sleep, but the Sandman sensed the visions of Hades bouncing in my brain and decided to bring me some of the most disturbing dreams I've experienced in years.

While scantily clad women seductively pose during the title credits (dammit, why didn't this part transfer over to dreamland?), the narrator infers that our lust may earn us a one-way ticket to Hell when he says, "Sins may escape the laws of justice, but religion imagines a world after death which deals punishment in place of the law." Our protagonist, a hard-working theology student named Shiro, has just become engaged to his girlfriend, and during a celebration with her and her parents, the mischievous Tamura pays them a visit. There's absolutely no backstory and it's never clear how he's connected to these people, so either Shiro is foolishly naïve for getting inside a creepy stranger's car or we're supposed to believe that these two incompatible men are friends for some bizarre reason.

The jovial night is ruined when Tamura hits an inebriated pedestrian in the middle of the street and speeds off, ignoring Shiro's pleas to return to the scene of the accident and check on the man's condition. It's later revealed that the man, who did not survive his injuries, was a member of the Yakuza (Japanese equivalent of the Mafia) and that his mother got a very good look at the vehicle that struck him. Shiro's week from hell continues when his fiancé is killed in a car accident (looking more like a graze than a crash) and his ailing mother takes a turn for the worse. He travels out to Tenjoen Senior Citizens Facility to visit her, while his father sleeps with another woman in the adjoining room. Questionable moralities continue to surface at this facility celebrating its 10th anniversary with a festival where everyone gets unbelievably sloshed and uninvited guests run amok.

After the first hour, I wasn't sure if *Jigoku* should be considered a horror film. But then people start literally going to hell and we still have 38 minutes left—38 minutes to spend in a depiction of hell that is artistic and ghastly, with shots of barren landscapes accentuating eternal loneliness (reminding me of favorite '70s progressive rock album covers) and intermingling with fiery pits and mammoth ogres carrying instruments of torture. We're also guided along Sanzu no Kawa, the Buddhists' answer to the Greeks' River Styx, leading to Sai No Kawara, the river bank where children are punished for the sin of dying before their parents. When even babies are sentenced to hell, it's safe to assume there's a lot of good real estate available in the clouds.

Out of the 104 films that Nobuo Nakagawa directed throughout his career, this was one of his most successful efforts in Japan but it was mostly ignored in the States until Criterion finally gave it a DVD release in 2006. This movie came out in 1960, eight years away from the intestine-chewing ghouls in *Night of the Living Dead*. This even precedes what is widely considered to be the first splatter film, Herschell Gordon Lewis' *Blood Feast*. And yet, *Jigoku* unflinchingly displays the inhabitants of Hell being decapitated, sawed in half, bludgeoned by large clubs, and in the most graphic image, even flayed! Horror fans, this is one you'll want to get your hands on, not tomorrow, not after breakfast, now! And what I want out of each and every one of you is a hard-target search of every gas station, residence, warehouse, farmhouse, henhouse, outhouse, and doghouse until you find a copy of the *Jigoku* soundtrack—which consists of nighttime lounge blues, film noir-ish jazz, and ethereal Japanese folk—and send it my way! Hey, I only slept three hours last night and dreamed of trying to awaken a mutilated and bloated corpse in Dante's Inferno, and so I'll quote *The Shawshank Redemption* and *The Fugitive* all I want, dammit!

NO FACE-HUGGING OR BODY-SNATCHING, BUT STILL SPONGEWORTHY SCI-FI HORROR

The Beast from 20,000 Fathoms (1953)
Director: Eugène Lourié
Writers: Lou Morheim, Fred Freiberger,
Ray Bradbury (story)
Cast: Paul Hubschmid, Paula Raymond, Cecil Kellaway, Kenneth Tobey, Donald Woods

For whatever reason I've been down in the dumps this holiday season, and with only 12 days remaining for Santa and Krampus to spread their versions of cheer and fear, it was looking very possible that this would be my first December without carols and a Christmas tree. I haven't wanted to prematurely force rewatches of *Christmas Vacation*, *Home Alone*, or *Mickey's Once Upon a Christmas* out of desperation because movie magic can only do so much, and watching those annual staples without possessing one iota of holiday spirit could worsen my mood. But still, it's important that I at least put in the effort to get out of my funk, and something that has reliably made my heart grow three sizes are those silly giant monster movies.

Predating *Godzilla* by 16 months, *The Beast from 20,000 Fathoms* practically invented the kaiju genre that has spawned over 75 films, and yet it remains mostly unknown to younger audiences. It's not exactly trending on Twitter, inspiring TikTok dances, or selling for $50,000 in unbelievably stupid non-fungible token pieces (hmm, maybe just learning about NFTs is what killed my holiday spirit). It's also not common knowledge how this film was the first colossal achievement for innovative artist Ray Harryhausen.

Harryhausen's first major movie credit was as an assistant animator in *Mighty Joe Young*, and just a few years later, he was put in charge of making a humongous prehistoric man-eating lizard creature look convincing as it tore apart lighthouses, skyscrapers, and rollercoasters. It was the ultimate challenge for an artist inspired as a child by *King Kong*, and he would modernize those pioneering stop-motion effects that made the impossible seem believable. While on the set, he was visited by his good friend Ray Bradbury who said the movie reminded him of a short story he wrote years ago about lighthouse keepers terrorized by a hungry dinosaur. Sensing opportunity, the producers quickly bought the rights to the story and incorporate some of its ideas into the script, which explains the unusual title credit "Suggested by the Saturday Evening Post story by Ray Bradbury."

A group of scientists are testing out atomic bombs in the Arctic Circle when they cause an avalanche and the awakening of a dinosaur that has been frozen in suspended animation for millions of years. Right away the movie looks awesome and provides some exciting winter wonderland vibes. Physicist Thomas Nesbitt witnesses the monster but is unable to convince anyone that it was more than just a panicked frostbitten hallucination.

Horror Galore

While recovering in New York and hearing reports of a sunken fishing vessel near Newfoundland, a toppled Maine lighthouse, and smashed buildings in Massachusetts, he persuades his paleontologist mentor to help investigate the path of destruction that is getting closer and closer to New York City; their fears are confirmed in a fantastic diving bell excursion scene in the Hudson River.

Some viewers might find themselves simply waiting for the next Rhedosaurus attack but I thought the human characters were entertaining enough, mostly thanks to Cecil Kellaway's performance as the sweet and self-deprecating aged professor and Paul Hubschmid's accent. Like it probably says in the Bible, "No line of dialogue is boring when spoken with a French-Canadian accent." I've seen several *Godzilla* movies where the humans are boring, have nothing interesting to say, and seem permanently glued to the floor of a dimly lit boardroom, and so I was appreciative of these characters who are always on the move and pepper the conversations with lines like "She makes coffee strong enough to enter the Olympics" and "This is such a strange feeling. I feel I'm leaving a world of untold tomorrows for a world of countless yesterdays."

The dinosaur then takes Manhattan in quite the cab-crushing, cop-chomping spectacle, where it's revealed how it can also create devastation by simply spilling its blood onto the pavement, making the act of fighting back much harder. The action then heads to Coney Island in a scene straight out of my wildest dreams, and wouldn't you know it, all it took was a dinosaur battle atop the Jack Rabbit Racer rollercoaster to make my Christmas season a little less blue. I wasn't exactly jumping on my bed upon realizing there was still time like Ebenezer Scrooge, but I did finally bring in the tree from the garage and decorated it better than ever. And I might also ask Santa for a poster of the Rhedosaurus' silhouette preparing to take a big bite out of the lighthouse—being able to stare at that shot every day would be the gift that keeps on giving the whole year, Clark.

Galaxy of Terror (1981)

Director: Bruce D. Clark
Writers: Marc Siegler, Bruce D. Clark
Cast: Edward Albert, Erin Moran, Ray Walston, Bernard Behrens, Grace Zabriskie

Five years before James Cameron directed *Aliens*, which grossed $180 million worldwide from a $18 million budget, he was working as a production designer for the Roger Corman-produced *Galaxy of Terror*, a blatant *Alien* rip-off, but one with such style and ingenuity that it's no wonder why he was rewarded with such a meteoric rise. These futuristic sets and vast matte paintings were such a pleasure to get lost in, and if I'm ever decapitated as a result of my severed arm throwing a temper tantrum or crushed by tentacles so tightly that my head explodes (such an amazing scene!), I only hope it's somewhere as aesthetically pleasing as this galaxy.

I was told this was essential viewing for fans of cheesy exploitation cinema, and right from the start I was all in because it's not every day when you see Robert Englund and Sid Haig's names grouped together in title credits, bathed in blue against an eerie purple backdrop while music plays in the vein of *2001: A Space Odyssey's* stargate sequence. They both play astronauts who are ordered by the glowy-headed Master to rescue any survivors from a spaceship that crashed on planet Morganthus. Along for the ride are other dynamic cast members including Grace Zabriskie, Ray Walston, Zalman King (who fans of cult cinema might recognize from Jeff Lieberman's *Blue Sunshine*), and Erin

No Face-Hugging Or Body-Snatching, But Still Spongeworthy Sci-Fi Horror

Moran (Joanie from *Happy Days*). "It doesn't look friendly but you should be able to breathe," Zabriskie's Captain Trantor tells her crew as they land in a desolate area close to the doomed, dark aircraft, now resembling piles of scrap metal. Their expectations of a heroic rescue are further tempered with the gruesome discovery of dead bodies, brains occasionally exposed, and no signs of life inside the aircraft until an unhospitable lobster-like creature shows up and attempts a scalping.

The deaths become more elaborate as the monsters increase in size, and before you know it, a female crewmember is raped by a giant worm in the film's most famous sequence, which had to be trimmed to lose its initial X-rating. As the crew dwindles down to a few, they are beckoned by a mammoth pyramid that uses their personal fears against them as they struggle through its labyrinthine funhouse interiors, earning the film's "haunted house in space" gimmick. It even has the ability to redecorate on a dime, ensuring that the characters are separated in much more satisfying ways than the old "We'll save more time by splitting up" cliché.

Whenever I noticed the *Galaxy of Terror* VHS cover in video stores growing up, I always wondered if it inspired the controversial artwork in Guns N' Roses *Appetite for Destruction* depicting a skeletal alien hovering over a topless rape victim. Now it would only require a quick Google search to learn of any connections, but I think I'll just let this one remain a mystery, much like whatever the hell happened to one of the main characters whose fate was ignored to such an inexplicable degree that I had to re-watch the final 20 minutes to make sure that I hadn't blinked during a crucial reveal.

The Hidden (1987)
Director: Jack Sholder
Writer: Jim Kouf
Cast: Kyle MacLachlan, Michael Nouri, Claudia Christian, Ed O'Ross, Clu Gulager

Those in the mood for an intelligent and quick-paced blend of horror, science-fiction, and action should look no further than *The Hidden*. It's a rollercoaster ride that doesn't start with a slow uphill climb, but with a sudden launch that goes from 0-80 mph in just a few seconds. After robbing a bank and causing mass casualties, a man speeds through Los Angeles in his Ferrari while blasting his beloved thrash metal and blasting away anybody that gets in his way. It takes a police roadblock, multiple gunshots, and an explosion to slow him down, and as his charred body clings to life in the hospital, the alien being living inside of him deems it an opportune time to crawl out of his mouth and slither its way inside a new host who will continue the path of destruction and hard rocking excess.

With *Dune* and *Blue Velvet* in the rear-view mirror and a career-defining performance as Special Agent Dale Cooper just around the corner, Kyle MacLachlan got some invaluable rehearsal here portraying a Pacific Northwest FBI Agent trying to avenge the death of a loved one in *The Hidden*. His character works with the increasingly flabbergasted detective assigned to the strangest case the LAPD has ever experienced where law-abiding citizens suddenly go crazy and commit cold-blooded murders inside record stores, car dealerships, strip clubs, mannequin warehouses, and Senatorial campaign stops.

After directing *Alone in the Dark* and *A Nightmare on Elm Street 2: Freddy's Revenge*, Jack Sholder kept his relationship with New Line Cinema going with *The Hidden*, a movie that the studio was so confident in that the budget allowed for the destruction of several very expensive automobiles. It didn't turn out to be the *Terminator*-like hit they thought it would be, but being released on VHS, DVD, Blu-ray, and various streaming rental services has prevented its name from being too ironic. This was one of several videotapes I rented the morning before getting my wisdom teeth removed in 1996, and it provided so much entertainment, humor, and high-octane action that it was probably just as instrumental in my recovery as the painkillers and vanilla milkshakes from Steak 'n Shake. And since I had recently been shown the almighty Internet Movie Database by a classmate, I was able to dial into AOL and find out why the faces belonging to supporting cast members Clu Gulager, Ed O'Ross, William Boyett, Danny Trejo, and Lin Shaye looked so familiar.

Twin Peaks fans will also be rewarded with a performance from Chris "Hank Jennings" Mulkey and a funny moment involving Alka Seltzer that makes it seem like MacLachlan is channeling the childlike innocence of Season 3's Dougie Jones

I Married a Monster from Outer Space (1958)

Director: Gene Fowler Jr.
Writer: Louis Vittes
Cast: Tom Tryon, Gloria Talbott, Peter Baldwin, Robert Ivers, Chuck Wassil, Ty Hardin

With lots of corn for popping, beer for drinking, and Ed Wood-level '50s science-fiction schlock for watching, I was ready to celebrate this Saturday night in style, but it got off to an unexpected start when *I Married a Monster from Outer Space*, Gene Fowler Jr.'s follow-up to the Michael Landon-starring *I Was a Teenaged Werewolf*, defied all expectations. It's easy to imagine Joel, Servo, and Crow sitting down in the front row for what would surely be hecklevision heaven, only to find themselves uncharacteristically lost for words by strong performances, decent special effects, and an intelligent screenplay that addresses important issues like spousal abuse.

On the drive home from his somber bachelor party, Bill Farrell (played by Tom Tryon before he became a successful novelist) loses much more than bachelor freedom when he's literally swallowed whole by a mysterious thick cloud of smoke, but despite all that he still makes it to church on time ("church on time") the next day for the big ceremony and some "modern love." His beautiful bride equates his sudden detached presence and laconic speech to wedding day nerves, and his headlight-less nighttime driving (earning him a "Why don't you turn your lights on, you dummy!?" from another driver) to honeymoon jitters. His strange behavior, which now includes a sudden aversion to dogs and alcohol, carries on the following week, causing the understandably upset Marge to fear that she's married a complete stranger, and she hasn't even seen the way his face now flickers during lightning strikes to reveal a horrifying true identity.

The extraterrestrial that has taken over Bill's body discovers that he has also inherited the innate emotions. He admits to grappling with foreign concepts like love, rejection, and loyalty while trying to remain steadfast on the ultimate mission of impregnating the women of earth to keep his species from extinction after the sun's increased intensity forced them to leave their home planet. It's refreshing the way he answers all of Marge's questions thoughtfully during their first honest conversation as husband and wife, questions like "Does frightening a woman make you proud or is pride something monsters don't understand?"

I Married a Monster from Outer Space was well-liked upon its release in 1958 because not only was it paired with *The Blob* as a double feature, but it gave audiences more bodysnatching invaders just a couple years after Kevin McCarthy screamed "You're next!" into the camera. Among the greatest moments are when the annoyed bartender yells at his most loyal customers for not touching their drinks, and when a young woman seeks nighttime companionship in a hooded figure that refuses to take his eyes off a doll-themed window display.

Night of the Comet (1984)
Writer and Director: Thom Eberhardt
Cast: Catherine Mary Stuart, Kelli Maroney, Robert Beltran, Mary Woronov, Geoffrey Lewis

Today I was walking around Portland's Lloyd Center Mall for perhaps the last time seeing as how its lenders recently initiated foreclosure proceedings. Nobody knows yet if this mall, which opened its doors for the first time in 1960, will be demolished or transformed into something different, but for the time being it provides a surreal opportunity for Portlanders to let their imaginations go wild as they pass by one permanently closed store after another while the still-functioning speakers fail at their attempts to project normalcy. Making the experience even more unsettling and uncomfortable was how despite its ghost town façade and lack of activity, I was still required to wear a face mask the whole time as if I were the last man on earth and trying not to breathe in the same air that reduced everybody else into piles of dust, and so of course I was reminded of the witty sci-fi horror cult film *Night of the Comet* and its excellent use of a shopping mall in the apocalypse.

Originally titled Teenage Mutant Horror Comet Zombies, the film opens with a kickass soundtrack and people celebrating the arrival of a comet with the same excitement as if they were counting down on New Year's Eve. Our protagonist Regina couldn't care less about the celestial miracle though because she's in a movie theater trying to beat her best score on an arcade game while her projectionist boyfriend geeks out about acquiring a rare print of *It Came from Outer Space*. The comet's aftermath is revealed the following morning in a breathtaking series of shots depicting deserted streets, a store's mechanical clown (the same one that Pee Wee Herman regretfully tied his precious bicycle next to) waving to customers that no longer exist, and rubber duckies who are far too innocent for this new, intensely red-skied world. Fearing that she may be the last living person on earth, Regina returns home and is relieved to discover her younger sister Samantha is still her same peppy, enthusiastic, non-vaporized, and completely oblivious self.

Played by Catherine Mary Stuart and Kelli Maroney (who sports a cheerleading outfit similar to the one she wore in *Fast Times at Ridgemont High*), this sister duo is so likable and energetic as they make the town's radio station and mall their kingdom while defending themselves against all sorts of scary predators like evil scientists, a zombie with a wrench, and a psychopath who forces games of Russian Roulette. It's so refreshing how they project legitimate girl power attitude without being reduced to stereotypes of valley girls or action stars. One of the reasons why the film feels so authentic despite all the wackiness and apocalyptic weirdness is because writer-director Thom Eberhardt did his homework and asked many teenagers about how they would act and what they would do in this scenario. The casting director clearly did some homework as well because we also get appearances from Mary Woronov and her *Eating Raoul* co-star Robert Beltran.

Night of the Comet is one of the most visually striking horror movies of the '80s, so it was fitting that cinematographer Arthur Albert would be chosen decades later to shoot several episodes of *Breaking Bad* and *Better Call Saul*, a dream gig for any director of photography. His wide-ranging career also included the comedies *Billy Madison*, *Dirty Work*, and *Beverly Hills Ninja*, as well as a combined total of 200 episodes of *ER* and *The Wonder Years*!

Uh oh, I'm starting to feel really strange. Either the unhealthy vibes of a soon-to-be ghost mall managed to penetrate my St. Louis Blues face mask or my body isn't reacting positively to my first Auntie Anne's pretzel in over a decade, but I need to end this night. Anyway, go see *Night of the Comet*. It's rad.

Pandorum (2009)

Director: Christian Alvart
Writers: Travis Milloy, Christian Alvart
Cast: Dennis Quaid, Ben Foster, Cam Gigandet, Antje Traue, Cung Le, Eddie Rouse

Twelve years after making the masterpiece *Event Horizon*, director Paul W.S. Anderson took another voyage into the horrors of outer space by co-producing *Pandorum*, and among the many things these two films have in common is how they sadly both crashed and burned at the box office due to lousy marketing. It's a real shame this one didn't do better because its array of chilling set pieces and atmospheric dread could have inspired one of the coolest-looking haunted houses for Universal Studios' Halloween Horror Nights.

With Earth's population exceeding 64 billion people by year 2174, and with food and water supplies dwindling, Spacecraft Elysium is launched to colonize the recently discovered planet Tanis. To survive the 123-year journey, all 60,000 passengers are placed in hypersleep, with crew members scheduled to wake up every two years in shifts to operate the ship. Corporal Bower and Lieutenant Payton (played by Ben Foster and Dennis Quaid) suffer the most unenvious of wake-up calls when they're prematurely dispatched from their pods and have to contend with several layers of dead skin, slight amnesia, and a transmission from Earth that states "You are all that's left of us." And I don't even think they have access to coffee after a power outage leaves a crucial door stubbornly shut, forcing Bower to climb through the ventilation system to locate and repair the reactor while Payton stays behind to man the computer and feed information via walkie talkie.

The claustrophobic, pitch-black hell triggers a panic attack, made only worse when his flashlight reveals the corpse of another crew member, but once freed from the peculiarly angular shaft, Bower faces even more dire circumstances with the revelation that the craft is home to a race of snarling, growling creatures with fangs that sink into flesh like butter. Because they're so damn fierce and scary-looking, every action scene is an ass-kicking adrenaline rush, even with the hyperkinetic camera movements and generic music that invite comparisons to video games. When you have creatures that look and behave like the cave dwellers from *The Descent*, and give them Legion of Doom spiked shoulder pads, you could drown the soundtrack with Hootie and the Blowfish and still have viewers at the edge of their seats watching them tear some poor sap apart.

I can't say that I understood everything that happened in *Pandorum*—which probably has more to do with me being a moron than the script being needlessly complicated—but I was engaged from beginning to end. It even gave me that hopelessly doomed, existential outer space psychosis that films like *2001: A Space Odyssey* have conditioned me to crave every now and then. It remains to be seen if it will ever gain a passionate cult following like *Event Horizon*, but it's safe to say that fans currently lining up to meet Norman Reedus at conventions aren't asking him to sign 8 X 10s depicting his two minutes of screen time in *Pandorum*.

No Face-Hugging Or Body-Snatching, But Still Spongeworthy Sci-Fi Horror

Lobby card for **Planet of the Vampires** (1965), American International Pictures

Planet of the Vampires (1965)

Director: Mario Bava
Writers: Ib Melchior, Alberto Bevilacqua, Callisto Cosulich, Mario Bava, Antonio Roman, Rafael J. Salvia, Renato Pestriniero (story)
Cast: Barry Sullivan, Norma Bengell, Angel Aranda, Evi Marandi, Stelio Candelli

After firing on all cylinders with *Black Sunday* and *Black Sabbath*, Mario Bava decided to leave the comforts of gothic eastern European castles and small leaky-roofed apartments and explore the vast terrors of outer space, resulting in a film that has been long-rumored to have inspired elements of *Alien*. Originally titled Planet of Terror, it was financed by production companies in Italy, Spain, and the USA, and the culture club extended to the cast, who recited the lines in their native languages before being dubbed over, making some of the more gibberish dialogue sound extra campy.

It begins with a group of astronauts responding to a distress signal from the planet Aura, and as they attempt to land their spacecraft through the oppressive mist with the force of gravity rapidly increasing and automatic controls going berserk, their bodies become weak and their minds confused, resulting in a temporary lapse of sanity as they begin attacking each other without reason. Once their wits return, they venture outside to look for survivors, only to be greeted by corpses who don't take too kindly to being buried. Even with black leather spacesuits, cape-like collars, and a nighttime presentation of coffin lids slowly creaking open, this planet actually has much more bodysnatching zombie action than anything traditionally vampiric.

Shortly after moving to Portland, I started a weekly horror movie group in hopes of making new friends, and for our second gathering, somebody had brought *Planet of the Vampires*. Even while I was enjoying all the groovy sights and classic sci-fi soundscapes, there was a noticeable lack of energy in the room and so I wouldn't recommend this movie for a fun night with friends. But if you've just smoked a heavy dooby and want to be transported somewhere enchanting and surreal for 90 minutes, then you probably won't mind the lethargic pace and non-distinguishable characters. The members of Fright Flicks in Portland (which sadly only had about seven other meetings) unanimously agreed that the scene involving two crew members exploring an abandoned aircraft that's seemingly being guarded by an Andre the Giant-sized skeleton was out-of-this-world creepy!

Convincing miniatures, forced perspective camerawork, astonishing production design by Giorgio Giovannini (who also worked on *Black Sabbath* as well as multiple Federico Fellini films like *Amarcord* and *La Dulce Vita*), and the thickest of atmospheres make this inhospitable planet truly a sight to behold. I sure wish there was a place in town where I could march through blankets of rainbow-colored fog under a deep red sky with glowing stones melting in the distance.

Horror Galore

SWIMMING TO YOUR WATERY GRAVES

Black Water (2007)

Writers and Directors: David Nerlich, Andrew Traucki
Cast: Diana Glenn, Maeve Dermody, Andy Rodoreda, Ben Oxenbould, Fiona Press

Many bloodthirsty horror fans in 2007 were counting down the days for the release of *Rogue*, Greg McLean's follow up to *Wolf Creek*, to see if he would succeed just as well with crocodiles as he did with outback psychos. After several goofy gator flicks tarnished by terrible CGI and cliched characters, it was a wonderful feeling knowing that a no-nonsense, hard-hitting crocodile nightmare of bone-crunching brutality was possibly within reach. While *Rogue* certainly delivered the goods, I wish I had also been paying attention to the land down under around this time because *Black Water* is another winner.

While on vacation in northern Australia, Grace, her husband Adam, and younger sister Lee visit an attraction that offers crowds the chance to witness the powerful jaws of a crocodile close-up, and then pose for photographs inside the jaws of a model specimen. The next day they decide on a fishing tour at Back Water Barry's, and after they just missed the scheduled departure time, an assistant agrees to take them out on a considerably smaller vessel into waters less traveled. For a while they certainly get their money's worth because leisurely floating down this pristine river while birds chirp and sunshine pokes through the mangrove trees is about as peaceful as it gets, but then something rams into the boat and tips it over, and their tour guide is never seen again… well, in one piece.

A massive and tenacious crocodile then makes its presence known and chases the three frightened tourists up a tree, where they remain for most of the running time, suffering from oppressive heat, omnipresent mosquitos, open wounds, and memories of that painfully ironic nursery rhyme that goes "Three little monkeys swinging from a tree, teasing Mr. Crocodile, 'You can't catch me!' Along came Mr. Crocodile as quietly as can be and 'snap!' went the crocodile. Then there were two little monkeys swinging from a tree…"

Writer-director Andrew Traucki claimed in an interview to having been extremely impressed with 2003's *Open Water*, and the inspiration is evident from the use of real predators (neither film could afford a believable-looking safe substitute with their meager budgets) and a terrifying nighttime sequence in which hopelessly trapped and defenseless humans learn that the scariest things in the world are even scarier when intermittently lit by lightning. Unlike the doomed American couple in Chris Kentis' masterpiece who can do nothing else except float in the middle of the ocean where sharks could devour them at any given second, the characters here have more control of their fate, and the film does an excellent job in laying out all of their options and weighing the pros and cons of each, making us sympathetic for them and thankful that we don't have to make such a difficult decision. It's loosely based on a true story of two Australian teenagers who found temporary safety up a tree while waiting for the crocodile that killed their friend to finally go away.

It may have gotten lost in the shuffle because of the overabundance of horror movies titled (Adjective) Water, but this one is worth tracking down for its unflinching realism and nail-biting suspense. The 14-foot crocodiles used in this film were drugged by a qualified zoologist and then maneuvered up and down the river, and while none of the actors were harmed, there was a very close call with a $20,000 camera that resulted in an unplanned inside-the-mouth POV shot! A sequel titled *Black Water: Abyss* surfaced thirteen years later but it wasn't worth the wait due to its characters being painfully generic and uninteresting. If you want to see a modern sequel that takes full advantage of razor-toothed predators preying on hapless humans in labyrinthine subterranean caves, stick with the excellent *47 Meters Down: Uncaged*.

The Deep House (2021)

Writers and Directors: Alexandre Bustillo and Julien Maury
Cast: Camille Rowe, James Jagger, Eric Savin, Alexis Servaes

Only the bravest of horror fans subjected their eyeballs to what French filmmakers were unleashing in the late '00s. One of the bloodiest examples of this merciless movement was *Inside*, and despite all of its acclaim, the next project from filmmaking duo Alexandre Bustillo and Julien Maury would be only available in France for an absurdly long time. The trailer and early reviews had been so unbelievably promising that every six months or so, I couldn't resist checking on *Livid*'s status to see if a North American release had been announced or if some kind soul uploaded a version on YouTube with English subtitles. All I could ever find were blogs written by other horror fans who were livid at its unavailability. While it just sat in Dimension's studio vaults, collecting dust, they would make other horror films that actually got proper distribution like *Among the Living*, *Leatherface*, and *Kandisha*. Eleven freakin' years after its first screening, it was announced that this movie would finally be making its international debut on the streaming service Shudder, and just in the nick of time because the due date for this book was rapidly approaching.

It was almost a foregone conclusion that *Livid*, about an at-home-nurse-in-training who is pressured by her boyfriend to break into a mansion on Halloween night to search for its comatose owner's hidden treasures, would make the cut. Yeah, I know, my expectations were foolishly, impossibly high. But for a good portion of the running time, it was actually surpassing these expectations with its brilliant setup, evocative October atmosphere, and nail-biting suspense. Unfortunately, with about 35 minutes to go, it shifted its gears and grinded mine by cramming in so many nonsensical, unnecessary subplots that all seemed to belong in separate scripts. It's still a pretty decent movie overall but I'm not ready to call it a fantastic fright flick just yet, and so I had to leave the vacancy previously reserved for it open. Thankfully, Bustillo and Maury are still a hardworking collaborative team, and their latest film, *The Deep House*, has recently become available on Amazon and a bunch of other streaming services. The mostly tepid reviews reminded me to temper my expectations this time even while the description "underwater haunted house," three words I had never seen next to each other before, was making me giddy.

An underwater haunted house movie seems like the kind of insane gimmick that would look good on paper but could easily sink like a stone when captured on camera, but I'm thrilled to report that *The Deep House* looks sensational as it plunges us through new depths of aquatic horror. Ben and Tina are an engaged couple traveling through Southwest France to film themselves exploring supposedly haunted locations for their YouTube channel. Ben thinks he's finally found the dwelling that will earn them millions of views and influencer status, and it involves going to an isolated area in the forest of Chanteloup and diving deep into its lake. Much like the poor scuba divers who became trapped in the drowned, shark-infested Mayan city in *47 Meters Down: Uncaged*, they are wearing the most sophisticated of equipment that allows them to verbally communicate underwater. They follow a path leading to a mansion that was too powerful for floods to destroy, and once inside, they are greeted by an abundance of unnerving visuals like clown heads, mannequins, broken pianos, candelabras, and posters of missing children. A Jesus statue appears to protect a secret passageway and that is the final straw for Tina, who wisely wants to get the hell out of that house immediately, but Ben, sensing that whatever is behind that door will allow them to finally "break the internet," pleads for her to swim just a little bit further. What they discover are a couple of bodies, masked and in chains, who look just as miraculously preserved as the bones of the house.

Imagine if Nora were hooked up to an oxygen tank as she tiptoed around the House on Haunted Hill, and had to somehow keep her breathing under control while being scared senseless from elderly blind ladies, falling chandeliers, ghosts, etc. Being constantly reminded of dwindling air percentages is a tactic that *The Deep House* merrily exploits to make Tina and Ben's situation even more perilous. It also makes us thankful to be on land.

More people should be talking about this one. It's an underwater haunted house movie from the makers of *Inside*, for crying out loud!

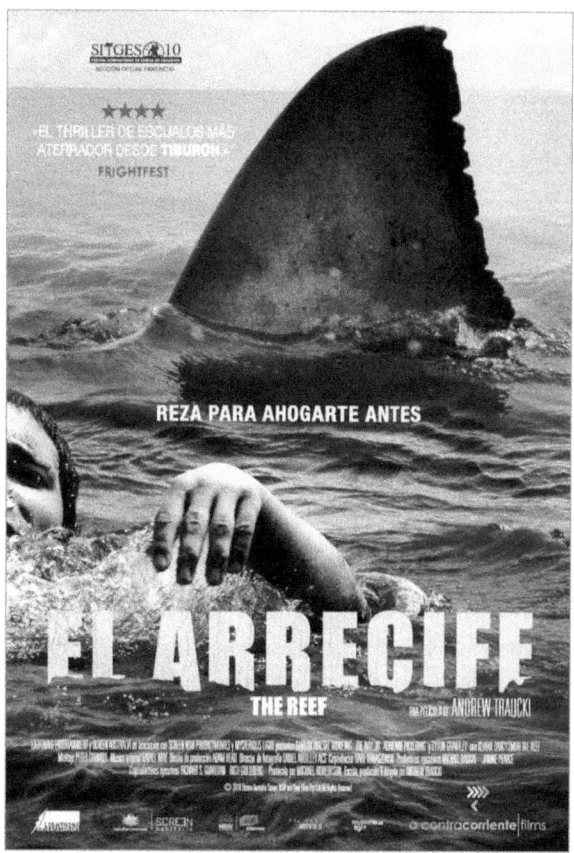

Spanish poster for *The Reef* (2010), Spain, Atlas Entertainment, Lightning Entertainment

The Reef (2010)

Writer and Director: Andrew Traucki
Cast: Damian Walshe-Howling, Gyton Grantley, Adrienne Pickering, Zoe Naylor, Kieran Smith

Florida's New Smyrna Beach (south of Daytona Beach) may be the shark attack capital of the world according to the National Geographic, but I would probably swim there before dipping my toes into

Horror Galore

any Australian waters because of all the terrifying man-against-nature films I've seen set in the land down under. The scariest one so far is *The Reef*, released seven years after the brilliant, realistic, and relentlessly bleak *Open Water*, and similar in how it places its characters in an unimaginably dangerous situation for most of the running time, where the most agonizing of deaths could happen any second. These characters are essentially floating shark bait, but they have enough personality to evoke our deepest sympathy, and due to the terrific camerawork, direction, editing, and performances, we feel like we're floating in the water along with them in an experience that is equally exhilarating and disturbing.

Damian Walshe-Howling (a dream name for any horror fan) stars as Luke, this charming man who invites four of his friends to accompany him on a yacht that he is set to deliver to a customer in Indonesia. After sailing under sunny skies and diving under crystal blue waters that provide a snorkeler's paradise, their idyllic vacation is cut short when the boat strikes a coral reef and rapidly fills with water. Luke collects supplies amidst a haunting medley of wood creaking and friends screaming from atop their overturned vessel, and once he joins them, he calmly describes their two equally perilous options. They aren't in a fly zone and haven't seen a plane for days, so they can either remain on a slowly sinking ship that's being carried further out to sea by the current with every passing minute in hopes of being rescued before a nasty dehydration death, or they can swim 12 miles in hopes of reaching Turtle Island. Warren, an experienced fisherman who knows everything that is potentially lurking beneath the surface, refuses to leave the boat, but Luke manages to convince everyone else to join him.

Long before the great white shark makes its presence known, the suspense level couldn't be higher as Luke and his friends attempt to swim as quietly as possible, avoiding any excessive movements that would draw attention. A half-eaten turtle and a sense that something is following them prompts Luke to put his mask on and check his surroundings underwater, a powerful motif that the movie uses repeatedly to great effect where shots of his nervous expressions are traded with what he observes in the abyss. A dorsal fin appears within inches of the defenseless and vulnerable quartet, but even after the shark swims away, one of the characters is reluctant to continue swimming because she doesn't want to stretch her legs out and feel them getting chomped off. These are easy characters to identify with because aside from one or two instances when they probably shouldn't bother swimming after certain objects, their decisions are all pretty rational given the amount of trauma they're under. It's the most nightmarish of scenarios made all the more upsetting in knowing that, just like in *Open Water*, it was based on true events. Another similarity is how the sharks in both films were absolutely real.

The Reef never made it to American theaters but received glowing reviews and streaming accessibility and so hopefully its reputation will continue to grow. My only complaint was how the perfectly lit nighttime scene lasted only a couple of minutes, which isn't enough time to sufficiently depict the most terrifying night a human being could ever experience. A sequel is currently in production and if it sees the light of day soon, then maybe this chapter can be a page longer. The bar has been set very high recently with the original along with *The Shallows* and both *47 Meters Down* films, but seeing as how it's from the same writer and director, I'm cautiously optimistic that *The Reef: Stalked* will at least fare better than the follow ups to *Open Water* and *Deep Blue Sea*.

COPYRIGHT INFRINGEMENT BE DAMNED TO HADES

Abby (1974)
Director: William Girdler
Writers: Gordon Cornell Layne, William Girdler
Cast: Carol Speed, William Marshall, Terry Carter, Austin Stoker, Juanita Moore

American International Pictures had a very green Christmas in 1974 when their blaxploitation horror film *Abby* was proving to be a hit, as it wasted no time in earning back its $500,000 budget. But its momentum was humbugged with a lawsuit from Warner Brothers, who claimed that the film blatantly plagiarized something they released exactly one year prior. While *Abby* had its fair share of original moments, the courts ultimately decided that it relied a little too heavily on the scariest film of all time, William Friedkin's *The Exorcist*, and as a result, it was pulled from theaters and Warner Brothers confiscated the copies and the rights, dooming the movie to obscurity and still to this day depriving it of a much-needed remastering. Considering just how many movies were ripping off *The Exorcist* at the time, it's a tad infuriating how the most severe legal actions were targeted at the one with the smallest budget, the campiest spirit, and blackest cast. If only Warner Brothers had put as much effort into making *Exorcist II: The Heretic* a watchable sequel.

William Marshall (Blacula himself, who would later be recognized as the King of Cartoons in *Pee Wee's Playhouse*) plays Bishop Garnet Williams aka Father Lankester Merrin, an archeologist doing research in Nigeria on a sect that worships the "black

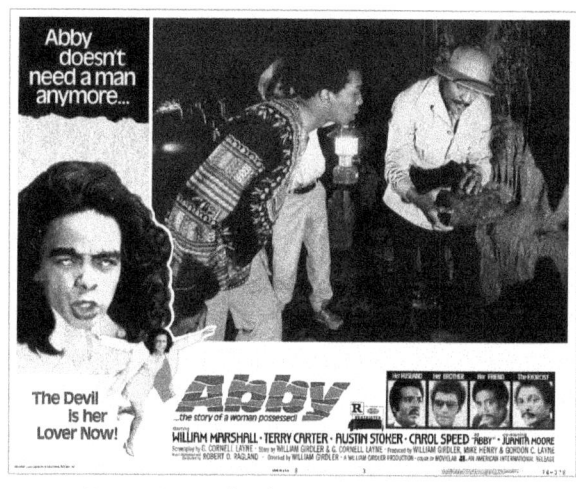

Lobby card for **Abby** (1974), American International Pictures

devil-god" Eshu that thrives on lecherous sexuality. He accidentally unleashes the demon in a cave, and despite the fact that it can travel anywhere in the entire world, it decides on Louisville, Kentucky, where the Bishop's daughter-in-law resides. A purer saint you won't find, as she sings in the church choir, volunteers at a soup kitchen, and has just gotten her license to work as a Christian marriage counselor. She is visited in the shower one afternoon by a shadowy figure who causes her to moan passionately over and over, and of course this was the very moment when my roommate and his girlfriend returned home, assuming I was watching 70's porn.

Unexplained gusts of wind, flashing lights, slamming doors, and broken glasses predicate changes in Abby's behavior; she purposefully slices up her arm while carving chicken, ruins a sermon with incess-

coughing and some pea soup action, and then scares the holy hell out of her husband (a pastor in the church) when her voice drops a couple octaves and spews sexual vulgarity. Neurological examinations produce no answers and when the doctor suggests a psychiatrist, her mother recoils in horror at the thought that her pure Christian daughter could be mentally unwell. Things only get worse for Abby's relatives when she escapes from the hospital and takes the super crazy evil up to 11, causing Bishop Williams to cut his Nigerian studies short and return home since he's apparently the only person that can free his daughter-in-law from Eshu, making the same kind of subliminal appearances as Pazuzu. Sure, similarities to *The Exorcist* abound, but did Pazuzu ever interfere hilariously in a marriage counseling session, engage in a genuinely chilling "Here we go around the merry go round" game, or prey on bachelors at a night club? This underwhelming club has orange and brown walls and is lit so brightly that the mirror ball serves no purpose, but its funky music is spot on and contributes to the uplifting experience of watching this hidden gem.

Abby was one of nine films directed by William Girdler, whose resume also included *Three on a Meathook* and *Grizzly*. Shortly after completing his final film, *The Manitou* (starring Tony Curtis), his life was tragically cut short in a helicopter crash in the Philippines at age 30.

Another *Exorcist* rip-off worth seeing is *Beyond the Door* (1974), which wasn't abruptly pulled from theaters like *Abby* was, but a portion of its hefty box office numbers had to be sacrificed to Warner Brothers as a result of a settlement. This Italian production opens with Satan himself lamenting about not having a single line of dialogue in the picture you're about to see, but he promises to make his presence known one way or another, even if it's by taking the form of the person sitting right next to

you. In all this lunacy you'll find toys that come to life, the interiors of a Safeway in the 70's, a glass of water that has eyeballs rather than ice cubes, a boy in the backseat of a car sipping cold Campbell's green pea soup through a straw, and an intrusive jazz musician playing the flute through his nose. *Beyond the Door*'s version of the classic Regan head-spin might be the scariest thing I've seen in months.

Cruel Jaws (1995)

Director: Bruno Mattei
Writers: Robert Feen, Bruno Mattei, Linda Morrison
Cast: David Luther, George Barnes Jr., Scott Silveria, Kristen Urso, Richard Dew, Sky Palma

Yeah, yeah, I know what some of you are thinking. Calling *Cruel Jaws* a hidden gem is an affront to the art of filmmaking. The database All Movie has referred to it as "The epitome of outrageous thievery cinema," and they are absolutely correct. Several *Jaws* imitators surfaced in the late '70s and early '80s and some were even met with lawsuits from Universal Pictures, but Italian schlockmeister Bruno Mattei must have sensed that in 1995, eight years after *Jaws: The Revenge* (the first horror film I ever saw in theaters) failed so spectacularly, the studio would no longer be interested in great white monsters of the deep. After brazenly borrowing elements of *Predator*, *The Terminator*, and *Dawn of the Dead* for his films *Robowar*, *Shocking Dark*, and *Hell of the Living Dead* respectively, he seemingly had balls the size of grapefruits when deciding to go the extra mile for *Cruel Jaws*, not only copying themes and lines from the Steven Spielberg classic, but also splicing in actual footage of Bruce the Shark. And why yes, that is Alex Kintner you see being pulled underwater! It directly steals even more from the 1981 movie *The Last Shark*, which is one of the movies that had to be yanked from theaters due to its *Jaws* similarities; however, it sadly didn't steal that insanely funny shot that comes up during your daily searches of *The Last Shark* gifs. It's almost as if the makers of *Cruel Jaws* were simply begging just to be noticed by Universal executives as an indication that they've reached the big time—either that or they stumbled upon some obscure clause pertaining to public domain or statutes of limitations. It's so very strange…and kinda awesome. It remains such an entertaining anomaly that I just had to include it.

Given how friendly Hollywood is to reboots and sequels, it has always surprised me how the *Jaws* franchise has managed to go untouched since 1987, especially after recent shark success stories like *The Shallows* and *47 Meters Down*. While I dread news of a remake like the plague, the idea of a Jaws 5 has always filled me with excitement and undeserved optimism, and so it was a genuinely fascinating experience watching a movie that tried very hard to convince the public that it was an official sequel by using the same iconic font for advertisements. It's safe to say that the three people who received writing credits have watched *Jaws* ad nauseum because every scene either contains a line reproduced verbatim or one slightly remixed. The familiar hits include "You're gonna need a bigger boat," "The doctor says he's OK, mild shock, he can go home in the morning," "This is not the place nor the time to cut open the shark's stomach," "I don't know what the shark's gonna do with it, eat it, I suppose," and "I've always acted in the best interest of the town," causing our heads to spin as we try to understand how this was allowed to happen. It's a shame we never get to hear the name of the dog on the beach because it surely would have rhymed with Pipit.

If you've repeatedly followed the Brody Family on their many triumphs and tragedies, then you'll be happy to know that the writers also watched Parts 2 and 3 diligently. It's fun spotting the many similarities like the helicopter attack, an exact reenactment of the most hard-hitting death, a teenaged girl asking her love interest if he does everything his daddy tells him to before telling him to meet her at the dock at 8:00, the inclusion of a pair of fun-loving dolphins, and oh so many more. The connections to *Jaws: The Revenge*, however, are mostly just limited to the choppy editing during certain shark attack sequences.

With Hulk Hogan already committed at the time to his action-adventure TV series *Thunder in Paradise*, the casting director found the next best thing in a legitimate Hulk Hogan impersonator (who has the right face but nowhere near the 24-inch pythons required to fool anybody) to star as a widowed owner of a bargain-bin Sea World attraction who finds out that he's being evicted by the corrupt mayor and his sleazy land developer. The mayor is also busy dealing with a half-eaten dead body that washed up on shore and trying to amend the autopsy report so that it lists the cause of death as a boat propeller accident, because if the media got word of a shark attack just days before the annual windsurfing regatta, they might not even be able to save August. There are half a dozen other storylines jostling for attention here, including one from Peter Benchley's original novel that, much like the romance angle involving Matt Hooper and Ellen Brody, was wisely omitted from the film adaptation, and the fact that they are all so clumsily written and acted keeps us fully entertained as we wait for the tiger shark ("A whaaaaaaat?") to continue its path of destruction and proudly flaunt the latest victim in its mandible.

Oh yeah, and there's also a direct rip-off of the *Star Wars* theme, with just a couple notes altered. *Cruel Jaws*, I don't know how the hell you're allowed to exist, on a remastered Blu-ray no less, but I'm thankful that you do because you're a hell of a lot more entertaining than *Jaws 3-D*.

Horror Galore

Mahakaal (1994)

Directors: Shyam Ramsay, Tulsi Ramsay
Writers: Y.V. Tyagi, Sayed Sultan, Kafil Azar
Cast: Archana Puran Singh, Karan Shah, Johny Lever, Mayur Verma, Reema Lagoo

With the atrocious remake of *A Nightmare on Elm Street* being Freddy Krueger's only adventure in nearly two decades, it's understandable to beg for a reason to lock your door, grab a crucifix, and stay up late; thankfully there's a bizarre and blatant Bollywood rip-off to fill the void and then some. Although it was made in the late '80s, the producers didn't want it to compete against 1989's *Khooni Murdaa*, which also borrowed heavily from the Wes Craven classic, and so it was shelved for a few years and released at the tailspin of an Indian horror boom spearheaded by the seven Ramsay brothers, who all collaborated in different pairings for their many films. At the time, Bollywood seemed to exist in its own bubble where intellectual properties on the outside were fair game, and the total lack of subtlety mixed with unparalleled tonal shifts and unexpectedly great production designs results in a viewing experience that will have fans of the *Nightmare on Elm Street* franchise, starved for more Freddy content, wondering just how *Mahakaal* has managed to remain so obscure.

It opens with a note-for-note replica of the musical score and the familiar sights of a distressed young woman wandering around a boiler room decorated with hanging chains. She's attacked by a severely burned maniac with a knife-glove and wakes up screaming and bloodied. Naturally her parents don't believe in the possibility of being physically assaulted in dreamland and having the injuries carry over to waking life, but it turns out her best friend has been having recurring dreams of the exact same man. He's not a wisecracker named Fred Krueger, but Shakal, a mulleted sorcerer who sacrificed children to become more powerful, and cackled sinisterly even while being buried alive by the father of one of his victims. With the exception of the effective closeup shots of his eyes, he bears a stronger resemblance to the monster in Hammer's *Curse of Frankenstein* or Leatherface's depiction in the must-see trailer for the third (and very underrated) *Texas Chainsaw Massacre* film, and his presence is undeniably unsettling.

Whereas Tina's brutal death in the original film occurs at the 16-minute mark, the friend in this movie doesn't get mysteriously murdered on a double-date sleepover until after 47 minutes, so rest assured that it's far from a shot-for-shot remake. Words simply can't describe how strange it is to see the bulk of the original's plot, as well as themes from the sequels, incorporated with cheerful musical numbers (the first of which is performed by a couple who sing things like "Nobody in the world is more beautiful than you" and "I am so lucky that I have your love" repeatedly to each other while dancing romantically on the beach), comic-relief characters like a Michael Jackson impersonator all played by the same actor, and attempted gang rapes thwarted by unconvincing martial arts battles. And c'mon, who among us hasn't mourned the fact that Freddy never stalked someone in a city aquarium? Or used 20 gloves instead of just one? Or that the underwater fantasy woman in Part 4's waterbed scene wasn't dressed from neck to toe in fine garments? Wait, scratch that last one. It's also easy to imagine Freddy feeling right at home inside a fog-filled temple with swinging lanterns, a Timmy-trapping well, and a massive skull sculpture festooned with corpses.

With its DVD release by Mondo Macabro out of print and not even available to buy used on Amazon or eBay at the moment, *Mahakaal*, also known as *The Monster*, isn't as accessible as another 1994 movie called *The Monster*, a slapstick comedy starring Roberto Benigni as a dimwitted gardener accused of being the sex maniac terrorizing the town, and so you might have to settle for a subpar YouTube transfer with numerous scenes muted.

Some reviewers have complained about the 2 ½ hour running time but I was grateful for every single second and would rejoice at the announcement of an even-longer director's cut.

Horror Galore

SPIRITS, DEMONS, AND ALIENS ATE MY HOMEWORK

Even the Wind is Afraid (1968)

Writer and Director: Carlos Enrique Taboada
Cast: Marga Lopez, Maricruz Olivier, Alicia Bonet, Norma Lazareno, Renata Seydel

All it takes is the opening shot of *Even the Wind is Afraid* to understand Carlos Enrique Taboada's reputation as a godfather of Mexican horror and major influence to the likes of Guillermo del Toro. While shrouded in darkness, a teenaged girl wearing a white lace nightgown stirs restlessly in her bed while ghostly moans of "Claudia, Claudia" call out to her. She sits up just as the camera pulls back to reveal a pair of bare feet dangling from the top of the frame, above her bed. Just as she's about to scream, a flash of lightning silhouettes the hanging body's profile against the wall, swinging ever so slowly. The camera then pans over to the window being forcefully swung open by a powerful wind, which blows through long strands of hair belonging to the still-shadowed deceased. These 30 seconds alone also make it easy to see how he went onto win two Ariel Awards, Mexico's equivalent to the Academy Awards, for his 1984 film *Poison for the Fairies*.

The following morning, a disturbed Claudia recites the details of her horrible nightmare to her friends at an all-girls boarding school, and then notices a startling similarity as they all walk to their first class: the door to the strictly-off-limits clock tower is unlocked and ajar. Entranced and curious, Claudia and her friends hope to discover the secrets of the tower and as they slowly ascend the spiral staircase, another crucial detail of the dream presents itself. When the strict headmistress learns of their trespassing, she punishes them by forcing them to remain at the school during the upcoming holiday break, even while knowing that a similar punishment resulted in an unimaginable tragedy on the grounds just a few years ago, and that the uncommonly violent winds that blew on that fateful night have made frequent revisits ever since.

There aren't a ton of scares in this classic ghost story but each one is methodically orchestrated and worth waiting for, especially the one where a lovesick girl has a late-night tiptoe excursion to the headmistress' desk to retrieve a photograph of her boyfriend. All of the characters, whether they are students or faculty members, are entertaining and will keep you invested during the slower scenes when it's merely a gentle breeze outside instead of a threatening storm. The film somehow even manages to retain its wholesome and innocent tone during a totally random scene when one of the girls educates the others on the art of strip-teasing.

Horror Galore

The House that Screamed (1969)

Director: Narciso Ibáñez Serrador
Writers: Narciso Ibáñez Serrador, Juan Tebar (story)
Cast: Lilli Palmer, Cristina Galbo, John Moulder-Brown, Maribel Martin, Mary Maude

Partially funded by the government of Spain, *The House that Screamed* became one of the first Spanish films to be shot in English for the international market, which is surprising given its semi-sleazy sensibilities. It's been said that Dario Argento was inspired by it when making *Suspiria*, but more noticeable is how it shares many of the tropes that would encompass the Italian giallo films and the "women in prison" subgenre throughout the following decade.

The House That Screamed takes place entirely within the grounds of a French boarding house for troubled wayward young women, run with an iron fist by Headmistress Senora Fourneau (Lilli Palmer). She punishes disobedient teenagers with solitary confinement and whippings, and even though she's taken drastic measures to improve security after a couple girls escape, this institution is surely no House of Whipcord, as the mademoiselles are generally well cared for and taught a wide variety of studies and pragmatic skills.

Running rampant in the institution are sexual urges conflicting with 19th century societal norms, and as a result, the girls compete over who gets to have a private encounter with the woodman during his weekly visit. Also, Headmistress Senora's allegedly asthmatic teenaged son becomes a daily peeping tom, and her protégé Irene (memorably played by Mary Maude) has an almost lustful reaction toward punishment and bullying. It's almost as if the director wanted the viewers to feel a similar shameful deprivation because even with a lengthy mass shower sequence, no nudity is shown as everybody keeps their gowns on (which cuts down on laundry expenses, I suppose).

Lobby card for ***The House That Screamed*** (1969), Anebel Films, American International Pictures

Even without the horror elements, this movie would be compelling for its forbidden lusts, lush soundtrack, and Oedipal overtones, but it goes for the extra credit by adding a mysterious killer with a sharp blade to the mix. The violence is minimal but it packs a powerful punch due to inspired choices with unexpected timing, freeze-frames and music rendering. The highlight of the film comes when our protagonist, newly admitted Teresa, tip-toes through the dark house looking for an exit, candelabra in hand, as deafening crashes of thunder and tick-tocks from the grandfather clock follow her every move.

While it made a killing in its native Spain, it didn't fare all that well in America, where it was mostly reduced to late-night double features at the drive-ins. Eventually it would be sold into syndication along with many others titles from American International Pictures, resulting in many TV showings of varying qualities and running times; many horror fans including yours truly had the "Mistress of the Night" Elvira to thank for the introduction.

Prom Night III: The Last Kiss (1990)

Directors: Ron Oliver, Peter R. Simpson
Writer: Ron Oliver
Cast: Tim Conlon, Cynthia Preston, Courtney Taylor, David Stratton, Dylan Neal

In an impossibly foggy cemetery under lightning and a full moon lays the tombstone of Mary Lou Maloney, who in the previous entry was crowned and damned to Hell for not forgiving those who trespassed against her burning body. Her sentence involves being shackled and robotically performing a kick line with other deceased women adorned in torn prom presses. The horned wardens of the underworld must have been lax in their inspections because she uses a nail file to escape from the chains and then she's off and running through the hallways of Hamilton High in a dizzying POV shot. Meanwhile, in the boiler room, the school custodian is charmed by a '50s jukebox that inexplicably appears and as he's checking his pockets for change, the charred Mary Lou surprises him and uses a term of endearment he hasn't heard in 30 years before she gets revenge on one of the many people who watched her die.

Everybody in the school gathers in the gymnasium the next morning, not for a memorial to their dear deceased custodian, but for an assembly featuring the school band playing "La Bamba" and the principal giving a witty speech about how all of the renovations will finally put to rest all of the ghosts of Hamilton High, the strange noises, the mysterious earth tremors, the vanishing students, and the unexplained fires. He then proceeds to chop off one of his fingers during a ribbon cutting ceremony. Hot damn, this movie is off to a good start!

After finding out that his medical school ambitions are in serious jeopardy due to his average grades, Alex cuts his anniversary date with his girlfriend, Sarah, short so that he can study for his biology exam the next day, but first he'll need to pick up his books at school. Realizing that a high school is even scarier at night than during the day, he wanders the hallways in trepidation before running into the beautiful Mary Lou, who seduces him in a tryst atop the American flag while the "Star Spangled Banner" plays in the background, because why not? If waking up to the morning school bell to find yourself completely naked in the hallway wasn't mortifying enough, poor Alex is totally unprepared for the big biology exam, but fortunately, his mysterious new lover has a way of turning F's into A's, as well as brutally murdering anyone that gives him a hard time. Alex soon finds himself a popular honor roll student and football star, but at the expense of a deteriorating relationship with Sarah and an unpleasant nighttime ritual that involves burying people in the football field.

If you haven't figured out by now, *Prom Night III: The Last Kiss*' sole aspiration is to put a big, goofy grin on your face and boy does it ever succeed with its care-free attitude, amusing sight gags, and Freddy Kruegerish post-kill one-liners. Sure, it might not be the least bit scary and perhaps it's ten minutes too long, but you'd have a hard time finding a direct-to-video '90s sequel that was this charming. Tim Conlon and Cynthia Preston make an endearing couple, and Courtney Taylor is so bewitching as Mary Lou that it's no wonder she was chosen to portray the applicant that George Costanza couldn't hire as his secretary because she was too sexy. "I would give up red meat just to get a glimpse of you in a bra. I'm terribly sorry."

This third entry has still not been released on DVD in its unedited glory, only sharing a disc with Part 4 in a bullshit TV version that maddeningly trims the gore. It's also the only *Prom Night* entry that my smart TV couldn't find a single record of. However, a good Samaritan was kind enough to post the full version on YouTube to the delight of everyone who enjoys watching biology teachers get turned into banana splits. It's also fortunate that writer-director Ron Oliver's impressive work in his low-budgeted inaugural film wasn't unnoticed, as he would be selected to direct several episodes of *Are You Afraid of the Dark* and *Goosebumps*.

The Substitute (2007)

Director: Ole Bornedal
Writers: Ole Bornedal, Henrik Prip
Cast: Paprika Steen, Ulrich Thomsen, Jonas Wandschneider, Nikolaj Falkenberg-Klok

Bedridden with the flu and always feeling either too hot or too cold, I spent most of the day watching TV when I wasn't drifting in and out of sleep. Just like in my early sick days, I relied on a string of game shows to lift my spirits, but then two obnoxious feuding families left an even nastier taste in my mouth than the medication, and so I decided to watch a movie instead. The Danish film *The Substitute* proved to be fever-soothing comfort food much like episodes of *Supermarket Sweep* and *Press Your Luck*, and part of that might have to do with my nostalgia for those books about discovering that your elementary school teacher was some kind of an alien or monster.

Because I wasn't sure how long I'd be able to keep my eyes open, I eschewed the subtitles for the English-dubbed version and it really added to the fun because some of the voice acting bordered on the ridiculous, especially the 6th grade girl who sounded just like comedian Maria Bamford when reminding the principal that they weren't assigned homework (to a chorus of groans). Her class is celebrating the fact that the teacher's salmonella poisoning means they'll get to take advantage of a clueless substitute teacher for several weeks, but the young Ulla Harms takes full command of the classroom the moment she taps her pencil repeatedly on the desk and states in a matter-of-fact tone, "I'm not used to being around so many idiots."

She leaves her students further rattled with belittling insults like "soggy cornflakes" and for mocking one boy for his large teeth and another for his deceased mother. She also proves her superiority by reading their minds, answering the most difficult of mathematical questions even faster than a calculator, and somehow manipulating their speech so that insults like "cruel monster" comes out as "cool hamster," which she's absolutely flattered to be called. Despite all of their differences and petty rivalries, everyone in class unites in their opposition to her, understanding that their claims will fall on the deaf ears of their parents without hard evidence of her alien status, which they hope to obtain by sneaking into her house of horrors one eventful evening.

An unlikely addition to the Ghosthouse Underground collection, this is a really fun sci-fi-horror movie for the whole family to enjoy, free of gore, nudity, and foul language, and so pure at heart that the characters even sing "99 Bottles of Milk on the Wall." As the substitute teacher from hell, Paprika Steen's smile is every bit as wicked as Angelica Huston's in *The Witches*, and while her physical transformation isn't nearly as elaborate, traumatic, or artistically executed, she will remind you a bit of Large Marge at one point. She's also a joy to watch when she attempts to brainwash the parents into agreeing on a field trip to Paris.

MANIC-KIN-ETI-CUTS: LET'S SEE ANDREW MCCARTHY SEDUCE THESE MANNEQUINS

Mill of the Stone Women (1960)
Director: Giorgio Ferroni
Writers: Louis Sauvat, Pieter van Weigen
Cast: Pierre Brice, Scilla Gabel, Wolfgang Preiss, Dany Carrel, Herbert A.E. Bohme

August 1960 was a fruitful time for Italian horror because just a couple weeks after the premiere of Mario Bava's gothic masterpiece *Black Sunday*, Italy released its first horror film shot in color, and thankfully the *Mill of the Stone Women*'s plot didn't require brown-suited businessmen to sit in a beige, windowless office for many scenes. Set in the scenic Dutch countryside, this movie makes excellent use out of its vibrant colors and knows just the right times to strip them all away so that every shadow appears as ominous as possible.

A fresh-faced researcher named Hans is on assignment at the home of Professor Gregorious Wahl to document the 100-year-anniversary of a most peculiar tourist attraction: a carousel of creepy waxworks powered by a windmill. His arrival makes for a superb opening scene, as he's waiting for the professor in the front room when he gets a glimpse of a mysterious woman with eyes of desperation peeking from behind the curtain, but before he can get a closer look, the stern caretaker directs him to the study—decorated with skulls and mannequin parts—and locks the door behind him. Professor Wahl has been restoring his great grandfather's

Lobby card for *Mill of the Stone Women* (1960), Vanguard Films, Parade Pictures

array of lifelike statues depicting notorious women throughout history and adding a few new additions of his own, where they are paraded on a track by creaking mechanisms. While calliope music cheers them on, these waxworks are hung by nooses, twisted and contorted by the blow of an axe, trapped in a torture device, or in the act of committing ghoulish atrocities of their own. It's a well-thought-out set piece, as is the dwelling that it inhabits.

The mysterious woman from before is introduced as the professor's daughter Elfy, who suffers from a debilitating illness that prevents her from leaving the house. Even the slightest mental turmoil can be fatal, something like falling madly in love with a new houseguest and finding out he's in love with somebody else. Hans soon experiences the same level of emotional fragility when he loses himself in a twisted web where nothing is as it seems. Any film that mixes themes from *Eyes Without a Face*, *House of Wax*, and *Lust of the Vampire* (aka *I, Vampiri*) is bound to be rich with intrigue and *Mill of the Stone Women* does not disappoint, even if it's occasionally marred by a slow middle section and plenty of unconvincing dubbed dialogue.

A strip mall in my neighborhood that included a K-Mart, an Indian restaurant, a glow-in-the-dark pirate-themed miniature golf course, and most importantly, the best Halloween haunted house in Oregon was recently demolished, now reduced to piles of rubble enclosed in fences. I have no idea what's going to take over the lot…condominiums, most likely, but you never know, maybe it will be the new home for the world's largest and most macabre carousel!

Update: Yep, condominiums. A whole bunch of them. And the world's largest and most macabre carousel is inside The House on the Rock in Spring Green, Wisconsin. Go there now. Trust me.

Mister Designer (1987)

Director: Oleg Teptsov
Writers: Yuriy Arabov, Alexander Grin (story)
Cast: Viktor Avilov, Anna Demyanenko, Mikhail Kozakov, Ivan Krasko, Vadim Lobanov

Artsy and occasionally open to interpretation, *Mister Designer* has the look of a feature film debut from someone fresh out of film school and anxious to show off a multitude of tricks, but never once does it come across as pretentious because right from the start Oleg Teptsov creates a certain off-kilter aura and uses single-scene anomalies like a sepia-tinted flashback or slow-motion psychedelia to intensify a strong story rather than overcompensate for a weak one.

Even when a shot demonstrates impressive production design, costumes, and sound design (all of which received individual nominations at Russia's equivalent to the Academy Awards), chances are that whenever Viktor Avilov is on screen, you won't be able to concentrate on anything else. Not handsome in the traditional sense, his face has a Klaus Kinski-like magnetism that draws us in and keeps us on guard with every disdainful expression. He plays the egomaniacal Platon Andreyevich, a famous artist in early 1900s St. Petersburg who is rehearsing his latest bizarre performance piece while preparing to create the most like-life mannequin for a jewelry store's window display. After being dissatisfied with the local morgue's latest inventory, he eventually finds a tuberculosis-stricken 14-year-old girl living in squalor who would make the perfect model for his latest creation. We later find out he suffers from the same obsessive traits as both Dr. Frankenstein and Jimmy Stewart from *Vertigo*.

He loses favor with the public thanks to his delusions of creating something even better than what God made and his "transformations of a vulgar living matter in a creation of art," and is reduced to a morphine-addicted shell of his former self just six years later. Despite being broke, he turns down an offer to redecorate the island mansion belonging to a wealthy businessman, but then changes his tune once he meets the man's wife, Maria, who looks just like the girl who exhilarated his creative spirit and captured his heart while she was on death's door. With a mysterious demeanor, a wink, and a smile, she denies that their paths have ever crossed before but through old sketches, confessions, searches through a cemetery rich in thimbleberries, and one of the most intense poker games in film history, the pieces of their strange union slowly come together.

My pen was very active during these 109 minutes, and the person whose contributions received the most capital letters and exclamation points was composer Sergei Kuryohkin. It was riveting the way he would strike during simple actions like flipping through an artbook or playing a game of cards and make it seem like the forces of evil were about to have their turn; he always found the perfect times to incorporate opera, progressive rock, classical, new wave, metal, and even a Pennywise-pleasing circus number.

Pin (1988)

Director: Sandor Stern
Writers: Sandor Stern, Andrew Neiderman (novel)
Cast: David Hewlett, Cynthia Preston, Terry O'Quinn, John Pyper-Ferguson, Helene Udy

Shortly after learning about the world of internet chat rooms and AOL's member directory, I made a friend on the West coast who shared my passion for horror and metal, and in one email she recommended a Canadian film called *Pin*. To my delight, it was available at my local video store, but even if I had to endure frustrating eBay bidding wars, an expensive special order at Suncoast, or the act of calling every video store in Missouri to ask, "Hi, do y'all have the movie Pin? P-I-N," it would have been well worth the trouble to see this smart and ultra-creepy psychological thriller. It impressed the hell out of me but for some reason I allowed more than 25 years to go by without a rewatch, and in that time had forgotten everything about it except what the titular dummy looked like. Reunited and it feels so good… icky, but good. I've also sadly forgotten just about everything about my early AOL pen pal, but I hope she's OK and still a proud admirer of this film.

The first surprise appeared in the credits because I hadn't remembered Terry O'Quinn playing the dad, and while he's certainly strict and authoritative like in his *Stepfather* role, at least he never comes close to swinging an axe at his family this time. The movie begins with a group of kids lying on the leaf-covered lawn of an expensive home, staring at the strange motionless figure that's always sitting by the third-story window and wondering if it's a paralyzed man, a mannequin, or something different. In the first of many suspenseful moments, the bravest of the bunch slowly climbs the trellis up to the window, where the curtain eventually flutters just enough to give him a glimpse of the mysteriously still person yelling at him to "GET OUT!"

Fifteen years earlier, Terry O'Quinn's character was living there with his wife and two blonde children, Leon and Ursula. He worked as a doctor and used his medical dummy, the fleshless kind with exposed tissue, to not only educate his patients, but to serve as an altruistic source of advice for his kids thanks to impressive ventriloquism skills. Leon and Ursula, who named him after Pinocchio, believed him to be a sentient, important member of the family, even if they were only allowed to converse with him while father was also in the room. Pin was even used to teach them about the birds and the bees, but Leon ended up learning a whole lot more when he spied on the nurse using it as a sex doll.

When the film jumps forward a few years, Ursula is pregnant at 15 and too terrified to confide in her parents, and so a session with Pin is recommended by Leon, an overly protective older brother and borderline schizophrenic whose condition only worsens after their parents die in an automobile accident. He moves Pin inside the house and provides him with a wig, one of his father's suits, an epidermis, a new speaking voice, and a seat at the dinner table, much to Ursula's horror. Not wanting to see her dear brother institutionalized, she does her best to pacify him while also attempting to live a normal teenaged life, even picking up a steady job and new boyfriend, which Pin interprets as an act of dissent and betrayal.

Psychosexual overtones, incestuous confessions, and inappropriate parenting make certain scenes awfully uncomfortable, but it's all in the service of a magnificent screenplay from Sandor Stern (*The Amityville Horror*), and so nothing feels exploitative or unnecessary. Sometimes it's just a genuine pleasure to be creeped out to this extent…and to also have a final shot disturb you this much! As Leon, David Hewlett (who went onto play Dr. Rodney McKay in *Stargate: Atlantis*) does a great job at channeling the sexually repressed, isolated, needy, and tragic spirit of Norman Bates as he mentally unravels and discovers new ways of terrifying his houseguests. The cast also includes a couple of *Prom Night* alumni, with John Pyper-Ferguson appearing the previous year in *Prom Night II* and Cynthia Preston going into battle with Mary Lou in 1993's underrated *Prom Night III: The Last Kiss*. But by far the biggest surprise on the IMDb page was learning which actor provided the voice of Pin—probably the least likely of every single cast member in the *Breaking Bad/ Better Call Saul* universe! Don't wait for a personal recommendation from your new AOL pen pal—just take my word and give this creepy Canadian cult flick a try.

Tourist Trap (1979)

Director: David Schmoeller
Writers: David Schmoeller, J. Larry Carroll
Cast: Chuck Connors, Jocelyn Jones, Jon Van Ness, Tanya Roberts, Robin Sherwood

Out of all of the movies in this book, this is probably the one I wrestled with the most in whether to call it a hidden gem or a straight-up gem. Needing some additional market research, I decided to ignore my antisocial tendencies and take a poll while attending the All-Night Horror Marathon last night at the Hollywood Theatre. Every time I was waiting in line for pizza, beer, coffee, donuts, or the

Watch out for tourist traps, Mr. Marbles Tigerpants!

slowest water cooler in the history of the world, I said to whoever was in front of me and behind, "Hi, I am taking a little survey, and I was just wondering if you've seen the movie *Tourist Trap* from 1979." Out of 12 people, five of them said yes, five said no, and for the two people who said they weren't sure, I'm just going to move them over to the no column because how the hell could anyone forget a movie like *Tourist Trap*? Its popularity may have grown over the years but based on these numbers, it's clear that more work needs to be done.

This was one of several films introduced to me as a child by *USA Saturday Nightmares*, and I loved it so much that when I spotted it at a video store during a family trip to Naperville, Illinois to visit relatives, I asked my mom if she could find out if it was available to purchase. She received a call from the store manager the following day, and I believe the magic number was in the $40-45 range. A bit steep, but it helped that my tenth birthday was just days away, and so before I knew it, I was clutching that plastic hard shell VHS in my tiny hands, probably screaming something like "It's mine! *Tourist Trap* is mine! Mwahahaha!" This jubilation would be reenacted about 25 years later when I was browsing through the horror section of Suncoast Motion Picture Company at St. Louis' dearly departed Crestwood Mall and spotted a DVD I never knew existed: a 20th Anniversary Special Edition DVD of *Tourist Trap*, with special features including a David Schmoeller commentary track! After this very special purchase, I was probably walking like Cosmo Kramer after a few café lattes to get to my car so I could drive to the also-deceased Best Buy location on Watson Road and buy my first DVD player.

Rather than run through the plot of a movie most of you have hopefully seen, I think I'll just make a list of 20 Reasons Why *Tourist Trap* Rules.

1. It has one of the creepiest opening scenes ever, with an exhausted young man named Woody pushing a deflated tire down a dusty road in the middle of nowhere until he comes across a gas station seemingly operated by cackling mannequins.

2. Woody's friends are a likable bunch and we genuinely worry for them when their vacation takes one nightmarish turn after another.

3. Chuck Connors, looking like a weathered version of The Rifleman, gets a grand introduction when he startles a trio of women bathing underneath a waterfall. He plays a relic of the past who laments about how he rarely gets visitors anymore because "everyone is in such a damn hurry these days." Much like the Bates Motel, Slausen's Lost Oasis was doomed after the construction of a new highway.

4. Connors' performance as kindly, kooky, terrifying, and ultimately tragic Mr. Slausen shows that he had the charisma and the dramatic range to become the next big horror icon, but sadly Tourist Trap's unjust failure at the box office led to a detour from the path paved by Vincent Price, Peter Cushing, and Christopher Lee.

5. The music! In the DVD commentary track, writer and director David Schmoeller commented on how the music ended up being one of the costliest expenses for the film, but every penny was well spent because it's impossible to imagine this film without the contributions of Italian composer Pino Donaggio (Carrie, Don't Look Back, The Howling, Piranha, etc), who shows his proficiency with breaking hearts in one scene and stopping them in the next. The "love theme" rivals Jerry Goldsmith's Psycho II score as the most achingly beautiful piece of music in horror cinema, whether it's performed by a piano, flute, string section, Moog synthesizer, or music box.

6. Several reviewers described it as "Carrie meets The Texas Chainsaw Massacre."

7. Forget Quint's death in Jaws or the face peeling in Poltergeist, because this movie has the most disturbing scene of any PG-rated release, and it goes on for several minutes where your heart could burst from fright at any moment. I know the ratings system was different back then but seriously, the officials must have been wasted on Billy Beer the day they gave Tourist Trap a PG.

8. No list counting down the 100 scariest movie moments is truly complete unless it includes the "see my friend!" scene with poor Molly.

9. Mr. Slausen's laugh is endearing.

10. The nighttime scenes are dripping with atmosphere and occasionally resemble a dark

fairytale when characters are chased through moonlit forests and moccasin-friendly ponds.

11. Because it uses its dreamlike logic so masterfully, you can't fault a character for screaming "THIS IS NOT HAPPENING!"
12. The vocalizations of the mannequins are beyond unsettling, especially whenever they find amusement in the misfortunes of others.
13. You know you have a great villain when he takes a time out just to play with his dolls.
14. It's not afraid to go full-on bonkers, evidenced by that surreal soup and crackers scene.
15. Right around the time Richard O. Helmer was helping knives, dishes, and mannequin mouths move on their own, he was also lending his special effects to another violent and maddening masterpiece: Francis Ford Coppola's Apocalypse Now.
16. One of the many reasons why this movie lingers in your memory is because of the art direction of Robert A. Burns, whose previous movies were The Texas Chainsaw Massacre and The Hills Have Eyes.
17. It's no surprise that the sound effects make our skin crawl, considering Ted Nicolai (future director of TerrorVision) also worked in the sound department of The Texas Chainsaw Massacre.
17. Tanya Roberts is at her va-va-voomiest!
18. General Custer approves of a sickening tomahawk smack to the back of someone's skull.
19. The final shot is absolutely perfect, and not just because the vulture unfurls its wing at just the right time.
20. Did I mention that it's also one of Stephen King's personal favorite horror movies?

Tourist Trap has been the victim of a couple unfortunate technical snafus in recent years, the most frustrating one being when it made its Blu-ray debut in 2018 through Full Moon Entertainment. There have been lots of conflicting reports and excuses regarding this controversy, but for whatever reason, five whole minutes of footage were mysteriously missing from this edition. They have since righted their wrongs by re-releasing it on Blu-ray in 2021 with the cover textually emblazoned with "uncut" and "remastered from the original 35mm." They have also made available Pino Donaggio's amazing soundtrack and a Mr. Slausen action figure with removable mask!

The other technical blunder occurred on a night when it would have reached possibly its widest audience ever, as it was chosen by Joe Bob Briggs to kick off his 24-hour horror marathon on Shudder—his first television event since the final airing of TNT's *MonsterVision* in 2000. But there was such overwhelming interest that Shudder's servers crashed immediately, and by the time most people who had been clamoring for more Joe Bob content were able to tune in, the ending credits with Donaggio's melancholy score were scrolling. Thankfully, his entire *Tourist Trap* treatment, along with all of the other movies included in this historic marathon, became available to stream soon after to allow all participants to complete the marathon at their leisure.

I have recommended 300 fantastic fright flicks in this book, but *Tourist Trap* is the most essential one of them all, and so if you haven't yet had the pleasure of getting lost in Mr. Slausen's oasis, then put this book down right now and treat yourself to a nightmare like no other.

Wax Mask (1997)

Director: Sergio Stivaletti
Writers: Dario Argento, Lucio Fulci, Daniele Stroppa
Cast: Robert Hossein, Romina Mondello, Riccardo Longhi, Gianni Franco, Valery Valmond

Seven years after teaming up with George A. Romero for the scary gruesome twosome *Two Evil Eyes*, Dario Argento collaborated with another master of horror (and fellow countryman) in Lucio Fulci, who was in poor health at the time and needed an exciting, spirit-lifting new project. Even though the horror community will forever revere these two filmmakers, it's safe to say that only the most diehard of fans, at least in North America, were actively following their careers in the 1990s, and so this movie's obscurity is no surprise. I don't even recall ever seeing *Wax Mask* in video stores, and it wasn't until just a couple hours ago when I learned that Argento and Fulci—whose reported long-running feud was likely nothing more than an entertaining myth—ever even worked together.

After completing their screenplay, loosely based on Gaston Leroux's short story "The Waxwork Museum," Fulci unfortunately landed on his deathbed before the director's chair, and since Argento was already slated to direct a remake of *The Phantom of the Opera* starring Julian Sands, he passed the reins to first-time director Sergio Stivaletti, who previously provided special effects to Argento's *Opera*, Lamberto Bava's *Demons* and Michele Soavi's *The Church* and *Cemetery Man*, and seemed to learn a lot from each director. His debut shot, lengthy and unbroken, is an absolute juggernaut, allowing us to be front and center for a New Year's Eve 1900 fireworks show in Paris that re-introduces the lurid colors synonymous with Italian horror of the 1970s, before the camera floats through an open window as lights bounce off the walls to strike the efficiently butchered bodies strewn throughout the apartment. Police officers then enter the apartment to find a man whose heart has been ripped out lying on the bed, and underneath is a horrified little girl hiding just inches away from his severed hand.

The story picks up 12 years later when in Rome, a new wax museum is the talk of the town—well, at least the talk of a local brothel. A customer is double-dog-dared to spend the night alone with those life-like waxworks depicting the most notorious crime scenes throughout history, and he fares far worse than Don Knotts in *The Ghost and Mr. Chicken*. He is examined the next morning by investigators who conclude that he died of fright, most likely after coming face to face with Medusa. Before bad publicity has a chance to reach potential applicants, museum owner Boris Volkoff (a perfect name if you hold Boris Karloff and wrestler Nicolai Volkoff in equally high regards) hires a beautiful woman named Sonia to be his new costume designer and wisely excludes the cavernous laboratory from orientation.

First impressions imply that this is just another modern retelling of *House of Wax*, but the story is actually pretty ambitious and weaves a tapestry of forbidden love, childhood trauma, delusions of grandeur, superhuman metallic claws, kinky S&M sex (not something I would naturally associate with early 20th century Rome), women being tied down and sliced in front of a sounder of swine, and much more. Decades may have passed but the horrendous dubbing attributed to Italian horror is still alive and well, and it only adds to the fun.

It's practically in my DNA to appreciate movies that take place in strange wax museums, and the one in *Wax Mask* is beyond impressive, almost castle-like. Not only does it offer waxworks so unnerving that only the bravest of souls would stand within an arm's reach away, but the simple mistake of going down the wrong hallway could lead to pendulums, steampunk gadgets, and classic mad scientist machinery with the staticky electrical volts. The scenes outside of the museum offer a nice contrast, as pleasant activities like canal boat rides, cotton candy consumption, Punch and Judy puppet shows, and misty nighttime strolls in the park are gorgeously shot.

To be honest, I wasn't expecting much out of *Wax Mask* but after 98 minutes of face-melting entertainment that both titillated and terrified (a murder scene that makes more use out of opera than *Opera* is the standout scare), I feel like I owe it to Argento and Fulci to check out more of their '90s offerings, while also delving further into the filmography of Sergio Stivaletti. There's even a character that looks like the evil twin brother of the curly-haired member of Color Me Badd, and that alone should have given this film several Academy Award nominations!

SOMETHING BONKERS FOR YOUR 4/20 VIEWING PLEASURE

Bloody Muscle Body Builder in Hell (2009)
Writer and Director: Shinichi Fukazawa
Cast: Shinichi Fukazawa, Masaaki Kai, Masahiro Kai, Aki Tama Mai

Well, I guess there comes a time in every man's life when he grabs the wrong bottle and accidentally pours half a cup of mango-flavored rum into the crockpot instead of the red wine the recipe called for. It still turned out to be pretty good, maybe because dinner's entertainment was Shinichi Fukazawa's decades-long labor of love about the bloodiest damn body builder that ever stepped foot in hell, and it put me in such an agreeable mood.

Fukazawa started writing the script in 1995 and then spent several years shooting on 8mm, until he was ready to start the editing phase in 2005. It wasn't until 2009 when the movie was mostly finished, but then it would take another four years before anyone got a chance to see it, and even longer until it was actually screened in a movie theater. That's a considerably longer timeline than even Guns N' Roses' *Chinese Democracy* but it was well worth the wait because while Fukazawa certainly doesn't get a medal in efficiency, he does win a Best in Evil Dead Show for capturing blood-spurting, Stooge-scuffling theatrics similar to Sam Raimi's classic, ratcheting up the carnage as well as the severed foot kicks to the crotch. "The Japanese Evil Dead" may be inscribed on the official poster and DVD cover, and a character might even utter "groovy" right after cocking his boomstick, but it pays homage more with its youthful, unabashed artistry (including the use of stop-motion animation) and sick sense of humor than it does with its narrative.

Wasting no time with small talk, this 62-minute movie bypasses exposition to show a man defending himself against a psychotic, potentially possessed lover by driving a knife into her chest (which opens a geyser of blood) and entombing her beneath the floorboards. Decades later, the man's son returns to the scene of the crime with the hopes of converting the house into a gym, and he brings along a former flame who is working on an article about the paranormal. Completing the trio is a psychic who believes that "exercising with ghosts is a good hobby." The Victorian mansion from *The Changeling* this house is not, as it's so small that the characters appear crammed together no matter what room they're in, but that's OK because it makes it easier for blood to splatter against the walls and severed body parts to reunite in ways you can't believe. Fortunately, the 8mm camera had just enough room to sweep around impressively and capture every act of hilarious dismemberment.

The next time I hang out with this bloody muscle body builder and his eye-popping, brain-crushing barbells, it will be with a group of friends in what could be my most successful movie night in years because its short running time and unlimited energy

Horror Galore

will force everybody to stay for a double feature. Not only is it top-notch entertainment, but there might be some medicinal value as well because it seems to have alleviated my weeklong eye twitch for the time being. Or maybe I have the mango-flavored rum beef stew to thank.

Poster for *Blue Sunshine* (1977), Cinema Shares International

Blue Sunshine (1977)

Writer and Director: Jeff Lieberman
Cast: Zalman King, Deborah Winters, Mark Goddard, Ray Young, Robert Walden

One of the first movies that scared the absolute bejesus out of me was *The Peanut Butter Solution* (1987), a Canadian freakfest wearing the guise of a harmless children's fantasy. It's about a kid who enters a supposedly haunted house on a dare and becomes so terrified that he loses all of his hair at once, leading to the titular remedy that works a little too well. Other films that terrified me around this young age, like *Jaws*, *Poltergeist*, and *Night of the Living Dead*, I would happily revisit time and time again to relive the thrills, but still to this day the thought of revisiting a single frame of *The Peanut Butter Solution* makes me uncomfortable. Being scarred from a scene in which the school bully pulls off the kid's wig (in punishing slow motion) probably made the opening of Jeff Lieberman's *Blue Sunshine* all the more shocking.

Released a year after Lieberman's killer worm debut *Squirm*, this '70s psychedelic shocker begins at a party that takes a strange turn when a man, in the middle of a charming song and dance routine, has his hair casually removed by one of his friends. He reacts not with embarrassment, but with a total psychotic breakdown resulting in some pretty nasty murders. One of the other guests, Jerry, is falsely accused of the massacre for some crazy reason and while evading police, he tries to solve the mystery that extends to other people in the city who are also losing their hair as well as their minds. What links them all together is a pretty creative piece of storytelling that's routinely spoiled in the synopsis, and so it's best to go in as blind as possible.

I had the pleasure of watching this movie again at the Hollywood Theatre on July 27, 2018 as part of a Jeff Lieberman double feature with the camping nightmare *Just Before Dawn*, and while the audience clearly felt hometown pride seeing a slasher set in one of Oregon's finest treasures, Silver Falls State Park, the applause at the end of *Blue Sunshine* was deservedly more thunderous. Being able to enjoy that bombastic shopping mall disco climax on 35mm with surround sound and Jeff Lieberman himself seated just a few rows back was quite a thrill. And

Something Bonkers For Your 4/20 Viewing Pleasure

I'd like to think I wasn't the only one who required a walk around the neighborhood afterwards to come down from this sunshine trip before driving home. Just thinking about this movie years later is putting me in a weird state of mind, so maybe I should get some hot tea and break out my Pure Moods compilation CDs or something.

Brain Damage (1988)

Writer and Director: Frank Henenlotter
Cast: Rick Hearst, Gordon MacDonald, Jennifer Lowry, Theo Barnes, Lucille Saint-Peter

In the auspicious opening scene of Frank Henenlotter's long-awaited follow-up to *Basket Case*, an elderly couple have a meltdown for the ages when they aren't able to find "Aylmer" for his nightly feeding of brains. They tear their apartment apart while screaming hysterically, and their inability to locate this mysterious character results in them writhing in pain on the floor while foaming at the mouth. In another apartment, a young man named Brian wakes up from a nap feeling unusual, and has to cancel plans to see a concert with his girlfriend. It's not your typical cold, however, but an escaped phallic parasite that has chosen the back of his neck to latch onto. Once injected with a dose of Aylmer's cerebellum-stirring neon-blue juice, Brian starts having hallucinations of his ceiling light taking the form of a pulsating eyeball and of his bedroom slowly filling up with the same blue liquid until he's completely submerged.

With the culprit identified with the help of a bathroom mirror, the slug-like creature with a mouth and a tiny pair of googly eyes introduces himself with a hilariously distinguished, smooth cadence (courtesy of east-coast horror host John Zacherle) and agrees to keep the good times rolling just as long as Brian keeps him well-fed—followed by maniacal laughter. A ghoulish symbiotic relationship forms, and pretty soon Brian is tripping at a car junkyard, experiencing euphoric bliss of lights and pleasures, and hooting and hollering at full volume. The orgasmic hallucinations are so strong that he doesn't even notice that right in front of him, Aylmer is chewing on the brains of a screaming security guard.

He's similarly oblivious in a later scene when a woman he meets at a punk/new-wave club performs outrageously ill-advised fellatio on him—a scene that caused multiple walkouts on set from offended crew members—but the cold light of morning signals that things are spiraling out of control and that he's losing his grip on reality. Desperately needing a change of scenery, he heads to the grittiest New York City neighborhood and checks into the seediest of motels to recover from the addiction and prove that he's the one in control, all while Aylmer mocks his pain with joyous showtunes and gloats about how Brian's chemistry has changed and that soon he'll be begging for his juice to cease the unbearable pain.

Brain Damage works as both a shocking drug allegory and as a wickedly entertaining horror-comedy, and much like *Basket Case* and *Frankenhooker*, is also full of charming characters who exhibit decency and kindness in the strangest of places—everyone is so damn nice in Henenlotter's worlds even with all the poverty and unpleasantness. In one of the cleverest of cameos, Brian rides a subway at night and exchanges glances with the man sitting directly across from him, who tries looking inconspicuous while an enormous locked basket rests on his lap and another passenger reads a newspaper with a front-page headline indicating a serial killer loose in the city.

Bonus points go to an appropriately spacey synth soundtrack, a bedroom adorned in rock posters (Siouxsie and the Banshees, The Cramps, Suicide, Slayer, Bauhaus, etc.), the world's most boring cereal box, the puppet's goofy expressions that reminded me of the meatball from *Aqua Teen Hunger Force*, and a scene in which actual meatballs turn into bite-sized vibrating brains.

Horror Galore

Dust Devil (1992)

Writer and Director: Richard Stanley
Cast: Robert Burke, Chelsea Field, Zakes Mokae, John Matshikiza, Rufus Swart

Don't confuse them with everyone's favorite handheld vacuum cleaner. These dust devils are whirlwinds of sand or dust common in dry, hot areas, and they dot the breathtaking desert terrain that encompasses Richard Stanley's follow-up to the dystopian cyberpunk cult classic *Hardware*. Once again featuring cinematography from Steven Shivers, the red-tinted majesty of the Namibian desert—so desolate that even one of the producers got lost during pre-production—is a sight to behold no matter which version of the film you end up seeing.

Dust Devil is one of those sad examples of films that were ultimately despised by their executive producers for being too unconventional or tricky to market, resulting in the reels of celluloid being ripped from the director's hands and hastily re-edited without his permission; in this case, it was the Weinstein Brothers and the cut material totaled 33 minutes. Thankfully, none of these missing scenes went ablaze or into a wood chipper, and Stanley would eventually purchase the rights with his own money and re-re-cut the film so audiences could see his original vision that included intense dream sequences and a supernatural-heavy backstory where Zakes Mokae (from Wes Craven's thrilling *The Serpent and the Rainbow*) requires the help of a shaman.

It's a violent and haunting ride with Sergio Leone spaghetti western imagery and a sweeping score from Simon Boswell, and while it was even more divisive to audiences than *Hardware*, I was on board right from the opening scene that unfolds with a house and cut-up remains of a woman's corpse burning to the sounds of a televangelist hellfiring and brimstoning on the radio.

The hitchhiking man of mystery is played by Robert John Burke, a face I should have easily recognized considering how many times I've seen Tom Holland's very underrated *Thinner*, and he's always on the move searching for young women so depressed that maybe the ritualistic killing would be doing them both a favor. In a segregated and dry-as-a-bone town where several people get on the train but hardly anyone gets off, he spots his next target, a suicidal woman named Wendy who's been driving toward the edge of the world after leaving her husband. One minor moment caused her to be such an ungrateful and unlikable protagonist in my eyes that I couldn't help but root for the devilish man using his powers to play the ultimate mind games while she's driving, but this unintended shift of alliance only made the movie more fun.

Dust Devil is also worth seeing for the pretty kitty resting on top of a pinball machine, the insane car crashes, and abandoned homes in the desert in which the collective mounds of sand inside create a disorienting funhouse aesthetic.

Hausu (1977)

Director: Nobuhiko Obayashi
Writers: Chiho Katsura, Chigumi Obayashi (story)
Cast: Kimiko Ikegami, Miki Jinbo, Kumiko Ohba, Ai Matsubara, Yoko Minamida, Mieko Sato

This candy-colored, psychedelic horror-fantasy from Japan makes a strong case that more children should be allowed into the writers' room. When Nobuhiko Obayashi was hired by the studio Toho to produce a movie with the same level of excitement as the recently released *Jaws*, he asked his ten-year-old daughter what would be as scary as Bruce the Shark, and she responded with a flurry of fanciful and inexplicable horrors including being eaten alive by a piano, pulling up a severed head from the well instead of a watermelon, and being attacked by a futon monster and by your own reflection. Screenwriter Chiho Katsura came up with just the right script where these zany, absurd visuals could coexist with themes influenced by the atomic bombing of Obayashi's hometown of Hiroshima.

Upset that her widowed father has brought home a new fiancé, a schoolgirl named Gorgeous decides to spend summer vacation at her aunt's house, and she brings along her giggly friends who also share strange names like Fantasy, Melody, Prof, and Kung Fu. The aunt may have some serious issues and the large-tongued house may be hungry for young girls, but on the bright side, they do get to meet a cute cat named Blanche. The film uses freeze-frames, chroma key compositing, color tints, superimpositions, stop motion animation, painted backdrops, and just about every other cinematic trick you can think of to create a whirlwind of psychedelia and silliness as the schoolgirls try to stay alive to experience another summer vacation with more sunflower field frolicking and less watching humans turn into bananas. There's nothing quite like seeing it for the first time; it's one that I love introducing people to so I can live vicariously through their virgin eyes. This delightful and wacky haunted house adventure is like the ultimate mind trip without any of the danger or repercussions.

Another genre-defying masterpiece from a first-time feature filmmaker was blowing audiences' minds in 1977, but unlike the midnight American stoners that were flocking to David Lynch's *Eraserhead*, the audiences for *Hausu* mostly consisted of Japanese children since it was marketed as a fantasy film despite the nudity and severed body parts. It took much longer for this movie to amass its sizeable cult following but it eventually got there, largely thanks to a Criterion Collection release and a remastered print that toured North American theaters in 2010.

After a lengthy duration of campaigning for the job, producer Obayashi persuaded the studio executives to let him direct the movie despite only having experience in short films and commercials. After *Hausu*'s surprising success, Obayashi didn't have to beg for opportunities anymore and would go onto direct 50 other feature films all the way until his death in 2020.

The Mask (1961)
Director: Julian Roffman
Writers: Frank Taubes, Sandy Haver, Franklin Delessert
Cast: Paul Stevens, Claudette Nevins, Bill Walker, Leo Leyden, Anne Collings, Martin Lavut

Smart moviegoers in 1961 were able to cope with their post-Halloween depression by venturing out into the November rain to their local theater and seeing Canada's first ever horror movie. They were even given a mask in the lobby for their troubles, a "miracle movie fright mask" that a well-dressed man who owns the world's most comprehensive mask collection promised in the movie trailer would take them to the very limits of their nerves and the very boundary line of sanity. Channeling the gimmicks of William Castle, he instructs moviegoers in a no-nonsense tone to follow the protagonist's lead and put their own masks on at crucial moments in the film to "share an adventure into the darkest hidden recesses of the human mind, where you'll see dread and secret desires lurking in that darkness." It's safe to say that nobody who saw *The Mask* back then could accuse him of hyperbole when he guaranteed "the weirdest nightmare world that man has ever dreamed or the screen has ever dared show" because these surrealistic and macabre montages are still enchanting and disturbing new generations of horror fans more than 60 years later.

Horror Galore

The movie opens in a rainy forest as a woman runs for her life only to be caught and strangled by a madman bearing a resemblance to Anthony Perkins. The next morning, this man, with scratches on his face and only vague memories of what transpired the night before, visits Dr. Allan Barnes and explains how, once again, he experienced a living nightmare where horrible acts of violence were committed. He attributes the strange phenomena to a mask he recently stole from a museum that gives him addictive powers and is further enraged by the concerned doctor's natural skepticism.

The man commits suicide later that night and shortly after, Allan Barnes receives a mysterious package in the mail. With a bedazzled skull mask now grinning at him from the desk, he reads the note from his deceased patient, telling him to conduct the experiment to see how strong his mind really is. Pulsating tribal drumming and narrated shouts to "put the mask on now, put the mask on now!" cue the audience to participate in Allan's first descent into foggy caverns of cobwebs, skeletons, strobes, lasers, flames, and sacrificial rites, where everyone either looks like mannequins with darting eyes full of fear or zombies with eyeballs hanging over the cheeks. It is here where we also see a monstrously sized version of that grinning mask, a visual that made my eyes pop out with excitement when I first saw it printed in an issue of *Rue Morgue* magazine several years ago.

The movie, which was given a 2015 Blu-ray release from Kino Lorber, treats ownership of the mask as a metaphor for drugs, causing the doctor's personality to change after his first trip. Obsessive over his new possession, he lashes out when his girlfriend suggests telling someone else about the mask, and later goes into a blind rage when she confiscates it and returns it to the museum where it was originally stolen. There are some people who would tell you that this movie has little to offer outside of those three ridiculously cool hallucinatory montages, but to me they were icing on a cake that was already pretty tasty in its simplest form. Paul Stevens, looking like Ralph Fiennes mixed with Martin Landau, makes for a compelling protagonist who risks self-destruction to get closer to understanding the mysteries hidden even deeper than the subconscious, and his journey should be identifiable to anyone who has ever suffered from an addiction.

LOVECRAFT ADAPTATIONS FOR YOUR CTHULHU CONVENTION

Dagon (2001)
Director: Stuart Gordon
Writers: Dennis Paoli, H.P. Lovecraft (stories)
Cast: Ezra Godden, Francisco Rabal, Raquel Merono, Macarena Gomez, Brendan Price

The website Spain This Way described Combarro, Spain as a "small, simple village but with a charm and uniqueness that make it well worth a visit," a sentiment shared by Trevor Huxman, who wrote on his travel blog that "it definitely ranks high on my list of prettiest Galician towns, so if you're ever exploring Galicia's western Atlantic coast, do try to slip over there for a visit!" This fishing village may be breathtaking on a sunny afternoon, but if it's overcast and taken over by Stuart Gordon and a dedicated crew, it looks like a foreboding cesspool of evil that could only exist in your worst nightmares. This was a perfect location for an H.P. Lovecraft adaptation, and might have made even the most decrepit and atmospheric fishing village in New England look like Disney World in comparison. *Dagon* is based on the short story "The Shadow Over Innsmouth," and is introduced by its final line: "We shall swim out to that brooding reef in the sea and dive down through black abysses to Cyclopean and many columned Y'ha-nthlei, and in that lair of the Deep Ones we shall dwell amidst wonder and glory for ever."

Had this movie been made in the '80s like Stuart Gordon intended, the role of Paul would have gone to Jeffrey Combs, but instead, it went to lookalike Ezra Godden in his film debut, and he does such a good job that not for one moment will you pine for what could have been. After a hellacious thunderstorm ruins Paul's attempts of a relaxing and luxurious vacation at sea, he and his girlfriend Barbara are forced to downgrade to a lifeboat and row with all their might to Imboca, a village that at first seems inexplicably deserted, but which only gets more chilling with each resident it introduces: a masked man hobbling down an alley, a webbed-fingered-priest lurking inside a pitch-black church with the most mystifying of creeds, a hotel concierge with clammy skin and what appears to be gills. Anyone reading this book has surely seen their fair share of creepy hotels in films, but the one in this movie would undoubtedly receive the harshest Yelp reviews! It is inside this outrageously filthy hotel room lit entirely by lightning where Paul, waiting for Barbara's return, realizes just how much trouble they are in after an innocent glance out the window attracts the attention of a large mob whose dialect consists solely of grunts, croaks, snorts, and growls. This sets up a grueling chase scene for the ages that places him in one seemingly hopeless situation after another, all while perpetual rain slams against the frames of his glasses and obscures his vision.

He finally gets a chance to catch his breath after encountering an elderly native living in a constant state of inebriation to numb himself of the horrors that have befallen his once-Christian village and whose story is briefly told through flashbacks. In one of the best scenes, Paul is creeping around a mansion to hide from a zombie-like horde when he meets the mysterious woman from so many of his dreams and nightmares, and now for the first time she's above water. As his night of terror goes on with possibilities dwindling and body counts rising, she pleads with him to submit to a destiny that may include his girlfriend being sacrificially fed to their ancient god of the sea. Those with a low tolerance for gore might want to keep their eyes closed during a particularly nasty scene, easily the most brutal and agonizing in Gordon's repertoire, and thankfully it's built up enough to give you ample warning.

Dagon was one of those criminally underrated gems that I never thought would ever be playing at a theater near me, but shortly after moving to Portland, Oregon, I learned that no film is off limits thanks to the beautiful Hollywood Theatre. Its annual H.P. Lovecraft Film Festival was taking place on a weekend while my parents were in town, and since my mom has an aversion to films like this, she explored the beautiful Japanese Gardens on a crisp autumn afternoon while my dad and I enjoyed a double feature of *The Unnamable* and *Dagon*. As if seeing *Dagon* in a sold-out theater with enthusiastic masses chanting along to "Iä! Iä! Cthulhu fhtagn!" wasn't cool enough, following the film was a highly entertaining and informative Q&A with Stuart Gordon himself, who seemed to be overjoyed that a movie that had been floating around in his magnificent brain for decades before making it had finally been given the warm reception it deserved.

About five years later, I got home from work to find that my copy of the brand-new *Dagon* Blu-ray had arrived, and that excitement was parlayed into a long night of watching one special feature after another until I decided to use the power of the mythical sea creature to call in sick the next morning.

The Haunted Palace (1963)

Director: Roger Corman
Writers: Charles Beaumont, H.P. Lovecraft (story), Edgar Allan Poe (poem)
Cast: Vincent Price, Debra Paget, Lon Chaney Jr., Frank Maxwell, Leo Gordon

Today I received a wedding invitation in the mail and reacted as if it were a violation from one of Portland's 10,000 speed/red light cameras. These days, the only marriages I want to witness are the kind that occur in movies like *The Haunted Palace*—marriages between the stories of H.P. Lovecraft and poetry from Poe, between elder sea gods and a cobwebbed New England mansion, and between Vincent Price and Lon Chaney Jr. sharing the screen for the only time and reciting incantations involving Cthulhu and Yog-Sothoth. I had known of this movie for years but wasn't aware of its distinction of being the first ever feature film adaptation of an H.P. Lovecraft story, and this is largely due to American International Pictures insisting that the title be changed from Lovecraft's The Case of Charles Dexter Ward to *Edgar Allan Poe's The Haunted Palace* so that it could fit in snugly in the Corman-Poe saga from a marketing perspective rather than confuse the moviegoing public who had never heard of this H.P. fella. Against the wishes of Corman, they tried to justify this misleading title change by simply including a couple stanzas from Poe's "Haunted Palace" poem in the opening and ending credits.

On a stormy night in 1765, a young woman in a trancelike state is spotted traversing through rolling fog and forested paths of Arkham to reach the mansion owned by Joseph Curwen (Price), rumored to be a warlock by the townsfolk. The suspicions are confirmed when he leads her through secret passageways to perform the unholiest of ceremonies that is cut short by a torch-wielding mob descending on the property. The proud owner of the Necronomicon is burned alive but not before he places a curse on their ancestors and a promise to return one day with a vengeance.

Price also plays Charles Dexter Ward, great great grandson of Curwen, who shows up in Arkham 110 years later with his wife Anne to look at this infamous piece of property they have just inherited. Despite their politeness and good intentions, they are given a cold reception by the distrustful locals who warn them not to step foot inside that evil, cursed place built from European stones. The consequences of Curwen's final words are exposed through a number of inhabitants with mutated malformations converging at the Harbor Supplies store, as well as a portrait still hanging on the mantle that casts a peculiar spell on Charles, making him susceptible to a spirit searching for a new host. "One grows accustomed to the dark here," warns the palace's caretaker (Lon Chaney Jr.), but does one grow accustomed to the breeding of ancient sea deities and sacrificial women to create a new race to take over the world? There's only one way to find out!

While incredibly spacious, this haunted palace is so crammed with ideas that a couple of the most interesting subplots aren't given room to breathe and…wait, why am I complaining about anything? Two hours ago, I thought I had seen all of the essential Lovecraft adaptations, but then this one comes along that happens to star the velvet-voiced horror god Vincent Price playing a Jekyll and Hyde duality to perfection! Art director Daniel Haller was a huge factor in all of these Corman-Price pictures being well-received, and he was rewarded with a directing career of his own where he would also attempt to interpret unnamable horrors with *Die, Monster Die!* (based on "The Colour Out of Space") and *The Dunwich Horror*.

Poster for ***Necronomicon: Book of the Dead*** (1993), August Entertainment, New Line Home Video

Necronomicon: Book of the Dead (1993)

Directors: Brian Yuzna, Christophe Gans, Shusuke Kaneko
Writers: Brent V. Friedman, Christophe Gans, Kazunori Ito, H.P. Lovecraft (stories)
Cast: Jeffrey Combs, Bruce Payne, David Warner, Millie Perkins, Signy Coleman, Don Calfa

I'm assuming that by the time you're reading this, some distribution company will have finally come to the rescue and given this underrated gem a physical release with all the bells and whistles, and that horror bloggers everywhere will be singing its praises much like I've been doing ever since a VHS rental back in 1993. But as of right now, *Necronomicon: Book of the Dead* is still unavailable on DVD, Blu-ray, or a single legal streaming service. How can the almighty Cthulhu allow this kind of injustice to continue year after year?

Jeffrey Combs excelled for years on stage playing Edgar Allan Poe in a one-man show, and is also very convincing here as H.P. Lovecraft despite the two men looking nothing alike. His believable prosthetics are a sign of what's to come in this horror anthology loaded with top-notch makeup and practical effects. It's set in the fall of 1932 (just five years before Lovecraft passed away from intestinal cancer at the age of 46) when the author is determined to do some "fact checking" inside a monastery where the Necronomicon is guarded by monks. "My work is wrongly construed as fiction by the lesser minded—in fact I take great pride in presenting fictional possibilities. It's my duty, after all, as a human being to enlighten the darkest depths of experience, to expose certain secrets unjustly hoarded by others," he tells one of them before stealing a set of keys that opens the secret reading room.

With the book that unlocks the mysteries of the universe now in front of him, he sits down and starts reading a chapter titled "The Drowned," or as the IMDb synopsis currently calls it, "The Drawned." Directed by Christophe Gans (*Silent Hill*, *Brotherhood of the Wolf*), this is very loosely based on Lovecraft's short story "The Rats in the Walls" about a downbeat man named Edward De Lapoer (Bruce Payne in a moving performance) visiting the New England cliffside mansion he's just inherited. It used to function as a prosperous hotel but has been empty and decaying for 60 years, ever since his uncle Jethro reacted to the shipwrecked deaths of his wife and child by throwing the Bible into a fire and accepting another book into his heart, one that had the capability of reviving his loved ones in twisted and monstrous Monkey's Paw-like stipulations. Despite the grave warnings, Edward is so blinded by grief from a reckless driving accident that killed his wife Clara that he conducts the same evil ceremony in hopes that he can see her one more time. This moody and merciless segment, probably my favorite of the three, succeeds at making this house—towering above water-filled caves that threaten to drown it at any moment with the help of a perpetual storm—an evil presence even before monsters show up to reveal their slimy tentacles.

Next up is "The Cold," directed by Shusuke Kaneko from *Death Note* and multiple Kaiju entries. It's inspired by Lovecraft's "Cool Air" story and centers around a woman who moves into a new home to escape her abusive stepfather. She is told to not bother the reclusive physician living on the third floor, who suffers from a rare skin condition that requires inordinately cold temperatures and maybe a vial of spinal fluid every now and then. I always found this segment to be slow and uninteresting as a kid, but that was before I truly appreciated the magnetism of veteran actor David Warner, who gets lots of screen time to shine.

And because this ancient Necronomicon is apparently able to encompass the past, present, *and* future, the final tale "Whispers" is set in modern times where a pair of police officers, Sarah and Paul, discuss their intimate relationship while also speeding after an enigmatic criminal known as "The Butcher." After losing control and wrecking the car, a barely conscious Sarah watches as Paul is pulled away and dragged down a tunnel into a warehouse, his blood leaving a terrifying path for her to follow. As she desperately tries to rescue the father of her unborn baby, she descends further and further into this building that starts resembling the underground lair at the climax of *House of 1000 Corpses*, where she meets a resident played by Don Calfa (*Return of the Living Dead*, *Weekend at Bernie's*). He's justifiably bonkers from spending so much time in this kind of environment, which "has a bad habit of swallowing things up like they never existed." If you wanted to create an early '90s horror dream team, then look no further than this powerful segment where the great Brian Yuzna worked with cinematographer Gerry Lively, who also shot *Warlock: The Armageddon*, *Waxwork II: Lost in Time*, *Return of the Living Dead III*, and *Hellraiser III: Hell on Earth*, as well as production designer Anton Tremblay, who lent his talents to *Leprechaun 3*, *Ticks*, and *Army of Darkness* before Rob Zombie hired him for *The Devil's Rejects* and *Halloween*. Together they created a vision of hell so bleak, artistic, and disturbing that when "Whispers" comes to end, we can't blame Mr. Lovecraft for being so affected that he lays his head on the table and massages his temples for relief, unaware that he's about to confront more unnamable horrors inside the library.

The Resurrected (1991)

Director: Dan O'Bannon
Writers: Brent V. Friedman, H.P. Lovecraft (story)
Cast: Chris Sarandon, John Terry, Jane Sibbett, Robert Romanus, Laurie Briscoe

Despite winning a Fangoria Chainsaw Award for Best Independent/Low-Budget Film, featuring the talents of Dan O'Bannon and Chris Sarandon, and for being one of the most faithful H.P. Lovecraft adaptations, *The Resurrected* went decades with very little fanfare but now has a small cult following and a special edition Scream Factory Blu-ray.

The late, great St. Louis native Dan O'Bannon got his start by collaborating with John Carpenter on the science fiction cult film *Dark Star*, and with the horrors of outer space still lurking in his mind, he penned the screenplay for *Alien* and endeared himself to the horror community forever. After writing another horror masterpiece in *Dead & Buried*, the Roy Scheider-starring action film *Blue Thunder*, and the best segment in *Heavy Metal*, he decided to add directing to his repertoire and was remarkably skilled at it. There are only two feature films that Dan O'Bannon directed: one is *The Return of the Living Dead*, which he also wrote, and the other is *The Resurrected*, based on the Lovecraft tale "The Case of Charles Dexter Ward."

Hopefully one of these days, a city will boost tourism by constructing a Mt. Rushmore for vampires, and obviously Bela Lugosi and Christopher Lee would have to be positioned in the center. Max Schreck's Nosferatu would probably have to be on one side, and on the other, I'd like to see Jerry Dandridge from *Fright Night*! Played by Chris Sarandon, he's not only one of the most suave, charismatic, and menacing vampires in cinema history, but with sad eyes and moments of melancholy, he exhibited how being a creature of the night can really suck in between the bloodsuckings. Sarandon continued to warm the hearts of horror fans in *Child's Play* and as the voice of the Pumpkin King himself, Jack Skellington, but if *Fright Night* left you wanting more Scary Sarandon, then *The Resurrected* is your very best bet because he gets to play a personification of eeeeeeeevil with ghoulish makeup and gnarly teeth, hissing lines like "I must have raw meat! Not disgusting, seared, burnt flesh. It is blood, I must have the blood! Your kitchen drains the blood from the meat!"

Originally titled Shatterbrain—a Middle English term for the crazies—this slow-burning nightmare rewards you generously for your patience. Jane Sibbett (*Herman's Head*, *Friends*) plays a concerned wife who hires a private investigator to find out just what is going on with her husband, well-respected chemical engineer Charles Ward, who has left home and locked himself in an eerie building neighboring a cemetery to conduct secretive experiments. When the private investigator stops at a gas station and asks for directions to this new home, the attendant simply instructs him to roll his windows down and follow the horrible smell that has infiltrated the whole damn town.

If the Fangoria Chainsaw Awards had included the category Most Terrifying Set Piece, then *The Resurrected* would have taken home a second trophy for sure because very few locations can measure up to these labyrinthine catacombs, which beckon you to press pause so you can closely examine every detail and catch the breath that was stolen when characters descend into this subterranean hellishness with diminishing light sources and confront vast pools of utter darkness where impressive animatronic elephantiasis-afflicted skeleton monsters await.

The Unnamable (1988)

Director: Jean-Paul Ouellette
Writers: Jean-Paul Ouellette, H.P. Lovecraft (story)
Cast: Charles Klausmeyer, Mark Kinsey Stephenson, Alexandra Durrell, Laura Albert

I learned at an early age that Saturday night was the best time of the week, because that's when USA's series *Saturday Nightmares* would take me on a dark ride; this was an invaluable service to someone still wearing their horror water wings and eager to explore the deep end. The H.P. Lovecraft adaptation *The Unnamable* was shown on one especially memorable episode, and it scared the living daylights out of me and made such an impression that afterwards I tried drawing a picture of Alyda Winthrop, only to learn that my complete lack of artistic ability was almost as frightening.

Mark Kinsey Stephenson plays Randolph Carter, a recurring character from seven different Lovecraft stories, who tells two of his Miskatonic University companions the true story of what happened to one of his ancestors inside the very house that currently towers over them. The three scholars have a philosophical debate that ends with Joel, a science major, deciding to spend the night alone in the long-vacant house just to disprove Carter's theories of unnamable creatures; Carter and Howard aren't willing to take the risk and head back to the campus. Once inside, the door slams shut and locks Joel inside, and for the next several minutes, he just explores the creepy old house by candlelight, passing by peeling wallpaper and centuries-old bloodstains in total silence with the exception of his footsteps and the occasional creak echoing in the distance. He reminds himself that he has nothing to be afraid of before removing the chains from a door leading up to the attic, and then his screams awaken the sole resident of the house.

When Joel doesn't return to campus the following day and misses a scheduled visit with relatives, Howard takes the matter very seriously, and after lots of coaxing, convinces Carter to assist him on a search and rescue mission. In a one-in-a-million coincidence, that same night a couple of fraternity guys volunteer to give two cute freshmen girls a little sneak preview of what their sorority initiation will look like. A setup like this might indicate plenty of silly misunderstandings, jock stereotypes, and hazing buffoonery, but *The Unnamable* plays it straight and is far more concerned with suspense than fun. On my most recent watch, this time finally in high-definition and widescreen thanks to a painfully long-awaited and beautifully remastered 2019 Blu-ray release from Unearthed Films, I tried taking off my rose-tinted nostalgic glasses to attempt objectivity, and I will admit to there being one too many meandering scenes of people simply crawling and tip-toeing all around a house where every room pretty much looks the same, but still, I would call them pleasantly boring as opposed to "let's see what else is on" boring, because I know it won't be long until Alyda makes her presence known again and tempts me to cower under the covers.

Thanks to sources like *Fangoria* and *Saturday Nightmares* shaping my youth and preparing me for a lifetime of horror fandom, a sizeable chunk of my brain hosts a dusty crypt in which creatures, demons, and ghouls roam, and out of all I have seen, none has looked as breathtaking and haunting as Alyda Winthrop. The film wisely keeps her offscreen for most of the running time because it knows that the final reveal will not disappoint. Her otherworldly shrieks, sounding equally ferocious and tragic, as well as a backstory of a man whose hair turned white after seeing her reflection permanently etched in a window (a result of her staring into it for many years) arouses our curiosity and makes us so damn anxious to see her, but in the meantime, we're more than happy to be teased with blink-and-you'll-miss glimpses of her hoofs, horns, wings, and claws. This cat-goat-bat-gargoyle-dragon-albino lady that occasionally moves as gracefully as a ballerina can effortlessly claw throats apart, pull hearts out, and bash heads against the floor until brains splatter, but the moment she starts to feel physical pain of her own brings unexpected pathos, a sign of a classic monster.

Stephenson's Randolph Carter makes for a compelling and unlikely heroic character because rather than confront the creature face to face or come to the aid of his screaming schoolmates, he just sits there and reads, his eyes gleaming with every ancient dust-covered scroll he discovers in the house. As his dweebish, sad puppy dog-eyed sidekick Howard, Charles Klausmeyer is also very charming, and I was so happy to see them reunite four years later in T*he Unnamable II: The Statement of Randolph Carter.*

Horror Galore

GHOSTS AND DEMONS THAT PREFER TO DOWNSIZE TO APARTMENTS

Lurkers (1988)
Director: Roberta Findlay
Writers: Ed Kelleher, Harriette Vidal
Cast: Christine Moore, Gary Warner, Marina Taylor, Roy MacArthur, Peter Oliver-Norman

Roberta Findlay wasted little time in making a name for herself in the world of exploitative cinema and hardcore pornography in the '60s and '70s, collaborating with her then-husband Michael Findlay (who would die tragically in a freak helicopter accident in 1977) and amassing credits as an actress, lighting technician, composer, cinematographer, editor, writer, producer, and director all before turning 25. A decade after her *Angel Number 9* screened in theaters and was publicized as the first major porno film directed by a woman, she shifted gears and directed a string of low-budget horror films set in the grimiest of New York City streets.

With a script from Ed Kelleher, a writer she crossed paths with on the set of the so-bad-it's-amazing *Invasion of the Blood Farmers*, *Lurkers* seems to tread the same waters as movies like *The Sentinel* and *Rosemary's Baby* by focusing on the psychological trauma of a young woman named Cathy who had the misfortune of growing up inside a cursed New York City brownstone apartment. The film opens with her as a little girl, tears rolling down her face as she's verbally abused by her despicable mother who forces her to go outside even though "they" are right on the doorsteps. Immediately after stepping outside, Cathy is invited by a couple other girls to play jump rope, and even creepier than their nursery rhymes is the way they fling the rope around her neck and squeeze with stone-faced pride. Poor Cathy can't even read under the covers at night without being mercilessly abused because hovering directly above her bed are spirits that look so goddamn creepy it's no surprise to learn that among the makeup artists was Ed French, whose credits include *Amityville II: The Possession*, *Sleepaway Camp*, *C.H.U.D.*, *The Stuff*, *Creepshow 2*, *Hellraiser: Bloodline*, and perhaps most nightmare-inducing of all, *White Chicks*.

Jumping forward many years, we learn that both of her parents met grisly fates and her brother joined the priesthood and wants absolutely nothing to do with her, but Cathy still managed to become a surprisingly content adult, working as a classically-trained musician and engaged to a successful photographer named Bob. But then the fear begins to take over once again with nightmares, visions of the ghosts from her childhood, and the paranoia that her fiancé is being unfaithful with his business partner and former model Monica. After lots of kissing scenes, including one that won't make you hungry for pepperoni pizza anytime soon, Bob convinces her to go to a swank party at Monica's place, but Cathy refuses to step inside once she discovers in horror that it's taking place inside the same building responsible for all of her long-term trauma. However, just like in her childhood, she's not so safe standing outside on the steps either. She eventually joins the party just so that she can call the police about a sledgehammer-swinging brute, a gang of punks, a blood-caked phonebooth, and a live chicken in a cemetery, and that's when the really weird stuff begins. You can't help but get pumped up every time she's about to open a door because there's always something shocking waiting for her on the other side.

Cathy is an easy character to root for because in addition to being sympathetic, she also stands up for herself and refuses to be patronized by Bob when he mocks her visions. Her psychic friend is another strong female character, criticizing Cathy's prehistoric plans of giving up her career for Bob and staying at home with future children. Even the women who exist solely for gratuitous nudity are interesting; instead of squealing about boys and parties, they're taking their tops off while casually discussing taxes, inside traders, and how "the junk bonds were used for the acquisition of an undervalued corporation." There's a Faustian subplot that doesn't make a whole lot of sense, but both the eventual explanation of Cathy's visions and the ending are grand-slam homeruns.

Plot-wise, it's not far off from the first horror film Findlay directed, *The Oracle*, in which drop-dead-gorgeous Jennifer moves into an apartment recently vacated by the death of an elderly woman and inherits the planchette she used to communicate with spirits. This stone hand gripping a feather pen is a nice alternative to the standard Ouija board, and after it makes quite an impression at a dinner party, to have it startle its new owner with middle-of-the-night scribbling is an even worse wake-up call than a vomiting cat. And when another character yells, "Come on you stupid piece of shit, you ain't got no power" after it ignores a request for tomorrow's lottery numbers, you just know that his autopsy won't be mentioning "natural causes." While rough around the edges and occasionally lagging, *The Oracle*, full of gore and scary visuals, tells a compelling story about a woman who can't get a single mustached man (of which there are oh so many) to believe her visions of a *Double Indemnity* victim seeking vengeance from beyond the grave. But an even better selling point might be its Christmastime setting in a NYC neighborhood littered with quirky details like a burlesque show sign reading "Where's the beef? It's here on stage! 4 Hunky Guys." Also, much like *Lurkers*, this film contains a party scene that is a thousand times more fun to watch than most real parties are to attend.

Under the Shadow (2016)

Writer and Director: Babak Anvari
Cast: Narges Rashidi, Avin Manshadi, Bobby Nederi, Arash Marandi, Aram Ghasemy

Many reviews have referred to this film as Iran's *Babadook* because it's about a woman whose inner turmoil is exacerbated when demonic forces prey on her and her only child, but it doesn't feel derivative in the slightest and is a must-see for fans of slow-burning psychological terrors. Co-produced between the nations of Qatar, Jordan, and the United Kingdom, it's a Persian-spoken film set in post-revolutionary Tehran during the Iran-Iraq War which lasted for almost all of the 1980s.

When we meet former medical student Shideh, she's being interviewed at a university but is told that due to her participation in left-leaning political protests years ago, she will never be allowed to return. Her dreams being crushed lead to jealousy and resentment toward her husband for his doctoral practice, and they are further driven apart when he receives his annual draft notice and has to serve in one of the most dangerous military areas. With rumors of missiles targeting Tehran, he advises Shideh to take their daughter Dorsa to his parents' house in a safer part of the country, but she stubbornly refuses to leave her home in which she feels safe and independent, even as emergency evacuations to the apartment complex's basement become just as elemental to her evening routine as her Jane Fonda aerobics video workout. She also has to frequently deal with her daughter's fanciful imagination and frightening visions of the djinn. One of her neighbors is also a believer, insisting that these supernatural creatures straight out of Arabian folklore travel on the wind from place to place until they find someone to possess.

Under the Shadow is yet another recent example of films not needing an R-rating to be scary-as-hell, but even without the supernatural horror elements, this would still be riveting cinema due to family struggles during wartime and the compelling dynamics between the many residents of the apartment complex. Iranian actress Narges Rashidi gives an unforgettable performance as Shideh, a character who is so vulnerable that a hasty escape from demonic forces could be punishable by lashes if she forgets to bring her Hijab with her. She's also committing a crime simply by watching the music video for Yaz's "Don't Go" because owning a VCR is against the law. Her strength is further tested as more and more of her neighbors leave, as the cracks in her ceiling get bigger and deeper, and as her daughter succumbs to fever and violent outbursts (there's only so much that a ball of magical cat fur

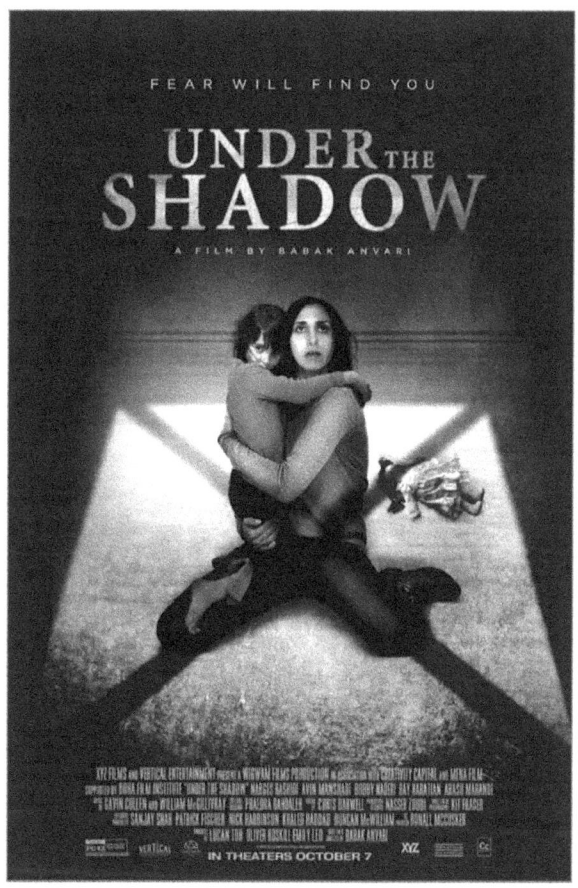

Poster for **Under the Shadow** (2016),
Wigwam Films, XYZ, Vertical Entertainment

can do). She even wakes up one morning to find a man who is not her husband sleeping beside her!

Under the Shadow made its premiere at the Sundance Film Festival, earning rave reviews, and was chosen as Great Britain's selection to the Academy Awards that year, but since it's a horror film, of course it was ignored by the voters.

Horror Galore

ENGLISH GHOST STORIES TO SCARE THE DICKENS OUT OF YOU

Haunted (1995)

Director: Lewis Gilbert
Writers: Timothy Prager, Bob Kellett, Lewis Gilbert, James Herbert (novel)
Cast: Aidan Quinn, Kate Beckinsale, Anthony Andrews, Anna Massey, Alex Lowe, John Gielgud

I was about 16 years old when *Haunted* first caught my eye on a Saturday night at Blockbuster Video, a night when I must have craved "a romantic ghost tale with a twist" like the critical blurb promised. The first viewing gripped me with its mysterious storyline involving dark family secrets and insanity-inducing visions, and even with all those mysteries solved and visions explained, I would rent the same videotape just a few weeks later. I wanted to be back at the charming estate of Edbrook in the 1920s, with its brightly-lit rooms and decadence, with sunshine, gentle breezes, and a rope swing facing a beautiful lake. The estate takes on a completely different personality when nighttime approaches but it's just as appealing. It's a perfect setting for a ghost story, and it even likes to show off every now and then by transforming into what it once was, or what it will eventually become. I wanted to visit all the characters again and replay their interesting discussions about death, longing, love, and traumas. And because this was before I could purchase a soundtrack on Amazon or listen to the songs on YouTube, I absolutely had to hear Debbie Wiseman's majestic, swooning, achingly

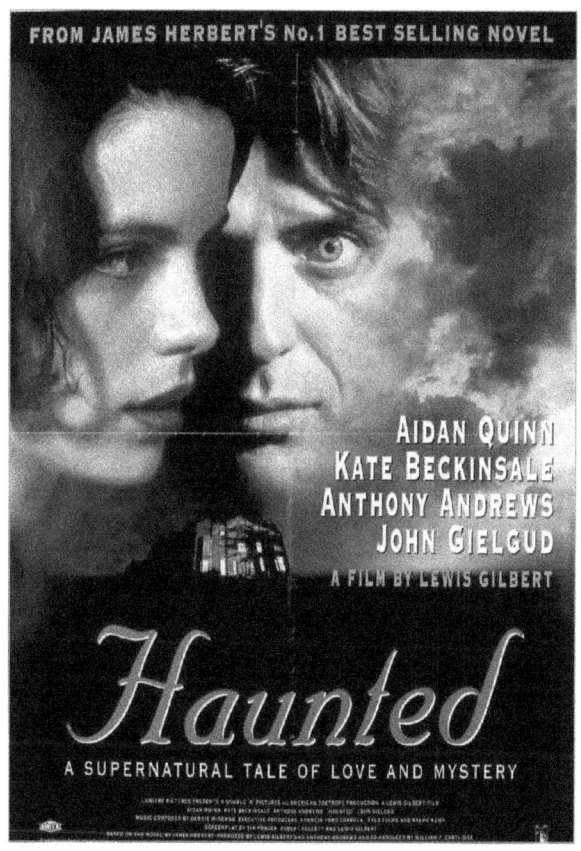

Poster for *Haunted* (1995), American Zoetrope, Entertainment Film Distributors

beautiful music once more, in which a sad piano melody tugs at the heartstrings before a full orchestra ties them into a beautiful bow. And just like our protagonist, I was finding the bewitching Christina, played by Kate Beckinsale, impossible to stay away from for very long.

The always-reliable Aidan Quinn (known mostly for *Legends of the Fall*, *Benny & Joon*, and *Practical Magic*) plays a professor of psychology named David Ash who believes "there are no ghosts or spirits, just the longing that there should be to ease our pain and our fears," and he's been harboring a tremendous amount of pain since childhood with the death of his twin sister. The publication of his latest book has resulted in several invitations to supposed haunted houses, the most disturbing and desperate ones coming from an elderly woman names Mrs. Webb who's convinced that spirits are tormenting her inside the isolated large mansion where she's worked as a housekeeper and nanny for the Mariell family for decades. He decides to investigate her peculiar claims, and after interviewing her, the three grownup Mariell siblings, and her affable doctor (the late great John Gielgud), he's convinced the woman needs a psychiatrist and not a paranormal expert. Still, he decides to stick around a bit longer to try to help with her delusions, but mostly to spend more time with Christina, much to the chagrin of her protective older brother Robert, played with devilish charm and the most masculine of British baritones by Anthony Andrews (who also served as one of the film's producers). Alarmed by the strange family dynamics and succumbing to unexplainable visions of his own, an increasingly fragile David struggles with a new reality that involves either loss of sanity or proof of the paranormal.

Haunted is a classic, period piece British ghost story like *The Turn of the Screw* or *The Innocents*, with high production values and sophisticated special effects, like when a cloud of dust spins in the howling wind and shapes itself into a distorted ghost, crying uncontrollably and beckoning David toward a lake made angry by a ferocious thunderstorm. Even though the movie could definitely use a widescreen remastering, it's still a feast for the senses because of Lewis Gilbert's direction, authentic 1920s Sussex costumes and cars, lovely music, and atmospheric touches like fog blanketing a cobblestone road and then mingling with the smoke from a train. It chills your bones but also has the courtesy of warming them up by showing lots of fire.

The Woman in Black (1989)

Director: Herbert Wise
Writers: Nigel Kneale, Susan Hill (novel)
Cast: Adrian Rawlins, Bernard Hepton, David Daker, Pauline Moran, David Ryall

While the 2012 remake starring Daniel Radcliffe was earning more than $20 million in North America on its opening weekend, the far-superior 1989 original could only be seen by shelling out a couple hundred dollars for a VHS copy. This widely beloved made-for-TV movie is still not easily accessible a decade later, although a pristine special edition Blu-ray was recently released in its native England. It's based on a 1983 novel from Susan Hill that also inspired one of the longest-running stage plays in London's West End as well as two BBC radio adaptations.

The plot is simple and familiar, with loving family man and London solicitor Arthur Kidd traveling to handle the estate of a recluse whose name captures the imagination and fear among the locals. But what is not common is how affectively this movie transports us back to 1925 with its Bentley automobiles, new innovations like spinning wheel electrical generators and voice-recording wax cylinders, and fashions at the coastal market (where a falling log nearly takes the head off of a child). Location, location, location serves as this movie's strongest weapon, with the characters having to navigate the real-life causeway to Osea Island to reach the impressive estate at Stanlake Park in Berkshire. Having to rely on the tides' cooperation makes an overnight stay at this haunted house—with its swinging chandeliers and secret rooms full of creepy dolls—extra intimidating, especially when one wrong step through the dense fog makes you easy prey for the sea. Past victims can still be heard wailing through the night in a ghostly purgatory.

Having a cemetery directly outside the house is another excellent touch, and it's where the titular character gives Arthur his first of many frights. It's only the first of October as I write this, but it's difficult to imagine receiving a bigger scare for the remainder of the Halloween season than the one this woman in black provided later in the movie. Making it extra special was how it came just after someone says my first name.

Adrian Rawlins is extremely likable as Arthur, and we can't help but root for him as he tries putting the pieces of the mystery together, especially after he shows genuine concern and affection for a sweet dog named Spider. And considering who would replace him in the remake, it's all the more fitting that Rawlins would appear in *The Goblet of Fire* and *The Deathly Hallows: Part 2* as Harry Potter's dad. Screenwriter Nigel Kneal also wrote the popular 1953 series *The Quartermass Experiment*, *The Stone Tape*, and an early draft of *Halloween III: Season of the Witch*. And given the strength of the music throughout, it's easy to see why Rachel Portman has composed for more than 100 other films, many of which were major Hollywood hits.

"They'll be scary ghost stories and tales of the glories of Christmases long, long ago," Andy Williams crooned on one of the more irritating Christmas songs, and the Brits who celebrated this lost tradition probably had their scariest Christmas Eve ever when *The Woman in Black* first aired in 1989, entangling them in a web so merciless that it could only be broken by the arrival of Saint Nick and dreams of sugarplums.

Horror Galore

SERIAL KILLERS AND PEOPLE WHO JUST GO A LITTLE MAD SOMETIMES

Alone (2020)
Director: John Hyams
Writer: Mattias Olsson
Cast: Jules Willcox, Marc Menchaca, Anthony Heald

With the film industry in complete disarray and distributors shuffling their decks as they stare at a bleak forecast with no prudent release dates in sight, smaller independent studios have been trying to take advantage of a stalled Hollywood and give audiences some much-deserved escapism in these uncertain times. The survival wilderness thriller *Alone* was released in September 2020 in very select theaters and on digital platforms, and was considered a success story by insiders like *Variety* since it cracked the iTunes top 10 and wowed the critics, but a film this thrilling and expertly crafted deserved so much more.

The underrated Jules Willcox stars as Jessica, who opens the film by playing Tetris as she struggles to maneuver all of her possessions inside a U-Haul. Needing to escape and start a new life, she says goodbye to the Portland streets and heads up north. Having spent almost two decades in this city, it was nice being able to spot the various locations of her drive and to see it filmed so beautifully, without any graffiti or homeless camps in sight. Few things in life are as liberating as a solo road trip through the Pacific Northwest, but Jessica doesn't get any enjoyment out of it due to coping with a heartbreaking end to a marriage and being weirded out by another motorist, played by *Ozark*'s Marc Menchaca, who makes his presence known one too many times for it to be merely coincidental. The actor recently played Klansman Joe in an episode of *Curb Your Enthusiasm*, but here he initially comes across as your average Joe with just enough coldness to his smile to make us breathe a sigh of relief every time she smartly speeds away from him, especially when he's using Ted Bundy's tactic of wearing a sling to appear vulnerable as he stands beside his immobilized vehicle in the middle of the road.

Jessica's hellish ordeal is broken up into five segments: The Road, The River, The Rain, The Night, and The Clearing, and all of them are so plentiful with visceral thrills that it would be impossible to rank them in order of suspense. She contends with not only a ruthless killer leading a double life, but also with a landscape that's every bit as dangerous as it is majestic. As this cat-and-mouse chase goes on, we become so invested in her survival that we'd all give up ice cream for a year if we could just personally give this bastard one good kneecap smash with a crowbar.

For nearly its entire runtime, *Alone* had my stomach in knots and my knuckles whiter than ever, and maybe in a few months when my cardiologist says my nerves have fully recovered, I'll seek out the original Swedish film *Försvunnen* from 2011 to see how Mattias Olsson's two scripts compare and contrast. The only time this movie seemed unrealistic was when Jessica had the audacity to pump her own gasoline in Oregon, breaking a state law that earns us much-deserved mockery from every other state besides New Jersey.

The Black Room (1935)

Director: Roy William Neill
Writers: Arthur Strawn, Henry Myers
Cast: Boris Karloff, Marian Marsh, Robert Allen, Thurston Hall, Katherine DeMille

Just three months after Universal Pictures wrapped up production on *Bride of Frankenstein* and Boris Karloff got to remove his electrodes and 11-pound boots, he headed to Columbia Pictures to star in a movie in which he played two characters, neither of which required extensive makeup or uncomfortable wardrobes—just a heck of a lot more lines to memorize! *The Black Room* opens inside a castle on a night that was intended to be a celebratory occasion, but when it's revealed that the Baron's wife has just given birth to twins, a sudden sternness takes over him as he reflects on a prophecy that has been embroiled in the family for generations. Being stubborn and superstitious, he's absolutely convinced of the inevitability that someday, the younger brother will murder the elder inside the black room of the castle, just like before.

Decades later, the elder brother, Gregor, has taken over the reins as baron and rules with an iron fist, but after multiple young women he courts mysteriously go missing, the angry peasants are preparing to make his head go missing. At the request of Gregor, younger brother Anton returns home after spending the past many years traveling throughout Europe, and he's given a nice welcome by the villagers who have always trusted and admired him. Gregor is incapable of expressing warmth and appreciation (unless he's praising his favorite type of fruit) and his only smile is a cruel one, whereas Anton possesses an aura of serenity and has mustered so much goodwill that he can't fathom the idea that so many people view his twin brother as a monster.

After yet another woman enters the castle and never comes out, the villagers swarm the property and surround Gregor, who in an effort to save his own life, announces that he will leave the country at once and relinquish the title to Anton. He signs the proper documents and packs his bags but before leaving, decides to show his brother the remodeling of the forbidden black room.

Karloff gives a remarkably nuanced performance and through the most subtle of mannerisms and movements, we never struggle with telling the twin brothers apart. The castle which they call home is oppressive in its gothic gloom, and the set dressers worked just as hard on the nearby cemetery, in which no two gravestones are alike. Add in some thunder, lightning, man's best friend, and a few murders, and you have a product even juicier than Gregor's beloved pears.

Frailty (2001)

Director: Bill Paxton
Writer: Brent Hanley
Cast: Bill Paxton, Matthew McConaughey, Matt O'Leary, Jeremy Sumpter, Powers Boothe

The closest I've come to having a movie theater entirely to myself was in May 2002, when it looked like my then-girlfriend and I would be the only ones at a screening for *Frailty*, Bill Paxton's directorial debut. But then during the short time between the final trailer and Lionsgate's logo, an older gentleman walked into the theater with a soda, the kind of cartoonishly sized tub of popcorn that's impossible to forget, and a surprising number of empty seats to choose from. Perhaps he was one of the few other people in Rindge, New Hampshire who caught the latest episode of *Ebert & Roeper* and wanted to see first-hand why their two enthusiastic thumbs practically ruptured the ceiling. Any of you who managed to see this movie in theaters probably had a similar experience because in a weekend where *Panic Room*, *Changing Lanes*, and *Ice Age* dominated the box office, *Frailty* opened in 9th place and only raked in $4 million dollars. This movie didn't get the rousing ovation that it deserved at our screening, but it's still impressive that 100% of the audience remained in their seats during the credits and didn't stand until the lights came on.

"Well, I'm tired and so weary but I must go along till the Lord comes and calls, calls me away, oh yes. Well, the bear will be gentle and the wolf will be tame, and the lion shall lay down with the lamb, oh yes. And the beast from the wild will be led by a child. And I'll be changed from this creature that I am, oh yes." Nowhere has a Johnny Cash tune felt more appropriate than in this Southern Gothic nightmare where two boys suddenly have a lot more to worry about than deciding whether to see *The Warriors* or *Meatballs* at the theater when in the middle of the night, they are awakened by their hardworking widowed father (Bill Paxton) who tells them that he was just visited by an angel with a very specific message: that they have been personally chosen to serve God's will by slaying demons that are masquerading as ordinary humans. Whereas Adam, young enough to have believed in Santa Claus until very recently, is blindly devoted to their new mission of conquering evil like superheroes do, older brother Fenton is terrified that his dad might not be right in the head and does whatever he can to prevent an innocent person from being slaughtered in the name of God. It's a thought-provoking and deeply disturbing nail-biter that is ubiquitous on lists concerning the most underrated horror gems,

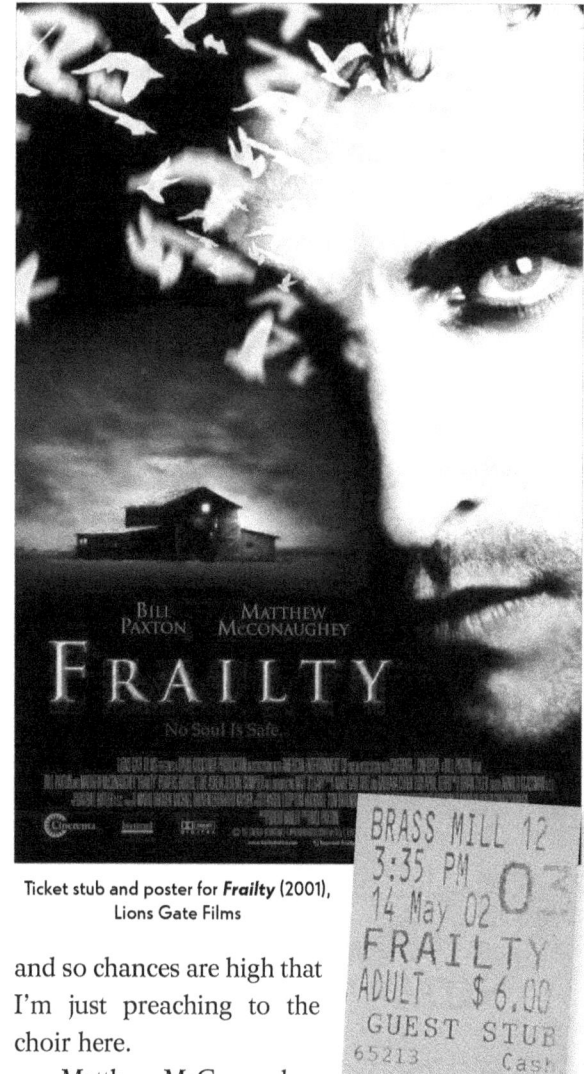

Ticket stub and poster for *Frailty* (2001), Lions Gate Films

and so chances are high that I'm just preaching to the choir here.

Matthew McConaughey was undoubtedly much prouder of his appearance here than in his previous horror movie, the much maligned but oddly fascinating *Texas Chainsaw Massacre: The Next Generation*, and every moment he gets to share on screen with the skeptical, gravelly-voiced Powers Booth is riveting. It's hard to top his performance in Sam Raimi's crime thriller masterpiece *A Simple Plan*, but Bill Paxton comes mightily close here playing a father whose love for his children is just as earnest and sincere as his desire to swing the axe down on those who happened to magically appear on his list; a good juxtaposition of a rain-splattered window dissolving into a Christian stop-motion after school special is one of many examples of him being just as commanding behind the camera. The two child actors are also terrific as the real heart and soul of this movie, and I'm happy to see on the IMDb that both of their careers seem to be doing well.

Pop culture connoisseurs sometimes feel numb by how frequently they have to mourn over beloved artists, but Bill Paxton's passing at the age of 61 hit especially hard because he was a uniquely gifted actor and because his damaged heart valve hadn't been well-publicized. It's rare to find an actor whose body of work could have earned him a spot in the Cult Movie Hall of Fame, if such an institution existed, due to appearing in movies like *Boxing Helena*, *One False Move*, and perhaps the most insane movie ever, Adam Rifkin's *The Dark Backward*, but who was mostly known for mega-blockbusters like *Titanic*, *Twister*, *True Lies*, and *Apollo 13*. And as legendary as his appearances in *Aliens* and *Near Dark* are in the horror community, he graced our preferred genre on many other occasions with *Mortuary*, *The Vagrant*, *Future Shock*, *Club Dread*, and the witty *Tales from the Crypt* episode "People Who Live in Brass Hearses," but to me, *Frailty* was his greatest gift to the world of cinema.

Homicidal (1961)

Director: William Castle
Writer: Robb White
Cast: Jean Arless, Glenn Corbett, Patricia Breslin, Eugenie Leontovich, Richard Rust

William Castle quickly capitalized off the success of *Psycho* by producing and directing *Homicidal*, and to refer to it as just a cheap knock-off would be doing it a grave disservice. Ever the effective spokesman, he even introduces this bizarre and psychosexual tale with a cigar in one hand, a threading needle in the other as he reminds us of our excursions to haunted hills, tinglers, and ghosts (referencing his three previous movies which also happened to be his most popular) and promises an even stranger journey this time around.

A mysterious femme fatale going by the name Miriam Webster checks into Hotel Ventura (now known as the Ventura Inn) and offers the bellboy a generous $2,000 tip just as long as he agrees to something outside of his job description: getting married at the midnight hour. Perplexed by the offer (which also mentions a fast annulment), but entranced by her beauty and the cash, he meets up with her later that night and admits on the drive that "this is the strangest thing I've ever been through." The woman wakes up the justice of the peace at his home and pays extra for an after-hours ceremony, but before the bellboy can kiss the unhappy bride, she takes out a surgical knife from her purse and brutally stabs the justice in the chest multiple times before fleeing the scene alone.

She only becomes more enigmatic in subsequent scenes where we wonder why she's a caretaker to an elderly mute woman who clearly despises her, why she throws a temper tantrum at the sight of a wedding cake, why she seems determined to break a couple apart, why she used the alias of a romantic partner's sister, why she traveled to Denmark, and most importantly, why she thinks a bowl of milk is a suitable breakfast. The plot is dizzying and convoluted, and while I can't say that all your questions will be answered, it's a lot of fun trying to put the pieces together.

Among the obvious influences to the Hitchcock masterpiece is a law-breaking blonde woman who nervously glances at the police car reflected in her rear-view mirror, a violin-heavy soundtrack, a killer who wields a knife but who also ignores the dosage recommendations on a bottle of strychnine, and a bombshell of a twist ending that probably caused theatergoers to inspect the sticky floors for their jaws during the credits. Sophisticated modern audiences will probably be quick to solve the mystery but this doesn't make the film any less entertaining, or the big reveal any less impressive. William Castle waited until there were less than ten minutes to go before unleashing a trademark gimmick, making the "Fright Break" ridiculously jarring but also adorably hokey. While a timer appears on screen, he narrates to the audience, "Do you hear that sound? That's the sound of a heartbeat. A frightened, terrified heart. Is it beating faster than your heart? Or slower? This heart is going to beat for another 25 seconds to allow anyone to leave this theater who is too frightened to see the end of the picture." And anyone who chose to leave would be immortalized in "The Coward's Corner."

Much like the installed seat buzzers in *The Tingler*, the inflatable skeleton emerging during a key sequence in *House on Haunted Hill*, and the dorky "illusion-o" glasses for *13 Ghosts*, it's easy to imagine this Fright Break giving theater audiences an exhilarated camaraderie and permission to be rambunctious with their reactions, and since Stewart Gilligan Griffin hasn't allowed me to use his time machine, all I can to do is close my eyes and imagine just how loud the theaters got when a certain wheelchaired character traverses down a certain flight of stairs for the last time.

Killing Spree (1987)

Writer and Director: Tim Ritter
Cast: Asbestos Felt, Courtney Lercara, Raymond Carbone, Bruce Paquette, Joel D. Wynkoop

If you're curating a horror marathon for strangers in a theater or for friends in a living room, then one movie you should definitely consider is *Killing Spree,* because it's the kind of outrageously gory and genuinely funny shot-on-video curiosity that will surprise and delight audiences, and keep the energy level high all the way to the closing credits.

A bushy-bearded, wild-haired man named Tom isn't coping with his new suburban life very well because he's struggling to pay the pills but also dead-set against his wife having to work. He's also struggling with a heightened state of paranoia and jealousy, stemming from a previous relationship, which causes him to lash out when his best friend makes the mistake of sitting just a little too close to his wife or looking at her a second too long, even though this friend is considerably older and pre-occupied with an 18-year-old prostitute named Angel. The following day, after flipping through the new edition of *Fangoria*, Tom decides to read something else that's on the coffee table: his wife's diary. It turns out there may be some validity to his suspicions when the latest entry is all about how she slept with her husband's best friend.

Tom grows increasingly unhinged in the following days when each subsequent peek at his wife's diary reveals new hot and streamy liaisons with seemingly every electrician, repairman, deliveryman, and lawn maintenance worker she comes in contact with, causing him to shout "WHY IS SHE WRITING ALL THIS DOWN?!" and "THREE IN ONE DAY? THAT BITCH!" Through the irate voice in his head, we learn that he doesn't necessarily blame her, and so the killing spree will be directed at all of the men who have been coming to the house. His violent acts, often preceded by pink-tinted lighting to accentuate his mania, involve lifting someone up to a dangerously modified ceiling fan, dropping a screwdriver from the roof through a skull, tearing off a face with the backend of a hammer, ripping open a torso with a chainsaw and then using the intestines to electrocute the body, etc. In one of the funniest scenes, not even an afternoon stroll at the beach can calm his nerves since he keeps attacking random men.

The main reason crowds will be howling with laughter is due to Asbestos Felt's (what a name, what a name) commanding performance, with his over-the-top crazed delivery, absurd Val Venis laughter following every sentence, and even more absurd choice of underwear. *Killing Spree* lets the supporting cast have a lot of fun with their roles as well. The fact that the most serious character is nicknamed "Stewmaster" makes me love the film even more, as does the 45-second shot of an old woman checking her neighbor's home for dust while the soundtrack seemingly gets hijacked by a cat walking across a Casio keyboard to the most unpleasant of settings. Another bit of music is a blatant rip-off of that amazing "Something to Tide You Over" score from *Creepshow*, appropriate enough since the film features the ocean as well as articulate zombies.

When Tom is flipping through his Fangoria ever so slowly, we can't help but notice the back-cover advertisement of Tim Ritter's previous movie, *Truth or Dare? A Critical Madness*, which is apparently the first ever direct-to-video title. It's also curiously about a man driven crazy by his wife's extracurricular activities, but this time he takes his aggression out on everybody he sees rather than just gentlemen callers—not even a little leaguer walking down the sidewalk is off limits from a possible chainsaw drive-by encounter. It has been championed by Elijah Wood, no stranger to the horror genre, on talk show appearances and a recent episode of the enormously popular YouTube series *Hot Ones*, and if any movie is suited to be praised by someone sweating bullets in a mad-spice delirium, it's *Truth or Dare*, with its directors, editor, composer, sound mixer, and cast competing over who can make the oddest choices.

The Leopard Man (1943)

Director: Jacques Tourneur
Writers: Ardel Wray, Edward Dein, Cornell Woolrich (novel)
Cast: Dennis O'Keefe, Jean Brooks, Margo, Isabel Jewell, James Bell, Margaret Landry

When RKO Pictures introduced a horror division to their repertoire, they gave a Russian "jack of all trades" named Val Lewton a chance to produce a string of low-budget films in an arrangement where they would provide the movie titles and the money (approximately $150,000 for each), and he would take it from there. Working closely with screenwriter DeWitt Bodeen and director Jacques Tourneur, they struck gold at first swing with *Cat People*, RKO's most profitable film of 1942. Lewton and Tourneur teamed up again for *I Walked with a Zombie*, which wasn't as successful, and for their next film, they were given the title *The Leopard Man* in an obvious attempt at recapturing the magic of *Cat People*. They even used the same leopard, Dynamite!

Right from the opening scene we're seduced by a small New Mexico town and its intriguing residents, as a friendly rivalry intensifies between two female nightclub entertainers. When more and more customers cheer for the dancing of Latin beauty Clo-Clo—commanding attention everywhere she goes with a confident stride, radiant smile, and handfuls of bone-clacking castanets—showbiz agent Jerry orchestrates a publicity stunt for his client and love interest, Kiki. During one of Clo-Clo's routines, Kiki steals the show by making a grand entrance with the leopard Jerry rented from a fellow entertainer. But the large cat manages to free itself from the leash and storm into the night much to the consternation of everyone living nearby.

Later that night, a teenaged girl is forced by her mom to buy cornmeal for supper. The local market is closed by the time she arrives, so she has to venture to the other side of town, underneath train tracks, and through deserted streets that trigger her lifelong fear of the dark. Such a vast pool of darkness would give any dangerous feline many places to hide. The tension continues to build when water slowly drips and shadows play around her, setting her up for a confrontation with a pair of glowing eyes that belong to a beast that's famished for much more than cornmeal.

Always the professionals, Jerry and Kiki maintain their calm demeanors but deep inside are wracked with guilt over the girl's death, showcasing how one of the film's greatest strengths lies in its character development. It seems that every single person living in this town has a compelling story to tell, like the maudlin fortune teller, the grocer who tells the teenaged girl, "The poor don't cheat one another, we're all poor together," the leopard's owner whose alcoholism exacerbates the terror of a rising death count, and the undertaker who when asked about his social life, points to the tombs and says "I have many friends, but they don't bother me with talk." It's presumed that the leopard is stalking the town in insatiable midnight snacks, belying its history as a gentle cat and its natural tendencies to escape to the countryside and roam free, which makes Jerry and Kiki wonder if something else could be causing the murders.

I watched this movie after getting home from work on my birthday and it proved to be a suitable choice because in one scene, a young woman wakes up to the scent of fresh flowers, her bed flanked by loved ones singing a birthday song far lovelier than the abrasive "Happy Birthday to You." She says shortly later, "Oh no! I must go to the cemetery! It's my birthday," and since *The Leopard Man* doesn't overstay its welcome at 66 minutes, I had more than enough time to steal her itinerary. But rather than deliver flowers to a loved one and wait for a scheduled romantic rendezvous only to find myself trapped inside, I just walked around and listened to albums from Cocteau Twins and Sonata Arctica before leaving unobstructed through the open cemetery gates.

Poster for *Mr. Sardonicus* (1961), Columbia Pictures

Mr. Sardonicus (1961)

Director: William Castle
Writer: Ray Russell
Cast: Ronald Lewis, Audrey Dalton, Guy Rolfe, Oskar Homolka, Vladimir Sokoloff

This movie, which incorporates themes from *The Phantom of the Opera, Dracula, The Man Who*

Laughs, and *Eyes Without a Face*, was recommended to me by my mom's friend Sue Simpson, who said it frightened her tremendously when she saw it as a child at a drive-in. I can certainly see why! It is introduced by director and master of gimmicks William Castle, cloaked in thick London fog as he asks us, his homicidal friends, if we know about ghouls. After accidentally looking up "ghoum" in the dictionary, he transports us to the year 1880, where distinguished physician Sir Robert Cargrave receives a handwritten letter from his ex-girlfriend Maude after she was forced by her destitute father to marry Baron Sardonicus. The contents cause him to cancel all of his appointments indefinitely.

She says in the letter that the Baron has expressed an interest in meeting him, and that it's most urgent to her well-being that he arrive at their Gorslava castle within a fortnight. After sharing a carriage with the Baron's one-eyed servant Krull through barren regions where the trees are surely skeletons all year round, Robert arrives at the castle and sees pictureless frames and a woman covered in leeches, but a far more unsettling visual awaits him at dinnertime.

We learn that a couple years ago, a poor farmer named Marek discovered that his family had won the lottery, but the jubilation was cut short upon realizing that the winning ticket was inside the jacket pocket of his recently-deceased father, now buried six feet under. "You said you loved me. This is your chance to prove it! Prove it!" screamed his miserable wife, and so the farmer desecrated his father's burial site to strike it rich. Wracked with guilt and shame, he forced open the coffin lid and became so shocked by what he saw that he brought upon the most grotesque of curses upon himself.

These two suspenseful stories come together to create even more suspense in a gothic cacophony of forbidden love, self-hatred, desperation, torture dungeons, miracle healers, untested medicine, and "soul-shattering smiles." As someone who only knew him from *Dolls* and the *Puppet Master* series, I enjoyed seeing a brown-haired Guy Rolfe playing Mr. Sardonicus as if he were a classic Universal monster, serving as both the tormenter and the tormented. Equally commanding is his devoted servant played by Oskar Homolka, a Viennese actor who fought for the Austro-Hungarian army during World War I and who fled Germany in 1933 during Hitler's rise to power. His career continued in Paris and then later in Hollywood, where he was even nominated for an Academy Award for *I Remember Mama* (1948), when for once he wasn't playing a villainous European.

It wouldn't be a William Castle film without a gimmick and the one here is a lot of fun, saved until the end of the movie where he asks the audience to vote on the fate of a key character by using the glow-in-the-dark "Punishment poll" cards that they were handed upon entering the theater. This movie is mostly known for a major plot point and a shocking reveal that I won't spoil here, and so if you go in blind like me, not having seen any film stills or trailers, you'll be in for quite a treat, my fellow ghouls! And maybe I was just excited for the Seattle Kraken's very first game in the NHL next week, but the S on the doorknob to the Sardonicus castle reminded me of the team's logo.

Psycho III (1986)

Director: Anthony Perkins
Writer: Charles Edward Pogue
Cast: Anthony Perkins, Diana Scarwid, Jeff Fahey, Roberta Maxwell, Katt Shea, Hugh Gillin

In terms of horror's all-time greatest sequels, *Bride of Frankenstein*, *Evil Dead 2*, *Aliens*, and *A Nightmare on Elm Street 3: Dream Warriors* are usually the ones that poll the best within the horror community, but no top 5 list would be worth a hill of beans without the inclusion of *Psycho II*. I've always considered it a perfect film and one that somehow gets even more artistic, frightening, sincere, creative, beautiful, and emotionally devastating with each revisit. As daunting a task as it was to make a worthy sequel to one of Hitchcock's most revered masterpieces 23 years later, it also couldn't have been easy to follow up a surprise box office champion and critical darling like *Psycho II*, but Anthony Perkins felt up to the challenge to not only reprise his iconic character once again, but to take over directing reins for the first time in his life.

The third installment ended up a failure at the box office and with most critics (the most notable exception being Roger Ebert, who awarded it three stars and praised Perkins's performance in front of the camera as well as behind it), and has always been overshadowed by its predecessors, but at least it's no longer collecting dust in the vaults due to the fantastic retrospective documentary *The Psycho Legacy* and a special edition Shout Factory Blu-ray. It's always redeeming to see an unfairly maligned film get a second life, and hopefully its reputation will continue to blossom over time much like *Halloween III* and *The Exorcist III*.

The few people who caught *Psycho III* in theaters might have believed they wandered into the wrong room when the picture opens not at the Bates Motel, or anywhere in the sleepy town of Fairvale, California for that matter. Instead, what we get is a suicidal young nun named Maureen screaming "There is no God!" in a fit of hysterics that results in the accidental death of one of her sisters. She leaves the convent and roams through the desert, carrying a single suitcase and choking back tears as composer Carter Burwell continues the streak of *Psycho* movies having truly exceptional soundtracks. She manages to escape death by dehydration and exposure by hitching a ride from an attractive young drifter named Duane (friends can call him Duke), but after he gets a little road weary and rapey later that night, she takes her chances with a torrential downpour. "Stupid bitch! You could have been coming instead of going," shouts Duane before speeding away.

The next morning, Duane stops at the Bates Motel and asks about the Help Wanted sign in hopes of earning enough money to get his car fixed and continue the journey to Los Angeles to become a rock 'n roll star. Despite having 12 cabins and 12 vacancies, Norman foresees a bright future for the motel and hires Duane on the spot, and as fate would have it, the next customer happens to be an exhausted ex-nun that's been walking all night desperately looking for a place to stay. The fact that she bears a resemblance to Marion Crane only complicates things further.

Psycho III is a very strange film, loaded with goofy comedy and sleazy sexual relations that might elicit WTFs, and its kills are more graphic than the previous entries, but it still stays true to the character of Norman Bates and his sympathetic lapses into insanity. It forges its own path and never plays it safe, which is something modern part threes have a very hard time doing because of excessive studio involvement and market research. Among the things I adore in this movie are Sherriff John Hunt (Hugh Gillin) and diner owner Ralph Statler (Robert Alan Browne) appearing once again as Norman's kind defenders, the sleazeball charisma of Jeff Fahey, Donovan Scott's contagious giggles (it warmed my heart to discover that this lovable actor has played Santa Claus in countless family films), the abundance of rain, the ambient choir chants accentuating the terror, the way Norman uses the same spoon for stuffing birds with sawdust and spreading peanut butter on crackers, his touching romance with fellow damaged soul Maureen, that memorable theme song and its multiple incarnations (Norman playing it on the piano was especially lovely), the way Mary Loomis' copy of *In the Belly of the Beast* from Part II is flapping in the breeze outside, the "Missing" signs for Mrs. Spool posted all over town, the underwater tour of Norman's favorite swamp, the strong winds creating funnels of dust, the guitar smash to the head, the candy corn bag smash to the counter, the way Norman naps in a suit on a dreadfully hot afternoon, the communal freezer and its bloody ice cubes, and Duane's unorthodox use of lampshades.

Psycho IV (1990)

Director: Mick Garris
Writer: Joseph Stefano
Cast: Anthony Perkins, Henry Thomas, Olivia Hussey, CCH Pounder, Warren Frost

The Back to the Future, E.T., Jaws, and King Kong rides were really fun, but even more memorable on my day at Universal Studios in the early '90s was the unexpected sight of a certain dwelling off in the distance. Due to how much I loved the *Psycho* series, it took all of my will power not to jump the barrier and get as close as I could to the gothic gloom and fading elegance of the home of Norma and Norman. I assumed it was the real deal going all the way back to Hitchcock's original, but my eyes deceived me because it was a replica constructed just a few years prior for Universal Studios Florida's first feature-length film production, *Psycho IV: The Beginning*.

Even though it was destined for Showtime instead of cinemas, this was a highly ambitious project penned by original *Psycho* screenwriter Joseph Stefano, who chose to ignore the fairly convoluted Mrs. Spool storyline and focus on Norman's traumatic upbringing and the horrors that still torment him. Nighttime radio talk show host Fran Ambrose (wonderfully played by CCH Pounder with a soothing voice and cigarette often in hand) is discussing the topic of matricide with a psychologist (*Twin Peaks'* Warren Frost) who deems it "the most unbearable of crimes, and most unbearable to the son who commits it." They receive a phone call from a man named Ed who claims he can provide insight, and as he reveals personal stories about his childhood and the horrible crimes he committed, the psychologist begins to suspect they are talking to Norman Bates, and that his confessions about having the urge to kill again must be taken extremely seriously.

Through a series of flashbacks, "Ed" recounts a wide variety of childhood stories so disturbing that the radio hosts and their producer (played by John Landis) find themselves in uncharted waters and bicker off-air about how to best handle the situation. Henry Thomas, who grew up to become one of horror's most capable leading men, was the perfect choice to play a young Norman Bates with his boyish charm, nervous mannerisms, and intensity that cuts just as well as a trusted butcher knife. When picturing Mother Bates, people probably weren't imagining a drop-dead-gorgeous woman with a British accent, and so Olivia Hussey's casting was more surprising, but she does a fantastic job. It's a multi-faceted performance in which she effortlessly goes from saccharine sweet to abusive monster on a dime—it's as if her character in the *It* miniseries woke up from the coma but still had the malevolent spirit of Pennywise hiding inside her.

It's a real shame that such a gifted actor like Anthony Perkins became typecast as an unhinged killer, but here in one of his final performances before passing away at age 60, he reminds us of his astonishing range and inimitable on-screen presence as he sends Norman's story out on the highest note possible. He repeatedly clashed behind the scenes with director Mick Garris (one of the most kindhearted and likable personalities in the industry by all accounts), but right after the initial screening to the cast and crew, he warmly and enthusiastically approached Garris to tell him that it was the finest of all the *Psycho* sequels, an uncommon sentiment also allegedly shared by Stephen King and Steven Spielberg. And it wouldn't be a *Psycho* film without a fantastic soundtrack, and here composer Graeme Revell finds just the right notes for forlorn rainy afternoons in springtime and middle-of-the-night spirals into impending doom.

Much like how 23 years separated *Psycho* and *Psycho II*, it would take just as long for the *Psycho* legacy to extend beyond *Psycho IV*, but it was well worth the wait because AMC's five flawless and unforgettable seasons of *Bates Motel* surely would have made Hitchcock and Perkins proud.

The Sadist (1963)

Writer and Director: James Landis
Cast: Arch Hall Jr., Helen Hovey, Richard Alden, Marilyn Manning, Don Russell

A pair of maniacal eyes pierces through the darkness at us while an intense narrator states, "To have complete mastery over another, to make him a helpless object, to humiliate him, to enslave, to inflict moral insanity on the innocent, that is his objective, his twisted pleasure," and then the camera zooms in quickly on the eyes as they are growing even wider for a very dynamic opening title card.

This is the only time you'll see darkness for the whole movie because it plays out in real time on a sunny afternoon where three high school teachers (dressed like Mormon missionaries) are driving through the desert landscapes of southern California's Antelope Valley to get to the newly constructed Dodger Stadium for a game against the Cincinnati Reds. They experience car trouble and pull off the road at a gas station for assistance. The film then plants the seeds for *The Texas Chainsaw Massacre* by having them poke around the property that is cluttered with abandoned vehicles. They find warm plates of food on the kitchen table but no signs of life. But rather than getting bludgeoned over the head by a towering cannibal, here they face off against Charlie Tibbs and his teenaged girlfriend Judy, who have murdered the property owners to extend a killing spree that has spilled blood across multiple states. These sadistic lovers are based on real-life serial killers Charles Starkweather and Caril Fugate, who would later inspire Terrence Malick's 1973 film *Badlands* (starring Martin Sheen and Sissy Spacek) and also *Natural Born Killers*.

Arch Hall Jr. attempted to emulate Elvis Presley with his first stabs at acting, earning him notoriety on *Mystery Science Theater 3000*'s treatment of *Eegah*, but in this movie he trades in his "wild" guitar and teen heartthrob persona for a Colt .45 (in which he reportedly used cost-effective live ammunition since he was an expert sharpshooter) and a goofy giggle that is just as exaggeratedly unhinged as his facial expressions. It's a polarizing performance, but it sure kept me entertained as he terrorizes the three educators who are doing their best to reason with him, outsmart him, and to live to see another beautiful day for a ballgame. On the surface it would seem like *The Sadist* was intended to be just another cheap piece of exploitation for drive-in double features, but instead it punches far above its weight and delivers the kind of realistic and gritty nihilism that still resonates almost 60 years later. It's superbly shot by Hungarian cinematographer Vilmos Zsigmond, making his feature film debut in a career that would give him much more expensive equipment to work with for *Close Encounters of the Third Kind*, *The Deer Hunter*, *Heaven's Gate*, and *Blow Out*.

In presenting the danger so quickly, *The Sadist* has to sustain a high level of tension for nearly 90 minutes, and the degree to which it succeeds is debatable, but nobody can argue about the merits of a cat-and-mouse chase scene that gives the movie an out-of-the-park grand slam home run kind of ending.

Symptoms (1974)

Director: José Ramón Larraz
Writers: José Ramón Larraz, Stanley Miller, Thomas Owen (story)
Cast: Angela Pleasence, Lorna Heilbron, Peter Vaughan, Nancy Nevinson, Ronald O'Neil

Often compared to Roman Polanski's *Repulsion*, *Symptoms* made its debut at the Cannes Film Festival in 1974, and in several ways, it could be interpreted as the yin to the yang of another José Ramón Larraz film that was screening in theaters around the same time. While his erotic *Vampyres* relished in unrestrained, carnal lust, *Symptoms* depicts the mental turmoil caused by sexual repression.

This turned out to be a perfect movie to watch in the dreary mid-January stretch when the inevitable dismantling of the Christmas tree weighs on the mind but keeps getting pre-empted due to lack of energy and motivation. Its joyless nature feels appropriate, and yet, the gorgeous and calming cinematography reassures brighter days are up ahead. Sunbeams stab through a canopy of trees. A boat lazily floats down a lake to the sounds of singing birds and oars gently swishing the water. A fire provides warmth and comfort to a rain that started soft and now pounds with a vengeance. A leisurely bike ride through fading autumn foliage becomes the perfect activity for when the rain finally relents. Characters in soothing British accents wait for the perfect time to light a cigarette, tempting you to buy your first pack of smokes in many weeks, months, or even years.

But don't think for a moment that this film is all roses and Jack Handey "Deep Thoughts" imagery, because the other side of the coin disrupts the serene mood with dread-mounting visuals of a dead naked girl floating gently down the stream, logic-defying mirror reflections, and the occasional feral stabbing. John Scott's soundtrack is diverse enough to magnify both the meditative afternoons and restless nights, and along with impressive sound mixing, guarantees that *Symptoms* is also an auditory treat. In one of his last film credits, Scott collaborated with the Royal Philharmonic Orchestra for *The Wicker Tree*, Robin Hardy's 2011 sequel to the legendary *The Wicker Man*, and while I was a little let down with the film like most people were, I remember thinking the music was really strong even if it couldn't hold a candle to "Willow's Song."

Angela Pleasance (daughter of Donald) stars as a soft-spoken, childlike, and inquisitive young woman named Helen who arrives at her family's country estate along with her friend from London, Anne (Lorna Heilbron), who has a sophisticatedly short hairstyle and a craving for some peace and quiet following a difficult breakup with her boyfriend. They connect on a deep level where Helen can have the most maudlin of episodes where she cradles a doll on the staircase and pleads not to be left alone, and Anne will remain unshaken, understanding, and nonjudgmental. This dynamic creates a lot of freedom with their dialogue because the most casual of conversations can turn weird on a dime with a non sequitur from Helen involving death, drowning, and how she can hear things that nobody else can—making these scenes even more engaging is the way she stares at Anne longingly the whole time. Even under the best circumstances, the dark side has a way of finding Helen and it often involves the framed photographs of former best friend Cora, a lake full of secrets, and the presence of Brady, an elder handyman on the estate that is anxious to talk to her attractive new lady friend.

Scenes of Helen psychologically unraveling coalesce with classic haunted house motifs like ticking clocks, earth-rattling thunder, swaying chandeliers, and attics full of restless shadows, which creates an arresting atmosphere and engrossing mystery while we wonder if the whisperings are from manor ghosts or voices in her head. Anne also struggles to get a good night's sleep, waking up to the sounds of laughter one night and sounds of masturbatory moaning the next.

When the widescreen negative was circulating the globe during a limited theatrical release in 1974, it seemed to get infuriatingly rerouted to the Bermuda Triangle, resulting in *Symptoms*' inclusion on the British Film Institute's 75 Most Wanted list. In 2016 it was finally uncovered—much to the delight of its two talented stars who have remained close friends over the decades—and given a proper Blu-ray release from Mondo Macabro. José Ramón Larraz, whose final horror films were the American-set *Edge of the Axe* and *Deadly Manor*, sadly didn't live to see his long-lost masterpiece resurrected from the dead, but I'm sure many people around him made it known just how impressive it was.

Horror Galore

VIDEO NASTIES TELLING YOU NOT TO DO SOMETHING

Don't Go in the Woods (1981)

Director: James Bryan
Writer: Garth Eliassen
Cast: Nick Cleland, Mary Gail Artz, James P. Hayden, Angie Brown, Ken Carter

Had the critics in 1981 watched this bizarre movie with friends, pizza, and beer, they probably wouldn't have been so harsh in their reviews because while it's certainly not a good movie by any conventional means, its charm oozes with as much abundance as its cheap-looking blood. Released in the heyday of American slashers, *Don't Go in the Woods* mostly focuses on a hiking-camping trip that hits a sour note when one of the group members throws a temper tantrum after being teased and scampers off. Thanks to a grunting and cackling maniac resembling Grizzly Adams decked out in rags, furs, and Mardi Gras beads, reuniting won't be easy.

Recommended to me by my friend "Monster Mailman" Mike, this movie boasts an impressively high body count by repeatedly introducing characters out of nowhere just for them to be killed seconds later, a strategy that avoids coming across as lazy, desperate, or redundant by keeping the deaths varied and the victims entertaining. They are kept on screen just long enough to win you over with odd wardrobe choices and hilariously inept voice dubbing. The newly married couple of Dick, who "ain't afraid of nothin' on two feet" and Cherry, who ain't sure how to properly close the RV doors, are my personal VIPs, with an honorable mention going to the girl who enters the woods on roller skates and is completely forgotten about. Our four leads don't get much character development whatsoever, but they're fun and likable enough to root for, and I admired their loyalty and unselfishness when faced with increasingly dangerous situations. I also admired the way both of the leading ladies sport such short hairstyles.

Much like another 1981 slasher, Jeff Lieberman's *Just Before Dawn*, filmed in Oregon's Silver Falls State Park, *Don't Go in the Woods* (filmed in Utah) benefits from stunning natural locations and a lot of cost-cutting daytime shoots. The crystal-clear water looks inviting and the gossamer fog beautifully blankets the mountains on Vinegar Syndrome's remastered Blu-ray, but a grainy VHS version has its advantages too because without all those pixels, you might be convinced that the police officer is none other than Gary Carlston's Sheriff Gene Freak from another Utah production, *Troll 2*.

While most of the deaths are very comedic, there's a pretty shocking machete attack inside an unkept cabin, and another scene depicting a little girl watching her artist mom being impaled through an easel, which is probably why this movie got invited to the Video Nasty Party. Or maybe someone took offense to a wheelchair-bound man getting decapitated after wailing in such an exaggeratedly pathetic

Horror Galore

manner that even Franklin from *Texas Chainsaw Massacre* would have laughed at him.

You'll definitely want to stay for the credits on this one because not only does Angie Brown's name inexplicably appear inside of a square (either an editing error or an absurd request from an actress), but a charming little ditty serves as a final reminder of why you shouldn't go out in the woods tonight. Apparently, composer H. Kingsley Thurber wrote it as a joke, but director James Bryan deemed it too enjoyable to keep to themselves.

Don't Look in the Basement (1973)

Director: S.F. Brownrigg
Writer: Tim Pope
Cast: Bill McGhee, Robert Dracup, Michael Harvey, Gene Ross, Camilla Carr, Betty Chandler

"The makers of *Last House on the Left* warn you again: to avoid fainting, keep repeating 'it's only a movie, only a movie, only a movie.' A line between sanity and madness can be crossed in a single step, and with this step, you enter the nightmare world of terror." This ominous narration accompanying closeups of women screaming and axe massacring makes the trailer for *Don't Look in the Basement* seem like it's strictly for the most hardcore horror fans out there, those who equate a Video Nasty categorization as a badge of honor. However, out of all 72 movies that the Director of Public Prosecutions banned in the United Kingdom, believing they violated the Obscene Publications Act of 1959, this is quite possibly the least offensive of them all. I was surprised to learn of its inclusion on this list because the only things I remembered from my first viewing as a teenager were the noticeably low budget, a character's fondness for popsicles, a woman that sort of resembled Marilyn Burns from *The Texas Chainsaw Massacre*, and an asylum that looked more like an ordinary country house without air conditioning or

Advertisement for *Don't Look in the Basement* (1973), Hallmark Releasing Corp.

medical equipment—none of the supposed ultraviolence or vulgarities stayed with me for some reason. Revisiting it more than 20 years later, I realized that it's because this movie isn't hardcore in the slightest; it's raw and unnerving, but it really shouldn't have enraged the wanker censors the way it did.

Popular among the grindhouse drive-in crowds upon its release, this movie concerns a young nurse named Charlotte who arrives at Stephens Sanitarium for her first day at work, just hours after its chief doctor (and the man who hired her) was slaughtered by one of his patients. The facility runs not with strict doctor-patient guidelines, but as a wholesome family environment in which nobody is locked inside of their rooms, meaning that poor Charlotte has to get used to being spooked in the dead of night by senile Mrs. Callingham warning her to get out and never ever come back before regaling her with a stanza from William Allingham's poem "The Fairy Folk." Among the other residents are a former sergeant suffering from PTSD, a nymphomaniac who veered further off the deep end with each failed relationship, a schizophrenic woman who won't accept the fact that her baby is made of plastic, and a childlike man whose heart is bigger than his brain (as Clark Griswold would say).

I enjoyed the earnest performances and sheer weirdness on display with every scene. Anne MacAdams shines in her role as the doctor quickly seizing authority the moment her superior gets an axe lodged in his back, and is effective at providing sympathetic backstories to The Forgotten (alternate title) and being a royal pain in the neck to the telephone repairman who simply wants to do his job and get the hell out of there.

Heavy on closeups where beads of sweat converge on every forehead, this is the kind of micro-budgeted, claustrophobic movie that will make you want to shower afterwards, and it's also the kind that benefits from a grainy VHS presentation. A climax full of carnage and a most charming ending credits sequence guarantees a happy exit from the drive-in or your living room.

I started to feel as unbalanced as the Stephens Sanitarium patients when researching this movie because all these years I could have sworn it was called Don't Go in the Basement, giving me a Berenstain/Berenstein phenomenon when attempting to log it on Letterboxd with a 3 ½ star-rating. Then I spent about 30 minutes researching the screenwriter because IMDb told me it was Tim Pope, the music video director from London mostly known for his many, many collaborations with my favorite band, The Cure, but who's also worked with The Style Council, Talk Talk, Soft Cell, David Bowie, Siouxsie and the Banshees, etc. This small production in Tehucana, Texas would have been his only screenwriting credit and only dip into the horror waters unless you count The Cure's cobwebbed-covered "Lullaby" video, and so it didn't make much sense to me. Turns out that IMDb was wrong because Don't Go in the Basement, dammit, Don't LOOK in the Basement was actually penned by an uncredited Thomas Pope, who also wrote *The Manitou*, and that is much easier to swallow.

Horror Galore

SO BAD IT'S ESSENTIAL

Hobgoblins (1988)
Writer and Director: Rick Sloane
Cast: Tom Bartlett, Paige Sullivan, Steven Boggs, Kelley Palmer, Billy Frank

On one New Year's Eve, I was combing through the IMDb message boards for *Critters* because that's what all the cool Portlanders in their late 20s did, and saw a thread devoted to other miniature monster knock-offs that tried to piggyback off the success of *Gremlins*. Someone mentioned that the movie *Hobgoblins* was even sillier and more cheaply-made than *Munchies* and *Ghoulies*, and that it veered into *Troll 2* levels of ineptness. A quick drive to Movie Madness followed and suddenly this New Year's Eve was shaping up to be a winner.

Hobgoblins was certainly loaded with hilarity and utter nonsense, but it doesn't actually belong in the same conversation as *Troll 2* due to the fact that Claudio Fragasso and his crew were legitimately trying to make a good, respectable film, and *Hobgoblins* creator Rick Sloane was clearly in on the joke and had no pretenses that it would be anything more than just silly shlock. A decade later, he would even introduce the movie to *Mystery Science Theater 3000* writer Paul Chaplin, who included it on a popular season 10 episode and went onto say that "it shoots right to the top of the list of the worst movies we've ever done."

While I enjoyed watching this as a party of one, these monsters feed off of energy and would probably benefit from larger audiences and with caffeinated drinks flowing like Yosemite Falls. Under the correct circumstances, even the most innocuous of lines such as "he's just looking for a place to park" could be met with howling laughter. Long before we're introduced to the hobgoblins, an elderly security guard named Dennis makes the nightly rounds at a defunct movie studio with his new partner and gives him explicit instructions that the vault is considered off limits and that there's nothing to see down there. The punk kid lets his curiosity get the best of him and at first, the vault does seem to be as desolate as the rest of the studio, but then the rock 'n' roll adoring kid finds himself transported to a stage with lights and a microphone. The roar of a rapt crowd prompts him to prance around on stage like a twit until he loses his balance with exaggerated gyrations and falls to his death. Cue opening credits!

After being scolded by his boss, dressed immaculately despite working late at night at a studio that's been closed for 30 years, Dennis hires a responsible, hard-working, and polite young man named Kevin, who hopes that a dangerous occupation like a security guard will impress his perpetually uptight girlfriend who enjoys emasculating him at every opportunity. In one of the funniest scenes in the movie, a mutual friend having just returned from two months of army training decides to teach Kevin some hand-to-hand combat using garden tools for no clear reason. With

Horror Galore

their girlfriends cheering them on, they battle for what seems like five minutes, with a loud musical stinger synchronized to every gentle touch between the rake and the hoe; the masked man in black and Inigo Montoya they are most certainly not.

During his shift Kevin accidentally releases the hobgoblins, and a panicked Dennis tells him that that these evil monsters are attracted to bright lights and if they are not destroyed before dawn, then it will be too late…whatever that means. It's also unclear if they should be forbidden from eating after midnight, but that's OK because they couldn't eat even if they wanted to since they are merely creepy-looking stuffed animals incapable of biting, walking, talking, or doing anything besides rhythmically wobbling behind oblivious characters. The smartest thing this movie does is give them a psychological edge since they aren't physically threatening—they can tap into a person's brain and prey on weaknesses by presenting their ultimate fantasy.

In another moment that needs to be seen to be believed, Kevin's friends participate in an impromptu dance party in a tiny living room (which will satisfy those with a soft spot for extremely dull-looking interiors in movies), and even though they don't turn off any of the house lights, the strobe light attracts the attention of the hobgoblins who must have been miles away. And I doubt any New Year's Eve hotspot in Portland could compete with Club Scum, where the movie pads out the running time by having the post-punk group The Fontanelles perform their song "Kiss Kicker" (or as the MST3000 guys call it, "Fish Licker") in its entirety.

Invasion of the Blood Farmers (1972)

Director: Ed Adlum
Writers: Ed Adlum, Ed Kelleher
Cast: Bruce Detrick, Norman Kelley, Tanna Hunter, Paul Craig Jennings, Jack Neubeck

After a draining weekend spent with the ghoulish horrors of *Found* (2012) and *The Eyes of My Mother*, I desperately needed therapy in the form of gentle May breezes and the kind of rare film that must have benefitted from a certain alignment of stars that transformed incompetence into accidental genius. Then I remembered somebody on Twitter recommending *Invasion of the Blood Farmers* and within minutes I was no longer wallowing in the dirge of headless and eyeless victims, but sailing the seas of cheese (thanks Primus) and startling the neighbors with howling laughter. This film definitely wears its flaws like badges of honor.

Much like how the power of the magic Stonehenge gave Spinal Tap their well-choreographed comedy number, here it allows a group of Neolithic druids to flee the comfort of Salisbury Plain and acclimate in a hick town in Westchester County, New York, to perform their ancient rituals. Replacing their ceremonial robes with overalls and

Poster for *Invasion of the Blood Farmers* (1972), NMD Film Distributing Co.

straw hats, the druids make sneak attacks on the townsfolk and drain their blood in hopes of bringing their queen, catatonic in a glass coffin, back to life.

It's easy to see why nearly the entire cast has never acted in another movie, and hard to pinpoint the worst performance because there are so many to choose from. The most capable one probably belongs to our leading man, played by Bruce Detrick, giving off the same kind of boyish charm and gosh-golly innocence that made Howard from *The Unnamable* so likeable. Don is a former university student that has spent the past year studying under Dr. Roy Anderson while also romancing his daughter Jenny. Their dynamics give the movie a lot of heart because they're all so nice and deferential, even while having to witness their sleepy town in which nothing ever happens suddenly become rampant with even bigger tragedies than poor television placements inside their "first class" hotel rooms.

The curiously excitable and loud-spoken Dr. Anderson secures a blood sample from one of the victims and discovers that the homeostatic balance was so disturbed that it promoted cellular growth at a rapid rate, and soon that one drop of blood requires multiple buckets. He also discovers that an old friend and colleague has been secretly renting the house down the street to conduct important experiments with a group of grunting bumpkins, but because the doctor is such a trusting fellow, he doesn't see how the two could possibly be related.

Invasion of the Blood Farmers was created on a $24,000 budget and has the rare distinction of acquiring a PG rating in the United States and "Video Nasty" status in the United Kingdom, both of which are equally baffling. No PG-rated film should show battered women chained up in a barn and having to watch all of their blood be removed through a tube at an agonizingly slow rate, and no Video Nasty should be this inoffensive and downright hilarious. Characters repeatedly say "Goodnight" in broad daylight, a man on his honeymoon uses soap on his hair in a hopelessly awkward shower scene, a woman strangely contorts her body to "comfortably" relax on a large riverside rock, and not a single actor is capable of using a telephone naturally. Static direction and sloppy editing only add to the charming experience of this film that I really hope to watch one day in a theater—the fact that I've gotten to see *Rock 'n' Roll Nightmare* and *Burial Ground* on the silver screen recently gives me hope.

Night Killer (1990)

Writer and Director: Claudio Fragasso
Cast: Tara Buckman, Peter Hooten, Richard Foster, Mel Davis, Lee Lively, Tova Sardot

If *Troll 2* were any closer to my heart, the viscus liquid coursing through my veins would be chlorophyll green, the color of sap, the color of goblins, and yet it was never a priority of mine to see what director Claudio Fragasso made right before or after, because I just assumed he wouldn't be able to catch lightning in a bottle twice in a row. I was wrong because *Night Killer* is loaded with the same kind of sincere, lovable nonsense that made *Troll 2* the best worst movie of all time, and it confirms that in the early '90s, Fragasso (this time going under the pseudonym Clyde Anderson) had no idea how normal human beings speak, react, or behave, and the world is a much better place as a result. Much like how the troll-less *Troll 2* tried to capitalize on the name recognition of *Troll*, this movie was released in Italy under the title *Texas Chainsaw Massacre 3* despite not having any chainsaws. Shamelessly attaching itself to the *Silent Night, Deadly Night* franchise would have made more sense given the Christmas setting.

I was shaking my head in confoundment almost immediately, as a flustered dance instructor on the brink of a nervous breakdown watches a hopeless rehearsal. One student arrives late and while she's changing backstage, a maniac wearing a dime store Freddy Krueger mask barges in and thrusts his penny store glove of long rubbery claws completely through her torso (a special effect that is utilized with every single murder scene), even though it's obvious that these claws wouldn't even be able to penetrate a marshmallow. I had to watch this scene twice out of pure delight, but I needed three views to try to understand why in the next scene, a man shows up at our main character Melanie Beck's house and kisses her cheek before escorting her little girl down the street hand-in-hand to another house, where he kisses another woman that precedes to drive the girl to some random place. *Night Killer* is only 90 minutes long but it took me over two and a half hours to finish because of all the scenes I watched repeatedly, either for clarity or amusement. In trying to think of the last movie that made me laugh this hard, I may have to go all the way back to 2010 with *Tucker and Dale vs Evil*.

Melanie is typing away at her word processor when her rotary telephone chirps instead of rings. On the other end is a man with the weirdest voice ever, who we presume to be her ex, and literally two seconds after she calmly says, "Anyway, Clarissa has gone to the country with Annie," she shouts "LISTEN! I DON'T HAVE ANYTHING TO SAY TO YOU EXCEPT DON'T CALL ME ANYMORE!" Her phone rings again but this time it's an obscene call from a heavy breather. She makes the classic mistake of locking herself *inside* the house when a masked maniac emerges with a string of taunts and deep thoughts like "I'm crazy about your body. I love your skin. Your breasts. The way you smell. I'm so horny." She also, for some reason, only loads a single bullet into her gun's chamber even though there are several more right in front of her and she has plenty of time.

She somehow survives the ordeal and winds up in a hospital with no memory of the attacker. Her doctor claims that she's the only person to have seen the maniac without his mask on, but because of her dissociative schizophrenia triggered by trauma, she's unable to assist law enforcement. Even with her severe amnesia, she manages to either escape from the hospital or be prematurely released because in the next scene, she's driving a white convertible when a jeep pulls up beside her and the driver makes cat calls while chugging from a whiskey bottle. This man, named Axel, is played by Peter Hooten in an unforgettably bewildering performance. Somehow resembling both Thom Mathews and Lance Henriksen, he gets his comeuppance in the ladies' room where Melanie forces him to strip at gunpoint and flush all of his clothes down the toilet. He then chases her down to the beach, where she is guzzling booze and swallowing pills by the shore, and they have this exchange: "What in the hell do you think you're doing?!" "Committing suicide!" "Well, you gotta drink seawater so you can throw up all that shit you've been taking!" "Are you crazy?!"

The movie shifts from goofy slasher to goofy psychosexual thriller as Axel keeps Melanie hostage in her hotel room, telling her that it'll be on his terms when and how she dies, and she begins to exhibit characteristics of Stockholm syndrome; it's a fascinating duel of overacting that both performers are determined to win. Basic human behavior is anathema to the supporting characters as well, especially to the police officer that has finally located where the maniac that's been terrorizing the city is hiding. He then tells his partner (and only backup) to take the car back to the station for no reason whatsoever, and so even if he somehow apprehends the psychopath all by himself, he won't have anywhere to put him. This is just one of many Olympic-level leaps in logic that will leave you howling with delight, and some of the most egregious are saved until the end. For Christmas this year I'll be asking Santa Claus for the Blu-ray that Severin put out in hopes that the special features will answer at least one of the many, many questions I have.

GLOVES ON, KNIVES OUT, A GIALLO WE WILL GO

All the Colors of the Dark (1972)

Director: Sergio Martino
Writers: Ernesto Gastaldi, Sauro Scavolini, Santiago Moncada (story)
Cast: George Hilton, Edwige Fenech, Ivan Rassimov, Julian Ugarte, George Rigaud

It was dreadfully hot in Portland today and while it would have been sensible to spend the daylight hours at the coast, the Columbia River Gorge, a movie theater, or a supermarket like the Bundy Family in one of the funniest *Married with Children* episodes, I had neither the energy or motivation to leave the house despite its lack of air conditioning. So instead, I traveled back in time to the disco era in Italy to watch people get stalked by a mysterious knife-wielding maniac. The search for a hidden giallo gem got off to a rough start because the first two movies on my list started out great only to wallow in halftime mediocrity. With deflating spirits, I began to wonder if the heat was making it impossible to enjoy any movie. Then I grabbed a Gatorade slush from the freezer and started movie #3, and quickly became as excited as Al Bundy being announced as the supermarket's one millionth customer after he cut in front of Marcy Darcy in line.

After a lakeside opening credits sequence that resembles a Calm App bedtime scene, *All the Colors of the Dark* shatters your tranquility with a barrage of shots alternating between the gross and

Poster for ***All the Colors of the Dark/They're Coming to Get You*** (1972), Lea Film, Variety Distribution

the surreal, made even more unsettling with the fast editing and perspective-manipulating camera lenses. Once again Jane is having her sleep disturbed with visions of a man with impossibly blue eyes swinging a knife, a possible side effect of a recent traumatic incident where a car accident terminated her pregnancy. She questions her sanity once the maniac in her dreams starts appearing in the waking hours in broad daylight, and this causes a rift between her pharmaceutical salesman boyfriend Richard and her sister Barbara. He believes rest and vitamins are the best cure, but Barbara chooses to schedule an appointment for her with a psychoanalyst.

Jane takes both of their advice but the problems only get worse, and after an encounter where she was only an inch away from the madman's knife, she puts her trust into a third person: a beguiling woman who insists that she knows how to free her from her demons. All she needs to do is drink canine blood with a Satanic, talon-fingered cult leader and then lie down bare-chested while his haggard-looking worshippers hover around her and take turns forcefully kissing her. This scene is made all the more harrowing and psychedelic by one of many great scores from composer Bruno Nicolai.

Misdirections and red herrings are staples in the giallo subgenre, and they are handled particularly well here with so many characters seemingly harboring secret agendas and a distressed narrator who's not the most trustworthy source. She's so batty that she even sits right next to complete strangers on a train when there are empty rows all around! This movie just seems to get better and better with each new reveal, setting up a thrilling, fist-clenching finale where we pray the right person is victorious. By this point, I was so impressed with *All the Colors of the Dark* that even if Barney the Dinosaur suddenly appeared on the rooftop to teach the characters about forgiveness, I still would have given it a glowing recommendation, but man oh man was I relieved when the ending proved to be just right! Also noteworthy is a very strong cast, evocative seasonal presence with winds that cut through beds of decaying leaves, hints of Roman Polanski's *Rosemary's Baby* and *Repulsion*, and a suspenseful "release the hounds" chase scene.

Sleepless (2001)

Director: Dario Argento
Writers: Dario Argento, Franco Ferrini, Carlo Lucarelli
Cast: Max von Sydow, Stefano Dionisi, Chiara Caselli, Gabriele Lavia, Rossella Falk

If you've been guzzling Hate-orade and talking trash on online message boards about how Dario Argento hasn't made a good movie since *Opera*, then you probably slept on this one, in which the maestro welcomed the new millennium with a return to his roots by structuring a giallo like a greatest hits collection. I'm sad to say that it had been at least seven years since I saw one of his films, but on the bright side, such an absence caused my arms to fill with goosebumps as it began with an unfamiliar Goblin score and the great Max von Sydow telling a traumatized, bloodied boy in 1983 that he was going to find out who killed his mother, even if it takes him his whole life.

Jumping forward to present day, a prostitute inadvertently steals incriminating evidence from her creepy john, and for the next 15 minutes, the two embark on a sensational cat-and-mouse chase aboard a train on a stormy night, lurid colors and masterful camerawork following their every step; this is easily one of the most exciting scenes in Argento's repertoire. When the police discover a couple of blood-drenched bodies later that night with similar calling cards to that of the infamous "killer dwarf" murder spree from 17 years ago, a now-retired Detective Moretti is notified that the case may not be closed after all. He reunites with the kid he made the promise to, and together they follow a long path of blood that seems to be inspired from a children's nursery rhyme.

Max von Sydow, in his seventies and looking just like Father Merrin, is such a calm and warm presence in between the acts of gratuitous, but never mean-spirited violence. It's a joy watching him smoke his first cigarette since 1966, lament about modern technology without a hint of cantankerousness, and make sure his pet bird is privy to all the investigative updates. Science has proven that any movie is an automatic winner if in a ten-minute span, a person gets stabbed through the mouth with an English horn and Max van Sydow gets to say the following to a bird: "Take a look at the weapons and the way he uses them. So, pruning knife, a musical instrument English horn, rope, drowned, bashed against the wall, and a hatchet. The English horn, why, what a strange choice. The rooster's cock-a-doo-dle-doo, the instrument for this fine song." *Sleepless in Seattle* may have made over $200 million at the box office, but it didn't have a single *Exorcist* star or mentioning of cock-a-doodle-doo like *Sleepless*, and all of its grisly face-stabbings probably came from boring items like meat cleavers.

Add in some ludicrous twists, a couple of hilariously over-the-top performances, a colorful smorgasbord of red herrings, and an incredible tracking shot during a Swan Lake theater production and you have one hell of a fun movie to watch outside on July 5th while leftover neighborhood fireworks provide another layer of percussion to the Goblin soundtrack.

The Strange Vice of Mrs. Wardh (1971)

Director: Sergio Martino
Writers: Ernesto Gastaldi, Eduardo Manzanos, Vittorio Caronia
Cast: Edwige Fenech, George Hilton, Conchita Airoldi, Manuel Gil, Ivan Rassimov

With soaring summer temperatures depleting our energy, I couldn't blame my girlfriend for struggling to stay awake during *Mausoleum* or *Only Lovers Left Alive*, but to my surprised delight, she didn't struggle whatsoever with *The Strange Vice of Mrs. Wardh*. This was the first giallo she's ever seen and it seemed to hit the spot like an Oreo Blizzard. Yawning just doesn't come naturally when you're staring at so much beautiful Austrian scenery, straight-razor slashing, hyper-stylized cinematography, and so much nudity of the highest quality.

Sergio Martino opens this film with a quote from Sigmund Freud that reads:

"The very emphasis of the commandment, 'Thou shalt not kill,' makes it certain that we are descended from an endlessly long chain of generations of murderers, whose love of murder was in their blood as it is perhaps also in ours." Those words aren't lost on a man wearing black gloves who picks up a prostitute and just seconds after she becomes the first of about a dozen women to casually bare their breasts, he kills her with a razor while an ascending airplane drowns out her screams. Known simply by the press as "Sex Fiend," he's been terrorizing the city of Vienna and leaving many of its beauties to bleed to death in alleys, showers, and even on the peaceful grounds of Schönbrunn Palace.

Having recently seen Samantha Robinson in *The Love Witch*, I wonder if its casting director was instructed to find a young actress who looks identical to the star of this movie (as well as *All the Colors of the Dark*), Edwige Fenech, whose magnetic presence is evident the moment we see her riding down a crowded escalator at the Venice airport. Her character, Julie, is much more distressed by the state of her marriage than she is with the string of grisly murders. Not only is she no longer in love with her boring diplomat husband, but she also begins to loathe the possessive man she'd been having a sado-masochistic affair with. He responds to her sudden rejection by including increasingly cryptic notes inside of her daily flower deliveries—not the most surprising reaction from a man who prefers his sexual trysts with broken glass and hard slaps to the face, memories of which haunt Julie every day.

Horror Galore

At a party that includes two women tearing each other's paper dresses off and wrestling around on the floor, Julie meets yet another man who refuses to take no for an answer, even after she pleads with him not to add even more complication to her life. But George, with his charisma, wealth, and perfect face you can't resist gazing at with a sigh, eventually wins her affection and a pivotal spot in her web of crazy drama.

With *The Strange Vice of Mrs. Wardh* (the silly "h" was added to Ward because of an even sillier litigation from a Mrs. Ward), you not only get all the giallo trademarks cooked to perfection but also a fancy restaurant with whole apples on the menu. There are also dangerous-looking motorcycle stunts, snorkelers in Spain, dizzying Magic Eye pattern wallpaper, and choruses of maniacal laughter to keep us fully engaged in between scenes of Hitchcockian suspense that are executed in time-honored locations like empty parking garages, elevators, and gloomy mansions with pet bats. As much as I hummed along and enjoyed every single note of Nora Orlandi's out-of-this-world soundtrack, I also appreciated when it was muted to allow dead silence (with the occasional footstep, bird chirp, wind gust, and heartbeat) to make these scenes all the more nerve-racking. And dessert comes in the form of a deliciously, deliriously weird whirlwind of an ending in which each twist has its own twist.

SCREAM AT THE BEACH

The Beach House (2019)
Writer and Director: Jeffrey A. Brown
Cast: Liana Liberato, Noah Le Gros, Jake Weber, Maryann Nagel

On an idyllic afternoon with the water glistening like diamonds, Randall and his girlfriend Emily arrive at his parents' beach house and feel like they have the entire neighborhood to themselves since the season doesn't officially start until Memorial Day. With their relationship on the rocks due to emotional absence and diverging career paths—he has recently dropped out of college and she intends on going to grad school to study astrobiology—they hope that this weekend away will relight the spark and put things in perspective. They discover after a startling and suspenseful encounter that they aren't alone in this house, and that an older couple named Mitch and Jane had arranged to stay there as well. There's plenty of room for the four of them, and they even share dinner together and bond despite the generational divide. Jane, who has filled the medicine cabinets with her many prescriptions, even gets teary-eyed and tells the kids how fortunate she is to be spending time with them. After the wine bottles quickly dry out and with no local stores still open, Randall comes to the rescue by asking, "Are you familiar with edibles?"

The elder couple deliberate briefly and decide they are up for the magical candy bar adventure, and it appears to be of the highest potency because while Randall succumbs to couchlock instantly and becomes lost in the vinyl collection, everyone else ventures outside to watch the world transform around them: trees glow with droplets of luminous lava, the winds carry twinkling blossoms, fairy dust emerge from sunspots, and thick fog saturates in neon hues. When pressed on her passion for science, Emily describes how she's in awe of life's fragility, and how we're just the right combination of elements, temperature, and distance from the sun, but would crumble to dust if just one of these factors was slightly off. Much of her intellect goes over the head of Mitch, who admits to being so overwhelmed by modern technology and the changing times that he prefers to just keep his head down and focus on the baseball team he coaches.

Because the first act of *The Beach House* does such a tremendous job in establishing these four characters, we're all the more impacted by the horrors that the next day brings, starting with Randall and Emily getting up on the wrong side of the bed. Before they can even relax with a cup of coffee, they're frightened awake by the state of Jane and the realization that maybe they hadn't been hallucinating after all.

2020 has not only been a year for corona horror, but also cosmic horror, as this film from first-time director Jeffrey A. Brown was released shortly after Richard Stanley's monumental comeback, *The Color*

Horror Galore

Out of Space. Both of these powerhouses get straight A's in the subjects of body horror, psychedelia, sci-fi soundscapes, and making sure that its characters die in agonizingly slow ways courtesy of a mad-as-hell-and-not-going-to-take-it-anymore world.

Don't let the breathtaking scenery fool you, this is a world every bit as merciless and suffocating as a Sawyer household, a Centobite ritual, and Paris catacombs, and while it's not quite as shocking as the "those aren't pillows" reveal from *Planes Trains and Automobiles*, the "it's not fog" line packs quite a punch. So does the line, "Fine, fine, just fine, I think I'll go for a swim," due to its lackadaisical reading that carries just a hint of devastation. Some horror fans will notice similarities to *Alien*, *Invasion of the Body Snatchers*, *The Blob*, *The Mist*, and *The Fog*, some will press pause to research why the actor playing Mitch looks so damn familiar (the answer is the *Dawn of the Dead* remake!), but just about every single one will be thankful for having fingers that they can peek through during a particularly nauseating, goo-soaked shot or two.

Horror of Party Beach (1964)

Director: Del Tenney
Writers: Richard Hilliard, Ronald Gianettino, Lou Binder
Cast: John Scott, Alice Lyon, Ellan Laurel, Eulabelle Moore, Marilyn Clarke, Augustin Mayor

This hybrid of teen beach comedy and rubber-suited monster horror was featured on an episode of *Mystery Science Theater 3000*, but it's best enjoyed sans robot commentary because the ridiculous dialogue deserves your undivided attention and because something legitimately creepy occurs on screen once or twice. The trailer takes a page out of William Castle's playbook and opens with large, shivering white text reading, "Urgent warning: You will not be permitted to see this shocking program unless you agree to release this theater of all respon-

Lobby card for *The Horror of Party Beach* (1964), 20th Century-Fox

sibility for death by fright!" It's also advertised as being the first monster horror musical, but I don't think that's accurate since none of the characters break out in song to advance the plot, but rather simply shake, rattle, and roll on the sand while The Del-Aires perform their surf-rock tunes on stage.

A young woman named Tina is particularly responsive to numbers like the "Zombie Stomp," hopped up on alcohol and the motivation to prove to her boyfriend, a scientist named Hank, that if they go their separate ways, she would be the one getting more out of life. Just before she's able to disrobe to the delight of a motorcycle gang, Hank intervenes and has an entertaining fist fight with its leader that shockingly ends with a handshake and with Tina running to the ocean and finding out that it's not safe to swim in waters where radioactive waste barrels were carelessly dumped over the watery grave of a shipwreck. The skeleton passengers undergo a bizarre metamorphosis and resurface looking like a cross between Hedora "The Smog Monster" and a store-brand Creature from the Black Lagoon. These googly-eyed monsters would look ridiculous even without the dozen hot dogs crammed into their mouths, representing teeth I reckon. And even though the actors underneath probably had a very difficult time doing things like seeing and moving, they succeeded in making the monsters a serious threat because they attack in numbers and quickly go for the jugular.

The greatest scene in the movie comes when a large group of "teenagers" gathers at a slumber party. After engaging in the obligatory giggly pillow fight, they suspect that a few boys might be coming over and so they play the timeless prank of placing a water-filled bucket on top of a door slightly ajar. With footsteps outside getting closer and closer, the girls turn the lights off and try their hardest to control their laughter while waiting for the door to open and the water to spill, but another liquid ends up spilling instead.

Another highlight of this fun and breezy so-bad-it's-good movie, which was filmed for about $50,000 in the unlikely party beach town of Stamford, Connecticut, sees a trio of potentially stoned female travelers stopping for gas immediately after this bizarre exchange: "Listen, we better skip this town. This is the place where they're having all the trouble. Murders by the hundreds. Some kind of monsters killing people and drinking their blood. Ooooh, it gives me the creeps." "Imagine…being that thirsty."

The Mutilator (1984)
Directors: Buddy Cooper, John Douglass
Writer: Buddy Cooper
Cast: Matt Mitler, Ruth Martinez, Bill Hitchcock, Connie Rogers, Frances Raines

New Yorkers who walked down 42nd Street with nothing to do in early 1985 were given one hell of an invitation with a theater marquee advertising a double bill of *Pieces* and *The Mutilator*, and it's hard to ask for a more enjoyable gruesome twosome to enjoy in a group setting. With absurd plots and questionable performances sparking contagious howls of laughter, and impressive kills eliciting "oooh's and "ahhh's," there must have been a unique level of camaraderie from the gorehounds who left that grimy theater with sticky shoes and the goofy, toe-tapping tune of "Fall Break" stuck in their heads. That song is probably the most renowned detail of directors Buddy Cooper and John Douglass' one and only film, and the fact Arrow Video has it playing on a loop for their Blu-ray main menu screen means that it has probably crept into the dreams of many who fell asleep during one of the boring parts.

In a bizarre prologue, a woman icing a birthday cake falls to her death after her son, Ed, accidentally shoots her while cleaning daddy's gun collection. The patriarch returns home to find the worst birthday surprise ever, and he reacts by pushing his little boy to the ground and drinking whisky on the couch next to the corpse of his wife, all without saying a single word. Jumping forward 15 years or so, a grown-up Ed is drinking beer with his buddies and lamenting how they have no plans for their upcoming week off, but as luck would have it, he and his friends are then invited to the cabin belonging to his estranged father for a little pre-winter maintenance.

It's rare to come across a non-shark horror movie with this much action on the coast. Having dark ocean waves stir in the background adds so much power to typical slasher scenes like youngsters searching for their recently mutilated friends. But the most memorable scene of characters searching for each other takes place inside the cabin with the nighttime game Blind Man's Bluff, where someone has to turn off all the lights and hide in a pitch-black house while everyone else does the seeking. It sounds like a pretty fun game to play but not a fun one to film. They might as well be playing this game at noon in Death Valley, California, because the amount of natural light in the house is insane when the characters are staggering around with eyes open and arms outstretched, somehow unable to see what is directly in front of them. It's also really strange why they only brought a dozen beers for six people, and if it wasn't for some senior citizens discount scheme (which I still don't understand) at the convenience store, they only would have bought six.

But what this movie lacks in lighting techniques, alcohol distribution, and appropriate bedtime attire for Ed, it makes up for with blood, lots of blood!

And the killer—whose identity is never kept a secret—has an arsenal that includes battleaxes, large fishing hooks, outboard motors, and pitchforks, guaranteeing that no two deaths are the same. His motive is quite stupid but I like his style as well as his ability to disrobe, climb in a swimming pool, drown a woman, and then drag her out without her macho boyfriend even noticing despite being in the same pool!

LET'S ALL DIE LAUGHING LIKE VIZZINI FROM PRINCESS BRIDE

Funny Man (1994)
Writer and Director: Simon Sprackling
Cast: Tim James, Benny Young, Ingrid Lacey, Christopher Lee, Pauline Black

A surefire way for a film to immediately hook in viewers is putting an intense and devilishly dressed Christopher Lee in a poker game with moody lighting and such high stakes that he places atop a pile of cash the keys to his ancestral mansion. Filthy-rich record producer Max Taylor isn't the least bit intimidated because he happens to be holding the greatest hand in poker with the help of a Joker card that hadn't been removed from the deck. Lee's character seems unphased by his measly pair being royally flushed out and tells the new homeowner, "You're a funny man, Mr. Taylor, but I've met funnier, and so will you."

While his younger brother/ lackey John Taylor (looking much more like Faith No More's Billy Gould than Duran Duran's John Taylor) is driving a van loaded up with expensive studio equipment and a zany assortment of hitchhikers that include a Jamaican tarot priestess and a live-action Velma from *Scooby Doo* (although listed in the credits as "Thelma"), Max is already exploring his new property with his wife and two children. It's more like a giant funhouse of horrors with no rhyme or reason, seemingly constructed by a very talented team of set designers given carte blanche to do whatever the hell they wanted. Inside one of these rooms, reminiscent of *TerrorVision*'s "Pleasure Palace," the wife is studiously gazing at statues and oblivious to the fact that a court jester goblin is creeping up behind her; this is one movie monster that knows how to make a grand entrance and toy with his prey long before vital organs are removed! The way he nonchalantly stands beside her to admire the same artwork and make small talk while she tries her hardest not to panic is a stroke of mad genius from the filmmaker.

Throughout the film this evil jester played by Tim Janes uses a variety of costumes, accents, and cranium-exploding weapons while frequently breaking the fourth wall to mug at the camera and tell us lame one-liners. He shares qualities of fellow 90's funny men like the Leprechaun, Wishmaster, Uncle Sam, and Rumpelstiltskin. I learned tonight that being in constant befuddlement for 93 straight minutes can really take a toll on one's facial muscles, and no scene was more eyebrow-raising than when Funny Man takes the time to set up a futuristic strip club in the middle of nowhere to overcharge one of the hitchhikers and then try to arouse him with a "sexy" musical number…just because. Long before we even get to the oceanside Punch and Judy puppet show massacre, this movie has proven to be such a wild and dazzling ride that it's easy to identify with a character who finds himself spiraling head-first down a cocaine-filled slide.

Adding to the charm are cameos from a stuffed Gizmo strapped to a van's grill, plastic vampire fangs scattered along the dashboard, and *Super Mario Brothers* on Game Boy.

Leprechaun 2 (1994)

Director: Rodman Flender
Writers: Turi Meyer, Alfredo Septien
Cast: Warwick Davis, Charlie Heath, Shevonne Durkin, Sandy Baron

Leprechaun 3 (1995)

Director: Brian Trenchard-Smith
Writer: David DuBos
Cast: Warwick Davis, Lee Armstrong, John Gatins, Caroline Williams, John DeMita

Warwick Davis as the jovial but vengeful leprechaun is so iconic that I hadn't considered including any of the movies in this book celebrating "rare" horror. But far too often, it seems that whenever people talk about the *Leprechaun* series, they mention the 1993 original and the trips to outer space and the hood, completely glazing over what are the best two entries by an urban galaxy mile. It gets my 14.6% (according to Ancestry.com) Irish temper boiling and so I'm going to let them share one of my 300 fantastic fright flick slots.

The original *Leprechaun* is a pleasure of mine that I'm not the slightest bit guilty about, and Part 2 is superior in just about every way. It's funnier, faster, bloodier, and rather than hang around a dimly lit farmhouse in need of a fresh coat of paint, here the leprechaun gets to leave a trail of blood that crosses continents and centuries as he tries to reclaim his bride and also a gold shilling that he drops along the way. My personal favorite scene takes place at a bar during St. Patrick's Day, where Lep foolishly tells a slippery, scheming, alcoholic Jack Klompus, "Drink all you can, drink all you're able, if you're drinking with me, you'll be under the table" and then with all of his supporters cheering him on, gets so plastered that he momentarily loses all of his powers. This forces him to recover in a hipster espresso bar to get his mojo back before continuing the chase (and the rhyming wisecracks) through go kart tracks and cave tunnels. And where else are you going to see Clint Howard and *Twin Peaks'* Kimmy Robertson bicker in the backseat of one of those dark side of Hollywood tours?

Since Part 2 only made a measly $2.3 million during its theatrical run, plans to continue the saga with Leprechaun's bride were scrapped in favor of a standalone story set in Las Vegas and destined for a video store debut. The twinkle in Warwick's eyes never shone brighter than in this entry packed with creative kills and a wicked sense of humor, where he gleefully raises hell in Sin City while taking breaks to play casino games, chat with an Elvis impersonator, and interrupt a magic show to perform an impressive chainsaw trick, and so it was no surprise to learn that this is his personal favorite *Leprechaun* film. Lee Armstrong (who sadly quit acting after the movie) and John Gatins lead a charismatic and endearing cast who play off each other wonderfully and seem to understand that *Leprechaun 3* is the definition of a fun time at the movies. Cult cinema icon Brian Trenchard-Smith even invited some of his *Night of the Demons 2* cast members to briefly reprise their roles around a craps table!

Psycho Goreman (2020)

Writer and Director: Steven Kostanski
Cast: Nita-Josee Hanna, Owen Myre, Matthew Ninaber, Steven Vlahos, Adam Brooks

Well, tonight I decided to finally see what this whole *Psycho Goreman* movie was all about after seeing multiple people gush over it on Twitter and Letterboxd. The comparisons to *Mighty Morphin*

Power Rangers had been keeping me at arm's length because for whatever reason I never went through a superhero phase whatsoever growing up. Now that those Marvel movies come out seemingly every single weekend and are the only ones breaking box office records, my mere indifference has mutated into alienation and a contempt stronger than kryptonite, which I understand is totally unfair seeing as how I'm apparently the last person on earth who doesn't watch them. But after a week where I subjected myself to five of the nine movies nominated for Best Picture at next month's Academy Awards—all of which were unbearably depressing and void of escapism—what I desperately needed was something silly, loud, and action-packed. *Psycho Goreman* delivered everything I craved on a platter splattered with blood and brains. I know it's only January, but I'm already going on record calling this the most entertaining movie of the year, and if there were any justice in the world, Glenn Close and Robert Redford would be on stage next month saying "And the Oscar for Best Picture goes to… Psycho Goreman, or PG for short!" Had I known that this was from the co-writer and co-director of *The Void*, one of my favorites of 2016, I wouldn't have waited so long. Steven Kostanski is also known for his work in Astron-6, the Canadian production company behind *The Editor* and *Father's Day*.

Siblings Mimi and Luke are out in the backyard playing Crazyball, a game they made up using a hilariously convoluted set of rules, and Luke's punishment for losing is having to dig a giant hole to be symbolically buried in. The final swing of the shovel makes an unexpected clank, prompting Mimi to reach beneath the soil and pull out a glowing gem that happens to control the heart and soul of a long-dormant intergalactic evil overlord known as the Archduke of Nightmares. After bedtime, when brother and sister are tapping on the walls in their secret language (which they have mastered to the point where "I told you, Grandma is in hell forever" is effortlessly communicated), the space monster emerges overnight and shows off a little of his awesome powers when he encounters a couple of suburban drug dealers, giving one a horrible death and the other one a fate worse than the most horrible of deaths.

Mimi discovers the next day that as long as she has the gem, the towering and English-speaking creature can't harm her and has to do whatever she says. It's like if a bratty, bullying, fearless, spazzy little girl had the ability to make Pinhead her pet, shrugging off his impolite threats like "The longer we play these childish games, the more horrifying your deaths will be" and then forcing him to play drums in her band. It's a brilliant concept cooked to perfection in *Psycho Goreman*, as the monster has no choice but to go along with the shenanigans until the Paladins from planet Gigax heed his call and tear the earth children to shreds.

Not even the most versatile and spectacularly designed army of space warriors can compete with the natural charisma and over-the-top manic energy of child actor Nita-Josee Hanna in her film debut. Mimi wouldn't be the best sister to have since she'd boss you around and steal your freedom fries, but boy is she fun to watch, especially when she's interacting with PG and becoming mad with power.

Every scene is executed with so much imagination, artistry, and vigor that this movie might have felt a little exhausting, even at only 95 minutes, if it weren't for the relatable family drama balancing out the outrageous visuals and making us care about the characters. If it ends up taking the horror community by storm by the end of the year and loses its "underseen" status, then I'll probably delete this entry. If it remains, then consider this your responsibility as a fun-loving horror fan to hop aboard the *Psycho*

Horror Galore

Goreman train and bring some friends. You know what, this movie put me in such an agreeable mood that I think I'll watch my very first episode of *Mighty Morphin Power Rangers* now just for the hell of it.

25 minutes later:

This is proving to be a very fun-filled Friday night. My ignorance showed right away because for some odd reason I thought *Mighty Morphin Power Rangers* was an '80s Saturday morning cartoon staple taking place in another galaxy. While perusing the episodes available on Netflix, I chose "I'm Dreaming of a White Ranger" because, even though it's been two weeks since Santa Claus slid down all of the chimneys in the world, my tree is still up for a couple more days at least. I was also curious to see how the worlds of superheroes and Christmas would mesh. Going in blind in an episode from season 3 proved to be a mystifying experience, as I didn't know what the hell was going on, but the corny holiday cheer and unintentionally funny reaction shots really hit the spot. I couldn't tell from a single episode if the *Psycho Goreman* comparisons were remotely valid, but similar to PG's self-reflection when he angrily dismissed Mimi's magazine and shouted "I DO NOT CARE FOR HUNKY BOYS...or do I?," tonight I was having the same kind of doubts regarding my opinion of '90s-era television teen superheroes.

Return to Horror High (1987)

Director: Bill Froehlich
Writers: Bill Froehlich, Mark Lisson, Dana Escalante, Greg H. Sims
Cast: Lori Lethin, Brendan Hughes, Alex Rocco, Scott Jacoby, Andy Romano, Philip McKeon

Considering how much the skeleton cheerleader VHS cover always popped out in video stores, I'm surprised I never joined in on the "Killer to the left, killer to the right, stand up, sit down, fright, fright, fright" cheer and took her home with me. Maybe the title suggested that it was a sequel to a movie that needed to be seen first for clarity but confusingly never sat beside it on the shelves. That assumption turned out to be incorrect as no original film exists, and I was also dead wrong in thinking that just because it was a late '80s slasher set in a high school, it would recycle the same old "tormented and possibly disfigured man gets revenge on high school bullies" plot. Ignorance sure turned out to be bliss tonight because this is a movie chockfull of surprises that I was more than happy to fall for. In a night where the gods blessed us by having a fly land on Mike Pence's head for two whole minutes while the whole world was watching, *Return to Horror High* kept the party atmosphere going.

It does begin like a sequel would, however, as we're treated to the aftermath of a long night of butchering, with police officers struggling to match up the body parts with the corresponding victims outside of Crippen High School. The only survivor is a shellshocked screenwriter who was working on a film inside the school that has been abandoned ever since a previous massacre took place back in 1982. Told in a nonlinear timeline and acutely aware on how the viewers will sometimes puzzle over whether this is past or present, movie or movie within a movie, *Return to Horror High* plays its viewers like a fiddle over and over and makes us feel like the most popular citizens of a town that takes its April Fools' Day seriously when certain scenes turn on a dime at the most unexpected of times.

It feels so far ahead of its time by how it playfully skewers slasher tropes (like characters who insist on exploring a dark basement without a flashlight) and the state of the slasher subgenre by having the screenwriter, director, and producer clash over what kind of movie they should be making. The director takes a cursory glance at the screenwriter's new scenes before crumpling up the papers right in front of him, while the crass producer shuns both of their arthouse, psychological aspirations because people pay money to see blood and boobs in cheap pictures like this that shouldn't even pretend to have redeeming qualities. Alex Rocco as the male chauvinist pig producer succeeds in making the most inappropriate behavior hilarious, even in the "me too" movement, as he interrupts the most dramatic of scenes to make absolutely sure the actress is topless, and after she complains about how degrading, objectifying, and exploitative these movies are to women, he compromises by telling the screenwriter to write "a new scene for Kelly. I dunno, two girls talk about love, marriage, babies, make it redeeming, you know, life is wonderful crap, give them a lot of hope. Set it in the locker room shower so they're naked."

The strong meta factor was inadvertently increased even more thanks to an early appearance from George Clooney, playing an actor who prematurely leaves the production for greener pastures after being cast in a TV series, but we'll never know if it was a blue-collar progressive comedy like *Roseanne* or medical drama like *ER* because he gets lost in the school looking for an exit and is the first of many to run into a maniac wearing a mask that merits a 7/10 on the creepy scale. Had this movie within a movie been a real movie, it would have made for the most fascinating episode of Shudder's *Cursed Films* series because additional cast members have their heads lopped off, their bodies turned into slush via industrial fan collision, and their windpipes blocked inside a dangerously deep sandbox. Oh yeah, and their old high school lockers get desecrated by ominous cupid arrows.

Even though I've only seen a few episodes of *The Brady Bunch*, I couldn't help but get excited when I realized the blonde policewoman who gets sexually aroused at bloody crime scenes was Maureen "Marcia Marcia Marcia" McCormick.

Tammy and the T-Rex (1994)
Director: Stewart Raffill
Writers: Stewart Raffill, Gary Brockette
Cast: Denise Richards, Theo Forsett, Paul Walker, Ellen Dubin, Terry Kiser

Inexplicably trending on Twitter in late June 2019 was *Tammy and the T-Rex*, a mostly forgotten PG-13-rated comedy from 1994. It was always intended to be released as a goofy horror film with a hard R-rating until producer and co-writer Gary Brockette decided at the last minute that it might have a better shot at the box office if it appealed more to kids and had taglines like "This tyrannosaurus rex just wants to be a party animal" and "He's the coolest pet in town." And so every second of skull-drilling, intestine-chewing, head-exploding, torso-disemboweling, blood-vomiting, and Savini-inspired splatter was removed to the heartbreak of writer-director Stewart Raffill. It would take over 25 long years before the original cut of *Tammy and the T-Rex* saw the light of day in theaters (starting with the Chicago festival Cinemapocalypse), on streaming services like Shudder, and with a pristine-looking Vinegar Syndrome Blu-ray loaded with extras to answer many of your burning questions, but not even the director had the foggiest idea why the title card reads "Tanny and the Teenage T-Rex."

With its release a year after *Jurassic Park*, some probably assumed this would be every bit as shameless and derivative as Raffill's *E.T.*-inspired disaster *Mac and Me*, but Tammy had a very unorthodox journey that began when Raffill was notified by a friend that for just a few weeks, he could have access to a life-size animatronic dinosaur before it was transported to a Texas theme park. Despite having no story, cast, or crew, he jumped at the opportunity to work for the first time since *Mannequin: On the Move*. Most everyone else involved shared in his excitement, leading to much camaraderie on the set as they braved actual wildfires in Calabasas, California to tell that old timeless Hollywood story of a romance between innocent teenagers Tammy (Denise Richards in one of her earliest roles) and Michael (an unrecognizably baby-faced Paul Walker) that faces some tough hurdles when her psychotic boyfriend kidnaps Michael and leaves him stranded in a wild animal sanctuary to be preyed upon by lions and jaguars, where he's later declared dead by a mad doctor (Terry Kiser of *Weekend At Bernie*'s fame) who proceeds to transplant his brain into a T-Rex robot. Retaining all of his memories inside of the dinosaur, Michael uses his super-strength to escape from the laboratory and exact revenge on his tormenters while also looking for his sweetheart.

As jaw-droppingly awesome as the gore scenes are, I have no doubts that the lucky audience members at the Cinemapocalypse festival popped just as loud, if not even louder, for the goofier, downright adorable moments in which the T-Rex uses a payphone, dusts off a friend's shoulders, plays a game of charades, and offers his opinions of the available bodies at the morgue. Seasoned horror fans probably also celebrated the appearances from Sean Whalen (who was riding high thanks to *The People Under the Stairs* and an enormously popular milk commercial), George "Buck" Flower, and *Leprechaun 2* star Sheyonne Durkin. When the pandemic is finally over and social restrictions are lifted, the first thing I'm going to do is send my friends a movie night invitation where Tammy is the main attraction, because after so many months of craziness of the bad kind, it's safe to say they could all use some craziness of the good kind.

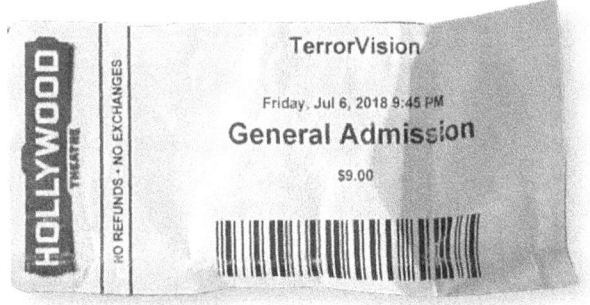

It's nice to have proof that my *TerrorVision* theater experience wasn't just a dream

TerrorVision (1986)

Writer and Director: Ted Nicolaou
Cast: Gerrit Graham, Mary Woronov, Diane Franklin, Chad Allen, Jon Gries, Bert Remsen

Shortly after 9:45 pm on July 6, 2018, I was on cloud nine watching the mutant creature disposal unit bounce against a series of planets in antiquated Pong style, because I knew any second the final boing would explode into the irresistible opening credits theme from the artsy post-punk band The Fibonaccis—it was a song I heard several times before but never quite like this. And then as the title card spun around frantically until landing on the center of 50-foot silver screen, the sizeable audience cheered and made it clear that I wasn't the only person insanely excited about finally seeing *TerrorVision* in an actual movie theater!

Ted Nicolaou, whose earliest credits include *The Texas Chainsaw Massacre* for sound recording and *Tourist Trap* for editing, was simply shown a promotional poster and the title *TerrorVision* by producer Charles Band, and then it was up to him to write and direct the film. Satirizing the excesses of the '80s way before it was trendy, this movie is a flashy, tacky, and wacky live-action cartoon where every single detail is deliberately exaggerated to your pleasure.

In a strike of dream casting for fans of cult cinema, Gerrit Graham (demonstrating his campiest facial expressions since the Brian De Palma masterpiece *Phantom of the Paradise*) and Mary Woronov play Stan and Raquel Putterman, who probably won't win any Parents of the Year awards due to their unabashed swinging lifestyle and large collection of erotic paintings that aren't restricted to the "Pleasure Palace" wing. After chastising his repairman for guzzling his Heinies instead of working (I guess Kyle MacLachlan's character in *Blue Velvet* wasn't the only proud Heineken drinker in 1986), Stan is proud to show off his brand new satellite dish to his family that also includes his son Sherman, new wave valley girl daughter Suzy, and survivalist father who complains about all the weirdos in the city while holding onto his handmade poster promoting lizard tails as the self-regenerating food that can be your salvation. Later that night, while Sherman and his grandfather fall asleep to Medusa's midnight movie marathon featuring *Robot Monster* and *Earth Vs the Flying Saucers*, their state-of-the-art satellite receiver attracts an actual space monster spiraling through the Milky Way who arrives at the Putterman household with hunger pangs.

In one of the goofiest scenes you'll ever see, Sherman and Suzy attempt to train the (absolutely amazing-looking) monster with the help of her heavy metal-obsessed boyfriend (Jon Gries from *Fright Night Part 2* and *Napoleon Dynamite*). It's oddly adorable watching this gooey, disgusting creature with cranium-crushing tentacles, a perpetual smile that shows off endless rows of fangs, a mega-sized tongue to slurp up brain matter from the floor, and one googly eye far larger than the other try to grasp concepts such as food, music, television, and the English language. Other scenes that make me so damn happy every time and which received monstrous-sized laughs at the Hollywood Theatre screening involve Mr. and Mrs. Putterman on a swinging date with a couple played by Argentinian actor Alejandro Rey (who sadly passed away the following year at the early age of 57) and Randi Brooks (*The Man with Two Brains*, *Hamburger: The Motion Picture*).

It had a spectacularly bad box office showing, was hated by critics, and didn't make much of a splash on the video shelves, but a horror film this creative, outrageous, artistic, and out-of-this-world entertaining could never hide in obscurity for long, and now it seems to receive weekly adoration from the horror websites I visit, podcasts I listen to, and many of the horror fans I follow on Twitter. Scream Factory gave it a pristine transfer with plenty of special features on a double feature Blu-ray with *The Video Dead*, which I thank my lucky stars for purchasing early because it's apparently out of print for some silly reason and going for almost $80 on Amazon.

Unmasked Part 25 (1988)

Director: Anders Palm
Writer: Mark Cutforth
Cast: Gregory Fox, Fiona Evans, Edward Brayshaw, Debbie Lee London, Kim Fenton

Eighteen years before *Behind the Mask: The Rise of Leslie Vernon* affectionately satirized the masked maniacs of the slasher subgenre, a British film called *Unmasked Part 25* also took a stab at conventions by imagining what a *Friday the 13th* sequel might have looked like had Jason Vorhees instantly fallen in love with someone he was seconds away from senselessly slaughtering.

It gets off to such a promising start with nighttime shots of London decorated with New Wave aesthetics popular at the time before taking us to a party set directly above the disgusting flat belonging to hockey-masked psychopath Jackson. The first victim of the night has his face peeled off and heart ripped out in five amazing seconds that signal right away the MPAA wasn't going to get its filthy paws on these kills like they did with many of Jason's. After more partygoers are gruesomely murdered for their debauchery practices, he seems to zero in on "The Final Girl" in record time, but Shelly happens to be blind and mistakes him for the date her friends arranged for her. They hit it off well and he decides to reveal that he's not just a hulking mute brute, but an intellectual man with the soul of a poet and a lot of appreciation for the literature of Lord Byron. He also feels comfortable enough to remove his mask (looking just like the one from *Friday the 13th Part V*'s second-rate poster art) inside her apartment since she's unable to see the severity of his deformities.

Unable to resist his killer instincts, especially with the unluckiest of holidays right around the corner, he keeps his extracurricular activities a secret while their romance blossoms. In one of the best scenes, Shelly takes him to a Halloween store so that she can buy a goalie mask of her own, in hopes that it'll make him feel less insecure about being seen in public, leading up to a romantic walk in the park that would be treated as just a ludicrous sight gag in any other movie, but here it feels deeply moving with the same tinges of tragedy from *Frankenstein*, *Beauty and the Beast*, *The Elephant Man*, and *The Phantom of the Opera* (which also comes to mind when organ music briefly takes over the soundtrack). The ludicrous sight gags are saved soon after, when Shelly wants to share her S&M proclivities in the bedroom to an embarrassed Jackson who hilariously consults the official guidebook.

With the future of the *Friday the 13th* series still bogged down in silly courtroom battles year after year over the rights, *Unmasked Part 25* (which also contains a Crazy Ralph and a summer camp backstory) will really hit the spot for those who've been missing the gruesome adventures of Camp Crystal Lake's favorite population control resource. The meaning behind the strange title, I'll leave for you to discover.

Vicious Fun (2020)

Director: Cody Calahan
Writers: Christopher Warre Smets, James Villeneuve, Cody Calahan
Cast: Evan Marsh, Amber Goldfarb, Ari Millen, Julian Richings, Robert Maillet, David Koechner

A more accurate title has never existed than *Vicious Fun*, a horror-comedy from Canadian filmmaker Cody Calahan (*The Oak Room*, *Let Her Out*) that enjoyed a successful international festival run before premiering on Shudder on June 29, 2021, hopefully to the appreciation of celebrity birthday boys Richard Lewis, Gary Busey, Don Dokken, and Deep Purple drummer Ian Paice. It's rewarding to latch onto at least a couple of horror podcasts that start out the new year by presenting their Top 10 of the Year lists because, assuming the hosts are trustworthy and have done their homework, you'll be left with multiple hidden gems to enjoy during the most depressing month of the year. *Vicious Fun* had flown under my radar but three hosts of the great podcast *Land of the Creeps* brought it to the surface by ranking it high on their respective Best of 2021 lists.

It ended up being one of those movies that I enjoyed so much that I couldn't bring myself to press pause or look away from the screen for a single moment to jot down observations. Being in prime relaxation mode with my feet up, a frosty mug of Ninkasi's Dawn of the Red IPA by my side, and an electric heating pad alleviating lower back pain also helped me fully immerse in this story about Joel, a young brash "deputy assistant editor" at a horror magazine who decides to follow the guy dating his roommate Carrie to a Chinese restaurant. He intends to strike up a conversation and secretly record him saying horrible things, just so she'll end up dumping the creep and date him instead. After his plan hilariously backfires and he becomes the victim of a Sea Bass bill scheme, Joel drinks so excessively at the bar that he mistakes the exit for a janitorial closet, where he spends the next few hours passed out on the floor.

When he wakes up and stumbles back into the lobby, he interrupts an after-hours support group already in progress, led by the always-entertaining David Koechner (*The Office*, *Anchorman*, *Krampus*, *Cheap Thrills*.) Joel is mistaken for the sole member of the group who hasn't shown up yet, and he learns that these people are not drug addicts trying to kick the habit, but serial killers who have formed a comradery with each other to discuss their various issues of dispatching victims and evading capture. Not wanting to anger the cannibal sous chef, the doctor who enjoys reviving his victims just to kill them all over again, or the 7-foot giant (played by former WWF wrestler Kurrgan!) that likes making his presence known at summer camps, Joel uses his horror expertise by telling everyone that he's a serial killing cab driver. Much like how he's done with his harsh movie reviews for the horror magazine, the smartest psycho in the group pokes holes into his flimsy story until the truth comes out and the night becomes a bloody adventure of mistakes, misunderstandings, and mayhem with nails pounded through foreheads, intestines spilled onto the floor, and the occasional arm hacked off. *Vicious Fun* works equally well as a comedy and a horror movie, an extremely rare feat, where one moment you'll be laughing at the meta humor and the next shrieking at the sight of Julian Richings' Fritz the Clown during a power outage.

Some people might be getting tired of all these retro pandering horror films coming out that are saturated in neon lights and vibrating with chilly synth beats, but yours truly is not one of them and so the '80s esthetics only added to my enjoyment. Those with nostalgia for drive-in theaters will also be greatly rewarded as the film ends on such a pleasing note that your hands won't be able to resist clapping even if nobody but your cat will hear.

Waxwork II: Lost in Time (1992)
Writer and Director: Anthony Hickox
Cast: Zach Galligan, Monika Schnarre, Martin Kemp, Bruce Campbell, Alexander Godunov

It's easy to imagine the sequel to *Waxwork* opening with the suburban wax museum rising from the ashes and rebuilding itself just in time to host a gathering for a new group of entitled rich brats, but fortunately, Anthony Hickox's imagination was way too active to play it safe. He didn't even bring back the wax museum, just a severed hand from the zombie waxwork that managed to crawl its way out of the inferno along with the two survivors, Mark and Sarah (played by a returning Zach Galligan and new addition Monika Schnarre, taking over for Deborah Foreman). Sarah returns home to get some much-needed rest after a night of losing her friends to vampires, werewolves, zombies, and the Marquis de Sade, but discovers her nightmare is far from over when the severed hand bludgeons her alcoholic stepfather (George "Buck" Flower in the first of many glorious cameos) with a hammer before attacking her with things like mustard and hot dog buns as an organ serenades us with "Take me out to the ballgame," a good indication that this movie is bonkers in the best possible way.

Sarah is arrested and put on trial for the death of her stepfather, and since it's unlikely that a jury will put the blame on a severed hand with a fondness for condiments, she and Mark embark on a quest of finding evidence to corroborate their story. Their first stop is the house of Sir Alfred, a family friend who helped them in the original. A film reel is cued up upon their arrival, where Sir Alfred speaks to them (and even amusingly anticipates their obvious questions) in riddles and leads them to a magical compass that was once used by angels to travel through other dimensions. Figuring they have nothing left to lose, they step into the portal and become separated while falling into the black void in which the only other inhabitant is a lizard bat creature. Mark and Sarah then explore different universes in hopes of gathering evidence and finding each other as well as a way home.

Several of these time travel destinations serve as warm hugs to horror fans because Hickox pays homage to beloved films such as *Dawn of the Dead*, *Alien*, *Dr. Jekyll and Mr. Hyde*, *Nosferatu*, and *Godzilla*, faithfully recreating the set pieces, film stocks, and wardrobes. As much as I enjoyed the *Frankenstein* segment in which Mark is hit by the extracted eyeballs and brains of the doctor after a monstrous squeeze, the best part of this movie is its tribute to 1960's *The Haunting*, because it's such an awesome pleasure to see Galligan (just a couple years after *Gremlins 2: The New* Batch) and Bruce Campbell step into the world of such an iconic haunted house and deal with the creaking doors, pounding, lightning, and mentally tortured Eleanor.

After taking horror fans on such an incredible ride for the first 40 minutes, the movie slows down…waaaaaaaaaaaaay down, when Mark and Sarah are reunited in King Arthur's medieval times and are in no rush to leave. The hallucinatory Renaissance party, David Carradine cameo, Mark's "Two Billion Bottles of Beer on the Wall" rendition, song reminiscent of Enigma's "Principles of Lust," and swordplay are enjoyable, but these scenes take up half of the damn running time and caused more than one of my friends to doze off during a horror marathon. Those of us who stayed awake were generously rewarded when *Waxwork II* burst back to life with a hell of a climax that parodied other horror favorites while also delivering more zany Looney Tunes-style shenanigans. Drew Barrymore supposedly makes a cameo near the end but I've managed to miss it each time.

CAMPING AND HIKING DISASTERS

Cheerleader Camp (1988)
Director: John Quinn
Writers: David Lee Fein, R.L. O'Keefe
Cast: Betsy Russell, Leif Garrett, Lucinda Dickey, Lorie Griffin, George "Buck" Flower

With such an eye-catching VHS cover displaying a female skeleton in mid-air, raising pom poms and exposing serious underboob, I feel a little ashamed that it took me this long to give *Cheerleader Camp* the time of day. I've devoted a huge majority of this three-day weekend to obscure slashers, and this was a definite highlight because even when my 3:30 am eyelids were getting heavy, my smile wasn't fading. Kudos to my buddy Michael for recommending it!

If a suspenseful and shocking slasher is what you're craving, then this movie won't fit the bill, but if you want more of a gory sex comedy whodunnit with lots of misbehaving, then it most certainly will. Ugh, sorry about that, but there's the absolute worst demonstration in the world of white men rapping in this movie, and I guess it put me in a rhyming mood, so sue me. It occurs when the two male crew members of the cheerleading squad introduce each cheerleader with a line that goes something like, "Next is Bonnie, she acts kinda funny, she'll steal your heart but not your money." Bonnie and her team are competing in a weekend cheerleading competition, where a victory would take them to the state finals, and teammate Alison is clearly feeling the pressure.

The film, originally titled Bloody Pom Poms, opens with Alison having a nightmare of being unable to locate her school locker (I was relieved to find out that many other people have this recurring dream as well), and when she finally changes into her uniform and runs out on the football field, she trips and falls to a chorus of boos and snarky commentary from the announcer. Her dreams get increasingly disturbing as the film progresses, a possible side effect of being overwhelmed at the thought of entering the real world without having any idea what she wants to do. She's also saddled by an unsatisfying relationship with her boyfriend Brent (played by 70's heartthrob Leif Garrett), who everybody fawns over and says he's the perfect guy, when in reality he's a loathsome piece of garbage without a single redeemable quality. His buddy, Timmy, is even more flagrant with his raging hormones, as he videotapes the girls in various stages of undress and even grabs a couple of their backsides while swimming, but I guess since he's obese and goofy, everyone just shrugs it off? The other cheerleaders in the squad are shallow, self-obsessed caricatures incapable of saying anything more profound than "If you don't look good, it ain't worth it!" And rounding out the squad is Cory (played by Lucinda Dickey of *Ninja III: The Domination* cult fandom), the frustrated team mascot who is forced to keep

Horror Galore

her alligator costume on while eating because the villainous administrator Miss Tipton reminds her, "You're a mascot, not a human."

Filmed in the serenity of Sequoia National Forest under a relaxed schedule, it's no wonder everyone involved appears to be in great spirits. I enjoyed my stay at Camp Hurrah, a place with infectious spirit, creepy employees, punk rock performances, and corpses falling on people who do something unsanitary like drink milk directly from the jug. As the dead bodies pile up and potential killers start to dwindle down, it takes a sudden turn to more straightforward slasher territory without losing any of its endearing qualities or inane dialogue. Some of the more quotable lines come from George "Buck" Flower (making yet another appearance in the book), who a month prior played a janitor in *Sorority Babes in the Slimeball Bowl-O-Rama* that was probably too lovable and wholesome to say something like, "She would make your pee-pee harder than a ten-pound bag of nickel jawbreakers."

The Forest (1982)
Writer and Director: Don Jones
Cast: Dean Russell, Gary Kent, Tomi Barrett, John Batis, Ann Wilkinson, Corky Pigeon

Once I heard the opening theme song to this movie, I couldn't help but get my hopes up because it sounded like an intriguing mixture of Yes keyboardist Rick Wakeman's beautiful score to another early '80s slasher, *The Burning*, and something you might hear from *Dr. Quinn Medicine Woman* or *Lassie*. Along with the soundtrack that continued to impress, *The Forest* also benefits from an imaginative script, a great setting, and lots of unintentional hilarity, resulting in a highly entertaining experience that isn't harmed by a complete lack of scares. When the first line is from a female hiker who says, "There's something following us!" and her husband,

Poster for *The Forest* (1982), Wide World of Entertainment, Fury Films Ltd.

without hesitation, insists, "There's nothing out there. It's your imagination," you know you're in for a jolly good time. After their slaughter, we're introduced to Steve and Charlie, who are at their wits' end because of all the Los Angeles smog, heat, and traffic, and decide that a camping trip would be the best way to rejuvenate. In a huge coincidence, their wives, Sharon and Teddi, have also made plans to go camping together, but as we soon learn, these four people are absolutely incompetent at making arrangements. The plans keep changing in dizzying fashion until it's decided that the wives will leave ten minutes before their husbands, as opposed to, I don't know, doing something that makes sense like all going together?!

When the guys experience car trouble, Sharon and Teddi's arbitrary ten minute head start increases by a couple hours, requiring them to put their backpacking, navigating, fire-building, and tent-pitching skills to the test while thunder ominously rumbles through a forest that has been harboring an inordinate number of missing people. On their first night, they are awakened by a pair of young siblings with heavily reverberated voices who warn them that their homicidal father is getting close. Sharon runs and hides but Teddi isn't so fortunate, as she's confronted by the madman who says he doesn't want to hurt her but hasn't had anything to eat for weeks. Armed with a knife, he promises that he'll make this quick, but when she fights back with a slash of her own, he angrily shouts, "What did you do that for?!"

There are many other head-scratching lines from actors playing it deadly serious, and I fully expect a plethora of howling laughter from my friends when I eventually show this at a movie night. "Hey Charlie, come here a minute, c'mon tell me, what do you make of that?" "It's wet dirt, sometimes they call it mud." "Yeah, yeah, I guess you're right" was another personal favorite exchange. But I also expect my friends to be at the edge of their seats when the men stumble upon a cave as a means of escaping the rain and find a candelabra and something strange cooking on the stove. It remains to be seen how they'll react when Steve (resembling both *Invasion of the Body Snatchers'* Donald Sutherland and *It*'s Harry Anderson with that mustache and hairstyle) sobs like a baby after twisting his ankle, but I sure as hell enjoyed it.

The villain might not be frightening or intimidating, but it's nice to see an articulate cannibalistic hermit for a change, and I loved the fact that he has unexplained teleporting skills and lives in a cave with the ghosts of his children and adulterous wife. This is a hidden gem begging to be seen in high definition so that the raging rivers, majestic groves, and granite formations at California's Sequoia National Forest can sparkle, but since I wasn't willing to shell out the $45 for a DVD courtesy of Code Red, I just squinted with a grainy version available at Internet Archive and tried my darndest to understand what the hell those echoey ghost kids were saying.

The Ritual (2017)

Director: David Bruckner
Writers: Joe Barton, Adam Nevill (novel)
Cast: Rafe Spall, Arsher Ali, Robert James-Collier, Sam Troughton, Paul Reid

The only time I've gotten to be on a panel of judges in any capacity was for *Horror Movie Podcast*'s third annual Horror Cinema Awards, and in a year that gave us *Hell Fest*, *Ghost Stories*, *Annihilation*, *Revenge*, *Apostle*, *The Endless*, *Hereditary*, *Mandy*, *Summer of '84*, *Incident in a Ghostland*, *Good Manners*, *Terrified*, *A Quiet Place*, and the obnoxiously titled *Halloween*, no decision was going to be easy peasy. For the last category, Best Horror Movie of 2018, I ended up going with *The Ritual*, an underdog for sure, but one that cohesively mixed the most satisfying aspects of several of its competitors together to create a mercilessly intense hiking excursion in beautiful Sweden (well, technically it was filmed in the Carpathian Mountains of Romania).

David Bruckner, who contributed superb segments in *The Signal*, *V/H/S*, and *Southbound*, made his first solo trek as a director with *The Ritual*. It made its debut at the Toronto International Film Festival in September 2017 before being sold to Netflix for international distribution the following year. Some would argue that the roughly 209 million global paid memberships disqualifies it from "underseen gem" status, but even on Netflix, a service that seemingly refuses to recognize any cine-

Horror Galore

matic achievement made before 2010, it's easy for a new movie like this to fall through the cracks.

We're introduced to five guys in their late thirties/early forties reminiscing in a pub while proposing options for their next big group adventure, something that's become increasingly harder to coordinate ever since being saddled with grownup responsibilities. Two of the friends, Luke and Rob, stop by a liquor store on the way home and unwittingly interrupt a robbery in progress. Luke immediately finds a place to hide while the thieves, brandishing machetes, target Rob and take his wallet. Gripping a bottle of vodka as a potential weapon, Luke desperately looks around and examines his options, but doesn't act fast enough to prevent Rob from being murdered after refusing to relinquish his wedding ring. The excellent filmmaking puts you right in Luke's shoes and forces you to imagine how you would react in the situation. Hopefully I'd be more effective than I was last night in a supermarket, when I almost had a panic attack trying to choose a box of cereal while other shoppers moseyed about.

Six months later, Luke, Phil, Dom, and Hutch embark on a four-day hike in Northern Sweden's Kungsleden trail to honor the memory of their friend, and it quickly becomes evident how the events of the tragedy have altered the dynamics of their close-knit team and created interpersonal conflicts. British actor Rafe Spall (*Life of Pi*, *Prometheus*) is especially sympathetic and convincing as Luke, a man so constantly racked with guilt and haunted by the fluorescent liquor store strobe that he's unable to find any solace in the breathtaking scenery around him. On the third day of the hike, Dom injures his knee and prompts a change to their itinerary: a short-cut through the forest. What follows are scenes that seemed constructed purely based on my personal horror preferences, as nothing makes me giddier than when lost hikers, who, after witnessing unsettling visuals like rune symbols carved into trees, stumble upon a creepy, abandoned house in the middle of the woods right at the moment when the thunder, lightning, and rain intensify. One of the guys jokes how this is the place where they will most certainly be murdered as they seek shelter inside. While a justifiably paranoid Luke stares out the window to locate the source of strange noises, he hears frantic shouting from Phil, who has discovered in the attic the statue of a beheaded man, made out of twigs and with antlers for arms. Even with a cozy fireplace, it's impossible for any of them to get some solid sack time in a cabin like this, festered by the type of evil that collaborates with personal demons to make sure that each individual wakes up screaming bloody murder.

This movie works so brilliantly as a survival-horror in the wilderness (loaded with *Blair Witch* vibes) and as a creature feature that when a Nordic cult subplot is introduced in the third act, it does lose a little momentum, but that's a very minor quibble. Even in a comfortable recliner chair with my feet propped up and a purring feline on my lap, I couldn't help but be green with envy at everyone at the Toronto International Film Festival, who were most likely un-reclined and catless, but who were the first to witness the amazing spectacle of this creature on a mega-sized screen, awing together as one and maybe even bowing to prove their devotion.

MORE DEMONIC POSSESSIONS TO SWALLOW YOUR SOULS

The Convent (2000)
Director: Mike Mendez
Writer: Chaton Anderson
Cast: Joanna Canton, Richard Trapp, Dax Miller, Megahn Perry, Adrienne Barbeau

OK, there are several different movies called *The Convent*, and so make sure the one you watch is from 2000 and depicts on the cover a woman who looks like *Pulp Fiction*'s Uma Thurman smoking a cigarette. It even starts out like a Tarantino film, with a badass dame kicking open the doors of a church to the tune of Leslie Gore's "You Don't Own Me," cigarette in mouth and whisky bottle in hand, and showing no emotion as she bashes in nun skulls with a baseball bat before setting the whole place ablaze.

On the 40th anniversary of this massacre, attributed by local legend to the woman's revenge over a forced abortion, a group of college students drive out to the abandoned seminary to smoke dope and get laid, but the gothic girl (terrifically played by Megahn Perry) who fenagled her way into the car seems to have ulterior motives. While exploring the building alone, she encounters more trespassers in the form of pretentious wannabe Satanists who hope that a human sacrifice will unleash the angry spirits of the sisters, and the fact that she's a virgin who's apparently saving herself for Marilyn Manson makes her all the more promising.

In many ways, *The Convent* feels like an honest-to-god spiritual successor to the *Night of the Demons* films, even though it sways heavier to the comedy side. An example of its good-natured humor comes when a frat boy, stereotyped to absurd degrees to the point where he becomes strangely endearing, decides to enhance the spooky setting by swallowing a stash of psychedelic mushrooms, causing him to react to real-life horrors with the same glazed over expression and goofy laugh inspired by crazy hallucinations like floating panties and a Jesus statue that turns his head and bellows, "Yo yo, get me down from here, motherfucker!" Just imagine if Stooge was tripping and told a possessed Angela that "You look all demonic and shit," before receiving that bloody kiss. Also appealing is the amount of pop culture references tossed around, as the characters mention The Misfits, Menudo, Daffney and Velma, *Sixteen Candles*, Elvira, etc. Even the character dumber than a doornail tries to join in by saying that "this place is all Amityville and shit, you know like, Redrum, redrum!" I was almost expecting someone to comment on how the nerdy fraternity pledge bears a resemblance to Courtney Gains from *Children of the Corn*, *The 'Burbs*, and *Can't Buy Me Love*.

Horror fans will have more reasons to celebrate with the appearances of Bill Moseley and Adrienne Barbeau; he plays a pot-smoking police officer (partnered with Coolio himself!) and she a gun-toting local legend with firsthand experience of demonic nuns and their bloodying yardstick strikes. Working against the movie is the overuse of shaky cam and terrible techno (the Tarantino soundtrack comparisons sadly died along with the nuns in the introduction) during all of the action scenes, but it won't stop you from marveling at the face-ripping and fluorescent blood gushing. It's also a shame that the two most entertaining college students didn't stick around longer because their facial expressions and line deliveries were as delightful as an improv Satan summoning set to the tune of "Silver Bells."

The Convent premiered at Sundance and went onto win the Audience Award at Fantafestival, but never really made much of a splash afterwards. Writer-director Mike Mendez later made the spooky and awesomely titled *The Gravedancers* and then began spending more and more time in the editing suite, splicing together horror anthologies like *Tales of Halloween* and *Nightmare Cinema*.

Head Count (2018)

Director: Elle Callahan
Writers: Michael Nader, Elle Callahan
Cast: Isaac Jay, Jay Lee, Ashleigh Morghan, Bevin Bru, A.J. Helfet, Billy Meade, Tory Freeth

"A Hisji is a vengeful thing, five times its name you never sing. With skin pale white and eyes of green, it's something you've already seen."

Elle Callahan's feature film debut will go down smooth for fans of recent mind-bending indie thrillers like *Coherence* and *Triangle*. It begins with a college student named Evan reluctantly turning down an invitation to spend the holiday break with friends so that he can visit his older brother Peyton, who lives in a trailer on the outskirts of Joshua Tree National Park. The two brothers lead very divergent lives but their lifelong bond is evident when they go on their first hike, the first of several occasions when the film takes full advantage of the stunning scenery. When Evan catches the eye of attractive photographer Zoe chilling out at the summit with her large group of friends, he is invited to join them for some freshly-rolled joints, while straight-edge new-age guru Peyton stays behind and smiles with his head in the sky.

With nighttime rolling in, Evan chooses not to go back to the trailer with his brother, but to spend more time with Zoe in the swanky house she and her friends are renting. Tequila shots and ghost stories around the firepit fill the cool air with possibilities and bring the two new lovebirds closer together, but then strange occurrences keep truncating hot tub soaks, subsequent hikes, and games of Never Have I Ever and Kings Cup. Some people speculate that their shroom-obsessed friend might have slipped something special into their cinnamon whisky, and others blame Evan for reading out loud a passage from a random creepypasta that was initially dismissed as just another lame Bloody Mary/Candyman knockoff where repeating a name multiple times will unleash a vengeful spirit.

Having so many characters limits our investment in them individually, but it does establish Evan's vulnerability as an outsider quite well as he tries to fit in with this close-knit group of people who haven't shied away from making disparaging comments about his strange brother. Their chaotic late-night shenanigans are fun to watch because the camerawork makes us feel as if we've been personally invited; you get the sense that many hours of rehearsal time were devoted to blocking because there's a ballet-like fluidity to everyone's movement. From the gunshots of NRA fanboys to the confusion of someone seemingly being in two places at once, the scares in *Head Count* are wide-ranging and effective. The Hisji is a vengeful thing indeed and it plays with a handbook that offers the ability to shapeshift and take over central nervous systems, and it's a good thing that the movie is far more interested in showing these powers than attempting to explain them. This movie also provoked nostalgic memories of a time not that long ago when I would go to parties and socialize with large groups of strangers, a simple concept that now seems strangely alien and difficult to retain.

The Shrine (2010)

Director: Jon Knautz
Writers: Brendan Moore, Trevor Matthews, Jon Knautz
Cast: Aaron Ashmore, Cindy Sampson, Meghan Heffern, Trevor Matthews, Vieslav Krystyan

Poster for *The Shrine* (2010), Brookstreet Pictures

This has been one of those weeks where my list of movies to consider for this book has reminded me of The Blob with how it's grown to mammoth proportions, but instead of devouring theater patrons and Lovers Lane teens, it snacks on horror websites and movie podcasts. As I scanned the list for a movie to watch tonight, it was hard not to feel defeated and overwhelmed by how after two years of writing about hidden gems, the finish line might as well be thousands of miles away in a small Polish village guarded heavily by a scary religious cult. I closed my eyes and pointed to *The Shrine*, a boring title that I couldn't remember adding. Cursory research led me to unappealing cover art (it's a shame I hadn't stumbled upon the much-cooler "theatrical" poster) and a ton of absolutely scathing reviews on Letterboxd, and so it was a little tempting to just delete it and move onto a title more enticing like *Lake Michigan Monster* or *Blood on Satan's Claw*.

Fortunately, I stuck to my guns because *The Shrine* ended up being my most satisfying horror viewing in weeks, and being able to hold a holy candle up to its good name has already made me feel energized and enthusiastic about this project once again. It was also an important reminder that quickly scrolling through Letterbox reviews beforehand can allow some real treasures to slip through your fingers as you assume that much greener pastures will be found elsewhere. So yeah, ignore all comprehensive audience scores and don't even think about watching the trailer for this Canadian slice of folk-cult horror, and hopefully you'll be as pleasantly surprised as I was.

After a brutal opening that sees a young man tied to a table and killed by a sledgehammer to the face, we're introduced to a journalist named Carmen who believes she's on the cusp of the most important story of her career when she hears that yet another American tourist has vanished without a trace in a remote area of Poland. Defying her boss who gives her a writing assignment about bees in Nebraska (or maybe it was Tennessee), she instead convinces her intern Sara and photographer boyfriend Marcus to accompany her somewhere much farther away. I immediately recognized the actor who plays Marcus from *The Ruins*, one of the most intense films ever about the dangers of stepping too far off the beaten path while traveling abroad, but it turns out that I was thinking of actor Shawn Ashmore, his twin brother. They travel to a small Polish village named Alvania—which was mentioned in a journal belonging to the latest missing person—but are greeted by stares and ominous warnings from the secretive locals, some of whom are spending the afternoon butchering pigs and bowing down to their medieval-looking religious leaders.

Carmen refuses to return home empty handed, so she persuades her boyfriend and intern to stick around a little longer and at least investigate that dense and still fog in the hills that is unlike anything they have ever seen before, and where a bleeding Pazuzu-style statue awaits with a grin that grows more sinister the closer they get and the more photographs they take.

This was Jon Knautz's follow-up to his feature film debut *Jack Brooks: Monster Slayer*, a bombastic and fun monster-hunting adventure, and while *The Shrine* lacks unforgettable-looking creature effects and a big name like Robert Englund, it succeeds as a no-nonsense exercise in suspense and misdirection. It treads similar folk-occult ground to *Apostle* and while it's nowhere near as powerful, it will probably earn more repeat viewings for being less punishing and 45-minutes shorter. In fact, it made me feel like Goldilocks because while so many movies this week had too much exposition or none at all, too much violence or not enough, and twists that were either too implausible or too predictable, everything in *The Shrine* felt just right.

At times you'll be reminded of *The Wicker Man*, *Evil Dead*, *Hostel*, and *The Exorcist* because this movie is confident enough in its storytelling ability to allow many themes to join the nightmare and fit right in. Taking a page out of *Midnight Express*, it also makes the risky decision of depriving audiences of subtitles whenever the villagers speak, which is often, so that we identify more with our vulnerable protagonists. Not having any idea what these strange people were saying probably contributed to many of the negative reviews, but it also confirmed its smart "show, don't tell" attitude.

SUFFERING FOR YOUR ART

Deadline (1980)
Director: Mario Azzopardi
Writers: Mario Azzopardi, Richard Oleksiak
Cast: Stephen Young, Sharon Masters, Marvin Goldhar, Jeannie Elias, Cindy Hinds

Shot and set in Toronto in the dying days of the '70s but not released to the masses until 1984, *Deadline* is about a famous horror author and screenwriter named Steven Lessey whose career and family life are competing over which one can put more bats in his belfry. The two worlds clash early on, when his wife attends one of his college lectures and laughs when the surprisingly conservative students lash out with venomous lines like, "You write horseshit horror, you exploit it for money, you expose society to your horseshit to grab off a few bloody bucks," and "You don't comment on blight, you are blight!"

Steven desperately wants to write a screenplay with more substance and meaning than his previous works, but his sleazy producer, unwilling to stray off a path that has proven to be safe and lucrative, tells Steven to leave the artsy horror films to the Europeans because they are good at it. "Pages! I need pages!" he often reminds Steven, which results in countless days sitting in front of the typewriter and only acknowledging his three children (one of whom bears an uncanny resemblance to *Poltergeist*'s Heather O'Rourke) with a shout for breaking his concentration. His wife feels similarly dejected and prefers spending evenings at parties with socialites and cocaine, dreaming of a white Christmas.

As Steven wrestles with the war inside his head, gruesome vignettes from his movies are sporadically spliced in and are probably what the few people who have seen *Deadline* remember most, especially since the gore is surprisingly impressive. As much as I liked the family drama, it's awfully hard to compete with a telepathic goat that uses a threshing machine to mangle and decapitate a man, two little kids playing a game with their grandma that involves tying her to the bed blindfolded and setting her on fire, a Nazi punk band using some sort of a frequency modulator to cause their fans' stomachs to explode, a woman taking the bloodiest shower of all time, and a vicar reacting violently to the body and blood of his savior and then having his organs feasted upon by nuns!

After a horrific tragedy, Steven dishes out more verbal abuse to his family and then invites a group of prostitutes over to his house for a party. And just when we think that he couldn't possibly be any more loathsome, he totally redeems himself by pulling down a gigantic projection screen and showing reels of spooky celluloid to his guests, which is the truest testament of a great host. But much like the character of Dani in Ari Aster's brilliant *Midsommar*, he probably isn't in the best frame of mind for hard drugs. *Deadline* is sometimes uncomfortable, sometimes hilarious, but always weird as hell and so I was happy to hear that Vinegar Syndrome will be releasing a remastered 2K Blu-ray/DVD in April 2020.

Fatal Exposure (1989)
Director: Peter B. Good
Writer: Christopher Painter
Cast: Blake Bahner, Ena O'Rourke, Dan Schmale, Julie Austin, Renee Cline

I'll surely experience some unpleasantness when I take down all of the Halloween decorations in a few days, but as of right now, I've managed to escape post-Halloween depression because the weather has been very pleasant and because I still have six full-sized 5th Avenue candy bars to enjoy since there were only nine trick-or-treaters last night. Spending 83 minutes with the shot-on-video *Fatal Exposure* also helped a lot because its nutritious balance of sleaze and cheese prevented lethargy and allowed me to focus on the present rather than lament on all of the Halloween festivities I didn't have enough time or inspiration to participate in.

World Kickboxing Champion Blake Bahner stars as a professional photographer named Jack T. Rippington, who is following in the footsteps of his notorious great grandfather by murdering his modeling subjects in wildly imaginative ways and then profiting off their agony. In an early scene, Jack is visited by a Southern Baptist couple who serve as the welcome committee to his new town of Prairieville, and he uses his charm and charisma to persuade them to pose for his latest magazine assignment. While the sexually repressed wife eagerly slips into a corset in another room, Jack straps the husband to a guillotine in front of a camera and places the camera clicker in his hands so that his twitching body will be able to take pictures even after his severed head rolls around on the floor. Wondering if he's finally found the right woman to carry on his diabolical bloodline by birthing him a son, he asks the man's wife three very important questions: Are there times in her life when she's ever been obsessed with death and dying, what does she think about when she hears the word "blood," and whether she's ever thought about killing someone. Heartbroken by her responses, he sticks a syringe through her neck that causes such a skin-sizzling, pus-pouring reaction that it was no surprise to learn that the makeup effects were provided by Scott Coulter, who dazzled us with similar body horror in *Street Trash*, *Slumber Party Massacre 2*, *Slime City*, *Friday the 13th Part VIII: Jason Takes Manhattan*, *Tales from the Crypt: Demon Knight*, and about a hundred other kickass flicks. He shows off many other tricks when Jack's subsequent victims are electrocuted, poisoned with hydrophosphoric acid, shot in the face, slit in the neck, stabbed in the mouth, and separated from minds and bodies via power saws. But the best spectacle is saved for last, and heavens to Betsy, is it ever a doozy!

Jack breaks the fourth wall by speaking directly to us in the graveyard where he disposes of bodies, and in a very creative framing device, is interrupted by a woman asking if he talks to himself often. Played by the charming Ena O'Rourke, this cemetery regular has a wonderful smile, morbid imagination, and most importantly, the correct responses to his three questions. Their burgeoning relationship is very entertaining and unpredictable, and in one scene, it might even trigger nostalgia for anyone who spent late nights with Cinemax. The inexperienced supporting cast members, with their thick southern accents, are also a ton of fun, especially when the Prairieville undertaker threatens Jack and the sheriff just wants to challenge him to a beer-chugging contest. *Fatal Exposure* certainly doesn't reinvent the wheel but it's one that I'll surely look back on and smile, and who knows, maybe I'll revisit it exactly a year from now to cure any blues left by Halloween's passing.

Sean Byron from the essential cult film podcast *Junk Food Dinner* kindly outlined director Peter B. Good's (yes, that's his real name) strange journey in Hollywood, which started at the age of 2 when he acted alongside Ronald Reagan in the dramas *Knute Rockne All American* and *Brother Rat and a Baby*. Perhaps feeling like he had nothing left to prove in the industry, he pursued other interests but eventually returned decades later to produce nature documentaries and serve as the cinematographer for episodes of *The Magical World of Disney* and sequences in the *Faces of Death* horror series. Johnny B. Versatile, more like it!

I, Madman (1989)

Director: Tibor Takacs
Writer: David Chaskin
Cast: Jenny Wright, Clayton Rohner, Randall William Cook, Stephanie Hodge

With a crew featuring the director of *The Gate*, screenwriter of *A Nightmare on Elm Street 2: Freddy's Revenge* and *The Curse*, and visual effects artist who worked on *The Thing*, *Ghostbusters*, and *Fright Night* before heading to Middle Earth with Peter Jackson, *I, Madman* makes itself known as a stylish and smart horror movie even before we're introduced to our main character, Virginia. She works at a used book store in Los Angeles that recently received an estate consignment from troubled author Malcolm Brand, and being a fan of '50s pulp horror, she takes home a copy of his first novel, Much of Madness, More of Sin. With the window open to fill the air with soothing sounds of rain and music from the pianist living across the street, she curls up on the couch and scares herself silly with this story of a mad doctor resembling Nosferatu conducting experiments in a hotel room and ignoring its policy of no pets and no stop-motion monstrosities.

The next day she receives a mysterious package containing Malcolm Brand's other book, I, Madman, which the author forced his publisher to classify as nonfiction. It's far more disturbing and concerns a psychopath slicing off his own face and using parts from murdered victims as replacements all in an attempt to prove his undying love to a woman. The graphic horrors leap off the page and into Virginia's world as the movie skillfully shifts back and forth between 1959 and 1989 and she becomes the new object of desire for the disfigured, razor-wielding madman vowing to steal her heart one way or another.

Ambition, imagination, a seriously scary villain, and the wonderful visual of a character swimming in a sea of paperbacks didn't translate to box office success or much fanfare whatsoever, and it didn't take long for its Shout Factory Blu-ray from 2015 to go out of print. I wasn't in a huge rush to drive to Portland to pick it up at Movie Madness because just last week when I was returning DVDs, somebody with the unenviable last name of Trumper smashed her car into mine, but thankfully, Tubi came to the rescue once again and had it available to stream.

Starry Eyes (2014)

Writers and Directors: Kevin Kölsch and Dennis Widmyer
Cast: Alex Essoe, Amanda Fuller, Noah Segan, Fabianne Therese, Pat Healy, Shane Coffey

Instead of driving home after work on April 4 2019, I went to a movie theater and because it was a special occasion, allowed myself to spend $10 on a beer. After years of waiting and reading all the updates on various horror websites, I was finally going to see the *Pet Sematary* remake. It's not usual to muster up much excitement over a modern interpretation of a childhood favorite, but this was only the second adaptation to arguably Stephen King's scariest novel of all time, and it was being directed by the same two gentleman who made *Starry Eyes*! I thought this new *Pet Sematary* was quite good (and about a bazillion times better than the most profitable Stephen King adaptation of 2019, *It: Chapter Two*), and it makes me very curious to see what the filmmaking tag team of Kevin Kölsch and Dennis Widmyer come up with next.

Starry Eyes sadly never got a wide theatrical release but it has steadily been available on popular streaming platforms and catching the attention of many due to strong word of mouth and for staying disturbingly relevant in the "Me Too" movement and the revelations of Hollywood figures like Harvey Weinstein. The concept of a talented young performer having to go to desperate measures in order to stand out among hundreds of equally talented competitors is nothing new and has been explored in multiple movies, but *Starry Eyes* takes it one step further and allows for plenty of buildup. By the time Sarah finally gets the opportunity she deserves, it's easy to sympathize with her and understand why she and so many other people in the world are willing to sell their souls.

A typical day for Sarah involves working a shift at Big Taters, a more family-friendly version of Hooters, meaning she not only has to wear skimpy uniforms but also sing songs to birthday boys. Then she'll attend an audition to chase after a dream of being a Hollywood actress, and if it doesn't happen to go well, then she'll instinctively escape to a private place for a mental breakdown, which usually involves screaming and pulling out her hair. Afterwards, she'll retreat to her bedroom adorned with screenshots of classic starlets, and eventually venture outside to join the large gathering of friends,

DVD cover for *Starry Eyes* (2014), Snowfort Pictures, Dark Sky Films

all of whom are also struggling to catch their big break in the city of dreams.

Sarah throws a particularly bad fit in a bathroom stall after a promising audition to a new Astraeus Pictures horror feature results in the dreaded, perfunctory "we'll be in touch," and is unwittingly eavesdropped upon by the casting director, who suspects that maybe she didn't see all that Sarah has to offer after all. The next audition, she is warned, will be quite different, and there she has to disrobe completely to a rhythmic series of strobe lights because as the casting director asks, "If you can't fully let yourself go, how can you transform into something else?" The next day, it looks like her big dream is finally coming true after she gets personally invited to meet with the head of Astraeus Pictures at his home. He explains that this new picture isn't simply a horror movie, but also a brutal examination about the city they both call home, and how once you cut through the fog, you get "desperation, plastic parishioners worshipping their deity of debauchery." He wants to capture the ugliness of the human spirit, and with that he asks something of Sarah that makes her wish she hadn't quit her day job just hours before.

Alex Essoe is, simply put, a revelation as Sarah, and will stay in your memory long after the credits roll. The supporting cast is also memorable, especially Maria Olsen (who will be appearing in a whopping 20 movies in 2020) as the casting director, and Pat Healy (*The Innkeepers*, *Cheap Thrills*) as the founder of Big Taters, who is humanized in a way that's refreshing because with only a couple scenes, he very easily could have just been a one-dimensional sexist pig. While it would have been nice to hear the Mötley Crüe song of the same name, the producers were wise to spend their limited means elsewhere, ensuring that *Starry Eyes* is not only a slow-burning and satirical psychological thriller, but also a fantastic-looking horror movie with the kind of makeup effects and violence that will satisfy the beasts among us–maggots are vomited, stomachs are stabbed, skulls crushed by dumbbells, etc. Kölsch and Widmyer have such a clear understanding of their characters and their target audience, and I love the delicate dance they play with the kills, keeping them nasty and shocking without coming across as mean-spirited in the slightest.

When a Stranger Calls Back (1993)
Writer and Director: Fred Walton
Cast: Jill Schoelen, Carol Kane, Charles Durning, Gene Lythgow

Most horror fans hold the opinion that the opening scene of *When a Stranger Calls* is a masterclass of suspense that the rest of the film can't even come close to holding a candle to, and few were excited by the thought of this story continuing 14 years down the road as a made-for-Showtime event. Once again written and directed by Fred Walton and featuring compelling performances from Carol Kane and Charles Durning, this sequel has no trouble surpassing the original, but what is most surprising is that its opening scene is every bit as nail-biting as the famous "Have you checked the children?" intro that's been featured in the majority of lists counting down the scariest movie moments of all time.

As a fan of *The Stepfather*, *Popcorn*, *The Phantom of the Opera* (1989), and *Cutting Cards*, I was happy to see Jill Schoelen be the one to knock on a suburban door for a traumatizing night of babysitting. With the two kids already asleep in their room, Julia entertains herself with MTV and literature before the phone rings. It turns out to be a false flag, however, because the movie has no intentions on replaying the greatest hits. Instead, it alarms its babysitter with repeated knocks on the door from a soft-spoken man who says his car has broken down. She makes all the smart moves at first, not allowing the stranger to enter the home and not letting him know that the phone line has just been cut, but he keeps coming back to the house with rising impatience. Walton puts on a clinic of suspense and because he's allowed us ample opportunities to familiarize ourselves with the house's layout (all while spooky shadows, ticking clocks, and thunder grumblings keep us on edge), he's able to translate seemingly innocuous household items like a notepad and a tea kettle into heart-stopping panic as Julia begins to suspect that somebody else is in the house.

Five years after the worst night of her life, Julia is a college student and volunteer for a crisis center for battered women. Her trauma resurfaces when she suspects that the man, who was never apprehended, has found a way to break into her triple-bolted apartment just to leave little calling cards. The male police officers chalk it up to mere hysterics but a counselor at the university, who knows better than anybody what she's been going through ever since that night of terror, takes her claims so seriously that she even brings in an old partner to help investigate a mystery that turns noirish when it leads to rainy back alleys, seedy theaters, and apartment complexes where horrible secrets are probably stashed beyond each door. Not even the holy grail of ludicrous plot developments in which a ventriloquist's skills are comically exaggerated can overcome the engaging alliance of Jill Schoelen, Carol Kane, and the kind-eyed Charles Durning (who has a knack for appearing in stellar made-for-tv horror movies). I kept praying for their safety and that they be rewarded with a long, relaxing vacation in the Bahamas if they somehow stopped the stranger's dialing days for good.

GAMES THAT ARE EVEN HARDER THAN MEGA MAN

Beyond the Gates (2016)
Director: Jackson Stewart
Writers: Jackson Stewart, Stephen Scarlata
Cast: Graham Skipper, Chase Williamson, Brea Grant, Barbara Crampton, Matt Mercer

Anyone whose happy place as a kid was a locally owned video store will feel waves of nostalgia at the beginning of Jackson Stewart's *Beyond the Gates*, where in the summer of 1992, a family of four celebrates the grand opening of their business that offers classics and hard-to-find titles, and even has a mural of Mount Rush-Monster! The rosy picture quickly withers when we discover that two decades later, the mother has passed away, the father has gone mysteriously missing, and the estranged brothers Gordon and John are reuniting at this dusty video store to start the exhausting process of transferring all 100,000 videos to moving boxes.

After finding a key to the office they were never allowed to enter as children, they finally explore the forbidden territory that mostly consists of more televisions and videocassettes. A handgun is the most interesting find until they notice that the last tape their dad watched was for a VCR game called Beyond the Gates—a loving tribute to early '90s horror-themed TV games like Nightmare. They decide to play the game after dinner with Gordon's girlfriend, and rather than a cloaked and gravelly voiced Gatekeeper shouting savagely and hurling

Poster for *Beyond the Gates* (2016), Destroy All Entertainment, IFC Midnight

insults at the players, here the host is an alluring and soft-spoken woman played by horror legend Barbara Crampton. With darting, unblinking eyes to put everyone in a state of hypnotic unease, she introduces the game with "Welcome, curious viewers, are you ready to step into the ultimate nightmare, a world of unimaginable horror?" before explaining that a series of challenges must be undertaken to acquire the four keys needed to unlock the gateway…and save their father's soul! From there the game takes on a life of its own, trapping the three participants and proving that simply throwing the tape in the trash can isn't going to put an end to disgusting feats like digging through the brain matter of exploded heads in hopes of finding a key.

Despite a budget of only $300,000, *Beyond the Gates* makes the most out of its "what if Jumanji was the horror movie it should have been?" concept, hitting hard with middle-of-the-night terrors and one of the best voodoo doll scenes ever. It's also a ton of fun (exemplified by the opening credits featuring catchy synth-pop and innerworkings of a VCR bathed in neon) and would make a perfect double-bill with *The Gate* for horror fans of all ages. The video store in the movie is actually Eddie Brandt's Saturday Matinee in North Hollywood, and even though they have over 100,000 movies, I'd like to think that *Beyond the Gates* has its own pedestal and spotlight, where customers can gaze upon the beauty that is Shout Factory's Blu-ray cover. The back of the case is just as appealing because among the many special features listed are a Premiere Q&A hosted by Stuart Gordon, a retro commercial for the movie, and a commentary track with the entertaining hosts of *Junk Food Dinner*.

Graham Skipper (looking like a younger and smaller Irwin R. Schyster) and Chase Williamson (star of *John Dies at the End*) are both very believable as brothers who drifted apart but who slowly begin to rekindle the bond they shared as kids. Jesse Merlin is an absolute scene-stealer as the cryptic, stylishly dressed owner of the occult store that sold the game to their father—it makes me wish I had witnessed him getting all pervy and decapitated playing Dr. Hill in *Re-Animator: The Musical*! It was also really nice to see Justin Welborn again, playing the polar opposite of his character in 2007's *The Signal* and not being the one on the receiving end of a baseball bat to the cranium.

The Most Dangerous Game (1932)
Directors: Irving Pichel, Ernest B. Schoedsack
Writers: James Ashmore Creelman, Richard Connell (story)
Cast: Joel McCrea, Fay Wray, Leslie Banks, Robert Armstrong, Noble Johnson

Easily one of the most adaptable short stories of all time is Richard Connell's "The Most Dangerous Game" (1924), its influence still palpable almost a century later with recent films like *Ready or Not* and *The Hunt*, in which ordinary people try to not to fall prey to bloodthirsty aristocrats hunting them for sport. But long, long before Mr. Burns hunted the citizens of Springfield in the amusing Treehouse of Horror segment "The Survival of the Fattest," featuring Homer almost immediately resorting to cannibalism despite the abundance of fresh bananas, there was a more direct adaptation that still holds up very well today and will be sure to satisfy anyone who saw *King Kong* and wished for more visions of Fay Wray running for her life through jungles. RKO Pictures shot both films simultaneously, using many of the same sets and two of the same stars—the other being Robert Armstrong, playing a very convincing drunk here because "if anyone has a right to his liquor, it's a victim of circumstance."

On the South American coast, the captain of a yacht is perturbed by how the channel lights aren't matching up properly with the charts, but the owner thinks his jitters are unwarranted and urges him to sail through waters known for their coral reefs and sharks. Also on board is a young man named Bob who's written successful books about his adventures of hunting animals in the wild, and just as the arrogant prick proclaims, "Listen here, you fellows, this world is divided into two kinds of people: the hunter and the hunted. Luckily, I'm a hunter and nothing could ever change that," the ship smacks into something, fills up with water, and explodes.

I was not expecting to see shark attack scenes in a 1932 film but the ancestor of Bruce has a good feast on those who survived the explosion, leaving Bob as the sole survivor, swimming to shore and traversing the jungles to discover a castle that might as well belong to Count Dracula. Bob is welcomed by its eccentric owner, the Russian Count Zaroff, and introduced to a pair of siblings who survived a similar shipwreck just days prior. In addition to food, drinks, shelter, and piano recitals, the Count also supplies his guests with tales of how the day he lost his love of hunting was the day he lost his lust for life, which should alarm them even more than the Satanic artwork. Their suspicions aren't confirmed until a late-night excursion to a basement that reveals a very unique trophy room, and had several scaredy cat audience members not walked out of the theater in revulsion during a test screening, some of the grisliest shots wouldn't have been cut.

The Most Dangerous Game fell into the public domain and so it couldn't be easier to track down, but chances are high that you'll be watching a crummy transfer unless you feast your eyes on the Criterion Collection DVD, which restored it to its former glory and gave full clarity to a magnificent game of hide and seek on a private island that offers waterfalls as well as hungry hounds.

Horror Galore

BLEAK AND BRUTAL

Bedevilled (2010)
Director: Cheol-soo Jang
Writer: Kwang-young Choi
Cast: Yeong-hie Seo, Seong-won Ji, Min-ho Hwang, Min Je, Ji-eun Lee, Jeong-hak Park

Much like fellow South Korean revenge thrillers *I Saw the Devil* and *Oldboy*, this is one movie you might want to watch in the company of none because its extreme nature and ability to enrage will put no one in a social mood. Scenes of rape and domestic abuse are tough enough to see without having to feed off the additional discomfort of others in the room. When it played the festival circuit, jury members were undoubtedly squirming in their seats but once the ending credits started to roll, were eager to reward it with prize after prize.

Bedevilled starts off in a busy Seoul neighborhood with a young woman being attacked by a trio of gang members and nobody bothering to come to her aid, and this disturbing theme will continue after our protagonist, 30-year-old loan officer and Guinness-chugging Hae-won, is ordered to take a vacation when she displays hostile mood swings at work. She decides to visit the island where she spent her childhood, and greeting her enthusiastically at the dock is her former best friend, Bok-nam, who has been sending letters on a regular basis that mostly go unopened. The female elders aren't as thrilled to see her again, believing that this city girl with pale

Poster for *Bedevilled* (2010), Sponge Ent, King Records

skin and high heels is stupid for taking trips instead of getting married and agreeing to a life of servitude and submission.

Bok-nam, who has never left the island, is trapped in a miserable marriage to a monster of a man who beats her daily and openly cheats (the kind of behavior that has always been accepted as status quo), and when she suspects that the sexual abuse extends to their young daughter, she pleads to Hae-won to take the little girl to Seoul where she can be safe, go to elementary school, and finally have a normal childhood. After Bok-nam experiences betrayal, a futile escape, and tragedy in under 24 hours, she finally snaps and takes bloody revenge using knives, scythes, and sledgehammers. Not only is it unbelievably cathartic, but it's a testament to incredibly strong filmmaking when you find yourself actively rooting for a defenseless old woman to die in a most horrible way.

Whether the camera is pointed at the ocean or a freshly sickle-severed head, the film never ceases to look spectacular, presenting this island like an ideal destination for a restful getaway, rich in both swimming holes and potatoes, but much like Las Vegas, you'd probably be eager to leave after a few days. If you're craving a descent into the pits of agony ruled by humanity at its most depraved, and you prefer to travel by means of an exciting rollercoaster ride, you can usually count on revenge thrillers from South Korea like *Bedevilled* to get the job done.

Black Death (2010)

Director: Christopher Smith
Writer: Dario Poloni
Cast: Eddie Redmayne, Sean Bean, Carice van Houten, John Lynch, Andy Nyman, Emun Elliott

Usually around this time of year I like to keep my viewing habits lighter and more uplifting than usual, but on this particular Black Friday I journeyed back to medieval England in the year of our lord 1348, perhaps the bleakest era of human civilization where everyone still with a pulse must have cursed themselves daily for simply being alive and having to put up with incomprehensible degrees of unpleasantness as a result of the bubonic plague. This is the last place I'd ever use a time machine to experience firsthand, but I was still very excited to see just how deep into hell Christopher Smith would take us, as the Bristol-born filmmaker showed enormous potential with *Creep* (2004), *Severance* (2006), and especially *Triangle* (2007).

Just a few years before winning an Oscar for his portrayal of Stephen Hawking in *The Theory of Everything*, Eddie Redmayne stars here as a young monk named Osmund who volunteers to guide a team of Christian mercenaries to a village close to where he grew up, in hopes that the journey will reunite him with the girl he loves. His bishop and father figure (David Warner) warns him that even if he survives the dangerous mission, the world outside will change him significantly, but given the stench of death that has surrounded them for ages, Osmund accepts any change whether it come from God or Satan. A stoic warrior named Ulrich is the leader of this group of knights, and looks very natural wearing a coat of arms and brandishing a sword since he's played by Sean Bean, known to most as Eddard 'Ned' Stark in *Game of Thrones* and Barimer from *The Lord of the Rings* series. The village they've been sent to has somehow remained free of pestilence despite the neighboring ones being completely wiped out, a phenomenon that he and other religious extremists are blaming on witchcraft, and so it's up to them to infiltrate the village, root out the necromancer, and see that he or she suffers a most unchristian death.

None of them would agree with Clark Griswold that getting there is half the fun, because along the way, heads are lopped off, stomachs disemboweled, and underarms revealed advanced stages of the plague. But when they finally cross the foggy marshes up their destination, they are welcomed by the Pagans and given food, shelter, and lots of attention from the females. Langiva, one of the leaders of the village, instinctively feels a connection to the young monk despite the slaying of her husband from another man of God, and as she treats Osmund's wounds, she attempts to find out the true intentions of the new visitors.

Unlike with similar-themed movies like *Witchfinder General*, *Apostle*, and *The Wicker Man*, here we aren't quite sure which side we should be rooting for since it makes the smart and compelling decision to be equally critical to the god-fearing and the godless. Our alliances may sway through the many twists and turns, but due to the atmosphere, production value, and performances, we're constantly reminded that everyone here is getting what no one deserves, and being pushed to the brink of desperation like this makes all of their decisions believable. The final sequences are especially dark but every bit of misery it inflicts on the characters and the viewers feels well earned. While it certainly didn't fill me with the sentimentality and good cheer necessary to put up a Christmas tree afterwards and commence the season, I didn't regret making this a Black Death Friday.

The Eyes of My Mother (2016)

Writer and Director: Nicolas Pesce
Cast: Kika Magalhães, Olivia Bond, Diana Agostini, Paul Nazak, Will Brill, Joey Curtis-Green

As seasoned horror fans, we occasionally feel the desire to step out of our comfort zone and wade in the depths of depravity to test our limitations. The thrill of these dangerous and unexplored territories impedes our inclination to look away even though we know it's going to leave an awful sting and probably show us things we wish could have remained unseen. *The Eyes of My Mother*, by first-time director and screenwriter Nicolas Pesce, isn't a film you'll want to watch with your friends on a lively weekend night, nor as casual dinnertime viewing; it's something you should save for when you're already in a somber mood and acquiescent to misery on its highest level. Wait until you're reeling from heartbreak, ravaged by the flu, or terribly annoyed that you drove three hours to see a concert only for it to be cancelled at the last minute. This won't punish you nearly as much as something like *Martyrs* (a film even more vicious than its French new wave counterparts *Frontier(s)* and *Inside*) because much of the violence is offscreen, but it similarly presents human suffering in unflinching detail while maintaining a high level of artistry.

Its beauty and power are evident from the lengthy opening shot, a monochromatic view from inside a truck traveling through isolated farmlands as a cheerful old-school country tune plays on the radio, sounding innocuous enough until you start to realize that this is probably the same kind of music Ed Gein enjoyed in the car. A woman is seen in the distance shuffling in the middle of the road like a Romero zombie and collapsing just as the driver stops his truck to assist her. The film is divided into three parts and her identity will be a mystery for the first two.

Francisca is a lonely little girl living a sheltered life inside a farmhouse with her parents. One afternoon in the kitchen, her Portuguese mother teaches her about anatomy and surgical techniques using a severed cow's head, and there's a strong nod to *Un Chien Andalou*'s most famous shot. They are visited by a peculiar young man with the artificial sanguinity of a Mormon missionary and within minutes, he's chopping up the mother in the bathtub while young Francisca sits in the kitchen and listens. Her father comes home and manages to incapacitate the deranged intruder, chaining him in the barn with unspecified injuries, and it's Francisca's responsibility to bring him food on a daily basis. Even though he massacred her mother and expressed what an extraordinary pleasure it was, she has no desire to return the favor because she views him as a friend, the first one she's ever had. Francisca has few people in her life, so she wants to do whatever it takes to make sure they stick around. When the next chapter begins, she is at least ten years older, and we see the horrifying repercussions of a childhood so fraught with trauma and devoid of treatment.

Beautifully shot in black and white, *The Eyes of My Mother* is such an intense experience that the 76-minute running time serves as an act of mercy. Few films are capable of being this ghoulish, hypnotic, and heartbreaking at the same time. For another intimate look at an outcast's desperate attempts to make friends, be sure to watch Lucky McKee's 2002 masterpiece *May* if you haven't already. Often described as "*Carrie* meets *Frankenstein*," it stars the always-magnetic Angela Bettis as a veterinary surgical technician with some of the poorest social skills ever. Jeremy Sisto and Anna Faris are also excellent in their roles in which they're initially attracted to May's awkwardness but aren't prepared for how she wants to spend Halloween night.

In a Glass Cage (1986)

Writer and Director: Agustí Villaronga
Cast: Gunter Meisner, David Sust, Marisa Paredes, Gisele Echevarria, Imma Colomer

Any movie inspired by the 15th-century Breton knight Gilles de Rais is not going to be an easy watch. After serving alongside Joan of Arc in the Hundred Years' War, he reportedly spent his time sodomizing and murdering hundreds of children—leading some scholars to speculate on whether he was the world's first serial killer—and was sentenced to death by hanging after confessing to the long list of crimes that also included necrophilia and delving into the occult. Seeing as how the last several films I watched were inoffensive and largely comedic, I figured it was time to sabotage an unusually sunny February weekend by exploring grimy territory and miring in hopelessness until I found something special to recommend to the bravest of souls.

In a Glass Cage was quick to inflict the misery—before a single word is uttered, a badly-beaten boy is chained up in a torture dungeon, barely clinging to life when a man named Klaus approaches and caresses his nude body tenderly before bashing him over the head with a board. Overcome by guilt, the man then ascends a spiral staircase (while moody Alan Hayworth-like synths drown the soundtrack) and plunges from the top.

Klaus's unsuccessful suicide leaves him paralyzed and dependent on an iron lung, much to the burden of his wife Griselda, who was probably already a cantankerous grumpy grouch long before the accident, what with being a Nazi and all. A young man arrives at the large gloomy Mediterranean villa in which they've been hiding since the war ended and insists on becoming Klaus's new nurse. Both Klaus and their young daughter Rena are supportive of the idea, but Griselda is skeptical of his motives and his ability to take care of her husband's medical needs. Her suspicions are justified when on his first night of duty, he purposefully separates Klaus from the machine that keeps him alive ever so briefly in order to show dominance, and then masturbates over him while reciting passages from the journal that Klaus kept during his concentration camp days to document all of his experiments on young boys. He later reveals his intentions to carry on the will of the fallen man he so admires, striving to make him feel whole again by bringing fresh young kids to his lair and forcing him to watch as the same methods from his Holocaust crimes are carried out. An even bigger concern is the close relationship forming between his mysterious and increasingly unhinged new nurse and his only daughter, clearly the most important person in his life.

Despite a myriad of the most uncomfortable taboos, writer and director Agusti Villaronga is thankfully far more concerned with his characters and with arthouse aesthetics than he is with exploitation and violence, and so it avoids entering *Salo* territory and making you wonder why in the hell you're subjecting yourself to such unspeakable ugliness. Throughout this cyclical examination of trauma and mistreatment, it's actually a great-looking movie, with the majority of scenes bathed in an icy cold palette of blues and grays, and with a production design that effectively mirrors the crumbling dwelling with the damaged psyche of those living inside. The ending credits assure that none of the young actors were exposed to anything inappropriate during filming and that a child psychologist was present, but still, you'll probably get the urge to take a long shower after watching this one.

I Saw the Devil (2010)

Director: Jee-woon Kim
Writers: Park Hoon-jung, Jee-woon Kim
Cast: Lee Byung-hun, Choi Min-sik, Jeon Gook-hwan, Ho-jin Chun, San-ha Oh

On a wintry night, a woman waiting in her flat-tired car for the tow truck driver is startled when another man approaches her window and volunteers to help. After she politely declines, he smashes his way inside the car, brutalizes her, and then drags her outside where she leaves a trail of red snow. The following day, her nude corpse is discovered in several pieces, starting with a severed ear by the river. With its unspeakable depravity from start to finish, this really isn't the kind of movie you want to eat a thin crust supreme pizza during. I should have known better because I first saw this devil nine years ago and so many moments have lingered in my memory ever since, but I was hungry, dammit.

The dead woman's fiancé works as a secret agent for the National Intelligence Service, and rather than help the police apprehend the serial killer played by Choi Min-shik (who knows something about grisly revenge films as the star of *Oldboy*), he decides to use all of his skills to enact a more sadistic and creative level of revenge. He locates the killer in a greenhouse where another nude woman is tied up and about to be slaughtered, and after beating him half to death in a stunningly-choreographed fight sequence, he places a capsule down his throat that contains a tracking device and a microphone. To inflict as much punishment as possible, he lets the creep go just so he can track him down and brutally attack him all over again the next day and the day after that. This catch-and-release strategy is so risky and doesn't always go as planned, but as viewers, we can't help but celebrate every time he bludgeons a hand or severs a tendon all while questioning just how far we would go if the person we despise the most were laying at our feet and at what point would we lose humanity by fulfilling a limitless lust for revenge, no matter how justified it may be. Due to how much we're rooting for the hero, we become just as bloodthirsty, so be mentally prepared to venture into some very dark territories, and don't expect to sleep peacefully afterwards. Just watching that electrifying car stabbing scene is probably the equivalent of chugging Bacchus F, which I'm told is the most caffeinated beverage in South Korea.

Director Jee-woon Kim, first catching the attention of horror fans with the moody ghost story *A Tale of Two Sisters*, spins the ultimate cat and mouse chase where both adversaries are wisely given equal screentime to show why they are both uniquely formidable, determined, and resourceful. It's an emotionally exhausting journey full of catharsis and heartache, and it manages to be absolutely riveting for every second of its 144-minute running time.

Killing Ground (2016)

Writer and Director: Damien Power
Cast: Aaron Pedersen, Ian Meadows, Harriet Dyer, Aaron Glenane, Maya Stange

Making his feature film debut as both writer and director, the badass-named Damien Power drew inspiration from the violent survival films of the '70s for *Killing Ground*, about a couple named Ian and Samantha who celebrate New Year's Eve by going camping in the beautiful Australian countryside only to fall prey to a couple of psychopaths.

This "don't go in the woods" story has been done to death, but strong cinematography, raw performances, and tense editing keep the material fresh and your eyes glued to the screen, all while the angel resting on your right shoulder persuades you to look away from the hellishness. Churning with malevolence, it's an uncomfortable film to sit through, but one that won't traumatize you with ugly images you'll spend years wishing you could unsee. It mercifully uses a "less is more" approach that keeps rape and much of the violence offscreen.

When Ian and Samantha arrive at the picturesque campground, they see two tents already set up with no trace of their occupants, and when a full day passes with the group still not showing up, they decide to investigate. One of the film's greatest strengths is its non-linear narrative, cleverly interconnecting the present and the past until the stories of Ian and Samantha, the pair of cold-blooded killers, and the other group of campers (consisting of a married couple, their teenaged daughter, and newborn son) all shockingly converge on a hiking trail. It's nasty and nail-biting, and definitely not for everyone, but I know a few of you are always up for the challenge of descending into an ultra-realistic, blood-soaked nightmare where not even a baby is safe. Those brave souls willing to stay on the mean and sick corner of horror for a little longer should also seek out *Incident in a Ghostland* (2018).

WON'T TRAUMATIZE THE KIDDIES

Attack of the Demons (2019)
Director: Eric Power
Writer: Andreas Petersen
Cast: Thomas Petersen, Katie Maguire, Andreas Petersen, August Sargenti, Eric Power

For the first time in thirteen years, tonight I watched a movie on the couch without a friendly orange feline purring on my lap or diverting my attention away from the television with his adorable antics. It had been five emotionally exhausting hours since my ailing sweet prince, Mr. Marbles Tigerpants, was euthanized and I just wanted to glue myself to the couch, stare straight ahead, and do absolutely nothing. I'll always be appreciative to the team of Eric Power and Andreas Peterson for helping me through this most difficult of nights for providing such a warm, sincere, and inviting world to get lost in for 75 minutes with their animated movie *Attack of the Demons*. After earning positive buzz with its initial festival screenings, it serendipitously made its streaming premiere on Shudder just when I needed it the most. Nothing could fill the void of a cat as special as Mr. Marbles, but the room would have felt so much colder and emptier tonight had this movie not been playing.

In the cold opening, the deep thoughts of an evening fisherman are rudely interrupted by the incantations and spurting blood of a cultist with ambitious plans for Barrington Colorado's annual harvest festival. In a town that welcomes its travelers with a sign proclaiming "big things can happen in the smallest places," just about every citizen attends this festival except our three lovable protagonists, Kevin, Natalie, and Jeff. Their paths never really crossed in the years when they attended the same high school, but tonight they have a brief and charming interaction in a Barrington bar before their individual passions for the arts gives them different itineraries and new opportunities for alienation. Diehard horror fan Kevin rushes to the Tower Theater in hopes that there will still be a ticket available for the 70's Italian horror film *The Grotesque Mirror*, and after the ticket booth attendant has a little fun with him, he enters the theater only to discover that the sacred reels of celluloid will be spinning for nobody else but him. While Natalie's pretentious music journalist boyfriend, who previously made fun of her shoegaze proclivities, is seeing a popular band perform at the festival, she goes to a depressingly empty bar to swoon alone to a live performance from her favorite indie group, Teek. Jeff, meanwhile, feels a little better about his version of paradise being completely deserted tonight because it makes the mission of playing the most obscure games in a video arcade easier to accomplish.

As much as I love experiencing obscure cult films in theaters, playing arcade games, and attending a live performance from a shoegaze group

Horror Galore

(although it doesn't appear that Teek is on the level of Slowdive), this harvest festival, with its haunted mine ride and Halloween decorations as far as the eye can see, is where all the fun seems to be; that is, until the cultist takes over the stage and recites a spell (where the word "Bava" is peppered throughout) that spreads a demonic infestation upon the town. Hopefully everyone got a chance to at least enjoy the delicious pumpkin funnel cake before transforming into disgusting, oozing creatures whose only instinct is to spread the infections by amalgamating with each other to take up more real estate. The danger escalates for our three social outcasts, who reunite and decide that their best chance of escape is to venture deep into the scary woods at night, but hot on the case is a scholar appropriately named Stuart Combs who may know how to send the demons back to hell.

Comparisons to *South Park* are unavoidable given the small-town Colorado setting and how it uses the same stop-motion style of animation as its pilot episode, before Trey Parker and Matt Stone realized that much of the artistry would have to be jettisoned to produce hundreds of episodes. The characters in *Attack of the Demons* were created out of colorful pieces of construction paper and given layers of texture, and seeing as how maddeningly painstaking it must have been to give so much fluidity to their movements using this technique, it's easy to forgive this movie for its one weakness that's impossible to ignore: the lackluster voice acting. I could praise this film for several more paragraphs but I should probably save some material just in case there's ever another edition of *Pumpkin Cinema*.

Swedish poster for *Hold That Ghost* (1941), Universal Pictures

Hold That Ghost (1941)

Director: Arthur Lubin
Writers: Robert Lees, Frederic I. Rinaldo, John Grant
Cast: Bud Abbott, Lou Costello, Joan Davis, Richard Carlson, Evelyn Ankers, Marc Lawrence

While I haven't seen all 36 feature films that Bud Abbott and Lou Costello made together from 1940-1956, it's hard to imagine one dethroning *Hold That Ghost* as their finest hour and a half. It proved that their superb comedic timing and priceless chemistry were suitable to spooky situations, paving the way for their meetings with the Universal monsters seven years later.

After their stint as waiters at a swanky nightclub (where a full-course dinner with entertainment costs three whole dollars!) is cut hilariously short, Chuck and Ferdie are given a new opportunity when they learn that they've inherited a motel from notorious gangster Moose Matson who had an unorthodox clause in his last will and testament. They take a cab to their new property on a dark and stormy night, only to be abandoned there along with the other passengers by a crooked driver who speeds away with their luggage. Ferdie is a scaredy-cat from the moment he lays eyes on the hotel ("I don't like this, Chuck, any place painted dark brown, I never care for"), earning him the disapproval and a few hard slaps from his bossy partner, who also doesn't appreciate childish antics like playing choo-choo train with the noisy kitchen faucets.

The shutters collapse, the soup tastes weird, the puddles of rain complicate a "Beautiful Blue Danube" dance routine, and Ferdie accidentally breaks a bed instead of making it, but a far graver concern comes with the discovery that one of the travelers has been strangled ("Is that serious?") and stuffed in a closet. The motel continues to show off an endless supply of menace throughout the night with its stark shadows, secret passageways, doors that mysteriously lock, possibly fanged owls, and ordinary bedrooms that transform into gambling parlors with the tug of a coat hanger. These reveals are happily exploited by an intense soundtrack that sure gave me a case of the frights as a youngin.

I'm a huge fan of *Abbott and Costello Meet Frankenstein*, also penned by the same writing trio, but I don't think it can hold a moving candle to *Hold That Ghost* in terms of laughs. This was a favorite of mine growing up and a strong contender for that painstaking question of "If you could only watch one movie for the rest of your life, what would it be?" Lots of laughs are had and lots of ghosts are held in this irresistible black and white horror-comedy that hits the spot, warms the heart, and tickles the funny bone every time whether it's a lazy October afternoon alone or a crowded movie night with friends.

Considering how much joy Joan Davis has given me over the decades playing Costello's potential love interest Camille Brewster, I feel great shame in not having done a deep dive of her career sooner. It doesn't surprise me that her immense talents were honored with two different stars on the Hollywood Walk of Fame, one for her contribution in film and the other in radio. *Hold That Ghost* also features a brief appearance from The Three Stooges' Shemp Howard and two lovely musical numbers from The Andrews Sisters, who also performed songs in Abbott and Costello's previous films *Buck Privates* and *In the Navy*.

Advertisement for *Mr. Boogedy* (1986), Walt Disney Television, ABC

Mr. Boogedy (1986)

Director: Oz Scott
Writer: Michael Janover
Cast: Richard Masur, Mimi Kennedy, Benji Gregory, David Faustino, Kristy Swanson

Considering I was only five years old when *Mr. Boogedy* aired on the ABC network's *Disney Sunday Movie* on April 20, 1986, it was pos-

Horror Galore

sibly the first horror film I ever saw, and it may explain why I've always had such a fondness for the haunted house subgenre. For decades I was apprehensive about revisiting it because I held it in such high regards as a kid and didn't want to risk tarnishing those memories in any way because of my overcritical, curmudgeon tendencies, but it turns out I had nothing to worry about because its goofy humor, playful spooks, and likable characters will win over anyone who is still young at heart. My trip down memory lane was made even more nostalgic thanks to a crisp version on YouTube that contained the original commercial breaks; it was weird when an ad for an ABC Afterschool Special starring Malcolm-Jamal Warner (*The Cosby Show*) about teen suicide was followed up by a Kudos commercial with a jolly Randy Newman-esque tune. Also included was an amusing introduction from then-Disney Chairman Michael Eisner, warning us about the ghosts, evil spirits, and very haunted house in this weird family comedy, all while his office appears to be hosting a phantasm party.

Richard Masur (mostly known to horror fans for playing the grownup Stanley in the *It* miniseries) stars as a salesman of gag gifts who relocates his family to a New England fixer-upper that was sold to him by C.B Karloff at "Devil May Care" Realty. Playing his three children much to my delight are Kristy Swanson (who would soon have even worse luck with moving into a new home in *Flowers in the Attic*), David Faustino (a very young Bud Bundy), and Benji Gregory (about to be busy for the next four years playing Brian Tanner in *ALF*). Since the movie is only 45-minutes long, they don't have to wait long for the ghost of Mr. Boogedy to show his yucky, grilled-cheese sandwich face and for haunting female sobs to echo through the halls in the middle of the night.

As if the cast wasn't already reeking of awesomeness, the great John Astin even emerges from the house's dark shadows to give the family one last chance to escape—he only gets a hand buzzer handshake for his troubles. He informs the children in a later scene that Mr. Boogedy—whose name was allegedly inspired by the middle segment of Stephen King's *Cat's Eye*—used to be a cantankerous pilgrim who sold his soul to the devil to win the affection of a beautiful widow named Marion. He ended up botching the spell that led to both of their deaths, as well as the death of her son (pretty heavy themes for five-year-old eyes!). Even in the afterlife, he is a miserable jerk and has used his magical powers for 300 years to prevent a reunion between ghost mom and ghost son, causing a dilemma to the new homeowners who have one foot out the door forever and the other wanting to kick Mr. Boogedy as hard as they can.

It was an ingenious decision to make the family's prosperity rely on practical jokes because not only does it allow for funny breakfast shenanigans, but it gives the apparition-denying father another explanation for the strange happenings. After all, why wouldn't his little boy want to follow in the old man's footsteps by rigging up an expensive sound system and showing off the kind of special effects you'd see in the Haunted Mansion dark ride? The only thing missing from this mini-movie is an appearance from Don Knotts, whose eyes would have grown impossibly wide while confronting cabinets that opened and closed by themselves, disembodied monster hands giving a round of applause, and once again, an organ with an invisible player.

Tonight, I also watched the sequel, *Bride of Boogedy*, which I only caught a minute or two of when it premiered on April 12, 1987. I was over at a friend's house and his mom was channel-surfing when I saw something on TV that stayed with me forever: a ghostly woman levitating off the ground of a carnival and floating in the sky while everyone below looks on in horror. It was nice to get the context of this enduring image 34 years later, even if the rest of the movie didn't quite match the fun of the first one. It definitely has its moments though, like the awesome "beware the spiders" opening where the violin plays itself, the sight of a possessed and cackling Richard Masur floating down the hallway in his pajamas, and all of the scenes with Eugene Levy, playing such a meanie that he can't resist pushing a baby carriage while the mother is distracted. It's also pretty cool to see little Bud Bundy dressed as the devil. The biggest problem with *Bride of Boogedy* is how it's twice as long and has to pad out the running time with about five different séance/fortune telling scene and at least 200 shouts of "Boogedy! Boogedy!" It also wasn't able to bring back Benji Gregory, Kristy Swanson, and John Astin, who were committed to other projects, and their replacements fail to make much of an impression.

Horror Galore

LEARNING IS FUN WITH THESE DOCUMENTARIES

Best Worst Movie (2009)
Writer and Director: Michael Paul Stephenson

With plenty of vacation time banked up, I took an impulse solo trip in November 2009, and I chose Denver for the sole purpose of seeing a very special documentary that was screening at the Starz Denver Film Festival with both the director and star in attendance. I arrived well before the theater doors were open, and so I entertained myself by walking laps around the Auraria Campus, making sure not to stray too far in case I got lost at the worst possible time. At one point I froze, not because of the bitter cold that was carrying the potential of flurries, but because there were two instantly recognizable people walking in my direction, whom I had seen many times for years, but only on a television screen. It was such a surreal moment being that close to Michael Paul Stephenson and George Hardy, the stars of the cult classic *Troll 2*. Being the awkward dork that I am, I accidentally called Michael by his middle name, but at least I was able to form complete sentences under pressure. They were both very gracious and appreciative that I flew all the way from Portland for this event, but I doubt they were all that surprised because after attending so many late-night, sold-out screenings of *Troll 2* (and even a weekend festival dedicated entirely to it) since its inexplicable, unprecedented comeback, they were well aware of the dedication and enthusiasm from fans all over the world.

Poster for *Best Worst Movie* (2009), Magic Stone Productions

Long ago when Stephenson was cast to play the lead role of young

Horror Galore

Joshua Waits in a horror movie titled Goblins, the child star thought that this would be his big break that would elevate him to stardom like *Labyrinth* did for Jennifer Connelly. It was filmed in the summer of 1989 in Morgan, Utah, and with an all-American, inexperienced cast and a crew consisting of Italians that spoke very little English, there were many lost in translation occurrences. On Christmas morning 1990, Stephenson unwrapped a VHS copy of his movie, now mysteriously titled *Troll 2*, and with the family gathered around the television in anticipation, it didn't take long for Santa's special gift to became the equivalent of a lump of coal. After just the first two scenes, the boy's dreams were crushed to smithereens because this wasn't just your average failure of a movie—it was quite possibly one of the worst movies in the history of the world. He was utterly embarrassed and wanted nothing to do with the film until many years later when he was all grown up and receiving messages on Myspace from hopeful fans inquiring on whether he was the real Joshua Waits. He had no idea that every time this movie aired on television, there were weirdos like me out there who were mesmerized, entertained, and above all else, in stitches, and who were also very eager to spread this special infection to our friends!

The miraculous *Troll 2* cult kept growing and on September 14, 2006, several cast members reunited for the first time in 17 years for a special screening at New York City's Upright Citizens Brigade Theater. It was a dream come true for fans and also a real opportunity for Stephenson, now a filmmaker himself, who realized that there was a quite a compelling story to be told here. Rather than simply exist as a testament to *Troll 2*'s fascinating and unlikely journey, his documentary takes some surprisingly profound and poignant turns when it focuses on key cast and crew members who are, for a variety of reasons, unable to celebrate the Nilbog festivities. Some of the most enlightening scenes come with the participation of Italian director Claudio Fragasso, who is overjoyed to see the long lines forming outside the theater at one Los Angeles screening, but becomes annoyed inside when everyone laughs hysterically at scenes that weren't meant to be funny.

Most of the attendees at *Best Worst Movie*'s screening in Denver had never seen *Troll 2* before, but it didn't stop them from howling with laughter and falling in love with this documentary. Same goes for Roger Ebert and many other impressed critics who helped make its journey a success for lovers of cinema and not strictly Nilbog devotees. George Hardy's Facebook page surely reached its capacity limit as a result because, as the main focus of this documentary, he encapsulates all that is genuine, sincere, and inspiring about the Utah-based horror movie that has absolutely nothing to do with the original *Troll*, or any trolls for that matter. This small-town Alabama dentist has such an affable and happy-go-lucky presence, it's no wonder that even his ex-wife has nothing but the kindest of words to say about him.

It can be awfully difficult to find a documentary these days that doesn't make you want to take a bath with the toaster, but this one will make you want to reach out to an estranged loved one, show hospitality to a stranger, create a piece of art, or at the very least, go to bed in a good mood. I also highly recommend Michael Paul Stephenson's follow-up documentary, *The American Scream* (2012), which explores the tortured artistry of those who put their hearts and souls into home-decorating for the Halloween season. That movie also received a thumbs up from Mr. Ebert.

In Search of Darkness: A Journey into Iconic '80s Horror (2019)

Writer and Director: David A. Weiner

I'm speaking from experience here. After returning home from a late-night stroll in the snow that would have been even more joyous had the winter wonderland occurred in December instead of the dreadful mid-February slog, you can forget about cat cuddles, electric blankets, hot chocolate, or even clothes straight out of the dryer, because there is no better way to warm up than curling up in front of the TV and experiencing the ultimate nostalgia blanket that is David A. Weiner's "journey into iconic '80s horror." I assumed with the running time that this documentary was intended to be viewed in multiple installments, but even when the midnight hour suddenly morphed into 4 am, there was no mothertrucking way I was going to turn this off. This was my happy place and I was in no rush to leave. For all of the misfit kids whose video store habits helped shape their futures, this documentary is the greatest love letter, but it also serves as the ideal gateway to less-seasoned fans of the genre and younger audiences who will walk away with a beautiful list of titles to watch for the first time.

Whether you've never seen a horror documentary before or have gorged so extensively on similar talking-head projects like Bravo's *100 Scariest Movie Moments*, *Never Sleep Again: The Elm Street Legacy*, and *Crystal Lake Memories* that some of these stories sound familiar, this slick presentation feels like attending the ultimate horror party where all the invitees searched for the dark side and found a very special and unbreakable camaraderie.

The list of participants is massive and consists of horror icons, actors, celebrities, artists, scholars, and even popular YouTube personalities (giving me the rare chance to actually see what Cecil Trachenburg looks like after listening to him for years on the impressive Goodbadflicks series). The decade's most notable horror movies are celebrated chronologically, and interluding each year is a conversation piece devoted to different horror topics such as innovative practical effects, the "final girl" trope, holiday slashers, sex and nudity, and VHS cover artistry. The way the camera pans over VHS cover art before centering on the next film for dissection is part of what makes this documentary so much fun because while the heaviest hitters are predictably in force, there are plenty of lesser-revered titles thrown into the mix as well, and it feels like cheering for your favorite sports team when an underrated gem like *Psycho III*, *The Company of Wolves*, *Night of the Comet*, and *Society* finds itself front and center.

Joe Bob Briggs, John Carpenter, Tom Atkins, Cassandra Peterson, Joe Dante, Barbara Crampton, Alex Winter, Mick Garris, Keith David, Doug Bradley, Tom Holland, Heather Langenkamp, Greg Nicotero, Lloyd Kaufman, and about 100 other effective spokespeople sharing their reverence for the genre is pure comfort food, but it's not without some poignancy since this is some of the last footage we'll ever see of beloved figures in the horror community like Stuart Gordon and Larry Cohen.

Update: AHHHHHHHHHH!!!! THEY MADE A PART 2! AND IT'S JUST AS AWESOME!

Another Update: WE'RE NOT WORTHY! WE'RE NOT WORTHY! *In Search of Darkness: Part III* comes out in 2022! I can't wait! Something tells me that *Spookies* will make the cut this time.

Yet Another Update: HOT DAMN! They just announced that they'll be covering '90s horror in the near future as well! What a time to be alive!

Horror Galore

Just Desserts: The Making of 'Creepshow' (2007)
Director: Michael Felsher

If you see Michael Felsher's name listed on any horror featurette, then chances are high that it'll be worth your time because his passion projects are consistently of the highest quality and he always seems to get the most out of his interviewees. It was exciting to learn one day on Bloody Disgusting that he was attached to a feature-length documentary about one of my all-time favorite movies, *Creepshow*, especially since the only North American DVD release of the popular George A. Romero/Stephen King collaboration had not a single bonus feature. The road to *Just Desserts* proved to be windy and torturous, with *Creepshow*'s US distributor Warner Bros rejecting the offer, and Felsher unable to find a new home for it in the States. For years, it was only available in the United Kingdom as part of a 2-disc special edition DVD of *Creepshow* that never made the intercontinental leap to Region 1. Synapse Films eventually ended our misery in 2016 by giving the documentary its own Blu-ray release with plenty of bonus material to sink our teeth into, and it was well worth the wait.

It may not be over six hours like *Crystal Lake Memories: The Complete History of Friday the 13th* or reveal jaw-dropping true tales of behind-the-scenes chaos like *My Best Fiend*, but it traces all aspects of *Creepshow*'s cycle, from the moment Stephen King and George A. Romero met to discuss adapting *Salem's Lot* and *The Stand*, and discovering they had a mutual love for the '50s horror comics to the day when the finished film hit theaters in November 1982 to audiences that were practically levitating off their seats in excitement.

Cursed movie productions are fascinating to hear about but every now and then it's refreshing to learn about shoots when everything went as planned and everyone got along, believing they were making something special. I'm glad that the cast and crew of *Creepshow* had just as much fun making it as we've had watching it over and over for decades, and that their memories are sharp enough to describe in great detail what it was like to be in the abandoned high school which contained their sets, on the New Jersey shore where Ted Dansen and Leslie Nielsen had the crew in stitches when they weren't obsessing over sunlight and footprints in the sand, and in a confined area where 18,000 cockroaches from Trinidad were unleashed in a way that even had the professional entomologist running away in screaming terror. As Tom Savini, who cherished the opportunity to create creatures instead of carnage, lovingly recalled, it was like five months of Halloween.

As great as this documentary is, it's missing such an important component because for whatever reason, Stephen King chose not to participate. Still, there are more than enough energetic contributors, entertaining tidbits, behind-the-scenes footage, and sparkles in George A. Romero's eyes (who was so proud of the finished project that he wished he could have made half a dozen sequels) to fill the void and make us eternally grateful for Felsher's efforts. There aren't any mentions of the great *Creepshow 2* and so I recommend pairing this up with Arrow Video's Blu-ray extras.

Lost Soul: The Doomed Journey of Richard Stanley's Island of Dr. Moreau (2014)
Writer and Director: David Gregory

Even though I hadn't yet been introduced to enigmatic South African filmmaker Richard Stanley's otherworldly horror offerings *Hardware* and *Dust Devil*, and barely remembered my one viewing of the much-reviled *The Island of Dr. Moreau* decades ago, I was excited about this documentary because similar treatments like *Hearts of Darkness: A Filmmaker's Apocalypse* proved that few things are more entertaining than hearing what happened behind the scenes during notoriously troubled and cursed film productions.

It's a blessing that we got a full-length documentary here instead of a condensed DVD special feature because of the sheer number of strange twists and turns that befell *The Island of Dr. Moreau* from the moment Richard Stanley, whose great grandfather shared a personal connection to the H.G. Wells novel, was hired to direct his first film for a major Hollywood studio. So many important players jumped at the chance to one-up each other with their personal stories from the set in which every day was utter madness.

As talented, passionate, and brilliant as Stanley is, he quickly found himself way over his head having to contend with Australian hurricanes, suicides, divorces, Marlon Brando's hounds, producers who wanted Roman Polanski all along, spider bites, flesh-eating parasites, the very difficult Val Kilmer, and oh, so much more, causing the young director to wonder if his attempt at a witchcraft spell backfired and summoned a cruel test to see whether his sanity or his dream job would be stolen first.

Among the many compelling witnesses are actress Fairuza Balk, who threatened to quit the production if Stanley was replaced; German actor Marco Hofschneider, whose screen time was slashed in half after Marlon Brando (competing against Kilmer to see who could sabotage the production more) preferred working with the smallest man in the world; and New Line Cinema Chairman Rob Shaye, who was awakened in the middle of the night multiple times by cast and crew members tearfully begging to be released from their contract and sent home. Storyboards, Stan Winston sketches, and pages of Stanley's original screenplay provide stirring glimpses as to what this *The Island of Dr. Moreau* version could have been had the universe been a little kinder, but even if nothing had gone wrong during production, there's no way the final result could have been as interesting or entertaining as this documentary. An ending that sees the disillusioned visionary doubting he could ever step behind the camera again after the traumatic experiences in the island of lost souls was depressing to witness in 2014, but thankfully there's now a blissful addendum in the form of *Color Out of Space*, which was tied with the St. Louis Blues capturing their first-ever Stanley Cup as the most incredible comeback story of 2019.

Nightmares in Red, White, and Blue: The Evolution of the American Horror Film (2009)

Director: Andrew Monument
Writer: Joseph Maddrey

No matter if you're still relying on your horror training wheels and under the impression that Jason Vorhees was in *A Nightmare on Elm Street*, or if you're an MVP at horror trivia and have amassed an impressive collection of signed 8x10s from a multitude of conventions, this documentary will entertain the hell out of you from start to finish, guaranteed. My girlfriend is in the former camp, so it was helpful to have such a well-rounded and succinct vehicle to take her on a trip through horror history and explain the cultural significance of each decade better than I ever could. She might not have been geeking out over appearances from the likes of Mick Garris, Joe Dante, Brian Yuzna, John Carpenter, George A. Romero, Roger Corman, Larry Cohen, and Tom McLoughlin like I was, but she did learn a heck of a lot and was pleased to hear that the narration

Horror Galore

was done by Lance Henriksen from that excellent *Tales from the Crypt* episode "Cutting Cards" that we watched last night.

Rhythmic editing and a fun collection of movie clips keep the energy level high as a century of American horror cinema is recounted chronologically—beginning with a piece on the 1910 adaptation of Mary Shelley's *Frankenstein*—and showing why each decade was distinctive based on the historical events and cultural opinions that shaped some of the most notable films. A few examples are how Lon Chaney's *Phantom of the Opera* reflected the fascination and repulsion that people had when severely injured soldiers returned home from World War I, how xenophobic attitudes infiltrated films like *Invasion of the Body Snatchers* and *War of the Worlds*, how the fear of the atomic bomb resulted in all those mutant bug films of the 1950s, and how a post-Vietnam America psychologically prepared people to confront new evils with *The Texas Chainsaw Massacre* and *The Last House on the Left*.

Also briefly discussed are America's racist past, the films of Val Lewton, Adolf Hitler's favorite film, the striking contrasts between Alfred Hitchcock and Herschell Gordon Lewis' early '60s work, the Vincent Price-led adaptations of the works of Edgar Allan Poe, Stephen King's "Norman Rockwell horror," Satanic fever, '80s slashers, *The Silence of the Lambs*' Oscar successes, and new millennium torture porn. Mick Garris proves once again why he's one of the most articulate and insightful horror voices we have, whether he's commenting on the works of Guillermo del Toro or sharing his vivid memories of the Vietnam draft dodge. Joe Dante is another fount of knowledge, and it was really enjoyable hearing him talk about his experiences at the theater seeing the radiation-afflicted giant insect movie *Tarantula*, as well as how *Gremlins* was originally going to be much more disturbing. He even gives the donkey transformation scene in *Pinocchio* some attention because of how shocking it was to youngsters, many of whom would decide to tough it up and explore the darkness some more. It was also refreshing to see obscure hidden gems like Bob Clark's *Deathdream* and Tom McLoughlin's *One Dark Night* stand alongside the all-time classics.

You might have to go all the way back to 1984's *Terror in the Aisles* to find a documentary about the genre that received even a semi-theatrical release, and so I was happy to see a screening of this in Portland in 2009. It was attended by only three other people, all of whom were also men who came to the theater alone—perhaps we should have exchanged numbers after the movie and started a podcast or something.

The Psycho Legacy (2010)
Writer and Director: Robert V. Galluzzo

I was floating on cloud nine when a certain package arrived on the third week of October 2010 because the wait was finally over. In the two and a half years since *The Psycho Legacy* was first announced, I had been following its journey every step of the way from various horror websites because having "the ultimate retrospective of the most influential horror series of all time" would more than make up for the DVD releases of the *Psycho* sequels not containing a single measly special feature, except perhaps "chapter selection." I practically salivated when the DVD case was finally in my hands and I saw the long list of special features with titles such as "The *Psycho* Reunion Panel," "Full Panel Discussion with Anthony Perkins," "Revisiting *Psycho II*," and "A Visit with *Psycho* Memorabilia Collector Guy Thorpe," but even without these three hours of extras, the 87-minute documentary still delivers everything I could have asked for. Director Robert V. Galluzzo took his time sorting through all of the archival footage, tracking down the majority of key cast and crew members to interview, and allowing prominent horror figures like Stuart Gordon (who is the first to appear) to reflect on the series' importance and share personal stories. He gives equal representation to all four films and wisely doesn't waste a single second on Gus Van Sant's ludicrously pointless shot-for-shot remake.

Among the many fascinating bits of trivia that I heard for the very first time were how Anthony Perkins, after many rehearsals of the interrogation scene with Martin Balsam, managed to convince Alfred Hitchcock to abandon his storyboards for this pivotal scene, how Alfred Hitchcock was being lured at the time by producers to direct the first 007 film instead of *Psycho*, how Jerry Goldsmith's initial score for *Psycho II* was rejected and then resurrected for *Twilight Zone: The Movie* (resulting in a second attempt that was so beautiful it moved Anthony Perkins to tears), how actor Donovan Scott's infectious laugh from a commercial three years prior led to him being cast in *Psycho III*, how Perkins arranged a screening of the Coen Brothers' *Blood Simple* right before sitting in the director's chair for the first time, and how all of the men on set were in love with Olivia Hussey and grappling with the realization that Norman's mom was breathtaking.

After so many years of waiting for these criminally underrated sequels to finally get their due, *The Psycho Legacy* made me feel as special as those Universal Studios tram passengers felt when they passed the iconic Bates property during filming and were waved to by Anthony Perkins, Jeff Fahey, and other *Psycho III* cast members. Shout Factory continued to paint the fictional small town of Fairville, California, red in the years following the documentary's release by giving Blu-ray releases to the sequels and filling them with even more special features, and then the universe expanded profoundly and brilliantly with AMC's series *Bates Motel*, which ended up being a thousand times better than anyone could have expected. Now all we need is some reasonably priced soundtracks to the sequels (Part II's is currently going for $119.99 on Amazon) and we'll be all set.

The Shark is Still Working: The Impact & Legacy of Jaws (2007)
Director: Erik Hollander
Writer: James Gelet

Even if you've already seen other retrospectives like *The Making of Jaws*, *In the Teeth of Jaws*, and *Jaws: The Inside Story*, you should still go out of your way to check out *The Shark is Still Working* because for these 100 minutes, you get the head, the tail, the whole damn thing, and so much more. This documentary was completed in 2007 and made sporadic festival appearances for what felt like forever until it was finally available to the masses in 2012 as a special feature on a new Blu-ray/DVD of *Jaws*.

Some of the stories you might have heard before, like Steven Spielberg filming one final scare in a swimming pool and splicing it in just hours before the first screening, John Williams coming up with that perfectly simplistic and primal score, or Bruce's mechanical problems causing one specific message to echo ad nauseum on the crew's walkie talkies, but everyone involved seems so excited to participate, it's like they're telling them for the first time. *The Shark is Still Working* is a documentary made by diehard fans for diehard fans, and so it relishes in exploring uncharted waters and tracking down important individuals who might not have gotten their moment in the sun in the other documentaries. It's honestly hard to think of a single surviving member of the alumni who was absent. In addition to all of the biggest names, we also get to hear from Percy Rodriguez, the man whose voice sent shivers down our spines with the words "It is as if God created the devil and gave him…jaws" in the trailer, the child actors all grown up, the oceanographers who recount just how close one of the stuntmen came to losing his life, the extra whose amazing line reading of a "a whaaaaaaat?" has earned him local legend status, and the list goes on and on.

The behind-the-scenes footage makes us feel like we're right out there in the unforgiving waters during one of the most tumultuous productions of all time, riddled with so many problems that the press mocked it by calling it Flaws instead of *Jaws*, and so it's such a gratifying feeling to witness the excitement building and the lines forming around the block for the initial screenings, when all of the hard work was about to pay off in ways nobody could have imagined. We're even given a seat on the couch next to Spielberg and his friend Joe Spinell (the "Maniac" himself!) as they react in real time to the Oscar nominations.

To chronicle *Jaws*' universal importance, director Erik Hollander has also invited an impressive group of modern filmmakers (including M. Night Shyamalan and Robert Rodriguez), prop collectors, historians, members of the band Anthrax, and fans who have permanently inked Roger Kastel's iconic artwork onto their bodies to tell how their first viewing of *Jaws* was such a defining moment of their lives. Similar sentiments are expressed at present-day Martha's Vineyard, which has made a conscious effort to keep Amity looking absolutely frozen in time to the relief of tourists, especially those attending the JawsFest events.

There are moments of sorrow as well, like when Spielberg recalls how devastated he was upon hearing that the actual Orca, which he would secretly visit from time to time on the Universal lot to reflect on his life and career, was casually dismantled by park staff members one day, and how a crew member never knew the unspeakably horrible details of the U.S.S. Indianapolis tragedy, in which a dear member of her family perished, until she heard Quint's speech. There was also a little in memoriam segment at the end to pay respects to the several participants who passed away in between the documentary's completion and release date, such as Peter Benchley, David Brown, and Roy Scheider, who died just a few months after he provided such stirring narration.

Universal Horror (1998)
Director: Kevin Brownlow

Those tuning into TCM on the evening of October 9, 1998 got a healthy dose of Halloween cheer with the premiere of Kevin Brownlow's 95-minute tribute to the iconic Universal horror movies of the '30s and '40s; sadly, I was not among that fortunate group and wouldn't learn of its existence until it became a special feature on *Frankenstein*'s 75th Anniversary Edition DVD. Given instant credibility by the narration of Kenneth Branagh, this documentary does a terrific job at speaking to both diehard horror fans who've ingrained Frankenstein, Dracula, The Invisible Man, The Wolf Man, and The Creature from the Black Lagoon into their hearts (and permanently onto their skin in some cases), and those who haven't yet graduated from horror history 101. Some will geek out to rare technicolor footage of Boris Karloff's Frankenstein playfully choking out makeup artist Jack Pierce, while others will experience iconic images like Lon Chaney's phantom reveal for the very first time.

It could have easily just been a congratulatory tribute to Carl Laemmle Jr.—who took a chance on horror at the age of 21 in hopes of saving the struggling studio his father created—and to all of the artists responsible for the monsters' enduring legacy, but *Universal Horror* is equally interested at exploring horror's origins in the silent era with films like *The Cabinet of Dr. Caligari*, *The Man who Laughs*, and *The Cat and the Canary*. It also covers the memorable contributions from rival studios Paramount and RKO, and as a result, comes across more as a definitive classic horror retrospective. With compelling bits of trivia abounding, it explains how the genre was impacted by events such as disfigured World War I veterans returning home, Hitler's rise to power, and America's film censors being pushed to the limits by the implied violence of *The Black Cat* and *The Raven*. It also takes viewers on rare tours of Forrest J. Ackerman's horror and science-fiction memorabilia museum in Griffith Park, and the Universal Studios backlot where the Paris Opera House set still stands.

In between the still-shocking movie scenes are testimonies from film historians, authors, and surviving cast and crew members who got to witness the magic in person. I especially enjoyed the insight from author David Skal, who should be everybody's phone-a-friend when it comes to classic horror trivia; Gloria Stuart, who shares her stories of *The Invisible Man* and *The Old Dark House* with the same appreciation as her most famous character did regarding her love affair with Jack on the "unsinkable" ship; screenwriter Curt Siodmak, who penned the script for *The Wolf Man* just three years after emigrating from Nazi Germany; actress Fay Wray, who vividly recalls what it was like to be pawed by King Kong and later rip the face off of the sculptor in *Mystery of the Wax Museum*; and the one-and-only Ray Bradbury, who said he wouldn't be the writer he was without the universal horror movies scaring the hell out of him in the theater as a young child. But being a huge fan of *The Return of the Living Dead* (1 and 2) and *Poltergeist*, I perhaps found no participator more welcome than James Karen, who somehow became even more likeable thanks to his contagious enthusiasm for horror's black and white legends.

I'll be flying to St. Louis in the morning and hopefully I can figure out a way to watch *London After Midnight* on my recently purchased Fire tablet. After learning how a serial killer blamed his sudden insanity on the transgressive makeup effects of Lon Chaney's character, this 1927 film has shot up to the top of my watch list.

Wolfman's Got Nards (2018)
Director: Andre Gower
Writers: Andre Gower, Henry Darrow McComas

When Austin's Alamo Drafthouse announced a special 25th anniversary screening of *The Monster Squad*, there was plenty of excitement and trepidation. The last-known 35mm print would be there, and so would several cast members seeing each other for the first time since 1987, but would anybody else be showing up to celebrate this relatively obscure horror-comedy that still hadn't been available on DVD? After all, everyone involved in Fred Dekker's follow-up to *Night of the Creeps* (an all-time favorite of yours truly) knows what it's like to have dreams and high expectations crumble to pieces when the public pays little attention at the moment of truth. Mercifully, their worries of history repeating itself were short-lived because this special event sold out faster than anything the Alamo Drafthouse had hosted before. It was just a sign of things to come for this movie that first came to life when Dekker and co-writer Shane Black (shortly before his career took off with *Lethal Weapon*) collaborated on a story that could be summed up as "Little Rascals meet the Universal Monsters," and which seemed destined to rise from the ashes of a truly disastrous theatrical run due to how many hearts it touched in the following 25 years. The fascinating rebirth is covered in this heartfelt and sentimental documentary which deserves a much better title than *Wolfman's Got Nards*—good grief, I can't believe they actually went with that.

In the documentary, Dekker recalls how he drove around town on opening night to visit seven different movie theaters that were screening *The Monster Squad*, and every time the rows upon rows of empty seats provided disbelief and devastation. After years of pouring his heart and soul into this movie, it became apparent on this night that it would become an even bigger flop than *Howard the Duck* from the previous year. My brother and I convinced our mom to take us to an afternoon screening, but we left after only a few minutes because the action-packed opening in Dracula's Castle proved to be too intense and loud for these kids aged 4 and 6 who had never seen a remotely scary movie in a theater before. So we abandoned *The Monster Squad*, creating yet another empty row of seats, and joined an already-in-progress adaptation of *Snow White and the Seven Dwarfs*, and I haven't forgiven myself since even though in retrospect I'm thankful that my introduction to the Universal Monsters was such an intimidating experience.

My first initiation into this exclusive club was a failure, but a year later, I caught it on HBO and of course went over the moon for it. And a week before Halloween 2014, I got to finally enjoy a theatrical screening of *The Monster Squad* in its entirety at Portland's Hollywood Theatre, and it meant a lot to be a part of that sold-out audience cheering as loud as they could when Fred Dekker walked down the aisle and took center stage for a Q&A. Receiving standing ovations like these for a movie that pretty much killed his career 25 years ago is something Dekker thoughtfully reflects upon.

Director Andre Gower, who portrayed the leader of the Monster Squad as a child actor, went the extra mile in making sure this would be a complete standalone documentary rather than merely a simple fan service lovefest. Making up his impressive assembly of participants are cast and crew members, modern creatives, horror journalists, film critics, college professors, memorabilia collectors, and the most passionate fans from around the globe, and together they've created something that will delight all monsters at heart, whether you're a Monster Squad virgin, a casual fan, or could instantly spot a red "Stephen King Rules" t-shirt from a sea of thousands. In one touching sequence, fans in their 40s recount how the movie came along just when they needed it most and helped them endure extreme challenges like testing positive for the AIDS virus, being friendless in a new country, or suffering from physical disabilities. A special tribute is also given to fallen squad member Brent Chalem, whose performance as Horace inspired many heavyset misfit youths; he would sadly pass away in 1997 at just 22 years old.

Wolfman's Got Nards (ugh, that title gets worse every time I see it) is also essential viewing for fans due to its treasure trove of unearthed behind-the-scenes clips, my favorite one featuring the young director coaching five-year-old Ashley Bank just before filming her emotional farewell to her pal Frankenstein. We also get to see how they filmed the scene in which Dracula (played by Duncan Regehr with an impressively sociopathic edge) approaches her slowly and shouts "GIVE ME THE AMULET, YOU BITCH!" The pint-sized actress knew that she was supposed to scream at some point during this scene but didn't know when—Dekker would only smile and say "Oh, you'll know." Other goodies include promotional material designed to look like Wanted posters with The Mummy's crimes listed as "armed bandage" and "statutory wrap," the coolest garage of all time, a group of female fans with exaggerated New York accents, an interesting connection to *The Shape of Water*, and in the background of one particular interviewer, a memorable prop from the *Amazing Stories* episode "Go to the Head of the Class," which I've probably already mentioned in this book is ESSENTIAL VIEWING!

You're So Cool, Brewster! The Story of Fright Night (2016)
Director: Chris Griffiths
Writers: Chris Griffiths, Neil Morris, Gary Smart

For so many years, fans of Tom Holland's masterpiece *Fright Night* could only display a bare boned DVD in their physical media collection while just about every other groundbreaking horror movie of the '80s was being honored with remastered special editions jam-packed with hours of special features. Making up for that frustration was how the horror convention circuit kept the film's legacy growing by hosting cast and crew reunions, which resulted in other goodies like a pair of online commentary tracks in 2008 courtesy of Icons of Fright and Shock N Roll—one with writer/director Tom Holland, Chris Sarandon, and Jonathan Stark, and the other featuring Holland with William Ragsdale, Stephen Geoffreys, and FX Artist Randall William Cook.

The studio Twilight Time released a 30th Anniversary Blu-ray of *Fright Night* in 2015 with the bonus features that we had been craving for so long, but it was a limited edition and very costly. My cheapness overpowered my fandom at the time and I didn't put down the big bucks, but a couple years later, I did contribute to a Kickstarter campaign that appeared to be the ultimate gift to fans, much like how Tom Holland wrote *Fright Night* as the ultimate gift to fans of classic horror cinema. The finished project was the 217-minute documentary *You're So Cool Brewster! The Story of Fright Night* and it turned out better than I ever could have dreamed.

After the success of *Psycho II*, screenwriter Tom Holland reunited with director Richard Franklin for the action-adventure family film *Cloak & Dagger*, starring the greats Henry Thomas and Dabney Coleman. During the production of this film, Holland had a brainstorming session that caused him to wonder what it would be like if a horror fan suspected that his next-door neighbor was a vampire. The documentary opens with Holland describing how excited he was to begin writing this story that had elements of *Rear Window* and some wish fulfillment thrown in due to how much he envied Charley's predicament. After years of vampires being satirized, he was determined to make them scary again. He takes us through the process of pre-production and the first draft of the screenplay, which didn't have the Amy character nor a happy ending, and then we're treated to some interesting stories about the casting process, like how Charlie Sheen was dismissed immediately for being too handsome in the Hollywood sense, how a misunderstanding led Stephen Geoffreys to a casting director who was expecting Anthony Michael Hall to show up, and how Art Evans was seconds away from walking out of a slow-moving audition for the Detective Lennox role until the person next to him in line made a wise observation.

British actor Simon Bamford, looking much more handsome than when he portrayed the Butterball cenobite in the first two *Hellraiser* films, serves as the documentary's host by recreating the character of Peter Vincent in wraparound vignettes that separate the many topics. Another *Hellraiser* connection is how producer Gary Smart's previous documentary was the 476-minute *Leviathan: The Story of Hellraiser and Hellbound: Hellraiser II*, which was criticized by many for missing the most important ingredient: the participation of Clive Barker himself. You certainly can't make a similar complaint about this documentary because it catches up with just about everybody and leaves no stone unturned. In addition to new interviews, we're also treated to clips from press kit interviews during production, with fresh-faced youngsters thrilled with the opportunity and completely unaware how the movie would carry a legacy growing for decades. The only person that director Chris Griffiths and Tom Holland were unable to track down is actress Dorothy Fielding, and even though her whereabouts are unknown, they still devoted a nice little moment to her because of how delightful she was playing Charley's mother.

As a kid I once recorded the songs from the movie onto a cassette so I could jam out to Sparks and J. Geils Band with my Walkman on the school bus, and so the chapter devoted to the soundtrack was a definite highlight. It was a real treat to hear composer Brad Fiedel (hired due to his work on *The Terminator*) share his inspirations and memories, especially in regards to the song "Come to Me." And seeing as how I laughed uncontrollably at a recent episode of *Family Guy* in which *Fright Night* was spoofed with a dance scene between Meg and a cat set to Ian Hunter's "Good Man in a Bad Time," I also appreciated how they delved into the concerted effort to find just the right synth pop music to fill the pivotal dance club scene.

The mad scientists working in the makeup and special effects departments provide extensive tours inside their laboratory, where they magically transformed a wolf into Evil Ed, melted Billy Cole into a skeleton, and turned the most sophisticated and suave late-sleepers into a grotesque spawn of Satan, long before the conveniences of CGI. We also get entertaining stories about a cast member breaking a foot during a casual scene, Chris Sarandon researching why his character would experience fruit cravings, dissatisfaction over the trailer, late night phone calls from diehard fans, what it was like to see the movie for the first time in theaters during its opening weekend, and so much more.

As irritating as it was for *Fright Night* fans to go so long without a respectable physical release, fans of the 1988 sequel have suffered far worse. As I mentioned in the vampire chapter, *Fright Night Part 2* faced horrible luck in theaters and on DVD, but it has found considerable redemption and long overdue respect thanks to this documentary devoting an hour to it and gathering insights from its principal players. Even the 2011 remake gets its time in the moon. The first half of that movie was pretty good in my opinion, and so I'm glad it wasn't totally torn to shreds by Holland and company. Hearing about Colin Farrell's love for the original and how William Ragsdale and Jonathan Stark saw the remake in a (nearly empty) theater together and screamed at the top of their lungs for Chris Sarandon's cameo made my smile even larger than Amy Peterson's shark mouth.

FUN-SIZED HORRORS OF 21 MINUTES OR LESS

Dear Beautiful (2007)

Director: Roland Becerra
Writers: Roland Becerra, Meredith DiMenna, Candace Rose
Cast: Nathan Smith, Erin Schultz, Tom DiMenna

Earning positive buzz and some awards on a festival circuit that included stops at Cannes and Toronto After Dark, *Dear Beautiful* is the result of five and a half years of hard work. Roland Becerra creates a wondrous world of his own with his blending of flash motion, stop motion, and live action to tell the story of Paul and Lauren, a young couple whose marriage is on the rocks after weeks of squabbling and unhappiness, and now faces the ultimate hurdle when an exotic, non-native species of flower starts sprouting all over New Haven, Connecticut, causing horrific side effects to anyone who gets too close.

Shortly after Lauren admires the beautiful and strange new flower in their backyard, she forgoes sleep just so she can stand and stare out the window all night. The following afternoon, she has a meltdown in the living room that causes an overwhelmed Paul to just sit alone in the kitchen and numb himself with a bottle of wine before moving onto something stronger. But things are about to get a whole lot worse when she quickly deteriorates both mentally and physically to the point where she's barely still human, and no matter how much he drinks, he's unable to block it out. This tragic and awe-inspiring short film really struck a nerve with me when I saw it seven years ago in preparation for a panel at Seattle's Crypticon convention about animated horror, and so I'm thrilled to be able to sing its praises once more.

For further explorations into the world of short horror animation involving living dead ghouls, be sure to revisit *Heavy Metal* for the segment titled "B-17" (written by Dan O'Bannon!) in which a World War II bomber is fired upon at night and the horrified pilot not only has to deal with mechanical issues but also the deceased soldiers turning into zombies.

The Haunted House (1921)

Writers and Directors: Edward F. Cline, Buster Keaton
Cast: Buster Keaton, Virginia Fox, Joe Roberts, Edward F. Cline

Buster Keaton plays a bank clerk having a miserable day at work. He falls from a high distance trying to adjust the clock and spills the open container of glue he keeps on the desk, which creates all sorts of comedic problems with people getting stuck to cash, floors, and each other. His absurd attempts to remedy the situation keep backfiring, resulting in him losing his pockets and some of his hair in the process, but he finds himself in an even stickier situation when he's wrongfully accused of a bungled robbery involving a group of gangsters and his corrupt boss. Running from the law, he breaks into a house to hide but as luck would have it, it's been boobytrapped and gimmicked to fool others into thinking it's haunted. A group of theater actors also seek shelter in the house after being chased through the woods by angry ticketholders because of their disastrous performance of "Faust."

Giving Scooby Doo inspiration for decades, what follows is a madcap medley of visual gags, physical comedy, and misunderstandings, as poor Buster finds himself unable to find a safe place in the house with all these ghosts, skeletons, devils, invisible men, and headless men running around. But his biggest tormenter is a collapsible staircase that gets the better of him each time, despite his many ingenious ways to outsmart it, and it even results in an encounter with Satan himself!

Had a new season of *Curb Your Enthusiasm* not commenced just a couple of weeks ago, this 100-year-old silent movie would have given me my loudest laughs in months, and so it's obvious that I need to finally make a point in seeing more from the uniquely talented Buster Keaton.

Horror Brunch!!! (1987)

Director: Rik Carter
Writers: Rik Carter, John Jockinsen, Bill Parsley

Dear readers, I can say with confidence that you'll have a blast with *Horror Brunch!!!* It starts off like a casual Sunday brunch at Hill's House restaurant, but then the waitress suddenly grows fangs, knives fly around hacking off hands, and plates go on a decapitation spree, all while a few oblivious diners continue sipping their coffee and eating soup. Norman Bates, Leatherface, and the Alien chestburster even show up to help paint the walls red and guarantee that even at just 4 minutes, this goes down like the most satisfying all-you-can-eat buffet for genre fans.

Right from the start when a man reveals the punchline of a joke to his friends, I had a smile on my face that kept getting bigger and bigger. While I wasn't able to find any joke online that ends with, "So the other guy says, 'What, no onions?!'" I did find out that Rik Joel Carter made a couple other short films shortly before working on *A Nightmare on Elm Street 4* and *5*, as a makeup artist and sculptor respectively.

I Dare Ya was filmed in sunny Santa Barbara and stars three children from the local theater group Peanut Gallery Productions, run by Carter's mother Jan. Just as much fun as their colorful late 80's outfits is their banter, as one of them is dared to approach the spookiest house in the neighborhood and ring the doorbell, a reliably exciting premise. "I'm not ascared of that old house," says the kid with the biggest Walkman of all time, and whether it was written that way or the young actor just mixed up "scared" and "afraid," it's so precious. With a great buildup and payoff, *I Dare Ya* fills you with the same exhilaration as going ding-dong-ditching for the very first time.

His final short film, *Closet Case*, about an old man hiding from the monster that's invaded his home, is also worth seeing for the inspired creature design and the way its snakelike claws slither their way through the closet cracks.

Other Side of the Box (2018)

Director: Caleb J. Phillips
Writers: Caleb J. Phillips, Nick Tag
Cast: Nick Tag, Teagan Rose, Josh Schell, Tyler Pochop

Ben and Rachel are having a romantic Christmas eve in their spacious, beautifully lit home when they are visited by their estranged friend Shawn. The details of their situation aren't spelled out but it's alluded that a love triangle is what drove them apart.

A nervous Shawn drops off a present and once it's unwrapped and opened, he apologizes and gets the hell out of there, leaving Ben and Rachel to wonder how a cardboard box could seemingly contain a bottomless pit. It's the understatement of the year when Rachel remarks "Well, that's odd" after Ben tests it out by dropping a pencil inside.

Not much clarification is given on Shawn's handwritten note but it contains one piece of helpful information: "I don't have it all figured out but I know it can't move while you're watching." If you watch this film on YouTube, please do your best to blur your eyes while clicking on the thumbnail because it sadly spoils what else is living inside the box's endless black void. *The Other Side of the Box*, which won the Grand Jury Award for Best Midnight Short at 2019's SXSW festival, concluded a self-curated 3-hour short horror marathon in my living room, and I couldn't have asked for a grander, spookier finale. While this high concept piece straight out of the "Outer Limits" left me begging for more in the form of a feature length adaptation, perhaps this fascinating story works best by keeping things open to interpretation and letting the impending doom envelop you the entire time without grasping for some kind of logical conclusion.

The Pendulum, the Pit, and Hope (1983)
Director: Jan Švankmajer
Writers: Jan Švankmajer, Edgar Allan Poe (story), Auguste Villiers de l'Isle-Adam (story)

My introduction to Edgar Allan's Poe most famous killing machine was at a cool tourist attraction in Florida called the Mystery Fun House, where one of the rooms depicted a screaming animatronic man sucking in his gut every time the swinging pendulum whooshed by him. I stared at the scene for several minutes, wondering how long a man could possibly keep himself alive under those circumstances (he'll have to fall asleep sometime), what acts could possibly warrant such extreme punishment, and why all those rats were intent on getting so close to him and that gigantic blade.

This short film was made by Czech master of surrealism Jan Švankmajer, and much like his feature length films *Alice* (1988) and *Faust* (1994), it innovatively blends live action with his signature stop motion to create an otherworldly sensation. It filled me with the same morbid fascination as the Mystery Fun House's display, but rather than watching someone about to have his chest sliced apart, this time I was the trapped victim staring up at the pendulum that gets faster and lower with each swing. Decades before it was trendy with the found footage subgenre, this film uses a POV approach to immerse the viewers in this impossibly frightening situation. Adding to the realism is the lack of score, so that all we hear in this underground inquisitional torture chamber are footsteps, drops of water, the pendulum's gears grinding away, that most distressing whoosh, and of course, our heavy breathing. By the end of this seriously scary short, we're biting our nails and practically begging for an act of mercy, a miracle, or to just feel sunlight on our skin one more time. Even without a word spoken, this onslaught of madness somehow feels like one of the more faithful adaptations of Edgar Allan Poe.

Possibly in Michigan (1983)
Writer and Director: Cecelia Condit
Cast: Jill Sands, Karen Skladany, Bill Blume

The TikToking "Gen Z" often get my "Xennial" eyes rolling, but tonight I feel nothing but gratitude after learning how they gave a second life to the experimental short musical *Possibly in Michigan*, which now has over 5 million views on YouTube because of their memes, gifs, and Reddit posts. Before that, the most publicity it ever received was when it was ridiculed in 1985 on the Christian program *The 700 Club*. The fact that Pat Robertson and company were so appalled that The National Endowment for the Arts and the Ohio Arts Council funded this movie that supposedly promoted violence, homosexuality, and sinful acts makes me adore it even more.

Director Cecilia Condit, who recently retired from serving as the professor and director of graduate studies in the Department of Film, Video, Animation, and New Genres at the University of Wisconsin-Milwaukee, was still processing a great deal of trauma during the making of *Possibly in Michigan*; it's a life-altering event to learn that the person you are dating is "The Unicorn Killer" who has been hiding the murdered corpse of his ex-girlfriend in a closet. In a plot that must have been therapeutic, two women turn the tables on their shopping mall stalker wearing a tuxedo and an elderly mannequin head with a terrifyingly wide-open mouth.

Shot on video and featuring artsy superimpositions, dozens of *Wicker Man*-esque ceremonial masks, and worms crawling in and out of corpses, *Possibly in Michigan* looks strange but it sounds even stranger, thanks to its perky Casio keyboard soundtrack and operatic approach in having the actresses sing all of their lines, even the most mundane and abstract ones. The result is a viewing experience unlike any other, so I encourage everyone to take 15 minutes out of their day and see why Condit's surrealism has become part of the permanent collection of the Museum of Modern Art. If you're anything like me, you'll be left with so many pressing questions and a strange desire to hear from everyone involved in the making of the film, as well as the mall shoppers and neighbors who were probably weirded out to the max.

The Sandman (1991)

Director: Paul Berry
Writer: E.T.A. Hoffmann (story)

Before lending his macabre stop motion animation skills to *The Nightmare Before Christmas* and *James and the Giant Peach*, Paul Berry put a very dark and twisted spin on the Sandman, a mythical character from European folklore who visits sleepy children and sprinkles magical dust on them to help them dream.

A young boy is happily playing with his drum while his mother knits in her rocking chair, but then the most ominous of cuckoo clocks signals bedtime's arrival. Guided by candleflame, he nervously ascends the twisting, bending staircase and maneuvers down the menacingly long hallway (meticulously angled to German expressionism proportions) to his bedroom. Sleep doesn't come easy when wind blasts open the window and the clouds make horrifying shapes while passing the crescent moon. After seeing what happens next, I'll probably be doing some tossing and turning tonight as well.

If the darkest elements of *Coraline* had you clamoring for more sinister puppetry, then you should definitely take the hand of this sandman off to never-never land. Given how disturbing some of the imagery is, I was a little surprised to see that it was nominated for Best Animated Short at the 1992 Academy Awards, but not surprised to see that it lost to something so joyous and whimsical as Daniel Greaves' *Manipulation*, a six-minute magic show on paper.

Suckablood (2012)

Writers and Directors: Jake Hendriks, Ben Tillett
Cast: Holly Jacobson, Samuel Metcalf, Robin Berry

The German children's book *Struwwelpeter* featured a collection of cruel and terrifying morality tales, the most memorable one being about a little

Fun-Sized Horrors Of 21 Minutes Or Less

Poster for *Suckablood* (2012), Bloody Cuts

boy's refusal to stop sucking his thumbs leads to them getting chopped off by a giant pair of scissors. For the six glorious minutes tonight when I watched the award-winning fairytale horror short *Suckablood*, it was as if I had gone way back in time and was reading it under the covers with a flashlight all over again, reliving some of my earliest spooks.

On the darkest and stormiest of nights, the Suckablood comes when a wicked stepmother summons the glowing-eyed demon to punish a little girl for her bad habit. In addition to being the co-writer and co-director, Ben Tillett also provides the nursery rhyme narration, channeling his inner Boris Karloff and James Earl Jones by delivering lines like "Suckablood, Suckablood, I beg you, come do slaughter my daughter should she suck her thumb!" with just the right amount of menace in his baritone.

This movie was produced by Ben Franklin, founding father of British horror anthology series *Bloody Cuts*, and features the kind of cinematography, music, makeup effects, sets, lighting, atmosphere, and sinister trees that would make Tim Burton drool. It's a dark gothic fairytale perfect to kick off a movie night during the Halloween season.

The Ten Steps (2004)
Writer and Director: Brendan Muldowney
Cast: Jill Harding, William O'Sullivan, Paula Lee

While mom and dad are out having dinner with another couple to discuss business opportunities, young Katie is put in charge of babysitting her younger brother who enjoys scaring the daylights out of her with his collection of masks. But Katie gets a much bigger fright when the power suddenly goes out in this large, creepy house with a troubled history, and she has to go down to the basement to change the fuse. Because she suffered a severe panic attack the last time she was down there, her father stays on the phone with her for support as she very slowly descends the staircase while gripping a candle, its flame in perpetual danger of being blown out by invisible forces.

It's a very simple premise that anyone who had an irrational fear of their basement growing up will have no trouble identifying with. Tonight, I've watched so many horror shorts that ended with a cheap and bombastic jump scare, and so it was such a treat to see what *The Ten Steps* does with its eventual payoff. Good god almighty, now that's how you go out on a high note! That's the kind of brilliantly executed scare that keeps a person restless all through the night and so it's lucky for me that tomorrow is Sunday and I can sleep until 2:00 if I want to.

Horror Galore

3 Verses (2016)

Writer and Director: Antonio Yee
Cast: Laura Mariscal, Edvan Galvan, Daniela Lopez, Dayhana Garcia

This Mexican film from first-time director Antonio Yee is often cited as one of the scariest shorts of the past decade and it only takes about 30 seconds of its 13-minute running time to understand why.

Two frightened, bloodied girls call a psychic named Margery late at night, believing that this seer of the past, present, and future could be the only one who can rid them of a vengeful spirit. Margery, wearing an unsettling paper mache doll mask and speaking in a deep, scratchy grumble, invites the girls into her candlelit home for a séance that takes a dangerous turn when one of them breaks the circle in a panic, filling the apartment with what looks like the monochrome citizens of "The Further."

The stylish production design, costumes, camerawork, and makeup effects give *3 Verses* such a timeless quality that when The Phantom of the Opera makes his big reveal on a character's television screen, it seems perfectly appropriate despite the two films being released 90 years apart. It also orchestrates a tantalizing double twist at the end that sure took me by surprise and made me love the film even more.

Toe (2019)

Writers and Directors: Neal O'Bryan, Chad Thurman
Cast: Cassie Carey

The beginning of my holiday break officially started a couple hours ago, but after a stressful 48-hour workweek, I wasn't feeling invigoration but rather pure exhaustion mixed with lingering humbuggery. I was practically mimicking the *Arrested Development* gif of George Michael doing his sad Charlie Brown walk and collapsing on the floor the second he enters the house. In fighting my age and stubbornly refusing to go to bed early on a Friday night, I hoped a fresh pot of coffee and a few snowman-shaped sugar cookies would lighten my eyelids, but it turns out another combination proved to be far more effective: a pair of headphones and the short film *Toe*.

Filmmakers Neal O'Bryan and Chad Thurman flipped through a copy of Alvin Schwartz's *Scary Stories to Tell in the Dark* one day in search of a collaborative effort, and decided that "The Big Toe" was the terrifying tale from their childhood they were most eager to recreate. They also said in interviews how despite having no animation in their repertoire, they agreed that stop motion was the only suitable way to bring Stephen Gammell's unforgettable imagery to life. Thankfully they are both quick learners who possess the infinite patience required for the artform.

Being the introductory story in the original book meant that "The Big Toe" was, for many children, the first scary story told to them in the dark, and so it was nice of 2019 to offer us two different film adaptations—*Toe* premiered at Chicago's Cinepocalypse Genre Film Festival a few months before André Øvredal's *Scary Stories to Tell in the Dark* hit theaters. Rather than a mother impulsively tossing a severed toe into a pot of stew for supper, this seven-minute short eliminates her character entirely so that her emaciated child is alone and forced to look after himself in a barren field where nothing grows. It never occurred to me that the characters in the story might be starving but here there is no question that if the boy refuses cannibalism, he might not survive another day. The bleak and gothic visuals are perfectly partnered with a soundtrack that echoes the whirring machinery and drones of despair from *The Texas Chainsaw Massacre* and *Eraserhead*, and by the time the little boy is awakened to rotting, garbled cries of "Where is my toe?" I felt like a little kid shivering under the covers with a flashlight and my favorite book all over again.

SOMETHING SPECIAL TO MAKE YOU FEEL LIKE YOU'VE JUST BOWLED A PERFECT 300

Phantom of the Paradise (1974)
Writer and Director: Brian De Palma
Cast: William Finley, Paul Williams, Jessica Harper, Gerrit Graham, George Memmoli

Last night I counted all of the films I've written about so far for this book and saw that I was just one away from finally reaching the magic number of 300. Then, in a moment of serendipity, I logged onto Twitter and immediately saw a poster for Brian De Palma's *Phantom of the Paradise*, where underneath the image of a screaming Winslow Leach was the tagline "The Most Highly Acclaimed Horror Phantasy of Our Time." My eyeballs zeroed in on the word "horror" with such power and precision that it was like DePalma himself was directing them. *Phantom of the Paradise* is a horror movie? Rotten Tomatoes, Wikipedia, Letterboxd, Horror Movie Podcast host Gillman Joel, and a never-ending list of critics seem to think so, and I really don't need any more coaxing to include what is probably the greatest movie I've watched for the first time over the past decade, with second place going to William Friedkin's follow-up to *The Exorcist*, the Roy Scheider-starring *Sorcerer*. It doesn't fit snugly in any genre, but even if people out there believe that it's more adjacent to drama, comedy, thriller, or even musical, I seriously doubt anyone would complain about its inclusion here because it's such a bizarre and powerful experience that you can make it out to be whatever you want.

Poster for ***Phantom of the Paradise*** (1974), Harbor Productions, 20th Century Fox

Released just a couple years before De Palma's *Carrie* and sharing similar visual techniques like the lurid split screens, this movie hearkens back to *The Phantom of the Opera*, but also integrates themes of *Faust* and *The Picture of Dorian Gray*. An introduction by none other than Rod Serling takes

Horror Galore

us to a concert hall where the crowd goes wild for retro-pandering act The Juicy Fruits, and then quiets down and shuffles about once Winslow Leach takes the stage and plays on his piano a beautiful tune from his cantata, with lyrics that would prove to be heartbreakingly prophetic. Nobody seems to be paying any attention to him except Swan, a record producer who believes he has finally found the right music to open his decadent new club, The Paradise. He uses his power and influence to steal the music and cause nothing but misery to the dorky, unmarketable artist who created it. It's really upsetting to see such terrible things happen to poor Winslow when he unwittingly makes a deal with the devil, but once he embraces his new horrifying persona and becomes hellbent on revenge, the film piles delightful layers of camp, comedy, and catharsis into the tragedy. Providing the most laughter is the androgenous shock-rocker Biff (Gerrit Graham), personally chosen by Swan to perform Winslow's music on opening night in his own outrageously over-the-top style, rendering the heartfelt songs unrecognizable in a biting satire of the innerworkings of the music industry. Another familiar face in the cast belongs to *Suspiria* star Jessica Harper, playing a backup singer named Phoenix who Winslow prays doesn't succumb to the same traps he did.

As much as we detest Swan, *Phantom of the Paradise* only reaffirms our love and appreciation for the talents of songwriter, actor, and 70's television staple Paul Williams, especially since he also delivered that sweet soundtrack (which I purchased immediately after my initial viewing). I've lost all interest in karaoke over the past several years but one thing that could bring me back is an uncrowded bar that offers "Faust" or the Oscar-nominated closing theme "The Hell of It."

Bombing in theaters amidst many negative reviews and being overshadowed in the midnight cult scene by *Rocky Horror Picture Show* wasn't enough to silence this phantom, as it would find a devoted following over the years leading to cast reunions and anniversary screenings. The only place in the world that got it right from the very beginning was Winnipeg, and the ways in which this freezing cold (even by Canadian standards) city responded to Brian De Palma's weird, flashy, dramatic horror-comedy-musical are affectionately shown in the 2019 documentary *Phantom of Winnipeg*. For this fact alone I always root for the Winnipeg Jets, except of course when the team on the other side of the ice is the St. Louis Blues.

Thank you for making it to the end of this book, and for your reward, here is the best piece of advice I can offer: watch the *Amazing Stories* episode "Go to the Head of the Class" this Halloween season!

Nathaniel Tolle graduated from Webster University in St. Louis with a degree in Film Studies, and is the author of *Pumpkin Cinema: The Best Movies for Halloween* and *Amazing Amusement Park Stories*. He currently lives in Beaverton, Oregon, which is less than 200 miles away from the fictional town of Twin Peaks. He is of no relation to bestselling spiritual guru Eckhart Tolle.

Horror Galore

ACKNOWLEDGMENTS:

Sincere thanks to my father Michael (who edited the book), mother Julia, brother Nick, Michael Aloisi, Cheryl Zion, Kelsi Schreiber, Joel Robertson, Peter Nielsen, Michael Griffith, Devon Arnold, Parker Bowman, Summer Violett, Ben Zurawski, Sue Simpson, Barb Niebruegge, Greg Morgan, Dave Becker, Jenne Campo, Steve Sabellico, Julia Schafermeyer, Aaron Matthews, Raif Hoffman, Matt Faure, Mathew and Catherine Holland, Jason Edward Davis, Tara Vermette, and the talented hosts of Retro Movie Geek, Land of the Creeps, Junk Food Dinner, Slime and Slashers, Horrorble Podcast, The Haunted Davenport, Horror Movie Podcast, Monster Kid Radio, Deadpit, and Monster Men.

To the staff of Movie Madness, The Hollywood Theatre, Raven's Manor, and The Freakybuttrue Peculiarium, thank you for making Portland, Oregon such a suitable place for horror fans to call home.

I'd also like to extend my appreciation to the following music groups for creating such beautifully haunting soundscapes to type along to.

- My Dying Bride for their 3-disc special edition of *Evinta*
- The 3rd and the Mortal for the albums *Painting on Glass* and *Tears Laid in Earth*
- Slowdive for *Pygmalion*
- Ulver for *Shadows of the Sun*
- Bohren & Der Club of Gore for their entire discography
- Kauan for their entire discography

www.ingramcontent.com/pod-product-compliance
Lightning Source LLC
Chambersburg PA
CBHW041409300426
44114CB00028B/2964